# The Chicago School of Political Economy

*Classics in Economics Series*
Warren J. Samuels, Series Editor

*The Chicago School of Political Economy*,
edited by Warren J. Samuels,
with a new introduction by the editor

*Economic Semantics*, Fritz Machlup,
with an introduction by Mark Perlman

*Economists and the Public*, William Harold Hutt,
with a new introduction by Warren J. Samuels

*Epistemics and Economics*, G.L.S. Shackle,
with a new introduction by the author

*Essays in Economics*, Joseph A. Schumpeter,
with an introduction by Richard Swedberg

*Evolutionary Economics*, David Hamilton,
with a new introduction by the author

*Institutional Economics*, John Commons,
with an introduction by Malcolm Rutherford

*Inventors and Moneymakers*, Frank W. Taussig,
with an introduction by Warren J. Samuels

*Main Currents in Modern Economics*, Ben Seligman,
with an introduction by E. Ray Canterbery

*Philosophy and Political Economy*, James Bonar,
with a new introduction by Warren J. Samuels

*The Place of Science in Modern Civilization*, Thorstein Veblen,
with a new introduction by Warren J. Samuels

*The Political Element in the Development of Economic Theory*,
Gunnar Myrdal, with an introduction by Richard Swedberg

*Politics, Economics, and Welfare*, Robert A. Dahl and Charles E. Lindblom,
with a new introduction by the authors

*The Professionalization of Economics*, John Maloney,
with a new introduction by the author

# The Chicago School of Political Economy

*Edited by*

**WARREN J. SAMUELS**

*With a New Introduction by the Editor*

Routledge
Taylor & Francis Group
LONDON AND NEW YORK

Originally published in 1976 by the Board of Trustees of Michigan State University.

First published 1993 by Transaction Publishers

Published 2020 by Routledge
2 Park Square, Milton Park, Abingdon, Oxon OX14 4RN
52 Vanderbilt Avenue, New York, NY 10017

*Routledge is an imprint of the Taylor & Francis Group, an informa business*



Library of Congress Catalog Number: 92-15711

Library of Congress Cataloging-in-Publication Data
The Chicago school of political economy / edited by Warren J. Samuels.
p. cm.
Material from the Dec. 1975 and Mar. 1976 issues of the Journal of economic issues which largely comprised a two-part symposium.
Originally published: University Park, Pa. : Association for Evolutionary Economics, 1976.
Includes bibliographical references.
ISBN 1-56000-633-1 (paper)
1. Chicago school of economics. I. Samuels, Warren, J., 1933-
HB98.2.C45 1993
330.15—dc20

92-15711
CIP

ISBN 13: 978-1-56000-633-6 (pbk)
ISBN 13: 978-1-138-53465-0 (hbk)

To the advancement of self-awareness by economists and thereby of the profession

The role of the intellectual is commonly exaggerated in its importance and misunderstood in its workings. But nothing I have said, or could say, would becloud the difference between great intellectuals and the rank and file, between the men who make ideas and those who peddle them. Milton Friedman refuses to accommodate himself to nice dichotomies, for he also is a masterful peddler. He is above all, however, the great theoretician, the discoverer of powerful systematizations of reality.

George Stigler
"The Intellectual and His Society"

The standpoint of the classical economists, in their higher or definitive syntheses and generalisations, may not inaptly be called the standpoint of ceremonial adequacy. The ultimate laws and principles which they formulated were laws of the normal or the natural, according to a preconception regarding the ends to which, in the nature of things, all things tend. In effect, this preconception imputes to things a tendency to work out what the instructed common sense of the time accepts as the adequate or worthy end of human effort. It is a projection of the accepted ideal of conduct. This ideal of conduct is made to serve as a canon of truth, to the extent that the investigator contents himself with an appeal to its legitimation for premises than run back of the facts with which he is immediately dealing, for the "controlling principles" that are conceived intangibly to underlie the process discussed, and for the "tendencies" that run beyond the situation as it lies before him.

Thorstein Veblen
"Why Is Economics Not an Evolutionary Science?"

"The institution of property" is a kind of shorthand notation for an infinitely complicated political-economic system and, indeed, for almost any possible alternative system. Meaning both nothing and everything, it naturally is the subject of much loose talk and impassioned rhetoric, among both stupid reactionaries and romantic radicals. To say that liberal democracy rests on private property is almost pure tautology. To discuss policy problems of "property" would be to discuss almost all economic-policy problems of our society.

Security of property, moreover, implies a flexible institution of property and persistent, progressive resolution of problems as they obtrude themselves into the democratic discussion process. Radical movements . . . may mainly serve merely to keep us properly busy with the small, manageable problems which are the grist of the democratic mill. Whether radicalism is excessive or inadequate at any period is not for contemporaries to judge with confidence. . . . Radicals jeopardize the security of property less by attacking the institution than by neglecting it. . . . The way to multiply big problems is to neglect small ones. There is nothing seriously wrong with our institution of property or our institutional system save our proclivity to waste time in attacking or defending it and to neglect proper tasks of changing it continuously by wise collective experimentation.

Libertarian prophecies of impending doom, save from global war, are as romantic as adolescent-radical notions of how all social problems can be solved. The development of political-economic institutions, if not altogether like that of language, is not altogether different either. Hysteria is unbecoming to liberals; they must have faith in social process and in the durability of liberty; for their kind of society simply cannot be promoted by revolutions or by counterrevolutions. A liberal screams (or despairs) only as an apostate.

Henry Simons
*Economic Policy for a Free Society*

And so at the Chicago of my student days it was, ironically enough, the socialist Oskar Lange who extolled the beauties of the Paretian optimum achieved by a perfectly competitive market—and Frank Knight who in effect taught us that the deeper welfare implications of this optimum were indeed quite limited.

Don Patinkin
"Frank Knight as Teacher"

# Contents

# Introduction to the Transaction Edition

In the decade and a half since this volume was first published, the Chicago School has maintained its almost hegemonic position in the discipline of economics. Its vitality has remained almost entirely intact, despite the retirements of several of its leading and most dramatic and effective figures, Milton Friedman and George Stigler (who died in 1991). Members of the School, both at the University of Chicago and elsewhere, continue to be honored with the Nobel Prize in economic science, most recently James M. Buchanan (at George Mason University) and Ronald H. Coase, and Gary Becker is a certain bet in the near future. The political and economic philosophy of the School found a home in the ideology and policies of the administrations of Ronald Reagan and George Bush. Whether the success of the School is due to the merit of its ideas, the hard work and/or personality of its members, or the spirit of the age, or some combination of these, the School is arguably the most successful in economics since World War Two.

The story that the Chicago School tells performs several specific functions. It attempts to describe, explain, and understand the economy. It seeks to perform the role of social control, in part, through its reenforcement and channelling of the dominant ideology and through influencing government policy (its ostensible noninterventionist ideology notwithstanding). It attempts to provide a psychic balm by which people can accept the market economy and its results without serious question, thus countering the, shall we say, natural tendency of people and groups to seek government solutions for common problems. And it attempts to legitimize economics as the putative queen of the social sciences, that is, to further enhance the status of economists and the social role of economists as persons of expert knowledge. The Chicago School has deliberately attempted to perform these roles, and it has done so very effectively, in both microeconomics and macroeconomics and in the various specialized fields of economics, by advancing its particular story. So-called new classical economics, is a logical extension of the fundamental Chicago School paradigm—though it also has sources outside of the School.

One of the themes of my contributions to this volume was the role of the received paradigm as the test of disciplinary value. Chicago School economists continue to be unreceptive to ideas and hypotheses that are not consonant with their fundamental paradigm, as manifest, for example, in the theory of tight prior equilibrium.

Part of the success of the School has been due to the tenacity with which it has advanced what Melvin W. Reder has called "tight prior equilibrium." This is "the hypothesis that decision makers so allocate the resources under their control that there is no alternative allocation such that any one decision maker could have his expected utility increased without a reduction occurring in the expected utility of at least one other decision maker."[1]

Notice some of the component elements of tight prior equilibrium theory: methodological individualism, an expected-utility maximizing theory of human behavior, given preferences, and the Pareto-optimality conception of collective welfare. Notice also that the theory is advanced as a hypothesis. A hypothesis is a conjecture offered as an explanation or a description. A hypothesis is a tool. The economic theory of the Chicago School is a set of tools with which to analyze the economy, and tools are not themselves either descriptions or explanations of reality.

During the last decade, in large part due to the work of Arjo Klamer and Donald McCloskey, and reflecting and absorbing postmodernist work in philosophy (for example, that of Richard Rorty), two arguments have become prominent in methodological discussions in economics. The first is that traditional epistemological beliefs in economics—in which, for example, hypotheses are subjected to tests within a prescriptive positivist protocol—exaggerate the conclusivity of the results of positivist science. The second is that all disciplines and all schools of thought within individual disciplines tell stories—stories that are not necessarily reflective of the object of analysis—and, moreover, that more than one story can properly be told about a common object. The Chicago School, therefore, must be understood as telling a story, a good story, but a story nonetheless, and not necessarily the absolute truth about the political economy. That, too, is one theme of this collection.

Another theme which runs throughout this volume is the limits of doctrines of the School. No theory can answer every question, though particular schools attempt to phrase their questions in a manner consonant with their particular perspective. So it is with the Chicago School. Every idea, every theory, every concept, every tool or technique has its limits; its meaningfulness is a function of both what it can and cannot do. But it seems typically incongruent with human nature, and the quest for status and social space, for scholars readily and effectively (except haltingly and largely only either pro forma or when prodded) to acknowledge and give credence to the limits of what they do. So it is with the Chicago School—and with all schools in economics.

Other than wishing, in retrospect, that the Reder article had been included, I generally have been satisfied with the collection. This may not mean much since I assembled it, and naturally should have both pride and bias, but if I were dissatisfied in any material way, I would say so. Yes, there could have been more attention to the economic imperialism led by Stigler and Becker (I tried but was unsuccessful) and to the offshoots of the Chicago School at other universities (I did not try). But no one book can cover everything. My greatest disappointment was my inability to recruit someone from within the School to contribute—though perhaps that might have been awkward.

The late Harry Johnson, of the University of Chicago, indicated that he was pleased with the job done, and the late George Stigler told me that he liked it. I had the impression that Stigler liked the attention given the Chicago School; to be given a critique is indeed a form of recognition, even of flattery. Perhaps a book that would have raised more hackles would have been preferable! But this one largely did what I wanted it to do, namely, present a constructive critique of its doctrines.

Chicago School theorists extol rigor and consistency. These criteria pertain to the exercise of deduction. That a conclusion correctly follows from its premises as a matter of logic means that the conclusion is valid. Its truth (meaning correct explanation or accurate description) is another matter.

It may be that in matters of government policy one cannot be consistent: Anti-interventionism does not mean the absence of government, generally only no legal change of law (and is only selectively followed). For example, deregulation is the functional equivalent of regulation in that both assign rights to parties, only different parties. And economists do tend to substitute their preferences for those of actual economic actors and to foreclose, in their analyses, the working out of actual economic processes, Chicago School economists no less than and perhaps more than others.

But the School tends to be consistent in another respect, and candid too, namely, its nonpandering attitude toward government. When the announcement came in October 1982 that Stigler, a sometime advisor to Ronald Reagan and a very candid person (even brutally so), was to be awarded the Nobel Prize in economic science, he was invited to the White House and gave, or was given, a press conference. Asked what he thought of "supply-side economics," the theory advanced by the administration, Stigler repled that it was "a gimmick, a slogan that was used to package certain ideas." After also saying in response to questions that his grade for Reagan-administration economic performance was "maybe an incomplete" and that the economy (contrary to official pronouncements in a period now recognized to have been a recession) was "bumping along the bottom, I assume," the power to the microphone was cut off. Just as one cannot properly charge against Karl Marx the excesses of Stalinism (and perhaps of central planning) of the former Soviet Union, which claimed him, and Lenin, as its philosophers, one cannot attribute to the Chicago School the economic, financial, political, and military scandals and blunders of the Reagan administration. If anything, those scandals lend credibility to the Chicago School critique of government, however ironically.

But the central tenets of the Chicago School are not about government; they are about the market. The tenets are that markets are ubiquitous and that markets by their very nature are competitive (other tenets involve the a priori acceptance of decision making through markets and the adverse consequences of government "intervention"[2]). There remain serious problems with these tenets, especially with regard to an economy which is arguably principally a vehicle of corporate interests. At various points in this volume the question of the role of Chicago School doctrines as social myth is discussed. The very notion of a "market" is at least a metaphor. The idea of the "market economy" may well be a myth,[3] and may simply represent a sterilized idealization of a set of economic arrangements in which business has power (going far beyond, though definitely not excluding, control over price) and that power—what would otherwise be the visible hand of business—is mystified, obfuscated, and legitimized by invocation of the invisible hand of the market. (The Pareto of Pareto optimality is, ironically, the author of a powerful analysis of the economy, including the market economy, as a system of power and mutual manipulation and of the role of ideologically driven theory in that process.[4]) Still, the microeconomic and macroeconomic analyses of markets is justifiably a central part of economics, though it cannot—it should not—be all there is to economics. Chicago School doctrine may serve nicely as psychic balm but there are other stories to tell, perhaps even better grounded in experience, though such a judgment is essentially subjective.

This volume has been out of print for some years. The Division of Research of the Graduate School of Business Administration at Michigan State University was a casualty of recession in 1981. The Division of Research also published the *Journal of Economic Issues* for the Association for Evolutionary Economics, the society of institutionalist economists, in whose pages some 60 percent of the contents of this volume originally appeared (see p. xvii). I continue to be thankful for the efforts of all who contributed to be the production of the book, especially, of course, the authors of the several chapters, and to Elizabeth Johnston, my production editor. And I am newly thankful to Transaction Publishers and to Irving Louis Horowitz, its president, for agreeing to this reprint edition. Horowitz is a distinguished political sociologist; perhaps it is scholars in that discipline who can best appreciate the social role of the Chicago School of political economy.

*Warren J. Samuels*

## *Notes*

1. Melvin W. Reder, "Chicago Economics: Permanence and Change," *Journal of Economic Literature*, vol. 20 (March 1982): 11. Reder's article is a gem of historical and analytical interpretation and should be read in conjunction with this volume.
2. It may well be that the fundamental limitation on Chicago School doctrines with regard to government is that they render nugatory the principles and perhaps the very existence of liberal representative democracy, the system of government which has tended to replace the predatory dynastic state in the modern world (including that of the Soviet Union, which mixed its Tsarist heritage with the economic doctrines and practices of a command economy), and thereby diminish the capabilities of a major institution of collective action—except, ironically, in military affairs.
3. William Lazonick, *Business Organization and the Myth of the Market Economy*, (New York: Cambridge University Press, 1991).
4. Vilfredo Pareto, *The Mind and Society*, 2 vols. (New York: Dover, 1963). See also Warren J. Samuels, *Pareto on Policy*, (New York and Amsterdam: Elsevier, 1974).

# Preface

This volume brings together articles, review articles, and book reviews from the December 1975 and March 1976 *Journal of Economic Issues,* which largely comprised a two-part symposium on the Chicago School. I have substituted an expanded introduction developing the type of constructive critique intended here and treating certain problems arising in the study of contemporary intellectual history. I also have added two chapters which constitute a comprehensive interpretation of the Chicago School's doctrines, and a note on socialism *vis-à-vis* the Chicago School.

I am deeply indebted to many persons, especially in connection with the preparation of the interpretation given in the chapters and note by me: to the JEI Editorial Board for suggestions; to all the contributors, including substantive correspondence with several of them; to James Buchanan and George Stigler for past correspondence; to Walter Adams, Bruce Allen, Byron Brown, Paul Ginsburg, Daniel Hamermesh, Glenn Johnson, Charles Larrowe, Carl Liedholm, Nicholas Mercuro, James Ramsey, Robert Rasche, Daniel Saks, Allan Schmid, Victor Smith, Robert Solo, and Daniel Suits for discussions both directly and indirectly bearing on the meaning and status of the Chicago School; and to Royall Brandis, John Henderson, Abraham Hirsch, Glenn Johnson, Carl Liedholm, Nicholas Mercuro, Allan Schmid, Paul Strassmann, and Harry Trebing for their reactions to an earlier draft of chapters 1, 16, and 17. I am especially grateful to Harry Trebing for his sage advice and cooperation in planning and executing the symposium. I would like to acknowledge reading and benefiting from papers by M. L. Myers, "Adam Smith's Concept of Equilibrium," and H. M. Thompson, "Economics: Universal Theory or Sacred Tale." I am indebted at every turn to Elizabeth Johnston for her stylistic and other suggestions. Finally, I must acknowledge my wife Sylvia's constant good humor and understanding during the several months that she lost her husband to this project.

The references cited in chapters 1, 16, 17, and 22 are listed on pages 519–25. Quotations cited in the epigraph may be found in the following: Stigler [quoted in Selden 1975, p. 321]; Veblen [1948, pp. 224–25]; Simons [1948, pp. 27, 33, and 318, n. 8]; and Patinkin [1973, p. 801].

# 1

# The Chicago School of Political Economy: A Constructive Critique

***Warren J. Samuels***

The purpose of this volume is to provide an interpretation of the Chicago School of political economy through constructive critique of its doctrines.[1] It is an inquiry into the nature, role, and significance of the school and its doctrines within both the economics profession and the larger world of ideas and action.[2] Central to the inquiry is an understanding of meaningfulness in terms of the combination of strengths and limits. I understand by "constructive critique" what in literary circles is thought of as criticism: the attempt to bring into focus the meaning of the nature, strengths, and limits of a body of ideas. In some respects the present effort may be deemed sympathetic; in others, unsympathetic. The school's affirmative contributions are recognized, as are the limits of its capacity to ground policy conclusions and recommendations. Implicit consideration is given to the reasons for acceptance and rejection of Chicago School doctrines, either of which must be largely a matter of faith. More important, the aim is to understand what is being said, what is not being said, and the bases and limits thereof. Hopefully, this volume will provide a deeper understanding of the Chicago School, of its strengths and weaknesses, and of the tasks of any body of thought which hopes to comprise an alternative.

The primary substance of this volume resides in the essays by other contributors. The purpose of my contributions is to provide personal conclusions concerning the interpretation and constructive critique of the Chicago School. Not all contributors will agree with everything I say, and it is unlikely that they would agree among themselves as to their own respective analyses, although their interpretations and conclusions converge on a number of important points. My conclusions are tentative, incomplete, and schematic. Only generalizations of lines of reasoning can be given, and references are held to a minimum. Nonetheless, I have some confidence that more elaborate presentation would sustain the interpretation. I acknowledge my desire to balance circumspection and accuracy, in part because of my wide areas of ignorance and lack of expertise and in part because of my strong feeling that it is beyond the capacity of any one interpreter fully to capture and articulate the meaning of a school of thought. The analysis given in my contributions is thus offered as one perspective on the Chicago School.

At this point it seems appropriate to elaborate on the philosophy underlying the objective of this venture. First, one of the roles of heterodoxy[3] is to unmask and to question the deepest levels of analysis and argument.[4] Its role is to promote the open discussion of deep and essential questions, to bring to the level of awareness critical elements of the cognitive system within which we operate willy nilly.

To present an interpretation and/or a constructive critique is not necessarily to agree or to disagree, to indict or to praise. Rather, such an effort should tend to elicit concurrence by both those who agree and those who disagree with the doctrines in question. Interpretation and critique should make explicit what each side respectively accepts and rejects. A correct interpretation ideally would present the doctrines and the limits assumed by virtue of the acceptance of the doctrines themselves. This is so although no single writer can fully capture the meaning of the body of doctrine.

No polemical broadside is intended here. Shrill criticism and slavish, patronizing idolatry are both to be avoided. The aim is to interpret doctrine through the articulation of strengths and limits which combine to produce the meaning of the Chicago School.[5] Distance without alienation is sought in order to produce understanding, not intellectual assassination. The symposium should raise more questions than it answers: questions concerning the substance upon which the Chicago School takes a position(s), questions of interpretation, and questions as to whether the authors have achieved the accuracy (not necessarily the objectivity) sought.

The very existence and the present interpretation of the Chicago School raise fundamental issues about economics as a profession, economics as a science, and the economy. These are questions with no ready answers, and each economist must work them out to his own satisfaction. Needless to say, Chicago doctrines, at their deepest level, provide a set of more or less unambiguous answers.

I should also indicate my belief in the complementarity of neoclassical and institutional economics. I have elaborated somewhat on this opinion elsewhere [Samuels 1972b], and Abraham Hirsch [1968] has presented this view quite cogently. In addition, there appear to be wide areas of substantive agreement between such seemingly conflicting writers as John R. Commons and Frank H. Knight.[6] More specifically, price theory *is* important for an understanding of resource allocation through market exchange, notwithstanding its limits and its capacity to serve as an ideological rationalization of the system. I would cast aside the rejection of orthodox economics (and economists) as the enemy (an unfortunate preoccupation of some heterodox economists); I share its pluralistic, free society values.[7]

The basic ideas stated by the Chicago School deal with such fundamental concerns and are often so attractive and congenial that some effort and pains are required to transcend them and envision reality as it is and as it would be if Chicago programs were put into effect: Conflicts as to specification of ideals and of visions of reality force one down to earth and to consider the deepest problems of social choice. Thus, Horace Gray [1973, p. 732] reports Oscar Wilde's comment on the French Communards of 1871:

> Those Christs upon the barricades!
> God knows I am with them—in some things!

The critique of libertarian thought creates the danger that one will appear statist,[8] although I hope that the analysis here is on such a level and is sufficiently clear that no such careless inference will be made.[9]

### *Neoclassical and Chicago Economics*

One problem which impinges upon the subject of this symposium concerns the relation of the Chicago School to neoclassical economics. It seems clear that Chicago (as the term is used) is neoclassicist. The school sees itself, however, as heterodox within or *vis-à-vis* the rest of (orthodox) economics. It is fair to say that certain beliefs held by members of the Chicago School also are held by a wider range of economists [see Wall 1972, p. vii]. Regardless of the range of individuals contemplated, there are always general characteristics or uniformities of analysis coupled with individual idiosyncracies [again see Wall 1972, pp. vii–viii]. The Chicago School represents the extreme vanguard of neoclassicism. It is the foremost ideological extension of that area of economics, representing its most conservative tendency, manifest in part by its emphasis upon Pareto optimality. It is characterized by a greater-than-average belief in the neoclassical analysis and therefore by its substantial efforts to push that analysis into newer applications. In comparison with general neoclassicism, however, the work of the Chicago School comes closer to institutional economics in its attention to the problem of organization and control of the economic system.

Some of the interpretation and critique which follows applies to neoclassical orthodoxy as a whole as well as to the Chicago School. (Chapter 3, by Robert Solo, attempts to place neoclassicism in perspective as prelude for further consideration of the Chicago School.) Just how the application is to be made must be left to the individual economist. Neoclassical economics is a meaningful cognitive system which largely governs the consciousness of most English-speaking economists, and it, too, as a whole requires the type of constructive critique here given its Chicago variant.

The potential fecundity of neoclassical economics is indicated by the recent applications of its basic concepts and theory, through the addition of, perhaps, more realistic assumptions, to produce quite different conclusions. In particular, the work of Randall Bartlett [1973] is a brilliant example of how neoclassical economics can be used to produce Galbraithian if not Marxian conclusions. That is, quite aside from such labels, Bartlett offers a penetrating analysis of how economic and political markets operate in a context of inequality, following the leads of Mancur Olson and Anthony Downs.[10]

To emphasize the ideological character of the Chicago School and general neoclassicism is to state a characteristic of all intellectual systems in the social sciences. Each is a mixture of description, heuristic capacity, and selective ideological and/or personal idiosyncratic preferences.

The Chicago School is not (or is not yet) the mainstream of economics or even of neoclassicism, but it does bid to dominate in matters of both theory and policy. The impact of the Chicago School is represented by the wide influence enjoyed by Pareto optimality in general neoclassical economics as more than an interpretive pricing rule (even though it is but one way of formulating or interpreting an equilibrium condition), as well as by other salient ground which enterprising Chicagoans have marked out and which has come to represent the profession's most conspicuous treatment of the relevant topics (for example, externalities, information theory, human capital, crime). The rise in prominence of the Chicago School may be an indication of crisis or anxiety within neoclassicism regarding the viability of the economics profession or the Western economic system. In any case, elements of the Chicago conservative defense account for many theoretical contributions and constitute important differences between it and general neoclassical economics, however many of the contributions are accepted or even cited by other neoclassicists.

### *Is There a Chicago School?*

A second problem which impinges upon this venture concerns the designation of "Chicago" as a school of economic thought. Is there a Chicago School? What is the relation(s) between the old and the new Chicago School? Who is to be included in the current (as well as historic) Chicago School? These are questions which are impossible to resolve conclusively, and while the position taken here is very simple (and question-begging), they do deserve some consideration [see Miller 1962; Stigler 1962; and Bronfenbrenner 1962].

The older Chicago School included most notably Frank Knight, Henry Simons, and Jacob Viner. For present purposes, their relation to contemporary Chicagoans includes not only much fundamental common doctrine, but also significant differences in practice, policy recommendations, theory, and methodology. The heart of the matter is that the older Chicagoans recognized complexities and problems which are denied, minimized, forgotten, and/or ruled out of bounds by contemporary Chicagoans. The fundamental Chicago doctrines apparently are maintained even while recognizing these complexities and problems. In part this is a result of subtler (or cleverer) articulation of fundamental doctrine; in part, it is a result of tactical adoption of more defensible positions given the new context of argument and debate. (In juxtaposing the old and the new Chicago, one cannot overstress the extent to which the style of the rest of the profession, as well as its intellectual and policy environment, has changed.)

As for the problem of the Chicago School's current membership, here the term will apply to all who subscribe to and practice its fundamental doctrines; in short, to all whom it fits and to the extent that it fits, whatever their place of employment. Needless to say, many and significant variations on details are to be expected, especially when dealing with the fundamental problems of economic control and change which are the generic substance of Chicago doctrines. "Chicago" is multifaceted and even kaleidoscopic: It includes many individuals, each typically working in several specialized areas of economics, each with distinctive angles of approach and twists of analysis. The outcome is a complex set of results, even for any one individual of any breadth of professional activity. The school's members are working out a body of thought, not rehearsing a given body of revelation. As Knight might say, the school is engaged in an exploration, and the results are emergent, however great the continuity and hold of fundamental doctrine.

But the overriding question is whether or not there is in fact *a* Chicago School. On this point, one can only agree with common usage and acknowledgment. Milton Friedman has said: "The term is used sometimes as an epithet, sometimes as an accolade, but always with a fairly definite—though by no means single-valued—meaning" [Friedman 1974, p. 11; see Selden 1975, pp. 2–4, and below]. The existence of a Chicago School can be treated as a hypothesis, and here it is taken as an operating premise. (The school is already in the history of economic thought texts; see Spiegel [1971, pp. 641–42].)

Apropos the notion of a "school," in passing it should be noted that the sociological character of science is a seriously neglected topic. At least insofar as economic inquiry is concerned, the insight of Thomas Kuhn [1962] in this regard (*vis-à-vis* his work on paradigms and scientific revolution per se) has not been pursued as far as it might [see Ward 1972, pp. 7–13 and passim]. On the subject of recruitment, membership is a function of several variables: professional training; political posture; the professional incentive and reward system governing career advancement, such as publication; and so on. Some economists are attracted by the perceived explanatory power of Chicago economics and practice it scientifically without conscious effort to adopt or apply its normative elements. Chicago fanaticism, so-called, is a function of a number of behavior patterns: ego involvement, professional identity, political preferences, and, *inter alia,* the debater or adversary mentality. In short, recruitment is a function of several selection mechanisms. (One might say that recruitment through the market is always optimal.) The school obviously centers at the University of Chicago, but there are several satellite departments in other universities, and acolytes, sympathizers, and kindred spirits, both conscious and unconscious, are scattered throughout the profession. Many provide mutual reinforcement, in part through mutual citation.[11]

A "school" does have relatively homogeneous views on important questions, including what is considered to be important, forming a fairly coherent philosophy or position on relevant issues which differs somewhat from most others [Stigler 1962, p. 70]. For present purposes, then, there is a Chicago School, possessing a distinctive paradigm, a general metaphysical orientation or point of view, and a conceptual framework of research that influences the nature of the problems and types of questions it will consider and the terms of that consideration. As a school of economic thought, it manifests a general attitude and a body of doctrine concerning the organization and control of the economic system. Although there is much conflict within the school as to how and where to develop its doctrines (as well as between egos), there nonetheless is a dedicated belief in the rightness of those doctrines.[12]

With regard to the members of the Chicago School, they obviously are not to be castigated as evil and mean-spirited persons; nor are they saints. They are typically individuals of intelligence, skill, and ability. There are the great and the rank and file. Their writings arc mixtures of charm and abrasiveness, solidity and cleverness, brilliance and disingenuousness, analysis and propaganda. But all are describing the world as they see it, and they sincerely believe that their ideal is not only practicable, but also likely to serve the interests of all, including the least advantaged persons in society (to use the Rawlsian formulation). In most, if not all, of these respects, the Chicago School is like any other.

Apropos the problem of "Chicago" as a school, then, the interpretations to follow apply to all whom they fit. The contributors to the symposium were left free to define and populate the school as they individually chose, and there undoubtedly is some (and perhaps much) heterogeneity of viewpoint among them.

### *Problems of Interpretation*

There are two aspects of interpretation upon which I should briefly expand. First, it is my general view that the highest level of understanding or meaning is ultimately a function of the matrix formed by the intra- and extrasystemic interpretations and cross-critiques provided by advocates of rival systems; in other words, the matrix is formed by the ways in which each school sees itself, is seen and criticized by others, and criticizes others in return [Samuels 1974b, pp. 319–20 and passim]. It is beyond the capacity of this symposium, and certainly of my contributions, to achieve such a complete composite result. One can only hope for a set of solid contributions thereto, with no pretense of exclusivism or finality. The Chicago School ultimately must be understood in terms of the totality of different conceptions of economy, economics, and "the social problem." Such understanding is obviously complicated by the heterogeneity of the status quo and the diversity of perspectives from which to view both the school and the status quo [Samuels 1974b, pp. 306–18]. For example, Solo's analysis below with regard to *essence* can be seen as indicating that some of us perceive certain economic phenomena as market adjustments, while others see them in terms of power and power play. These are different specifications of the world and are *not necessarily* better or worse, correct or incorrect, or, for that matter, mutually exclusive! What can be said in terms of one often can be said in terms of the other, given appropriate translation formulas [Samuels 1974b, pp. 320–22].

Second, I believe there are three inevitable dimensions of economic thought: Economics is a blend of knowledge (of one epistemological type or another), social control, and psychic balm.[13] Economics caters to our need for certainty, order, and coherence; to our need for a philosophy of social control, an ideology providing a selective attitude toward the status quo, as social criticism and legitimation (a fundamental social process). This view of economics is a key to the interpretation of the Chicago School which I offer.

### *Chicago Doctrine*

In part because I was unable to secure an article more or less authoritatively articulating the Chicago view of its doctrines, it seems that a general summary of the Chicago position should be provided. It may be left to others to decide, if they feel the need, whether or not it is objective, accurate, and sympathetic or unsympathetic.

Friedman's own summary of Chicago's "fairly definite—though by no means single-valued—meaning" provides a useful starting point:

> In discussions of economic policy, "Chicago" stands for belief in the efficacy of the free market as a means of organizing resources, for scepticism about government intervention into economic affairs, and for emphasis on the quantity of money as a key factor in producing inflation.
>
> In discussions of economic science, "Chicago" stands for an approach that takes seriously the use of economic theory as a tool for analyzing a startlingly wide range of concrete problems, rather than as an abstract mathematical structure of great beauty but little power; for an approach that insists on the empirical testing of theoretical generalizations and that rejects alike facts without theory and theory without facts.[14]

Some of these beliefs have been discussed by David Wall: "First, that theory is of fundamental importance; second, that theory is irrelevant unless set in a definite empirical context; and third, that in the absence of evidence to the contrary, the market works."[15]

In matters of political economy, then, the Chicago School would establish a presumption in favor of the market, that is, for market solutions. The market is, for all practical purposes, equated with the economic, as opposed to the political, order. Chicagoans do recognize government policy as an important factor in the operation of the economy, for example, in the rate and structure of economic development [Wall 1972, p. ix]. They are aware of ostensible limits to markets and market solutions, of nonmarket bases of the market, and of the role of legal and moral rules. Nevertheless, they believe in the power of market organization and its virtues in comparison with nonmarket (namely, governmental) organization of economic activity. They believe that market theory (price theory) adequately represents fundamental economic reality on both positive and normative grounds. They are antagonistic to the use of government as reformer and panacea for ostensible "problems." They believe in the market system and voluntary exchange as the most efficient and most widely equitable modes of organizing human activity. They believe that the power of business and personal wealth in the market is greatly exaggerated by critics; that especially in comparison with alternative power concentration in government, such power in the market is in fact quite diffused. In a sense, the ultimate Chicago position is that the market system, whatever its structure of power (say, within a reasonable range), possesses *inherently* more power diffusion than any alternative system. Thus Aaron Director wrote of Simons's belief in "the decentralization of power inherent in a free-market system" [Simons 1948, p. vi]. Chicagoans believe that the forces and organization of the market system do not require independent (conscious) control, yet produce productive and optimal allocations of resources and the highest levels of economic welfare. Alongside the foregoing is a presumption in favor of status quo arrangements insofar as they contribute to a viable market economy and a belief that maintenance of such a status quo would minimize coercion (defined as legal change or social change through law) in order to permit voluntary choice and exchange.

In considering these ideas it is necessary and important to avoid stereotype, caricature, and straw men. The Chicago School takes subtle positions on complex intellectual problems, both positive and normative, dealing ultimately with basic social questions relating to but also transcending the status quo and the economic role of government [see Buchanan and Samuels 1975]. Yet, fully avoiding caricaturization here is difficult for several reasons: (1) the size and complexity of the subject matter; (2) the emotional content, that is, the heavy ideological element;[16] (3) limited space; and, *inter alia,* (4) the ease with which the

Chicago School position does in fact reduce to stereotype, in part because of the self-admitted and intentional propaganda role of Chicago spokesmen.[17]

It is easy to charge the Chicago School with "neglecting" this or that qualification, but two points should be made. First, such neglect should be seen not as a failure necessarily to consider the objection, but as a result of Chicagoans having opted for a consideration deemed weightier, more important, or more strategic to their cause, perhaps only simply more interesting. Second, this neglect means that there are limits to the Chicagoans' doctrines which follow from their own choices and viewpoint. In a profound sense they "know" and "accept" the problems of and limits to their analysis and argument. Although they often will readily deny them, on the deepest level they seem ready to count them as so many opportunity costs, or so can be inferred if Knight is juxtaposed to the current members of the school, who must be presumed to "know their Knight."

The positions they take thus open them to charges (say, of "neglect") which, while they may be denied or rejected as a matter of tactics or argument, they must be and (one strongly presumes, after much thought and some interaction) are prepared to accept. The critical point is that on things which they seem to neglect they really are taking a position, perhaps typically with the effect of minimizing or defining away its importance.[18] One must get to the fundamentals of their doctrines, that is, below the level of stereotypes (including those of their own manufacture), to see this. Needless to say, I am not fully convinced that I have completely done so.

### *Chicago's Contributions*

The work and doctrines of the Chicago School have not only limits but also strengths, and these not solely in the school's own terms. Chicago has made substantial and rigorous, if controversial, contributions to theory and empirical work. Members of the school are among the master technicians and major innovators of the profession.

Chicagoans have contributed to a greater and more explicit sense of coherence of economic theory, in part by placing great stress on internal consistency and empirical verification, to the point of clarifying—at least to the relatively objective observer—the limits of the theory.

Another contribution has been the fecundity of Chicago's normative system in generating scientific hypotheses which do not always depend upon the school's normative position, such that its descriptive and explanatory analyses can be integrated with the constructive work of others.[19]

Notwithstanding the general disrepute of explicit paradigm development work in economics, the Chicago School has contributed to the formulation of a paradigm of economic order.

The school has contributed a spirited defense of orthodox neoclassical economics, helping the latter become cemented as the dominant body of economic thought,[20] thus enhancing, also, the status and identity of economics in the neoclassical mold.

Chicago has contributed to our understanding of the operation of markets. Prices *are* important in choosing. Also, while it has overidealized the market, which is not a magical black box, it has nonetheless shown how static resource allocation theory can contribute to the understanding of system evolution: Both system operation and evolution are a partial function of allocative short-run decision making affecting the structure of opportunity sets over time and thereby the structure, direction, and rate of institutional and input-output growth and development.

The school has made fecund applications of the micro model of market or market-like adjustments to a wide range of institutional and other arrangements in which calculations of advantage—considerations of constrained maximization—seem to permeate and help explain both their adoption and operation. According to the Chicago view, perhaps all areas of life are subject to the analysis of maximizing or calculations of advantage.[21] Thus the school has stressed, in its own way, that the economy operates within and is profoundly influenced by legal and moral rules which are themselves a function of considerations of advantage. In this scheme, maximization is not necessarily of some economic quantity (say, profits) but of whatever goal(s) or advantage the individual or subgroup has in view, reduced for technical purposes to expected net wealth increase or the like. As part of this the Chicago School has made interesting positive analyses of the role or use of government, as well as other institutions. For example, the legal system is shown to have market-like features (and not always the intended or anticipated ones), and legal change is examined as producing behavioral reactions and adjustments. Chicagoans thereby have contributed to our understanding of political behavior and performance, underscoring the realistic insight that government is subject to constrained maximization analysis, that it is not a black box, but is subject to analysis as an economic alternative and arena of constrained maximization decision making. Although their analysis has severe limits, they have brought to light and subjected to critical inquiry important elements of legal-economic interrelations, for example, political influence, the demand for and supply of regulation, and transaction costs. The Chicago analysis of institutions has extended to crime, the family, and, *inter alia,* the demand and supply of ideological behavior [Stigler, in Selden 1975, pp. 314ff]. If anything, the Chicago School does not go far enough in this direction, generally stopping short of analyzing the genesis of extant property rights and business arrangements with regard to the past economic use of government (see Martin's chapter 13 and chapter 17), something I attribute to a lack of interest derived from their normative orientation.

The school has articulated the philosophical-ideological bases and (in its view) essential features of the market economy and society. In developing the rationale of the market system it has helped clarify how that system operates and what acceptance of it means. In so doing, it has forced consideration of deep aspects of the socioeconomic fabric, while emphasizing the need for the proper legal system and set of institutions deemed necessary to make markets work.

Chicago has contributed a sophisticated, if sometimes evasive and merely clever, defense of the market system. It thus has made important contributions to the social valuational process as a voice of libertarian and conservative[22] (ostensibly nineteenth-century liberal) social thought and of the normative neoclassical paradigm. An example is its stress on inflation, one of the social problems of greatest substantive and strategic importance to conservatives, as well as others. It has articulated an idealized version of the status quo, projected as the market system, as the putative basis for social critique and policy.

Through its distinctive blend of positive and normative analysis, the Chicago School has made interesting if not always important, as well as controversial, contributions to both the analysis and strategy of economic policy. Often ingenious proposals have been made for directing government policy to increase opportunities for private gain or choice and intended thereby to increase the scope of the market's working. Members have not been above suggesting possibilities for manipulating the incentive system to engage private calculations of advantage in the achievement of some goal deemed socially desirable (say, greater agricultural output in less developed nations). Conversely, Chicagoans have pointed (often with unconcealed delight) to deficiencies in government policies and programs—deficiencies which should be important from the viewpoint of the programs' partisan advocates.

The contribution of perhaps most profound significance has been Chicago's emphasis upon the use of the market as a regulatory system. Markets exist, and they may be, in a sense, a cheaper and freer mode of organizing activity and solving problems than likely alternatives. Whatever the limits of a presumption in favor of the market, or of market solutions, Chicago doctrines emphasizing the freedom of the market *vis-à-vis* all alternative systems, the avoidance of information and other problems of centralized decision making, and so on, serve to remind us of the possibilities of the market. Not all institutionalists, for example, find these possibilities repugnant [see Martin 1974b].

The contribution of most immediate or practical significance is corollary to the emphasis on the market: frequently reiterated cautions against reliance upon governmental solutions to problems. In particular, the Chicago School has emphasized the following: the dangers of permitting the venting of all prejudices and narrow interests through government; the likelihood of incongruity and failure to achieve desired results; the sensibleness of an opportunity cost analysis *vis-à-vis* emotional wishful thinking about government policies; the dangers of relying upon a crisis approach to problems, since the perception of crisis tends to induce ill-advised resort to government, among other things; the *non sequitur* of implying the desirability or necessity of government intervention from a perception of market failure; government policy and its changes are a function of alterations in political and economic power which are not necessarily desirable; skepticism as to the possibility of changing people and overcoming problems by altering the form of economic institutions through law; and so on. Chicagoans have caused us to pause in our ready acceptance of government solutions. In reminding us that government may be a nemesis and is not a neutral black box, they have played a great role in demythicizing government and have produced a greater and more healthy skepticism concerning its economic role.[23]

## *Notes*

1. The title intentionally uses "political economy" and not "economics": Chicago is not a school solely of economics (meaning economic theory) or of economic science (notwithstanding its pretensions of positivism), for it is self-admittedly (1) heavily infused with certain values and (2) directed at prescribing certain legal-economic relations, that is, the economic role of government. The school recently has been referred to as "the Chicago school of libertarian economics" [Foley 1975, p. 231].
2. An analysis of the Chicago School of sociology is given by James Carey [1975].
3. On the hallmarks of orthodoxy, see Richard H. Day [1975, pp. 229–31].

4. I am not fully convinced that orthodox economics, which (as the recent flood of articles from within the ranks of eminent neoclassical theorists attests) badly requires critiquing, is totally insensitive to reasoned criticism and interpretation.
5. The spirit of the symposium is indicated by the following excerpts from the letter sent in 1974 to invited contributors.

> The December 1975 symposium of the JEI will be devoted to a constructive critique of the Chicago School. This letter is written to explore your possible participation in the symposium.
>
> The meaning of any analytical technique or school of thought depends upon its particular strengths and weaknesses, however equivocal. The combination thereof defines what it can and cannot do, its limits. Each school of thought poses and answers questions on its own terms; its heuristic value—part of its meaningfulness—is governed thereby. A school of economic thought, given the heterogeneity which marks most if not all schools, has its limits governed by its ideological structure and role, by the range and structure of its admitted variables, and, *inter alia,* by the problems which it defines as interesting and the way it formulates and goes about their analysis. The planned symposium will attempt to provide a constructive critique—identify and interpret the limits—of the Chicago School's economics.
>
> Each article must be comprehensive and highly sophisticated in its area. It must avoid narrowness and minutiae and deal directly with fundamentals. Above all, it cannot be a polemical broadside; rather, it should be constructive in identifying the limits and their significance. I must reserve the right to reject manuscripts that do not conform to the intended critical standards.

6. It is my intent eventually to write a book interpreting and exploring the areas of agreement and grounds of disagreement between Commons and Knight. To the same end, for example, compare the following. Edwin Witte wrote: "To find the solution of economic policy problems, the institutional set-up must be understood. Institutions cannot be taken for granted, as they are man-made and changeable. Changes in the working rules are possible and occur frequently, although normally only slowly. Institutional economists . . . do not rule out the possibility of changes in institutions [Witte 1954, pp. 134–35]. Frank Knight wrote: "Human society must always be largely of the original institutional character; custom and habit must rule most of what people feel, think, and do. Institutions . . . are more or less explained historically rather than scientifically and are little subject to control" [Knight 1957, p. 20].
7. See Hirsch [1968, pp. 81, 82, 86]. Also see Trebing [1969, p. 90, n. 6]; and Knight [1960, p. 82; 1952 pp. 46, 50, 51, 52, 53]. For exam-

ples of recent institutionalist critique of neoclassicism, see Martin [1974] and Melody [1974]. For an institutionalist use of neoclassical tools, see Klein [1973].

8. See James Buchanan's [1972] reaction to an earlier article of mine.
9. For my own views on the state, see Samuels [1974c] and Buchanan and Samuels [1975].
10. The close historical association of neoclassical (especially Austrian) economics with conservative (nineteenth-century liberal) or libertarian philosophy has produced the idea that neoclassicism per se is an apologetics for the status quo capitalist system. Benjamin Ward [1972, pp. 72, 77, 84, 85, 87] and Howard Sherman [1975, p. 247], among others, have identified or labeled neoclassicism as a ruler economics, or an establishment economics, suitable for whatever status quo is taken for granted. There *is* a general tendency for mutual luster to be cast between a theory and the system it purports to explain, but this need not be the case, as the work of Bartlett [1973] and others attests. There is a heavier proportion of apologetics in the Chicago version of neoclassicism than in neoclassicism in general. There is also a neoclassical underworld (from a Chicago perspective) of critical accounts of status quo phenomena, for example, A.C. Pigou on exploitation and externalities (to which, of course, Chicagoans object; *per contra,* many criticisms were well known to and in a sense accepted by the older Chicagoans such as Frank Knight and Henry Simons).
11. This is but one example of the tendency noted by Joseph Spengler "of like-minded economists to take in one another's verbal wash" [Spengler 1974, p. 529]. Spengler also quotes George Stigler: "Perhaps their most common error is to believe other economists" [Spengler 1974, p. 542]. Mutual citation is, of course, one practice which enables the charting of invisible colleges.
12. Friedman [1974, p. 14] insists that the Chicago School is not a closed-minded cult. I would say that schools are generally religious, that is, absolutist, in their analysis, at least in that they do not overdo the public discussion of the limits of their doctrine. They also tend to be sectarian, at least in their condescension toward those who do not share their views and in their evaluation of the work of others. This evaluation is done largely if not wholly from their own point of view and on their own terms, for example, restating conflicting work (assuming it is dealt with in public at all) in a manner intended to make it safe for the school's doctrine or (to use the lawyers' expression) as a "distinguished aside." These remarks apply generally (and I hope not unfairly) to the Chicago School, but by no means do they fully describe the professional posture of its members. The remarks also apply generally (and again I hope not unfairly) to institutionalists.

    Following the school's own proclivity to apply demand and supply analysis wherever it can, I hope it is not considered gratuitous (or worse) to say that the members of the school, by their own doctrine, seek and enjoy acclaim and professional and worldly status (a key argument of professional utility functions), although this does not suffice to explain the adoption of their ideas, no more than does the use of constrained maximization analysis in formal theory fully identify the substance of utility functions.

Apropos what I have to say below concerning the school's doctrinal activism and adversary role, I am taken by the statement that "Frank Knight was one of the last prominent economists to avoid all significant connections with the political and business worlds" [Anonymous 1973, p. 1048].

13. See Samuels [1974b, pp. 314–18]; Shackle [1967, chapters 1, 2, and (especially) 18]; Robinson [1962, chapter 1 and passim]; and many other sources, including works by John Dewey, Karl Mannheim, and John Kenneth Galbraith.
14. "These denotations of the Chicago school of economics are of long standing. They have prevailed for decades, with only minor, though not negligible, changes in meaning, despite a complete change in the persons regarded as the 'leaders' of the school" [Friedman 1974, p. 11]. The article quoted was given as an address to the Board of Trustees of the University of Chicago.
15. Wall [1972, p. vii]. Wall later cautions against

> the common error of assuming that the third component of the Chicago "credo" is a belief that "the market mechanism always works,' when in fact the relevant belief is that "*in the absence of evidence to the contrary* the market works." In this context the phrase "the market works" should be taken to mean that in specified situations, unimpeded competitive forces will lead to the most efficient and *potentially* most equitable allocation of the world's scarce resources. In general this implies that normal economic behavior will usually ensure that competitive forces will lead to levels of output, from given resources, which will reduce the distortionary effect of given absolute amounts of socially desired income transfers [Wall 1972, pp. xv–xvi].

(The latter of course must be read in the context of his discussion, but the general point is clear, if controversial. Wall's statement about potentiality is a good example of the need to juxtapose stress upon the market to recognized limits.) I give a somewhat different interpretation to the "market works" principle below. On Wall's qualification (to the same effect), see Knight [1956, pp. 16, 17]. The Chicago position is also summarized in Selden [1975, pp. 2–4 and passim].

16. I feel that I must repeat an earlier caution: The identification of the ideological character of the Chicago School or of its limitations does *not* (1) deny the ideological character or limits of schools holding the opposite or different doctrines; (2) mean that I agree with some presumed opposite view; or (3) with respect to critique of the Chicago School doctrines concerning government, necessarily signify belief in interventionism.
17. I should say, and again hope it is not thought gratuitous or offensive, that I find Knight's many writings more satisfactory (notwithstanding disagreements with him) than Friedman's *Capitalism and Freedom*, largely because the latter seems designed as a propaganda tract and the

former were not. I suppose, too, that the meaning or message of a school tends to be reduced, perhaps through an equivalent of Gresham's law, to its epigrammatic formulation. The Chicago School, through its propaganda activity and facade of ideological purism, tends to encourage this.

18. Many phenomena are played down because of a belief that the market will better promote economic welfare notwithstanding such facts, for example, class, than any alternative system.
19. This is essentially Joan Robinson's [1962] theme of metaphysical doctrine enabling the formulation of scientific hypotheses. The main point has been made in connection with the Virginia branch of the Chicago School by Mancur Olson and Christopher Clague [1971, p. 754].
20. In discussions with colleagues on the status of the Chicago School and its relation to general neoclassical economics, I found this range of opinion: Chicago is different from general neoclassicism; it is perhaps an extreme, almost freakish, version; it may come to dominate (and should or should not); it has come to dominate; and it *is* neoclassicism.
21. Hopefully, it is not gratuitous (again!) to say that I feel the Chicago extensions and applications of the micro model to the so-called noneconomic areas is intended and certainly functions to strengthen and legitimize the neoclassical fortress.
22. It may be somewhat disingenuous but certainly understandable for the Chicago School to emphasize how radical (and not conservative) it is with regard to institutional change: The institutions it wants to change or eliminate (whatever else can be said about their functioning) are seen by many others to moderate the asymmetrical and unfair operation and performance of the economic system to which the Chicago School would ostensibly return [see Baran 1963, p. 593]. Friedman's negative income tax would substitute for the welfare state; like the latter, it would not directly strike at the unequal structure of social power. It is only a cheaper—more efficient—way of attempting to buy off (keep docile) the poor.
23. Yet their own doctrinaire posture opens them to the charge that they suffer from a lack of adequate skepticism about their own beliefs. Criticism of government ineptitude is an important critical role; defining problems away through the manipulation of definitions and assumptions is something else. The Pareto rule, for example, functions to eliminate or abort the important issues of policy, the ones involving negative sum and uncompensated changes. Their adoption of the rule seems coupled with a willingness to accept the usual criticism, for example, that it canonizes the status quo. George Stigler [1965, chapter 4] has emphasized, if not boasted, that professional training in economics makes one conservative. Yet, a case can be made that it need not do so (although it may attract conservatives), only create cautious or constructive skeptics. Thus Chicago's emphasis on inept government policy, say, that policies ostensibly designed to help the poor or disadvantaged tend to help the rich or advantaged and actually may hinder and further disadvantage the former, a lesson reinforced by Boulding and Pfaff [1972], may serve, without the Chicago catechism, of course, to under-

score the necessity for truly fundamental change in property and legal relations in order to effectuate meaningful revision of the hierarchical power and distributive structures and processes of society. Inadvertently, Chicagoans point to the necessity of fundamental rather than cosmetic or dissembling change.

# 2

# What Is Structuralism? Piaget's Genetic Epistemology and the Varieties of Structuralist Thought

***Robert A. Solo***

This article will attempt to survey and interpret *structuralism,* or, as some would have it, "French Structuralism," an amorphous, multifaceted, and complex phenomenon, without a disciplinary boundary or any established authority to settle controversies concerning it. This interpretation will be based, alas, on the limited experience of one who can claim expertise neither in linguistics, psychology, nor anthropology, where structuralist thought has had its greatest impact.

The essay will be divided into five parts. The first will suggest the rationale of the conscious, partially organized structuralist movement with its recognized masters and committed disciples, research centers and institutes, and niches in university curricula. The second will consider the need for a structuralist movement in economics. The third will examine those bodies of thought that have developed spontaneously and independently here and there over the spectrum of the disciplines sharing an analytic approach or outlook that can be identified as structuralist; that is, abstracting from the structuralist movement, the character of structuralist thought will be specified, with Jean Piaget's psychology taken as its prototype. The fourth part reviews and compares structuralist thought in anthropology, linguistics, the history and philosophy of science, and literary criticism. The fifth suggests the peculiar relevance

---

*The author is Professor of Economics, Michigan State University, East Lansing.*

of structuralist thought in postindustrial societies, with particular reference to the economic situation and the situation in economics.

### *The Structuralist Movement*

Our starting point in considering both structuralist thought and the structuralist movement is the career of Jean Piaget. Born in 1896, he began his scientific work studying marine life in the lakes of his native Switzerland. Papers published in his early teens earned Piaget an international reputation as a marine biologist. In due course he became a professor of the history of science and a professor of philosophy in Swiss universities. It was, however, through his studies of child learning that Piaget has become recognized as perhaps the greatest living psychologist.

Ours is a time of proliferating new sciences, each with its peculiar problem locii, assumptions, presuppositions, conventions, and established fields of controversy. Most of those who travel one of the many avenues of science are oblivious to what is said, thought, and done by others on another path. Not Piaget. Wearing at once the hats of philosopher and experimental psychologist, he could not help but know that what the philosophers of knowledge, that is, the epistemologist, pronounced as true, ruled out *a priori* his psychological findings. What he had to say as a psychologist was shut off from the philosopher's discourse on the mind. It was this contradiction that led him to organize the structuralist *movement*. His rationale for doing so is developed in *Logique et connaissance scientifique*.[1] He holds that the split between epistemology, that is, the disciplined reflection on the character of knowledge, and empirical science, that is, the disciplined effort to generate knowledge, is relatively recent. It is at one with the general fragmentation of thought into specializations without link or overlap, but is in this instance peculiarly pernicious because it denies to reflection that experience necessary for the challenge and test of epistemological theory and doctrine. Those philosophers who greatly contributed to epistemological thought, such as Aristotle or Descartes, were scientists as well; they derived their ideas concerning knowledge in general from their experience in producing it in the particular. In modern times, too, it is from empirical science, even though denuded of the disciplined capacity to reflect upon itself, that significant advance in epistemological thought has come. Philosophical reflection, detached from the feedback of experience, has been sterile.

Piaget divides the subject matter of epistemology into three parts.

There is, first, logic, specifying the conditions of coherence and consistency and developing systems of inference. Logic merges into and becomes mathematics. It is mathematics and not epistemology that has extended significantly the modern understanding of the conditions of coherence and that has developed important new systems of inference.

A second facet of epistemology, associated with the philosophy of science, involves the scientific method, the manner of conceptualizing experience, the character of "scientific" truth, the means of verifying or falsifying statements and, hence, establishing their credibility. In this regard the thought of academic philosophers has long been impaled on an idealized image of classical mechanics.[2] Meanwhile, empirical science has changed its forms. Confronted with new dimensions of experience, such as subatomic phenomena, it has developed different criteria of credibility and another conceptualizing apparatus. Not the epistemologists, but historians such as Herbert Butterfield, Thomas Kuhn, and Michel Foucault have advanced significantly our understanding of the real nature of this scientific enterprise and its constraints.

The final facet of epistemology is thought concerning thought itself, that is, the process of learning and the character of knowing or becom-
understood as a theory of the mind. Here it suffices that, inasmuch as hy-
ing aware, which can, at the level of the individual at least, be
pothesis can be put to experimental test, the matter belongs not to philosophy, but to experimental psychology.

Thus, according to Piaget, mathematics is best equipped to determine the conditions of coherence and to develop systems of inference, the conceptualization of phenomena and of the means of determining the verity of statement absolutely requires a feedback of experience that only empirical science can supply, and the character of learning and knowing are properly the subject of experimental psychology. Therefore, nothing of epistemology remains as a domain proper to academic philosophy, speaking *ex cathedra* on the theory of the mind, or pronouncing with Olympian detachment on what is and what is not properly "scientific." Instead, Piaget argues, a disciplined thought concerning thought and a systematic reflection on the source and character of knowledge should be integrated back into each of the empirical sciences with a new, overarching epistemology. This latter will help the empirical sciences to learn from each other, act as a nexus between them, and seek to generalize upon and find a more universal expression for that which comes out of disciplined self-reflection.

Thus, the structuralist movement can be understood as the demand for, and an effort to create, a new epistemological inquiry, geared into, and organized as, a disciplined reflection upon the epistemological concerns of each of the empirical sciences. Following this rationale, locii of epistemological inquiry have been established in a diversity of academic disciplines in France, and in Geneva, the Institute of Genetic Epistemology, organized under Piaget's direction, brings together representatives of virtually all the sciences to collaborate on matters of general epistemological concern.

Piaget has strong ideas as to the substantive content of the epistemology he envisages as a bridge overarching the disciplines.[3] No doubt he conceives it as a vehicle for his own brand of thought, focused on the common and universal structures underlying human thought in its many manifestations. But, after all, the substantive content of such epistemology cannot be foretold: It well might be of a wholly different order. What is immediately at issue is a different question: How should science organize its self-reflection and its disciplined thought upon thought itself? Is there the need to incorporate a disciplined epistemological inquiry into each of the empirical sciences? Are thought concerning thought and disciplined reflection on the character of inquiry and the nature of knowledge merely esoteric and peripheral matters, so far as the practicing scientist is concerned, best left to specialists in the distant, self-contained domain of the academic philosopher? To that question, I can only respond from the perspective of a practitioner in the social sciences, an economist speaking from the experience of that discipline.

### *A Structuralist Movement in Economics?*

For half a century economics has been in a state of epistemological crisis, and there is no end in sight. The crisis has involved what economics must know of itself, the basis of its statement, the appropriate test of its verities, and the boundaries of its inquiry. And the substantive inadequacies and failures of economics, evidenced by the bankruptcy of economic policy today, raise this epistemological question: What is the character of testing and the basis of acceptability that permits the perpetuation and preservation intact of a core theory, over generations, irrespective of the massive changes in the social universe to which it refers and of the policy disasters to which it leads?

Consider some of the oustanding epistemological issues that confront today's economist. Paul Samuelson's *Foundations of Economics,*[4] written in the late 1930s and published after the war, was an epistemological treatise pure and simple. It was not *about* the world of phenomena and event. Of itself, it could lay no claim to empirical verity. It neither challenged and tested nor developed and extended the implications of the established (neoclassical) theory in predicting event or explaining phenomena. Rather, it gave accepted theory another form of statement. It did so on grounds that were strictly epistemological, following the convention that mathematics is the properly "scientific" medium of expression. For subsequent generations the mathematization of statements became the major preoccupation of the discipline, and this course has been paralleled in other social and behavioral sciences. And what has been its effect? Has it exposed theory to test and refutation through concrete prediction? Or has it simply removed the corpus of thought from the purview of many who might observe and judge it from their living experience? There are certainly rumblings of discontent even at the heart of the Establishment. Wassily Leontief, who by the measure of achievement may be regarded as our greatest econometrician, in his inaugural address as President of the American Economic Association denounced the sterility of what he called the mathematical model building factories, including virtually the whole of the modern endeavor.[5] Another world renowned econometrician, Nicholas Georgescu-Roegen, mounts in his most recent book a total attack on the epistemological foundation of mathematizing statements about the economy and society.[6] Clearly, the game is not over. The epistemological issue has not yet been settled.

In another effort launched in the late 1930s, following the lead of Sir John Hicks, economics undertook to purge itself of the notion of cardinal utility. Here, too, anathema was pronounced on grounds that were purely epistemological. It came down to us as an imperative from on high that "cardinal utility" was not "scientific"; all interpersonal comparisons were epistemologically improper, and all value judgments were forbidden in the name of science. Alas, the only way that economics could have followed this new command was to have severed its every connection with economic policy; that the economist was unwilling to do, and those who pay for the upkeep of the discipline did not cease to expect social guidance. Hence, a second preoccupation of postwar economics became the creation of a system of social evaluation that would be free of social values, a welfare economics that would not compare the well-being of one with that of another, or take any stand on what was good and what was ill. That effort, of course, had to fail, and few now would deny that it has been a total failure and a gigantic waste. After so many futile decades, we find suddenly that cardinal utility as a criterion of the good is in favor again. It has been brought in by the back door or swept out from under some rug, while a conspiracy of silence prevails, blotting out any mention of all prior pronouncements of anathema upon it. This restoration explains the new rage in economics for John Rawls's *Theory of Justice,*[7] inasmuch as Rawls has invented an imaginative device that permits orthodoxy to leapfrog cardinal utility and, hence, any need for public recantation, and yet land back at a point very close to where it was four decades ago.

I do not mean to make a case for or against the worth of cardinal utility, or the propriety of interpersonal comparisons, or the appropriateness of mathematics as a medium for the expression of general theory in the social sciences; I only insist that these have been, and continue to be, critical issues. In respect to them, economists have moved in one direction or the other, this way or that, on the road to glory or up the garden path, without reasoned argument, without critical response, without true dialogue, without search and selection, and with never an effort to test and evaluate the consequences of an action taken. Epistemologically untrained and unsensitized to the problems at issue, without the competence to judge or the self-confidence to challenge, oppose, or question imperatives delivered from on high or the whims and fashions of the instant, economists have moved like sheep in panic. The total concern of each has not been with where he or she is going, but only with not being left behind in the movement of the flock.

It is clear, then, why Piaget's call for a new epistemology built into the practicing sciences, developing thereby the capacity of each systematically to reflect upon itself, appeals to me. Economics and the other social and behavioral sciences face epistemological issues of critical importance. We need a rational discourse, a process of systematic learning, and we need practitioners trained to a sophisticated understanding of root problems concerning the nature of the discipline, its objectives, its preconceptions, the propriety of its statements, the scope of its inquiry, and its criteria of credibility and coherence.

The discussion thus far has dealt only with the structuralist "movement," not with structuralist thought. This latter transcends the movement and most often owes nothing to it. Rather, it is the irruption of an idea that blazes as scientific revolution on certain of the frontiers of discourse, or is elsewhere to be found in the undergrounds of science or in the hidden zones of heresy.

### *Psychological Structuralism: The Work of Jean Piaget*

Piaget's clash with the philosopher's opinion reveals not only what structuralist thought is, but also, and equally important, what it is not; indeed, what it is in opposition to.

The structuralist idea confronts and breaks away from (what can be called) the neoclassical conception of man and mind. That conception views man as an autonomous being, acting in freedom and a kind of splendid isolation, with a mind that absorbs impression through sensation, replicates reality in the mirror of consciousness, and learns through imitation, association, and accumulation of impressions in the storehouse of memory. In effect, the neoclassical idea of mind is of a cross between a sponge and a calculating machine, or, using a more current analogy, of a self-programming computer precipitately absorbing, storing, logically manipulating, and replicating the inputs of image and sensation. Rationality serves as the needle of the mind's compass, perpetually pointing true north, fixing the ultimate, unilinear path of self-interest and social development.

In opposition, Piaget uncovers in his studies of child learning a sequential emergence of identifiable, explicable cognitive structures, formations within the unconscious that put boundaries upon observation and awareness and determine the possibilities and the character of thought.[8] The infant in its groping realizes the geography of the blanket and the space of the crib; within that cognitive structure it observes the events of the world. On the frame of that fundamental cognitive structure another then can evolve through the questing volition of the mind. That other is the comprehension of continuities extraneous to one's own sight and sensation, that is, of the independence of the object in the realization that the toy tucked under the blanket before the nap will be there upon waking and that all other things have a life or existence continuing outside and apart from the mind's eye. In the frame of that structure of cognition, transforming sights and sensations into independent things and existences, the patterns of relationships between these objects and existences can be perceived and thought upon. This could be understood as the analytic-experimental realization of the Kantian *a priori*. Yet, in another sense, there is no *a priori* in Piaget's schemata. For him, a cognitive structure is itself formed through a structured system of development following an invariable (and necessary) sequence, operating through experience produced through energies and volition expressed in seeking and purpose, impacting as action upon the universe of objects and being coupled with an innate learning capacity. True learning, then, is the process through which new cognitive structures are developed, thereby extending the scope of volition and the framework of observation and thought.

In Piaget's work can be found the characteristics of all structuralist thought, no matter where expressed. That thought is always in opposition to the neoclassical idea of man and mind: of the rational and autonomous individual, free in his powers of observation and choice, learning through the random accumulation and association of information via a stream of impression, with consciousness as a mirror upon the world.

Structuralist thought is opposed as well to another theory of the mind (*mind* meaning the locus of knowledge, thought, and decision) that derives not from the classicism of the seventeenth and eighteenth century, but from the romanticism of the nineteenth. It is the transcendental "mind" of Race, Nation, Class, Life Force; the expression of an autonomous super-being, detached from the universe of individual interest and striving, in motion through the vast open stretches of historical time, in Hegelian conception; or expressing the interest of the globalized group, defined by functional role in an economic order which is, in turn, determined by the character of technology, in the perpetuum of class warfare, in the Marxist. In either case, the classical rationale of man is projected as a global, transcendental image. The dialectic of Hegelian spirit operates, after all, as one might fancy a civilized discourse would between learned philosophers, and the Marxist dialectic globalizes and projects in the immortal form of class, the self-interested greed of the economic man of neoclassical conception. The same projection of the neoclassical idea of individual mind and man into a global, unitary, transcendental image is commonplace today in the way that economics conceives the great corporation, or in the way that most of us think, for example, of science.

Opposed both to the neoclassical idea of mind and its romantic (transcendental, globalized) counterpart, structuralist thought in all its manifestations explains thought and behavior, of the individual or the group, as the operation of volition within the determinant structure of a cognitive system. The structure of that system, whose ultimate locus is always the unconscious individual mind, determines, hence is reflected in, hence is deducible from, the potentials, the boundaries, the character of thought and behavior.

There is another way of seeing this difference between the structuralist and neoclassical theory of the mind. Both accept the elements of rationality, autonomy, and volition. Nor would the modern neoclassical thinker be bothered to deny a Kantian *a priori*. If he were an economist, he certainly would impute a structure at least of tastes and proclivities within the framework of which volition and logic operate. But for him these are parameters outside the locus of inquiry, neutralized in an analytic that conceives the mind in the rational catalysis of information or sensation into choice and behavior. For the structuralist, on the other hand, the framework of the unconscious is the key variable and the central locus of inquiry. The cognitive structures that are his concern may be, as we have seen, genetic formations in the mind of the child, or they may be the accumulation and product of the experience of the race or the society or the group embodied in ritual and institution, preserved and perpetuated in the unconscious of successive generations.

Such structured cognitive systems may be closed, transforming inputs in the manner of an algebraic equation, that is, they may be synchronic systems. Or they may be open, developmental, generating new structures, and hence new capacities, for observation and thought, in other words, diachronic. Nevertheless, they always are *cognitive,* operating through individual volition acting within the structured unconscious of the mind.

It becomes then the task of structuralist inquiry to explicate those structures of the unconscious. The normal method for so doing is to read back from observed thought and behavior, or from the institutions and artifacts in which these are embodied, to the structures that determined the boundaries and shaped the character of that thought and behavior.

### *Varieties of Structuralist Thought*

Such is the character of structuralist thought. Consider its manifestations in disciplines other than psychology.

In his anthropology, Claude Levi-Strauss rejects the idea of society as a neutral ground with more or less rational arrangements for ordering the competition, the interaction, and cooperative endeavors of autonomous persons.[9] He rejects as well the comparison of societies as the globalized prototypes of rational man at certain stages in his formation with primitive society, thus understood as a less awakened, less knowledgeable, less aware stage of our modern selves. Both of these ideas, rejected by Levi-Strauss and long dominant in anthropology and sociology, easily can be recognized as variants upon the neoclassical and romantic theories of the mind.

Instead, Levi-Strauss conceives of society as a thought and behavior producing system; the patterns of behavior and the character of thought deriving from the determinant structure of that system. His analysis, in his own words, "dissolves man," dissolves, that is, the autonomous pleasure-seeking, satisfaction-optimizing, profit-maximizing, interest-pursuing machine, that imitating, impression-assimilating, word-regurgitating, knowledge-accumulating, isolable robot of neoclassical conception; it dissolves as well those global, man-like entities of Marxist class or Hegelian spirit. Instead, there are volitions, constrained and shaped by the complex, integral structure within which they operate. Everywhere, human capabilities and the logical capacities of individuals are the same. One group is as rational as another. Every society accumulates and organizes a vast fund of knowledge. What differentiates one from another is that structure which gives to logic a particular direction and to knowledge its form and character. Nor is there any common scale by which systems and the behavioral patterns and forms of awareness they produce can be evaluated. Like rosies and posies, they are incommensurable.

How does one discern and explicate that understructure of thought and behavior? It is expressed and embodied in customs, laws, conventions, and institutions, but ultimately its location is the unconscious mind of those who think and act, in a way of thought that has found the means of perpetuating itself from generation to generation. Thus Levi-Strauss, as does Piaget, focuses on cognitive structures, although these belong to a wholly different system of genesis and learning. As does Piaget, Levi-Strauss reads back from expressed thought and observed behavior to the system of cognition that produced them. He chooses to study the myths of a people as that body of thought that is least shaped by the exigencies of circumstances and the requisites of function and hence best suited to reveal the key structure of cognition in the depths of the unconscious.[10]

In addition to Levi-Strauss, there is the structuralism of Thomas Kuhn[11] and Michel Foucault[12] in the history and philosophy of science.

The neoclassical view of science projects the image of rational man onto a continuum of centuries. An endless, indefatigable, unilinear learning process produces an accumulating fund of information, ever increasing in breadth and in the precision with which it follows the contours of reality. As does the rational mind, science operates through perpetually testing its ideas against its experience of reality. When an established theory, extended beyond its power to comprehend and explain observed phenomena, fails the test of prediction, it is rejected. In its place a new theory is installed, one that cannot be so refuted within the present range of information, until once more the quest for information goes beyond the powers of theory to explain and to predict. That theory, in its turn, is refuted, discarded, and replaced by another, more adequate theory. So the process continues in the unending construction of a more encompassing system of scientific laws.

Thomas Kuhn's *Structure of Scientific Revolutions* denied this very process. Science does not and never has worked that way. Rather, each of the sciences operates within a given set of related generalizations and theories, attitudes and expectations, conventional assumptions and experimental models, which Kuhn calls a paradigm. What is a paradigm? It is the partially institutionalized expression of a cognitive system, structured in the minds of scientists, preserved and perpetuated through the instrumentalities of the discipline. Within the frame of that cognitive system theories are formed, experiments are undertaken, and observations are made. The paradigm that encloses a science and shapes its thought is tough, resistant to challenge and change. It exists, so to speak, as an island in a sea of anomalies, that is, of the contradictory and, in its terms, the inexplicable. Very occasionally the paradigm is shattered and totally replaced by another under pressures that neither Kuhn nor anyone else has yet explained, producing what later generations see as the great breakthrough, the discontinuous "revolutionary advances" of science.

As a measure of the devastating impact of Kuhn's structuralism, Karl Popper, currently the great man of the neoclassical tradition, has, under Kuhnian attack, fled the old stronghold and taken refuge in what could be construed either as a return to Plato, or an entry through the back door to a structuralist philosophy.[18] (Popper postulates three interacting "worlds." One of physical relationships, another of psychological responses and individual thought, and a third of objective knowledge. It is not clear what constitutes this third world—Platonic essences, or cognitive structures as Levi-Strauss, Kuhn, or Piaget have analyzed them, or, more probably, something of both.)

The work of Michel Foucault in France parallels that of Thomas Kuhn in the United States, although Foucault's is of an incomparably greater depth. Kuhn delivers a slashing attack on an old position and proposes an alternative hypothesis; Foucault produces a massive analytic and the positive basis for an integral new discipline. In his major work, translated into English as *The Order of Things,* covering the period from the Renaissance to date, Foucault studies the changing character of the sciences concerned with life, language, the economy, and, in other of his works, disease and insanity. For every point in the periods of history covered, Foucault articulates the cognitive structure that shapes and is expressed in each one of the aforementioned areas. He digs deeper, to uncover the understructure of cognition that encompasses all of these discursive systems, that shapes and is expressed in them all. He calls this understructure an "episteme." His work reveals the quick collapse and sudden replacement of the prevailing episteme and the way that the new one works its way up from the deep layers of thought, to transform, in its own image, each of the particular disciplines, appearing in history as a cluster of "scientific revolutions."

Indeed, the very irruption of structuralist thought described in this article, transforming one body of scientific thought after another, is an example of such epistemic change.

And then there is the structuralist revolution in linguistics, associated with the work of Noam Chomsky,[14] Roman Jacobson, and Fernand de Saussure. The science of language is peculiarly suited to the expression of structuralist thought. For that reason, linguistics may be destined to be the model, similar to the role the biology of Charles Darwin and Georges Cuivier played in the nineteenth century and the "Natural History" of Jean-Baptiste Lamarck and Charles de Linnaeus and the cosmology of Isaac Newton played in the seventeenth. Why so?

Language is itself a structured system introduced into the unconscious, one that contains and shapes the individual's thought and behavior. It is, moreover, an immensely complex, marvelously effective, collective creation. The product of the unconscious, not of an individual but of a people in their evolution through millenia, it must reflect the deepest structures of the human mind.

The new linguistics emerges in contrast to philology, which was born in the nineteenth century. The latter belongs to the romantic rather than the neoclassical tradition, and it views language as the distinctive voice of Nation, Race, and Folk, expressing the spirit of that transcendental subject.

In opposition to this view, Fernand de Saussure, working in Switzerland at the turn of this century, conceived of language as a structured system, indeed, as a set of systems nested one within the other: *Parole* exists at the level of personal volition; it nests within *langue,* or the social system of vocal discourse in the sense of the French or English languages, which in turn nests within *language,* understood as the human physical and mental potential for speech. All these linguistic systems are nested within a more encompassing system of signs that would include symbolic rites, gestures, body signals, pictures, and mathematics.

Linguistic systems, as products of the unconscious, must reflect the structures of the minds that shaped them. In being learned, languages are incorporated into the structure of the unconscious of successive generations, to contain and constrain individual volitions and to shape the social capacity for communication and for discourse.

What is particular about *this* cognitive structure is that it is totally revealed, made overtly and explicitly manifest, so that its structures and rationale can be studied directly, without being dredged from the unconscious or deduced from patterns of thought and behavior. For that reason linguistics need not and linguists may not take the relationship of language to cognitive processes into account. But for the revolutionary thinker such as Noam Chomsky, the link between language and the unconscious mind is the very heart of the matter. He relates the learning of language to the genetic unfolding of cognitive structures. He locates the generative (diachronic) development of linguistic systems to the creative use by the speaker-hearer of an "internalized . . . system of rules that determines the semantic interpretation of an unbounded set of sentences," and he seeks for a "fixed and innate scheme" in unconscious depths as the ultimate source of all grammars.[15]

The fact that most of those U.S. academics who are aware of "structuralism" think of it as a species of literary criticism possibly can be explained as a consequence of the link between linguistics and literary studies. The two are so closely related that a spillover of thought from the former to the latter is inevitable. While linguistics has been the main center of structuralist achievement in the United States, it is, after all, a small and esoteric field that does not flow easily into the cultural mainstream, while literature is the very stuff of the common culture. How then can structuralist thought be expressed in literature or in literary criticism? Presumably books or plays can take as their theme the cognitive structure that frames the volition of individuals, and some have done so.[16]

Jean Genet's *The Maids* is surely an example of structuralist literature.[17] It is without a plot in the sense of a problem that engages and is to be resolved by an individual. Its characters are ambivalent and tenuous. But as an analytic of the cognitive structure within which a segment of humanity is or might be entrapped and their volition formed, a cognitive structure that is expressed by their thought and is revealed in their behavior, it is a work of art.

It is the structure of cognition proper to the universe of the servant, specifically the French servant, a near destitute body of humanity, naked in its weakness, inextricably coupled with (in the anthropological term the "moiety" of) the very rich, the aristocratic, the powerful, the most secure. Hence, the servant's world is a cognitive subsystem institutionally enclosed by, perpetuated through, and functionally bound to another.

The truth of *The Maids* is universal in all human volition—in the craving for virtue, the energies of ambition restless for an object and an outlet, the need to identify with and hence to find identity, the force of fantasy that fastens upon an object of hope and a source of power, the drive for transcendence—as these elements of the human volition are or would be expressed in the closed universe of the servants: those who sleep at night in the meanest garrets with a water spigot and a bare, dim, and fitful light in the filthy corridor, uglier than a prison, and who dwell by day in the casual luxury and magnificence of the very rich; those whose whole devotion focuses on the infinite vanities and the sacrosanct egoism of the mistress, the "beautiful" mistress, the "kind" mistress, capricious, weak, and yet all powerful; those who exist solely for her convenience and pleasure and hence can find a meaning for their existence and a recognition for their being only in her indifferent glance and uncomprehending eye. Coupled to the world of the aristocrat and haute bourgeoisie, the servants are the underside of the grand hierarchies, arranging the props, sweeping the stage, and manning the rear choruses in perpetual and magnificent rituals of power.

In that system of mind there is no other object of hope and hatred than patron and patroness, who render final judgment, those upon whose kindness, caprice, and cruelty everything depends. Necessarily, the virtue of the soldier is courage, and the virtue of the servant is servility, hence the servant's craving for an absolute virtue finds its fulfillment and ecstacy in absolute self-abasement. The servants identify and can only identify with the master and the mistress, which means finding identity in that which holds them in contempt and mirrors their abasement. What heroism is then possible, what act of nobility, for those whose volition exists within this structure of mind? None other, says Genet, than to kill the mistress or the master, or murder the maid, or destroy one's own self in proxy for them: No other transcendence is possible, says Genet. And as the maid dreams of her apotheosis through murder, it is in the image of the grand ritual. She mounts to the guillotine as to a moment of ultimate glory, "and behind me will march the butlers, and behind them the footmen, and behind them the valets, and behind them the maids, and then the porter, all marching."

Literary criticism in the structuralist mode surely will lead to no critique of the quality of literature, but rather to an understanding of the standards by which literature is judged. It would constitute a study of, or a reflection upon, the cognitive or aesthetic system within which a work of literature is created, understood, communicated, and evaluated.[18] The same would hold for structuralism in the criticism of art.[19]

Thus, linguistics asks: What is language? In literature, the structuralist critic asks: What is *poetic* language? He searches for an answer in the system of signs and signals, that multilayered context in which the word is spoken, and in the cognitive-emotive structures that characterize the psyche of listener and speaker.

Structuralist thought, of course, has been made manifest elsewhere, for example, in Gregory Bateson's "Ecology of the Mind" and the forms of psychology and therapy related to it.[20] Physicists may find it in the subjectivism of Max Planck or in Einsteinian relativity, mathematicians in the parent structures of Nicholas Bourbaki.[21]

Structuralist thought, moreover, is but a species of a large genre; it is but one element, a particular paradigmatic cluster as part of a more encompassing episteme. Certainly structuralism is not alone in opposing the neoclassical and romantic conception of mind: That opposition was launched in the revolutionary work of Sigmund Freud and C. G. Jung. Although psychoanalytic theory is related to the structuralist irruption, the two are not the same. The former is no more geared for and equipped to explain the path of normal learning or the rationale of diverse individual and social patterns of thought and behavior than is the latter to disentangle the roots of neurosis in hidden psychic depths.

The focus on the structure of cognitive systems, moreover, parallels the current emphasis on structured systems over the spectrum of science from microbiology, crystalography, geology, and atomic physics to operations research and so-called systems analysis.

### *Structuralist Thought and Economics*

So far as economics is concerned—that field of study that I know best—structuralist thought is still outside the gates. Yet, a look at those forces which press those concerned with economic phenomena to take cognitive structures into account will reveal the same objective circumstances that give to structuralist thought a peculiar importance in our time.

There are two coherent and powerful systems of discourse concerned with economic phenomena, the liberal and Marxist. About the latter, especially in its more recent manifestations, I can speak only tentatively. Both have a theory of mind, understood as the center of calculus and decision and as the nexus of thought into action.

For liberal economics, mind is the pleasure-calculator of autonomous man, geared to the rational pursuit of a self-interest determined by "wants," "desires," and "preferences," with these inscribed as a map (a "preference map") upon the brain.

Aside from the question of its intrinsic verity, this version of the neoclassical idea of mind is operational (it works) as a cog in a plausible theory for explaining behavior in competitive markets where the entrepreneur runs his own factory for his private and personal ends, every laborer bargains as an individual, and each consumer searches the stalls of the open market to higgle and haggle with the sellers there.

Whatever once might have been, such no longer is the nature of our economy. We are now confronted with, we ourselves are the very elments of, an economy (and a society and a polity) of vast corporate and public organizations. Autonomous self-seeking has ceased to be relevant because individual autonomy is gone. Ownership of property, that once gave to the individual will its solid base in the exercise of control, has lost its old meaning. The activities of thousands and hundreds of thousands must now gear together in multipurposed, yet integral, extremely complex, yet flexible and adaptive, patterns where coherence absolutely requires a mass perception and a shared commitment. Shared cognition defines the group, and cognitive structure is the key to organizational form and behavior. The neoclassical theory of man and mind cannot explain, indeed excludes any explanation of, development, variations in behavior and performance, policies and decision processes, inertia, stagnation, dynamism, or creativity of large public agencies and corporate organizations. With respect to the corporate-organizational part of the economy, economics draws a blank. That "blank" is one reason for the spectacular failures of public policy during this decade.

The omnipresence of organization, and the passing of the world of individual autonomy, gives structuralist thought its centrality in our time.

It is not only the need to think in a world of organizations that drives us to a consciousness of cognitive structure, but also the urgent need to understand the phenomenon of learning—individual, organizational, and social. For that we must encounter cognitive structure, as Piaget did with the learning child, as Levi-Strauss did in formulating boundaries and forms of social learning. Indeed, what else are the works of Michel Foucault and Thomas Kuhn if not an analysis of how science learns?

The process of social and organizational learning is at the heart of two current and crucial economic problems. One is the need to raise the so-called underdeveloped societies from the ruts of an ancient and endemic poverty. The economist's perceptions of sound budgeting and capital accumulation have failed, for economic development (as is any form of social development) is inescapably a process of social learning, and underdevelopment is the consequence of the failure of spontaneous social learning. The second is the need to accelerate and direct technological advance to satisfy the rising tides of human want in the face of an ever-diminishing natural resource base. Technological advance is the product of a multifaceted cognitive system operating through a complex of cognitive structures, and research and development build a part of this learning function into the operation of large public and corporate organizations.

Economics has failed to understand either economic development or technological advance, and it must continue to do so as long as it rests on the neoclassical theory of mind, since that theory excludes the very questions that must be asked in order to understand individual, social, or organizational learning.

I do not mean that there are no economists who have thought on these questions. In a beautiful little book that he himself considers to be his best and most successful work, *The Image,*[22] Kenneth Boulding displays before us the working of a mind as it moves out under the impulsion of whim or will, unrolling the topography of its thought in diverse regions of speculation, anticipation, response, and decision. Thereby Boulding cleared the way to a search for cognitive structures in explaining the intermeshed expectations, the integration of purposes, the coordination of behavior that constitutes the phenomenon of group, corporate, and social behavior. No one followed in the path he had opened.

I am myself a structuralist through and through. My work relates alternative forms of economic organization to their requisite cognitive structures; the pathways of economic transformations and of economic revolutions to the topography of culture and cognition and the processes of ideological disintegration and creation to the formation of the law and of policy.[23]

There are those of us who think as structuralists, but our thought has not yet entered into that system of discourse that constitutes the discipline. Therefore, our numbers cannot be known or our impact measured. We belong to the science underground still.

Marxist theory also has its theory of mind, again meaning by *mind* a center of calculus and decision and the nexus of thought into action. Its rationale is familiar: The group becomes conscious of its place in an economic system, and an ideology forms as the superstructure of that group's function and functionally determined interest. The group expresses that ideology in its behavior. Thus the globalized mind of a functionally determined class operates, for all intents and purposes, like the mind of economic man in the neoclassical theory blown large, deciding and acting in the rational pursuit of self (read, class) interest. Nothing intervenes between directly perceived (group) interest, as given by a functional situation, and behavior.

Yet, among the Marxists also there is an irruption of structuralist thinking, analogous to Boulding's and mine, in the work of Louis Althusser, who was, incidentally, a teacher of Michel Foucault. Althusser, as a Communist, operates in a more theological atmosphere than ours, one charged still with the sensed need for solidarity of a group that considers itself besieged. His analytic starts not with Marxist theory, but with the theory of Marx, as part of the ongoing controversy as to which Marx was the true one—the young, the transitional, or the mature Marx. Here Althusser poses his concept of a "problematic," by which he means the cognitive structure that frames and shapes the volition and thought of the individual or the group that shares it. It is through the problematic that the questions arise and ideologies are formed. It is as the action of Marx's volition within and then its escape from a particular problematic that Althusser traces the troubled path of Marx's thought.[24] Marx was born into the German philosophical problematic, already centuries old, shared with Hegel. As a "Young Hegelian" Marx tried to reorient; as a Feuerbachian he struck out against Hegel's philosophy, but his opposition remains within the same problematic. Then came a fundamental "Epistemological Break," in which he tore himself away from that structure of cognition and created (according to Althusser) a new problematic, another cognitive structure to shape and frame thought and volition, which would offer another bounded field of controversy.

If the initial problematic—not bourgeois but German, different from that which prevailed in France or England—was indeed so critical in determining Marx's own thought and behavior, how can Althusser exclude cognitive structures as an autonomous force in the analysis of social behavior generally? In fact, he cannot, yet he must tread with care, for his theory departs from the classic Marxist idea of mind. It is with his "problematic" in the background that he asks precisely the questions that cannot be answered when thought and behavior are understood simply as expressing the rationale of class interest. How does one account, he asks, for the so-called survivals continuously troublesome for Marxist theory and communist practice? How does one explain why "the proud and generous Russian people bore Stalin's crimes and repression with such resignation; how the Bolshevik Party could tolerate them; not to speak of the final question—how a Communist leader could have ordered them?"[25] How does one explain why revolution came "in Russia, in China, in Cuba . . . and not elsewhere."[26] He also might have asked: How else can one account for the making of Mao Tse-tung's Little Red Book into a catechism, or indeed for the Chinese cultural revolutions, except as a massive and systematic effort to re-create the cognitive understructure of a vast and ancient society? Indeed, it is upon the capacity to re-create the structure of cognition, a task beyond any rationale of class interest, that the success and significance of socialism must depend.

The neoclassical paradigm concerns us more directly and immediately. It is the structure for too long embedded in the unconscious of the Western economist's mind through which he has tried to comprehend the world and to interpret policy and behavior. Hopefully, the articles of the symposium to which this journal has devoted its pages will raise the elements of that mental structure to the level of consciousness, will expose them to a critical reexamination, and will set in motion the the dynamic of a long overdue reconstruction.

## *Notes*

1. Jean Piaget et al., *Logique et connaissance scientifique* (Paris: Gallimard, 1967), *Histoire et methode,* 2d ed. (Paris: PUF, 1967), and *Les théories de la causalité* (Paris: PUF, 1971). See also the following by Piaget: *Épistémologie des sciences de l'homme* (Paris: Gallimard, 1972); *Épistémologie mathematique et psychologique* (Paris: PUF, 1961); *Études sociologique* (Geneva: Droz, 1965); *Introduction à l'épistémologie génétique* (Paris: PUF, 1950); *La structuralisme* (Paris: PUF, 1968; English ed., *Structuralism* [New York: Harper Torchbooks, 1971]); and *Biologie et connaissance* (Paris: Gallimard, 1967).
2. Nicholas Georgescu-Roegen, *The Entropy Law and the Economic Process* (Cambridge, Mass.: Harvard University Press, 1971).
3. Piaget, *Structuralism.*
4. Paul Samuelson, *Foundations of Economics* (Cambridge, Mass.: Harvard University Press, 1947).
5. Wassily Leontief, "Theoretical Assumptions and Non-Observed Facts," *American Economic Review* 61 (March 1971): 1–7.
6. Georgescu-Roegen, *Entropy Law.* See also my "Arithmomorphism and Entropy," *Economic Development and Cultural Change* 22 (April 1974): 510–17.
7. John Rawls, *A Theory of Justice* (Cambridge, Mass.: Belknap Press, 1971).
8. Jean Piaget, *La construction du réel chez l'enfant,* 3d ed. (Neuchâtel: Delachaux and Niestlé, 1963), *La formation du symbole chez l'enfant,* 3d ed. (Neuchâtel: Delachaux and Niestlé, 1964), *Études sur la logique de l'enfant* (Neuchâtel: Delachaux and Niestlé, 1962), and *La psychologie de l'intelligence* (Paris: A. Colin, 1967). See also Jean Piaget and Barbel Inhelder, *Le developpement des quantités physiques chez l'enfant,* 2d ed. (Neuchâtel: Delachaux and Niestlé, 1962), *La genèse de l'idée d'hasard chez l'enfant* (Paris: PUF, 1951), *L'image mentale chez l'enfant* (Paris: PUF, 1966), and *De la logique de l'enfant à la logique de l'adolescent* (Paris: PUF, 1970); Jean Piaget and Alina Szeminska, *La genèse du nombre chez l'enfant* (Paris: PUF, 1964); and Jean Piaget, Barbel Inhelder, and Alina Szeminska, *La géometrie spontanée de l'enfant* (Paris: PUF, 1948).
9. See the following by Claude Levi-Strauss: *Anthropologies structurale*

(Paris: Plon, 1958; English ed., *Structural Anthropology* [New York: Basic Books, 1963]); *La pensée sauvage* (Paris: Plon, 1962; English ed., *The Savage Mind* [London: Weidenfeld and Nicolson, 1966]); *Les structures élémentaires de la parente* (Paris: PUF, 1949; English ed., *Elementary Structures of Kinship* [Boston: Beacon Press, 1969]); *Le totémisme aujourd'hui* (Paris: PUF, 1962; English ed., *Totemism* [Boston: Beacon Press, 1963]); *Triste tropiques* (Paris: Plon, 1955; English ed., *Tristes tropiques* [New York: Criterion Books, 1961]); *A World on the Wane* (New York: Criterion Books, 1961); *Du Miel aux Cendres* (Paris: Plon, 1963; English ed., *From Honey to Ashes* [New York: Harper and Row, 1973]); and *Le cru et le cuit* (Paris: Plon, 1964; English ed., *The Raw and the Cooked* [London: Harper and Row, 1969]).

10. For general discussion see: Howard Gardner, *The Quest for Mind: Piaget, Levi-Strauss and the Structuralist Movement* (New York: Vintage, 1974); and *Structuralism* (New Haven: Yale French Studies, 1966), which includes essays on structuralism in anthropology and psychiatry and a bibliography on anthropology.
11. Thomas S. Kuhn, *The Structure of Scientific Revolutions* (Chicago: University of Chicago Press, 1962).
12. Michel Foucault, *Les mot et les choses* (Paris: Gallimard, 1966; English ed., *The Order of Things* [New York: Random House, 1970]), *The Archeology of Knowledge and the Discourse on Language* (New York: Random House, 1972), *The Birth of the Clinic* (New York: Random House, 1973), and *Madness and Civilization* (New York: Random House, 1965).
13. *Objective Knowledge: An Evolutionary Approach* (Oxford: Clarendon Press, 1972).
14. Noam Chomsky, *Syntactic Structures* (The Hague: Mouton and Co., 1957), pp. 6–24, *Current Issues in Linguistic Theory* (London: Mouton and Co., 1964), *Language and the Mind* (New York: Harcourt, Brace & World, 1968), *Topics in the Theory of Generative Grammar* (London: Mouton and Co., 1969), and *Problems of Knowledge and Freedom: The Russell Lectures* (New York: Vintage Books, 1971). See also Gilbert Hartman, ed., *On Noam Chomsky: Critical Essays* (New York: Doubleday Anchor, 1974). For a general bibliography of structuralism in linguistics, see Yale French Studies, *Structuralism.*
15. Noam Chomsky. "Persistent Topics in Linguistic Theory," *Diogenes,* no. 15 (Fall 1965): 113.
16. Althusser refers to the work of Carlo Bertolazzi and Bertolt Brecht in this sense. See Louis Althusser, *For Marx* (New York: Vintage Books, 1970), pp. 129–51.
17. Jean Genet, *The Maids and the Death Watch* (New York: Grove Press, 1962). For the quotations I have relied on the arrangement of the American Film Theatre.
18. Robert Scholes, *Structuralism in Literature* (New Haven: Yale University Press, 1974), also contains a good general bibliography.
19. Jack Burnham, *The Structure of Art* (New York: Braziller, 1971), includes a bibliography, as does E. H. Gombrich, *Art and Illusion* (Princeton: Princeton University Press, 1969).

20. Gregory Bateson, *Steps to an Ecology of the Mind* (New York: Ballantine Books, 1972).
21. Nicholas Bourbaki is the collective pseudonym of a group of French mathematicians who publish under that name.
22. Kenneth E. Boulding, *The Image* (Ann Arbor: Ann Arbor Paperback, 1968).
23. Robert Solo, *Economic Organizations and Social Systems* (Indianapolis: Bobbs Merrill, 1967), and *The Political Authority and the Market System* (Cincinnati: Southwestern, 1974).
24. Althusser, *For Marx.*
25. Ibid., p. 116.
26. Ibid., p. 207.

# 3

# Neoclassical Economics in Perspective

*Robert A. Solo*

It will be the purpose of this article to put neoclassical theory into perspective as an historical force, as a conceptualizing and analytic apparatus and a blueprint for policy.

### *The Theory in History*

1776 saw not only the publication of the Declaration of Independence, but also another great statement attacking the self-same mercantilist doctrines against which the colonies were in rebellion: the *Wealth of Nations*. In it Adam Smith was a propagandist, a policy seeker, a moral philosopher, seeking to influence social choice. He opposed a disintegrating mercantilist statism where the ministers of the crown treated the economy as though it were a vast feudal domain to be administered and drained of its surplus for the sake of the royal treasury. In its stead he projected the vision of a free-exchange economy. He was in the vanguard of a new (burgher, bourgeois, entrepreneurial) class and of the industrial revolution that was carrying that new class into a position of economic and political dominance.

The *Wealth of Nations* was one with the credo of that new entrepreneurial class. It drew upon their experience, reflected their values, and responded to their interests. But it was certainly not the whole of their credo. Their outlook and attitudes simultaneously were being expressed in respect to every aspect of individual and social activity—

*The author is Professor of Economics, Michigan State University, East Lansing.*

developing as the new ideology of liberalism of which the laissez-faire policies preached by Adam Smith were an inextricable part.

Subsequently, the message of Adam Smith and his followers was transformed because the role and the position of the newcomers to power were transformed. From outsiders they became insiders; from those who pressed for a share in the temporal power they became its prime possessor; from those who sought to escape the domination of an entrenched aristocracy, they became themselves dominant and entrenched.

No longer the banner of protest and the credo of reform, the new economics was to serve other purposes. It was instrumental in solving knotty problems of social choice. Thus, in spearheading the fight against the Corn Laws, David Ricardo established, to the satisfaction of his generation, that the contribution of land to production did not in any way depend upon rental payments. Eliminating the tariff on domestic grain would reduce the incomes of an idle, landowning aristocracy without affecting production. But lowering the costs of imported materials and, by reducing the price of bread, reducing wages would increase profits, thus stimulating the accumulation of capital, and through capital accumulation bring about a rise in production and wealth. Through unrestricted trade England would specialize in those outputs in which it had a comparative advantage. This also would increase the surplus available for capital accumulation, further augmenting production and wealth. The new industrialists, supported by Ricardo's arguments, carried the day—indeed, they carried the century. The defeat of the Corn Laws ushered in an epoch of free trade for Great Britain and of rapid growth and industrial supremacy.

In the course of his analysis, Ricardo explained the distribution of income as between the factors of production, and he also established the mutual advantages of trade between high wage, high productivity, and low wage, low productivity economies. In addition to this problem solving, policy formulating function, the new economics had another purpose. Industrialization produced great private wealth, but for many among those who labored, perhaps even for the majority, the level of life positively deteriorated from what it had been before. Reformers and revolutionaries speaking for the impoverished in the name of Christian charity, or social justice, or proletarian solidarity demanded a redistribution of wealth and power. Sometimes they called for a socialist economy.

In response, neoclassical theory developed as a defense of the status quo and of the policies of laissez-faire, becoming an apologia for capitalism. Such was the economics of Thomas Malthus and of Eugen von Böhm Bawerk.

Malthus argued against the redistribution of wealth or, indeed, against relief for the hungry, on the grounds that any amelioration of the condition of the masses would result only in an increase in population. Lower class misery was a social necessity, or else the poor in their numbers would grow until the whole society was forced to the edge of starvation. That self-same argument would be used again and again to explain the failure of colonial regimes and of economic development programs in India, Latin America, and elsewhere.

Marxists argued that production was solely a function of labor (including, of course, the labor of management). Capital, they held, was simply "frozen labor." Since labor alone was responsible for all production, all production rightfully should accrue to labor. In response, Böhm Bawerk and those who followed him developed a theory of capital which holds that higher productivity, that is, a larger real output per unit of labor input, is brought about through "lengthening" or making more "roundabout" the processes of production. Greater lengthiness or roundaboutness required capital accumulation, or a greater quantum of labor inputs immobilized as producer durables. To divert resources into capital accumulation, thereby raising productivity, consumption must be curtailed. The abstentions (savings) of the rich made possible the diversion of resources into the accumulation of capital, and profit and interest were justified as a reward for such abstentions and risks.

Through the eighteenth and nineteenth century the theory continued to develop, primarily in England, Austria, and the United States. Alfred Marshall's *Principles of Economics,* first published in 1890, remains its viable synthesis. Although many of the propositions of what Marshall called his "organon" since have been translated from common English into an esoteric mathematics, price theory remains essentially what it was in the Marshallian synthesis: The two significant exceptions are the theory of monopolistic competition, associated with Edward H. Chamberlin, and indifference analysis, developed by J. R. Hicks.

### *Hicks and the Flight from Moral Philosophy*

Utilitarianism was a perfect match to the liberal outlook. It found the totality of value in the consumption satisfactions of the individual; *ergo* consumer sovereignty and the process of exchange are the touchstone of well being. It constructed a moral world out of a universe of autonomous individuals, each the self-seeking locus of all choice, each the impermiable, irreducible, beginning and end-all; *ergo* individualized choice was sanctified as "liberty," and collective choice was diabolized as tyranny. There was, alas, in this moral philosophy a hidden trap. From the law of diminishing marginal utility it could be deduced that the sum of satisfactions would be greater if income was shifted from the rich to the poor, and that the sum of satisfactions would be greatest if income shares were equal. This proposition did not unduly trouble the propertied in those Victorian days when they had a monopoly of political power. The moral philosopher might preach the ultimate value of equal shares, just as the clergyman might preach the ultimate value of brotherhood, but what was to be done was left to the conscience of the rich. There was not the slightest danger that such philosophizing would upset the institutional applecart. After World War I all that was changed. From the 1920s onward the Labour Party and organized labor were forces that must be reckoned with. The levelers were leveling. The utilitarian idea had become a positive threat to the interests of that class whose power, diminished in Parliament and weakened in the factories, was unshaken still in the British universities (which at the time dominated the academic outlook in the United States), and economists and philosophers there severed their connections with this subversive doctrine by declaring anathema on cardinal utility. On the grounds that interpersonal comparisons and value judgments are unscientific, Sir John Hicks replaced the utilitarian understructure with an "indifference analysis" without disturbing the superstructure of the theory. Now, however, it no longer could be deduced from the theory in its dessicated form that an equalization of wealth would increase well being, nor could neoclassical economics any more claim to guide the distribution of income or the allocation of resources.

The ready acceptance of indifference analysis reflected a pervasive desire to make economics into a science such as physics, free as physics is free from "value judgments." Comparing Mr. A's utilities to Mr. B's was ruled out as a value judgment. Despite confused and confusing arguments to the contrary, the supposition that Mr. A has a psychological-cum-physiological response (call it utility, or satisfaction, or what you like) from a given increment of income that is substantially the same as the response of Mr. B to the same increment of income under comparable circumstances, that is, the notion of cardinal utility, is *not* a judgment of values; rather, it is an hypothesis concerning the psychological-cum-physiological facts. As with many such statements, it is very difficult to establish by empirical test and measurement, although certainly no more so than is the Hicksian allegation of an indifference map etched on the consumer's brain. Since neither notion can be disproven, neither one can be established by reference to the observed responses of consumers. But if the assumption of cardinal utility is not a value judgment, it is indeed associated with one, namely, that utilities, or "satisfactions," or "human happiness" *should* be maximized for the community as a whole even though this means that some members of the community are worse off than before. The interesting question then is the right to make value judgments. Must economics, in the name of Science, become as free of value judgments as physics is supposed to be?

True, physics is free from value judgments, but physics is not, never has been, and never claimed to be a guide to social choice, whereas economics has been and claims to be just that. Economics has evolved as an instrument of social decision. It was shaped in the effort to differentiate between more and less desirable policies and more and less desirable forms of economic and political organization. Brainchild of moral philosophers, it came into being as a moral philosophy, and this it must remain so long as it puts itself forward as a critic of social choice. There can be no standard for social choice, no guide to social policy, that does not rest upon value judgments. It is logically impossible to offer guidance, or to evoke a criterion for social choice, except in the expression of some set of values. What is really at issue is not the "unscientific" nature of value judgments, but the role of economics. Should economics cease to be an instrument of social decision making and a criterion of social choice?

The very economists who clamored against cardinal utilities, who urged the purge of value judgments, who sought to make economics pure and scientific, never have been willing to detach themselves *qua* economists from the processes of social choice. They never have ceased to criticize and censure or to suggest and to support policies and institutions on the basis of their alleged professional competencies and the truths of the trade. As a consequence, the economist acts the part of the pure scientist, but he plays the role of a moral philosopher. His value judgments are not purged, but hidden. The value judgments of economics have become covert and equivocal. Such was the case with those who proposed Pareto optimality as a kind of covenant among economists to support only such change as might be to the advantage of some, and to the detriment of none, supposing that this would permit them to contribute to the formulation of policy without engaging in value judgments. Alas, a decision to avoid such action as might be to anyone's disadvantage is as much a value judgment as any other. Moreover, the criterion of Pareto optimality turns out to be indeterminable in theory and inapplicable in practice.

The role of economics as moral philosophy is yet to be reconciled to its role as a science, and the manner in which it should deal with value judgments remains an open question.

*Chamberlin and the Disintegration of Neoclassical Theory*

The other important change in the Marshallian synthesis is represented by Edward Chamberlin's *The Theory of Monopolistic Competition*, a positive and important statement concerning the organization of exchange and the determinants of price. It proposes that monopoly should not be considered as an anomoly, with the monopolist as an occasional and lonely robber astride a lane of commerce to whom a toll must be paid; rather, the exchange economy should be conceived as a spectrum ranging from the extreme of "pure competition," where individual sellers and buyers have no influence whatsoever upon price, to another extreme, where the selling or procuring agency can impose a change of price without significant retaliation by competitors. Between these poles is a continuum in the form of control over price and product and in the degree of competitive constraint and interaction. The element of monopoly is held to be pervasive and significant throughout the economy.

Chamberlin's conception is certainly in closer accord with commonplace observation of the modern economy than is that of the traditional theory of decentralized market direction, but his theory is gravely subversive of the symmetrical and universal determinism of "general equilibrium," crowning glory of neoclassical economics. Hicks warned his fellow professionals of the danger.

> Yet it has to be recognized that a general abandonment of the assumption of perfect [read "pure"] competition, a universal adoption of the assumption of monopoly [read the "theory of monopolistic competition"], must have very destructive consequences for economic theory [read "for the traditional theory of decentralized market direction"]. Under monopoly [read "monopolistic competition"] the stability conditions become indeterminate; and the basis on which economic laws can be constructed is therefore shorn away. . . . It is, I believe, only possible to save anything from this wreck—and it must be remembered that the threatened wreckage is that of the greater part of general equilibrium theory—if we can assume that the markets confronting most of the firms with which we shall be dealing do not differ greatly from perfectly competitive markets. . . . At least, this get-away seems well worth trying. We must be aware, however, that we are taking dangerous steps, and probably limit-

> ing to a serious extent the problems with which our subsequent analysis will be fitted to deal. Personally, however, I doubt if most of the problems we shall have to exclude for this reason are capable of much useful analysis by the methods of economic theory [read "by reference to the traditional theory of decentralized market direction"].[1]

Hicks was correct to advise his peers against accepting Chamberlin's ideas, not because they were invalid (he did not question their validity or relevance), but because they threatened the very heart of neoclassical economics. Theorists have followed Hicks's advice. They have dealt with the problem by disregarding it. The theory of monopolistic competition is tucked away in every text, but its relevance and its implications are ignored.

It is incomparably easier for economics than for physics wholly to ignore an observation that is unpleasantly out of accord with orthodox theory; unlike physics, economics and the other social sciences have no institutionalized system for the continuous, experimental verification or refutation of hypothesis and statement.

How then are we to judge the credibility of a statement in social science? Either we accept the pronouncements of those who speak with "authority," or we ourselves compare the statement and its implications with what we can observe of phenomena and events in the real world.

One fact of history should cast strong *a priori* doubts on the validity and relevance of neoclassical theory. The theory was formulated a long time ago, and things have changed since then. Its essentials were laid down in the mid-eighteenth century; its last great synthesis was at the end of the nineteenth century; we live in the last half of the twentieth.

The validity of a proposition in mathematics is not affected by the passage of time; neither, within the range of the human experience on earth, can the passage of time affect the validity of a theory in physics. Of course, in time, a proposition in mathematics may be disproven, and a theory of physics may be superseded—but not as a consequence of what happens to the universe of relationships to which that proposition or theory refers. Those real relationships are constant and continuing. Not so with a proposition of economics. The universe to which such a theory refers, the relationships it seeks to explain, these change, vanish, and are replaced by newly created forms of organization, functional interactions, and individual responses. The goals and the values that are expressed in policy and that motivate choice also change. Conclusions may follow logically from premises, but the *premises,* hence the deductions and conclusions which can be drawn from them, cease to be relevant or acceptable.

### *Fundamental Presuppositions and Assumptions*

Generally it is the case, and certainly it has been true for economics, that theory nests within ideology. Furthermore, both theory and ideology rest upon what Jean Piaget, Claude Levi-Strauss, and Noam Chomsky might call a *cognitive structure,* what Michel Foucault calls an *episteme,* Kuhn a *paradigm,* Althusser a *problematic,* that is, upon a system of conceptualization and a body of presuppositions that frame the field of controversy, shape outlook and the character of inquiry, and determine the meaningfulness of the question and the significance of the problem. The theory is different from these deeper strata of thought in the degree that the latter are embedded in the unconscious. They belong to the realm of the self-evident, of the unquestionable, parameters not simply of sets of thoughts but of the process of thought itself. It is with certain of these fundamental presuppositions, indigenous to the age when neoclassical theory took its essential form and, hence, inextricably imprinted upon the character of that theory, that this section will be concerned.

#### *The Notion of Equilibrium*

At one level, *equilibrium* can be understood as metaphor drawn from classical mechanics, of forces in balance, at a point or in a position or in a state from which there is no tendency to deviate, a finally, fully realized position, so to speak.

But, more than a convenient bit of imagery, the metaphor is central to the approach of neoclassical economics in its organization of observation, in its effort to encompass and to comprehend phenomena. Equilibrium is an idea that limits and defines the scope of the economist's outlook. Equilibrium is what the economist is looking for, what he expects to find, and what he asserts must be there. Equilibrium is what neoclassical theory is all about. Equilibrium is the end point of all tendencies, and that which perpetually pulls all straying elements in its direction is the cosmic glue that coheres and patterns the whole economic universe.

The dynamic of neoclassical theory is the movement toward or around a point of equilibrium. Equilibrium is always there, yet never there, separated from the observable facts by the length of time that would be required for the flux to settle and for all tendencies to have found their place. Thus, a "market," a "short-run," and a "long-run" equilibrium each are defined by the time that it would take for more or less slowly maturing forces to detach themselves from where they happen to be and to find their proper place in a vast, forever changing, configuration. Equilibrium suggests a magnetic force that draws events toward a coherent pattern and determines the form of economic change and movement *through time*. There is movement in the neoclassical system, but not development. The neoclassical system moves perpetually; it never comes to rest. And it does not develop.

In his biographical sketch of Alfred Marshall, John Maynard Keynes singles out from among Marshall's "more striking contributions" his extension of "the proposition that value is determined at the equilibrium point of Demand and Supply . . . so as to discover a whole Copernican system by which all the elements of the universe are kept in their places by mutual counterpoise and interaction."[2]

The analogy is apt. As in the Copernican, so in the Marshallian universe all is preordained, "all the elements of Marshall's . . . universe are *kept in their places.*" The paths of the orbiting bodies are given, as are their velocities. Each itself revolves in fixed phases. There is movement, but there is no development.

Neoclassical economics was formed as, and in substance remains, an analytic of the parts. It focuses on fragments of exchange carved out within the boundaries of *ceteris paribus*. Without an equilibrating force that holds output, prices, and demand in persisting patterns, partial equilibrium disintegrates. An industry demand function, for example, referring to a relationship existing at an instant in time, says that everything else remaining equal (*ceteris paribus*), *then* such and such numbers of (say) houses will be purchased at the indicated prices. If everything else remains equal! But what are the other things that must remain equal for this demand function to retain its integrity?

The whole pattern of consumer demand must remain "equal," including the demand for the complementary goods that are needed along with houses and for the substitute goods that will be purchased instead of houses, or else the numbers of houses purchased at the indicated prices also will change. And the whole pattern of resource availabilities must remain the same since these determine the relative costs of complementary and substitute goods. And the distribution of income must remain the same or else expenditure patterns and hence the demand for houses as well as for other goods also would change. All must remain "equal," *ceteris paribus,* if this (or any) demand function is to retain its integrity.

Granting *ceteris paribus,* that is, that everything remains in a state of suspended animation *except that which specifically relates to a movement along a given demand function,* the question remains as to whether the demand function then could retain its integral and determinant character. Or will the very movement from point to point along a demand function change the understructure upon which the form of the curve depends? The answer must be that it will. Given a movement along the demand function, things cannot remain as they are and the curve as it was.

A significant shift from one point to another must reshape that whole substructure. The movement from one point of the demand function to another must redistribute income between those who sell houses and those who buy. Simultaneously, as income is redistributed, the wants and tastes of different groups come into play, necessarily changing all patterns of demand. Similarly, the movement along the demand function increases the input of resources into or releases resources from the production of the item demanded. This release or in-migration of resources necessarily changes the pattern of resource availabilities and product costs. The costs and prices of complementary and substitute goods must change, and so too must consumer expenditures on these goods.

Any significant movement up or down any supply or demand function sets in motion forces that simultaneously change its entire shape. The curve drawn with mathematical precision dissolves under the very movement it is supposed to describe. The posited functional relationship turns out to be incompatible with the assumption upon which it is based. And if the economist should propose the specified demand function as an instantaneous representation of the whole adjustment of the entire economic system to a significant change in the price-output of a single product, then *ipso facto* no two demand schedules could ever be operational simultaneously. The clear lines fade and vanish into a mist of indeterminacy.

Demand or supply functions as conceived in neoclassical economics are inherently indeterminant even with the assumption that there are no extraneous changes whatsoever, that is, no changes other than those tied into the demand or supply change itself.

This paradox can be resolved only if it can be assumed that powerful forces hold everything more or less continuously in equilibrium and particular deviations from equilibrium are only marginal and infinitesimal. Under such conditions, where output or demand changes are marginal, hence too small to have significant effect on the economy at large, only then do the supply and demand functions of microeconomics become conceptually viable as practical approximations. It does not matter then that those functions would crumble under the impact of large and significant internal change, for such change is excluded from the system. In this system changes are infinitesimal, trembling around the needlepoint of equilibrium, unable to shake the formidable force that holds everything more or less in place.

There of late have been gales of controversy in British economics over the notion of equilibrium, with Cambridge University as the center of the storm. Nicholas Kaldor and others have attacked the idea,[3] and F. H. Hahn has defended it,[4] except that the equilibrium that Hahn defends has ceased to have predictive value or, indeed, to be even a statement about what happens in the world. It has lost its role as the focal configuration toward which the realities of the economy forever must tend. It becomes for Hahn a conceivable state, the value of which would seem to be that by determining the preconditions of such a state, it becomes possible to rule out observed realities as being *not* in equilibrium. Kaldor's rejection of equilibrium rests on his contention that the declining cost function is the general condition of modern industry. What is the sense of his argument? In the first instance it is that the price-competitive market must then be unstable, with the size of firms increasing and their numbers declining until oligopoly prevails. Given oligopoly and following the line of neoclassical thought, the game that oligopolists would be obliged to play would be set by three incommensurable objectives: to maximize the profits of the industry, augment the share of the firm, and reduce costs through a continual increase in an integral output or through merger. Under those conditions there is no predetermined point of equilibrium. Should all industries be monopolized and under state control, a universal condition of declining costs would itself be no barrier to an optimizing allocation of resources and, in that sense, to an equilibrium imposed by plan and command.

### *Essence*

This conception of a universe in perpetual movement toward the hidden patterns of equilibrium carries with it an even more fundamental presupposition. All science turns on this question: Why should a statement be judged as true or accepted as credible? A philosopher-physicist such as Karl Popper would have replied that the statement of science is to be accepted because in its many permutations and following numerous lines of deductive prediction, it has been tested by reference to the concrete and specific facts and not yet been found wanting. Although continuously assailed by experimental prediction, it has not yet failed to conform with predicted results and measured facts. "Any form of statement," he would have said, "that cannot be so tested and falsified is not scientific and belongs to some other category of thought than that of science."

Although the basis of credibility in physics is by no means so clear-cut as Popper has supposed, this much can be granted. Its statements *conceivably* at least can be falsified through the test of concrete prediction. Not so for economics. Its statements cannot even conceivably be falsified by the measure of predicted event, for the fundamental statements of economics are not about concretely measurable events or measurable facts. Because they refer to a reality underlying the flux of observable event, they cannot be reached by the measurement of such event. As with equilibrium, there is implicit the notion of a definitive configuration beneath the ceaseless and confusing flux of day-to-day experience, where every element has a proper resting place, an end-point of all tendencies, that is itself never witnessed or achieved. Such truth is of another order than that of physics; it is akin, rather, to what the ancient Greeks called "essences," by which they meant ideas existing in the mind of God that find diverse, confused, and partial expression in human thought and in the artifacts of man's world. So too the equilibrium configuration belongs to the never-to-be-precisely-known or specifically observed essence of things. That the statement of essence is not scientific in the sense that those of physics are is not to say that it is false or useless. It can be most illuminating and useful, and probably it is the only possible way of generalizing upon the transitory events and contradictory phenomena of the economic universe or wherever phenomena and event are functions of ideologies and imagries.

On what basis then are we to accept or reject a theory that attempts to capture the essence of things? Only by a considered judgment based on personal observation and a weighing of the evidence pro and con; there is no rational alternative.

Having this epistemological character, neoclassical theory is vulnerable to at least two sorts of obscurantism. It has in fact succumbed to both.

First, in an age when science is the normative ideal, statements of any other order are falsely disguised in the forms of science. Neoclassical economics, pretending to that high status, recast its statements into the mathematical symbolism associated with physics. This introduction of mathematics into economics has heuristic value. It serves as a means of precisely stating simultaneous relationships that cannot be expressed in natural language except through metaphor. It also provides the most powerful means of deducing the measured consequences of an interacting complex of measurable events, when such problem solving is the task of the economist. But what of the establishment or disestablishment of the "truth" of general theory? In that regard, the mathematical formulation of physical theory is to be justified because it facilitates the determination of credibility through the test of prediction. In neoclassical economics, where general theory has the character of essence, statements cannot be so falsified and in fact have never been seriously challenged through the tests of specific prediction. On that account the recasting of its general theory into mathematical form has been obscurantist and profoundly antiscientific; such recasting never has served the purpose of test through inferential prediction, but has vitiated all possibility of common sense comparison of theory and event or the evaluation of statement by reference to living experience. Robert Heilbroner's "greater rigor, correspondingly mortis" has its roots in epistemological necessity.

Second, on rational grounds, statements of essence should be accepted only tentatively and continuously reevaluated in the light of new experience. The paradox is this: Necessarily resting on the fallibilities of judgment, partisans choose to accept the statements of essence as articles of faith, as total and exclusive, crowding out other directions of thought and blinding neoclassical or Marxist zealots to the variety of existing social forms. Even those who are sensible to the limitations of neoclassical theory seem unable to recognize the variety and coexistences of economic forms. I recall Wassily Leontief's Presidential Address before the American Economic Association,[5] where he condemned the mathematical model-building factories that constitute virtually the whole endeavor of modern economics. The only oasis that he saw in this wasteland was the achievement of agricultural economics. Yet, he failed to see the evident reason for this: Only in agriculture is there a relationship of reasonable approximation between the neoclassical model and the form of organization to which it refers. Even there, a decentralized, price directed economy survives and prospers only through the socialized organization of technological advance and the exercise of governmental control of price and output. Outside of agriculture, and particularly in that part of the economy dominated by the modern corporate enterprise, economic activity has a different form and rationale, requires a different conceptual framework and a different theory than neoclassical economics.

### *Individual Autonomy and the Theory of the Mind*

Two other presuppositions belong to the framework of thought in which neoclassical theory took form.

The first is a conception of the social universe as made up of autonomous individuals, independent decision makers, each operating in a kind of splendid isolation. With that idea of the world as its reference, neoclassical thought gives inevitable primacy to those values that attach to individualized choice and exchange, for example, "liberty" and the satisfactions of private consumption. Thus, it also is able to conceptualize and to accept the legitimacy only of those institutions and social arrangements that are selectively perceived as protecting and projecting individualized choice and mutually advantageous exchange, for example, property, contract, and competitive markets. It is a paradigm that hardly can take into account the economy of large organizations, or an analytic of organizational (as opposed to individualized) choice; neither can it recognize the values of community, the structures of society, nor the table of collective values.

The second is a conception of mind, the mind of the autonomous individual who, in his numbers, populates the economy of private choice and free exchange. Mind is understood as approximating the perfect instrument of pleasure and pain, work dissatisfaction and consumption satisfaction, utility optimizing, preference balancing, cost minimizing calculus with cost differentials, opportunity sets, wants, utilities or preference relationships taken as given. It is an idea of the mind which is wholly unable to explain and in consequence rules out of account (1) culture based differences in behavior, (2) significant variations in the levels of economic performance, and, most important, (3) the process of individual, group, or social learning. This is the reason for its incapacity to go beyond the naïve mystique of capital accumulation in any analysis of technological advance or technology transfer, hence of economic growth or development.

### *Marginalism*

Marginalism, closely associated with neoclassical theory, is at once an analytic technique, a normative guide, and an hypothesis of behavior, conveying the idea of an economy where all choice has the character of incremental adjustments from established positions. Empirical studies dating from those by Charles Hitch in the early 1940s have challenged this hypothesis, while theorists have defended it as an underlying rationale. The question remains as to whether the marginal calculus is truly rational. Even assuming pure competition, its logic will depend upon whether product outputs and resource inputs are minutely variable and upon the costs of measuring the costs of small variations. When choice is between integral processes requiring particular sets of resource inputs, or when outputs are fixed in relation to resource inputs, marginalism becomes irrelevant. The element of monopoly adds to the difficulties of measuring the cost effects of marginal variations in factor inputs, the probable insurmountable difficulties of anticipating the price effects consequent upon marginal changes in any significant range of offerings. Nor has the marginal calculus anything to do with the games that oligopolists play for market share and power. When we leave the assumption of individual autonomy, the marginal calculus becomes less meaningful still in any effort to account for corporation policy and behavior as a species of organizational (hence quasi-political) choice. For the engineering choice between technologies, or in the big, sustained, irreversible jumps from product to product, or market to market, or operating structure to operating structure, marginalism is irrelevant. Even further from its scope is the process of innovation in which the creative venture in uncertainty is the crux.

### *The Disappearing Quanta*

The edifice of classical and neoclassical economics was erected on the three quanta: land, labor, and capital, once considered a solid and unshakable foundation. That erstwhile solidity is now dissolving as our conception of each one of these three fundamental factors disintegrates or is transformed.

Land, the domain of nature, once understood as immutable and fixed forever, is conceived now as a limited stock, extendible through technological advance and depleting with enormous rapidity as the sheer consequence of industrial existence. Both extension and depletion are outside the scope of the theory.

Labor, once understood as the homogeneous sea of muscle and belly springing forth from the womb of Eve so long as a wage was sufficient to sustain it, has been transformed into the human resource whose economic worth is a function of learning (signalled by such catch phrases as "investment in human capital") and of culture. Both learning and culture are outside the scope of the theory.

Capital, once the conceptual axis upon which Marxist and neoclassical theory turned, has been the most completely disintegrated. Its viability was undermined by Moses Abramovitz's studies in the 1950s.[6] Elsewhere I have demonstrated the circularity inherent in its measurement and the falsity of its *a priori* claims.[7] Cambridge economists, particularly Luigi Passinatti, A. J. Fischer, Piero Sraffa, and Joan Robinson, have made the attack upon it into their credo.

### *The Policy Blueprint*

Whatever it is worth as a statement about the real, neoclassical theory also has served as a normative ideal. This is legitimate. We need utopias in order to select our goals and to guide our choice. What is not legitimate is to pose this form of economic organization as the ideal without objectively comparing its virtues and defects with those of alternatives. Finally, then, let us suggest something of what is involved in contrasting the neoclassical blueprint with alternatives.

There are various possible criteria of comparison. Economic organizations might be compared as ways of life or as systems for technological progress and economic growth. Since our purpose here is simply illustrative, the traditional criterion of efficiency will suffice. It could, on *a priori* grounds, be claimed that an economy organized according to the neoclassical blueprint would be sensitive to shifts in consumer priorities and would respond spontaneously to relative resource scarcities registered in the indexes of price. Such an economy, moreover, would have the great advantage of a built-in incentive to work and to organize efficiently and would provide as well for the automatic weeding out of inefficient operations and recruitment of a leadership of proven talent. It would, on the other hand, be burdened by the following: (1) extreme and pervasive uncertainties; (2) extreme price instabilities with detrimental consequences upon time-extended contractual arrangements; (3) the need to rely on windfall profits and loss to guide the reallocation of resources, with consequent distributional inequities and a random selection of economic leadership; (4) to the maximum degree, the "externalization" of costs and benefits, with a consequent distortion of economic choice; and, as well (5) the externalization of options and opportunities with the consequent limitation on transformation and development. Cost and benefits are externalized by separating the agency of choice from responsibility for or concern with the diffused effects of its choice; opportunities are externalized by reducing the resources available to any decision maker—both species of externalization are functions of decentralized power.

Again for the sake of illustration, consider the consequences of one sort of externality, recognizable in the apparatus of neoclassical theory. The upward or downward slope of industry supply curves and cost functions are entirely functions of economies and diseconomies external to the firm. Therefore, the response of an industry in pure competition to a change in demand takes no account of the *marginal* costs of going from one level of industry output to another. It follows from the neoclassical rationale that, given an outward shift in market demand, the industry always must overrespond when its cost function is rising and underrespond when its costs ride downward. This leads to a curious paradox.

If neoclassical theorists have seen pure competition as a kind of paradise on earth, hell would be a world of monopolies. Some have held that the great value of socialism is that the economy then could be commanded to follow the rules of pure competition.[8] Permit us the converse of that fantasy. Consider an economy where a single enterprise controls production at each market juncture, and that enterprise is instructed to act as the pure monopolist of neoclassical theory. Neither labor nor the consumer would have any countervailing bargaining power, and resource prices and wages would be allowed to fall until all were employed. The huge profit residuals of these great monopolies then could be siphoned off without affecting managerial decision or work motivation; and those profits, constituting the whole "surplus product," would be transferred into a general fund to (1) supplement earned incomes, (2) support collective goals, and (3) promote the advance of technology and hence the rise of productivity.

How then would such an economy of pure monopoly compare with one of pure competition? In both cases resources would be fully employed and at the level of the enterprise, economized in about the same way. In the allocation of resources, *incremental* costs or savings consequent upon a change in the output of the industry would be taken into account in the economy of monopolies and not in the economy of pure competition. As an instrument for the efficient allocation of resources, the economy of monopolies would on that account be preferred.

Economic choice is guided not only by cost considerations, but also by revenue anticipations. Under pure monopoly, not average but marginal revenue would guide the comparative response of industries to shifts in their demand. The converse is true for pure competition. If it were possible to offer the two output conglomerates as alternative packages on the market, the pattern of outputs produced in the universe of pure monopolies would command the higher price since, in responding to marginal rather than average revenue, it would be more fully sensitized to relative intensities of demand.

The universe of pure monopolies would have the advantages also in achieving a "just" distribution of income. Windfalls would not be required by its dynamic of transformation and change. Hence, a great part of the economic product could be siphoned off without affecting the operations of the economy to be redistributed according to whatever criterion of justice might prevail.

Granted, this game of imaginary worlds is an uncertain and dangerous one; nevertheless, it says something about the neoclassical blueprint that, playing the game by the neoclassical rules, we find the very antithesis of pure competition to more closely approximate the neoclassical welfare ideal of efficiency and distributive justice.

## *Conclusion*

This has been a critique. But if I came not to praise neoclassical theory, neither did I hope to bury it. It is a body of thought deeply embedded in the social and political outlook. It is deeply embedded in my own outlook as well, and it has been useful to me in making sense of observation and experience. As the most evolved of all social theories, it sensitizes those who master it to the complex and subtle webwork of relationships of which observed events are only surface nodules. It has played an important role in history, in ideological controversy, in the formation of institutions, and in the development of policy. For all these reasons it needs to be studied and understood—but in perspective.

## *Notes*

1. J. R. Hicks, *Value and Capital* (Oxford: Clarendon Press, 1946), p. 43–85.
2. J. M. Keynes, *Essays in Biography* (London: Macmillan, 1933), p. 223.
3. Nicholas Kaldor, "The Irrelevance of Equilibrium Economics," *Economic Journal* 82 (December 1972): 1237–52; and Jonas Kornai, *Anti-Equilibrium* (Amsterdam: North Holland, 1971).
4. F. H. Hahn, *On the Notion of Equilibrium in Economics*, an Inaugural Lecture (Cambridge: Cambridge University Press, 1973).
5. Wassily Leontief, "Theoretical Assumptions and Non-Observed Facts," *American Economic Review* 61 (March 1971): 1–7.
6. "Resource and Output Trends in the United States Since 1870," *American Economic Review: Proceedings* 46 (May 1956): 5–23.
7. *Economic Organizations and Social Systems* (Indianapolis: Bobbs Merrill, 1967), chapter 7.
8. A. P. Lerner, *The Economics of Control* (New York: Macmillan, 1946).

# 4

# The Heterodox Methodology of Two Chicago Economists

*Eva and Abraham Hirsch*

In the area of methodology, the "old" and "new" Chicago School seem literally poles apart. Frank Knight, spokesman for the old, was the archenemy of positivism; Milton Friedman, representative of the new, is its great champion.[1] Yet, in at least one respect they are alike. In relation to the Nassau Senior/J.E. Cairnes tradition which has dominated mainstream Anglo-Saxon economic methodology,[2] both Knight and Friedman are heterodox. It is this heterodoxy to which major attention will be devoted in this article. First, the major characteristics of the Senior/Cairnes methodology will be considered as a context for what follows. Knight's views, and then Friedman's, will be examined. It is not our purpose to cover the subjects' work comprehensively, nor to undertake a detailed critique of their views on methodology. Occasional reference is made to the work and ideas of Knight and Friedman which fall outside the area of methodology, but only where this material is relevant to methodology. Where questions are raised it is primarily for the purpose of illuminating differences between vision and its rationalization. The last part of the article will consider whether Knight and Friedman are as far apart as they appear to be and whether, despite any difference, there can be distilled from their work a set of ideas

*The authors are, respectively, Associate Professor of Economics, Rutgers University, Newark, New Jersey, and Professor of Economics, Brooklyn College, Brooklyn, New York.*

which might be characterized as the methodological preferences of the Chicago School.

### *The Senior/Cairnes Methodology*

Methodologists in the Senior/Cairnes tradition argue that economics is a "science."[3] Skeptics dismiss this as window dressing, and in a sense the criticism hits the mark. What skeptics overlook, however, is that the association of economics with science shows a real intention, a choice to follow a predictive rather than an assumptive approach and to make economics one of the family of predictive disciplines.[4] The assumer determines validity by correct logical deduction from premises which are necessarily true, the predictor in the correspondence of the predictions of theory with the real world. The assumer may feel that his work has predictive relevance since true premises lead to conclusions which are at least part of the truth. The predictor is not necessarily unconcerned with the truth of his premises since untruth affects the quality of predictions.[5] But an assumer does not judge theory on how well it predicts, nor does the predictor on the basis of self-evident premises. Thus methodologists compare economics with physics rather than with metaphysics because, reflecting a view that long has prevailed in the community of economists, their objective is to attain the kind of predictive power the physicist has, rather than to derive the kind of explanations that are characteristic of metaphysics.

But having chosen the predictor family, methodologists have found it very difficult to remain inside its bounds. First, they generally ruled out the possibility of deriving premises for theorizing from detailed observation of specific experience, as is done in the other predictive disciplines.[6] This choice could be defended on the ground that what counts is not how the premises are derived, but how well they predict.[7] Fair enough. But having ruled our the a *posteriori* method,[8] they then appealed to the truth of their premises in defending economic theory! Nassau Senior, J. E. Cairnes, John Neville Keynes, and Lionel Robbins all followed this course.[9] They did so because economics is really political economy, and if the economist had offered policy proposals and given as his authority the record of his past predictions, he would have looked rather silly.[10] It was easier to be disloyal to the prediction family and appeal to the truth of premises. (Not so John Stuart Mill. He was a reasonably consistent predictor who earned a reputation as black sheep of mainstream methodology because of it.[11])

This inconsistency in the position of mainstream economic methodology posed a problem. Since theory oversimplifies, even if premises are unqualifiedly true, as Mill pointed out, the conclusions will predict only if "disturbing causes" are unimportant.[12] In other words, in order to be able to predict, the premises not only must be true but also must include all the forces that "operate in a predominating way," as J. N. Keynes put it.[13] Few mainstream economists today believe that this condition is fulfilled,[14] but until relatively recently most economists felt that it was, and methodologists reflected their consensus, including Lionel Robbins [50, p. 152] in 1933 and Benjamin Higgins [17, p. 27], in a work on methodology, as late as 1951.

### *Frank H. Knight*

Frank Hyneman Knight was reared in the same rigid, narrow-minded, dogmatic environment as the institutionalists, an environment in which the common prejudices of the community were elevated to the status of premises for academic ("common sense") philosophizing,[15] and the foundations of economic thought were said to be on a par with the teachings of Christianity.[16] It was an environment in which contradictions between what economists did and what they said they were doing appeared to a sharp observer even greater than generally has been the case. Institutionalists, such as Wesley Clair Mitchell, saw through the methodological inconsistency of the Senior/Cairnes tradition, wrote off economic theory as mostly a misguided enterprise, and opted for an economic theory that was truly predictive.[17] Knight recognized the inconsistency, too, but reacted differently. He saw value in the theory, finding fault only in its misuse.[18] To achieve consistency, Knight removed economics from the predictor family altogether,[19] a bold stroke which had much to recommend it as far as representation of what actually prevailed in the past was concerned, and perhaps even as guide for the future. But being so out of line with the trend of the times put Knight beyond the pale, a philosopher who had insightful things to say on assorted subjects, but hardly one to follow in the area of methodology.

The benefits that Knight could show from putting economics into the assumer family were impressive, among them the fact that he unselfconsciously could appeal to premises and argue about them in a most persuasive fashion. The thesis that the validity of the behavioral foundations of economic theory could be established by observation might be relatively easy to demolish.[20] The notion that there is an aspect of our behavior which corresponds to the behavioral assumptions of neoclassical economic thought and that is necessarily true cannot be so easily controverted.[21] One could ask, of course, whether this made for a discipline which is very meaningful or useful, but that is another question, and one to which Knight had an answer.

The reason Knight could deal so adeptly with the question of significance was that he viewed economics as being an assumer rather than predictive discipline. A true assumer does not see a contradiction between theory which is both positive and normative, nor need he avoid introducing his own value scale in building his system. Thus, Knight saw the chief role of economic theory—what he called "pure theory"—as the clarification of value choices in a liberal society. He did not argue that economic theory "proves" the case for liberal policies. Quite the other way around. It is only in a liberal society, Knight felt, that economic theory finds its true significance.[22] Belief in liberal society rests upon freedom as value, according to Knight, and it is supported by an understanding of how limited is our ability to predict human behavior.[23] Knight did not apologize, as did Alfred Marshall, for example,[24] for the intrusion of political values into the economic theorizing of his predecessors. He felt that it was the correct procedure, and one that should be carried on in the present.[25]

This was only one side of Knight's views on methodology. He also believed that economic theory has instrumental value, that is, that it can help us find the means to achieve desired ends.[26] In this, the portion of his methodology which deals with what generally is regarded as the province of methodology as such, Knight comes closer to the Senior/Cairnes tradition, but even here there are significant differences. As already observed, Knight is more direct and unselfconscious in basing his arguments on the self-evident nature of the premises. More important, being very well aware that we deal in economic theory with only part of man's nature, a part which may not predominate in any situation or area, and recognizing that there are "disturbing causes" which cannot be identified and measured in any systematic and objective manner, Knight does not give "verification" of theory any role in his system, nor does he need to duck the issue. This, of course, follows to a large extent from Knight's unashamed assumer stance. It gives his methodology, even the part dealing with the instrumental side of economics, an entirely different flavor. Although economists until quite recently pretty much neglected the verification aspect of the methodology to which they supposedly subscribed, methodologists either had to give it a definite role or gloss over the issue, else economics would have lost its link with the predictor family.[27] Knight was under no such constraint.

Since Knight makes economics an assumer discipline, and since the term *science* generally has been associated with the predictor family, one might have expected Knight to argue against the notion that economics is a science. We find, in fact, that he does. In page after page Knight embellishes and reiterates this thesis. Man is an animal who responds in a predictable fashion to stimuli, he admits. But he is also a knower whose knowledge of predictions will upset predictions; he is a calculating animal whose calculation of the best means to achieve ends leaves its mark; he is a romantic searcher after new values, a problem solver, a maker of mistakes. As a consequence, Knight feels, one could not expect to deal successfully with human behavior in the way one deals with material which does not have these complicating characteristics. Knight observes, for example, that

> human phenomena are not amenable to treatment in accordance with the strict canons of science. They will not yield generalizations which can be used as the basis of prediction and the guidance of policy, because there are no generalizations about them which are true. . . . It seems to us that science is a special technique developed for and applicable to the control of physical nature, but that the ideal constantly preached and reiterated, of carrying its procedure over into the field of the social phenomena rests on a serious misapprehension.[28]

Yet, having said this much, Knight backtracks and argues that economics *is* a science. He states flatly that "there is a science of economics, a true, and even exact, science, which reaches laws as universal as those of mathematics and mechanics."[29] One is tempted to resolve the paradox by saying that Knight believed that in *form* economics is a science, but this would be incorrect; for a true rationalist such as Knight, form without content has little usefulness or meaning. In fact, we see no way of resolving this paradox, but we can note some of Knight's arguments and observe why we feel they are unsatisfactory in the context of his own frame of thought.

One argument Knight uses is that the laws of economics are like the laws of mathematics, which are "characteristics of the world we live in, but characteristics so obvious that it is impossible to escape recognizing them and so fundamental that to think them away would necessitate creating in the imagination a different type of universe." One could argue with this conception of mathematics, but more to the point is the purpose for which Knight uses it. Were he unconcerned with practical usefulness, the matter would be academic. But the very purpose for which the relation is made is to show that since mathematics is useful, although abstract, economics must have the same kind of usefulness. Of mathematics he says that "its conclusions are descriptive of reality and are indispensable in predicting and controlling the phenomena of the physical world."[30] The problem here is that mathematics as such has no usefulness whatsoever; a particular calculus (or model) of mathematics may be useful when applied (or interpreted) in a particular area, but it must be *demonstrated in each area* that the application works. We have by now had enough evidence of the usefulness of different calculi of mathematics to agree *in general* that mathematics is useful. But does this carry over for economic theory, a specific calculus? Above all, what does the whole argument tell us about economic science, particularly economics as an *empirical* science?

A second argument Knight uses is that economics is like classical mechanics (and theoretical physics generally) because the conclusions of mechanics hold true only for an "ideal" universe, in the case of mechanics a frictionless world.[31] Friction, of course, is identifiable and measurable, and it can be demonstrated that the less friction, the better the predictions. This makes it possible to give "verification" of predictions such a central role in physics. In fact, the role is so fundamental, as Knight himself seemed to believe, that theory in physics which did not predict would not be given an important place in the science for very long. As Knight observes, "science, then, is merely the *technique of prediction*."[32] Arguments that premises are necessary truths are not convincing to the physicist. As a result, economists such as Mill, impressed with this state of affairs and desiring to make economics a "true" science, have argued that theory should be judged on how well it predicts.[33] Not so Knight, of course, who grounded theory on necessary truths.[34] Then what sense does it make to argue that economic theory is like theoretical physics?

It is true, of course, that both theoretical physics and economic theory oversimplify and therefore must be supplemented when applied. But the significant point is that the way theory is applied is so different, according to Knight himself. Knight was annoyed because economic theory was criticized for oversimplifying, whereas physics was not,[35] but such criticism against economics arose at least partly because its theory, no matter how applied, did not yield reliable predictions. The criticism of oversimplification was merely an attempt to find reasons for the failure. To answer the criticism Knight would have had to demonstrate that if simplifications are properly allowed for, the theory does give reasonably good predictions which are not dependent upon the unique intuitive skill of the particular predictor. As Knight observes, "in general, truth cannot be considered scientific unless it is demonstrable, which means that it must be alike for all observers and accurately communicable."[36] Knight instead gives the distinct impression in most of his writings that he felt that, even if properly applied, economic theory could not do this. Typical are statements such as these: Applied economics is inherently "at least as much an art based on general knowledge and sound judgment as a science with accurate premises and rigorous conclusions," and "it is not conceivably possibly to 'verify' any propositions about 'economic' behavior by any 'empirical' procedure, if the key words of this statement are defined as they must be defined to be used with relevance and precision."[37]

Knight uses still another argument in this same area, a thrust apparently aimed at the common criticism that physicists generally agree, but economists do not. Knight observes that, even in physics, "truth" is determined by the consensus of the fraternity of competent physicists, as in agreement on the results of experiment.[38] Of course, this is true. Yet to say that the difference between economics and physics in this respect is a matter of degree, even if it is admitted that the degree is large, does far more to mislead than to point up a significant connection. In the predictive disciplines such as physics, some disagreement does occur, of course, and in the rationalistic disciplines such as metaphysics, men in the field sometimes do agree about what is supposedly self-evident. What seems significant about this, however, is the difference in kind between the two processes of trying to reach agreement, not the fact that agreement and disagreement are possible in both areas.

More can and should be said about Knight's views about economics as science. The questions asked here, however, merely were raised to show that this is the most vulnerable portion of Knight's methodological formulations, to suggest that it is not an inherent element in the methodological vision which Knight was trying to rationalize, and to argue that even an admirer who accepted all else that Knight taught, but came of age a generation or so later and absorbed notions about science which were taken for granted by then, likely would have had difficulty going along with Knight in this area. We only can speculate whether Friedman found himself in this position as a student of Knight's and note that the conjecture that he did does not seem incompatible with the available evidence.

## *Milton Friedman*

At first glance Friedman's methodology seems to represent a revolt of student against teacher, for Friedman does nothing less than turn Knight's methodology inside out. But more careful reading shows that this is not at all the case. In fact, Friedman in his methodology is manning the same barricades in defense of economic theory. The common enemy is the critic of traditional theory who attacks the validity of premises.[39] A major mission of Knight's from the first was to parry such threats by admitting that the premises of economic theory were "unrealistic," but then going on to argue that it was the very unrealism of the theory which made it valuable. Thus, as Knight saw it, "the makers and users of economic analysis have in general still to be made to see that deductions from theory are necessary, not because literally true—that in the strict sense they are useful *because not* literally true—but only if they bear a certain relation to literal truth and if all who work with them constantly bear in mind what that relation is."[40] Friedman, too, argues that unrealism can be a virtue,[41] a feature of his methodology which has generated a great deal of argument, but he modifies its character by putting the argument in a different context, as will be shown in what follows.

Friedman, too, came of age when traditional economic theory was under attack, but the critics were now not institutionalists attacking from the "outside"; they were members in good standing of the economics fraternity who had begun to have doubts about the assumptions of traditional theory. Since the ability of theory to predict, according to mainstream methodology, depends not only upon the truth of the premises, but also upon whether the forces taken account of in the premises have a predominating effect, it seemed clear that what was needed was to erect new theory on more adequate premises. The result, as everyone knows, was a series of revolutions which have made economic theory very different from the way it was in Alfred Marshall's day. Not only was new theory developed, but also the way theory was envisaged underwent radical change. Theory now tended to be seen as "models" which were entirely analytic (not empirical or synthetic), and it was posited that such models could be fruitfully applied only where the assumptions of the model corresponded with what prevailed in fact.[42] That Marshallian theory as such did not have the requisite "realism"—much as it might be useful in some undefined way as "analysis"—generally had come to be accepted. It was to show that the new trends represented retrogression rather than advance that Friedman's methodology was formulated.

Knight himself had argued against the new trends, but his arguments lack the force of his earlier broadsides.[43] Perhaps this is because weapons fashioned for one purpose do not serve as well for another. It may also be that the arguments seem less effective because we ourselves have been affected so directly by the new trends that arguments against them do not convince so easily. In any case, Friedman resumed where

Knight left off, and instead of renovating the Knightian structure, he chose to erect a new, more contemporary one, a methodology which was consistent, as Knight's was not, with the prevalent view that economics was a mature science. In developing his methodology Knight used science negatively; his positive references are peripheral and, as we have tried to show, somwhat puzzling. Friedman puts "science" at the center of his analysis.[44] As did Knight, Friedman rejected the Senior/Cairnes methodological tradition, wherein economics takes on the dual character of being ostensibly predictive, but mostly assumer in fact. But whereas Knight resolved the dualism by putting economics squarely into the assumer family, Friedman resolved it by making economics a member of the predictive group. His methodology, in effect, attempts to draw the implications from this choice.

Friedman downgrades analysis as such to the status of mere language,[45] which is its role in the predictor family. He argues that theory be judged primarily by how well it predicts. He even goes so far as to welcome back the *a posteriori,* which had been banished from economics since before Mill's time, and seems to be suggesting that the derivation of theory from specific observation is not only the way it should be derived, but also the way it always has been derived. He tells us that

> Theory can be used in two very different ways in the development of a science. The approach that is standard in the physical sciences is to use theory to derive generalizations about the real world. The theorist starts with some set of observed and related facts. . . . He seeks a generalization that will explain these facts. . . . He tests this theory to make sure that it is logically consistent, that its elements are susceptible of empirical determination, that it will explain adequately the facts he started with. He then seeks to deduce from his theory facts other than those he used to derive it and to check these deductions against reality.[46]

All of this is fully consistent. Problems arise when Friedman begins to argue within this context, as Knight had within his, that the lack of realism of premises can be a strength rather than a failing.

Critics of Friedman point out that he gets himself into fundamental problems of logic,[47] that he seems to rule theory out altogether in favor of empirical generalizations,[48] that contrary to his argument there is a vital connection between the truth of premises and the ability of a theory to predict.[49] Friedman's formulations invite such criticism. A more sympathetic reading, however, suggests that, *within the context of the predictive disciplines,* theory that does not in time yield testable predictions is considered of little value, that theory whose assumptions are not entirely true (or whose truth or falsity is not known) may yet be exceedingly valuable,[50] that the choice between a theory which has more realistic assumptions and one which gives better predictions probably would be made in favor of the latter. But since so much debate has ensued in this area, it would be to little purpose to cover this ground yet once again.[51] There are, however, other questions that Friedman's formulations raise which have not been asked and that are more germane to our purpose.

First, Friedman presents his methodology not only as an ideal, but also as the rationale of economic science which is implicit in work of the past.[52] It is an intriguing thesis and worth more attention than can be devoted to it here. Suffice it to note that, at least on the face of it, it does not seem to be borne out by the facts. For example, do we judge advance in economics by theories' power to predict? Is neoclassical considered to be superior to classical theory because of its greater predictive power? The solution of the "paradox of value" is considered a matter of some importance in the history of economics. Does it represent much of an advance in the power to predict? If we reject Friedman's references to the past and argue that this is the way things should be rather than the way they have been, his thesis stands on firmer ground, but questions still remain.

If economics is taken to be a member of the predictor family, we must be able to demonstrate objectively that the theory which we accept does, indeed, have some minimum of predictive power. It was the failure to be able to do so, we have suggested previously, which led methodologists of the Senior/Cairnes tradition away from predictive moorings. Has the situation changed that much today? Not on Friedman's showing. In arguing for the maximum-of-returns hypothesis, for example, Friedman does not demonstrate predictive power; rather, he admits that "this evidence is extremely hard to document; it is scattered in numerous memorandums, articles and monographs concerned primarily with specific concrete problems rather than with submitting the hypothesis to test."[53] If the data are really there, and if we are committed to Friedman's methodology, would it not be of vital importance to gather it together as the only real support for the hypothesis? When we do, of course, we might be in for a surprise. Until more work is done, might not the declaration of a methodological revolution be premature?

Not having the data, Friedman resorts to the classic argument in favor of the maximum-of-returns hypothesis. He argues that it is inconceivable to think differently from what we know about the world.[54] Here is an assumer argument somehow lost in the midst of Friedman's predictive methodology.[55] In this instance the matter is not merely one of formulation; it points up a fundamental question: Is a true predictive economics an attainable ideal? Fritz Machlup, staunch defender of mainstream economic thought, admits that "the test of most of our theories will be more nearly of the character of *illustrations* than of the kind possible in relation with repeated controlled experiments or with recurring fully identified situations."[56] Under such circumstances is the kind of "mature" science of economics, which Friedman ostensibly champions, attainable? Some of Knight's arguments certainly leave one in doubt. One wonders, in fact, about Friedman himself. Might he, in his enthusiasm to formulate a methodology that was consistent with prevailing views in philosophy of science, have made statements whose implications he would not be ready to accept?[57]

## *The Chicago Core*

So far we have tried to show how the methodologies of Knight and Friedman differed from those in the Senior/Cairnes tradition and how they differed from each other. The latter difference is obviously great, and we here can reiterate the observation made in the introduction, since examination does indeed show that the two are poles apart.[58] Yet, it could be argued that on a deeper level the basic feelings about the character of economic theory of Knight and Friedman are essentially the same and to suggest as an hypothesis that these notions validly can be described as belonging to that group of economists who have been identified as members of the Chicago School.[59] The two basic notions are: (1) Mainstream economic theory, which was developed from Adam Smith to Marshall, is not mere analysis; it has empirical significance, that is, it tells us what actually happens in the real world. It may be only part of the truth, but it is the truth nonetheless; and (2) while economic theory tells us what actually happens, it gives us a picture that is true only in the most broad and general terms. Thus, if we hold the theory too closely to account for detailed observation, it may appear to be falsified, even though, on a broader view, it is generally valid.

Friedman's emphasis is stronger on the first point, Knight's on the second, but one finds evidence that Knight and Friedman adhered to both. Thus, Friedman argues very vigorously against abstract theorizing and holds up Marshall as an example of one who properly developed the kind of theory which helps us to discover tendencies in the real world.[60] That Marshall himself half succumbed to the sin of mere analysis in his formulations of demand theory, Friedman admits, but Friedman tries to convince us of the superiority of a side of Marshall on demand which is more empirically oriented.[61] Friedman's criticism of Léon Walras, Oskar Lange, and Abba P. Lerner, specifically, and of most trends in contemporary economic thought, generally, centers on this point.[62] Furthermore, Friedman takes on a defense of the maximum-of-returns hypothesis even though, as we have shown, it gets him into difficulty. Such a defense was necessary because without it neoclassical thought is left mostly an analytic shell. Some would say that even as analysis this theory can be exceedingly useful, but not Friedman. His criterion of acceptability is that theory be in some sense descriptive of the real world.

There is less obvious stress in Knight on the first point, but it is quite clear that he adheres to it just as fervently. As assumer he has no use for analytic bones without the flesh of reality attached to them.[63] That is at least one reason why very early he dissociated himself from mathematical economics.[64] His arguments for economic "science," if they have any purpose at all, are to support the contention that economic theory is as "real," even if abstract, as is theoretical physics.[65] Telling, too, is Knight's association with his fellow Chicagoans during the Great Depression in urging government action through spending to increase the money supply. Knight was not as explicit as were others who more directly concerned themselves with money,[66] but at Chicago, according to Friedman, "the quantity theory was connected and integrated with general price theory and became a flexible and sensitive tool for interpreting movements in aggregate economic activity and for developing relevant policy prescriptions."[67] Methodologically, this contrasts sharply with A.C. Pigou's view, for example, that "the 'quantity theory' is often defended and opposed as though it were a definite set of propositions that must be either true or false. But in fact the formulae employed in the exposition of that theory are merely devices for enabling us to bring together in an orderly way the principal causes by which the value of money is determined."[68]

With regard to the second point—that is, the one having to do with the limitations of theory—little need be added to what already has been said concerning Knight. From the beginning to the end it was a central theme in his work. Friedman has said little directly on this score, and one must admit that the spirit of his positivism on the face of it does not seem to go very well with notions about limitations. However, a careful reading of Friedman does show that he is very specific about the need to explore where and to what extent the theory does or does not hold,[69] and it is hard to believe that his general endorsement of Marshall as guide in today's times does not have attached to it implicitly the kind of cautions about which Knight was so eloquently explicit. Friedman's policy conclusions from his monetary work are also pertinent in this regard. Although a fervent believer in the relationship between changes in the quantity of money and income, he does not draw from the (positivist) results of research the conclusion that there is a basis in this for close control. Rather, he urges that the results best can be used as general guide in the formulation of policy in a manner which is reminiscent of the use of the quantity theory by others from Chicago in the 1930s.[70]

Both Knight's and Friedman's methodological formulations founder on their attempt to link up economics with science. Knight got into difficulty because the rationale of economics he developed does not fit with science; Friedman is unconvincing because he established an ideal from which he himself, even at this late date, is forced to back away. One must distinguish, however, between a vision and its rationalization. The vision that seems common to both men needs more careful formulation by its adherents and more serious scrutiny by its critics. We strongly suspect that further examination will show that it was this vision which guided mainstream economic thought until relatively recent times. The vision was accepted too uncritically at one time and tends to be rejected too cavalierly today. To judge it more intelligently and more fairly we must try to understand what the vision is. Knight and Friedman not only can help us understand, but also can show why understanding in this area is so difficult to achieve.

## Notes

1. Knight and Friedman use the term *positivism* somewhat differently. To Knight [24, p. 226], positivism involves using the methods of physical science, which excludes the kind of concern with means-ends calculations with which economic theory deals. Friedman [12, pp. 3–7] uses the term merely to exclude concern with norms. As will be seen in what follows, however, the difference in methodological formulations is more than a matter of semantics.
2. Lionel Robbins [50, p. 82] speaks of the Senior/Cairnes tradition, with which he identifies. J.N. Keynes [21] differs from the others in some respects, but on the whole is in conformity with it. John Stuart Mill [43; 44], for reasons suggested below, does not belong. T.W. Hutchison [20, p. 745], too, refers to the Senior/Cairnes tradition.

3. For example, Cairnes [5, pp. 16–20]; Keynes [21, pp. 149–52]; Robbins [50, pp. 78–79]; and Higgins [14, pp. 9–22].
4. We would have preferred to use more familiar labels, but terms such as *rationalist* and *positivist* have too many meanings and too many complex associations attached to them to serve well for our purposes. John Dewey [8] makes the comparison we have in mind when he analyzes what he calls "the natural history of thinking," referring to the first (assumer approach) as the "discussion" mode and to the second (predictor) as the "inference" mode. He observes (p. 844): "What makes the essential difference between modern research and the reflection of, say, the Greeks, [is] the presence of conditions for testing results." However, Dewey has no doubts but that the "inference" approach is superior to that of "discussion"; so far as theoretical economics is concerned, we feel that this is very much an open question. The reason for our doubts will be apparent in the part of the article dealing with Friedman's contribution.
5. Melitz [41] shows this clearly.
6. Cairnes [5, pp. 60–87]; and Robbins [50, pp. 104–21]. Mill [43, pp. 423–35] argues this point persuasively. Keynes [21, pp. 227–36] is somewhat ambiguous, but in the areas of traditional theory (pp. 207–15), he is very much in line with the others.
7. Popper [49, p. 31].
8. Mill [43, pp. 423–24] stacked the cards, so to speak, by defining the *a posteriori* method as one in which only empirical generalizations are derived from detailed investigation of the facts. We include the derivation of postulates for theorizing. Both uses conform to the traditional philosophical conception of the term, but ours, we feel, is more in conformity with common usage.
9. Bowley on Senior [1, p. 43]; Cairnes [5, pp. 39–45]; Keynes [21, pp. 223–26, 240]; and Robbins [50, pp. 78–80].
10. Senior notes, as quoted in Cairnes [5, p. 51]: "No one listens to an exposition of what might be the state of things under given but unreal conditions with the interest with which he hears a statement of what is actually taking place." This illustrates, if indeed illustration is needed, that methodologists were not unconcerned with the policy issue in formulating methodological principles.
11. For criticism of Mill see Keynes [21, pp. 233–34, 115–19]; and Robbins [50, p. 150]. Mill particularly irritated Alfred Marshall, who spoke of "the baneful spell of Mill's logic." (The quote is from an unpublished letter by John Whittaker in an article to appear in the *Journal of Political Economy*.)
12. Mill [43, p. 429] introduced this term.
13. Keynes [21, pp. 223–24].
14. For example, J.R. Hicks [16, p. 23] talks of "the assumption, at the beginning of every economic argument, that the things to be dealt with in the argument are the only things that matter in some practical problem." He adds: "This is always a dangerous assumption, and nearly always more or less wrong—which is why the application of economic theory is such a ticklish matter."
15. Compare, for example, Dorfman [10, chapter 2].

16. For example, Laughlin [34].
17. For example, Mitchell [45, pp. 342–55].
18. See, for example, for the earliest statement, Knight [32, pp. vii–ix]. (Since Knight keeps repeating the same themes in his writings, sometimes almost verbatim, we cite only examples of his views. The reader who is interested in more complete citations is referred to the very excellent article by Gonce [15].)
19. For example, Knight [22, pp. 105–35]. Knight [30, p. 751] notes: "I, for one, do not particularly care whether economic theory is regarded as science or not."
20. For example, Hutchison [19].
21. Methodologists often have appealed to "consciousness" as the basis for premises in economic theory, but they do not make clear what they mean by this and invariably go on to fudge things up by speaking of assumptions as "facts," running together different aspects of behavior, and not recognizing the implications of what they are saying. Knight is in a class by himself for clarity and consistency.
22. Knight [22, pp. 286–88].
23. Knight [28; 21, chapter 11].
24. Marshall [39, p. 756].
25. Knight [22, pp. 285–86, 279].
26. Ibid., pp. 135–47.
27. Cairnes [5, pp. 80–81]; and Keynes [21, pp. 232–36]. With Mill [43, pp. 431–33], for reasons that have been indicated, verification has a more genuine role. (This does not mean that Mill's practice necessarily was consistent with his methodology. Compare De Marchi [7].) Robbins is quite definite in the belief that economics is a science like physics [50, pp. 104–106] and has no doubts whatever about the predictive power of economic theory [50, pp. 121–26], yet he says nothing about verification. The omission is either an oversight or an irrationality.
28. Knight [22, pp. 129, 133].
29. Ibid., p. 135.
30. Ibid., pp. 136, 137.
31. Ibid., pp. 138, 94.
32. Knight [25, p. 109, italics in original].
33. Mill [44, p. 585].
34. Knight seemed to have difficulty in making up his mind about verification and prediction. Three careful readers (Gonce [15, p. 555], Macfie [36, pp. 783–84], and Shackle [57, p. 65]) come to the conclusion, on the basis of good evidence, that it was Knight's view that prediction was impossible in economics. Yet, Knight [25, p. 260] does say that the principles of economic theory "have great value in the prediction of the effects of changes." It is not surprising that readers were thrown off. Statements about prediction such as the above come out of the air and are in a spirit quite opposed to that in Knight's work generally. One would expect that if theory can predict, it should be possible to verify such predictions. But verification is something Knight will have none of; he tells us [25, p. 163], for example: "It is not conceivably possible to 'verify' any proposition about 'economic' behavior by any 'empirical' procedure." Is it then on the *authority* of the economist that we must

rely? James Buchanan [4] tells us that Knight was not interested in prediction, which we think sums it up quite well.

35. Knight [32, p. 16].
36. Knight [22, p. 118].
37. Knight [22, p. 143; 21, p. 163].
38. Knight [23, pp. 264–65; 26, pp. 751–52]. We do not have to rely on the *authority* of a physicist on matters of prediction as, apparently according to Knight (see note 34), we do in economics.
39. Friedman [12, pp. 15–16].
40. Knight [32, pp. 14–15].
41. Friedman [12, p. 14] tells us that "the more significant the theory the more unrealistic the assumptions (in this sense)."
42. Joan Robinson [51, p. 2], for example, argues that "the best the economist can do is . . . to take the utmost pains to make clear what assumptions about the nature of the problem are implicit in his answer. If these assumptions are near enough to the actual conditions to make the answer serviceable the practical man can accept it."
43. Knight [27; 29; 25, chapter 9].
44. Friedman [12, pp. 3–12].
45. Ibid., pp. 7–8.
46. Ibid., pp. 8–9, 282–83.
47. Rotwein [52; 53]; and Samuelson [54; 55; 56].
48. Nagel [46].
49. Melitz [41].
50. Melitz (ibid., p. 59) admits this, and Nagel [46, p. 219] ends his critique with the statement that "I have therefore tried . . . to indicate why the main thesis he is ostensibly defending is nonetheless sound."
51. A very large literature on this issue has been created, and it continues to grow. Compare, for example, in addition to those cited above, Bear and Orr [1]; De Alessi [6]; Koopmans [33]; Lerner [35]; Machlup [37; 38]; Massey [40]; and Wong [59].
52. Friedman [12, pp. 41–42].
53. Ibid., pp. 22–23.
54. Ibid., p. 22.
55. Knight [25, p. 206] gives this kind of an argument, but it more appropriately fits with Knight's assumer orientation. However, the argument that "it suffices that men largely behave 'as if' they were trying to conform to the principles" seems to involve a switch on Knight's part from the notion that the premises of economic theory are necessary truths to the idea that they are a fiction needed for prediction.
56. Machlup [37, p. 191, italics in original].
57. We say this not only because of the lapses already noted, but also because there are a number of very significant escape clauses in Friedman which make it possible to come up with very different interpretations of his position. For example, as does Knight, he argues that only "experts" can determine whether predictions are consistent with theory [12, p. 25]; he has an impressionistic, empirical "rules of application or interpretation" part, telling us how and where the hypothesis legitimately can be applied, which he takes to be an integral part of the hypothesis; and he argues (p. 31) that "legitimate" criticism must be accompanied by

an alternative hypothesis which yields better predictions than the one criticized, implying that theory does not have to predict at all well, only less badly than any other. Such qualifications, we believe, while they make Friedman's position ambiguous, do make it more defensible. In effect, Friedman's qualifications can be interpreted to make him an aggressive disciple of John Stuart Mill, who felt constrained to show that economic theory was a mature science.

58. This is true even if, for reasons cited in the last footnote, we soften the sharp lines of Friedman's analysis.
59. Discussions about the Chicago School—for example, Miller [42]; Stigler [58]; Bronfenbrenner [3]; Davis [9]; Humphrey [18]; and Patinkin [47]—do not deal explicitly with methodological issues. Cursory examination suggests the proposed hypothesis, which we feel is worth exploring.
60. Friedman [12, pp. 11–12, 91, 283, 300; 13].
61. Friedman [12, pp. 47–99].
62. Ibid., pp. 91, 300, 319, and [11].
63. That is why, as noted above, Knight insists on a descriptive (rather than analytic) interpretation even of mathematics.
64. Knight [32, pp. 5–6].
65. Knight [28, p. 72] tells us: "The statement that economics describes the way the economic order works refers to its working as a mechanism; that is the meaning of being scientific."
66. Davis [9].
67. Friedman [11, p. 937].
68. Pigou [48, p. 38].
69. See note 57 above.
70. Friedman [14, p. 23].

## *References*


[1] Bear, D.V.T., and Orr, Daniel. "Logic and Expediency in Economic Theorizing." *Journal of Political Economy* 75 (April 1967): 188–96.

[2] Bowley, Marion. *Nassau Senior and Classical Political Economy*. New York: Augustus M. Kelley, 1949.

[3] Bronfenbrenner, Martin. "Observations on the 'Chicago School(s).'" *Journal of Political Economy* 70 (February 1962): 72–75.

[4] Buchanan, James. "Frank H. Knight." *International Journal of the Social Sciences* 8: 424–28.

[5] Cairnes, J.N. *The Character and Logical Method of Political Economy*. 2d ed. London: Macmillan, 1875.

[6] De Alessi, Louis. "Reversals of Assumptions and Implications." *Journal of Political Economy* 79 (July–August 1971): 867–77.

[7] De Marchi, N.B. "The Empirical Content and Longevity of Ricardian Economics." *Economica*, N.S.37 (August 1970): 257–76.

[8] Dewey, John. "The Natural History of Thinking." In *Intelligence in*

*the Modern World: John Dewey's Philosophy*, edited by Joseph Ratner. New York: Modern Library, 1939. Pp. 837–50.

[9] Davis, J.R. "Chicago Economists, Deficit Budgets and the Early 1930's." *American Economic Review* 58 (June 1968): 476–82.

[10] Dorfman, Joseph. *Thorstein Veblen and His America*. New York: Viking Press, 1934.

[11] Friedman, Milton. "Comments on the Critics." *Journal of Political Economy* 80 (September–October 1972): 906–50.

[12] ———. *Essays in Positive Economics*. Chicago: University of Chicago Press, 1953.

[13] ———. "Leon Walras and His Economic System." *American Economic Review* 45 (December 1955): 900–909.

[14] ———. *A Program for Monetary Stability*. New York: Fordham University Press, 1960.

[15] Gonce, R.A. "Frank H. Knight on Social Control and the Scope and Method of Economics." *Southern Economic Journal* 38 (April 1972): 547–58.

[16] Hicks, J.R. *Value and Capital*. 2d ed. Oxford: Clarendon Press, 1946.

[17] Higgins, Benjamin. *What Do Economists Know?* Melbourne: Melbourne University Press, 1951.

[18] Humphrey, T.M. "Role of Non-Chicago Economists in the Evolution of the Quantity Theory in America, 1930–50." *Southern Economic Journal* 38 (July 1971): 12–18.

[19] Hutchison, T.W. *The Significance and Basic Postulates of Economic Theory*. New York: Augustus M. Kelley, 1960.

[20] ———. "The Significance and Basic Postulates of Economic Theory: A Reply to Professor Knight." *Journal of Political Economy* 49 (October 1941): 732–50.

[21] Keynes. J.N. *The Scope and Method of Political Economy*. 4th ed. New York: Augustus M. Kelley, 1955.

[22] Knight, F.H. *The Ethics of Competition and Other Essays*. New York: Augustus M. Kelley, 1951.

[23] ———. "Fact and Metaphysics in Economic Psychology." *American Economic Review* 15 (June 1925): 247–66.

[24] ———. *Freedom and Reform*. New York: Harper, 1947.

[25] ———. *On the History and Method of Economics*. Chicago: University of Chicago Press, 1956.

[26] ———. "Immutable Law in Economics: Its Reality and Limitations." *American Economic Review, Papers and Proceedings* 36 (May 1946): 93–111.

[27] ———. "Imperfect Competition." *Journal of Marketing* 3 (April 1939): 360–66.

[28] ———. *Intelligence and Democratic Action*. Cambridge, Mass.: Harvard University Press, 1960.

[29] ———. "Realism and Relevance in the Theory of Demand." *Journal of Political Economy* 52 (December 1944): 289–318.

[30] ———. "A Rejoinder." *Journal of Political Economy* 49 (October 1941): 750–53.

[31] ———. "Review: Robbins, L.C. *The Nature and Significance of Economic Science.*" *Ethics* 44 (April 1934): 358–61.
[32] ———. *Risk, Uncertainty and Profit.* New York: Augustus M. Kelley, 1964.
[33] Koopmans, T.C. *Three Essays on the State of Economic Science.* New York: McGraw-Hill, 1957.
[34] Laughlin, J.L. "Political Economy and Christianity." In *Latter Day Problems.* New York: D. Appelton and Co., 1866.
[35] Lerner, Abba P. "Professor Samuelson on Theory and Realism: Comment." *American Economic Review* 55 (December 1965): 1153–55.
[36] Macfie, A.L. "Review: Knight, F.H. *On the History and Method of Economics.*" *Economic Journal* 68 (December 1958): 780–86.
[37] Machlup, Fritz. "The Problem of Verification in Economics." *Southern Economic Journal* 22 (July 1955): 1–21.
[38] ———. "Professor Samuelson on Theory and Realism." *American Economic Review* 54 (September 1964): 733–35.
[39] Marshall, Alfred. *Principles of Economics.* 8th ed. New York: Macmillan, 1920.
[40] Massey, Gerald J. "Professor Samuelson on Theory and Realism: Comment." *American Economic Review* 55 (December 1965): 1155–63.
[41] Melitz, Jack. "Friedman and Machlup on the Significance of Testing Economic Assumptions." *Journal of Political Economy* 73 (February 1965): 37–60.
[42] Miller, H.L. "On the 'Chicago School of Economics.'" *Journal of Political Economy* 70 (February 1962): 64–69.
[43] Mill, J.S. "On the Definition of Political Economy and on the Method of Investigation Proper to It." In *John Stuart Mill's Philosophy of Scientific Method,* edited by Ernest Nagel. New York: Hafner, 1950.
[44] ———. *A System of Logic.* 8th ed. London: Longmans, Green & Co., 1965.
[45] Mitchell, W.C. *The Backward Art of Spending Money and Other Essays.* New York: Augustus M. Kelley, 1950.
[46] Nagel, Ernest. "Assumptions in Economic Theory." *American Economic Review, Papers and Proceedings* 53 (May 1963): 211–19.
[47] Patinkin, Don. "On the Monetary Economics of Chicagoans and Non-Chicagoans: Comment." *Southern Economic Journal* 39 (January 1973): 454–59.
[48] Pigou, A.C. "The Value of Money." *Quarterly Journal of Economics* 32 (November 1917): 38–65.
[49] Popper, Karl. *The Logic of Scientific Discovery.* New York: Basic Books, 1961.
[50] Robbins, Lionel. *An Essay on the Nature and Significance of Economic Science.* London: Macmillan, 1949.
[51] Robinson, Joan. *The Economics of Imperfect Competition.* London: Macmillan, 1948.
[52] Rotwein, Eugene. "Empiricism and Economic Method: Several Views Considered." *Journal of Economic Issues* 7 (September 1973): 361–82.
[53] ———. "On 'The Methodology of Positive Economics.'" *Quarterly Journal of Economics* 73 (November 1959): 552–75.

[54] Samuelson, Paul. "Problems of Methodology: Discussion." *American Economic Review, Papers and Proceedings* 53 (May 1963): 231–36.
[55] ———. "Professor Samuelson on Theory and Realism: Reply." *American Economic Review* 55 (December 1965): 1164–72.
[56] ———. "Theory and Realism: A Reply." *American Economic Review* 54 (September 1964): 736–39.
[57] Shackle, G.L.S. "Review: Knight, F.H. *On the History and Method of Economics: Selected Essays.*" *Economica* 25 (February 1958): 65–66.
[58] Stigler, G.J. "On the 'Chicago School of Economics': Comment." *Journal of Political Economy* 70 (February 1962): 70–71.
[59] Wong, Stanley. "The 'F-Twist' and the Methodology of Paul Samuelson." *American Economic Review* 63 (June 1973): 312–25.

# 5

# The Chicago School: Positivism or Ideal Type

*Charles K. Wilber*
*and*
*Jon D. Wisman*

The economics profession recognizes the University of Chicago as the fountainhead and guardian of a distinct, although by no means homogeneous, school of thought (with branches at UCLA and VPI). It can be characterized by both its methodology for analyzing "what is" and its policy stance on "what ought to be." Its methodology is a form of logical positivism which strives to make economics as *Wertfrei* or objectively scientific as the physical sciences. Its policy stance is founded on the belief that the theoretical model of competition can be utilized to provide empirical proof that laissez-faire capitalism maximizes both personal freedom and economic welfare.

The purpose of this article is to investigate the degree to which the Chicago School's methodology and policy stance are related. We argue that hypotheses generated from a logical positivist methodology in economics are, in practice, nonfalsifiable. As a result, when combined with a commitment to a policy of laissez-faire, the "positivist" economic theory of the Chicago School tends to be transformed into an ideal type. As such, economic analysis becomes more a prescriptive than a descriptive theory. Ironically, what starts off as a *Wertfrei* positivism ends up a

*The authors are, respectively, Professor and Chairman, Department of Economics, University of Notre Dame, South Bend, Indiana, and Assistant Professor of Economics, The American University, Washington, D.C.*

value laden tool for the defense of a particular socioeconomic system. We conclude with a brief discussion of a certain paradox between the Chicago School's espousal of a positivist methodology and its commitment to laissez-faire. Furtherance of the former may be inimical to crucial elements of the latter.

Even though the Chicago School is characterized by both methodological and policy stance heterogeneity, its internal differences are less marked than its differences with the outside world. In fact, under scrutiny, many of the differences tend to disappear. For example, Frank Knight held that empirical verification of theory is unnecessary, that truth lies in the logic of the theory. Despite an explicit espousal of positivism, this is where, *de facto,* Milton Friedman ends up. This is our main argument. However, to avoid overly gross distortions of those internal differences, we confine our investigation principally to Friedman, the Chicago School's currently best known spokesman.

### *Positivist Methodology*

How can we know reality? How can we explain what happens in the physical and social worlds? Before the advent of modern science, the appeal was to authority. Sorcerers, popes, kings, and tradition were looked to for explanation of reality. With the growth of modern science two major opposing trends developed in the philosophy of science. On the one side were the rationalists, such as René Descartes, who argued that we can know the world through reason alone. For Descartes, the real world is characterized by order and rationality, and thus it is best apprehended through an appeal to human reason alone. Descartes's lineal descendants in economics include Ludwig von Mises, Frank Knight, and sometimes Lionel Robbins.[1] Truth about reality lies in the logic of the theory. Opposing the rationalists were the empiricists, such as John Locke, who argued that we can know reality only through experience. Direct descendants of Locke include the German Historical School in the nineteenth century and T. W. Hutchinson in the twentieth.[2]

Those economists in the rationalist tradition believe that economic theory is not amenable to verification or refutation on purely empirical grounds. Instead, they believe that economics is a system of *a priori* truths, a product of pure reason, a system of pure deduction from a series of postulates. The difficulty is that there is an infinite number of possible logical systems. Without some empirical means of choosing one over another, logical systems tend to degenerate into ideologies (or, less pejoratively, ideal types).

Empiricism also faces a telling objection, one that has become known as the problem of induction.[3] If reality can be known only through experience, then generalizations are impossible. Simply because *X* follows *Y* the first 1,000 times measured does not necessitate that it will follow the 1,001st time.

Immanuel Kant wanted to prove that scientific explanations are true and, at the same time, answer both the rationalists and empiricists. Rationalists *assumed* that reality is rational, and the empiricists denied that it is anything more than a collection of discrete experiences. Kant argued that to experience anything we must give it order by synthesizing those experiences in terms of categories such as time, space, substance, and causality. That is, we create synthetic, *a priori* truths. They are *a priori* assumptions, *but* they, or at least their implications, can be tested against experience.

The grand synthesis that Kant constructed serves as the foundation for logical positivism. The classic modern version of this logical positivism is found in the work of Carl Hempel and Paul Oppenheim.[4] They attempted to construct a model of scientific explanation that codified how, in effect, physical science explained reality. Their argument that scientific explanation always requires the use of general laws led them to develop what they call the covering law model. The following diagram will help clarify their model. The C's are statements of antecedent conditions, since they describe facts about the world which are relevant in explaining the observed phenomenon. The L's are general laws of the particular science (in economics, maximizing behavior would be one, for example) which form the core of the model used to explain the observed phenomenon. Using the rules of logic, an explanandum or hypothesis is deduced from the explanans. This explanandum is then subjected to empirical verification by either direct observation or statistical inference. The hypothesis is then either accepted as confirmed or rejected as disconfirmed. The result is that every explanation is covered by (subsumed under) one or more general law. This is what makes an explanation a *scientific* explanation instead of merely an *ad hoc* one.

COVERING LAW MODEL OF EXPLANATION

| | | |
|---|---|---|
| Logical deduction | $L_1, L_2, L_3 \ldots L_n$ General laws<br>$C_1, C_2, C_3 \ldots C_n$ Antecedent conditions | Explanans |
| | E Description of the empirical phenomenon to be explained (hypothesis) | Explanandum |

In the covering law model, explanation and prediction are seen as symmetrical. That is, explanation occurs when the explanandum is derived after the event, and prediction occurs when the explanadum is derived before the event takes place. Explanation is not considered adequate unless it could have served as the basis of prediction.

Logical positivism, with its covering law model of explanation, has found wide acceptance among economists since the publication of I.M.D. Little's *Critique of Welfare Economics* and Friedman's *Essays in Positive Economics* during the early 1950s.[5] Both Paul Samuelson's revealed preference theory and Friedman's demand for money function can be seen as attempts to restructure economic theory into a logical positivist form.[6] This acceptance has become so widespread that an overwhelming number of current textbooks contains an introductory chapter in which a positivist methodology is espoused.[7]

The goal of positive economics, according to Friedman, "is to provide a system of generalizations that can be used to make correct predictions about the consequences of any change in circumstances. Its performance is to be judged by the precision, scope, and conformity with experience of the predictions it yields."[8] Predictability, then, is the crucial element in positive economics. Since explanation and prediction are symmetrical, correct predictions imply correct explanations. Economic science is carried forth by logically deducing an explanandum from an explanans. These explananda or hypotheses act as predictions of correlational relationships in the real world. That is, the positive investigator pursues a testing of the degree of correspondence between his or her predictions and the empirical evidence provided by the real world. A high degree of correspondence, or a "good fit," acts to confirm or verify the theory. A low level or lack of correspondence indicates a flaw in the theory. It is by testing that disputes are resolved, and testing leads to the accumulation of general laws that constitute theory. If the predictions derived from one model prove "better" than the corresponding predictions drawn from another model, the former is tentatively selected as preferable. In every case the theory preferred is the one which best explains the observable phenomena of the economic world.

Furthermore, Friedman argues that the validity of an hypothesis is to be judged *solely* by its predictive ability, regardless of whether or not the initial assumptions are realistic. A model cannot, by definition, capture or reproduce the whole of reality. Therefore, assumptions and hypotheses must of necessity be unrealistic. Consequently, one hypothesis is to be chosen over another "not because its 'assumptions' are more 'realistic' but rather because it is part of a more general theory that applies to a wider variety of phenomena"; and the more general theory "has more implications of being contradicted, and has failed to be contradicted under a wider variety of circumstances."[9] Indeed, assumptions are often best presented "as if" they were true. For example, it may be sufficient to assume that economic agents behave "as if" they were maximizing.

A second related criterion for the selection of one hypothesis over another involves the principle of simplicity, or maximum use of Occam's razor. Thus, for Friedman, "the choice among alternative hypotheses equally consistent with the available evidence must to some extent be arbitrary, though there is general agreement that relevant considerations are suggested by . . . criteria [such as] 'simplicity'. . . . A theory is 'simpler' the less the initial knowledge needed to make a prediction within a given field of phenomena. . . . A hypothesis is important if it 'explains' much by little."[10] Theory, by definition, involves the simplification of reality, and thus in the interests of economy maximum simplification is justified. Simplicity also serves the function of warding off value judgments which might seep in unnoticed amid unnecessary complexity.

Although the goal of prediction is no mean task, especially in a social science such as economics, the end sought by positivism is notably a humble one. Positive methodology does not strive to assert causality. Rather, it is satisfied to establish a high probable correlation between two events. An event is explained by citing an earlier event with which it correlated and establishing a generalization which relates the two. The generalization is validated through repeated empirical testing. Causality cannot be observed empirically. The world of facts offers the investigator only events in contingent sequences. General laws can exist only as the consequence of repeatedly observed correlation.

The final major distinguishing characteristic of positivist methodology is that its orientation is ahistorical. Positive theory is conceived of as a timeless analytical construct. Not only does it deny values in its framework, it denies that as a method it represents values, or that it is culture bound. And, in addition to denying its own historicity, positive methodology relates to historical issues in a quite restricted manner. It is not concerned with either the evolution of ideas or the motivations behind historical events, since such phenomena are not amenable to empirical verification. Its interest in history is bound by the degree to which historical investigation promises to confirm ahistorical, general laws.[11]

### *Positivist Insularity*

The task of positive economics, then, is to apply to the realm of economic phenomena the same methodology which has yielded such impressive fruits in the physical sciences. The position of positive economics is that knowledge, whether in the physical sciences or in a social science such as economics, is to be distinguished solely on the basis of the empirical subject matter and not by the methodology. The crucial issue, then, is whether the subject matter of economics is of a comparable nature to that of the physical sciences, so as to permit profitable application of a positive methodology. In other words, is the subject matter of economics such that the generalizations which can be formulated about it lead to successful predictions?

The social sciences and the physical sciences are by nature different because of "the inherent instability of the data with which the discipline is concerned."[12] These data can be classified into two different categories: The first relates to "the physical nature of the production process," whereas the second relates to "the behavioral response to economic stimuli."[13] Robert Heilbroner argues that although behavioral responses tend to exhibit a significant degree of long-run stability due to the influence of " 'habits,' customs, traditions and usages of societies . . . the long-run production functions of the economy are . . . awkward or impossible to predict."[14] On the other hand, whereas it may be "within the bounds of plausibility that it would be possible to construct a set of production functions that would mirror with a fair degree of accuracy the actual production possibilities open to society in the short-run,"[15] short-run behavioral responses tend to be highly unpredictable.[16] Consequently, prediction in economics is severely limited because of the nature of the subject matter.

A related limitation on the possibility of deriving successful predictions of economic events stems from the fact that the discipline deals with open rather than closed systems.[17] In the physical sciences experiments can be controlled such that an "artificially closed system" is created in which it is possible to correctly identify the chosen variables. Because the subject matter of economics is not amenable to controlled experiments, "economics has resorted to the use of partial equilibrium analysis in an attempt to reduce the complexity of economic phenomena to manageable proportions."[18] The potential random behavior of certain factors requires extensive use of the *ceteris paribus* technique to give the model, although not the subject matter itself, a degree of determinedness.

Because of the reasons given above, we conclude that successful prediction is extremely difficult to achieve in economics. Experience in the past several years with unemployment, inflation, the energy crisis, and so on, highlights this inability to predict. However, positive economists have achieved a high degree of insularity from the failure of their predictions. This is due to the highly conditional nature of economic predictions, which are dependent upon the *ceteris paribus* clauses holding and upon the data's being representative of economic reality. These conditionals give the positivist an escape clause for rationalizing the failure of a prediction. When his model repeatedly fails to predict correctly, the physicist blames his model. The positive economist, on the other hand, is tempted to blame the *ceteris paribus* conditions, the data, or the specific testing procedure itself. Consequently, for the positive economist, hypotheses are seldom disconfirmed and general theory rarely or never disproved. Positive economics thus becomes perfectly insulated from refutation: It cannot be harmed by demonstrating its assumptions to be unrealistic, and it is not rejected when its predictions fail to fit the facts.

Since Friedman places so much weight on the ability to predict as the main verification of the truth of a theory, this insulation of predictions from refutation is worth exploring further. Why do positive economists resist disconfirmation of their hypotheses? At the heart of the issue is Thomas Kuhn's concept of a paradigm.[19] A scientist normally has some general theory that guides the choice of problems, provides the analytic tools, and supplies a general vision of how reality is structured. This general theory—whether it be neoclassical economics, Marxism, or some other—is usually so much a part of the very thought processes that empirical disconfirmation of some particular hypothesis is almost automatically rejected. Three specific problems, briefly mentioned above, make it easy to reject a disconfirmation as invalid and, thus, protect the scientist's basic theory or paradigm.

First is the *ceteris paribus* problem. Hypotheses in economics must always be stated in the form of "if . . . then" propositions. Since the "ifs" do change, an econometric test that disconfirms the theory can always be rejected as "misspecified."[20] In addition, since explananda or hypotheses are stated in probabilistic terms, a *non*occurrence of the predicted event cannot be used as a refutation of the general law from which the particular hypothesis was deduced.[21]

Second is the difficulty of constructing a clear-cut test of an hypothesis in economics. Most of the traditional statistical tests, for example, null hypotheses, are very weak ones which a large number of different theories are capable of passing. The choice among alternative theories, therefore, cannot be settled on empirical grounds. Instead, the desirable qualities of a logical model—simplicity, generality, specificity, and aesthetic quality—are used, and the relative evaluation of these qualities is probably determined by one's own paradigm.[22]

Finally, both the methods of collection and construction of economic data are unreliable. Furthermore, the data that are statistically constructed frequently are not conceptually the same as the corresponding variables in the theory. Therefore, econometricians engage in data "massaging." If a test disconfirms an hypothesis, the investigator can always blame the data—they have been "massaged" either too much or not enough.

### *The Ideal Type*

When a theory has achieved such a high level of insularity from falsification, we contend that it might be best termed an ideal type. Implicit in such theories (or abstract formal models, as Paul Diesing refers to them) "is an idealization of one facet of a complex reality, while the verbal language of the theory disguises the abstractions of the model and makes it look like a simple empirical description."[23]

When a theory becomes an ideal type it functions more as a prescriptive than as a descriptive device. That is, theory functions as a parable to elucidate the ideal toward which we should strive. For economists such as Paul Samuelson, Robert Solow, and Wassily Leontief, neoclassical economic theory has become the "grand parable" that is still defended against nonbelievers but is not taken too seriously as a scientific explanation of "what is."[24] Rather, attention is focused on the development of a set of "engineering tools"—linear programming, input-output analysis, cost-benefit analysis, and so on. Economics has come to be conceived in engineering terms: How do you maximize some objective function in the face of various constraints?

For the Chicago School, however, particularly as exemplified by the work of Milton Friedman, neoclassical economic theory (including the pure competition version), while in fact an ideal type, is treated as if it were a highly confirmed theory of "what is." Ironically, Friedman the avowed positivist ends up *de facto* in company with Frank Knight. Knight held that empirical verification of theory is unnecessary, and Friedman, through his insistence on prediction as the sole form of verification, renders empirical falsification virtually impossible. All that remains is theory as ideal type.

As an ideal type, Friedman's version of economic theory serves two essential and related functions. It acts to restrict the scope for "scientific" economic inquiry, and it serves as a policy stance for molding society in its image, while legitimating certain aspects of the status quo.

On the level of restricting or defining the scope of economics, the neoclassical theory of the Chicago School acts as a set of "exemplars" which guide the pursuit of normal scientific research. The complexity of the real world is to be viewed through the lenses of supply and demand, equilibrium, and maximization subject to constraints. As such, universally applicable hypotheses are devised which transcend institutional and historical variations. These lenses focus potential economic research upon and, in effect, constrain attention to the behavior of atomistic agents. Such agents are assumed to act rationally and exclusively on the basis of market given information. Hence, one of the most challenging areas for current economic theory—the issue of externalities—seldom merits more than a passing reference. Market generated data have the aura of value free facticity, whereas imputing valuations of extramarket phenomena is clearly more open to the influence of the researcher's own values. Thus, the challenges of social critics such as Ezra Mishan,[25] namely, that human welfare may be decreasing even as per capita market values increase, are excluded from serious "scientific" scrutiny.

But more important yet is that concentration on the presumed "rational" actions of atomistic actors camouflages the existence and exercise of power. The firm is assumed to be ultimately subordinate to the consumer. Advertising functions merely in providing the rational consumer with market information. And although some firms are admittedly larger than others, and some consumers richer than others, power is assumed to be widely diffused and vested solely in the atomistic, sovereign consumer. Firms do not collude and form cartels, nor do consumers exert power through social class membership. A perfect example of this myopia, induced by being a prisoner of an ideal type, is Friedman's attempt to connect personal and functional income distribution.[26] The latter is explained, of course, by marginal productivity theory, and the former is attributed to risk, chance, natural ability, and inheritance. Differences in power and sociocultural environment are never mentioned; differences in wealth play but a minor role. In fact, his conclusion seems to be that personal inequality is due to free choice—by the rich and poor alike.

The Chicago School's ideal type "explains" economic reality in a very restricted sense. Only those phenomena which can be represented in its laissez-faire, capitalist model merit investigation. For example, most members of the Chicago School have ignored the question of monopoly, both empirically and theoretically. Theories of imperfect competition have been dismissed out of hand,[27] and no real attempt has been made empirically to test noncompetitive theory.[28] Since the Chicago School's theory is left essentially unscathed by both the unrealism of its assumptions and its inability to provide successful prediction, the ideal type has an independent life of its own. Rather than repair the model to better conform with the real world, the burden of conformity is placed on the real world. Thus, the policy stance of the Chicago School is characterized by proposals to change the real economic world according to the requisites of its ideal type—laissez-faire capitalism.

This orientation is most clearly exemplified in the public policy pronouncements of Milton Friedman. This stance is commensurate with a neoclassical vision of an economic reality in which externalities are of minimal importance, power is widely diffused, and economic agents behave independently in a rational manner. Since externalities are "marginal," markets should be unfettered so as to provide optimally efficient resource allocation. Monopoly power, if existent, is not viewed as institutional or endemic to modern industrial society, but is largely traceable to governmental interference in the economic system. Indeed most, if not all, of the ills afflicting contemporary society are to be traced to the existence of an overgrown government. But the growth of government is not seen as functional to the economic system, that is, as stemming from an increase in externalities, as a force countervailing other growing power concentrations, or as representing particular class interests; rather, it stems from misguided political philosophy.

Individuals are viewed as self-interested maximizers who function with a timeless sort of reason, unbounded by any cultural or institutional artifacts other than the available choices provided by the market itself. Thus, it is not relevant that Americans might be culturally prone to seek fulfillment through consumption rather than in creative work environments. Since markets assume overwhelming importance in rational, individual decision making, maximizing behavior will eradicate all vestiges of racism and sexism in a laissez-faire capitalism. And failure to recognize that rationality is culture and class bound leads to a proposal that education also be allocated by the market system.[29]

Somewhat ironically, although Friedman's version of theory emphasizes both prediction and rationality, it places no faith in the possibility of discretionary, macroeconomic stabilization policy. Successful prediction is not deemed possible in this realm, and it is implied that policy makers are not quite capable of behaving rationally in the interests of society. In a *Newsweek* column on national economic planning, Friedman argues that "we are suffering from inflation and recession produced by government attempts to promote full-employment."[30] He goes on to say that government planning cannot work and then outlines his alternative.

> The central planners want planning by them for us. They want the government—by which they really mean themselves—to decide "social priorities" (i.e., tell us what is good for us); "rationalize production" (i.e., tell us where and how we should work); assure "equitable distribution" (i.e., take from some of us to give to others of us).
>
> Such planning, from the top down, is inefficient because it makes it impossible to use the detailed knowledge shared among millions of individuals. It undermines freedom because it requires people to obey orders rather than pursue their own interests.
>
> I am for planning, too, but planning by each of us separately in light of our individual, though shared, values, coordinated by voluntary exchange in free markets. Such planning, from the bottom up, enlists the interests of each in promoting the well-being of all. Government has its role—to provide a stable legal and monetary framework, enforce contracts and adjudicate disputes and protect us from coercion by our fellow citizens.[31]

Adam Smith could not have said it better. Two hundred years of change in the economic world is irrelevant to the economic theory of the Chicago School. No Rockefellers, no multinational corporations, no imperialism, no environmental destruction; just many small buyers and sellers engaging in exchange and thus maximizing their freedom and economic welfare. If we could only get government to tend to its proper business, all would be well. This vision of the world may be beautiful, but it *is* a vision. It has no established basis in empirical reality. Positivism becomes a facade; faith wins out.

### *Conclusion*

As seen above, positivism tends to insulate the Chicago School's version of neoclassical economics from falsifiability. What remains, therefore, is an ideal type from which policy prescriptions for the "good society" are derived. But this ideal type seems particularly inappropriate to provide solutions to today's socioeconomic problems. The modern economy is characterized by *interdependence* of its economic actors. Externalities are the rule not the exception. Firms are not simply price takers; they are dependent upon each other's price and quantity decisions. Power is necessary to market new products, attain government favors, and compete internationally. General Motors, ITT, and IBM, not the corner newspaper dealer, typify the "representative firm" of today.

The perfectly competitive model of the Chicago School has little of relevance to say in the face of today's urgent socioeconomic problems other than to exhort us to believe that they all will go away if we simply return to a laissez-faire government policy. Technological change will not undermine competition, external diseconomies will transform themselves into minor "neighborhood" effects, power will dissolve, bureaucracies will break up, and to eliminate job dissatisfaction people will equate the disutility of work with the utility of income.

Finally, we want to make some brief comments on an apparent paradox between the Chicago School's espousal of a positivist methodology and its commitment to laissez-faire. Ironically, the methodology of positive economics might be inimical to the social values which are so highly esteemed in the Chicago version of neoclassical economics.

Friedman, the Chicago School, and the liberal tradition which they represent place ultimate importance on the freedom of the individual to determine his or her own fate. However, free human choice is only emphasized within a given institutional framework. Thus, the approach tends to direct attention away from what could conceivably constitute the most important realm of human choice—creating meaningful changes in social institutions.

Perhaps more crucial yet, by striving for the predictability of economic phenomena, the methodology of positive economics creates a powerful instrument of social control. Predictability holds forth the potential for social control in two essential ways. First, predictions, when issued by those with power and authority, sow the seeds of their own fulfillment by influencing expectations. Humans, unlike atoms and celestial bodies, are capable of understanding predictions and changing their behavior in conformity with them. The success of such predictions may rely less on "scientific truth" than on the power—as represented by prestige, wealth, or politics—of those formulating them.

Second, prediction provides those possessing power with a more readily rationalized justification for social manipulation. Of course, it could be countered that prediction might provide the powerless with the arms to discredit the powerful. However, such a retort has overtones of a produce-bombs-for-peace argument, and such a stance presumes that there is a widely dispersed ability to gain access to data, generate predictions, and make them known. Such is not the case: Government and large corporate interests underwrite, either directly or indirectly, most of the social science research which leads to predictions. Furthermore, those who collect the data from which most economic predictions are made are generally either government agencies or corporate entities. Faith in the possibility of the successful prediction of social phenomena leads to an increased demand for data. Since data gathering probably admits of economies of scale, the industry might therefore be a case of "natural monopoly." Not only does the collection of data pose a serious threat to personal liberty, but also its potential for "scientifically" rationalized social control is more frightening yet. Thus, for example, whereas the Chicago School has persistently opposed the implementation of national planning, its epistemology promises to take us ever closer to it. This is not because predictability has been proven, but because an ever increasing portion of the American people have been led to believe that we can predict and thereby control our social destiny.

The glory of the Chicago School is its insistence on maintaining a vision of a "good society" and its refusal to become mere technicians at the service of whoever is in power. Thus, the ethos of the Chicago School would seem to plead for a methodology which, rather than providing us with predictions, would provide us with an understanding of our past and present such that we might more rationally and freely choose our own destiny. Our social sciences must not constitute what Ben Seligman referred to as a "mere scientism"—"the attempt to impose a unified method on all disciplines . . . that is confusing form with substance."[32] Ultimately, it is the intrusion of human freedom and responsibility that renders the social sciences different in substance from the physical sciences and thereby makes human behavior largely unpredictable.

## Notes

1. See Ludwig von Mises, *Epistemological Problems of Economics* (Princeton: Princeton University Press, 1960); Frank Knight, "The Limitations of Scientific Method in Economics," in *The Ethics of Competition* (New York: Harper, 1935); and Lionel Robbins, *The Nature and Significance of Economic Science* (London: Macmillan, 1935).
2. See T. W. Hutchinson, *The Significance and Basic Postulates of Economic Theory* (London: Macmillan, 1938).
3. See Martin Hollis and Edward Nell, *Rational Economic Man* (London: Cambridge University Press, 1975).
4. Carl G. Hempel and Paul Oppenheim, "Studies in the Logic of Explanation," *Philosophy of Science* 15 (1948): 135–75.
5. I.M.D. Little, *A Critique of Welfare Economics,* 2d ed. (Oxford: Clarendon Press, 1957); and Milton Friedman, *Essays in Positive Economics* (Chicago: University of Chicago Press, 1953).
6. Paul A. Samuelson, *Foundations of Economic Analysis* (Cambridge,

Mass.; Harvard University Press, 1947), chapters 5 and 6; and Milton Friedman, "The Demand for Money: Some Theoretical and Empirical Results," *Journal of Political Economy* 67 (August 1959): 327–51.

7. See particularly Richard Lipsey and Peter Steiner, *Economics* (New York: Harper & Row, 1966). Lipsey published an earlier version in England under the title *Introduction to Positive Economics*. Oddly, the ascent of positivism in economics has coincided with a decrease in its popularity among professional philosophers.
8. Friedman, "The Methodology of Positive Economics," in *Essays*, p. 4.
9. Ibid., p. 20.
10. Ibid., pp. 10, 14.
11. This can be seen in much of the "new" economic history, where history is treated as merely a laboratory for testing economic models. See, for example, Robert Fogel, *Railroads and American Economic Growth* (Baltimore: Johns Hopkins Press, 1964).
12. Alfred F. Chalk, "Concepts of Change and the Role of Predictability in Economics," *History of Political Economy* 2 (Spring 1970): 109.
13. Robert L. Heilbroner. "On the Limits of Economic Prediction," *Diogenes* 70 (April 1970): 36.
14. Ibid., p. 37.
15. Ibid., p. 33.
16. Note that Friedman's concept of "transitory income" in his permanent income hypothesis would tend to substantiate this view.
17. Chalk, "Concepts," p. 114.
18. Ibid.
19. T.S. Kuhn, *The Structure of Scientific Revolutions* (Chicago: University of Chicago Press, 1970).
20. See Fritz Machlup, "The Problem of Verification in Economics," *Southern Economic Journal* 22 (July 1955): 1–21.
21. Ibid.
22. See Jeffrey B. Nugent, "Methodology in Economics: Some Implications of Pessimism and Some Suggested Alternatives," *American Economist* 11 (Fall 1967): 49–55; and Jack Melitz, "Friedman and Machlup on the Significance of Testing Economic Assumptions," *Journal of Political Economy* 73 (February 1965): 37–60.
23. Paul Diesing, *Patterns of Discovery in the Social Sciences* (Chicago and New York: Aldine-Atherton, Inc., 1971), p. 121.
24. Under the onslaught of the theory of second best, the Cambridge controversy in capital theory, Koopman's dissection of econometric method, Little's attack on welfare economics, the competitive model as a theory of "what is" was quietly shelved. See Martin Shubik, "A Curmudgeon's Guide to Microeconomics," *Journal of Economic Literature* (June 1970): 405–34.
25. Ezra J. Mishan, *The Costs of Economic Growth* (New York: Praeger Publishers, 1967).
26. Milton Friedman, "Choice, Chance, and the Personal Distribution of Income," *Journal of Political Economy* 61 (August 1953): 277–90.
27. E.H. Chamberlin, *Towards a More General Theory of Value* (New York: Oxford University Press, 1957), pp. 296ff.

28. Ben Seligman, *Main Currents in Modern Economics* (Glencoe: The Free Press, 1962), p. 728.
29. See the essays in Milton Friedman, *Capitalism and Freedom* (Chicago: University of Chicago Press, 1962).
30. Milton Friedman, "National Economic Planning," *Newsweek*, 14 July 1975, p. 71.
31. Ibid.
32. Ben B. Seligman, "The Impact of Positivism on Economic Thought," *History of Political Economy* 1 (Fall 1969): 262.

# 6

# The Folklore of the Market: An Inquiry into the Economic Doctrines of the Chicago School

*Ezra J. Mishan*

According to a recent statement by Milton Friedman (1974, p. 11), "in discussions of economic policy, 'Chicago' stands for belief in the efficacy of the free market as a means of organizing resources, for scepticism about government intervention into economic affairs, and for emphasis on the quantity of money as a key factor in producing inflation."

"In discussions of economic science," the statement continues, " 'Chicago' stands for an approach that takes seriously the use of economic theory as a tool for analyzing a startlingly wide range of concrete problems, rather than as an abstract mathematical structure of great beauty but little power; for an approach that insists on the empirical testing of theoretical generalizations and that rejects alike facts without theory and theory without facts."

In this preliminary investigation into the validity and relevance of the economic presuppositions and the belief-system of the Chicago School, I shall concentrate chiefly on the arguments that bear on its belief in the efficacy of free markets in organizing resources, in extending individual choice, and in preserving political freedom.

---

*The author is Professor of Economics, London School of Economics, and Visiting Professor of Economics, University of Maryland, College Park.* *He wishes to thank George Borts for his comments and to record his indebtedness to Milton Friedman for detailed and trenchant criticism of an earlier draft.*

## I. Introduction

### *Definition of a Market*

In a press conference, an abridged version of which was reproduced along with the statement quoted above, Friedman replied to the question of whether market forces were capable of redistributing wealth throughout the world as follows: "Voluntary arrangements by people, voluntary giving of charity to other countries are market forces. Market forces means voluntary forces."

The equation above of voluntary action with market forces implies a concept of the market broader than that usually entailed in the professional literature; and it is entirely possible that Friedman put it this way in order to emphasize the link between private munificence and nineteenth-century capitalist freedom. To most economists, however, the word *market* suggests a voluntary exchange of goods; a *quid pro quo* is involved. And in the more familiar economic contexts the word is indicative of an *organized* market, which adjective conveys the notion of a number of people offering to buy and sell at a money price various amounts of a particular good—a good being defined as something having value and including, therefore, products or services, final or intermediate, and, consequently, also productive services or factors.

However, when the term "the free market" is used in a normative context, additional associations are invoked which purport to assess the social merits of the institution. As used by the Chicago School, at least, "the free market" can be identified with, or can partake of, each of the following institutional features:

(1) The private ownership of capital, or productive (nonhuman) assets;
(2) The private management of economic enterprise;
(3) The decentralization of economic enterprise;
(4) Competitive enterprise;
(5) A price system; and
(6) A market system.

These features, although distinct, are obviously not all mutually exclusive. But setting them out in this way has some heuristic value. It is possible to imagine the existence of (1), private ownership of capital, without (2), the private management of economic enterprises, or (2) without (1). It is no less possible to conceive an economy in which (3), enterprise is decentralized, without its being (1), privately owned, or (2), privately managed,[1] or (4), competitive. Again, (5), a pricing system, may be established in the absence of the remaining features, in particular without the existence of (6), a market system. On the other hand, it is hard to visualize a competitive enterprise system without a market system, and impossible to have a market system without prices.

An economy combining features (1), private ownership of capital, (2), private management of enterprise, and (6), a market system, can be expected to react to changes in the conditions of demand and supply. The more there is of (4), competition, the greater the sensitivity we should expect to changes in these conditions.

Since (4), competition, implies the existence of (5), a price system, and (6), a market system, and since (4) in the presence of (1) entails (3), we may conclude that the simultaneous existence of three features, (1), (2), and (4)—in which (1) and (2) have tended, historically, to grow together—forms the essentials of that economic system which is so attractive to the Chicago School. We may refer to this system as the "competitive private enterprise economy." Wherever the advantages to be considered are those flowing from private ownership or private management of enterprise, the terminology may be abbreviated to "the private enterprise economy" or "the capitalist system." Where, instead, the focus of our examination is upon the allocative merits associated with the competitive model, the term "competitive market" or "free market" will be used. But the reader must not expect rigor in this respect, and the terminology will vary not only according to context, but also according to any need to avoid monotony.

### *Terms of Reference*

The existence of a "competitive private enterprise economy" does not of itself, however, ensure smooth and rapid adjustment of the economy to changes in the underlying conditions of demand and supply. Whether market equilibria are stable, at least locally, is a question of fact in each case, one that depends on behavior and technological relationships. The productive efficiency of a competitive economy, and the speed of adjustment to changing patterns of demand, will vary from one type of good to another and will depend *inter alia* on the quality of management, the geography of the market, and the development of communications. Nonetheless, the clear belief of the Chicago School is that, in the absence of direct government intervention in the operation of free markets, the system will function at least as well as it would under any alternative economic arrangement. Moreover, when regard is paid not so much to the allocative properties of competitive equilibrium but to the dynamic consequences of the struggle for profits, the competitive economy, it is believed, can be vindicated by reasoning analogous to the Darwinian principle of natural selection: the inefficient do not survive long in a competitive economy.

Although this is legitimate conjecture, it does not suffice to establish a strong presumption in favor of the competitive market on these grounds. The inefficient go to the wall in a highly competitive economy, and they would go there more frequently if governments undertook fewer rescue operations. But how quickly would they go? And although, given enough time, the more efficient tend to survive, they are not necessarily as efficient as they might be. In a modern economy in which markets open up, close down, expand, and contract, from year to year, are there any forces at work to ensure that the most efficient firms are more than tolerably efficient? A more searching investigation would pursue such questions which (not because of limitations of space, but of competence) I can only raise here.

The tasks I set myself in this preliminary inquiry are the following: First, to examine the advantages commonly attributed to free markets; the extension of individual choice, the convenience offered to buyers and sellers of goods and factors, the tendency of resources to move in order to clear markets, and the resulting economic efficiency in the allocation of goods and factors. Secondly, to appraise the virtues attributed to a private enterprise economy, the encouragement it offers to managerial initiative, the continuing incentives it provides for service- , product- , and process-innovation, and its reinforcement of political freedom. Thirdly, to assess the social importance of other desiderata that are not claimed for the competitive economy, especially equity and the quality of life. Fourthly, to comment, in passing, on some of the better known canons of economic policy associated with the Chicago School, such as

(1) the removal of all legislation or government devices tending to strengthen monopoly among employers or employees;

(2) the removal of all impediments to the free movement of goods and factors, including the migration of peoples;

(3) the removal of government intervention in foreign exchange markets;

(4) the use of monetary policy rather than price controls in stabilizing prices; and

(5) the preference for transfers in cash rather than in kind.

*Criteria*

In appraising the virtues claimed for the competitive, private enterprise economy various yardsticks might be used.

First, it is possible to compare that economy with alternative economic systems, existing or seemingly feasible. Here, care must be exercised not to compare an existing imperfect private enterprise system with an alternative ideal hypothetical system; nor to compare an existing and imperfect alternative economic system, say, that of some socialist country, with a hypothetical ideal private enterprise system. Since this sort of comparison is a task better suited to those who specialize in comparative economic systems, I shall hardly do more than drop a stray remark here and there. It should be clear, however, that this sort of comparison is limited to answering the question: what sort of economic system, in a given social context, performs better in given respects?

Secondly, it is possible to engage in more immanent criticisms in the light of recent economic thought and to discuss how far from, or close to, realizing the virtues claimed for it is a competitive market economy. A supplementary question may then be posed: do these competitive market virtues, if indeed they are realized in existing societies, make a significant contribution to social welfare? A negative or uncertain answer to this question would cast doubt on the existing allocation of effort and ingenuity among economists to promote legislation and institutions tending to increase competition. Since, in the main, I shall be raising questions that are suggested by relevant theoretical developments in order, occasionally, to cast doubt on implied logical connections, the conclusions that emerge from this survey can only be tentative and impressionistic—an invitation to the profession to re-examine the validity of economic presumptions and the relevance of economic canons that have for so long exerted a dominating influence on the shape and content of economic literature, and to do so in the light of new knowledge and changing material circumstances.

As the reader will soon observe, I follow my exasperating habit of restricting social conjectures or factual judgments to the affluent countries of the world, although some of them may apply as well to the poor or—to use the popular inept euphemism—"developing" countries of the "Third World."

An outline of the structure of this inquiry is easily conveyed by the section titles that follow:

II. The Welfare Significance of Economic Efficiency
III. The Free Market and the Environment
IV. Risk and the Market Economy

V. Intergenerational Equity and the Market
VI. The Consumer Bias of the Market
VII. Consumer Tastes and the Free Market
VIII. Advertising and the Competitive Economy
IX. Individual Freedom and the Competitive Economy
X. Summary and Conclusions.

## *II. The Welfare Significance of Economic Efficiency*

### *The Optimal Conditions Again*

Since we are to examine briefly the welfare significance of the economic concept of allocative efficiency and, later, to make frequent reference to this concept, the first step must be to decompose a Pareto summit position arbitrarily into a convenient number of necessary conditions by reference to familiar simplifying assumptions.[2] The following four have been chosen: (a) The "Exchange Optimum," which is met for any distribution of a collection of goods, wherever it is not possible to make "everyone" better off.[3] When this necessary condition is met, the goods rate of substitution is (under the familiar behavior assumptions mentioned) the same for each person in the community. Since the condition can be met for an indefinite number of distributions among the community, a locus of optimal distributions can be generated which is represented geometrically as the "contract curve."

(b) The "Production Optimum," which is met for any collection of goods produced with a given factor endowment when it is not possible to produce any more of one good without producing less of another good. When this necessary condition is fulfilled the factor rate of substitution is the same in the production of each good. Again, the condition can be met for an indefinite variety of goods, the locus of which can be represented geometrically as a production frontier.

(c) The "Top-level Optimum," which is reached when it is no longer possible to make "everyone" in the community better off with the given endowment of factors. When this necessary condition is met, the goods rate of substitution common to each person in the community is equal to the economy's goods rate of transformation. The geometric analogue is the tangency of the community's indifference curve with the production frontier, or product-transformation curve—a construct which also implies the fulfillment of the exchange optimum and the production optimum respectively.

Finally, wherever the factors available to the economy are not fixed in supply, another condition has to be met; namely (d) the "Factor-use optimum." When this necessary condition is met, it is not possible to make "everyone" better off by varying the supply of any factor. Its fulfillment implies that the subjective factor-product rate of substitution for each person is equal to the "objective" factor-product rate of substitution with the existing technology. The corresponding geometric analogue is the tangency between the individual's factor-product indifference curve and the Knightian factor-product transformation curve.

Since a well-functioning market, whether competitive or not, tends to produce a common set of goods prices, the assumption of consumer maximization implies a tendency for the exchange optimal condition to be met. Inasmuch as it tends also to produce a common set of factor prices, the assumption that firms are cost minimizers—although perhaps less plausible—implies a tendency for the production optimum condition to be met as well. However, in the presence of monopoly, the factor-use optimum is not met. Even in the presence of universal competition, it is not met unless, at ruling factor prices, factor owners suffer no constraint on the amounts of factors they would choose to supply—which is unlikely to be the case in modern industry.

More interest is attached customarily to the top-level optimal condition, inasmuch as it is violated wherever goods outputs are such that one or more prices in the economy are not equal to their corresponding marginal costs.[4] Thus, although the general term *allocative efficiency* comprehends "lower level" optima such as (a), (b), and (d) above, its use in the economic literature has reference in the main to the top-level optimum condition, as for instance in the treatment of taxes, tariffs, price controls, and monopolistic pricing.

The Chicago School's concern with the allocative advantages of increased competition would seem to imply a belief in two things; first, a belief in existence of some significant social gain from fulfilling top-level optimal conditions alone, since, however imperfect the market, these lower level optimal conditions (a) and (b) could also be met. Nevertheless it could be argued that competition impels the economy closer to the production optimum. This belief in the social gains from increasing competition is obviously not easy to verify. There are difficulties enough in measuring such gains under the restrictive assumptions of partial analysis. As for the measurement of gains in a broader context, arising from a change to more competitive arrangements, the unlimited recourse to simplification and, often, to the fiction of a two- or three-sector economy, are such that nobody is inclined to regard the quantitative results as anything more than a bold guess, hopefully illustrative of the direction of gain.

The second implied belief is in the speed of adjustment in a competitive economy.

It is not enough to perceive a continuing *tendency* toward a better allocation of resources. The rapidity or otherwise of industrial adjustment to exogenous movements in demand and supply is also a determinant of allocative improvement over time. Factors other than the degree of competition—for instance, economic institutions, political and cultural features, the stage and pace of technological development, and the extent of state intervention—will influence the speed at which industry adjusts to such exogenous changes. It is altogether possible that, however competitive the economy is, industrial equipment is such that the actual changes in the pattern of outputs take place slowly relative to exogenous changes in the pattern of consumption so that the welfare significance of the tendencies toward optimality is slight. To put it otherwise, if in fact, for whatever reason, the economy responds so slowly as to leave it uncertain whether, at any moment of time, we are moving closer to or further from optimality, the belief that "distortions" can be eliminated by increasing competition is more tenuous, even though we ignore the problems of "first-" and "second-best" that are considered below. Casual judgments about the time factor may yet give way to methods for assessing the time-profile of "economic" welfare by comparing the optimal price-quantity adjustment at each point of time with the actual price-quantity adjustment that takes place under given institutions and with given policies.

The opposition to the use of price controls as an aid in combatting inflation on the grounds that, if effective, it creates allocative "distortions" in the economy, is weakened by doctrinairism of this sort. Until some plausible estimates can be made of the actual welfare significance of the alleged distortions over the anticipated period of time, and until such estimates of social cost can be compared with that of the temporary increase in unemployment associated with the alternative monetarist solution, the allegation of "distortions" raises an issue, but does not settle it.

### *Problems of Second Best*

The traditional goal of promoting competition throughout the economy suffered a severe blow from the formal articulation by Lipsey and Lancaster in 1957 of "The General Theory of Second Best." There it was demonstrated that the extension of marginal cost pricing in an economy in which some sectors were constrained to realize other pricing rules would not of itself increase social welfare and could, indeed, reduce it. Although it is not possible to infer from the theorem that, in the absence of a first best solution for the economy, any allocation was as good or as bad as any other,[5] it certainly took the wind out of the sails of many a competitive model notwithstanding some limited counterblasts.[6] Technological unemployment among economists is unthinkable, however, and predictably the procession of allocative propositions continued undiminished with only a respectful salutation in the direction of Second Best, which theorem continues to this day to be more honored in the breach than the observance.

The upshot of the theorem is that recommendations of marginal cost pricing can be strictly justified only if it is believed that, as a result of such recommendations, marginal cost pricing will be universally adopted; an unlikely prospect. True, the predilection of the Chicago School for a more competitive economy receives support from consideration other than allocation. But it is the allocative significance of the Chicago doctrine that concerns us in this section.

### *Problems of First Best*

Although economists are wont to distinguish with exaggerated care between allocation and equity—where equity includes distributional justice—we should recall that the original appeal of the Pareto principle, on which all allocation propositions are raised, was to a sense of ethical propriety: a change is deemed to be good if nobody is made worse off and at least one person is made better off. If the decentralized competitive economy could be depended upon to produce only these kinds of changes then—allowing for short periods of inconvenience—the esteem in which it is still held by many economists would be wholly vindicated. But the conditions for this outcome to obtain—a world of constant costs (in order to obviate the so-called "pecuniary" external diseconomies) and a market that captures all goods and bads that are generated in society—will never be realized. Just because these conditions are never met, practically every significant change occurring in the market economy acts to make some people better off and others worse off. Needless to remark, a change from a nonoptimal position to an ideal, or top-level, optimal position will also produce these mixed effects. What is more, some of those who are made worse off could be among the very poor just as some of those who are made better off could be among the very rich. Unless the economist can discover the distributional facts associated with particular allocative improvements, or unless he has reason to believe that any resulting inequities will be overcome quickly with the passage of time, he should be cautious in their recommendation.

The above remarks also apply to potential Pareto improvements, of the Kaldor-Scitovsky variety—or tests of hypothetical compensation as they are sometimes called—for which, if costless distribution were possible, everyone could be made better off. Put otherwise, such tests are met simply if aggregate gains exceed aggregate losses, even though it is explicitly acknowledged that some, possibly the poor, will be made worse off.

Indeed, it cannot be too often emphasized that all purely allocative propositions, whether made within a partial or general economic context, turn on the concept of a *potential* Pareto improvement only. For this reason their ethical appeal is limited.

Recognizing this possibility, the outcome of a conventional cost-benefit study (organized as it is around the notion of the algebraic sum of the compensating variations of everyone affected by the project) is not to be regarded as a decision criterion. Indeed, the magnitude of the excess of gains over losses is to be regarded only as one of the essential bits of information, along with other information about distribution and equity.

Of course, in the limiting case of so progressive an income tax that everyone is left with the same disposable income, all potential improvements become translated into actual improvements for everyone—unless the costs of the transfer exceed the net gains. It is not, therefore, unreasonable to argue that in a market economy without significant externalities the pursuit of allocative efficiency—though perhaps difficult in view of the problems of first and second best—could at least lead to the bulk of the population being made better off over time *provided* the tax system was both highly progressive and efficient. Couched in such terms, however, the statement reveals only too clearly the extent of our ignorance about relevant magnitudes, in particular the order of magnitudes of the actual gains and actual losses arising from seemingly efficient reallocations, their distribution through the existing tax system, and, indeed, the long-run costs to society in maintaining existing tax systems which are neither highly progressive nor highly efficient. In sum, it reveals the extent to which current presuppositions in favor of economic efficiency depend no less upon faith than upon knowledge of the facts.

A final deficiency of allocative propositions in economics also arises from our acceptance of their formulation in terms of potential gains. As demonstrated initially by Scitovsky (1941), and on innumerable later occasions by other writers, if a collection of goods $Q_2$ is allocatively superior to a collection $Q_1$, in that everyone could be made better off by a movement from $Q_1$ to $Q_2$, the same may be said for the reverse movement, from $Q_2$ to $Q_1$. This apparent contradiction depends upon a correspondence between each efficient distribution of a given goods collection and a set of prices. Thus, thinking in terms of the related price-index criterion, it is hardly paradoxical to state that at one set of prices the goods collection $Q_2$ is valued higher than $Q_1$, whereas for another set of prices $Q_1$ is valued higher.

But there are further implications of this line of analysis that make one pause. First, it is no longer possible to show, in general, that a top-level optimal position is unambiguously superior—on a potential Pareto test, that is—to a nonoptimal position (Mishan, 1957). Indeed, it is not possible in general to regard as unambiguously superior, in this same sense, a collection of goods $Q_2$ that has more of all goods than $Q_1$—even if, in addition, $Q_2$ is a top-level optimum and $Q_1$ is not only nonoptimal but is situated below the production boundary and, therefore, does not meet the production optimal conditions.[7]

The question of how important in the real world are these awkward possibilities is one which invites speculation. There may be important limiting conditions, but as yet they have not been discovered. I tend to think that it is less likely than it appears in the geometry of the two- or three-good case. Yet awareness of these possibilities does add something to the doubts about the welfare significance of allocative improvements and, *a fortiori* therefore, to the presumption that an extension of the competitive economy enhances welfare.[8]

*Interdependent Utilities*

This phenomenon comes under the category of externalities inasmuch as a person's welfare depends upon variables—the utility, or the income, or the amounts of goods purchased, of other persons—that he cannot control. They are less amenable to correction, however, than the more tangible externalities inflicted by pollutants.

The implication of Duesenberry's "relative income hypothesis" (1949) for social welfare in a growing economy, though of the utmost importance, is familiar enough today to warrant only brief mention before turning to the more recent exploration of other aspects of interdependent utilities. That people's satisfaction in life is not impervious to the wealth of their neighbors is an observation too banal to be worth the recording. Yet when nicely formalized and fed into the Pareto machinery, the resulting outcome gives economic respectability to current philosophical doubts about the value of sustained material growth.

If it is true that the higher the level of "real" per capita income the more does a person's well-being depend, not on his absolute income but on his income relative to those of others, the less the Pareto justification for further economic growth. People may continue, of course, to struggle to improve their position relative to others but clearly, in the limiting case in which individual welfare depends only on relative income, it would no longer be possible to make everyone better off: only redistribution possibilities would remain open to society. And, once real income were equally distributed, no rise in well-being would be experienced by anyone even though output per capita would continue to grow.

Although there is evidence from surveys of the increasing prevalence of this phenomenon,[9] much more needs to be known before any strong conclusion can be reached. The more prevalent it becomes, however, the more do the attractions of further economic growth diminish.[10] And although a disciple of the Chicago School may have no particular brief for economic growth *per se,* but only for that economic growth that is the collective result of individual decisions, the value of the growth of "real" income resulting therefrom is also diminished.

In general, it may be said that the more the relative income hypothesis operates the less value is to be placed on more goods satisfaction and on allocative improvements, even where free of all ambiguity.

In contrast to this negative relationship between a person's welfare and the income of others, in particular the income of those within his status group, recent writers have been paying more attention to the positive relation between a person's welfare and the incomes of those who are poorer than he. The first relationship can be referred to briefly as "envy," the second "benevolence." Needless to remark, the two hypotheses are not mutually exclusive: person A's welfare may rise with an increase in B's income until it exceeds some critical proportion of A's income, after which A's welfare declines with increases in B's income.

However, by reference to the Pareto criterion, the "benevolence" relationship has been employed to rationalize actual or possible patterns of distribution either in money or in kind.

Three kinds of argument bearing on distribution can be distinguished. (1) One argument, associated with Hochman and Rodgers (1969), confines itself to money transfers that are actual Pareto improvements. Thus, if it is assumed that a dollar received by Mr. Poor is valued by him at just one dollar, it is required of the donor, Mr. Rich, that he obtain more than one dollar's worth of satisfaction from "spending" the dollar on Mr. Poor. Following this line of thought some distributions, at least, can be regarded simply as an extension of the Pareto principle.

(2) It is to be noted that a potential Pareto improvement criterion would imply a larger transfer of income than an actual Pareto improvement criterion. For on the former criterion we could justify transferring a dollar from Mr. Rich even if the satisfaction he derives from its donation to Mr. Poor were less than a dollar. It is enough that Mr. Rich's satisfaction is not negative.

The distributional agreement associated with Thurow (1969) is, in fact, based on a potential Pareto improvement criterion. Classifying the structure of the income distribution as a collective good, each conceivable income structure (or tax structure) is assumed to affect the welfare of every member of the community. In consequence each person can place a value, or compensating variation, on each alternative structure. If it raises his welfare, this compensating variation is the sum he is willing to pay for the collective adoption of the structure in question. If it lowers his welfare, the compensating variation is the sum he must receive to restore his welfare. The largest potential Pareto improvement follows from implementing (costlessly) that distributional structure that commands the largest positive aggregate of compensating variations.

(3) A third argument linked with Daly and Giertz (1972) rests on a distinction between "utility externalities" (the dependence of A's welfare on the levels of income of others) and "goods externalities" (the dependence of A's welfare on amounts of specific goods consumed by others). In the former case, all the goods-exchange optimal conditions are met and, as indicated earlier, improvements can be effected only through transfers of purchasing power. In the latter case, however, since a person's welfare depends *inter alia* on the amounts of specific goods consumed by others, the existence of a common set of prices no longer ensures the existence of an exchange optimum: if negotiation were costless, person A, for example, might improve his position by bribing other persons to take more, or less, of those particular goods their possession of which affects his welfare.

From this implication, a case may be conceived for transfers in kind rather than in cash. The proponents of such a scheme agree that it costs to convert money into goods and to administer the distribution of the goods. They agree also that, as a rule, the recipients prefer cash to goods. Yet they conclude that to insist on cash transfers in all cases might imply a loss of possible gains in welfare. For if donors were not allowed to give transfers in kind, they might give away considerably less in cash than the value of the goods they would willingly have given. Not only would the donors be worse off if the cash-only doctrine were enforced, but the recipients also inasmuch as—though they prefer a dollar of cash to a dollar's wealth of goods—the value of the total cash they receive is less than the value they attach to the goods they would have received. Thus, although transfers in kind may be stigmatized as "paternalism," they can, it seems, be vindicated not only by the democratic process but also by the Pareto criterion which has some ethical appeal inasmuch as every one counts, donors as well as recipients.

I do not know whether adherents of the Chicago School were much impressed by any of these arguments.[11] But they do favor voluntary cash transfers which appear to be the policy implication of the first argument. However, Hochman and Rodgers also make use of their concept to rationalize the existing tax system, which is unacceptable to the Chicago School. Nor would the direct tax implication of Thurow's analysis appeal to it. The Daly and Giertz conclusions would go down no better. Although their analysis proceeds by reference to voluntary behavior, information and transactions costs are such that government action is necessary to implement the findings in favor of goods transfers. Indeed, not only are the required transfers to be compulsory, the sums raised are to be used for the purchase and distribution of specific goods, a policy which entails expansion of state bureaucracies.

### *Ethics versus Utility*

The three distribution arguments summarized above are examples of analyses that omit a vital distinction in connection with the way distribution enters into each person's utility: the distinction between the "Pareto efficient" distribution and the "just" distribution. A movement toward the former can, as indicated, be justified beginning from an existing real world position. The "just" or "ethical" distribution, on the other hand, is one that is conceived to emerge from a constitution that is framed behind Rawls's veil of ignorance. In other words, it is an ideal distribution that men might hope to agree upon if the matter were debated in some hypothetical state prior to their entering into the real world—a state in which no man could foresee his genetic or material endowment in the real world or the circumstances that would befall him. Insofar as men succeed, in their actual deliberations, in projecting themselves into this imaginary state, they are addressing themselves to the "just" distribution, not the Pareto efficient one (Mishan, 1971).

The traditional separation between economic efficiency and distribution entails, in my interpretation, a concern with the "just" distribution and not the Pareto efficient one. It should be clear, moreover, that insofar as there is conflict between the two approaches to distribution, the "just" distribution has the stronger ethical appeal.

Thus in the broader context of economy policy, the Pareto principle is not the only criterion acceptable to the liberal economist or, indeed, to the welfare economist. As I have indicated elsewhere (1969), the choice of a utility base for welfare economics can be rejected in favor of an ethical base, the ethics being those of the society for which the prescriptive statements of welfare economics are intended to apply. As indicated above, these ethics, however, are sometimes those that would emerge only from deliberations taking place behind "the veil of ignorance" and are, therefore, not always readily apparent from public expression. Nor then can they always be expected to be politically decisive. The most to be hoped for is that, in consequence of a continuing dialogue, they will ultimately prevail.

However, in some instances the ethics of an issue are more manifestly in conflict with the prescriptions flowing from a utility- or Pareto-based welfare economics. Excess benefits, for example, may arise from the expropriation by a majority of the property of a rich minority. Again, a project that raises the material well-being of a given group of people sufficiently to warrant the real resources involved, may be vetoed on the Pareto criterion if it inflames the prejudices of neighboring groups. Yet the ethics of society might forbid that a policy be rejected simply because—although it improves the material well-being of one group without damaging the material interests of any other group—it could be resented by others.

What is more, there can be accord among economists against resort to the Pareto criterion on a wide range of policy issues simply because the public lacks both the relevant knowledge and the training to foresee the likely consequences of the alternative policies being mooted. On such issues the economist would prefer that decisions be reached through the political process, not necessarily because he is impressed by the wisdom of the multitude as expressed through the ballot box. After all, the democratic process has come out in support of many policies rejected not only by the Chicago School but also by a majority of economists—tariffs, trade restrictions, farm price supports, wage and price legislation, to mention just a few. The economist may prefer the political process because he is averse to extending a criterion appropriate for the choice of market goods—where its justification depends upon the notion of given tastes and on the belief, or fiction, that people know their own interests best—to broader or more complex issues in which given "tastes" may be given prejudices, and which it is demonstrably untrue that people know their own interests best, much less those of the community at large. Employing the Pareto principle in such issues, assuming all measurement problems could be overcome, might well find in favor of existing and possibly higher tariffs, in favor of farm price supports, in favor of racial discrimination—and in favor of distribution in kind. In short, its wholesale employment, assuming its feasibility, would give the sanction of economic efficiency to policies that are today roundly condemned by liberal economists. Relegating such issues instead to the political arena, at least enables economists and others to participate in an ongoing dialogue in the endeavor to persuade an existing majority that it is not in their ultimate interests or desires to support policies they currently favor.

Thus, notwithstanding the recent analyses of Pareto-efficient distributions, the argument against proposed transfers in kind can draw upon ethical considerations touched upon in the paragraph preceding the above, as well as those of propriety mentioned in the preceding paragraph. The liberal economist may reasonably affirm that *in respect of market goods,* it is morally appropriate that all adults, even the poor and destitute, should be treated as if they knew their own interests best; they should be treated, that is, on a par with other members of society in this respect. Only exceptional circumstances warrant the implied indignity. And if it is true that donors prefer to give in kind because they believe that they know better what the recipients need than do the recipients themselves—or for whatever reason—then the liberal economist could well retort that it is quite improper for them to think in this way and would seek to convince them of the impropriety.

### *III. Free Markets and the Environment*

The proposition that the existence of perfectly competitive equilibria in all markets entails an optimal position for the economy always carries the standard proviso that there be no external effects. At the time Pigou was writing, the existence of such effects was thought to be more the exception than the rule. But with growing public concern over pollution after World War II and, in consequence, the vastly increased attention being given to environmental externalities in the professional literature over the last decade or so, the Chicago School could no longer avoid discussing some of the issues raised by their incidence.

#### *The Chicago View*

Not surprisingly, a more conservative approach was developed, in part inspired by Frank Knight's classic article (1924), and also perhaps by the no less celebrated paper by Jacob Viner (1931), which sought to weaken the popular arguments for government intervention, and to strengthen the presumption that unaided market forces would, or could be made to, bring about a proper allocation of resources, at least within the restrictive assumptions of a partial context. Caution against too ready a recourse to excise taxes or subsidies, or other controls, continues to be urged for a number of reasons.

First, and rather casually, members of the Chicago School maintain that the current preoccupation with pollution is out of proportion to the problems it poses,[12] and they vent their resentment against "environmentalists" by associating their articulate concern with elitist self-interest. "The quality of the environment" it is repeatedly asserted "is predominantly a middle-class interest," which interest, were it to prevail, would tend to have regressive distributional effects—through the raising of the prices of a range of products that forms a significant proportion of the consumption of the "poor," and through a possible slowing down of the rate of economic growth (as a result both of reducing resources otherwise available for new investment and of interfering with the decisions of private industry).

These allegations carry little conviction. It is not impossible that social marginal costs of a range of polluting goods exceed their prices and, if corrected, would reduce the "real" incomes (measured in terms only of man-made goods) of the poor by a greater proportion than those of the rich. Yet conservative economists do not favor subsidizing particular goods for distributional reasons. They favor direct transfers of money. On the difficulties of estimating the distributional effects of combatting a wide range of pollutants, see Kneese and Schultze (1973).

As for the concern with future economic growth, there is no apparent reason to suppose that allocative correction for environmental spillovers would act to reduce aggregate investment or innovation.

In the same spirit, caveats were uttered against state intervention in the attempt to improve the environment without careful thought of the consequences. If, for example, the measures taken by a government succeeded in improving the urban environment inhabited by the poor, the suburban rich might begin to move back to the urban area and, in the process, drive up rents so far as to displace the poor.

Secondly, a number of arguments found favor with these more conservative economists, many of whom disliked the tax solution associated with the writings of Pigou. There was a tendency, for example, to conclude that the calculation of an optimal tax was costly and its administration fraught with difficulties.[13] Another much favored maneuver was to discover circumstances in which an external diseconomy might warrant an expansion of output rather than a contraction.[14] These apparently perverse possibilities, however, do not rate as counterexamples to the broad Pigovian theme which, in the face of market failures, directed the state to bring about a "reshuffling" of resources as between economic activities in the endeavor to realize an ideal allocation, one identified by the necessary condition that in the production of all goods prices should equal corresponding marginal *social* cost.

In the same category can be found the rather lame proposition (Buchanan and Stubblebine, 1962) that an optimal excise tax levied on a good producing an external diseconomy could result in a suboptimal contraction of output if further bargaining between the affected parties took place.[15] Also, another more plausible assertion; that the market left to itself raises the costs of pollutant-causing products by the required amount inasmuch as industries established in polluted areas have to offer a premium to attract workers from, and prevent workers migrating to, less polluted areas.[16]

Thirdly, a more convincing argument against state intervention can be made by relating the operation of the market to the distribution of property rights in scarce resources. Thus, in contrast to Pigou's optimal tax solution to the congested highway problem, Knight (1924) explained the congestion itself in terms of the overuse of a scarce resource, highway space, this being the result of its being treated as a common property. Regarded in this light, the appropriate remedy was to treat the highway as private property and so to price traffic as to maximize the return to the highway.[17]

In effect, Knight's proposed solution emerged as part of his analysis. It was a solution, however, that produced the same output as Pigou's optimal tax. The pragmatic question, then, turns on a comparison of the social costs of collecting the appropriate tolls or taxes either by the highway owners or by the agencies of the state. Yet Knight's insight was impressive, and a *prima facie* argument against the necessity of state intervention was established—at least for those external diseconomies that result from treating as common property those scarce but appropriable resources associated with areas of land and water.

This seminal idea, however, was to lie in fallow soil until about 1960 when it began to produce much fruit after its kind. Coase's celebrated contribution of that year illustrated, among other things, the proposition that in the absence of income effects (or, more properly "welfare effects") and in the absence of all transactions costs, the bargaining solution to an external diseconomy problem would be optimal and uniquely determined.[18] Coase also sought to dispose of the popular notion of one party's inflicting damage on another, a notion that lends itself to policies that favor compensation for the victim. What modest success he had in this endeavor arose from his choice of examples in which conflicts of business interest were mutual and therefore were such as to make the question of equity difficult to determine.

Fourthly, the explicit consideration of transactions costs could be made to tell against state intervention.

In the absence of all transactions costs, mutual bargaining would, as indicated by Coase (1960), tend to produce an optimal solution—even if there were scarce resources involved that were being treated as common property. In fact, it is the existence of transactions costs large enough to prevent bargaining that requires the consideration of other solutions among which, needless to remark, the one most favored by Chicago is that which would direct the scarce appropriable resource to be managed as private property. Thus, it came to pass that the concept of transactions costs, along with that of property rights, inspired a number of thoughtful contributions, many of which appeared during the 1960s in the *Journal of Law and Economics,*[19] designed to strengthen the presumption favoring the free market even in the presence of significant externalities. Indeed, arguments were pushed to the point of suggesting that the mere existence of an unchecked market output of a good $x$, one generating external diseconomies, could be accepted as evidence that transactions costs, more particularly bargaining costs, must be in excess of the net social gains that would otherwise result from optimal correction of the output. The existence of a de facto optimum could then be legitimately inferred. On the other hand, the nonexistence of a market for a good $y$ could be interpreted as evidence that transactions costs, more particularly enforcement or policing costs, must be greater than the (otherwise) net gains to society. By extending the concept of transactions cost to encompass any inertia or lack of initiative in society, one comes uncomfortably close to the thesis that, in economics, whatever is, is best.

Fifthly, the conservative economist warns against premature action against pollution. Action must wait upon knowledge; and the eventual measures, if any, to be taken must be the fruit of prolonged and dispassionate research. Bearing in mind the costs of unearthing relevant information, the effect of such conservative advice is to put the burden of expense and proof on the antipollution faction.

Sixthly, although there is an absence of markets, in the conventional sense, for the more commonly recognized environmental goods, aesthetic amenity, quiet, fresh air, clean water, it may be contended that individuals retain some choice in the matter through the simple mechanism mentioned in the Tiebout hypothesis (1956). For environmental goods could be included in each of the packages of public goods offered by the different local authorities. In fact the extent of the choice in respect of environmental goods is limited by the size of the jurisdiction, by their number, by the pressure of business interests, and all too commonly, by the lack of initiative and imagination. Even if the differences in environmental goods as between locations were substantially greater than they happen to be, accessibility to them is limited by costs of movement, "real" and "psychic," which are likely to fall more heavily on the poor. There is, moreover, nothing in this mechanism to prevent a general erosion over time of environmental standards in all areas of a country, the direct result of the technologies and products associated with postwar economic growth.

Finally, by conceding the case, in principle, for the need of some form of property rights in environmental goods, it is seemingly possible to reconcile a concern over environmental disruption with a faith in the operation of free markets.

### *Assessment of the Chicago View*

I should not want to underrate either the ingenuity or the significance of the many contributions that served to strengthen the Chicago School's faith in the allocative virtue of the free market even in a society that is increasingly afflicted by external diseconomies. But there is a number of aspects of the problem, related to equity as well as to allocation, that the market cannot satisfactorily resolve. These appear more important as less attention is paid to interfirm or interindustry externalities and more attention to the overspill on the public at large from the processes or products of modern industry.

First, although the notion of some ideal distribution among the populace of property rights in environmental amenities—what I refer to more briefly as "amenity rights" (1967a)—is suggestive in understanding the nature of the problem, there are insuperable difficulties in implementing it. A vision of a decentralized market in which, for example, each member of the public can sell or rent his allotted volume of air-space—to be regarded by buyers of the amounts of air-space needed by industry as a substitute for the air-space owned by any other member of the public—to be used as a repository for containing pollutants such as smoke, particles, fume, noise, and so forth, can be counted on to provoke the imagination to grasp the limitations of our universe. But just because, in those cases where the scarce resource is not appropriable, such schemes are impossible, we are constrained to compare an inefficient market solution with a solution requiring some form of state intervention. For there are, indeed, social costs in extending a bureaucracy over and above the usual list of transactions costs. And the latter will be high if economists insist on calculating the magnitude of the ideal excise or effluent tax. Without being optimal, however, rough and tentative tax calculations can effect a substantial improvement. Certainly the use of taxes to enforce tolerable standards may yield significant social gains over and above the costs of enforcement.[20]

Secondly, although the bargaining outcome will be optimal if there are no transactions costs, it will not be uniquely optimal if there are nonzero welfare effects. The incidence of these effects on the outcome can be assumed negligible only if the impact of the decision in question on people's well-being is small, which is not generally the case for environmental spillovers. Assuming normal (positive) welfare effects, what a person in a noisy environment is willing to pay for continuing quiet may be only a fraction of the minimum sum he is willing to accept to put up with the existing noise, or with the additional noise expected to be generated by a highway or airport to be built near his home. Whether the airport or highway is sanctioned on economic grounds can then depend on whether the law requires compensation for the residents in question or whether, in default of a legal ruling, the economic cost of the noise is estimated simply by what the residents can pay to prevent it. Thus, in the absence of marketable amenity rights, the disamenities inflicted on the public are ignored by the entrepreneur who will be induced to modify his scheme only if the sums they can offer him in return will more than compensate for his incidental loss of profit. Furthermore, even if the building of a proposed highway or airport is contingent upon a thoroughgoing cost-benefit criterion, one taking into account compensatory variations for all disamenties incurred, the question of equity is neglected.

Thirdly, as for the conservative principle that no action be taken unless and until relevant information is available, it could be a recipe for disaster in a world of rapid change. It is, of course, true that the ideal tax cannot be calculated in the absence of detailed knowledge about the environmental impact of the good or process in question. It is also true, as indicated above, that worthwhile improvements can be implemented without recourse to an ideal tax. What is more to the point, however, is that such a principle amounts to the methodological rule: when in doubt, continue to pollute.

For a community living on the margin of subsistence such a rule might be justified—at least insofar as it would countenance the introduction of polluting goods or processes that otherwise make a substantial contribution to the community's welfare. But in an already affluent society, the case for adopting such a rule is far from obvious. And if we include in the term *pollution,* the risk of grave and possibly irreversible genetic and ecological consequences—a subject we touch on in the following section—the reverse methodological rule would seem more prudent; namely, that all processes generating, or products containing, substances about whose effects we have limited experience, should be withheld until prolonged research has uncovered their range of consequences beyond reasonable doubt.

Fourthly, if the law were to prohibit any new developments having manifestly adverse environmental effects without fully compensating all who were thereby injured, the outputs of some industries would tend to be smaller than they would in the absence of such restrictive environmental legislation. Indeed, if only because of the heavy costs also incurred in identifying and bargaining with potential victims, some industries would not be able to operate at all. Yet the equilibrium that the competitive market tends to, under this dispensation, would be no less of an optimal than the equilibrium it would tend to if, instead, the spillover victims had no rights whatsoever. The interesting question arises whether, in respect of net social gains and/or equity, the competitive equilibrium solution in the presence of this restrictive legislation is better or worse than the competitive equilibrium solution in the absence of any such restrictive legislation: or whether, perhaps, a mixture of the two, or else a system of effluent taxes that enforce environmental standards, is better than either—bearing in mind that the magnitude of transactions costs (which use up real resources) will vary from one solution to another. Without further reflection and some empirical study there is not much to be said that would command general assent. There are certainly no considerations that lead one to suspect that a pollutant permissive, competitive market solution is likely to be best in respect either of net social gain or of equity.

Fifthly, and most important of all, among the great virtues claimed for the market, one apt to be overlooked in a professional literature that lends itself too easily to formal allocation propositions, is that of the freedom to choose. Notwithstanding Machlup's arguments (1969), there is no necessary restriction of consumer freedom if, without reducing disposable incomes, excise taxes and subsidies are used to make good *x* dearer and good *y* cheaper. So far as the consumer is affected, the resulting change of market prices could have as well been the outcome of changes in the conditions of supply. Indeed, the only difference between these two cases is allocative: The tax-subsidy alteration of goods prices is potentially Pareto inferior to a situation in which the relative prices reflect their corresponding social marginal costs.

The case is quite different for expenditure or quantitative constraints. As Milton Friedman has persuasively argued, the more the public sector takes over from the private market sector the less choice remains for the individual. His money is used, allegedly on his behalf, in the production of public goods that may not interest him and, insofar as these goods are nonoptional, he is compelled to consume them in amounts other than those he would prefer.[21] If this is true of public sector collective goods, it is no less true of nonoptional collective bads, or external diseconomies. And it remains true whether or not allocative criteria are satisfied;[22] whether, that is, the optimal amounts of collective goods or collective bads are being produced.

Thus, if a person complains of smog or aircraft noise, it is not altogether to the purpose to remark the impressive growth of industry and its products, or the increase of travel opportunities. He may himself have little use for the smog-creating products or air travel services. And if he were observed to make use of them—if only because in the sort of environment developed in response to these products, and in particular to the growth in airplanes and automobiles, he is left with little choice in the matter—he still might not want to put up with the concomitant bads in the amounts he currently receives. Indeed, on balance, he may regard himself as worse off in consequence of the availability of such goods-cum-bads. In contrast, a tied sale (by which a person is compelled to pay for some items he may not want, or may dislike, in order to acquire the goods he wants) cannot make him worse off. For he can always refuse the tied sale offer if, on balance, it reduces his welfare. But where the package includes nonoptional collective bads, no matter how much or little he takes of the accompanying goods he cannot reduce the quantum of bads that fall on him—save, possibly, by incurring expenditures.

The point is not trivial. The virtue of extended choice claimed for the market resides in its ability, so to speak, to "decompose" composite packages of goods, or bads, or both, for individual consumption—packages that could result, say, from a state decree or from a popular vote—into its constituent parts among which the individual may freely choose. Insofar as the market is to be successful in this vital respect, all the goods and all the bads of any welfare significance must enter the price system. Changes over time operating through this market will then tend to realize[23] actual Pareto improvements; those in which everyone is actually made better off.

The significance of the above passage may be brought out by imagining a market economy without a labor market. Allocative criteria in these circumstances would be met by taking proper account of the "diswelfare," in terms of compensating variations, of all the labor forcibly directed into the production of amounts of goods being demanded; the costs of such labor being treated, quite properly in this economy, as an external diseconomy. In making the transition to an organized labor market in which, within the constraints of technology and custom, each worker can now choose for himself where among the alternative opportunities to place his labor, there will be a significant extension of individual choice which enhances social welfare. Its formal expression, however, is in terms of a movement from a potential to an actual Pareto improvement.

Now in the nature of things, one cannot literally set up a spillovers market, one in which each person can decide for himself how much of each spillover he will freely absorb at the going market price. The unavoidable treatment in economics of such spillovers as external diseconomies, or nonoptional collective bads, that is, entails the use of this more limited criterion—the potential Pareto improvement, and not the actual one. And the welfare significance of this limitation clearly depends upon the impact of the range of spillovers on individual well-being.

Considering the pace and scale of modern technology and the power of commercial interests,[24] it would be optimistic to anticipate much decline in the existing range of spillovers over the future. At best, we can expect new spillovers for old. Some pervasive spillovers, such as noise, visual distraction, urban litter and ugliness, are not likely to diminish much over the next decade. Bearing in mind the inertia of political processes, is it too pessimistic to conclude that, notwithstanding the operation of free markets, in all of that which is trivial the individual today has ample choice, but in much that is truly important to the state of his well-being—the environment in which he is enmeshed—he has very little choice? At any rate, if something like this conclusion is credible, the claims made for the virtue of the free market in purveying choice will, as a result of the technologies of economic growth, have to be considerably diminished. For the domain of its success in this respect, at least under existing laws, has come to exclude areas of great sensitivity.

The question then to be faced is whether any alternative economic organization can do better than the existing market system even when supplemented by effluent taxes. A fairly radical suggestion, one compatible with the operation of the market, has already been suggested: that in respect of a number of environmental spillovers suffered by the public at large legislation be enacted placing the burden of prevention or compensation wholly on the industries or persons responsible for them.[25] Enforcement costs may, of course, be so large that the optimum toward which the economy tends under this form of law, offers a smaller net social gain than the optimum toward which the economy tends under the existing laws. On the other hand, all adjustments involving environmental repercussions will, under the proposed law, tend to involve actual Pareto improvements: nobody will then suffer uncompensated damage. In effect, a trade-off between equity or justice, on the one hand, and (unweighted) real income on the other would be at issue, with society requiring some idea of the magnitudes and some criterion by which to assess these incommensurables. In a materially prosperous society, however, it may be easier to secure assent to the maxim, that it is more important to prevent injustice and unnecessary suffering than it is to provide opportunities for further material aggrandizement.

## *IV. Risk and the Market Economy*

Some of the risks run by private businesses can be insured against. Some of the risks that cannot be insured against arise from the uncertainty of future prices and can be hedged against on futures or forward markets. Yet others can be, at least, partly unloaded onto willing speculators. Employees may also be able to insure against sickness, unemployment, or loss of earnings. Through such schemes, a variety of risks can be costed into the economic system and, since such schemes, like the production of any new good, offer social gains, there is warrant for some economic ingenuity being directed into innovations of this sort.

In this section, the risks that concern us are not those arising from the ordinary vicissitudes of trade—that is, from the uncertainty about future prices and availabilities—but those arising in the production and use of goods that bear on the health and survival of members of society. The treatment of this problem, then, involves an extension of the treatment of environmental externalities in the preceding section.

Although the line between risk and uncertainty, and between knowledge and ignorance of potential damage, is very blurred, some arbitrary classification will help us to come to grips with the problems.

### *Voluntary and Known Risk*

The unchecked operation of the goods market will suffice wherever it can be supposed that each person knows from experience the probability of incurring particular disabilities from the consumption and use of the different goods, or else can acquire the relevant information at low cost and little inconvenience. As for those occupational risks that are correctly assessed, the operation of the market can be expected to produce factor prices that include the appropriate risk premia.

*Voluntary and Unknown Risk*

Exceptions always being allowed for the protection of minors, the position taken by John Stuart Mill continues to express the judgment of liberal economists today. In the absence of external effects,[26] the maxim, that no man should seek to improve the social welfare by interfering in any way in those individual choices directed to market goods, would also extend to any adult the freedom to imperil his life or health in any way he wished. Since knowledge of the kind of risks that are associated with the consumption of tobacco, liquor, or traditional drugs, such as opium, is fairly widely dispersed in society, the case in freedom for allowing a man to take what risks he will, provided they fall entirely on his person,[27] is buttressed by modern instances of the unhappier consequences of attempts by the state to control the traffic in liquor or drugs.

There is a case, indeed, for the freedom of any person to take drugs about which very little is currently known, either of the consequences or of their likelihood of occurrence, granted always that there is little chance of his hurting others. Suffice that he knows it to be a drug that could conceivably have dire consequences on his physical and mental health, there is a case in freedom for permitting him to experiment on his own person only if he so chooses.

*Involuntary and Known Risk*

If we accept this view, at least provisionally, we need concern ourselves in the remainder of this section only with instances in which risks fall on those who by their own activity do not incur them; in short with the externality aspects of risk-bearing. Where the external diseconomies that arise in the production or the consumption of the goods in question are those that increase the risk of damage to the health of others by a known probability, recourse to a system of excise taxes can, in principle, internalize the resulting social costs into the price system. No more need be said here about alternative solutions, however, since environmental damage, treated in the preceding section, includes any known health risks of intervention in the environment or biosphere.

*Involuntary and Unknown Risk*

In this category are those instances where the nature, magnitude, and, therefore, possibly the valuation of the damage that might occur are believed to be understood, but the probability of its occurrence is not; also included are those instances where we have no knowledge or very imperfect knowledge of the extent of the damage that could occur.

Game theory is one of the techniques favored by economists for dealing with such problems of uncertainty, especially those for which the magnitudes of alternative outcomes are known but not the probabilities of their occurrence. For the case where the magnitudes themselves are unknown, our greater ignorance can also be formalized along game theoretic lines by extending the spectrum of possible social costs from some negligible figure at one end to a figure at the other end that is large enough to shock anybody.

It is possible to make use of such techniques in social cost-benefit studies, although in fact they are seldom used in putting a value on the social hazards of large projects using complex technology. The greater the extent of our ignorance, the less satisfactory the outcome of a game theory exercise, bearing in mind also that it does not carry with it a rule for deciding which criterion to apply; whether, for instance, the more conservative *maximin* criterion or the more opportunistic *minimax* one. What can be said for sure, however, is that wherever such risks are borne involuntarily—wherever, that is, they are not confined to the individual, the firm, or the industry generating them—but instead fall upon the public at large, the free market cannot cope with them.

The popular examples of such hazards that spring to mind are, not surprisingly, the consequence of scientific and technological advance. Although in all cases it is possible (though not likely) that the full range of adverse consequences, and the probability distribution of each of them, will come to light with the passage of time, the social problem is that of somehow adjusting the economic system to the existence of our dangerous state of ignorance until we know more.[28] Recollecting the social consequences of the introduction of heroin at the turn of the century (advertised and prescribed for a while by the medical profession as a safe sedative), more recently those of Methadone, the genetic consequence of Thalidomide and, to a lesser extent, chemical food additives to say nothing of the far-reaching ecological effects of DDT and a growing range of chemical pesticides, it is obvious that no provision for them can be made by the mechanism of the market; nor, for that matter, by such traditional economic devices as a system of excise or other taxes.

The postwar cornucopia of drugs and synthetics about whose consequences, singly or in combination, we know next to nothing, now runs into many thousands. And although the probability of some genetic or ecological calamity in the production or use of any one of them might be very small indeed, as the number of such products continues to multiply, the resulting risk of some such calamity actually occurring increases to a point beyond which society is in grave peril. In these circumstances, measuring social gains against social costs with the aid of market prices is no longer that of a routine exercise in allocation economics. Indeed, any hope of translating these sorts of risk into money values that can somehow be internalized into the economic system is to be dismissed as chimerical.[29] The nature of many of the risks we are courting can be dealt with only at the highest political level and following considerable public debate.

In this connection one has only to think of the possible consequences currently associated with "genetic engineering," with supersonic flights, with the operation of nuclear fission plants, to appreciate the magnitude of some of the problems that the technological society is running into. To continue much longer, therefore, to allow scientists to make their own decisions about fields of research, to allow research departments of corporations to decide themselves whether and when a new product should be marketed, to allow government agencies, guided by the advice of enthusiastic technocrats, to make critical decisions about vast projects and policies that could conceivably endanger the lives and health of thousands or millions of ordinary citizens, would amount to a victory of traditional laissez-faire doctrine, and of faith in elected governments, over society's instinct for self-preservation, a victory that could pave the way for social disaster. In this new and more dangerous world we are entering, adequate legislation would entail a wide range of democratic controls, not only over the activities of private enterprise, but also over the research activities of scientists.

Whatever the outcome, however, the variety of apprehensions that afflict a society in consequence of the perils, real or imagined, that flow directly from new research or technologies, or indirectly from the social consequences of technological growth, can reach levels that swamp any contribution to social welfare arising from the operation of free markets in a growing economy. In the present state of technological development this is not an idle fancy. As we shall see anon, technology has yet other consequences that run counter to the beneficient effects of free markets, in particular those extending individual choice and personal freedom; consequences, therefore, that relegate to that felicitous institution a diminishing role in the preservation of society's welfare.

### *V. Intergenerational Equity and the Market*

In an ideal Irving-Fisher type of capital market, the volume of current new investment is the collective outcome of individual decisions, each one the result of weighing the inconvenience of postponing consumption against the gains (from investment) of doing so. Insofar as economic growth stems only from the accumulation of capital in this manner, its path is determined by a market that reflects individual desires. The contribution to economic growth of technological progress need not, however, be regarded as an independent factor. For the advance and diffusion of technology may reach a stage at which the returns to investment in research itself will continually be compared with the returns to investment in known techniques of production.

It is unnecessary to remark that the operation of capital markets is unlikely to produce this ideal result and that, for a number of reasons, we should expect current social yields on new investment to exceed individual rates of time preference: they include income and corporation taxes, possible external economies of investment, uncertainty about the future felt by lender and borrower, and the borrowing advantages of large corporations. Yet even if capital markets were to operate perfectly and, at any point of time, the rate of time preference were equal to the current social yield on new investment, its merit would consist only in giving expression, through the accumulation of capital, to the saving and investment decisions of the existing generation. And in this connection, it is hardly necessary to remark that many people today still choose to save for and leave wealth to their children and grandchildren, and would continue to do so whether, through its collective actions, society's real income were expected to increase or decline. However, inasmuch as intergenerational equity is a desideratum that economists are having to think about in consequence of our concern with technological growth and the depletion of natural resources, the extent of the market's inability to promote it is worth exploring.

In the belief that people were naturally impatient to consume, Pigou favored the idea of the state's acting as guardian for future generations. But apart from a general directive that the state should act to increase the rate of capital accumulation above that resulting from the free play of the market, no explicit criterion was offered for the ideal rate of investment through time.

If the welfare of the existing generation alone were at issue, there would be little difficulty since—allowing, for argument's sake, that people's capacity to enjoy goods does not alter over their lives—this "impatience" could be sensibly defined to exist if, at a zero rate of interest, people chose to consume more in their earlier years. Yet if such were the pattern of their behavior, the laissez-faire economist would perceive no justification for intervening in the market. Nevertheless, a case in justice or humanity for intervening in the market exists if there is reason to believe that the impatience or short-sightedness of present generations can imperil the survival of future generations.

### *Intergenerational Criteria*

Touching on this question of the welfare of succeeding generations, three distinct criteria can be discovered in the economic literature.

(1) The simplest criterion is an egalitarian one; per capita income should, ideally, remain constant from one generation to another. If it is believed that, even without positive net investment, per capita "real" income will grow over time as a result, say, of incidental innovation, possible economies of scale, and improved managerial efficiency, the ideal can be attained only by net consumption of capital at some rate over time. Each generation would then pass on a smaller stock of more productive capital than it would inherit from the preceding generation, a policy that would require considerable state intervention.

(2) An alternative criterion is the neoclassical one of maximizing the utility that accrues over time. By assuming equal capacity for enjoyment within a given society along with diminishing marginal utility of "real" income, aggregate utility *at any point of time* is maximized only when it is equally distributed among all members—each person (or family) having the same total utility as any other.

Once future generations are brought into the picture, however, the amount of goods to be consumed is not a fixed amount that can be distributed among a number of successive generations. Goods are produced continuously through time and their consumption, through the investment process, can be shifted in only one direction—forward into the future. Utility maximization which, under the above assumptions, requires that the *marginal* utility of consumption through time and, therefore, for each successive generation, be equal, is consistent with different patterns of aggregate and per capita consumption over time. Thus, if real output, per capita or in the aggregate, can be expected to increase over time, the utility maximization condition implies a rising level of per capita or of aggregate consumption respectively. Economic policy instrumental to this objective requires additional investment in any period for which the proportional expected (real) growth of a dollar invested exceeds the proportional expected decline in the marginal utility of a dollar of consumption. Thus, aggregate investment in any period $t_0$

has to be carried to the point at which the percentage yield on a dollar of marginal investment realized at $t_1$ is just equal to the percentage reduction in the marginal utility of a dollar consumed at $t_1$ compared with $t_0$.[30] Implementation of this policy, however, requires knowledge of the relation between aggregate consumption and utility, or—at any point of time—the elasticity of the marginal utility of money with respect to consumption.[31]

(3) For those economists who still eschew interpersonal and, therefore, intergenerational comparisons of utility there remains the Pareto criterion, the wellhead of all our allocative propositions. In any cost-benefit analysis, a potential Pareto improvement is the criterion, and it is met if the value of gains exceeds that of the losses. Yet those affected by the project in question are assumed to remain alive over the period so that the valuation they place on an item at any point of time is determined by reference to their own time preference. A person who anticipates a gain of $100 in 20 years time with virtual certainty might value its worth today at $40, an equivalence that would be incorporated into the cost-benefit analysis.

If, now, the composition of the community alters over time, so that the $100 can be expected to accrue to someone else yet to be born, its present value is not $40. For the gainer is to be a person who does not have the option of receiving it today. Evaluating the future gains of long-term investment by reference to those who later come to enjoy them could realize potential Pareto improvements with projects that would be rejected by the standard discounting procedure. Thus, extending the potential Pareto criterion to long-term investments having yields that are wholly, or partly, enjoyed by members of a future generation would act to favor future generations as against earlier generations.

None of these criteria will be realized by the market, however, even under the most simplifying assumptions. By reference to the (1) criterion, the market makes too much provision for the future. By reference to the (3) criterion, it makes too little. As for the (2) criterion, since in fact judgments about the validity of interpersonal utility comparisons, *a fortiori* of intergenerational utility comparisons, are apt to differ markedly, any rationalization of existing market rates of return, in terms of some assumed value of the elasticity of marginal utility of consumption, carries little conviction.

The (1) criterion clearly has stronger ethical appeal than the others, and is the one most likely to command a consensus at some imaginary constitutional gathering made up of representatives of different generations (Page, forthcoming). Although, as suggested, under the once common assumption that economic growth (in some "real" sense) will continue into the far future, the market makes too much provision for the future, there is today a countervailing consideration turning on the rapid depletion of natural resources for which no good substitutes may be available. It is then not impossible that, on balance, we are making too little provision for the future (Page, forthcoming).

*Depletable Resources*

Until very recently there was something akin to complacency among economists about current rates of exploitation of fixed natural deposits of minerals and fossil fuels, some of it arising from empirical studies of their relative prices over time (Barnett and Morse, 1963), perhaps more from general theoretical considerations of the sort advanced in Hotelling's classic (1931) paper. Defining an optimal rate of exploitation of a fixed resource as one that maximizes its present social value, the necessary condition follows that the discounted present value of the *net* price (marginal social valuation *less* marginal resource cost) for all years be the same. The question is then whether a competitive market can bring about this required optimal time path of exploitation: If so, the economist need concern himself only with possible externalities and those forms of government intervention (regulation, taxes, depletion allowances, and so forth) that imply a departure from the optimal path—at least in a first-best world.

Since the necessary condition is met if, through time, the percentage rise in the net price is equal to the rate of interest,[32] a competitive market, in which price is assumed equal to marginal social valuation, might seem on first thoughts to be an appropriate mechanism. For there would, indeed, be forces tending to bring the annual percentage net price increase into equality with the rate of interest. To illustrate with a 5 percent interest rate and a current net price of 100, if the net price next year is expected to be 105, competitive mining firms are indifferent as between producing ore this year or next year. If, instead, next year's net price happens to be 108, competitive firms will defer production until next year.[33] But as the amount of ore marketed this year diminishes in consequence, its net price this year will rise until the 5 percent differential is restored. *Per contra,* if next year's expected net price is 102, firms will switch to producing more ore this year.[34] The resulting decline in the current net price continues until, once again, the equilibrium 5 percent differential is restored.

This seemingly providential mechanism, however, ignores the formation of price expectations. If the elasticity of price expectations exceeds zero, so that a change in the current price of the mineral causes the market to revise its estimate of future prices—a not uncommon phenomenon—the rate of production will veer off the optimal path. Indeed, if the elasticity of expectations is equal to or greater than unity, the market response will be destabilizing:[35] any initial deviation from the optimal path, in either direction, gathers force—until, eventually, the elasticity falls below unity. There may, in addition, be autonomous revisions of future price expectations so that, even though the necessary condition through time is being met, the actual production path taken is above or below the optimal path. In fact, only if all future demand curves and all future costs happen to be known to the competing firms (or else to a perfectly competitive futures market) can there be assurance that prompt reaction by firms to profit opportunities will succeed in preventing the rate of production from straying far from the optimal path. Thus no assumption about the intelligence of producers, or about their incentives, can avail, when the required knowledge is not available to them. Nor would any expenditure on better forecasts enable it to be made available. We conclude that one of the prime virtues claimed for a competitive market; namely that the decentralization involved tends to reduce relevant information costs—although it seems to be valid enough for the more commonly considered case of inexhaustible inputs—is not valid for the case of exhaustible inputs.

Finally, we are to remind ourselves that this ideal production path has Pareto justification only for a community consisting of an unchanged number of people. For some person of a later generation, say a person yet to be born who is destined to consume the mineral in question in year 50 from now, the value of consuming a marginal unit will be equal to its then current price, say 100; and not $100/(1 + r)^{50}$ or the discounted present value at the time the investment decision is made. This consideration might not seem to matter much for those cases in which cost-benefit analysis is applicable—at least, those for which the political constraints are such that all the net benefits of the project are wholly reinvested at existing market yields—since, as the mineral is depleted it is replaced by productive assets having greater social value. But where, as the practice is in mineral and fossil fuel exploitation, the bulk of the net benefits are, in effect, consumed contemporaneously by the public—through its direct consumption of the minerals or fuels, or through the consumption of products into which they enter[36]—the popular belief, that in using up finite natural resources no specific provision is being made for future generations, is far from being erroneous.

The complacent view of the matter has now to rest its case, not on any specific provision for the future inherent in the market mechanism, but rather in a faith that the future will be much like the recent past in two related respects: (1) in the discovery of substitute resources for those being depleted and (2) in the continuing secular rise of living standards[37] (at least in the industrialized countries of the world). Ultimately, it amounts to a faith in the capability of science in overcoming a multitude of social and environmental problems that have begun to absorb our attention.

In connection with natural resource substitutes, there is one more thing to be said. Technical substitution is not enough to secure a continued rise of social welfare; not enough even to maintain it. To touch on a trivial case first, the market has not prevented a decline in the quality of some foodstuffs over time: perhaps it cannot reasonably be expected to do this. If in 30 years time, much of the food we shall be eating will taste more like plastic than it does today, the market may not be to blame. A lot of it may be chemical synthetics, time saving and much cheaper than more "natural" foodstuffs. Again, we may rightly refrain from blaming the market if, in consequence of the absence of enforceable property rights, or of the absence of other devices or institutions that would internalize the externalities into the economic system, vast areas of natural beauty and wildlife continue to dwindle rapidly so that our grandchildren come to inherit a more desolate and monotonous world. But, then, neither can we repose any faith in the mere operation itself of competitive markets in maintaining a satisfactory allocation of resources over time in this crucial regard.

Over time, the terms of trade as between natural goods and man-made goods can be expected to alter in favor of the former. And although future generations may well have much more of the latter, it may not be enough to compensate them for the apparently inexorable disappearance of the variety of wild life and natural beauty. Perhaps no amounts of manufactured goods and recreational opportunities will suffice for the diminished accessibility to unspoiled coastline, to mountain, lake, and woodland, much less for escape for the sensitive into a world of solitude and grandeur.

## *VI. The Consumer Bias of the Market*

In the absence of all externalities, universal perfect competition, as described in the textbooks, is neither a necessary nor sufficient condition for optimal allocation. Since marginal cost pricing can be pursued by other forms of economic organization—for instance, by the state or by discriminating monopolists—it is not necessary. And since free entry of factors into each industry does not entail the fulfillment of the factor-use condition (the fulfillment of which, in the case of labor, would imply opportunities for workers to choose the amounts of time to work in each of the occupations that utilize their labor), perfect competiton is not sufficient.

This proposition, however, is not of great interest. Much more important are the possible welfare losses that can be endured by workers subject to the "discipline of the market." Thus, if there were a shift of $10 million of consumption expenditure from good X to good Y which, in due course, was followed by a movement of, say, a thousand workers from industry X to industry Y, the market would have done its job well, and, assuming marginal cost pricing were restored, allocation criteria would also be met.

But the welfare of the workers qua workers is apt to be overlooked: in particular, their rents, arising from occupational or locational preferences, and their costs of movement[38] and retraining[39] are often neglected. Of course, it can be argued that if workers are to be attracted into occupations they do not like, they will have to be compensated by higher wages or better conditions. And this net-advantages doctrine is useful as part of a long-run explanation of wage differentials. But if we are not surveying the opportunities facing new entrants into industry, but are instead concerned with the fortunes of the existing work force in industry X, we cannot realistically suppose that workers always move out of X in response to attractions elsewhere. They may simply be discharged by industry X, and to that extent suffer a loss of welfare. Thus the gain to consumers from complete market adjustment to their shift in demand might well fall short of the losses in welfare suffered by the thousand workers.

Of course, a comparison of consumer welfare as between an equilibrium with the initial tastes and that with the new tastes is not possible. Once the new tastes are established, however, consumers become better off according as outputs adjust to the new demand pattern. But, as indicated, if workers who have to move from X to Y—not as a result of being attracted from X to Y so much as being laid off by industry X—they can be made substantially worse off.

In an imaginary world in which consumers' tastes remained constant, consumers also could be made worse off if workers moved voluntarily out of X into Y and, in consequence, output X were reduced leaving consumers perforce to spend more on Y; and they could be substantially worse off if X were important in their budgets. Yet the subsequent adjustment of consumer expenditure could be interpreted as consistent with marginal cost pricing in X and Y.

In sum, if the adjustment to an exogenous change in tastes (whether of consumers or workers) comes about wholly through price changes it does not reduce the welfare of the adjusters (whether they are workers or consumers). If, on the other hand, the adjustment comes about wholly through quantity changes (opportunities being withdrawn) it does entail a reduction in the welfare of the adjusters.

If the movements of labor necessary to implement the changing pattern of consumer demand lack proper allocative underpinning, once we turn from Pareto criteria to considerations of social equity, reservations about ideal market adjustments increase. For a dollar gained or lost by the consumer may have less welfare significance than a dollar lost or gained by the worker, and this without invoking differences in income. The average consumer in a wealthy economy is faced by a wide range of goods, substitution as between which causes him little inconvenience and no hardship. Indeed, a proportion of his purchases is aptly referred to as "impulse buying." Some may be the result of a recent advertising campaign, or seeing an item in a neighbor's home, or of being momentarily intrigued by some useless novelty, or of a bid to break the monotony of events. And though any frustration of his buying impulse at that point of time may elicit a protest,[40] the hardship he endures is negligible. On the other hand, the loss of welfare borne by workers who are displaced from the familiarity of their workplace and their neighborhood can reasonably be described as hardship.

Similar considerations apply to improved techniques of production. Even though labor's productivity and "real" earnings rise in consequence, workers ultimately have little choice in the matter. They must perforce adopt the new methods and adjust accordingly. There can, therefore, be no presumption of net social advantage in any specific instance simply because consumers gain from lower unit costs.[41]

The conclusion of this argument is that the operation of the market is consumer oriented. Ideal market adjustments are compatible with net social loss on the Pareto criterion, a loss that can be magnified by weighting the welfare content of money gains and losses. How important this bias is depends upon the vicissitudes of consumer demand and the extent to which shifting patterns of consumer demand impose significant welfare losses on workers. Increasing affluence, which implies a growth of "luxuries" and, consequently, of "impulse buying," is likely to increase the threat to the security of workers unless there are countervailing forces at work, some associated with the welfare state.

In the circumstances, a doctrine that favors free markets specifically on allocation or equity grounds poses some difficulty. There is now more to it than the appealing notion of a continuing movement of scarce resources to uses in which their social value is highest, if only because of this built-in bias toward consumer valuation. In any assessment, however, the question of alternative economic organizations arises, including, of course, the feasibility of corrective institutions.

Again, although the liberal economist is disinclined to favor any innovation that extends power to the state, a simple-minded case could be argued for sustained advertising (as in Britain during the war and beyond) for being satisfied with what is, in the endeavor to maintain the pattern of currently produced outputs, and to alter it only to accommodate changes over time in occupational preferences. If successful, the scheme would entail no loss of welfare to consumers while conferring a gain in the workers' welfare arising from their increase in occupational security. It may, of course, seem to some an absurd objective for society to pursue, but that is largely because of the disproportionate importance attached to the notion of continuing change by postindustrial man and his relative unconcern with social welfare *per se*. At all events, once we free our minds from the simple equation between well-functioning competitive markets and allocative merit, we are likely to become less censorious than the Chicago School of such restrictive organizations as monopolies, cartels, labor unions, and of such restrictive practices as trade controls and immigration quotas.

Although it does not produce enthusiastic "trust-busters," believing, as it does, that in the absence of active government intervention and legislation the extent and power of monopoly in the economic system would be limited, the Chicago School evidently looks on monopolies, cartels, price agreements, and government price supports with disrelish. Setting aside the question of the economic and political power wielded by large corporations, as discussed at length by Berle and Means (1933), we can recognize (in the light of the preceding remarks) that the allocative arguments against them are, on a general plane, inconclusive.

There is, moreover, another consideration. In a world of rapid change, in which the future is increasingly uncertain, the monopolistic propensities of employers and managers, their defensive advertising expenditures, their support for tariffs and price controls, can be understood as measures directed to stabilizing their markets in order to increase the security of their profits and personnel. Ostensibly, it is this same search for security in a highly uncertain world, as much as for higher real earnings, that inspires the formation of labor unions and of restrictive professional bodies. To the extent they reduce anxiety and increase security, such restrictive organizations and practices contribute to social welfare.

It may, of course, be possible to devise institutions that will afford to workers, professionals, business executives, and shareholders the sort of security that they seek in a world of increasing uncertainty, while at the same time encouraging them to alter their plans more readily to meet the requirements of changing technology and demand conditions. But until such institutions are operative, the belief in the paramountcy of consumer demand in calling the allocative tune, and the consequent opposition by conservative economists to any resistance of consumer expression by restrictive associations and practices, are open to challenge.[42]

### *VII. Consumer Tastes and the Free Market*

In the preceding section we have remarked on the consumer bias of the market and the bias, therefore, in the common interpretation of economic efficiency arising therefrom. Enquiry into this consumer bias can be carried further by broaching the question of consumers' tastes, which are generally treated in allocative contexts as an exogenous variable. More specifically, the question posed is whether the economist concerned with social welfare can be consistently indifferent to the changing pattern of consumers' tastes.

In order to distil the relevant issue from all extraneous matter, picture a competitive economy having an ideal distribution of income and free of all external effects. Everyone is buying and selling the amounts that he wishes, and at prices equal to unit costs that are as low as possible with the existing resource endowment and technology. In such an economic millenium, can the economist interested in welfare make any valid judgment about the effect of consumers' tastes or changes in tastes?

I have met distinguished economists who have declared emphatically, though seemingly without reflection, that their role as economists, insofar as it has any normative facet, consists only in making available to people what they (the people) want on the best terms possible. On this view, the task of the economist is discharged by facilitating the supply of goods for which people—preferably through the market mechanism—express a desire.

It is debatable whether those—and they are not economists only—who assert that "push-penny is as good as Pushkin," or words to that effect, personally believe this; whether they believe that others ought to believe it; or whether they simply think that people ought to act as if they believe it. What is certain, however, is that many people do not believe it; indeed, the idea of an educational establishment is raised on the contrary premise which, if accepted, is not without allocative significance, as we shall see.

Rather than argue about the proper role of the economist, it will be more useful, first, to assess the importance of the welfare contribution of the economist who, in respect of tastes, confines himself to the evidence of the market, and, second, to judge the adequacy of allocative criteria in the light of social welfare.

### *Allocative Assessment of Changes in Taste*

To the economist concerned only with the working of the market, any exogenous shift in demand that calls for a shift of resources is as important as any other. But to the welfare economist, more significance is to be attached to exogenous shifts of demand that are "price-inelastic" than to those that are "price-elastic"; more significance to demand shifts as between broad categories of goods, say, as between housing, transport, food, clothing, and recreation, than to demand shifts as within these categories; and more significance to the movements in international trade as between countries whose economies are highly complementary than to movements as between countries trading goods that are close substitutes.

If the welfare economist is prepared, once in a while, to cross the Paretian Rubicon and to make the journey back North to the old neoclassical homelands, he can, on arrival, say more. He may still maintain that interpersonal measurements of utility are not "scientific," or that fine judgments about the worth of a good, or a dollar's worth of goods, to different individuals or groups are unlikely to command universal support. But he will not be so far removed from reality as to persuade himself that the loss of $10 to a Rockefeller is no less important to him than the loss of $10 to a near destitute denizen of Calcutta, and that society ought to treat such losses as equally important. Such an economist will find no difficulty in believing that an additional $1 billion of consumption goods to a poor country yields more satisfaction than an additional $1 billion of consumption goods to a rich country. Following this reflection, he might surmise that a good allocation of resources is of greater importance in a poor society than in a rich one.

Indeed, without crossing the Paretian Rubicon, the economist can make sensible statements about the welfare significance of shifts in taste. If, as a result of the influence of fashion, or for any other reason, society is fickle in its tastes—consumer expenditure shifting from goods X to Y and, soon after, back to X again—the economist is inclined to accept this fickleness as a datum. In that case, it would seem to follow that social welfare is promoted by moving resources from X to Y and, soon after, back to X again. Nevertheless, the economist may also pertinently observe that, in the process, capital goods that are in good physical condition may thereby become obsolete. In comparison with a society in which tastes were less fickle, an effective loss of resources is incurred. More generally, in an economy in which goods are increasingly "fashion goods," the period of capital amortization is shorter, and, therefore, unit inclusive costs of goods are higher than they are in a more stable-taste economy. Thus, rapid changes of taste, whether spontaneous, fashion-created, or commercially induced, impose costs on the community inasmuch as in their absence—that is, if society had instead preferred to consume X continuously rather than X today, Y tomorrow, and X again the day after—it would have more goods at its disposal for the same resource endowment.

What follows? Were the economist truly indifferent as between a taste for X and a taste for Y, he would infer that welfare can be increased if the costs involved in persuading the public to stabilize their tastes (in favor, say, of their existing preference for X) are lower than the additional resource costs incurred in meeting the switch in demand from X to Y and, perhaps, back again to X. In an economy characterized by rapid changes of taste of this sort, substantial savings might be effected by the success of some organization in persuading the public to be less fickle in their tastes.

Of course, there can be trends in taste as well as oscillations. Insofar as demand shifts from X to Y, later from Y to Z, and then from Z to W, we cannot describe the change of tastes as wasteful in the preceding sense. Yet it is still meaningful to contend that some changes in the pattern of consumer expenditure have greater welfare significance than others, and that some changes in taste that are expressed through the market are more apt to reduce than to enhance social welfare—a judgment of fact, not of values. Thus, although Hayek (1961) is right to be skeptical of a distinction between "natural" and "artificial" wants, and right to associate the history of cultural advance with the invention of new wants, it is *not* right to conclude that all product innovation, or even the greater part of it, at any moment in time constitutes a welfare advance much less a cultural advance—at least, not when the word *cultural* is used in the approved sense in which Hayek uses it.

Finally, by restricting ourselves, provisionally, to the conventional allocative context, it is possible to show that the market, regarded as an indicator of current tastes, new or old, is misleading by reference to what economists now call "merit goods." A merit good can be defined as one whose aggregate consumption enters positively into the utility functions of individuals. By symmetry, the aggregate consumption of a "demerit good" enters negatively into individual utility functions. Clearly, merit and demerit goods fall into the category of external economies and diseconomies, respectively; in fact, they are a species of the "interdependent utilities" family of externalities, the utility of one person depending in some way on the goods possessed or used by others.[43]

Opera, ballet, symphony orchestras, art galleries, libraries—including, possibly, a Pushkin reading room!—are among the common examples of a merit good.[44] People who seldom or never attend cultural events, who prefer cinema or television entertainment, may yet agree that high culture is a good thing and derive some satisfaction from its visible manifestation and in the knowledge that cultural activities are being promoted. Indeed, if a value judgment is permitted, some cultural activities are important enough in the civilization of the West to warrant a risk of overprovision rather than underprovision.

There are, to be sure, voluntary organizations for promoting good causes and cultural events. But inasmuch as a person's willing contribution to a merit good depends upon the amounts others are believed to contribute, and a person's declared willingness-to-pay is influenced by the "free rider" opportunity open to him (especially where the number of beneficiaries is large), economists conclude that, whether such goods are provided through the political process or through voluntary action, their supply tends to fall below optimal (Olson, 1965).

On the other hand, pin-ball arcades, obscene literature, and pornographic theater are examples of a demerit good. People who willingly buy demerit goods, since they are available on the market anyway, may yet wish that there were less of them available to the public: they would think better of their fellow citizens if the demand for such things were to fall off.[45] Again, there will be voluntary organizations for combatting the spread of some of these demerit goods. Yet, for the reasons given above, contributions toward their diminution tend to fall below those necessary to reduce them to optimal.

Thus allegations of a deterioration in the quality of life may have reference, among other things, to the manifest increase in demerit goods. In these circumstances, the economist who accepts the existing demand for demerit goods as expressed by the market as indicative of what society really wants deceives himself, and accepts a misallocation of resources in these respects.[46] And the fact that the information required to correct the existing situation appears, at present, difficult to obtain does not detract from the extent of the market's misrepresentation of what society wants and the consequent misallocation of resources.

### *Welfare Assessment of Ideal Allocation in a Growing Economy*

A surprisingly common belief among students of economics is that in the absence of all externalities (including the absence of the aforementioned merit and demerit goods), a perfectly functioning competitive market will improve welfare in a growing economy—one in which productivity per capita increases over time.

The statement can be made to follow from restrictive assumptions that are useful enough in abstract models. Once the restrictive assumptions are discarded, and we turn to the real world, the preceding statement is not a tautology but a statement of fact and, therefore, open to dispute.[47] It may, of course, be very difficult or impossible to demonstrate conclusively whether such a statement is true or false, generally, or over any particular period of time. But it is always possible to adduce considerations that weaken the presumption that economic growth, even in a (competitive) externality-free economy, increases social welfare. I say *even* in an externality-free economy because there is no difficulty in weakening this presumption if account is taken of the variety of external diseconomies that, for technical or political reasons, are unlikely to be properly internalized into the economic system.

That a well-functioning market, under these postulated conditions, will enable choices to be made on "nature's terms" is, of course, true. But there is nothing in the machinery of the market to ensure that free choice is wise choice. In a world of rapid technological change and continuing product innovation, relevant information about quality and performance of consumer goods is increasingly costly to obtain. It is still more difficult—for society as much as for the individual—to be *au courant* about such arcane matters as the cumulative toxic or genetic effects of drugs and food additives. And it is all but impossible to foresee the ultimate consequences on society's well-being of the adoption of outstanding innovations—though it is also far from certain that their adoption would be resisted even if the range of adverse consequences could be foreseen. For there is an apparent momentum about technology that sweeps all before it. As Jacques Ellul (1965) has remarked with understandable exaggeration; it is enough for a technology to be feasible to ensure its adoption.

The end result of improvements in all media and means of communication could be to accelerate the pace of life to a frantic degree. The longer term effects on social well-being of a succession of labor-saving devices can be less impressive than the ingenuity that created them and the cost of resources used up in providing them. For instance, the trend in consumer innovation toward means of faster mobility, toward push-button gadgetry, toward physical self-sufficiency, may become subversive of welfare—at least, insofar as it is through our overt need of other persons that opportunities for human contact, kindness, and sacrifice arise in a community, as a result of which the seeds of mutual trust take root and friendships flourish.

## VIII. Advertising and the Competitive Economy

Our concern with the Chicago School's attitude toward commercial advertising focuses on two related aspects. First, whether commercial advertising is, as alleged by Henry Simons (1948), a "major barrier" to competitive enterprise. Second, and more important, whether the institution can be justified on economic and social grounds. These questions are dealt with in that order.

### *Advertising and Competition*

The sort of advertising expenditure that is the subject of our enquiry is other than that necessary to announce the existence of a firm, its premises, conditions of business, and so forth, or particulars of a sale—though even here, the size of the notice or repetition of particulars can influence taste beyond that warranted by the bare information itself. Clearly, it is not impossible for competition between firms to take place within an industry that is advertising the goods being sold by all the firms in that industry. It is also possible for the imaginative to conceive, as Telser (1964) does, of a large group of firms, each of which produces goods having identical characteristics, including identical kinds and amounts of advertising, and which are therefore in perfect competition with one another.

Now if one begins with a presumption against monopoly, a theoretic reconciliation of perfect competition with advertising, plus the finding that there is no marked relationship between advertising expenditure and industrial concentration, or between advertising expenditure and stability of sales (Telser, 1964), enables commercial advertising to evade discountenance. If, moreover, it is believed that continued "consumer experimentation" is a good thing in itself, or that rapid entry and exit of firms into and out of an industry is "a healthy sign," then insofar as commercial advertising fosters taste-switching and so facilitates entry of new firms into an industry, something might be said in its favor. However, such beliefs are ancillary to those traditionally invoked in the economic concept of allocating scarce resources as to best satisfy human wants and, indeed, seem to conflict with them. This older and, perhaps, more static view, accepts wants as a datum with resources being distributed so as to satisfy them, whereas these other and more recent beliefs are compatible with an institution that uses scarce resources, also, to change wants; in effect, at least in the affluent society, perpetually to create dissatisfactions with existing goods in favor of rival goods or new goods.[48] Such a process could be vindicated by the belief that, over time, commercial advertising succeeds in inculcating tastes and living habits superior to those that would prevail in its absence, so making a contribution to civilized living. However, I do not suppose many economists would feel comfortable arguing the case for modern commercial advertising along these lines.

On traditional economic premises, a respectable case for commercial advertising does not look to be possible. Even a hypothetical advertising-cum-perfect-competition economy does not answer. For it is not enough that all the relevant marginal equalities be met: total conditions also have to be met in order to ensure that there is no "waste" in the economy (in other words, that the optimal is not merely local but global). Thus, if resources were not used up in attempts to influence wants, they can always be used instead to produce additional goods which can be distributed as to make "everyone" better off.

### *Some Popular Rationalizations of Commercial Advertising*

Estimates of current advertising expenditures in the United States exceed $20 billion. Evidently there are people who believe that it is worth incurring such expenses, though from this belief alone one cannot infer social justification for the institution. The question to which much of the debate addresses itself is whether, and to what extent, commercial advertising influences consumers, a question that can be embarrassing to those who give it their blessing. For they have to steer their arguments carefully between Scylla and Charybdis. On the one hand, in order to justify advertising expenditures, they must not deny its efficacy—which is tantamount to an admission that consumers' tastes can be formed, unformed, and possibly deformed by business interests. If, on the other hand, they disclaim its effects, and insist that, on balance, it has little influence on consumers' choice,[49] it is hard to avoid the conclusion that commercial advertising is a colossal waste of resources.

Prior to a brief but more general statement in support of this latter conclusion, some of the more popular rationalizations for commercial advertising can be briefly disposed of.

There is, first, the oft-heard claim that advertisers help to pay for our newspapers and television programs. For instance, in addition to covering the real costs of an automobile advertisement, the manufacturers make a contribution to the costs of the newspaper which sum is to be recovered in the price of the automobile. In short, the buyers of the advertised car are made to subsidize newspaper readers.[50] But unless there is good reason to believe that the newspaper (together with its advertisements) confers benefits on the community which, at the margin, exceed the value of resources in producing the newspaper, there is no economic warrant for the subsidy.

Secondly, there is the suggestion that the newspaper advertisement or television advertisement should be regarded as an essential part of a joint product, the other part being entertainment. But advertising and entertainment are clearly not inseparable products as are, say, wool and mutton. No good reason is offered why advertising, which piques itself on being a valuable service to the public, should not be sold at a price that covers its cost. Advertisers may, of course, suspect that if they tried to sell pure advertising "by the yard" to the public at a price set to cover its cost, they would sell precious little of it; and that if they charged whatever addition was necessary to cover the costs of any "entertaining" bits thrown in with the "information," they would sell little more. Apparently they find it more profitable to provide advertising free, with or without entertainment, in the expectation of recouping these expenditures by selling enough of the advertised items at prices above their costs of production. The result is that the newspaper reader, or the television viewer, is subject to a "tied sale": he receives advertising (and "entertainment") along with his newspaper whether he wants them both together or not.[51]

A third rationalization is more cunning; it is to the effect that people actually prefer myth to truth. In connection with some aspects of life this is undeniable. Many people find solace and satisfaction in religious beliefs, in national myths, in a faith in the inherent goodness or ultimate wisdom of the people. Whether it is equally true for the mundane aspects of life, such as those that may involve a choice between one model of a television set and another, one brand of nylon tights and another, one can of peaches and another, is much more doubtful.

Finally, there is the justification in terms of information. Provided it is believed that the provision of information is desirable, in that it enables the public to make more satisfactory choices among the goods offered by industry, the critical distinction to bear in mind is not that between information and persuasion, which can be very tenuous, but between *partial* information and *impartial* information.

The advertiser is not concerned primarily with providing impartial information but with increasing the sale of the product. If the statements he makes happen to be accurate, this is incidental to his main task.[52]

If the buying public wants disinterested information about certain goods, then it is not reasonable for it to expect to obtain such information from those parties whose livelihood and success depend directly on the sales of such goods. Any advertising agency pledged to tell the whole truth and nothing but the truth about its clients' products would not be in business very long.

Consider, then, an alternative in the shape of one or more independent agencies, devoted to the task of providing impartial information, in the sense of providing "complete" and "relevant" information[53] from tests carried out under as objective conditions as possible. That the results of these tests, when published, can be very persuasive is nothing to the purpose. What is to the purpose is that the investigations be undertaken in a scientific spirit and free, therefore, from any conscious source of bias. It is not pertinent in arguing against such agencies that coverage of products is limited or that tests are not exhaustive. Such defects can be attributed to a lack of resources or to a lack of efficiency which, in the course of time, can be overcome. What matters is that such organizations operate on a principle entirely different from that of the advertising agency. The *aim* of the advertising agency is to promote the sales of his clients' goods: any information that is provided by the agency is selected to serve that end. The *aim* of the research agency, in contrast, is to provide impartial information to the consumer.[54]

Thus, if one accepts as a desirable social end, the provision of impartial and, increasingly, more accurate and complete information to the public, there does not seem much one can say in favor of continuing the present system of using substantial resources in providing the public with partial information at uneconomic prices and in tied-sale form that precludes choice. There is more to be said for the alternative of devoting the same resources to the provision of yet more and better consumer research services, the demand for which would be likely to expand if the existing tied-sale form of commercial advertising were to cease.

### *Is There a Political Case for Commercial Advertising?*

Having raised doubts about the present system of commercial advertising on economic grounds, let us now examine the popular view that the doctrine of freedom to propagate opinions should be extended to cover the contending claims of private firms as embodied in commercial advertising. Why, it may be asked, should any disability be placed on organizations that choose to spend their own income or "profits" in propagating a particular point of view?

First, in respect of goods such as drugs or slow poisons that are believed to damage the mental or physical health, an ethical problem arises wherever vast sums are spent annually to promote their consumption, in particular among the young and impressionable, who are led to associate its consumption with initiation into adulthood or fashion. In the absence of tobacco advertisements, for instance, new addictions would decline and thousands of deaths from lung cancer could be prevented each year. If, to look at the matter otherwise, heroin promotion campaigns became legal, a rise in sicknesses and death, among other misfortunes, could be confidently predicted.[55]

For goods that are not widely believed to be dangerous to consumers or third parties, there are yet other considerations. Perhaps a difference in the degree of social significance between, on the one hand, political and philosophical issues and, on the other, judgments about the durability of doormats and the quality of breakfast cereals might be conceded. Certainly there are differences in conviction with which opinions are held about these two categories of phenomena. Yet there is no need for the case against a political right of freedom to advertise merchandise to turn wholly on these different degrees of significance or conviction.

John Milton's eloquent plea for freedom of speech is raised on a utilitarian premise: that from the conflict of arguments, truth would surely emerge. If advertising supporters would conscript John Milton to their cause, they must embrace the belief that knowledge of the best kind of filter-tip cigarette or rubber sole will inevitably emerge from the counter-claims of competing advertisers.

More important, if we accept the utilitarian approach[56]—which conceives the public interest, in some sense, as the ultimate criterion of social policy—then, as with freedom of political expression itself, commercial advertising freedom has to be judged, not as an end in itself, but as a means of promoting the public interest. Thus, free political speech can be defended not only for the truths it uncovers, but also because it reduces the risk of violence in a context of continuing social change. For political ideas evolve over time and in the light of experience. At any moment of time, no political doctrine can be held as absolutely true, and if it were believed to be so, it is unlikely that the belief would remain unchallenged for long in the modern world. This being the case, it is a matter of political prudence to allow men openly to express their convictions on issues they believe to be of the highest moment; encouraging them always to try to persuade others rather than to coerce them.

Now such reasons cannot be invoked to justify the claims and counter-claims of competing manufacturers. The "opinions" they propagate are not motivated by deep convictions about their truth, but solely by the search for profits. And the questions they raise—whether, in fact, one detergent really washes "whiter than white," or whether one electric blanket is safer or warmer than another—are not those on which men are divided by deep conviction. In contrast to the conflicting claims of ideology, or to the conflicting opinions on social policy, there is very little about the competing claims of advertisers that cannot, in all relevant respects, be resolved simply by impartial testing—that is, by recourse to the facts.

### *IX. Individual Freedom and the Competitive Economy*

Let us turn, in this penultimate section, to that rooted belief in the social advantage of decentralized private enterprise, a belief that has exerted a lasting influence on the ideology and methodological presuppositions of Western economists. There is, first, the advantage of individual choice, itself a dimension of freedom, offered by the market sector of the economy. The smaller the public sector of the economy, the larger the area of choice remaining, at least for the consumer—a consideration which is decisive in the Chicago School's preference that any redistribution of income be effected through transfers in cash rather than in kind.[57] Secondly, there is the more general accession of freedom conferred on society by the competitive economy, not in virtue of its being a competitive market economy, but in virtue of its being a competitive *capitalist* economy. More specifically, a decentralized private enterprise system entails a dispersal of economic power throughout society that acts as a counterweight to the economic power of the state. And since economic power is also a means of implementing political purposes, the larger the private sector of the economy, the greater the constraint on the ambition of bureaucrats and the power of the state.

It is in arguing the case for competitive capitalism on both these grounds that the Chicago School is most persuasive. Taking its stand there, it recognizes its advocacy to be in line with the great classical tradition that can be traced back to the economic thought of British and Continental writers of the eighteenth century, that came to fruition in the nineteenth century, and that was seemingly confirmed by the harsh experience of the twentieth.[58] Nothing I could say would so well remind the reader of the powerful appeal to utilitarian predilection and libertarian impulse than a quotation from Milton Friedman, the most distinguished exponent today of the Chicago School of thought. "The kind of economic organization that provides economic freedom directly, namely, competitive capitalism, also promotes political freedom because it separates economic power from political power and in this way enables the one to offset the other" (1962, p. 9).

Declaring that *economic* freedom (in the sense of individual freedom to choose man-made goods) is best realized through competitive markets, Friedman goes on to observe that "what the market does is to reduce greatly the range of issues that must be decided through political means, and thereby to minimize the extent to which government need participate directly in the game. The characteristic feature of action through political channels is that it tends to require or enforce substantial conformity. The great advantage of the market, on the other hand, is that it permits wide diversity" (1962, p. 15). Yet this same competitive private enterprise system that extends to economic freedom acts also to promote political freedom. For

> the fundamental threat to freedom is the power to coerce, be it in the hands of a monarch, a dictator, an oligarchy, or a momentary majority. The preservation of freedom requires the elimination of such concentration of power to the fullest possible extent and the dispersal and distribution of whatever power cannot be eliminated—a system of checks and balances. By removing the organization of economic power from the control of political authority, the market eliminates this source of coercive power. It enables economic strength to be a check to political power rather than a reinforcement (1962, p. 15).

I confess that I am in sympathy with the broad sweep of this argument. Although, as indicated in the preceding section, the operation of a competitive private enterprise economy cannot of itself prevent a deterioration of the quality of life or erosion of moral values, it is surely more congenial to the exercise of effective economic and political freedom than the concentration of economic power in the hands of giant corporations or, worse, in the hands of the state.

Nevertheless, in spite of the increasing resentment of ordinary citizens at the scale and frequency of government intervention, in spite of the articulate apprehension of liberals everywhere, in spite even of the occasional resolutions of government spokesmen, the size of the public sector has continued to grow in all major Western countries since the turn of the century. True, the U.S. government does not yet directly control well over half the country's economic activity, as does the

British government, but there can be little doubt that it is heading in this direction. As late as 1930, the upsurge in the total expenditure of the U.S. government (federal, state, and local) following World War I had subsided to about 9 percent of net national expenditure, or what it had been in 1913. By 1940 the figure had risen to 25 percent: by 1950 to 29 percent, and by 1970 to 42 percent. To some, this phenomenon may not be surprising in view of the growth of democratic or, rather, egalitarian sentiment over the last 100 years, and, accompanying it, a demand not only for greater opportunity to compete for the economic prizes, but also, and increasingly since World War II, for a share in whatever prizes are won—this latter demand being met partly through increased income transfers, but more through burgeoning public expenditures on health, education, and welfare services generally. Such an explanation of events—in terms, that is, of misdirected humanitarianism and egalitarian aspirations—is not uncongenial to the liberal mind since it offers hope for the future. The good fight against persistent government encroachment could hardly be waged with conviction unless it were believed that this continuing trend could be checked, if not reversed; unless, that is, it were believed that the factors making for more government intervention in the economy are not decisive and, in the last resort, need not prevail against the expressed desires of that enlightened electorate which it is the task of the good liberal to bring into being.

From this liberal perspective, at any rate, the public sector in modern democracies grows in response to popular egalitarian sentiment which, as it happens, is linked to a strong preference for the government provision of specific services rather than for the straightforward money transfers favored by the Chicago School. What is more, this popular demand for more government services is directly facilitated by the operation of existing progressive tax systems inasmuch as, in a growing economy (especially in an inflationary economy), it enables the government over time to collect an increasing proportion of the national product. From time to time, of course, nominal tax rates are lowered. But they are not lowered enough to counteract the aforementioned trend; a fact that makes it easier for governments to expand their economic activities. For this reason alone there is a strong case for proportional taxation, though one that will not be presented here.[59]

However, apart from popular egalitarian sentiment, reinforced perhaps by the empire-building propensities of bureaucrats, which are, incidentally, facilitated by a progressive tax structure, may there not be also a secular trend, arising from the shape of economic growth, that favors the continued expansion of government control over the economy? The fact that such a possibility did not occur to the libertarian economist must be attributed in some part to an ideological commitment to that material progress which he continues to regard, despite the accumulating evidence to the contrary, as a potent solvent of all social frictions and personal frustrations; though in some part also to the economist's habit of thinking about economic growth in terms of a rise in the flow of an abstract "real" income.[60] As a result, they have paid too little attention to population growth and to the particular kinds of technology that, accompanying the process of economic growth, have come to increase the power and reach of the modern state. Thus the concomitant decline in personal freedom has to be regarded not only as a corollary of the reduction in the private sector of the economy, but also of a conscious surrender of personal rights and freedom, this being the unavoidable reaction of society to the consequences of population growth and of particular kinds of technology.

### *The Impact of Population and Technology on Freedom*

In general terms it may be affirmed that the slower the changes taking place in any civilized society, and the greater the degree of moral consensus within it, the smaller the scope for legislation. *Per contra,* the more rapid the changes and the less the moral consensus, the greater the amount of legislation required. It is in this latter situation that we find ourselves today.

Concerning population growth in a technological society, its continuance, according to Ronald Ridker

> forces upon us a slow but irreversible change in life style. Embedded in the folklore of what constitutes the American way of life is freedom from public regulation: freedom to hunt, fish, swim, and camp where and when we will; free use of water and access to uncongested, unregulated roadways; freedom to do as we please with what we own; and freedom from permits, licences, fees, red tape, and bureaucrats. Obviously we do not live this way now. Maybe we never did. But everything is relative. Americans of 2020 may look back with envy on what from their vantage point appears to be our relatively unfettered way of life, much as some today look back with nostalgia on the Wild West.
>
> Conservation of our water resources, preservation of wilderness areas, protection of animal life threatened by man, restrictions on pollutant emissions, and limitations on fertilizer and pesticide-use all require public regulation. Rules must be set and enforced, complaints heard and adjudicated. True enough, the more

> we can find means of relying on the price system, the easier will be the bureaucratic task. But even if effluent charges and user fees become universal, they would have to be set administratively, emissions and use metered, and fees collected. It appears inevitable that a larger proportion of our lives will be devoted to filling out forms, arguing with the computer or its representatives, appealing decisions, waiting for our case to be handled, finding ways to evade or move ahead in the queue. In many small ways, everyday life will become more contrived (1972, p. 31).

Turning to technology proper, among those features whose development acts to diminish the area of individual freedom, the following deserve special mention.

(1) The Computer Revolution. The growing use of computers in controlling the operation of chemical plants, telephone exchanges, and public utilities such as gas, electricity, water supply, and sewage disposal, means that breakdowns are likely to be costly if not disastrous. In consequence, closer checks and tighter controls on personnel involved in the day-to-day management, maintenance, and repair of computers will be exercised, which requires detailed psychological knowledge of employees. Such knowledge will be provided by agencies and will be facilitated by the cooperation of citizens inasmuch as economic opportunities will come to depend increasingly upon its availability.

(2) The Internal Combustion Engine. The postwar expansion of motorized pastimes, involving the use of such things as motorcycles, speedboats, snowmobiles, and so forth, has started a reaction among the more amenity-conscious citizenry which is manifestly on the increase and which is likely to result in substantial restrictions on the freedoms hitherto enjoyed by the motorized multitude. Again, the promotion of mass tourism, as a result of the popularity of air travel, has begun to run into the incipient resentment of populations in the host countries, or host regions within a country. Official attempts have already begun to limit the freedom of people to travel where and when they wish. Within countries, for instance, motorized travel to national parks and lake districts will soon have to be rationed, if not by price then by more direct measures.

(3) The Rise of Toxic Technology. The mounting concern during the last decade with air, water, and soil pollution arising from new industrial processes—in particular, over the destruction of forests, wetlands, everglades, over the dumping of sewage in estuaries and oil on the high seas, over the wanton use of pesticides and chemical fertilizers—has

been vociferous enough to precipitate a rash of restrictive legislation in the United States, both state and federal. The Environmental Protection Agency has recently been added to the several federal bureaucracies charged in effect with preventing businessmen from freely choosing their most profitable location and their most profitable type and scale of industrial plant.

(4) Technology in the Service of Crime. Whether or not the increase in the postwar incidence of crime and violence can be linked with economic growth, there can be no doubt of the increased power conferred on organized crime by technological innovation. It is by now abundantly clear that continued scientific research produces not only more expensive missile systems or deadlier rays, gases, and bacteria. It also produces critical simplifications in the design of smaller thermonuclear or bacteriological bombs that place them not only within the capacity of the smaller and, generally, less politically stable nation states, but also within the capacity of modern criminal organizations.

Furthermore, at a time when criminals and political fanatics—their effectiveness multiplied by air travel, radio communication, and other modern devices—are becoming active in intimidating the public by blackmail, kidnapping, and the torture or murder of hostages, the fear instilled into the ordinary citizen is the result also of the increased vulnerability of the large city or conurbation (itself a product of economic growth) owing to its dependence upon a single source of supply for its water, electricity, or sewage disposal. Once people come to recognize how vulnerable they have become in these respects, there will be less resistance to a closer monitoring of internal and international travel and to a surrender to the police of more arbitrary powers of search and arrest.

(5) The Techno-Military Spiral. In 1913 the U.S. national defence expenditure was about 0.7 percent of national income. In the 1970s it is over 10 percent. The arms race among the "superpowers" takes the form, not of expanding military personnel or the accumulation of military hardware, but of massive investment in developing more expensive and deadlier weapons. For every new weapon of offensive capability there will soon be designed a weapon of defensive capability, the response to which will be a yet more destructive offensive weapon, and so on.[61] The fears, real or imaginary, of ubiquitous enemy intelligence can sanction the use of special powers to be vested in government agencies, powers virtually to pry into the private affairs not only of government employees but also of every resident in the country. There is precious little a government, even a democratic government, cannot do today in the name of national defence or military necessity.

(6) Atoms for Peace. Of the several sorts of risk associated with nuclear fission reactors, one will suffice to illustrate the theme of this section; the production of biological poisons, in particular that of plutonium, one of the deadliest elements ever handled by man. In a fully developed U.S. nuclear economy some 200,000 pounds of plutonium will be generated annually. Bearing in mind that a mere half pound of it, dispersed into the atmosphere as fine soluble particles, would be enough to inflict every living mortal with lung cancer, bearing in mind also that the half-life of plutonium is about 24,000 years, a containment level as high even as 99.99 percent would hardly be acceptable. Yet inasmuch as plutonium is a necessary material for the fabrication of nuclear weapons, and is expected to be a lucrative item of illicit traffic, such a containment level is likely to prove unfeasible.[62]

The extent of the vigilance required by the planned expansion of a nuclear energy program will entail an unprecedented extension of the internal and international security system.[63] Among other measures, this security system will involve armed protection of the transport network along which move the containers of atomic materials, a vast increase in internal surveillance and, inevitably, a surrender to special agents of extraordinary powers of entry, arrest, detention, and interrogation if, as they will surely claim, they are to move fast enough to prevent highly organized criminals, fanatics, and psychopaths from capturing positions from which they can effectively blackmail a nation or cause, inadvertently or deliberately, irreparable disaster.

It is, in sum, difficult to avoid the conclusion that competitive capitalism—even were it able to resist the growth of egalitarian sentiment and what Daniel Bell (1974) calls "the revolution of rising entitlements"—will not suffice to shore up traditional freedoms against the continuing encroachment of the state. As we move into an increasingly dangerous world, the product of scientific and technical ingenuity, the instinctive desire for self-preservation, found in organized societies as well as in individuals, will prompt men, albeit reluctantly, to cede to governments far greater powers of surveillance, control, and repression, than are compatible with contemporary notions of personal liberty.

## X. *Summary and Conclusions*

The progress of a science, especially a social science, can derive inestimable benefits from a widely recognized school of thought that produces a body of coherent doctrine. Such a school can be influential in imparting a distinctive method to the discipline and in demarcating its scope, as a result of which it can suggest promising areas of enquiry.

The coherence itself of the doctrines held offers incentives to unify theoretical analyses, following which the original principles are extended to encompass a more diverse range of phenomena. In the last resort, it offers a framework for the discussion of new issues, and an edifice against which adversaries may try the strength of their unorthodox idea. With these considerations in mind, my own judgment is that the influence of the Chicago School of economics has, on balance, exercised a sobering and salutary effect on the profession.

However, with the passage of time and, partly in consequence of continuing theoretical developments, occasions will arise when the disciples of any school of thought may be ready to disturb the dust of complacency that inevitably settles on doctrines long held against assault, and to examine anew their relevance, especially in a world that is changing rapidly. The adoption of new concepts and the discovery of new relationships act to reopen avenues of enquiry that once seemed to have been sealed off. Arguments that were once forceful and clear begin to look less certain in the light of new developments. And once the empirical judgments on which they rest are challenged, prescriptive policies and general presumptions may begin to lose their appeal.

This preliminary and somewhat incautious commentary on my understanding of the belief-system of the Chicago School of economists suggests that it is not too early to initiate a systematic reassessment of the validity and the relevance of the *political* economy, at least, that inspires its attitudes and activities. Such a reassessment may result in an increased sophistication of some of its views along with the qualification or discarding of others. Clearly, there is always a risk that, at some point in this process, the acceptance of one more major modification will begin to raise doubts about the affinity between the resulting edifice and the original.

My own opinion is that, on examination, some parts of the structure will appear weaker than its defenders suspect. The main findings of this paper, a summary of which follows, may not ruffle their equanimity unduly. But they are enough to raise important questions about the current relevance of some facts of the Chicago School's political economy in the minds of those who are less committed to its tenets.

### *Efficiency of the Competitive Economy*

On these grounds the case for a competitive economy does not look so strong today as it did, say, before World War II. Although it may still be thought to have advantages over a strictly centralized economy, Western economists are today less complacent when comparing the merits of each. There is, of course, more scope in a competitive market economy for such dynamic intangibles as "the spirit of enterprise." But in highly industrial countries, this spirit of commercial enterprise may in fact confer little advantage in fundamental innovation, spending itself rather in the creation of consumer trivia. Moreover, a form of economic organization that nurtures the money-making instincts of a community, does not, for that reason alone, necessarily promote the social welfare.

Turning away from these less measurable consequences, however, the efficiency presumption favoring the competitive economy, at least when judged by standard criteria, looks weak today for a number of reasons.

First, the welfare significance of the concept of allocative efficiency, regarded properly as a normative criterion, is not compelling. The allocative "first best" itself entails a *potential* improvement only, and, as such, may also issue in unresolvable ambiguities.

Secondly, the old allocative prescription that favored an extension of the competitive market so as to extend the dominion of the marginal cost rule, has been confounded by the Second Best Theorem.[64]

Thirdly, the exceptions that suggest modification of the unchecked operation of competitive markets, in the shape of collective bads and goods, have begun to loom large with the spread of affluence and the progress of technology. In particular, the forms of industrial overspill that can be "corrected" within the framework of the competitive market are issues in current controversy.

Fourthly, insofar as Duesenberry's relative income hypothesis becomes increasingly applicable in wealthier communities, the impress on social well-being of allocative improvements becomes increasingly faint.

Fifthly, judgments about the efficacy of the working of the market are apt to be consumer biased, the constraints on the choices of workers, and the psychic and pecuniary costs of their involuntary changes of job and location, in meeting voluntary changes of consumer demand being generally neglected by the market and often by economists also. The fears that beset workers and producers, subject as they are to the unforeseeable vicissitudes of trade, offer some explanation for the persistence of movements to erect tariffs, to establish monopolies, and to promote labor unions: they are protectionist, that is, not only in a power-seeking sense but also in a security-seeking sense.[65]

### *Reconsideration of Some Chicago School Prescriptions*

These weaknesses in the concept and application of economic efficiency, reflected in the presumed merit of the competitive market, enter along with other factors into a brief reconsideration of the prescriptive policies of the Chicago School. To illustrate with three of the more familiar ones.

(1) Monetary restriction rather than price controls as a means of controlling inflation. As I understand it, the opposition to price controls is based on an aversion to any extension of government powers, on the inefficacy of such controls, and on the allocative damage of restricting relative price movements. Yet much depends also on the length of time over which it is widely believed the controls are to be retained and on the willingness of the public to cooperate. If prices, or some key prices, become easier to control; if, in their control, allocative losses are not large,[66] or their welfare significance is not large; if the unemployed required to abate the existing pace of inflation is thought to be heavy; and if there is some risk of losing control for a time of an incipient recession resulting from the application alone of monetary controls, there might be a respectable case in political economy for supplementing monetary restrictions with price controls for a period of time. In short, although a presumption against price controls is in order, it ought not to be held with a tenacity that precludes the exercise of judgment fitting to specific economic and political circumstances.

(2) The support of Chicago economists for freely floating exchange rates as the appropriate equilibrating mechanism in international exchange rather than, say, the gold standard, arises from a recognition of the difficulties of operating a gold standard in the absence of universal wage flexibility. Their arguments against government controlled exchange rates, which may or may not entail pegging the price of gold, turn on a general aversion to government intervention in free markets which, in the case of the foreign exchange market, causes inequities and distortions, prolongs a trade imbalance, and tempts governments into imposing trade restrictions.

Even if the aforementioned weaknesses in the concept of economic efficiency are conceded, therefore, the case for free exchanges appears to be strong on operational and political grounds. Thus, so long as free exchanges maintain current equilibrium in the balance of payments, each country is effectively insulated from variations in the aggregate employment and price levels of other countries: it neither "imports" nor "exports" unemployment or inflation.[67]

However, movements in the exchange rate will maintain balance-of-payments equilibrium only if foreign currencies bought and sold are chiefly for current transactions. The larger are speculative capital movements in a free market relative to current payments, the greater the influence they exert on the exchange rates. By analogy with price-stabilizing speculation on the domestic market for securities, which arises from a strong sense of a normal price (an alternative expression for a highly elastic liquidity preference), these speculative capital movements may tend to stabilize the rate of exchange in a free market, so putting a part of the burden of adjustment on changes of employment and price levels in the trading countries.

It follows that in order for complete freedom of international capital movements to be compatible with exchange rates that are flexible enough to prevent international transmissions of aggregate employment or inflation, the amount of speculative capital movements must be small relative to current international payments.

(3) A general presumption in favor of the removal of all political obstacles to international factor movements[68] includes a particular presumption in favor of removing all immigration quotas, which impede the free flow of international labor. In the absence of state welfare payments, this goal of policy would seem to fit easily into the political economy of the Chicago School: it extends personal freedom and improves the world allocation of resources.

The enlightened self-interest of the host country, however, does not point clearly in the same direction. Apart from the risks of short-term economic and social disruption from massive inflows of labor (which might be mitigated by government attempts to regulate the rate of immigration), the long-term implications for indigenous labor are not favorable. For a potential host country that is already worried about its population density, or about the growing congestion in urban areas, or about the erosion of environmental amenities, an awareness of the opportunities being offered to families in poor countries to better their material condition, or an awareness of the resultant expansion of world GNP, may not suffice to allay its apprehensions. Bearing in mind the immense populations of the poorer countries of Asia, Africa, and South America, and their current rate of increase, the prospect of an open-ended commitment to receive them in any numbers would strike Malthusian fears in many a liberal heart. To this one can add fears of a growing pressure on wages toward a subsistence level, and fears of social tensions that can arise at an apparent "invasion" of new peoples differentiated from the local populations by race, language, and custom.[69] The American "melting pot" splutters more than it melts, and Western European countries have already experienced difficulties in their attempts to absorb relatively small numbers of immigrant labor since the war.[70]

If enlightened self-interest is translated into an interest in the welfare of one's countrymen, the net advantages of a wide-open door policy are far from evident.[71] If, on the other hand, one's vision is universalistic, a case might be made in support of such a policy, albeit an uneasy one resting on beliefs about the magnitudes involved and about the ability of the world to escape from the Malthusian nightmare.

*Equity of the Competitive Economy*

Few orthodox economists since J.B. Clark have argued that the market tends also to promote distributional justice. Recent attempts (Thurow, 1969; Hochman and Rodgers, 1969) to extend allocative criteria so as to embrace distributional problems only serve to confirm the inadequacy of the market in this respect. Yet, if the meaning of the term *equity* is extended to cover a person's freedom to select or reject, the operation of free markets, according to the Chicago School, promotes equity in this sense.

As indicated earlier, this exercise of choice is more evident for the consumer than the worker. Yet it is no more evident for the worker than for those citizens who suffer a decline in welfare as a result of external diseconomies generated by industrial processes or their products. Indeed, since there are free markets in labor, the worker has some choice in the matter; certainly he receives some compensation for the "diswelfare" of his labor. However, inasmuch as environmental property rights are, in practice, difficult to distribute, and a competitive market for trading in such rights virtually impossible, the citizen is generally denied this choice. The sort of feasible solution that is common—either an unchecked competitive market or else a competitive market that is checked by excise or effluent taxes, or otherwise regulated—although it may meet allocative criteria is not such as to compensate the citizens for suffering collectively the residual bads. It entails a form of coercion no less onerous—and to many a sensitive citizen, far more onerous—than any arbitrary system of taxes. If, therefore, the incidence of these adverse spillovers tends to grow over time along with the conventional index of per capita growth, and if these spillovers come to be increasingly resented, the claims made for the market as an instrument for extending the area of individual choice will have to be seriously qualified.

Nevertheless, this defect is to some extent a consequence of the existing laws rather than wholly attributable to the market, which could operate well enough in a society pledged to pollution-repressive laws under which none of a range of pollutants could be incurred without paying adequate compensation. The case in justice for such laws is strong, but the enforcement and transactions costs could be heavy.

Touching on the question of intergenerational equity, we have already remarked, unnecessarily perhaps, that the market, even an ideal market, has no tendency to promote it. In respect of the amounts of man-made goods and their quality of efficacy, our descendents might well be wealthier than we. In respect of environmental goods, they will, if trends continue, be worse off. As for the depletion of natural resources, which is also related to man-made goods and environmental goods, the best outcome of a competitive market—which outcome, for reasons given, is not likely to occur—is the generation of an "optimal" time-path of consumption which, however, makes no provision for our descendents. There is only the hope, or conventional expectation, that this manifest deficiency will be made good by continued technological progress and by the discovery of substitute materials over time.

### *The Competitive Economy and the Quality of Life*

While it is true that the Chicago School does not consider the competitive economy to be a panacea for all social infirmities, it has, perhaps, been overimpressed by its economic and political virtues—by its potential for the creation and distribution of material wealth, for the extension of individual choice, and for the preservation of political freedom. Yet close attention to theoretical developments, to institutional constraints, and to the growing impact of modern technology, has served, as indicated, to uncover a number of weak connections that, taken together, must diminish one's faith in this soverign institution.

Finally and moving a little away from these familiar haunts, the import of the phrase "the neutrality of the market" can bear some comment. There is an obvious sense in which the competitive market is value free, or to put it otherwise, value blind. For it can serve a slave economy as faithfully as a free economy. So far as economic efficiency and consumer choice are concerned, it can work as well as, or perhaps better, in an authoritarian regime than in a democratic one. Few markets can ever have been as competitive as those that flourished in Britain in the first half of the nineteenth century, when infants became deformed as they toiled their way to an early death in the pits and mills of the Black Country. And there is no lack of examples today to confirm the fact also that well-functioning markets have no innate tendency to promote excellence in any form. They offer no resistance to forces making for a descent into cultural barbarity or moral depravity.

Over the past two decades, rapid economic growth in the West has been accompanied by rapid growth also in the visible signs of social disintegration, as borne out by indexes of divorce, drug-taking, suicide, vandalism, delinquency, homicide, and crimes of violence, especially among the young. City streets are increasingly unsafe to walk in. Anxiety levels among parents have never been higher. Without implying a causal relationship between postwar economic expansion and these unhappier features of contemporary society, their effects on society's sense of well-being have to be weighed against those arising from the accumulation of material conveniences. It is a bold man who will declare that, over the postwar period, the contribution of economics to social welfare has been decisive.[72]

But however this contribution is assessed, those who are concerned primarily with society's well-being no longer look, today, to competitive markets for salvation. As, willy nilly, we are ushered into the postindustrial era, the focus of concern is shifting inevitably from traditional controversies about the economic conditions under which goods are produced toward a new controversy, one that turns about the sorts of goods themselves, both capital goods and consumer goods, that are now being produced—and their far-reaching effects on our environment, on our character, and on our chances of survival.

## *Notes*

1. As in Lerner's *Economics of Control* (1946), in which there is state ownership of the means of production, managed by public servants in a decentralized economic system that is designed to simulate a competitive economy under certain conditions.
2. Namely, that all consumption and production functions have nonzero second derivatives; that each person consumes some amount of each good; and that the production of each good requires some amount of each factor. Obvious amendments apply if these conditions are not met, but they do not modify our conclusions in significant respects.
3. I follow my own convention in using the phrase "everyone" better off to include the case where one person or more are made better off and nobody is made worse off.
4. In the special case of fixed factor supplies, the optimal condition is violated if the price-marginal cost ratios are not the same for all goods. For further elaboration the interested reader is referred to Baumol and Bradford (1971) and Lerner (1971).
5. A first crude response to the theorem would be to include the price-marginal cost ratios of most sectors within a broad band, and to regard deviations from this range as being significant. See H.A.J. Green (1962) and Mishan (1962) for broad rules in the presence of second best problems.
6. See in particular Davis and Whinston (1965) and McManus (1967), P. Bohm (1967), and Negishi (1967).

7. I have shown in my 1973 paper that wherever such apparently contradictory cases arise, it is not possible to attach superior allocative merit to either collection of goods inasmuch as the welfare combinations associated with each collection can be reduced to alternative distributions of a third hypothetical collection of goods.
8. A related criticism of economic practices that evade the problems of value or translate them into mechanistic allocative problems is elaborated in a recent paper by Klein (1974).
9. For a recent survey see the article by Mark Abrams in *Encounter* (1974).
10. This statement is valid provided all goods and bads are available on the market. To the extent that some goods are not available on the market exceptions can be made. Thus the provision of some collective goods, in particular when they are designed to reduce collective bads (external diseconomies) such as pollutants, that are a simultaneous form of annoyance to many people, can raise social welfare even in the limiting case of complete equality of distribution.
11. On an abstract level, the analysis of (1) and (2) cannot altogether solve the distribution problem since it begins, in each case, with the status quo. Allowing that, in principle, there is a different Pareto efficient distributional solution corresponding to each initial distribution, society cannot escape having to make a choice among a wide range of alternative Pareto efficient distributions. And for this ultimate choice, no criterion is offered.
12. Indeed, by focusing on some particular form of pollution—such as horse dung, sewage, or smoke—in some locations at some point in history, economists have argued that "pollution-wise" we are better off today. For a recent example, see Beckerman (1972).
13. In this connection, see Coase (1960); see also Davis and Whinston (1962 and 1965), who managed to compound the difficulty by using a model in which two firms of industries inflicted external diseconomies upon each other.
14. See, for example, Plott (1966), Schall (1971). There are some brief comments on these models in my 1974 paper.
15. Clearly, if transactions costs were low enough to allow bargaining to take place in the first instance there would be no justification for an excise tax (in any case, the excise tax could be made conditional upon no further bargaining by the parties).
16. The assertion is unsatisfactory, however. It is not enough to show that the market can, in some circumstances, respond in the required direction. It has to be shown, also, that it will tend to respond by the *required magnitude*. For instance, congestion of itself tends to choke off traffic, but the resulting reduction of traffic falls short of that required by reference to the optimal condition.

    The conditions necessary for the market solution to be optimal in a polluted industrial area are: (a) that the level of pollution in the industrial area be unrelated to the size of the working population, (b) that the workers' costs of movement are negligible, and (c) that pollution levels everywhere are not rising over time.
17. The analysis is on all fours with private property in farmland. Rent, the

return to land, is to be maximized only through "exploitation" of the upward-sloping supply curve of corn. "Exploitation" of the demand curve, on the other hand, which is possible if land ownership is not diffused, produces monopoly rent and, therefore, a suboptimal output.

18. Useful insights into this proposition can be found in a short but valuable contribution by Calabresi (1968).
19. Particular attention should be given to the articles by Demsetz (1964 and 1966) and more recently by Cheung (1970).
20. The advantages of this approach are discussed by Baumol and Oates (1975, chapter 10).
21. The distinction between optional collective goods (such as a public park or a public broadcast) and nonoptional collective goods (such as "artificial rain," or internal security) is made in my 1969 paper.
22. For optional collective goods, exchange optimum is met inasmuch as ( in the absence of congestion) the marginal cost to each person is zero. For nonoptional collective goods, however, exchange optimum is unlikely to be met since the amounts people are constrained to absorb are unalterable (except, perhaps, by incurring costs).
23. At least in the absence of "pecuniary external diseconomies" or rising long-run unit costs.
24. In this connection see Freeman and Haveman (1972).
25. The suggestion does not, however, amount to the dictum that the polluter should be made to pay, which is ambiguous. Less ambiguous is the dictum that he who incurs the pollution should be made to bear the costs. Thus if a person chooses to move into a polluted zone, it is allocatively appropriate that he should be made to bear the environmental costs himself. Compensation in this circumstance is tantamount to a subsidy and can be shown to be allocatively unwarranted. If, however, he and others choose to move without pecuniary inducement, further social gains may be realized by curbing the activities of the polluting industries.
26. As a consequence of the spread of the welfare state into the field of medicine, the health risks that a person is ready to take can be partly spread among the taxpayers. But the "external diseconomies" on them that appear to arise from this financial arrangement are what Viner would call "pecuniary"; in effect, transfer payments only. Since the costs of any health damage fall in the first instance entirely on the risk taker, there is no purely *allocative* justification for invoking the concept of "social cost" in arguing a case for interfering with the individual's choice.
27. No man is an island unto himself, however, and there cannot be many persons whose health or survival is a matter of indifference to everyone else including the members of his family. Again, however, we are faced with a choice of grounding our welfare propositions in the Pareto criterion or in the ethics of society. The liberal welfare economist may consistently override the Pareto criterion—which attitude, in this instance, implies a disregard of the reaction of others—in order to safeguard the freedom of the individual, and in doing so may be giving proper expression to the ethics of the community.
28. Our ignorance is dangerous whenever we produce, and market, complex

chemical agents or new synthetic substances that are reasonably suspect of having genetic or ecological side effects yet to be discovered.

29. A sober account of the dangers accompanying the spread of breeder reactors is given by Kneese (1973).
30. Allowance being made for adjusting the base; so that, for example, a marginal dollar grown through investment to $1.25 is exactly offset by a 20 percent decline in the utility of the resulting $1.25.
31. If this elasticity were equal to −4, and if average growth in per capita income were 2 percent per annum, the use of 8 percent as discount rate for calculating the present value of marginal gains and losses over time can be rationalized as a device for transforming dollar increments scattered through time into present dollars of equal utility weight. This sort of rationalization for the use of a discount rate is clearly distinct from that conventionally associated with its use in public investment criteria; namely, that it represents the yield of alternative uses.
32. In this context, the relevant rate of interest is that equal to the current social yield on new investment (before tax).
33. For if the firm produces a unit of ore this year at a net price of 100 and invests the proceeds at 5 percent, it will realize 105 next year, whereas by postponing its extraction to next year a net price of 108 is realized.
34. For if the firm extracts a unit of ore today it fetches a net price of 100 which, when invested at 5 percent, realizes 105 next year, whereas if the firm postpones its extraction to next year it realizes a net price of only 102.
35. For a fairly popular treatment of such possibilities, see Solow (1974).
36. In general, that is, only a small fraction of the stream of net proceeds (or net benefits) is saved and reinvested in productive assets. For a treatment of the usual assumptions made about the reinvestment of returns from public investment, see Mishan (1975, Part IV).
37. This second belief depends, to some extent, on the first being true.
38. Included are those intangible costs of separating himself from a neighborhood in which he has made close friends and from a pattern of life full of familiar associations.
39. Sometimes taxpayers are made to subsidize a proportion of the costs of movement or of retraining, a policy that also suffers from allocative deficiencies.
40. If the actions of all others were similarly circumscribed, he would feel less injured. And if, for political reasons—as in Britain between 1945 and 1954—restrictions on consumer choice are accepted by society at large, his experience of welfare could, for a number of reasons, be as high or higher than it would be if such restrictions were removed.
41. There have, however, been recent reports in business journals of experiments that extend more choice to workers in respect of hours, or of work conditions, or of methods of production.
42. The suggestion that there can be considerations bearing on social welfare other than the seeming efficiency of markets that provide justification for some restrictive practices must not, however, be construed as blanket extenuation of extortionate pricing and dishonest dealings of many large corporations.

43. It is as well to remind readers at this stage that if transactions costs were zero, this interdependence would resolve itself through voluntary activity, which would produce the optimal amounts of these goods. But this ideal solution would require that merit good producers have costless information about which persons benefit, and by how much, from the consumption by others of particular merit goods. Since such costs are likely to be prohibitive (involving, as they do, the free-rider problem), the effective choice society has is either to attempt to produce an optimal amount of some merit goods, or at least more of them than would be forthcoming on the free market, through subsidies financed by income (or other) taxes, or do nothing. A person strongly opposed to taxes, as being coercive, will choose to do nothing.
44. They also happen to be collective goods inasmuch as, in the absence of congestion, the costs of such services cannot be economically allocated among the beneficiaries. But this is not a necessary characteristic of merit goods which can also be private goods—for example, classical records or history books.
45. Even though people, on being directly questioned, declare in favor of freedom for the pornographic theater, it may well be simply because in their confusion they now believe they ought to feel ashamed of their (natural?) feelings of shame, and because they fear to be thought illiberal or in favor of censorship. Yet despite their intimidation by fashionable views, they might still feel better off if carnal displays disappeared from cinema and theater.
46. The reader will recall that I argued earlier (in section II), in connection with the transfers in kind and other issues, that the liberal economist is not obliged to raise his hat to Pareto on all occasions, and, indeed, where there is a conflict between Pareto-based allocative propositions and the ethical norms of the community, priority be given to the latter. However, insofar as the categorization of merit-demerit goods arises from the application of the more transcendental values of a society, this possible conflict between ethics and Pareto efficiency is circumvented.
47. Unless the meaning of *externalities* is extended beyond its conventional economic definition so as to exclude, in particular, all unforeseen and adverse consequences. But if so, it would clearly be impossible to know how to "correct" externalities.
48. In private correspondence with me, Professor Friedman mentioned a Chicago study which found that the prices of identical optical goods were lower in the states that permitted advertising of opticians' services than in those states that did not. But this sort of advertising of services that the customer can judge for himself is more like simple announcements of place and terms of business. It is the sort of information that would or should be provided by consumer research agencies.
49. In support of such allegations, it is often remarked that a large proportion of competitive advertising is self-cancelling in its effects, and that the competitive firm's advertising mainly serves the purpose of maintaining its share of the market. However, it is not absurd to suppose that the market shares of the competitive firm would remain at least as stable in the absence of competitive advertising.
50. There is, in fact, both a distributional and an allocative effect. The dis-

tributional one involves no more than a shift of real income from car buyers to newspaper readers. The former pay more than the real costs incurred in the production of their cars, as a result of which the latter obtain the advertisement free and, in addition, pay less than the costs of the newspaper.

51. I do not think that Chicago economists would dissent from the above arguments. Some of them have long urged that TV and radio channels be sold by auction, and that those who buy the rights to them should be free to distribute their programs by any means they wish, including pay TV and pay radio.

52. I am not suggesting that advertising agencies are unscrupulous. They may well abide by what looks like a reasonable code of ethics. But the fact remains that, in virtue of his vocation, the advertising agent cannot be concerned primarily to disclose the whole truth (so far as he knows it) and nothing but the truth, but only those parts of it, along with some imagery, that would appear to him best able to promote the sale of the product.

53. By "relevant," I mean information that enters into the consumer's decision. If he thinks that looking like, or acting like, other people is important, then information on the numbers of people using, or likely to be using, the article or service becomes relevant. By "complete," I mean *all* information that is relevant in the above sense. Clearly, completeness must be regarded as an aim; the more of it for a given outlay, the better. Yet the investigations have to be limited by the resources available to the agency, both financial and technical.

54. Of course, it could be argued that consumers prefer partial to impartial information. But if the law were amended to require manufacturers to sell their advertisements to the public at full cost, the public would be able to choose as between buying impartial and partial information, buying each at a price that covers its cost to the economy.

55. In his *Newsweek* column (16 June 1969) Milton Friedman attacked the then proposed prohibition of tobacco advertising as constituting a form of censorship "hostile to the maintenance of a free society," a view we shall examine in the text. To this general view, however, he appends a particular objection to arguments favoring prohibition of cigarette advertising simply on the grounds of health risks. "Every time we take an automobile ride, or cross the street," says Friedman, "we knowingly risk our lives because we think that the gain from the ride or crossing the street justifies the risk."

True, risk in varying degrees and in a variety of ways, pervades our lives. The question at issue, however, is whether resources should be used in persuading people to take risks which otherwise they might not want to incur. Can there be no legitimate objection to advertising campaigns designed to persuade motorists of the joys of high-speed driving, or to persuade pedestrians of the exhilarations of running across city streets?

John Stuart Mill's argument for freedom of choice was reinforced by the consideration that the alleged ill effects on the consumers of drugs would themselves act as a deterrent to others once they became manifest to all. This deterrent effect, however, can be offset or overcome by sustained propaganda in its favor. It is hard to believe that tobacco and liquor addiction would be so widespread were it not for sustained propaganda by commercial interests.

Friedman's disappoval of the antismoking campaign of federal agencies on the grounds that "government has no business using the taxpayer's money to propagandize" certain views is hard to understand. If a government, local, state, or federal, receives a mandate from the electorate for just that purpose, it cannot be accused of a misuse of the taxpayer's money, in particular since the views in question are not political in the ordinary sense. The government propaganda is better regarded as a collective good designed specifically to counter the propaganda of interested parties who are attempting to induce people to increase their exposure to health hazards.

56. It seems only fair to point out, however, that the Chicago School does not accept a utilitarian approach in which personal freedom is but one ingredient, though an important one, in the promotion of well-being. If I may quote from private correspondence with Friedman: "We regard the virtues and role of freedom as not simply instrumental . . . for maximizing utilities, but far more fundamentally even in its instrumental role as a means for forming character and values and more basically as an ultimate end in itself derived from our lack of certainty about our own beliefs which seem to us to render it improper to try to impose these on somebody else."

However, even if this conception of the role of freedom is accepted it does not seem to me to upset the conclusion reached in the last two paragraphs of this section.

57. Although an ideal size of the public sector, judged on allocative grounds, may be related to the incidence and magnitude of the collective goods and bads emerging at some stage of technical progress, it is at least conceivable either (a) to have a public sector that embraces the entire economy even where all the goods produced are "private" on the conventional definition, or (b) to have a private sector of the economy that contains nothing but collective goods. In arguments about the best size of the public sector, however, considerations arising from economic efficiency and from political expediency may point in opposite directions.

58. The chief lesson that was drawn by Hayek from the collectivist experiments on the Continent in the interwar period as described in his arresting monograph (1944), was the imperative of a large private sector of the economy as a means of preserving individual freedoms.

59. The case is cogently argued in Friedman (1962, pp. 172–76).

60. At best, liberal economists have been satisfied to think about economic growth in terms of more, or better, consumer goods which, it is said, "expand the area of choice open to the individual."

61. A fascinating account of the process of self-generating expenditures of the defence establishment by Charles Schultz appeared in 1970. Schultz concluded that "continually advancing technology and the risk aversion of military planners, therefore, combine to produce ever more complex and expensive weapons systems and ever more contingencies to guard against" (p. 14).

62. According to the *London Observer* (9 March 1975), about 20 million Americans (on that date) were shown on their television screens how easy it was to steal plutonium and produce a home-made atomic bomb. If the report was accurate, the viewers were told that no nuclear plant in the United States—and probably in the world—is adequately protected against a well planned attack by terrorists.
63. Writing in the *Bulletin of Atomic Scientists,* May 1972, Dr. Hannes Alfven, Nobel Laureate in Physics, stated: "Fission energy is safe only if a number of critical devices work as they should, if a number of people in key positions follow all their instructions, if there is no sabotage, no hijacking of the transports, if no reactor fuel processing plant or reprocessing plant or repository anywhere in the world is situated in a region of riots or guerilla activity, and no revolution or war—even a 'conventional' one—takes place in these regions. The enormous quantities of extremely dangerous material must not get into the hands of ignorant people or desperados. No Acts of God can be permitted."
64. Nonetheless, the larger the discrepancy between the market price and the social marginal valuation of the product, the more certain is the standard correction to offer an improvement—a proposition that justifies treatment within a partial context of significant environmental diseconomies.
65. To be more obvious about it, losing one's market or losing one's job—even in "the short run"—is an upsetting experience against which, in the scale of social welfare, additional consumer satisfaction may weigh very little.
66. This can be the case if adjustments to changing conditions of demand come about less through the movement of prices and more through the movement of factors in response to economic opportunities.
67. Under fixed exchange rates, in contrast, a full employment economy having a rate of inflation above those of the countries with which it trades, incurs an increasing balance-of-payments deficit. Attempts to eliminate this deficit by devaluing its currency *without* first improving the internal balance (reducing aggregate investment and government expenditures relative to saving and tax revenues) can only aggravate its inflation and restore the deficit.
68. The proposition that the international exchange of goods is a substitute for international factor movements, and tends to bring about international equality of factor prices, depends not only on the relevant number of traded goods being no fewer than the number of factors (which invites conjecture on the appropriate definitions of goods and factors) and on the absence of factor-ratio reversibility but also and perhaps more important, on the assumption of identical linear homogeneous production functions in each country of the traded goods. The introduction of production functions having different degrees of technical progress (neutral or otherwise) is enough to vitiate the result that costless free trade equalizes factor prices.
69. An idea of the resentments felt by some people in Britain at the numbers of "Commonwealth" immigrants is conveyed by Lord Elton (1965).
70. An account of these difficulties can be found in J. Power (1974).

71. Even though analytic considerations may suggest that economic gains to renters and capitalists exceed economic losses to workers.
72. Nordhaus and Tobin (1971) were too intelligent to be that bold. Whatever results were established by their figures were effectively disestablished by their explicit doubts and qualifications.

## *References*

Abrams, Mark. 1974. "Changing Values." *Encounter* 43 (October): 29–38.

Ayres, Robert, and Kneese, Allen V. 1969. "Production, Consumption and Externalities." *American Economic Review* 59 (June): 282–97.

Barnett, Harold, and Morse, Chandler. 1963. *Scarcity and Growth*. Baltimore: Johns Hopkins Press.

Bator, Francis. 1958. "The Anatomy of Market Failure." *Quarterly Journal of Economics* 72 (August): 351–79.

Baumol, William J., and Bradford, David. 1970. "Optimal Departures from Marginal Cost Pricing." *American Economic Review* 60 (June): 265–83.

Baumol, William, and Oates, Wallace E. 1975. *The Theory of Environmental Policy*. New Jersey: Prentice-Hall.

Beckerman, Wilfred. 1972. "Economist, Scientists and Environmental Catastrophe." *Oxford Economic Papers* 24 (November): 327–44.

Bell, Daniel. 1974. "The Public Household." *Public Interest* 37 (Fall): 29–68.

Berle, Adolf A., and Means, Gardiner C. 1933. *The Modern Corporation and Private Property*. New York: Macmillan.

Breton, Albert A. 1966. "A Theory of the Demand for Public Goods." *Canadian Journal of Public Economics* 32 (November): 455–67.

Buchanan, James, and Stubblebine, W.M. Craig. 1962. "Externality." *Economica* 29 (November): 371–84.

Cheung, Steven. 1970. "The Structure of a Contract." *Journal of Law and Economics* 13 (April): 49–70.

Coase, Ronald H. 1960. "The Problems of Social Cost." *Journal of Law and Economics* 3 (October): 1–4.

Daly, George, and Giertz, Fred. 1972. "Welfare Economics and Welfare Reform." *American Economic Review* 62 (March): 131–38.

Davis, Otto, and Winston, Andrew. 1962. "Externalities, Welfare and the Theory of Games." *Journal of Political Economy* 70 (June): 241–62.

Demsetz, Harold. 1964. "The Exchange and Enforcement of Property Rights." *Journal of Law and Economics* 7 (October): 11–26.

———. 1966. "Some Aspects of Property Rights." *Journal of Law and Economics* 9 (October): 61–70.

Duesenberry, James. 1949. *Income, Saving and the Theory of Consumer Behavior*. Cambridge, Mass.: Harvard University Press.

Ellul, Jacques. 1965. *The Technical Society*. London: Jonathan Cape.

Elton (Lord). 1965. *The Unarmed Invasion*. London: Geoffrey Bles.

Epstein, Edward J. 1974. "Methadone, the Forlorn Hope." *Public Interest* 36 (Summer): 3–24.

Freeman, A. Myrick, and Haveman, Robert. 1972. "Clean Rhetoric, Dirty Water." *Public Interest* 28 (Summer): 51–65.

Friedman, Milton. 1962. *Capitalism and Freedom*. Chicago: University of Chicago Press.

———. 1974. "Schools at Chicago." *University of Chicago Magazine* (Autumn): 11–16.

Georgescu-Roegen, Nicholas. 1975. "Energy and Economic Myths." *Southern Economic Journal* 41 (January): 347–81.

Gaffney, Mason, ed. 1967. *Extractive Resources and Taxation*. Madison: University of Wisconsin Press.

Gofman, John. 1972. "Time for a Moratorium." *Environmental Action* 4 (November): 11–15.

Graff, Jan V. 1957. *Theoretical Welfare Economics*. Cambridge: the University Press.

Green, H.A. John. 1962. "The Social Optimum in the Presence of Monopoly and Taxation." *Review of Economic Studies* 29 (February): 66–78.

Hayek, Frederick A. 1944. *The Road to Serfdom*. London: Routledge & Sons.

———. 1961. "The Non *Sequitur* of the 'Dependence Effect.' " *Southern Economic Journal* 27 (April): 346–48.

Hicks, John R. 1939. *Value and Capital*. Oxford: Clarendon Press.

Hochman, Harold, and Rodgers, James. 1969. "Pareto Optimal Redistribution." *American Economic Review* 59 (September): 542–57.

Hotelling, Harold. 1931. "The Economics of Exhaustible Resources." *Journal of Political Economy* 39 (April): 137–75.

Johnson, Harry. *Man and His Environment*. British North American Committee.

Klein, Phillip. 1974. "Economics: Allocation or Valuation." *Journal of Economic Issues* 8 (December): 785–811.

Kneese, Allen. 1973. *The Faustian Bargain*. Washington, D.C.: Resources for the Future.

——— and Schultze, Charles. 1975. *Pollution, Prices and Public Policy*. Washington, D.C.: The Brookings Institution.

Knight, Frank H. 1924. "Some Fallacies in the Interpretation of Social Cost." *Quarterly Journal of Economics* 38 (August): 582–606.

Kaldor, Nicolas. 1939. "Welfare Propositions in Economics and Interpersonal Comparisons of Utility." *Economic Journal* 51 (September): 549–52.

Krutilla, John A., and Fisher, Anthony. 1975. *The Economics of Natural Resources*. Washington, D.C.: Resources for the Future.

Lerner, Abba P. 1970. "On Optimal Taxes with an Untaxable Sector." *American Economic Review* 60 (June): 284–94.

———. 1946. *The Economics of Control*. New York: Macmillan Co.

Lipsey, Richard G. 1957. "The General Theory of Second Best." *Review of Economic Studies* 24 (November): 11–32.

Machlup, Fritz. 1969. "Liberalism and the Choice of Freedom." In *Roads to Freedom*, edited by E. Streissler. London: Routledge & Kegan Paul.

Maddox, John. 1972. "Raw Materials and the Price Mechanism." *Nature* 236 (14 April): 331–34.

Mishan, E.J. 1962. "Second Thought on Second Best." *Oxford Economic Papers* 14 (October): 205–17.

———. 1965. "Reflection on Recent Developments in the Concept of External Effects." *Canadian Journal of Political Economy* 31 (February): 3–34.

———. 1967. *The Costs of Economic Growth*. New York: Praeger.

———. 1967. "Pareto Optimality and the Law." *Oxford Economic Papers* 19 (November): 255–87.

———. 1969. "The Relationship between Joint Products, Collective Goods, and External Effects." *Journal of Political Economy* 72 (3) (May): 329–48.

———. 1969. *Welfare Economics: An Assessment*. Amsterdam: North Holland.

———. 1971. "The Postwar Literature on Externalities: An Interpretive Essay." *Journal of Economic Literature* 9 (May): 1–28.

———. 1972. "The Futility of Pareto Efficient Distribution." *American Economic Review* 62 (December): 974–76.

———. 1973. *Making the World Safe for Pornography* (chapter 6). London: Alcove Press.

———. 1973. "Welfare Criteria: Resolution of a Paradox." *Economic Journal* 83 (September): 747–67.

———. 1974. "What Is the Optimal Level of Pollution?" *Journal of Political Economy* 82 (November): 1287–99.

———. 1975. *Cost Benefit Analysis*, 2d ed. London: Allen and Unwin.

Nordhaus, William, and Tobin, Joseph. 1972. *Is Growth Obsolete?* In National Bureau of Economic Research, *Economic Growth*. New York: Columbia University Press.

Olsen, Mancur. 1965. *The Logic of Collective Action*. Cambridge, Mass.: Harvard University Press.

Packard, Vance. 1972. *A Nation of Strangers*. New York: David McKay.

Page, Talbot. 1973. *The Economics of Involuntary Transfers*. New York: Springer-Verlag.

———. *The Economics of a Throwaway Society* (forthcoming).

Pigou, Arthur C. 1946. *The Economics of Welfare*, 4th ed. London: Macmillan.

Plott, Charles. 1966. "Externalities and Corrective Taxes." *Economica* 33 (February): 84–87.

Power, John. 1974. "The New Proletariat." *Encounter* 43 (September): 8–13.

Ridker, Ronald, ed. 1972. *Population, Resources and the Environment*. Washington, D.C.: U.S. Government Printing Office.

Schall, Lawrence. 1971. "Technological Externalities and Resource Allocation." *Journal of Political Economy* 79 (September): 983–1001.

Schultze, Charles. 1970. "Reexamining the Military Budget." *Public Interest* 18 (Winter): 3–24.

Scitovsky, Tibor. 1941. "A Note on Welfare Propositions in Economics." *Review of Economic Studies* 9 (November): 77–88.

Simons, Henry. 1948. *Economic Policy for a Free Society*. Chicago: University of Chicago Press.

Solow, Robert. 1974. "The Economics of Resources or the Resources of Economics." *American Economic Review* 64 (May): 1–14.

Telser, Lester. 1964. "Advertising and Competition." *Journal of Political Economy* 72 (December): 537–62.

Thurow, Lester. 1971. "The Income Distribution as a Pure Public Good." *Quarterly Journal of Economics* 85 (May): 327–36.

Tiebout, Charles. 1956. "A Pure Theory of Local Expenditure." *Journal of Political Economy* 64 (October): 416–24.

Turvey, Ralph. 1963. "On Divergences between Social and Private Cost." *Economica* 30 (August): 309–13.

Viner, Jacob, 1953. "Cost Curves and Supply Curves" (1931). Reprinted in *Readings in Price Theory*. New York: The Blakiston Co.

# 7

# Chicago Economics: From Individualism True to Individualism False

*Warren S. Gramm*

In a 1945 lecture, "Individualism: True and False," F. A. Hayek identified two streams in Western thought which he believed had led to political polar opposites—capitalistic liberalism and socialistic authoritarianism. The first stream, the true individualism which he defends, began with John Locke, Bernard Mandeville, and David Hume and reached "full stature . . . in the work of Josiah Tucker, Adam Ferguson, and Adam Smith."[1] The second, that of false individualism, is dominated by Cartesian rationalism. Developing primarily on the Continent, it appeared initially with "the Encyclopedists, Rousseau, and the physiocrats" and was extended initially by Auguste Comte and the St. Simonians.[2]

The conceptual base of Hayek's dichotomy on individualism is applied here to the evolution of the Chicago School of economics.[3] It is argued that development of the school presents a fundamental transition—a movement from individualism true to individualism false—and is a hyperindividualism opposite to that of Hayek. Analysis of the transition is based on (1) identification of the substantive, ethical, and methodological elements of major early and contemporary Chicago economists and (2) the interrelationships between this analytical base and their normative policy position.

True individualism is social, and deals with individuals as part of society, rather than as dissociated, independent atoms. It is, in Hayek's words, "primarily a *theory* of society, an attempt to understand the

*The author is Professor of Economics, Washington State University, Pullman.*

forces which determine the social life of man, and only in the second instance a set of political maxims derived from this view of society."[4] False individualism is characterized—is dominated—by rationalism and ethical pragmatism. It views human action as based on rules (commands), in contrast to general principles; it is supportive of elitism and economic man and views human behavior as essentially fatalistic and amoral. In addition, Hayek's individualism false incorporates the historicist "design theory" of social institutions—a deterministic view of history based on the assumed existence of inevitable laws of historical development. The intertwining of Cartesian rationalism and historical determination—the positivistic position of Comte with the historicism of St. Simonians (plus some Marxists and other socialists)—is the basis for Hayek's judgment that the nineteenth-century intellectual tradition of false individualism comes to rest in twentieth-century socialist rationality.

The normative-ethical base of both the early and late Chicago tradition (that is, individualistic liberalism) has remained formally the same, while method and related analytic substance and policy positions have undergone fundamental change. For both groups the major means to the end of maximizing individual freedom is the institutional base of private markets and minimal government restraint of individual choice. Freedom is equated with equality of opportunity, which is, in turn, a function of a socially operational equality of economic and political power. The existence of equal rights (legal and social) is consonant with significant—but not extreme—inequality in distribution of income and wealth.

In the true individualism of early Chicago, the substance of major analytic propositions, method, and policy is consistent with the liberal ethic. The individualism false of contemporary, ultrarationalist, hyperindividualist thought, method, and policy provides normative weight antithetical to liberal polity.

### *Individualism True and Early Chicago Tradition*

The major representatives of the early Chicago School were Jacob Viner and Frank H. Knight. Its normative peak is presented in Henry C. Simons's 1934 essay, *A Positive Program for Laissez-Faire—Some Proposals for a Liberal Economic Policy.*[5] Other major representatives are considered in particular contexts. While Milton Friedman is most appropriately included here, his methodology and significant qualification of the 1930s policy position of Simons and others suggest that he is at the same time a transitional figure.[6] All share the philosophy reflected in Simons's political credo, his "underlying position [that] may be characterized as severely libertarian or, in the English-Continental sense, liberal."[7]

*Predecessors of Early Chicago*

The social tradition of individualism true, of the early Chicago School, presents the convergence of English and continental liberalism—of John Locke, Adam Smith, Alfred Marshall, Karl Menger, and Friedrich von Wieser.[8] The English line is relatively unambiguous. The Scottish, classical tradition beginning with Smith runs directly through John Stuart Mill to Marshall.[9] It is manifested in "what might be called the Cambridge spirit of economics—the Marshallian conviction that there is an intimate link between social philosophy and economic analysis, which should never be severed."[10]

Adam Smith, in his two major works, presents the fundamental elements of individualism true in the blending of the social constraint of "sympathy" with individual self-interest which dominates—which creates—economic man. Smith's methodology is eclectic, incorporating broad principles that range from positivist, matter-of-fact analyses of markets and growth to his strategic metaphor, the Invisible Hand. The last is a metaphysical relationship (applied first to landlords in *Theory of Moral Sentiments* and then to the new commercial class) which expresses his optimism concerning the reality of natural harmony to reconcile equally natural elements of conflict between humans. The metaphysics of the Invisible Hand moves from naïve optimism to an element in a "theory of society" when its existence (for Smith) is seen to rest on the late-eighteenth-century realities of (1) social community constraints of greed and (2) the religious golden rule whose effect stems from fear of damnation as well as human conscience. This is social individualism. The rights of individuals exist in, and are constrained by, the given social setting. The maximum of individual liberty requires the socially based limitations of self that rest on recognition of the rights of others.[11] The greater the self-restraint engendered by social consciousness (sympathy, conscience, or codes of chivalry), the less the coercive restraints of government.

In its twentieth-century extension, there developed within neoclassicism a significant strain of false individualism, based essentially on the long-run effects of changing methodology. With Lionel Robbins playing a leading role, logical positivism became the dominant base of scientific economics. This involved "the purging from economics of a concern with ends which lead to an increased emphasis on the logical structure and abstracted from questions of morality and policy, which have been the traditional concern of Western economics."[12] Early leading neoclassicists, particularly W. Stanley Jevons, participated in and contributed to the methodological development of logical positivism; however, they maintained, on balance, the methodological eclecticism associated with scientific method.[13]

In Austrian neoclassicism the link between substance and method is presented in the theory of subjective value and the concept of natural value or price. Karl Menger's perception of marginal utility emphasized qualitative differences of consumer goods, both in the different uses of a particular good and in the hierarchical range between necessities and luxuries. The last relationship is particularly significant in Wieser's integration of market prices, human welfare, income distribution, and the proper role of government. The strategic proposition is his distinction between market and natural value. In market or exchange value, prices are based on a combination of marginal utility and purchasing power, while natural value is determined by marginal utility alone. In exchange value, luxuries tend to be overvalued and necessities undervalued, and the opposite is true with respect to necessities. "Exchange value, even when considered as perfect, is, if we may call it, a caricature of natural value."[14]

Wieser concluded that whenever the divergence between natural and exchange value is too great—when allocation of resources to production of luxury goods, compared with necessities, is larger than is socially desirable—it is appropriate for government to intervene. When there is a conflict between a given private interest and the public interest, the latter must come first. "In particular, where any considerable want is concerned while the power to pay is wanting, the service must be undertaken at limited prices,—that is to say, valuation according to exchange value must be replaced by valuation according to natural value. Thus, emerges the 'public enterprise.' "[15] Such intervention will have the effect of a real redistribution of income. Wieser's perspective concerning laissez-faire was essentially the same as that of the English classical and neoclassical schools.

### *Early Individualism True: Ethics, Method, and Public Policy*

In general, there is no difficulty in establishing the common philosophical and ethical ground of Viner, Knight, and Simons in relation to social individualism. The strategic base is the equality of opportunity ethic. In Simons's words, "liberal ideals include equality of opportunity—or steadily diminishing inequality. [Still,] hard questions arise of how and how rapidly egalitarian measures may be pursued without undermining the structure of voluntary associations at its foundation."[16] "Equality of opportunity is an ideal that a free society should constantly pursue even at much cost in terms of other ends. Freedom without power, like power without freedom, has no substance or meaning."[17] On this ethical base true individualism supports democracy as the necessary political norm. But emphasis on individual rights and the reality of great differences in individual interests and behavior necessitate restraint on the potential tyranny of the majority.

Perhaps the single most important issue concerns attainment of a broadly defined scientific method—of the appropriate balance between deduction and induction (quantification) with respect to varying economic-analytic problems. The goal is that of a golden mean, a balance between the two, appropriate for a given problem, rather than an exaggerated use of either.[18]

The methodology of individualism true is eclectic. Based on the norm of scientific objectivity, it emphasizes the interaction of deduction and induction, the faculties of imagination and rationality grounded on individual and social reality, in solution of social problems. Its eclecticism allows employment of whatever paradigms, models, or analogies—symbolic, mechanical, or organic—that promise better understanding of a given phenomenon. Generally, its analysis stems from general principles, from qualitative, evaluative propositions unconstrained by their quantitative properties.[19]

A major methodological thrust of individualism true in the interwar period (1920–1940) was opposition to the rise of positivism. In general terms, such opposition was based on the judgment that the positivistic, natural science based scientific method is not fully or directly applicable to social science. Analysis of problems of human beings cannot be expected to yield the definitive, deductive answers of mathematics, on the one hand, or the hard proofs of laboratory science, on the other. These are the bases of the skepticism of Viner concerning mathematics as a source of insight for economics and the fears of both Viner and John U. Nef concerning an economics dominated by—limited to—propositions that meet the criterion of empirical disproof.[20] Viner's important contributions to economic theory establish his recognition of the necessity of developing useful abstractions stemming from general principles of economic significance. His 1917 essay on methodology presented sympathetic recognition of the growing inductive, quantitative emphasis in economics.

Important, effective examples of scientific method are presented in the works of Wesley C. Mitchell and Paul H. Douglas. Mitchell's seminal work on business cycles, initiated in the early Chicago setting, reflected the continental historical and institutional stimulus to quantitative economics. Douglas showed how fruitful associations could be developed between a mathematical-deductive base and quantitative-statistical applications. His work involved functional integration of theory and application, of abstraction and empiricism.

Of the early Chicago economists, Frank H. Knight was the only one who wrote extensively on methodology. His position in this regard, as in the remainder of his thought, was broad and eclectic; hence, it is impossible to encompass in a given category or under a given label. His writing over some four decades reflects refinement, but no fundamental change. In his initial, major statement in 1924 he divided economic analysis into "three methods of treatment which must logically be sharply differentiated": pure, essentially deductive, theory (essentially short run or timeless, based on general laws or axioms of rational behavior); applied economics based on particular data and principles not appropriate for pure theory; and historical economics dealing with "cumulative changes of institutions."[21] In his 1943 review article, "Social Causation," he stated that economic theory deals with two very different dimensions of general principles. First, it analyzes individual choice in maximizing alternative means with given ends. But second, and much more important, "in its main content it is a social science. It deals with interindividual relations, with cooperation or organization between individuals for increasing efficiency."[22] Individual wants—the purpose or end of production—are given (independent variables) in the short run; the study of their long-run change "would seem to be the most conspicuous task of institutional economics."[23] In 1961 he stated that "there are social values that cannot be realistically dealt with or discussed in terms of individual interest; a society acts for the future, not merely in interests of its living members."[24] In the large, it is clear that Knight regarded the task of economic analysis as including a theory of social process within which individual values were paramount.

The normative, policy orientation of early Chicago economists was Smithian laissez-faire, the "market-plus" position of English classicism[25] and Cambridge and Austrian neoclassicism. This is clearly seen in their positions on both the macro and micro problems of mature industrial capitalism in the 1930s. The early "Keynesian" response of leading Chicago economists to the Great Depression in the early 1930s has been analyzed by J. Ronnie Davis. A January 1932 telegram to President Hoover recommending continued deficit spending for finance of public works expenditure was signed by 25 representatives of the

University of Chicago, including Douglas, Gideonse, Knight, Simons, and Viner.[26] In a 1932 letter to Senator Robert F. Wagner, Knight stated: "As far as I know economists are completely agreed that the Government should spend as much and tax as little as possible, at a time such as this."[27]

The strongest policy statement of the early Chicago approach to major microeconomic problems of the U.S. economy—the issues of market monopoly and inequality of income distribution—was presented by Henry C. Simons in 1934. His "positive program for *laissez faire*" marks the apogee of individualism true in the Chicago tradition. Simons argued that "the main elements in a sound liberal policy may be defined in terms of five proposals or objectives (in descending scale of relative importance): elimination of private monopoly in all its forms (including public ownership of natural monopoly and drastic reform of rules of incorporation), monetary reform, tax reform leading to greater equality, tariff reform, and, finally, limitation on expenditures for advertising and other selling activity."[28]

In general, in both its macro and micro policy orientation the early Chicago policies of individualism true presented a socially functional, internally consistent contact with the political reality of confronting the problem of equality of opportunity, which is the essence of liberalism. Since the 1940s, Chicago representatives of individualism true have presented significant qualifications of (elements of retreat from) Simons's unequivocal position. This modification is seen most clearly in Friedman's 1962 normative statement. Concerning monopoly, Friedman holds that the social cost of private monopoly is likely to be less than that of public ownership. On taxation, he judges that the redistribution via a progressive personal income tax is neither necessary nor desirable.[29] Acceptable tax reform is limited essentially to a negative income tax that will maintain minimum incomes. When combined with his positivist methodology, these concessions to existing concentrations of market power and wealth provide a significant basis for associating Friedman with the new Chicago of false individualism.

### *Individualism False and Contemporary Chicago Economics*

The basic attributes of false individualism are the exaggerated individualism that dissociates the individual from society and the hyperrationalism that sees individual behavior governed by rational choice rather than jointly influenced by feelings and intellect. The methodological and conceptual paradigm of rational choice as the strategic factor in human behavior is the dominant theme in a new, individualistic economics.[30] Insofar as this may be the beginning of an identifiable new focus of economics (analogous to the now defunct Keynesian revolution), it clearly includes important non-Chicago economists. The present discussion concerns the connection of contemporary University of Chicago associated economists with Hayekian attributes of false individualism; however, it cannot be overstressed (as indicated in note 6) that the focus is on ideas, not individuals.

A long, direct, precursory connection between the early Chicago School and the intellectual and political tradition of true individualism was presented earlier. There is no similar precedent for contemporary, ultrarationalist individualism false. It is perhaps best understood as a selective perversion of the tradition of individualism true. That is, the socially constrained rationality of Smithian self-interest (dominant solely in the economic sphere) is extended via "economic man" as the prototypical base of human behavior in general. Human actions stem from interaction of rational and nonrational elements (desires, impulses, drives). Domination of one by the other, at the extreme, is symptomatic of neurosis or psychosis for the individual as well as society. This is the general basis for the association by Hayek, Ben B. Seligman, and others of ultrarationalism (scientism) with authoritarianism (wherein liberal polity is judged "normal" or "healthy").[31]

### *False Individualism in Contemporary Rationalist Economics*

As with true individualism, judgment concerning the existence of false individualism is based on the three elements of ethics, method, and their normative associations. Since the formal, conscious ethic of contemporary Chicago economists is the same as that of their predecessors, the attributes of false individualism must be sought primarily in their method and normative weight regarding social policy. There are two fundamental issues with respect to methodology and individualism false. The first concerns the inapplicability of the scientific method, as such, to the social sciences. As noted above, leading early Chicago economists were in full agreement with Hayek in this regard. Second, in its application to economic problems, the extreme of rationalistic deduction or quantification as fetish must be avoided.

The dominant element of the new economics of individual choice is acceptance of the scientific method as appropriate for dealing with problems in social science. The standard of Karl Popper's positivism places formal emphasis on the wedding of formal hypotheses with quantifiable bases for disproof. But the new economics of choice is based primarily (perhaps solely) on the important, but truistic, relationship of opportunity cost, the least important of Knight's two components of economic science. This strategic element in the decision process—decision theory—has been extended from allocation of economic resources to provide the conceptual basis for an "economics of welfare, manners, language, industry, music and art [and] war . . . power [and] love."[32]

In standard texts on economic principles and price theory, opportunity costs now are commonly regarded as the *real* costs of production or consumption. While they are, indeed, real in significant metaphysical aspects of both objective and subjective reality, they are not real in the sense of inductive, statistical costs. They are not the real outlay costs that are conceptualized in the standard cost apparatus of formal equilibrium economics. Their only measurable reality is *ex post* when it is possible to measure (estimate) the actual values foregone. The quantifiable status of opportunity costs is the same as utility; both are vital, irreplaceable economic relationships, and both are nonmeasurable in positivistic terms.

Thus, the new economics of choice, nominally based on positivistic scientific method, is subject to the Hayekian label of scientism. In arrogating the hedonistic calculus of rational marginal producer and consumer equilibrium as a sufficient basis for analysis of all human behavior (the new economics of choice provides no links to other social, physical, or psychological elements in human choice), the new economics seems liable to the charge that "before it has considered its subject, [it] claims to know what is the most appropriate way of investigating it."[33] Deduction dominates; understandably, there is no serious attempt at quantification, at balanced application of scientific method.

This critical line applies as well to the economics of human capital, as it has evolved with leading Chicago economists, as an extension of individual maximizing behavior. On the pattern initiated by Gary S. Becker,[34] the genesis and valuation of human capital rests primarily—and solely, in analytical terms—on decisions or choices that individuals make concerning investment in themselves. Such decisions are assumed to be based primarily (solely) on individual anticipations and valuations concerning the relationship between such investment and future earnings. This approach to human capital has expanded into an economics of procreation and valuation of children (and related individual and social decision making, overlapping the general economics of choice).[35] The overall approach has culminated in Becker's presentation of "A Theory of Social Interactions," which "incorporates a general treatment of interactions into the modern theory of consumer demand."[36]

The fundamental question in the present context is whether or not such a theory of social interactions embodies the substance of social or true individualism; whether, in Hayek's words, it is a substantive "theory of society." Such an evaluation cannot be attempted here. The nature of the problem is seen in Harvey Leibenstein's observation that "the analogy of children as durable goods strains reality. Nevertheless, in the last decade a group of economists (Becker, Mincer, Willis, etc.) have used this analogy."[37] In his introduction to a symposium, "New Approaches to Fertility," Theodore W. Schultz anticipated that "many sensitive, thoughtful people will be offended by these studies of fertility because they may see them as debasing family and motherhood"; his assessment was based on similar earlier objections to applying the human capital concept to education.[38] These considerations are relevant to the issue of the humanist or non- or antihumanist substance of the particular method as well as this new Chicago economics. More directly relevant in the immediate context is whether or not the "new school" fulfills its methodological promise of yielding socially relevant, testable, refutable hypotheses.[39]

The opposite extreme, the exaggeration of quantification (in contrast to deduction) in the general area of contemporary individualistic economics, is seen in the development of the "new" economic history. Applying the positivist criteria and base of scientific method, the cliometrician selects his problems on the basis of availablity (or conceivable availability) of hard data. Historical interpretation is based on application of quantitative analysis to such data. The theoretical-conceptual base, when used, is that of orthodox micro or macro equilibrium theory. Hence, the conclusions often are severely vitiated by abstract, even metaphysical, elements of the theory. The possibility of a general association of this history with false individualism is seen in the critical response of Paul David and Peter Temin to *Time on the Cross: The Economics of American Negro Slavery,* by William Fogel and Stanley L. Engerman. The latter authors assume that they have separated economics and morality. Pointing out that the base of Pareto optimality is not ethically neutral, David and Temin conclude that the analysis is seriously deficient in its combination of orthodox welfare theory with quantitative data, thus providing a guide for "making coherent statements about the welfare efficiency of slavery from the standpoint of everyone but the slaves."[40] Clearly this work, and inferentially this method, is not based on, nor is it contributory to, a theory of society, to an economics of true individualism. The historical dimensions of such a theory were indicated by Nef in 1940 in viewing the demise of liberalism in the interwar period: "If the industrial historian is to help in guiding men into the ways of truth, justice, reason and virtue, he should consider industrial history in relation to the whole of history, including the history of thought and of the arts."[41] The "old" economic history developed by Nef, Chester W. Wright, and their contemporaries and students was seriously quantitative, but not to the exclusion of social, humanist perspective and content.

### *Normative Effects of the Contemporary Chicago School*

The major effects and social implications of contemporary Chicago-led economics are to displace an economics of ethics with efficiency, to dissociate economics from the process of historical and social change, and, most important, to lend implicit support to the authoritarian tendencies of advanced industrial capitalism. All of these elements stem from the base of rationality elevated to the overriding consideration—both the means and the end—in analysis and judgment of human behavior. The substitution of allocational efficiency for ethically based social welfare criteria is the strategic factor in the recent history of welfare economics. Positivist methodology rules out welfare analytics, given the latter's functional association with ethics.

The new individualist economics presents itself as humanistic in viewing choices of the individual—the consumer, the individual producer (worker, manager, saver, investor), and the family as an economic unit—as the strategic analytical factor. The business firm is not considered as an economic unit.[42] If this new economics is successful, the theory of the firm will become a peripheral element of micro analytics. The remaining vestiges of direct contact with normative, welfare issues—with the social performance of the private market, or capitalism as a system—will disappear from orthodox theory. Normative analysis of consumer welfare (sovereignty) and monopoly performance (consumer exploitation) will be relegated completely to the outer or underworld of institutional economics. With all its limitations, the welfare paradigm presented by the formal model of pure competition and pure monopoly provided a direct basis for judgment concerning the performance of private capitalism.[43] Given the limitations of Pareto optima, the new economics of rational choice provides no comparable welfare base.[44] In its support of the demise of market analytics it provides indirect support of existing monopoly market structures.

Contemporary individualism false—hyperindividualism—is unhistorical in that it assumes that market maximizing behavior, hence, the private market system, is the only thinkable institutional base. This is seen, for example, in Douglass C. North's reinterpretation of Western European history on the assumed dominance of market decisions.[45] The new economic history may be regarded as unhistorical insofar as it does not deal with the problem of explaining historical process or change, of involvement with historical dynamics as identified by Joseph A. Schumpeter.[46] In this regard, contemporary false individualism is the opposite of that identified by Hayek, wherein the historical process was characterized and dominant.

Contemporary hyperindividualist economics embodies a double paradox. Its ultrarationalist methodology and its retreat from public policy combine to encourage a result that is "no part of their original intent." Efficiency—rationality—carried to its logical extreme (as emphasized by Hayek) becomes antithetical to maximum freedom of choice. It is natural for an engineering perspective to come to dominate an economics of efficiency. The engineer, the efficiency economist, is concerned only with means to an externally given end. Necessarily, in the absence of analysis of or concern with larger ends, efficient means may be transformed into efficiency as a sufficient end.

Individual decision making, or free choice, tends to be reduced to a minimum when efficiency (as both means and end) is applied in the context of hierarchical organization. With contemporary technology, efficiency depends upon technicians, specialists overseen by the one, the supertechnician, the chairman, chief of staff, or coach, the leader who, having sole possession of the big picture, does the thinking and choosing. The players do not call the plays.[47] Ultrarationalism and hyperindividualism are manifested in the faith in competitive markets to accomplish the desired end of commutative justice (equivalence of exchange), the fear of bigness in government (and worker organization), and the related ignoring of the issues of distributive justice (appropriate degree of inequality) and bigness in business. Concerning the distribution of income and wealth in relation to a viable free market system, Viner observed in 1960: "No modern people will have zeal for the free market unless it operates in a setting of 'distributive justice' with which they are tolerably content. . . . [A free market position which ignores distributive justice is] glaringly unrealistic [regarding] its chances of political success and highly questionable also with respect to more exalted criteria of merit."[48]

In abstracting from these relationships, contemporary rationalist, individualist economics contributes to ignoring the implications of integration of government with private corporate planning—the conjunctive power of state capitalism. By abstention it provides an apologetic for monopolistic capitalism, for acceptance of the existing distribution of wealth.

### *Social Implications of Individualism False and Manifestations of Individualism True*

The strategic relationship is the association between false individualism and authoritarian polity. Just as the ultrarationalist tradition identified by Hayek contributed to authoritarian socialism, the similar pattern, stemming from hyperindividualism, is supportive of authoritarian capitalism, of fascism. Two points will be discussed in this regard: (1) the 1930s premonitions of Simons, Eduard Heimann, and others are linked to the contemporary reality of burgeoning corporate capitalism, and (2) the various ongoing manifestations of true individualism are noted briefly.

Humanistic social individualism evolved during the nineteenth century as a secular substitute for the waning Judeo-Christian ethic. True individualism, as in Hayek's view, provides a basis for human organization and action, a political philosophy, "a set of principles which, indeed, is implicit in most of Western or Christian political tradition."[49] In the large and with increasing intensity, the interrelated materialist ethics of science and efficiency have threatened to displace humanistic individualism during the twentieth century.

The early Chicago economists, proponents of true individualism, recognized the unavoidable reality of a monopoly sector in the private industrial economy. They believed that there were a limited number of industries in which scale economies might warrant monopoly structure; hence, the competitive private market would maintain the economic base for liberal society. Nonetheless, they clearly recognized the authoritarian potential of monopoly or state capitalism. In 1936 Simons observed: "Private monopolies with the blessing of regulation and the support of law are malignant cancers in the system" and lead inevitably toward fascism.[50] (Public ownership of natural monopoly did not carry this portent.) Friedman noted in 1962 that capitalism was a necessary but not sufficient condition for liberal polity.

When such recognition of the authoritarian potential of monopoly capitalism is joined with Heimann's judgment concerning the political implications of a dominant, ethically neutral positivism in social science, we have the bases for considering the paradoxical authoritarian potential of contemporary false individualism. Heimann stated: "Once the [classical economist's] belief in Nature's harmony and wisdom had been given up . . . the adoption of the same attitude of detachment connoted something else—indifference and irresponsibility. Once social science contented itself with merely describing class cleavages, depression and potential civil war, and refused in the name of objectivity to teach wisdom and provide leadership, people were plunged into the despair from which there seems to be no way out but forcible integration by Fascism . . . the counsel of despair to which people turn when democracy loses its socially integrating power."[51]

Hayek envisaged the rise of an authoritarian state whenever it became dominated by pursuit of any given end, rather than being limited with respect to particular kinds of action. "As Lord Acton pointed out long ago: 'Whenever a single definite object is made the supreme end of the State, be it the advantage of a class, the safety or the power of the country, the greatest happiness of the greatest number or the support of any speculative idea, the State becomes for the time inevitably absolute.' "[52]

The normative base of contemporary hyperindividualist economists is minimal government. Preservation of existing private property relationships, the private market, is the penultimate end of ends (the means to the final end of individual freedom). Private property is equated simplistically with minimal government. The strategic, related issues, such as structure of property holding and locus and uses of power, are ignored.

The critical contemporary dimension of interrelated economic and political power concerns oligopolistic and related conglomerate and multinational corporate developments rather than "classical" natural monopoly. It is within these contemporary structures that the issue of the social role and significance of private market power appears. The issue of social responsibility of the private corporation is strategic in judging contemporary economists (Chicago and others) as representing true or false individualism. Friedman, recognizing the liberal necessity of separating economic and political power, avers that "acceptance by corporate officials of a social responsibility other than to make as much money for their stockholders as possible . . . is a fundamentally subversive doctrine."[53]

The opposing position, the case for corporate responsibility, is represented by Henry C. Wallich. He argues that such responsibility promises great rewards for everyone: business executives, stockholders, and the public. "The job of improving the world . . . will get done at minimum cost instead of with maximum bureaucracy. The ultimate menace of Big Brother in Washington will be pushed back. . . . [This will mean] a genuine change in the system."[54] Lacking specification, the new system remains a utopian vision. The social reality is the symbiotic relationship between the large private corporate sector and government. There are strong indications that operational corporate social responsibility reflects a mix of voluntary action and compulsion (from both government and other private power centers).[55] Friedman, in accepting the conceptual possibility of liberal socialism, enjoined advocates thereof to consider seriously the real bureaucratic hazards that would confront such an institutional set.[56] This injunction to serious analysis of the "freedom problem" applies as well to contemporary hyperindividualists such as Wallich, who envisage a viable liberal free market resolution of the problems posed by advanced urban-industrial technology. Is their position more than an argument for "the advantage of a class"?

Based on faith in the beneficient liberalizing force of pluralism,[57] the prestige of the academy is placed in support of the existing public-private power mix, the state capitalism that has been characterized as Tory socialism. The "benevolent feudalism" that W. J. Ghent envisaged in the early 1900s as "the next step" is accepted as the operational base of advanced, industrial capitalist society. This is perhaps the logical end of the Manchester apologetic perversion of classical laissez-faire. It is the opposite of the policy perspective of the social individualism of Chicago economists of the early 1930s.

The argument that a cause-and-effect relationship existed between socialism and authoritarianism was the primary normative inference that Hayek drew from his association of ultrarationalism and historical determinism with individualism false. His concession that individual socialists such as H. D. Dickinson could be genuinely libertarian was overridden by conviction that liberalism required the voluntarism possible only in a spontaneous, free market setting.[58]

The world history of the past quarter of a century is inconclusive concerning the libertarian-authoritarian associations with capitalism and socialism. In the present context, however, it is important to note that there is a significant sense in which a meaningful contemporary manifestation of true individualism is found in the ongoing tradition of humanistic, liberal socialism.[59]

This position is based on the substance of the ethic, method, and policy of liberal socialism. The ethic is equality of opportunity, that is, a significant reduction in the inequality of distribution of income and wealth under industrial capitalism. As evidenced by its most notable proponents (for example, R. H. Tawney, Maurice Dobb, H. D. Dickenson, and Paul M. Sweezy), it does not displace ethics with efficiency. In 1912 Tawney noted the interrelationship between capitalistic efficiency and its authoritarian propensity: "The case for the existing industrial system is the case for autocratic government all the world over. It is efficient: it saves trouble: responsibility is placed in a few hands: there is no nonsense about consulting committees."[60] Tawney's full, 1931 statement of the problems of equality and equality of opportunity has not been surpassed.[61]

Socialist-Marxist analytical literature in the past fifty years clearly indicates an eclectic, nonpositivist methodology.[62] The historical orientation, the second pillar of Hayek's antisocialist argument, was denied by Marx during his lifetime (it was perhaps the major basis for Marx's declaration that he was not a Marxist), has been effectively rejoined in recent translations of Marx's historical work,[63] and is rejected by leading contemporary Marxian scholars. Flexible alternative use of scientific method, orthodox micro- and macro- ("capitalist") economics as well as the historical dialectic are characteristic of leading socialist economists such as Oskar Lange, Dobb, and Sweezy.

The transitional sequence between liberal capitalism and liberal socialism, in terms of their common ethical base, is epitomized in J. S. Mill, whose last major (incomplete) work was a sympathetic discussion of socialism. It is extended in the essentially Fabian, long-run perspective of J. M. Keynes, wherein the economic possibilities that he foresaw for his grandchildren included a significant reduction in the inequalities of nineteenth-century England and a Millsian, humanistic life-style that supervened the value base of materialism and efficiency. This is the social tradition of the early Chicago School.

True individualism envisages—defines—civilization as the development of human beings to their full individual potential. This means the actualization of the long-term liberal goal of equality of opportunity. Individualism false runs against these goals in its reinforcement of the elitist, statist potential of either capitalist or socialist economy.

## *Notes*

1. F.A. Hayek, *Individualism and Economic Order* (Chicago: University of Chicago Press, 1948), p. 4. It was most directly extended by Alexis de Tocqueville and Lord Acton.
2. Ibid.
3. The usage here is the same as H. Laurence Miller, Jr., "On the 'Chicago School of Economics,'" *Journal of Political Economy* 70 (February 1962): 64. Also see Henry W. Spiegel, *The Growth of Economic Thought* (Englewood Cliffs, N.J.: Prentice-Hall, Inc., 1971), pp. 641–42.
4. Ibid., p. 6.
5. Simons's statement was published originally in the University of Chi-

cago Public Policy Pamphlet series (No. 15). It is reprinted in Henry C. Simons, *Economic Policy for a Free Society* (Chicago: University of Chicago Press, 1948), pp. 40–77.

6. It is impossible in analyzing ideas to separate them from the individuals who develop and use them. Thus, it is difficult to separate the treatment of ideas from criticism of the individuals involved. The perspective here is the same as that expressed by both Adam Smith and Karl Marx in this context. In criticizing mercantilist thought and policy, Smith stated: "I mean not, however, by any thing which I have here said, to throw any odious imputation upon the general character of the servants of the East India Company, and much less upon that of any particular persons." *The Wealth of Nations* (New York: Modern Library, 1937), p. 605. Similarly, in the preface to *Capital*, vol. 1 (New York: Modern Library, Charles H. Kerr & Co., 1906), Marx stated: "Individuals are dealt with only in so far as they are the personifications of economic categories" (p. 15). The analysis concerns ideas—their sources and consequences—not individuals.
7. Simons, *Economic Policy*, p. 1. The vital interrelationship between individual freedom, effective equality, and power was recognized clearly by Simons. "Freedom and equality convey, among libertarians, similar and complementary meanings. Both imply responsible individuals or families, the rule of law, and great dispersion of power. And, equality imposed from above, or by remote authority, is a negation not only of freedom but of equality as well . . . . but the ultimate liberty obviously is that of men equal in power" (ibid., p. 7).
8. "The [liberal] intellectual tradition is intended to be that of Adam Smith, Herrmann, Thunen, Mill, Menger, Bretano, Sidgwick, Marshall, Fetter, and Knight, and of Locke, Hume, Bentham, Humboldt, Tocqueville, Burckhardt, Acton, Dicey, Barker, and Hayek." Simons, *Economic Policy*, p. 1.
9. Hayek's association of Jeremy Bentham and J.S. Mill with false individualism—as nonlibertarian—does not seem supportable. See, for example, Warren J. Samuels, *The Classical Theory of Economic Policy* (New York: World Publishing Company, 1966), pp. 220–22; and Jacob Viner, "Bentham and J.S. Mill: the Utilitarian Background," *American Economic Review* 39 (March 1949): 360–82.
10. W. Stark, *The Ideal Foundations of Economic Thought* (New York: Oxford University Press, 1944), p. viii.
11. Minimization of government coercion requires, first, that individual action and nonaction that will contribute to the general welfare be based on general rules, for example, that the individual "should have a clearly delimited area of responsibility." Second, there must be correspondence between the immediate benefits of an individual's actions and the remote and "to him unknown effects of his action." Hayek, *Individualism*, p. 17.
12. Lawrence Nabers, "The Positive and Genetic Approaches," in *The Structure of Economic Science*, edited by Sherman Roy Krupp (Englewood Cliffs, N.J.: Prentice-Hall, Inc., 1966), pp. 70–71. See notes 13 and 19 for brief interpretative comment on the evolution of logical positivism.

13. Jevons appears to be the first to argue effectively that the appropriate role of induction is in the *testing* or confirmation rather than the formulation of hypotheses. Laurens Laudan, "Theories of Scientific Method from Plato to Mach: A Bibliographical Review," in *History of Science,* vol. 7, edited by A.C. Crombie and M.A. Hoskin (Cambridge: W. Heffer & Sons, 1968), p. 35. Still, positivism became established on the Continent at an earlier date than in Great Britain.
14. Friedrich von Wieser, *Natural Value* (New York: G.E. Stechert & Co., 1930), p. 62.
15. Ibid., p. 225.
16. Simons, *Economic Policy,* p. 4. Also see Hayek, *Individualism,* pp. 16, 30; and Milton Friedman, *Capitalism and Freedom* (Chicago: University of Chicago Press, 1962), p. 195.
17. Simons, *Economic Policy,* p. 6.
18. For example, "Mill achieved a delicate balance between the inductive-deductive extremes in economic method [in his blending of the methods of Ricardo and Comte]." Robert B. Ekelund, Jr., and Robert F. Hebert, *A History of Economic Theory and Method* (New York: McGraw-Hill, 1975), p. 117. Here is an additional ground for associating Mill with true individualism. See note 9.
19. Thus, Hayek distinguishes between the method of science, "the general spirit of disinterested inquiry," which he unreservedly supports, and "scientism" or "scientistic" prejudice, which leads to the perversion of science. F. A. Hayek, *The Counter-Revolution of Science* (Glencoe, Ill.: The Free Press, 1952), p. 15. The subtitle, "Studies in the Abuse of Reason," provides the key to his argument concerning false individualism. In terms of method this abuse is most significant in the escalation of Comte's case for induction into a fetish of quantification. "The blind transfer of the striving for quantitative measurements to a field in which the specific conditions are not present which give it its basic importance in the nature sciences . . . is probably responsible for the worst aberrations and absurdities produced by scientism in the social sciences" (p. 51).

   The fundamental underlying methodological issue concerns the epistemological "life-cycle" of positivism in relation to valid methodology for social science. Positivism beginning with Comte and culminating in logical positivism of the Vienna circle (which evolved from Ernst Mach through Moritz Schlick, August Carnap, and others, strongly influenced by Ludwig Wittgenstein and Bertrand Russell), presents an evolutionary transition characteristic of major concepts and schools in economics. See Warren S. Gramm, "Natural Selection in Economic Thought: Ideology, Power, and the Keynesian Counterrevolution," *Journal of Economic Issues* 7 (March 1973): 3.

   Logical positivism was a critical, creative response to exaggerated use of deduction and a "Continental metaphysics [that] had become intolerably inbred and pompously verbose." Michael Scriven, "Logical Positivism and the Behavioral Sciences," in *The Legacy of Logical Positivism,* edited by Peter Achinstein and Stephen F. Barker (Baltimore: Johns Hopkins Press, 1969), p. 195. Its creative role is seen in its stimulation of development of computer science (John von Neumann), theoretical linguistics (Noam Chomsky), and the possibility "of a new science of human understanding [related to] the logical structure of our concepts and language uses." Stephen E. Toulmin, "From Logical Analysis to Conceptual History," in ibid., p. 53.

However, Hayek's critical position is reflected in the articles of Scriven and Toulmin, whose sympathetic perspectives on positivism are qualifications of their basic criticism. On the fundamental issue—the importance of the relationships that are inadmissable to the extreme positivist—Toulmin concludes: "Aesthetic appraisals or metaphysical declarations ... were regretfully (or cheerfully) written off as merely leading one into a linguistic morass or an intellectual junk pile.... What was not formalizable could no longer be deemed significant. The triumph of technique was seemingly complete" (ibid., p. 46). Also see Herbert Feigl, "The Origin and Spirit of Logical Positivism," in Achinstein and Barker, eds., *Legacy*, pp. 3–24; and Ben B. Seligman, "The Impact of Positivism on Economic Thought," *History of Political Economy* 1 (Fall 1969): 256–78.

20. Viner's position is well illustrated in his comment on critics of "Bentham's felicific calculus [as] merely one more manifestation of the inferiority complex which practitioners of the social 'sciences' had in the eighteenth century, and have reacquired in the twentieth, towards mathematics, towards the exact sciences, and towards quantification as one of the higher virtues. Since ... we now all accept without protest the derivation of measured 'propensities' from correlations between psychologically and otherwise promiscuous statistical aggregates compiled catch-as-can on anything up to a global scale, our readiness to laugh at Bentham's . . . gestures in this direction excites my propensity for amazement." "Bentham and J.S. Mill," p. 368.

Nef finds the essence of capitalism to be in "production for the sake of quantity, in the interest of private profits." *The Conquest of the Material World* (Chicago: University of Chicago Press, 1964), p. 212. He regards the rise and dominant role of quantification (measurement) as the strategic element in the rise of industrial civilization. But this creative aspect of the past is not the viable base for a humane future: It "has transformed the material conditions of life during the past century and a half and especially during the past fifty years. [Now] with figures collected by governments and private business enterprises dancing upwards before our eyes, sometimes in geometrical progression, we are almost hypnotized into considering our public and private problems in terms of quantitative hopes and nightmares" (p. 217). In direct contrast, "the future of industrial civilization ... [lies with] renewal of the search for the perfection of the human personality." *Cultural Foundations of Industrial Civilization* (Hamden, Conn.: Archon Books, 1974 [1958]), p. 154. The humane future lies with emphasis on quality of life rather than quantitative surrogates for human well-being.

21. Frank H. Knight, "The Limitation of Scientific Method in Economics," in *The Trend of Economics*, edited by R.G. Tugwell (New York: Alfred A. Knopf, 1924), pp. 264–65.

22. Frank H. Knight, *On the History and Method of Economics* (Chicago: University of Chicago Press, 1956), pp. 145–46. The impossibility of

briefly summarizing Knight's thinking in this area is spelled out in R.A. Gonce, "Frank H. Knight on Social Control and the Scope and Method of Economics," *Southern Economic Journal* 38 (April 1972): 547–48. For the interrelationships and differences between Knight and J.N. Keynes, on the one hand, and the Robbins-Friedman position on method, on the other, see Gerald Garb, "The Problem of Causality in Economics," *Kyklos* 27 (Facs. 4, 1964): 594–609.

23. Knight, "Limitation of Scientific Method," pp. 265–66.
24. Frank H. Knight, "Methodology in Economics," *Southern Economic Journal* 27 (April 1961): 282.
25. Samuels, *Classical Theory*, pp. 14–18.
26. J. Ronnie Davis, *The New Economics and the Old Economists* (Ames: Iowa State University Press, 1971), pp. 163–65.
27. Ibid., p. 16. The philosophical base for pragmatic policy was expressed by Paul H. Douglas: "[The] stirring flow of events during periods of upheaval and social change compel [economists] to turn their attention to the problems of practical adjustment" (ibid., p. 48).
28. Simons, *Economic Policy*, p. 57.
29. Friedman, *Capitalism and Freedom*, pp. 28–29, pp. 121–23 (monopoly), and pp. 163–65 (taxation).
30. For example, Gary S. Becker, Jacob Mincer, and Robert A. Mundell as well as Chicago-associated analysts such as Gordon Tullock.
31. See, for example, Seligman, *Impact of Positivism*, p. 258; and p. 766 concerning Hayek. The relationships are illustrated in Nazism, which presented the separate, compartmentalized extremes of ultrarationalism (hyperefficiency) and antirationalism (in emotional, metaphysical philosophy and the means of social control).
32. Robert A. Mundell, *Man and Economics, The Science of Choice* (New York: McGraw-Hill, 1968), Preface.
33. Hayek, *Counter-Revolution*, p. 16. The analytical status of rationality is a strategic issue. To qualify as positivist analysis the generality of human rationality in relation to individual maximizing behavior must be a "conceivably falsifiable" truth. Yet, such status has not been established beyond a reasonable doubt. For example, Martin Hollis and Edward Nell believe that "the statement that there are rational economic men . . . is a synthetic *a priori* truth; but no positivist will allow this for a moment. So is it a hypothesis, a theorem or an assumption?" *Rational Economic Man* (London: Cambridge University Press, 1975), p. 55. Also see note 42, below.
34. See *Human Capital* (New York: Columbia University Press, 1964).
35. See, for example, the two supplementary issues of the *Journal of Political Economy*: "New Economic Approaches to Fertility," 81, Pt. II (March/April 1973), and "Marriage, Family Human Capital and Fertility," 82, Part II (March/April 1974), edited by Theodore W. Schultz.
35. Gary S. Becker, "A Theory of Social Interactions," *Journal of Political Economy* 82 (November-December 1974): 1066.
37. Harvey Leibenstein, "The Economic Theory of Fertility Decline," *Quarterly Journal of Economics* 89 (February 1975): 1.
38. "New Economic Approaches to Fertility," p. S3.
39. With respect to the problem of quantification (the "serious data limita-

tions and ... econometric complexities that remain unsolved"), Schultz observes that "better data, however, for these purposes can undoubtedly be 'made.' " Skeptics will wonder about the scientific ethic of manufacturing data to meet the requirements of method. See note 19, above, for Viner's comment in this regard. Finally, the new economics of human capital seems nonconversant with the implications of Abner Shimony's observation that "the mind-body problem is a vast desert of ignorance in the sciences of psychology and physiology." *The Nature and Function of Scientific Theories,* edited by Robert G. Colodny (London: Henry M. Snyder & Co., University of Pittsburg Press, 1970), p. xiv.

40. Paul David and Peter Temin, "Slavery: The Progressive Institution?" *Journal of Economic History* 34 (September 1974): 783.
41. John U. Nef, *Industry and Government in France and England 1540–1640* (Ithaca, N.Y.: Great Seal Books, 1957), p. vi.
42. See, for example, Erik G. Furubotn and Svetozar Pejovich, "Property Rights and Economic Theory: A Survey of Recent Literature," *Journal of Economic Literature* 10 (December 1972): 1138. In very general terms this may be related to the proposition that "the gap between the theory of the firm and reality is enormous" (Oscar Morgenstern, "Thirteen Critical Points in Contemporary Economic Theory," *Journal of Economic Literature* 10 [December 1972]: 1183) and, somewhat more specifically, to successive qualifications of the fundamental behavioral and equilibrium adjustment maxim, profit maximization by the firm. Conceptually, the assumption of profit maximization moved from an empirical relationship (Robbins) or a self-evident truth (Knight) to empirical irrelevance (Friedman). Its operational significance has been reduced in recent decades by arguments of multiple or alternative maximization by the firm (for example, sales or growth) and the theory of the second best.
43. In a formal sense the early or transitional Chicago School won the battle of monopolistic versus perfect competition. George J. Stigler concluded in 1957 that "the concept of perfect competition is being used more widely by the profession in its theoretical work than at any time in the past. The vitality of the concept is strongly spoken for by this triumph." "Perfect Competition, Historically Contemplated," *Journal of Political Economy* 65 (February 1957): 16. Now, recognition of the limits of the competitive paradigm is coming to the fore again. With respect to the earlier controversy see Edward H. Chamberlin, "The Chicago School," in *Towards a More General Theory of Value* (New York: Oxford University Press, 1957), pp. 296–306; and G.C. Archibald, "Chamberlin versus Chicago," *Review of Economic Studies* 29 (October 1961): 2–28.
44. See, for example, Mark Blaug, *Economic Theory in Retrospect,* rev. ed. (Homewood, Ill.: Richard D. Irwin, Inc., 1968), p. 609.
45. The direct connection between the new economic history and the new economics of choice and human capital is indicated in his presidential address, "Beyond the New Economic History," *Journal of Economic History* 34 (March 1974): 4.
46. Acceptance of rationality as the behavioral dominant of mankind means that institutional change is constrained to variations on the

market theme. Methodologically, this is analogous to the analytic dynamics "that links quantities pertaining to different points of theoretic time . . . and not the theory of evolutionary processes that run their courses in historic time." Joseph A. Schumpeter, *History of Economic Analysis* (New York: Oxford University Press, 1954), p. 1160. Hence, early precapitalist societies are viewed, in absolutist terms, through market glasses. This is the opposite of Alfred Marshall's relativistic position that "every age and every country has its own problems; and every change in social conditions is likely to require a new development of economic doctrines." *Principles of Economics*, 8th ed. (New York: Macmillan, 1949), p. 37. In 1928 the distinguished physicist P. W. Bridgeman observed: "It is difficult to conceive of anything more scientifically bigoted than to postulate that all possible experience conforms to the same type as that with which we are already familiar." Hayek, *Counter-Revolution*, p. 207.

The phenomenon of historical change has been explained on at least four major grounds: (1) predetermined, natural laws; (2) deliberate, rational decisions; (3) nondeliberative social relationships; and (4) mysticism or mythology. In combination, (2) and (3) present the historical relationship of balance between rational and nonrational elements of social adjustment (that is, the operational characteristic of individualism true). See Samuels's discussion of this interaction with respect to classical economic policy in *Classical Theory*, especially pp. 13 and 22–24. The first and last categories tend to overlap in their common metaphysical dimension. The new economic history does not confront the difficulties presented by these relationships—the analysis of historical change.

47. See, for example, Ike Balbus, "Politics as Sports: The Political Ascendency of the Sports Metaphor in America," *Monthly Review* 26 (March 1975): 32. This is an excellent statement of the tendency of the rationalist efficiency perspective to dominate contemporary industrial society.
48. Jacob Viner, "The Intellectual History of Laissez Faire," *Journal of Economics and Law* 3 (October 1960): 68.
49. Hayek, *Individualism*, p. 2.
50. Henry Simons, "The Requisites of Free Competition," *American Economic Review* 26, Supplement (March 1936): 74–75.
51. Eduard Heimann, *History of Economic Doctrines* (New York: Oxford University Press, 1964), pp. 111–12.
52. Hayek, *Individualism*, p. 19.
53. Friedman, *Capitalism*, p. 133.
54. Henry C. Wallich, "How Business Can Rescue Capitalism," *Fortune* 85 (March 1972): 124.
55. See James W. McKie, ed., *Social Responsibility and the Business Predicament* (New York: Brookings Institution, 1975).
56. Friedman, *Capitalism and Freedom*, pp. 18–19.
57. For a brief, critical evaluation of contemporary pluralism see Warren S. Gramm, "Industrial Capitalism and the Breakdown of the Liberal Rule of Law," *Journal of Economic Issues* 7 (December 1973): 596–97.
58. See "Socialist Calculation: The Competitive 'Solution,'" *Economics* 7

(May 1940): 130, commenting on Dickinson's *Economics of Socialism* (Freeport, N.Y.: Books for Libraries Press, 1971 [1939]). See also Friedrich A. Hayek, *The Road to Serfdom* (Chicago: University of Chicago Press, 1944). Hayek's analysis is perhaps most vulnerable in the area of historical method and interpretation in connection with Marxism, socialism, and fascism. Most significant in the present context is his judgment that the major cause of Nazism was "socialism, particularly Marxian socialism," rather than the concatenation of German nationalism, depression, and/or reaction to military defeat. Harry K. Girvetz, *The Evolution of Liberalism* (New York: Collier Books, 1963 [1950]), p. 283.

59. Contemporary representatives of true individualism range from conservatives such as columnist George F. Will to moderates (for example, Michael Harrington) and radical socialists (for example, Paul M. Sweezy). Many conservative and moderate orthodox economists would be so judged under the criteria presented in the text. Perhaps the major common ground with respect to true individualism is genuine fear of authoritarian potential of monopoly market power.
60. J. M. Winter and K. M. Joslin, eds., *R. H. Tawney's Commonplace Book* (Cambridge: the University Press, 1972), p. 26.
61. Tawney stated: "Equality of opportunity is not simply a matter of legal equality. Its existence depends, not merely on the absence of disabilities, but on the presence of abilities. It obtains in so far as, and only in so far as, each member of the community . . . possesses in fact . . . equal chances of using to the full his natural endowments." *Equality* (New York: Harcourt, Brace, 1931), p. 125.
62. Contrast, for example, the orientation with respect to analysis of human capital of the new Chicago School and contemporary Marxism presented by Samuel Bowles and Herbert Gintis in "The Problem with Human Capital Theory—A Marxian Critique," *American Economic Review* 65 (May 1975): 74–82.
63. Introducing the recent English translation of *Karl Marx's Pre-Capitalist Economic Formations* (New York: International Publishers, 1964), E. J. Hobsbawm observes that Marx's general historical analysis "does not imply any statement about specific historical periods, forces and relations of production whatever" (p. 11). This work would appear to establish that the historicist label does not apply to Marx.

# 8

# Frank H. Knight and Chicago Libertarianism

*John McKinney*

The University of Chicago is unique among U.S. universities in having produced a genuine "school" of economists. Today this school is perhaps best known for its "monetarism," what seems to most post-Keynesian economists to be an exaggerated emphasis on changes in the quantity of money as causes of inflations or depressions.[1] However, more significantly, the members are adherents in varying degrees of a social philosophy, sometimes called Chicago "neo-liberalism" or, paradoxically, "neo-conservatism." The most distinguished figure in the development of this philosophy is Frank H. Knight (1885–1972), who, through a long and influential career, wrote extensively and provocatively about the nature of free society. It is his version of the philosophy we shall examine. Knight himself usually described it as "true" or "authentic liberalism" because he claimed it represented a return to the classic liberalism of the eighteenth and early-nineteenth century, in contrast to twentieth-century liberalism, which he said had substituted "government paternalism" for true individual freedom.[2] We prefer the term *libertarianism* because it seems more adequately to indicate the distinctive feature of this philosophy: its ideal of the autonomous individual.

---

*The author is Associate Professor of Economics, C. W. Post College of Long Island University, Greenvale, Long Island, New York.*

### *Economic Exchange and the Exchange of Ideas*

The central issue in an appraisal of the libertarian philosophy is the meaning of *freedom*, a protean word, as Knight points out, a term "used as a slogan by the most diverse ethical and social philosophers. . . . Ecclesiastical authoritarianism . . . and contemporary totalitarianism . . . claim to embody the 'real freedom.' "[3]

For Knight the fundamental meaning of *freedom* is "freedom of the will." This is what he calls "metaphysical" freedom, evidently meaning by this that it is the essential condition for all truly human existence: "To live, on the human plane, is to choose."[4] Most of Knight's teaching, not only as a social philosopher, but also as an economic theorist and a methodologist of social science, takes the form of elaborations of a dichotomy between *procedure*, the creative, problem-solving activity of man as rational or moral agent, and *process*, his term for the course of events in inert nature, "persistence and change, in accordance with cause and effect, or scientific law."[5] Freedom implies *possibility*, in contrast to scientific determinism, said to be a "denial of possibility." Rational discussion and the "validity of moral distinctions" presuppose metaphysical freedom, but the practical political problem is said to center on the idea of freedom as voluntary agreement among responsible individuals. This (social) freedom is held to be the opposite not of determinism, but of coercion. The latter includes persuasion, "a species of force, based on deception, and all coercion presupposes metaphysical freedom in both parties."[6] Individual freedom is expressed in undetermined choices, while social freedom takes the form of freedom of contract. The problem of classifying acts as free or unfree is one of locating those acts which are *voluntary*, that is, expressions of individual autonomy.

For the libertarian, orthodox economic theory provides a blueprint, the model of a perfect market, for an association of individuals (or families) whose only relations are those of voluntary cooperation. Each individual enters each transaction freely in the sense that for any economic choice there are alternatives. Knight holds that the conditions of the ideal market rule out all "personal" association between the parties, for these involve power relationships, and the individual under such influence is unable to act with true autonomy. Even the term *competition* is a misnomer if the market is truly perfect, for this suggests an awareness of other participants as personalities. "To realize its ideal character, the system would have to be operated through vending machines."[7] Each individual uses his own means to achieve his own ends, the advantage of the association consisting in his ability to use other individuals as means, under the principle of mutual free consent.

Given these logically ideal conditions, the perfect market achieves efficiency in the use of resources, as economists have demonstrated in their models of static general equilibrium.[8] Under such equilibrium conditions, it is impossible to make anyone better off without making someone else worse off. Reasoning along such lines, some of the older economists, particularly those under the influence of the utilitarian philosophy, argued the merits of free enterprise on the grounds of a "doctrine of maximum satisfaction." Insofar as actual markets approximate to the perfect market, they tend to provide the greatest possible aggregate of consumer welfare, under the given conditions of consumer taste and the distribution of income. The libertarian moralist rejects this line of argument. The utilitarian treats freedom as a means to an end, while the libertarian regards it as an end in itself.[9] If one could show that a centrally planned socialist economy could operate more efficiently to produce consumer satisfaction than could any conceivable free enterprise system, the utilitarian would be logically bound to prefer it, but the libertarian would remain unmoved. His commitment is not to "maximum satisfaction" but to "maximum freedom." The perfect market is "ideal" because it is the "embodiment of complete freedom."[10] It makes it possible for everyone to be "free as a Crusoe is free."[11]

However, it is impossible to organize a society exclusively on the principle of freedom, as exemplified in the free market. To begin with, there are the problems Knight calls "mechanical." These have to do with the practical feasibility—as opposed to the ethical desirability—of using the blueprint of the perfect market as the guide to social organization. Thus, if monopoly power is widespread, Knight believes the system will degenerate into chaos. In general, like most of the Chicago School, Knight holds that the problem of monopoly is exaggerated by critics of the enterprise system. "I still think Adam Smith is largely right; if the government would keep its hands clean of encouraging monopolies, much of the problem would largely take care of itself."[12] But he was also capable of writing of the need for "extensive legislation to prevent intolerable divergencies from free market conditions."[13]

Then there are externalities, activities whose costs and benefits must be reckoned collectively rather than individually. "At a minimum, rules must be made and enforced by some agency representing the whole market . . . and the policing must be paid for on a principle other than direct payment for service rendered."[14]

Third, there is the problem of the business cycle, which Knight regards as an inevitable accompaniment of free economic relations. Its control requires a "scientific monetary system," politically administered.[15]

It seems a fair account of Knight's position to say that he does not regard such "mechanical" problems as formidable obstacles to a system based predominately on free economic relations. Although it can be argued that this is too sanguine a view, we shall leave it unchallenged for the present discussion and turn to the problems that were of more concern to him, the ones he called "ethical."

The perfect market not only achieves efficiency in the use of resources, but also realizes one kind of justice in the distribution of the product, what Knight calls "commutative" justice, the exchange of equal values, so that each party takes out, in value equivalent, what he puts in ("What a man soweth, that shall he also reap."[16]). But the market does not guarantee the more fundamental "distributive" justice. For what a man puts in, and so takes out, depends upon the economic capacity at his disposal—his personal abilities and his ownership of property—and this is a legacy of the past. It depends upon the laws and institutions of the society, and if these are not just, there is no reason to think that the legacy is just. Although the market provides for "right relations between given individuals," this fails to dispose of the ethical problem because the individual with his capacities is not in fact "given," but created by the system. Therefore, it is an error when some laissez-faire advocates use "abstract economics" as an "absolute ethics." "The market is an agency of cooperation between . . . given units, it is no agency for improving tastes . . . it will not redistribute capacity, and hence product, to accord with any norm of ideal justice."[17]

Evidently such considerations as these led Knight originally (1921) to condemn attempts to justify the enterprise system on grounds that it provides freedom. It was held that there was "no more egregious error in the whole science of politics" than "the confusion between 'freedom' and 'freedom of contract,' "[18] or "the error of confounding freedom with free competition."[19] However, in his middle forties, Knight became convinced of the need to separate and treat as "distinct factors in conduct" freedom and the power that comes from the possession of economic capacity. The libertarian ethic emerges as a consequence of effecting this rigid separation of freedom to choose from power to act. "Freedom as a right presupposes, takes as given, both the means of power possessed by the individual and what he may want to do."[20] The moral quality of rational action is associated exclusively with the act of choice, a private, subjective event. It is the internal decision and not the external action that concerns the libertarian moralist. He can speak of a society with perfect "actual" freedom and yet with virtually no "effective" freedom.[21] This would be the case if, under a regime of laissez-faire, most economic power were centralized in the hands of a few ruthless individuals.[22]

So even in the most ideally functioning market system, there remain conflicts of interest which imply problems about rights and ideal ends. Free society must find ways to resolve such conflicts. The methods it uses constitute what Knight calls *social procedure,* discussion among free men concerning the making and changing of laws.[23] So long as laws are made and changed on the basis of voluntary agreement—there is no *enforced* law—the society remains as free as that of the perfect market. The ideal is "antinomian" (that is, lawless) anarchism, which, for the libertarian, is an extension of the principle of free choice, as exhibited in the perfect market, to discussion and debate about the law. Democracy is "government by discussion," and "discussion is inherently free—in fact it may be viewed as a form of exchange, and rather the most fundamental form."[24] Economic exchange and the "exchange of ideas" in free discussion "make up the ideal type which defines free association."[25]

A free society allows full participation of its members in the activities of making and changing the law. Since absolute unanimity usually does not exist concerning a proposed change, complete freedom includes the right to leave the group at will and form other groups. The ability to give up one's citizenship in a modern state and join another state or form a new one is sharply limited; therefore, all states must employ coercion in forcing some citizens to obey the law. Knight defines a group as *political* to the extent that it does not allow this freedom to give up one's membership in it.[26] Thus the political is, in this view, inherently *coercive.*

For the libertarian moralist, economic freedom is the basic freedom in two senses. First, Knight contends that it is essential to the existence of all other forms of freedom—religious, political, intellectual—"as historical fact and general considerations join in proving."[27] But, more fundamentally, economic choice gives the form of all free conduct. Individual freedom is expressed in voluntary choices. The ideal type of free association is the contract entered into by bargaining individuals. "It is unfortunate . . . that the term laissez-faire became distinctively attached to economic freedom. It means simply 'freedom' and was supposed to apply as a matter of course to all individual and social life."[28]

With economic action generalized to include the "exchange of ideas," we can say that the libertarian ethic is based on a distinction between free economic action and coercive political power. The problem of elevating the moral quality of social life is one of increasing the scope of mutual consent and restricting that of coercion, which is equivalent to saying we should seek to divide the space in which social life takes place so there is a maximum economic and a minimum political sector.

With some supplementation, we accept Knight's view of democracy as "government by discussion," but we shall argue against the attempt to assimilate social procedure to economic bargaining. More generally, we hope to show that Knight was correct in his earlier judgment, that it is an error to confound social freedom with the free competition of the market.

### *The Community of Inquirers*

The key concepts in Knight's social philosophy are *pluralism* and the related idea of *emergent evolution.* "The most important fact about man is that he is at the same time a number of kinds of being, which are not only different but in theory mutually incompatible. He seems to be the product of a 'emergent evolution,' in which many new traits have been successively imposed on an extending series without, in the main, eliminating the earlier."[29] The pluralist is one who believes in coexisting "realities," each with its own kind of truth, which may, confusingly, contradict the truths of other orders of reality. Between the various orders, "philosophy has so far built no adequate bridges, and does not seem in the way of doing so."[30]

Pluralism is related to a theory of knowledge which makes truth "practical" or "pragmatic" in that the particular order of reality to which one refers depends upon one's purpose. "Reality is not what is logical, but what it suits our purposes to treat as real."[31] Knight's pluralism is the philosophical basis of his *antiscientism,* his urging that the methods of science be confined to the order of reality to which in his view they are appropriate. He thus seeks to establish the credibility of the quite different kinds of truth expressed in aesthetic, moral, and "common sense" judgments, "to make the objects of scientific observation the only reality is merely to say dogmatically that scientific curiosity shall be the only legitimate interest in life."[32]

The pluralist not only separates the ethical from the physical order, but also insists on an ethical pluralism, which means that ethical values can coexist in a state of contradiction. We already have noted the conflict between freedom and justice. This conflict is held to be irreconcilable, simply to be accepted as a tragic human dilemma.

According to Knight, there are two different kinds of intelligence.[33] There are what he calls *instrumental rationality,* the ability to adapt means to *given* ends, and *critical judgment* in deliberating about ends.

Instrumental rationality is held to be "inherently individualistic" and even presocial.[34] "Human nature seems to have been produced by the subsequent socialization . . . of a species which first achieved a considerable degree of individual instrumental intelligence."[35]

The individual whose total conduct can be accounted for in accordance with the principles of instrumental rationality is Crusoe, the economic man, "a concept methodologically analogous to the frictionless machine of theoretical mechanics and essential to analysis in the same way."[36] The economic man is exclusively concerned with the most efficient use of means for the realization of given ends. Knight claims that every reasonable individual has intuitive insight into the nature of instrumental rationality, and it is this intuitive knowledge that furnishes the "axioms of economics." Crusoe's activity is a form of procedure, it is problem solving activity which, according to Knight, is in principle unpredictable and, therefore, beyond science. For if the solution to a problem can be predicted in advance, there is no problem. The economist meets this difficulty by abstraction from uncertainty and error and, therefore, from effort. In effect, he turns procedure into process and makes one kind of purposive activity the subject matter of science. Thus we have one of Knight's characteristic paradoxes: "At the limit, instrumental rationality runs over into the very different category of mechanistic cause and effect. It would be irrational to be . . . perfectly rational. . . . Analysis must simply ignore this element of self-contradiction."[37]

Instrumental rationality is found in its highest development in modern science. So Crusoe is not only the economic man, but also the "scientific man," the "individualist individual." He "knows . . . only useful facts . . . and would solve problems only in the instrumental sense. He would be a 'pragmatist' in the crudest meaning . . . our hypothetical Crusoe would have no interest in truth as a value, no intellectual curiosity . . . and, of course, no moral interests or values."[38]

Knight's antiscientist position can be expressed in the assertion that social and moral problems, in free society, are not "instrumental" in this sense; they are not problems in adapting means to "given" nonproblematic ends. While instrumental rationality "is necessary in our relations . . . to the physical environment . . . it must be *prevented* from carrying over to the social field if ethical society is to exist."[39] Most emphatically, the essential social activity, social procedure, discussion aimed at determining "right" ends, and the organization for their pursuit, is not a means-end problem: "Intelligent choice between ends is a very different thing from 'science.' "[40] The faculty that is relevant to social intelligence is critical judgment, not instrumental rationality.

Yet, despite the radical distinction Knight wishes to draw between the two kinds of intelligence, it turns out that there are interesting parallels between the activities in which they are engaged. Although the discussion of conflicts of values is said to be not a "scientific" activity, Knight nevertheless claims that the values to be established by social procedure are, like the facts of the scientist, "objective," not matters of mere preference. Otherwise, there can be no true discussion of them. "Discussion is a co-operative quest for an impersonal 'objectively' right (or best) solution of an impersonal problem."[41] Knight inverts the usual "there is no disputing about tastes" into the counterclaim that it is only tastes about which one can dispute as opposed to discuss and rationally debate.

How is the objectivity of "valid values" established? It is by the consensus eventually reached by the participants in social procedure. But some skeptics might question whether a mere meeting of minds is sufficient evidence of objectivity. In anticipation of these objections, Knight points to the natural scientist. According to Knight, the scientist purports to be concerned solely with coexistences and sequences among observed objects and events. In fact, the only evidence he has that he is dealing with such objective facts is a consensus, a meeting of minds precisely like that of the discussants in social procedure.

This is because of the nature of observation. In principle, so Knight claims, the natural scientist carries his explanations back to propositions about the "sensible objects" of the external environment. But the contact between the sense organs and the primary data is a far from simple procedure. "What is 'really' perceived, and what is 'only' inferred or seen because it is wished?"[42] The allegedly "sensible objects" present "the main perennial, unsolved and probably unsolvable problem of the theory of knowledge as a whole."[43]

In consequence of this elusiveness of the primary data, the natural scientist is forced to confine himself to data Knight describes as having been "tested," that is, other scientists report having seen the same objects. So it is that in scientific method, as in social procedure, a "conscious critical consensus is the essence of the idea of objectivity or truth." Scientific method implies a commitment to a moral code, the obligation of the scientific observer to tell the truth about his observations. "Without a sense of honor . . . among scientists . . . there could be no science."[44] At the end of analysis, we find that individualistic, amoral science involves a method that is both social and ethical. And Knight consequently makes the interesting suggestion that the appropriate model for free society is the scientific community. "The pursuit of truth . . . is the ideal type of ethical association, which is to say of all true society."[45] Yet he argues, in line with his pluralism, that the "spirit of discussion is the essence of the scientific spirit, but the antithesis of the scientific method."[46] It is the ethic, not the method, of science that provides the appropriate model.[47]

To appraise these views about an alleged "antithesis" between the "spirit" and the "method" of science, we must take a closer look at Knight's antiscientism. There are two reasons why he rejects scientific method as the appropriate model for social procedure. One is technical, the other ethical. We shall consider them in turn.

Knight holds that the observation and experiment essential to agreement among natural scientists have no counterparts when we are concerned with the social and moral order. Natural scientists reach agreement "without coercion," by appeal to observed facts, while such unforced agreement is rarely to be hoped for even among the best intentioned discussants of social problems or ethical questions.[48] The data of the social sciences consist of "meanings, opinions, attitudes, and values, not of physical facts."[49] This view is related to Knight's overexacting conception of "observation." He tends to identify "physical" reality with the schema of classical mechanics. Scientific observation is confined to forms of primitive contact between the sensory organs and the measurable properties of solid "external objects" ("data of sense observation"). So Knight taunts the physicist who speaks of "potential" energy as having abandoned the strictly scientific point of view.[50] Even "expression and communication" can be included in observable behavior only by "something of a *tour de force*."[51]

This has the consequence of throwing all social and moral aspects of existence over into a "mental" order, where they can only be known by some manner of intuitive insight: "Conscious states are certainly never observed through the senses, they are not directly observed in any other person; and it is far from clear just what it means . . . to say that one observes even his own conscious states as such."[52] For this reason, Knight maintains that economics is not an empirical science, for the economist deals with motivated activity, and the existence of motives and purposes "cannot be proved or argued or 'tested.' "[53]

But this conception fails to take account of the elaborately designed experimental procedures whereby natural scientists "observe"—in one sense of this ambiguous word—such entities as electrons of molecules. The order revealed by modern physics bears little relation to our everyday sensory experience. Indeed, scientific observation is a more complex affair, and the alleged "primary data" of the scientist, the so-called "sensible objects," are even more elusive than Knight's analysis suggests. Scientific observation is not the receipt of sensations by a passive mind; it is an "active" procedure, directed by theoretical conceptions.[54] An adequate account of it requires that we use "mind" as a verb rather than a noun and the "mental" as an adjective describing kinds of overt activity rather than a separate order of existence. In fact, we must reject the radical dualism between the physical and the mental which—despite some characteristic qualifications[55]—is so prominent a feature of Knight's discussion of social science methodology.

According to this reconstructed conception of mind, we must be skeptical about claims based on the intuitive self-knowledge Knight relies on to furnish the axioms of economics. But there is no reason to question that, through observing our own and others' conduct, we are able to form reasonable judgments about dispositions, capacities, habits, and patterns of motivation and make inferences about purposes and values.[56]

However, there is, from Knight's viewpoint, an even more important reason why social data are inappropriate for scientific treatment. This is the presence, in individual and social conduct, of unpredictable problem-solving activity, procedure. We have noted the necessity for the economist to abstract from uncertainty, and so from effort, in order to turn procedure into process and make the economic man an object of science.

Knight grants that, despite our inability to use "sense observation," it is still possible to have certain positive sciences of society, provided procedural activity is not involved. He gives as an example cultural anthropology, the study of the development of institutions. In fact, this is said to be "the" science of society, even though the data are derived through the unscientific method of "intercommunication and interpretation."[57] Cultural anthropology can retain its scientific status so long as the knowledge it provides is "useless." Knight gives as an example the development of a language which no one is interested in reforming. The point here seems to be that if the knowledge were used to some purpose, the knower and the known would interact, procedure would replace process, and the discovered trends cease to hold.[58]

This involves a singular view of science and of scientific prediction. The cultural anthropology example suggests that, by way of analogy, if we were to learn to predict and control the weather, meteorology would cease to be a science because the patterns on our present weather maps would no longer indicate the movements of air masses.

The contention that problem-solving conduct is in principle unpredictable seems to confuse scientific predictability with fatalistic predestination. Knight himself argues that economics provides more accurate prediction than the other social sciences.[59] But the subject matter of this science is rational conduct, and, of course, our predictions of responses to changes in prices or incomes will be the more reliable, the more nearly the market participants resemble rationally purposive economic men. Also, there is nothing self-contradictory about one's predicting the course of development of so purposive an activity as scientific investigation, even though one could not predict the solution to a single individual problem. Predictability hardly can be discussed outside the context of the particular problem under investigation.

Therefore, we hold that counterparts of the natural scientist's observation and experiment are available to help end disagreement among reasonable men about social and moral questions.

But the proposal to apply scientific method in resolving such questions also raises for Knight an ethical problem. This is a consequence of his identifying "science" with the Crusoe economy. The logic of scientific technology is demonstrated for the case of an isolated individual manipulating the objects of inert nature to his private advantage. How could such techniques be applied to society? One possibility is to have every individual attempt to manipulate every other—a recipe for chaos. Or, more likely, a dictator could attempt to manipulate and control the society—a recipe for tyranny. The "social problem . . . is one of rational *consensus* . . . not of control in the correct meaning of manipulation."[60]

There is much that is puzzling about Knight's assertion that a science of society has these insidious ethical implications. In the first place, as we have seen, Knight shows that Crusoe's amoral program of scientific investigation cannot be carried out. Moreover, there does not seem to be any convincing reason for arguing that scientific technology is appropriate only to serve invidious individualist ends. Is it not the case that scientific knowledge has served many purposes, from the profane to the sacred? It has been used not only to build nuclear weapons, but also to design programs of public health. The moral problem is one of directing the use of this knowledge to ends consistently humane, that is, we must apply the same kind of social intelligence to the choice among ends that has proved so successful in the perfecting of means. This is the task of social procedure.

To accomplish such a task, social procedure must be joined to a social technology. This will provide the counterparts of the natural scientist's observation and experiment. Without these, we are unable to confer on values that objectivity which Knight claims is required for true discussion. A mere "meeting of minds" without reference to the facts and possibilities of social life is not enough. Ethical judgments must be stated as hypotheses and tested through the rational reconstruction of institutions. In this way social and political knowledge accumulates, and we have the informed public opinion essential to the maintenance of free institutions. Adherence to the ethic of science—to truth as a value—rules out the deception and manipulation Knight fears from a social technology.

Therefore, we claim that ideal free society is most effectively characterized by the presence of social procedure, joined with a social technology. A free society is an open society, experimentally seeking the most perfect justice in laws and institutions.

But now we have two blueprints for free society. One is the perfect market, "the embodiment of complete freedom," the "society of Crusoes." The other is the scientific community. What is the relationship between them? Knight evidently wishes us to think of our constructing the second community by a simple extension of the principle of freedom expressed by the first. Social discussion is said to be a form of voluntary exchange, "rather the most fundamental kind."[61]

However, it seems a long road from the society of Crusoes, each selfishly maximizing utility, to the community of inquirers, selflessly devoted to truth and justice. Although we use such expressions as "the marketplace for ideas," this is a misleading metaphor if it is taken to imply a *quid pro quo* in the "exchange of ideas." The requirements for admission into the community of inquirers include ethical commitment, disinterestedness, public spiritedness.[62] In fact, Knight's "society of Crusoes" seems useful for providing the sharpest possible contrast to the community of inquirers.[63]

The freedom basic to social procedure is freedom of inquiry and expression. This freedom cannot be analyzed in the categories of a theory of free individual choice, or in terms of the libertarian dichotomy between an autonomous individual will and the collective coercive power. It requires for its expression the design of appropriate institutions—linguistic, educational, cultural. It is not the freedom of a Crusoe.

The essential feature that the society of Crusoes and the community of inquirers are supposed to have in common is that they are examples of voluntary association. The idea of the voluntary is therefore the basic principle of libertarian ethics, and to this we now turn for a closer examination.

### *The Elusiveness of the Voluntary*

Although most of us think we know what we mean when we say we act voluntarily—and no doubt often deliberate over choices among possible courses of action—it is a profound philosophical problem, with a history dating back to Plato, to define the voluntary and its opposite, the coerced. This is because coercion includes, as Knight emphasizes, persuasion by deception and, more importantly, conditioning. Individuals can be conditioned by political dictators, advertisers, fashion setters, and evangelists to accept "voluntarily" the most absurd beliefs and to act to achieve all kinds of ends that serve the conditioner rather than the actor. In the course of a discussion of freedom, Knight says he wishes to offer "in parenthesis" his view that the "real problem of defining freedom . . . is the matter of distinguishing between being free and feeling free."[64] But this is not a "parenthetical" problem for the libertarian. Social procedure requires objective values, yet he has no objective criterion for a free act. Of course, one cannot look into another's mind and see if an overt act was preceded by an exercise of will. But the matter is more hopeless than this. One can have no way of knowing, even after the fact, whether his own act of choice was free. To have felt free is not necessarily to have been free.

What the libertarian requires is an ability to locate a presocial ego and to identify situations in which such an individual chooses autonomously. Moral judgments require these identifications if we accept the libertarian contention that all moral life depends upon the individual's being "morally self-made."[65] Yet Knight's writings offer little to encourage us about the possibility of finding such autonomous beings in contemporary society. "In sociological terms it may also be said that the individual is unreal; any . . . society . . . is a complex of institutions . . . rather than an organization of independent individuals."[66]

So it is that Knight's ethical system involves a combination of radical moral individualism with sociological determinism. On the rule that "ought" implies "can," this must be rated morally repugnant. The individual is assigned a moral responsibility which the facts of social life disqualify him from carrying out. For Knight, this paradox is just another aspect of man's pluralistic existence. But it seems more reasonable to attempt to resolve it by looking for an idea of freedom which takes account of the inevitably social nature of the individual.

Let us consider the way we actually assign moral responsibility. If we are to blame an individual for committing an illegal or immoral act, it is said that we must determine if his "will was free," if he *could* have chosen to act other than he did. Yet we can never reach conclusions about prior acts of an autonomous will, or about choices that might have been made among past options. The relevant inquiry is into the individual's competence, his intellectual and physical capacities, and the opportunity he had for exercising these. If an individual is judged competent to act in accordance with certain rules of conduct, he is said to be responsible. If his performance fails to live up to expectations, and he is unable to furnish excuses, then his improper conduct is said to be "voluntary," and so subject to sanctions. Thus the voluntary is not properly used to indicate events taking place "in the mind." Its proper application is to judgments of blame concerning the acts of competent individuals. Indeed, we reasonably hold individuals responsible for negligent conduct, although there is no suggestion here of a prior volition or intention or of any thought at all.

Our proper concern in assigning responsibility is with the educability of the individuals whose conduct is under examination. One is made responsible for past conduct, and even subjected to punishment, if he or others are capable of learning from the experience, and so improving future conduct. The relevant question in the moral judgment is not whether the individual could have chosen differently in the past. Rather, it is whether making him responsible now will cause his future choices to be made with greater concern for their consequences. One does not punish the stone that accidently falls on one's head; there is nothing one can teach a stone. The parent does punish the child who amuses himself by throwing rocks at strangers. He believes the child is capable of learning, of changing his character. Insofar as this is so, the child is a free moral agent.

This view of responsibility goes along with a conception of freedom as personal growth. "The foundation of liberty is the idea of growth."[67] A useful definition of freedom will not be framed in terms of individual acts of choice. Not an isolated choice, but a sequence of such choices, each more intelligent than its predecessor, exemplifies free conduct. The free individual is one who is growing, developing his character, realizing his potentialities. To be sure, growth and development are not uncomplicated notions. But it is the function of social discussion in free society to clarify such ideas. So clarified, they are revealed in observable, therefore objective, attributes of character and personality. Thus, we must reject the libertarian conception of freedom as freedom to choose irrespective of power to act, as "freedom from" without regard for "freedom to."[68]

Certainly we cannot identify economic choices with an autonomous ego. It is not necessary to turn to radical critics of contemporary capitalism to read accounts of how the ends the system serves, rather than represent the spontaneous desires of the citizens, are in fact largely created by the system itself. This is one of Knight's favorite themes. The form of economic organization, he writes, "goes far to determine what is wanted, and to mold the attitudes of persons toward their work and toward each other."[69] So it is not reasonable, watching the housewife pushing her shopping cart through the supermarket, to suppose she is exercising free will in any awe-inspiring sense. Economic conduct is highly conditioned, the product of rigorous training in "the exact science of making change." Moreover, Knight does not regard this conditioning as morally uplifting. He writes of the "Machiavellian-Mandevillan standards which make intelligent selfishness equivalent to virtue, and power and cunning the main component of our human ideal."[70]

The case for the organization of economic life around the market had better be based upon the classical argument for the efficiency of this arrangement rather than upon the libertarian's freedom as "end in itself." Through each properly conditioned marketer following a simple rule of rational economic calculation—to maximize profits and minimize costs—the market decentralizes the decision-making process and effectively coordinates the participants' activities. What is impressive about the market is not the alleged autonomous nature of individual choice, but the powerful constraints imposed upon economic decision making. In the hypothetical perfect market—according to Knight, the "embodiment of complete freedom"—each individual buyer or seller must be so insignificant a part of the total market that he can have no effect on prices and costs; and it is the *powerlessness,* the opposite of individual autonomy, which is the basis of the market's efficiency. If income is inequitably distributed, then the market constraints will bear down unequally and unjustly on the citizenry. But even with an ethically ideal distribution, they will still operate, as indeed they must, given the omnipresent fact of economic scarcity. High school students who dream of becoming television stars, professional athletes, or political leaders will end up "freely choosing" to become bank clerks, filling station operators, or insurance salesmen. The economic order can be described more realistically as a realm of constraint rather than of freedom, although, of course, insofar as the constraints operate efficiently to organize economic life, they make possible a larger freedom in other areas, such as the political and the cultural.

If we are unable to accept the libertarian's view of economic choice as giving the form of all free conduct, what can we say of the identification of the political with coercion? We recall that Knight argues the latter proposition on the basis of an account of a perfectly free society, an antinomian anarchy, in which all laws are obeyed "voluntarily," and there is no enforcement. This state of affairs can be maintained as long as there is unanimous ethical consensus—universal agreement that the laws are just—or when dissenters are free to leave this society and join another. The society becomes political when there is dissent and the dissenters are not allowed to leave. Then they must be forced to obey the law.

First, we encounter in this analysis of the role of law the ambiguities we have noted about the term *voluntary*. As Knight would agree, it is possible to imagine a society with little or no law enforcement which we would regard as a slave state, for example, a caste society in which everyone knows his place and "freely" accepts it. Second, it is not the case that, when the law is enforced against violators, we associate their crimes with an ethical dissent. Thieves and killers are not usually by their acts offering dissenting views about the morality of laws against burglary and murder. On the contrary, the rationale of punishment assumes they are within the consensus, that they understand or are capable of understanding that their acts are wrong.

An alternative analysis of the political relates it to externalities of the kind Knight includes among the "mechanical" obstacles to a regime of perfect freedom. Let us substitute for Knight's antinomian anarchism a society in which all the relations among citizens are confined to private transactions. This implies that all the consequences of each transaction are realized by the participants in that transaction, and nonparticipants are unaffected. In such a society, there need be no public concern; political activity, as it seems most useful to define it, would not exist. In a society of moderate complexity, these conditions are not realized. Almost all transactions have some external consequences, and for many there is a broad diffusion, advantageous and disadvantageous, throughout the society. Even in Knight's society of Crusoes, insofar as there is an organized market, there is a public concern in the inviolability of contracts, and so a need for a public authority. In contemporary society there is a proliferation of externalities. A citizen's ownership and operation of an automobile are not purely private matters to be settled between the dealer and himself. The driver must be licensed and willing to follow publicly determined rules of the road. These serve as guides and restraints, but without such regulations, backed by sanctions, most would agree that motoring would become, not freer, but suicidal.

The most obtrusive fact about the public sector is the dominance of collective decision making. The libertarian position seems to be that all such decisions involve coercion, except in rare cases of unanimity. This follows from the ideal of antinomian anarchism and the definition of the political as coercive. If 95 percent of the citizens in a community vote to build a new school, taxes are levied on everyone, so the 5 percent who do not want the school are subject to coercion. But the rule of unanimity involves a paradox. It provides an irrational bias in favor of the status quo. Suppose in a community every citizen but one becomes convinced that a certain law is unjust or outmoded; that one dissenter could block change. The rule of unanimity invites a tyranny of the minority. Plainly, the citizens of free society must find a way to reconcile freedom with less than unanimous decisions.

Such a reconciliation can be effected in this way. We can imagine a situation in which we are able to realize the libertarian ideal of free contract among autonomous individuals. It is necessary for the contract to be entered into prior to social organization, among individuals equal in knowledge and power. Such a state of affairs was hypothesized in the seventeenth- and eighteenth-century doctrines of a social contract.[71]

Although Knight himself will have nothing to do with this fiction ("If there is any nonsense that surpasses the contract theory of the origin of society, I should like to have an example of it."[72]), it provides the only appropriate setting for the libertarian morality. Moreover, it gives expression to the liberal ideal. The state exists to serve the needs and desires of individuals; these individuals have the right to change laws and institutions to make the state a more effective instrument to these ends.

The social contract is the symbol for the moral consensus which is the basis of free society. Rational individuals with developed moral sensibilities and knowledge of the nature of social organization, but with a "veil of ignorance" hiding from each his particular opportunities and goals,[73] agree upon the broad principles of association, the principles of justice, freedom, equality. The veil of ignorance assures that the self-interest of each is in the welfare of all. Choosing rationally, they reach unanimous decisions. Within this ethical consensus, the rules for collective decision making are worked out, the constitution of free society.

When we come to particular collective decisions, then we must take account of the fact that each individual is aware of his own interests and values. Unanimity is rarely to be expected. Yet, each individual accepts the consequences of less than unanimous agreement, even when he is in the minority. This is because of his adherence to the moral consensus and his interest in preserving an orderly society.

Social procedure is the discussion of proposed changes in the laws and reforms of institutions, in accordance with the principles expressed in the moral consensus. It is what we should call political action. So defined, political action breaks down when force or coercion are employed. Individuals are punished, not to coerce them into the consensus, but because they have failed to live up to the ethical commitments implied by free citizenship.

The libertarian ethic is conservative. Since political action is defined as coercive, the cost of political intervention in the economic order, for however seemingly worthy an end, must be judged in terms of the inevitable extension of coercive power. So there is a presumption in favor of the status quo.[74] However, the opposition of free economic relations to coercive political power is a general idea, adaptable to a variety of positions on concrete issues. Knight himself on occasion writes of the inevitability of much coercion in modern industrial society.[75] On the other hand, some of the disciples, notably Milton Friedman, raise few questions about the feasibility of extreme laissez-faire.

However, if, as has been argued, economic choices are not voluntary in the required libertarian sense, and political action not coercive, then citizens of an ideal free society have no inhibitions about the use of politically organized power—experimentally, in an environment of free discussion—to bring about the appropriate background conditions for a just economic order.

### *The Difficulties of Pluralism*

It is Knight's pluralism that presents the greatest difficulty to his interpreters or critics, for it implies holding two or more inconsistent positions simultaneously. This philosophy may be useful as an antidote to a simple-minded monism that purposes to reduce all emotional and spiritual experience to mechanical interactions among lifeless atoms, but an overdose of pluralism calls for its own antidote. It is the function of intelligence to render our experience coherent, yet the pluralist finds the highest truths in logical contradictions. Much of Knight's analysis consists in showing how his conceptions, such as "freedom" or "rational action," lead to paradox and confusion when one attempts a consistent application of them–thus, "it would be irrational to be, or try to be, perfectly rational." Rather than going on to develop more useful conceptions, he stays to enjoy the reader's perplexity.

We have been especially concerned with contradictions involving man's dual existence as an individual and as a social being. We have science as amoral individualist instrumental rationality and as a social activity guided by ethical principles. Knight's antiscientism requires our confining ourselves to the first of these viewpoints, although when looked at from the second, a science of society has decidedly different significance.[76] It is this second viewpoint which provides Knight's most useful model for free society—the community of inquirers—a model, so we argued, that is the polar opposite of his other model, the association of instrumentally rational, "individualistic individuals," the society of Crusoes.

Then there are the contradictions between the ideal of the autonomous individual, "morally self-made," and the fact of the human being as "social as a termite." Indeed, Knight says that the fundamental objective of social action is to build "ideal institutions" which will create "ideal individuals."[77] So the individual is not self-made, and his individuality depends upon an appropriate structure of institutions. The idea of a conflict between individual autonomy and collective coercion is false. The basic freedom is realized within society. It is the right to participate in the reform of institutions, and it is political, not economic, freedom.

Finally, there are the difficulties of ethical pluralism. Freedom is an "end in itself." One debases it by assigning it a merely instrumental function. There is an irreconcilable conflict between freedom and other values, such as justice, order, and security. Yet it is surely the task of moral reasoning to find a suitable balance among the values in terms of some more general conception of social welfare, such as that implied by David Hume's principle of a "cool preference for what is useful and serviceable to mankind."[78] There is reason to suspect any less general "end in itself." This is especially true when freedom is conceived as the acts of an (invisible) autonomous will and in this sense is identified with economic choices. So economic activity is by definition free, although there is no independent, objective criterion for a free act. The analysis is readily adaptable to reactionary ends. A society cannot be both free and just, so we must acquiesce in injustice as the "price of freedom." It would be unfair to accuse Knight of carrying advocacy of laissez-faire to an extreme. Constitutionally incapable of zealotry in any cause, he was inclined to be as severe with doctrinaire laissez-faire advocates as with doctrinaire "planners." But the potential for obscurantism remains.

## *Notes*

1. See Milton Friedman, ed., *Studies in the Quantity Theory of Money* (Chicago: University of Chicago Press, 1956).
2. *Intelligence and Democratic Action* (Cambridge, Mass.: Harvard University Press, 1960), p. 15.
3. "The Sickness of Liberal Society" (1946), reprinted in *Freedom and Reform* (New York and London: Harper and Brothers, 1947), p. 371.
4. "Economic Psychology and the Value Problem" (1925), reprinted in *The Ethics of Competition and Other Essays* (New York: Augustus M. Kelley, 1951), p. 88.
5. "Science, Philosophy and Social Procedure" (1942), reprinted in *Freedom and Reform,* p. 205. Readers familiar with Knight's writings will recall that his best-known work, *Risk, Uncertainty and Profit* (1921)

(New York: Harper and Row, 1965), presents a theory of income distribution which replaces the classical (Ricardian) tripartite division between classes. Knight substitutes a division between the "procedural" decision-making entrepreneur and the passive suppliers of productive resources, whose function can, through abstraction from uncertainty and error and therefore effort, be described in terms of "process." His extensive writings on social science methodology are largely devoted to his doctrine of antiscientism, which claims the futility and even the immorality of attempting to contain man and his creative mind within the categories of deterministic science. As a libertarian moralist, he finds the highest ethical value in undetermined choices.

6. "Liberalism and Christianity" (1945), in *The Economic Order and Religion* (London: Routledge, 1948), p. 55.
7. "The Role of Principles in Economics and Politics" (1951), reprinted in *On the History and Method of Economics* (Chicago: University of Chicago Press, 1956), p. 268.
8. See, for example, Francis M. Bator, "The Simple Analytics of Welfare Maximization" (1957), reprinted in William Breit and Harold M. Hochman, eds., *Readings in Microeconomics,* 2d ed. (New York: Holt, Rinehart and Winston, Inc., 1971).
9 See Knight's criticism of the classic liberals for their utilitarianism in "Ethics and Economic Reform" (1939), reprinted in *Freedom and Reform,* p. 55.
10. "Principles," p. 258.
11. Ibid., p. 263.
12. *Intelligence,* p. 99.
13. "Abstract Economics as Absolute Ethics," *Ethics* 76 (April 1966): 163–77. It is largely a matter of polemical orientation. In this essay Knight is dealing severely with the laissez-faire simplism of Henry Hazlitt, although he acknowledges a basic agreement with Hazlitt's views. The essay is of particular interest as the vigorous expression of an eighty-year-old iconoclast.
14. "Principles," p. 268.
15. *Intelligence,* p. 105. It is interesting to note that Knight believes this administration must be by "authority" rather than "rules," unlike some of his colleagues at the University of Chicago.
16. "Free Society" (1948), reprinted in *History and Method,* p. 292.
17. "Principles," p. 271.
18. *Risk, Uncertainty and Profit,* p. 351.
19. "The Ethics of Competition" (1923), reprinted in *Ethics of Competition.* In this well-known essay, Knight argues that no persuasive ethical justification of the enterprise system can be given.
20. *Intelligence,* p. 124. The separation of freedom from power seems to have been made first in "Freedom as Fact and Criterion" (1929), reprinted in *Freedom and Reform.* See footnote, pp. 4–5.
21. *Intelligence,* p. 113.
22. Although, as Knight notes, great inequalities are a threat to the maintenance of a competitive order. "Ethics and Economic Reform," p. 67. This raises the question of our ability to separate definitively commutative from distributive justice.

23. "Science, Philosophy and Social Procedure," pp. 205ff.
24. *Intelligence,* p. 2.
25. Ibid.
26. "The Sickness of Liberal Society," p. 391.
27. "Ethics and Economic Reform," p. 52.
28. "Free Society," p. 288.
29. Ibid., p. 285. The idea of pluralism comes from William James, emergent evolution from Henri Bergson. See James, *A Pluralistic Universe* (New York: Longmans, Green and Company, 1909); and Bergson, *Creative Evolution* (New York: Henry Holt and Company, 1911). These two philosopher-psychologists were the principal spokesmen for a turn-of-the-century "neoromantic" reaction to what they regarded as the excessive materialism of nineteenth-century thought. They energetically defended man's free will from what they conceived as insidious threats from scientific determinism. Both preceded Knight in the use of the term *scientism* in a deprecatory sense. Knight acknowledges his debt to James and Bergson. See, for example, "Economic Psychology," p. 97.
30. "Fact and Value in Social Science" (1942), reprinted in *Freedom and Reform,* p. 230.
31. "Economic Psychology," p. 95.
32. Ibid.
33. *Intelligence,* p. 17.
34. "Free Society," p. 283.
35. "Science, Philosophy and Social Procedure," p. 211.
36. "Social Science" (1941), reprinted in *History and Method,* p. 127.
37. *Intelligence,* p. 72.
38. "Science, Philosophy and Social Procedure," p. 211.
39. "Pragmatism and Social Action" (1936), reprinted in *Freedom and Reform,* p. 37.
40. Ibid., p. 39.
41. *Risk, Uncertainty and Profit,* Preface (1933), p. xxxv.
42. "Economic Psychology," p. 93.
43. " 'What Is Truth?' in Economics" (1940), reprinted in *History and Method,* p. 259.
44. Ibid.
45. "Social Science," p. 132.
46. *Risk, Uncertainty and Profit,* Preface (1933), p. xxxvi.
47. In his essay, "Virtue and Knowledge: The Views of Professor Polanyi," *Ethics* 59 (July 1949): 271–84, Knight criticizes Michael Polanyi's proposal to use scientific method as ideal type for the political process in Polanyi's *Science, Faith and Society* (Oxford: the University Press, 1946), although he notes that Polanyi's conception of scientific method is quite different from his own. He thinks that Polanyi neglects the role of "sense observation and manipulation" in obtaining agreement among natural scientists. See also James M. Buchanan, "Politics and Science: Reflections on Knight's Critique of Polanyi," *Ethics* 77 (July 1967): 303–10.
48. "Salvation by Science" (1947), reprinted in *History and Method,* footnote, p. 228.

49. "Fact and Value in Social Science" (1942), reprinted in *Freedom and Reform*, p. 228.
50. "Economic Psychology," footnote, p. 86.
51. "Fact and Value in Social Science," p. 229.
52. "Economic Psychology," p. 79.
53. " 'What Is Truth?' " p. 160.
54. Compare Thomas S. Kuhn, *The Structure of Scientific Revolutions* (Chicago: University of Chicago Press, 1962), chapter 5.
55. This is a characteristic expression: "Physical causation also ultimately needs mind, of a sort, to be 'real'; and social causation does not need it and cannot use it for purposes of 'science,' properly interpreted." "Social Causation" (1943), reprinted in *History and Method*, p. 139.
56. The seeds of a "functional" view of mind are contained in the psychology of William James. These were nurtured and developed by John Dewey and George Herbert Mead. See Dewey's essay, "The Vanishing 'Subject' in the Psychology of William James" (1942), reprinted in *Problems of Men* (New York: Philosophical Library, 1946), and especially *Experience and Nature* (2d ed., 1929) (New York: Dover Publications, 1958), chapters 6 and 7. A similar view is part of the philosophy of Ludwig Wittgenstein; see his *Philosophical Investigations* (New York: Macmillan Co., 1953). See also Gilbert Ryle, *The Concept of Mind* (New York: Barnes and Noble, 1949). When scientific laws are stated in their correct, conditional, "if-then" form, they refer to potentialities in situations. Ryle shows that statements of motives have a similar logical form. They are *dispositional* statements, reporting tendencies to act in observable ways. Such a statement is objectively true if it enables one to predict or explain the conduct of another.
57. "Fact and Value," p. 242.
58. "Social Science," p. 126.
59. *Intelligence*, chapter 6.
60. "Science, Philosophy and Social Procedure," p. 224.
61. Milton Friedman attempts the same extension of the idea of economic exchange to free discussion. See his contribution to Sidney Hook, ed., *Human Values and Economic Policy* (New York: New York University Press, 1967), p. 90.
62. Charles Sanders Peirce, perhaps America's most profound interpreter of scientific method, emphasized the social and moral elements in scientific research. He stressed the contrast between the moral commitment of the scientist and the "Gospel of Greed," characteristic of the nineteenth-century marketplace. See, for example, "The Fixation of Belief" (1877) and other essays by Peirce in Philip P. Wiener, ed., *Values in a Universe of Chance* (Garden City, N.Y.: Doubleday and Co., 1958).
63. Knight's society of Crusoes is the extreme individualist order. Alexis de Tocqueville argued that such individualism was a prescription for tyranny. See *The Old Regime and the French Revolution* (1856), translated by Gilbert Stuart (Garden City, N.Y.: Doubleday and Co., 1955), Part Two, chapter 9. A similar view is repeatedly expressed in the political writings of Hannah Arendt. See, for example, "What Is Freedom?" in *Between Past and Future* (New York: The Viking Press, 1968). Moreover, Knight apparently agrees with these judgments. He

writes of "intolerable consequences that would prevail if society were organized solely through exchange by individuals." "Abstract Economics as Absolute Ethics," p. 177. Thus, freedom as he defines it is worse than "inherently unattainable"; it is self-destroying.

64. *Intelligence*, p. 116.
65. "Sickness of Liberal Society," p. 382.
66. Ibid., p. 383.
67. L. T. Hobhouse, *Liberalism* (1911) (New York: Oxford University Press, 1964), p. 66.
68. Sir Isaiah Berlin has shown how philosophies based on "freedom to" while neglecting "freedom from" are easily adapted to the purposes of maintaining a totalitarian state. See "Two Concepts of Liberty" (1958), reprinted in *Four Essays on Liberty* (London and New York: Oxford University Press, 1969). In a later essay he notes that a similar purpose can be served by confining liberty to "freedom from." In this latter form, it can be used to justify ruthless economic exploitation. See the introduction to the above volume.
69. "Economic Psychology," p. 102.
70. Ibid.
71. Immanuel Kant made clear that the social contract was a hypothetical not historical event. Recently the theory of a social contract has been generalized and refined by John Rawls in *A Theory of Justice* (Cambridge, Mass.: Harvard University Press, 1971), chapter 3.
72. *Intelligence*, p. 47.
73. Compare Rawls, *Theory*, chapter 3.
74. See "Ethics and Economic Reform," where Knight writes: "Empasis on the necessity of an *onus probandi* in favor of conservatism, and against change, must stand as our last word" (p. 74).
75. "Abstract Economics as Absolute Ethics," and see also "Laissez-faire: Pro and Con," *Journal of Political Economy* 75 (December 1967): 782–95.
76. John Dewey is often taken as the prophet of that scientism Knight wishes to disavow. See "Pragmatism and Social Action," in *Freedom and Reform*. But when Dewey proposes applying scientific method to social problems he means something not so different from what Knight has in mind when he suggests using the ethic of science as guide for social procedure. Dewey protests the uncritical importation of natural science techniques into social inquiry. See *Logic* (New York: Holt, Rinehart and Winston, 1938), chapter 23. He also makes the same point Knight does about the immorality of a social science designed to manipulate and control the citizenry. *Freedom and Culture* (New York: Capricorn Books, 1939), chapter 7. Knight is given to obliterating arguments his adversaries—Marx, Dewey, Veblen, Keynes—would have difficulty recognizing, although perhaps even better men (Dewey, himself) are not above this practice.
77. "Social Science," p. 133.
78. *An inquiry Concerning the Principles of Morals* (1751), reprinted in Ralph Cohen, ed., *Essential Works of David Hume* (New York: Bantam Books, 1965), p. 254.

# 9

# Bargain and Contract Theory in Law and Economics

*S. Todd Lowry*

There has been expanded interest in recent years in the formal analysis of legal problems in economic terms. This work has been greatly influenced by R. H. Coase and the *Journal of Law and Economics,* published at the University of Chicago, which has provided a forum for investigations radiating out from Coase's classic article, "The Problem of Social Cost."[1]

It is the purpose of this study to examine the definitions and premises underlying the concept of bargain, upon which theories of transaction costs such as Coase's are predicated. It also will be necessary to examine the concept of contract, the economic implications of which deserve more specific attention. It is hoped that this approach will frame the diverse literature in the field in a clearer perspective.

Since so much of the current discussion has been provoked by the formulation that has come to be called the "Coase theorem," it will be desirable to use this specific formulation of the issues as a point of departure even though some of Coase's premises have not been conspicuous in subsequent literature purporting to be in the same tradition. In general terms, the Coase theorem states that individual bargaining will result in similar allocations of resources regardless of the presence or

*The author is Professor of Economics and Administration, Washington and Lee University, Lexington, Virginia.* *He would like to acknowledge useful comments on an earlier draft of the manuscript by Professors Lewis H. Larue and Andrew W. McThenia, Jr., of the Washington and Lee School of Law.*

absence of legally enforced rights or liabilities if there are no transaction costs. Coase's classic illustration for this analysis is the confrontation between a farmer and a cattle rancher where the increase in the rancher's herd results in a higher income to the rancher but increased damage to the farmer's crop caused by straying cattle. The theorem holds that, in the absence of liability, optimum social efficiency will not be altered when a more remunerative economic activity is being damaged by a less remunerative activity because a rational decision maker will pay or bribe the operator of the less remunerative activity to have the activity discontinued. This illustration, as well as that of the railroad spark problem, has been used by Coase, and others,[2] to develop the thesis that, given rational individual behavior, the prime social concern in such situations *from the point of view of economics as the analysis of social cost and efficiency,* is whether or not there are transaction costs which must be countered by legal intervention to replicate a competitive market situation. In other words, it is socially desirable to favor whichever arrangement involves the lower transaction costs. A situation which involves tort liability with consequent legally assertable rights resulting in less than optimal allocation of resources, according to the Coasians, results in higher transaction costs since rights which are successfully asserted against another party can then be sold back as a property right. This arrangement is deemed to be socially inefficient compared to private bargaining.

Without becoming involved in the technical validity of this formulation,[3] it should be pointed out that the overriding result of the Coase theorem is to provide a base line or fundamental premise to the effect that there is a natural plateau of socially uniform, rational behavior generated by individual bargaining. Therefore, rational negotiations between competing economic interests will result in the same social costs and benefits, minus the costs of the transaction necessary to the adjustment. The prime economic objective thus becomes the elimination of unnecessary transaction costs. The legal burden, where transaction costs are unavoidable, is to replicate the ideal results of the rational bargain and to use this measure of social efficiency as the basis for conflict resolution and regulation. It seems pointless from the Coasian viewpoint to create legal rights simply to have them bought back, a procedure which introduces the costs of two transactions as a double hurdle in reaching economic efficiency.[4] The Coase theorem thus accepts the rational two-party bargain as the basic unit of social welfare and treats this plateau of two-party bargaining as the potential measure, or definition, of social cost. The two-party bargain is presumed to capture the same rational essence as more general social determination.[5]

It will be remembered that Adam Smith decried mercantilist policies which prohibited practices such as forestalling on the grounds that such regulations interfered with individual bargaining.[6] (Forestalling involved waylaying peasants on their way to the supervised public markets and buying their produce in an isolated bargain.) Smith's justification for permitting isolated bargains was that the greater flexibility thus made possible would result, in the long run, in a superior allocation of resources in the public interest. However, he placed little reliance on individual rationality in isolated exchange as a method of achieving economically equitable results. Instead, he looked to the workings of the natural market to ensure the furtherance of economic and social welfare and assumed that such a natural, competitive market would make unnecessary the cumbersome, governmentally structured market system through which mercantilist officials tried to keep private transactions consistent with the public interest.

Coase, unlike Smith, appears to be prepared to rely on subjective individual rationality as a means of minimizing social costs and to substitute unregulated bargaining for the legal system's use of tort liability to optimize resource allocation in unique or imperfect market situations. Gary Becker, however, retreats from reliance on the rationality of the individual bargain to a concept of the *average* of transactions as constituting an expression of optimum rationality.[7] He thus puts into question the usefulness of the assumption of rationality in individual bargaining by limiting the assumption to an aggregate market situation. It is important to make a clear distinction here between the derivation of socially or economically rational behavior from individual rationality, on the one hand, and the derivation of the rationality of individual transactions from general social or economic processes such as the market, on the other. The notion of a common optimality assumes the identity of individual values and purposes expressed in the bargain with those of society expressed in the market. Once it is conceded that the measure of optimality is derived from an organized, socially sponsored system drawing on the aggregate intelligence of the community, that is, the market or a political consensus, the individual bargain can no longer be defined as a generative unit but is seen in large part as a result of that process. This distinction also will be important in the discussion which follows of the theory of the social compact and of the bearing of contract on unique or specialized relationships.

As a first step in analyzing Coase's approach to the legal structure, it will be necessary to explore the assumptions implicit in the idea of a bargain between two rational individuals engaged in conflicting activities as being necessarily consistent with maximum social welfare where there are no transaction costs and in the absence of social prescriptions, entitlements, or rules of liability. Setting aside for the moment the question of individual rationality, let us examine the concept of bargain in Coase's system by pursuing the ramifications of his cattle and crop example. Suppose that Farmer A, who raises corn, suffers damage from Rancher B's growing herd of cattle. The Coasians argue that Farmer A, being a rational individual, will offer to pay B to curtail his herd if corn raising is sufficiently profitable. On the other hand, if cattle raising is more profitable, he will not be able to do so and will abandon corn farming where it conflicts with cattle raising and instead direct his efforts to some other more remunerative pursuit. In either case, the highest level of social production is assumed to be automatically forthcoming as a result of the bargaining process. There is no *causa* or reason for society to offer a remedy to either individual in furtherance of a social interest.

But let us examine another scenario equally plausible given the stated premises of the Coase theorem. Farmer A raises corn. Rancher B's expanding herd of cattle does $x$ dollars damage on A's land and provides $y$ dollars return to B. A then takes his 30-30 deer rifle, which constitutes an investment already written off to recreation, and communicates to B that he has invested 25 cents in a rifle cartridge with which he intends to shoot one of B's steers. This cost, $z$, where $z$ is less than $y$, in the absence of liability, immediately sets up new criteria for bargaining. B stands to lose $q$ dollars, where $q$ is the capital value of the steer, while A stands to incur a cost of $z$, with $z$ less than $q$. Social welfare will potentially be reduced by the cost of a dead steer spoiling in the field. Rancher B thus will be under bargaining pressure to pay A any sum up to the salvage value of the steer, minus $z$ (25 cents), to avoid suffering an even greater loss. B will then fence his cattle on the assumption that A will not shoot them if they do not stray into A's field, or he will rationally be inclined to pay A nearly full value of any steer that does stray, minus A's cost of shooting it, plus salvage value.

But once A learns how vulnerable B's cattle are, he might threaten to shoot all of them unless B pays him the profit received from his ranching operation. If this bargain is struck, A will then recognize that, in the short run, if he wishes to liquidate this apparently captured ranching operation, all he need do is to threaten to shoot all of B's cattle unless B sells them and pays him the price for which the cattle can be sold, minus the transaction cost and potential cost of shooting them, plus some nominal recompence to B greater than zero. If B is rational, he will prefer to be left with any small amount of money in preference to the total loss of having his entire herd shot without recompence. However, B eventually may realize that shorter run pressures are even more remunerative and notify A that unless A liquidates his corn raising operation and pays the money to him, B, he will shoot A. If our premises include the absence of liability for breaches of legally defined rights, we need postulate no restraint on the exercise of rational self-interest by either party to a bargain.[8] That is to say, in the context of a relationship composed of only two parties, each of whom is guided *only* by self-interest, we may not define *any* action as antisocial behavior since a social reference has been excluded by our definition.[9] We leave A and B maneuvering in A's cornfield, each trying to shoot the other in self-defense in a modern version of Thomas Hobbes's "solitary, poor, nasty, brutish, and short" presocial compact state of nature.

The latter scenario demonstrates an unstated premise in the Coase theorem vitally important in the definition of bargain as a basis for social welfare: Only marginal or incremental transactions superimposed upon an established system of enforceable order are being considered. Moreover, the theorem takes for granted that only economically productive activities (and not willfully destructive ones) will be undertaken by a rational individual. Thus *rational* in terms of the Coase theorem actually means conformity with socially accepted and legally reenforced objectives, at least up to some unstated threshold. However, if individual rationality and the two-party bargain are to be the sole criteria for determining optimum social welfare, they would have to be deducible from a state of nature, that is, a condition prior to the existence of the social compact (the farmer and rancher stalking each other in the partially destroyed cornfield). This is nothing more than Hobbes's state of man as "a condition of war of everyone against everyone." We will leave aside for the present the premise of absolute rationality. It is the origin and nature of a social perspective which must be analyzed if bargain and contract are to be understood in the social context which is the *sine qua non* of their existence.

### *From Bargain to Contract and from Transaction to Relation*

Since ancient times theorists have attempted to explain the social process in general and the economy in particular in terms of a self-generating system of atomic or individual relations based upon subjective rationality. Plato, in Book II of *The Republic*, presented two formulations of mutually advantageous bargains that have come to be known as the "social compact." The first is that society grew from two isolated individuals meeting in the forest and agreeing, out of rational, subjective self-interest, to enjoy the mutual advantages of peace by refraining from destroying each other's property since the gain to the destroyer was minor compared to the loss to the owner of the destroyed property. Based upon reciprocity, this essentially negative compact produced a great mutual advantage at a minor mutual cost.

After such a relationship has been established, the premise of subjective mutuality and rational self-interest may well serve to justify the continuation of such a relationship. But this begs the question of how, in the absence of the level of trust which would make such reasonable behavior automatic, the relation necessary to support the transaction began. Where did the level of trust or the threshold of good faith necessary for such a relation originate? In the absence of a perfect equilibrium of fear and immobilizing uncertainty, the first savage to catch another unaware and hit him on the head would most rationally serve his own self-interest and solve the whole problem without the stress of presuming on the other's good faith. This problem is not limited to ancient rationalizations of the origins of society. In our own time, when world community apparently must be re-rationalized with every generation of Department of Defense whiz kids, lack of a sense of mutual respect for world society leads directly to the rationality of the pre-emptive strike.

The second formulation of the social compact doctrine in Plato's *Republic* is based on the premise of affirmative benefit or mutual increment as a result of compact. This view suggests that the increased productivity resulting from cooperative activity and barter makes the crossing of the threshold of the social compact a nonzero sum game, where both parties stand to gain more than they lose or, more important, to gain more than they ever had before. This contrasts with the first statement of the social compact where both parties stand only to cease losing more than they gain from reciprocal, destructive activity. This recognition of a social welfare fund beyond the capacity of isolated individual efforts traditionally has been viewed as the binding force that holds a rationalistic society together.

The problem remains of the derivation of an established threshold of trust or enforcement—in short, society—for a relation cannot be logically derived from subjective individual rationality, but requires a comprehensive social rationality.[10] Once such a threshold of trust or presumption is established, there is no longer a surplus or relational benefit which can be attributed to the two-party transaction, and the bargain reverts to a zero sum game in which one party's gain is the other party's loss.[11] The general potential of relation therefore must be attributed to the relational fabric or setting which makes the bargain or transaction possible, and not to the bargain itself. Bargaining is essentially only a distributive or allocative process. The problem being explored here is the relationship of bargain or transaction to contract or relation.[12] Can bargains exist as atomized transactional units prior to the development of relation or contract, or must the requisite relations, rationalizations, and a threshold of social stability and trust provide a frame of reference before bargain or transaction can occur?

And how is the initial sense of relation developed? This brings us back to a basic anthropological questioning of the perspective of the social compact itself. The premise that two adults, presumably aggressive males, meet in the forest in a cultural vacuum to begin the formation of rational society seems to overlook the fact that human beings necessarily have a mother and father in whose care and under whose training they must subsist for a rather long period during their formative years. These simple facts of biology suggest a more plausible basis for a sense of society or community with its institutionalized sense of trust than bargaining based on natural rationality. At the very minimum, a sense of trust in human good faith is implicit in the mother-child relation. The extended family, with its institutional arrangements, is surely a better starting point for understanding social and economic relations than is the rationality of isolated individuals.

The basic relation in terms of which bargaining takes place is socially derived and involves limits and guidelines which keep it consistent with social goals. In this sense, bargaining can be viewed as taking place in a social or institutional arena rather than providing the natural base for society. Liability and entitlements are implicit in the fabric of relations which supports transactions.[13] The Coasian theorem, on the other hand, introduces an inversion of this perspective when it attempts to predicate social benefit on nominally independent, laissez-faire transactions. Its assumption of an implicit, socially desirable rationality distilled from individual bargaining provides a justification for minimizing transaction costs or liability rules for individual transactions, thus ignoring the role of transaction costs and liability rules as part of the necessary framework of the social structure in which transactions occur. The thesis of this article is that rules for transactions must be developed as values defined in terms of ongoing social relations, not as a problem of minimizing social costs where social welfare is deducible from an aggregation of individual bargains or transactions.

### *The Theory of Relation and Contract*

Three facets of the problems being developed here may serve as organizing perspectives in terms of which the literature can be analyzed and kept in common focus. These are the concept of bargain, sale, or transaction versus contract or relation; the concept of a threshold between the presumptive or legally institutionalized aspects of social organization and the negotiative or individually arranged aspects; and the problem of individual rationality versus social rationality and the accompanying dilemmas of interpersonal utility comparisons.

As has been noted previously, the rationalistically defined bargain justified from the point of view of individual, subjective self-interest commonly regresses to a shorter and shorter calculation of advantage, with concomitantly more defensive and hostile gestures of self-interest unless the bargaining relation is crystallized in a setting of relational premises which define the boundaries of the arena of interaction for both parties. Entitlements and liability rules are the legal expressions of these institutional relations which confine the transaction. This set of relations is the social or economic threshold that is the necessary condition for the particular society or economy to function in its customary manner. Although the deduction of the basic social fabric has been attempted from the subjective mutuality of the isolated bargain under the social compact premise, the problem of deducing a relational setting as the necessary precondition for a bargain cannot be solved by postulating an initial bargain.

Several other approaches have been made to the problem of defining the foundations of this fundamental social or economic relation which has provided the stability necessary for constructive mutuality. Plato, as did later writers such as Hobbes and the nineteenth-century legal scholar John Austin, argued that stable social relations are an outgrowth of the assertion of authority or sovereignty by a king or head of state. There is in this tradition an echo of the authority implicit in the power focus of the Aryan patriarchal family. This view postulates the rationality of the sovereign imposed upon society in order to develop a framework of social benefits which secondarily may improve the lot of the individual in his role as a member of society. The guiding principle is the assertion of sovereign or administrative discretion as opposed to traditional institutions as a means of setting the threshold above which individual bargaining must operate.[14] The basic premise of the sovereign norm, whether an expression of the self-appointed ruler, philosopher-king, or legislative assembly, has produced the positivist approach to law which can be only vaguely paralleled with what Milton Friedman calls "positive economics."[15] The real parallel in both systems is the abiding faith in the consistent cogency of the rational individual.

Another view of the derivation of the relational threshold assumes an emergent institutional framework or body of custom which results from the steady crystallization of routine, habit, and ritual in a setting where large numbers of individuals follow consistent patterns of behavior or conduct unless interrupted. The emerging benefits of stable interaction tend to be reenforced by the stress brought to bear on deviant behavior in a conformist society. While this may not be a fair statement of the views of such diverse writers as John R. Commons, C. E. Ayres, Karl Polanyi, and even the game-oriented, multiple participant analyses of J. M. Buchanan, it summarizes a common thread which runs through all their theories, namely, the idea of a cumulative base line or threshold of relation which results from the crystallization of custom and working rules.

A last view is of interest because it specifically calls into question the premise of rationalism upon which most arguments are based which attempt to derive a social compact from bargaining among rational individuals. The social compact-oriented Greek Atomists, as represented by Epicurus, found it logically impossible to explain atomic interaction in terms of independent propensities by self-sufficient atomic particles and therefore developed a theory of sympathetic attraction or a cohesive force, the "swerving of the flow of particles."[16] The same dilemma was developed by Plato in the following terms. The purely subjective, self-interested individual requires only the effective *appearance* of social responsibility in order to benefit from society's protection. There is thus no necessary coincidence between individual rationality and social efficiency or between individual benefit and service to society. Adam Smith, who, like David Hume, found the social compact thesis unsatisfactory, developed a doctrine of human sympathy in *Theory of Moral Sentiments* in order to explain how rationally self-interested mankind could build a moral structure or cross the relational threshold that provides the infrastructure for individual bargaining.

The purpose here is merely to indicate that there historically has been considerable concern for the components of a relational threshold for constructive social arrangements. This threshold has been presumed to set social values or purposes and includes entitlements and liability rules. Our next step is to examine the conceptual framework in terms of which the details of social and economic interaction can be characterized as bargain, contract, or administrative decision.

By failing to recognize the relational threshold as a precondition for bargain, the distinction between bargain (transaction) and contract (relation) has been obscured in some discussions of legal and economic process. Many writers have followed a natural law approach, which assumes that the market emerges from an aggregation of individual bargains in the same way that some suppose the common law emerges from individual decisions. The common law, however, is the expression of a core of common judicial principles applied to an accretion of individual cases and not simply an averaging of unrelated, empirically derived opinions. So, too, the role of the legal system in setting up detailed rules defining property rights, enforcing transfers of title, and establishing liability suggests that the market in our society is a publicly structured, relational threshold defining the arena in which individual bargains, sales, or transactions take place. This structure serves the role of generating a consensus of economic opinion and current values (prices) which indicates the public's anticipation of others' needs and their potentiality for production. In the market relation built by the legal and customary framework, all that is needed is the simple sale. The average view, the average rationality, and the average anticipation of the future, all function to provide the social statement of aggregate intellectual judgment, and the ordinary buyer and seller can rely on the general safeguards of average price in this structured relation.[17]

The market, in other words, creates a forum for consensus economizing which requires for the exchange of goods only the legal device of the sale. The sale or individual bargain is supported by legal rules regarding the technicalities of the bargaining process, such as warranties of merchantable quality and valid title. In this setting, speculators may of course anticipate future market conditions different from the general consensus and make bargains for future delivery. Although this type of arrangement may involve the traditional form of contract, it is essentially a bargain or sale in a market context to take place at some time in the future. It is a future bargain relying on the socially structured market arena for its relational significance.

An increasingly detailed literature has directed attention in recent years to the difference between transactional arrangments and relational contract and to the difficulties created when relational contract is analyzed in transactional or exchange terms.[18] In this context, it is useful to examine the concept of contract from a specifically economic point of view. Suppose a shepherd with a flock of one hundred sheep is ready to sell them. The market is four days' drive from his pastureland. If the market is stable and effectively represents the willingness to buy and sell on the part of the buyers and sellers of sheep, the general set of economic relations between sheep raising and sheep buying exists as an established threshold which can be taken for granted. Where there is such a customarily or publicly structured relation, the shepherd would be content to drive his sheep to market and negotiate a bargain, transaction, or sale in the context of the established relational or market process. This would be a transaction within the relational structure provided by law, custom, or administrative fiat. If, however, the sheep herder believed the market price to be capricious and that he had superior quality sheep whose value would not be adequately protected by the market structure, he could go to individual buyers and discuss specialized terms for the sale and delivery of his specific sheep.

This system of building private specifications as the setting for bargain has elements of the structuring of relation which society provides through the market. This private negotiation has the potential of making special arrangements of mutual advantage to both parties and improving efficiency in terms of reduction in social costs, for example, by bypassing the trip to the market and thence to the buyer's processing facilities.[19] Moreover, the sheep may be more usefully delivered to a particular buyer in smaller lots at two-week intervals, and leeway for delivery dates may be allowed depending upon the weather. If there are mutual advantages in such arrangements, both parties will be influenced by the anticipation of future transactions of this type. With the increased complexity of the economy, the detailed structuring of individual relations would be expected to emerge as an even more desirable practice. The failure of the organized market to permit such unique arrangements is the type of problem Adam Smith was dealing with when he marshalled his natural market arguments in opposition to the unwieldy, publicly arranged market structures of the mercantilist period, which were partially designed to protect the peasantry from exploitation by foreign merchants.[20] In an economic sense, contract can be viewed as a form of individualized economic planning where voluntary initiative is permitted to organize its own relational structure supported by public recognition of the desirability of lending legal force to such arrangements. E. Allan Farnsworth summarized the legal history of contract by saying: "[Private] parties . . . were viewed as acting in a kind of legislative capacity, so that the enforcement of a contract by the state merely implemented a form of private law established by the parties."[21] This process is primarily premised upon economic voluntarism as a recognized source of public benefit.

Executory agreements to sell were not enforced in ancient Greek law, thus making all exchanges volitional up to the point of the actual transfer of goods or money by both parties.[22] That the economic significance of voluntarism was, however, appreciated in Hellenic times is evidenced by the importance accorded the concept in the following story from

Xenophon's *Cyropaedia.*[23] Cyrus the Great, while still a boy, was assigned the role of judge when quarrels broke out among his schoolmates. A dispute was brought before him that arose out of the following transaction. A tall boy with a short cloak spied a short boy with a long cloak and, when the shorter boy refused the proffered rational trade, forcibly exchanged cloaks with him. Cyrus ruled that, since both boys were better off as a result of the exchange, a case of reciprocal mutuality and higher social benefit, the forcible exchange was fair. Similarly, under the Coase theorem, without liability and in the absence of some defined threshold of accepted transaction costs, if the shorter boy had no significant advantage from the longer cloak and was unwilling to pay a bribe or share such an advantage to keep his cloak, social cost would be minimized by the exchange since the tall boy would not have to get a longer cloak elsewhere. Cyrus's teachers, however, rebuked him and told him that he had made an incorrect decision, since the primary social value involved in the issue before him was whether the exchange was voluntary. It should be noted that the Persian empire was built upon a peasant agriculture and apparently recognized the superior productivity of voluntary efforts in contrast to the emerging Greek and Roman reliance upon slave labor. The release of initiative through voluntaristic exchange was also one of Adam Smith's concerns. In modern times voluntarism is recognized as an indispensable measure of justice and as a major element in evaluating fairness in individual transactions. Reenforced with principles of disclosure and liability, it has supported the private generation of arrangements which structure future economic relations where the market does not provide the detailed specificity necessary for a complex commercial and industrial society.

### *The Legal Theory of Contract and the Economic Theory of Exchange*

In discussing the current literature in which attempts are made to carry economic theory into law by superimposing bargain and exchange analysis upon the legal formulation of commercial transactions, it will be necessary to take cognizance of new developments in the legal theory of contract. First, it should be reiterated that the traditional economic analysis of exchange in a market setting properly corresponds to the legal concept of *sale* (rather than contract), since sale presumes arrangements in a market context and requires legal support primarily in enforcing transfers of title. Contract, on the other hand, evolved out of the need of individuals for structuring unique patterns of commitment and obligation over a period of time *in the absence of market alternatives.*

The concept of contractual commitment in the form of *obligatio* existed in Roman law, and various forms of long-term commitment were brought into the mainstream of English common law through the Law Merchant during the seventeenth and eighteenth centuries. However, the legal form for *enforcing* a promise to do something in the future in the English tradition grew out of the earlier action of assumpsit, which was essentially a tort action, a civil action available to the individual empowering him to seek redress for certain forms of malfeasance considered civil wrongs. This, in essence, meant that the state did not take the initiative in punishing this kind of misconduct in the general public interest as in the case of criminal law, but the injured individual was given the right to obtain redress in a public forum, thus punishing the culprit and alleviating the wrong simultaneously. This tradition involves the notion that a publicly desirable standard of behavior is to be enforced, but the penalty/award is assessed in light of the particular circumstances and injuries to the plaintiff. The enforcement of contract therefore provided a structure whereby individuals could design patterns of future relations upon which they could rely in the absence of readily available, dependable market alternatives. In other words, economic planning could then be developed at a complex level beyond the capacity of the individual enterprise because enforceable commitments permit the coordination of others' activities in specialized areas not supported by a general market.

Although these early planning contracts were mainly exchanges of commitments to make deliveries of goods in the future or to perform services in the future, it was tempting for the courts to deal with these agreements, designed to set relational patterns beyond the limits of individual ownership at a more detailed level than was possible in the open market, as simple sales of future commitments. Moreover, the emergence of Smithian and Ricardian economic theory seems to have contributed to a positivistic retreat from the broader and, in some respects, more advanced decisions made in some commercial law areas by Lord Mansfield in the latter half of the eighteenth century.[24] Mansfield, in an essentially pragmatic approach, tended to follow the customs of the merchants in providing legal reenforcement and support for the rapidly developing commercial economy of eighteenth-century England.

The quantitative *quid pro quo* analysis which deduced exchange commitments from sale seems to have dominated the thinking of nineteenth-century jurists in both England and the United States so that no broader legal formulation of what contract was about was able to develop. Morton Horwitz has argued that early nineteenth-century intellectual influence contributed to the formal rigidity and narrowing of the legal doctrines used in handling contract problems.[25] Grant Gilmore, in a detailed analysis of the strained emergence of a formal theory of contract in the United States under the influence of Langdell, Holmes, and Williston, contended that these legal scholars felt the need to reduce contract law to a consistent body of theory derivable from some common core of rational, internally consistent, transactional patterns occurring in the economy.[26] It would appear that this rational element being sought is the economic concept of exchange. The exchange of promises regarding future actions was treated in their writings as essentially exchanges or sales of commitments or rights. The title of Gilmore's book, *The Death of Contract,* indicates his contention that the notion of a logically coherent theory of contract deducible from some body of transactional principles is no longer a viable basis for handling modern economic problems. Piero Mini has suggested that this penchant for assuming the existence of an internally consistent, rational explanation for social phenomena in economic writings was derived from Locke and Descartes.[27] Rationalism, in general, of course, has much older roots.

The problem for the economist is to analyze the economic activities and relations comprehended by contract. Expectations and futurity are, of course, concepts with which economists have long been familiar, and they parallel the kinds of contract which some legal scholars have characterized as agreements which transfer anticipated risk.[28] In a smoothly working, competitive market context, the only reason for an individual to agree to deliver goods at a future time at a given price is because he anticipates the price will fall. The buyer of this promise, of course, anticipates that the price will rise. This partakes of both gambling and insurance, neither of which is relevant in a stable, perfectly competitive market where prices neither rise nor fall significantly, where both buyers and sellers have perfect knowledge, and where no individual can significantly affect supply or demand. Rationally anticipatable changes in price are systematically discounted by the competitive market so that only in the case of perishables is futures trading necessary. The view of contract as a transfer of anticipated risk therefore does not explain the building of economic relations characteristic of interactions in imperfectly competitive business. If economists are to make a contribution to the modern legal analysis of contract as relation, they will have to develop an analysis in terms of actual economic processes to which contract law applies.[29]

As a clarification of the traditional view of contract, the most provocative and imaginative formulation is Ian Macneil's concept of "presentiation."[30] In the flexible framework of modern jurisprudence, what is needed is a generalized picture of the economic impact of business relations so that judges may develop working principles of what social purposes are being achieved by the enforcement or nonenforcement of various types and levels of commitment dealing with future events. Macneil argues that traditional Willistonian contract theory approaches the planning of future business relations by creating rights which are bargained for in the present, thus assimilating planning into a current transaction. In other words, contracts "presentiate" the future, or bring the future into the present where it is arranged. At first glance it would appear that this formulation does nothing more than reduce contract to a special form of sale in a market context, but the future exchanges being presentiated are being formulated in terms of rights which can be legally accepted as *faits accomplis*. This approach to molding the future and structuring relations in terms of current transactions based on consent limits the ability of the law to deal properly with the dynamics of business relations by tying contract theory to the transaction or bargain.

In an institutionally stable, traditional society with limited market exchange, the future, the present, and the past are all structured by an established system of relations or institutions. This relational structure, although differing from society to society, provides the arena in which barter or sale takes place as exchange transactions. As economic life becomes more complex and the commercial phase of society dominates a larger and larger fraction of its activities, traditional stability is eroded, and social and technological change comes to be an expected phenomenon. In this context, it becomes apparent that the emerging future can be influenced or organized in better or worse ways through the exercise of human imagination and intelligence. Persons engaged in productive activities are thus not satisfied to count on future exchange on the open market when the relational context of the market is constantly changing. Those who can aggregate more control over the economic processes subject to being structured and manipulated are better able to plan their affairs, a form of planning by owning. As noted in Coase's 1937 article, the prime ownership institution for supplementary market planning in our day is the firm (corporation), which has largely replaced individually owned enterprise. The other form of economic planning in the private sector is one structured through commitments (contracts) which permit individuals and firms to create relational stability and achieve efficiency from planning in areas where there is no market or where the market is not a sufficient source of stability to foster planning of economic processes.

Where there is a perfected market, the going market price is not only an expression of the cumulative rationality and aggregated factual information available, but also a social consensus that can be self-validating.[81] Under such circumstances, the individual has little need to make private commitments regarding the future unless he doubts the stability of the market or has a penchant for gambling, of pitting his estimate of the future against those of professional forecasters. It is only when an individual or business is involved with an increasingly complex economic process with more and more unique and specialized problems that there arises a need to develop a private relational structure. It is in this context that contract can be thought of not simply as anticipating the future, but as actually organizing and planning future economic relations. What is going on is economic decision making which structures events in the scale of time similar to planning which structures relations in the scale of space and size. The market exchange system can thus become secondary or ancillary to the actual planning and organizing of the complicated and important processes that go on in a modern economy.

### *The Political Economy of Relational Contract*

The concept of the competitive, two-party bargain as conceived by the Coase theorem falls short of providing an economic formulation to parallel the new legal analyses being developed in the modern theory of contract. Although the two-party bargain may superficially resemble the two-party contract, the burden of this article has been to show that bargain is a regressive, adversary transaction in which individualistic self-interest is paramount and that either party's gain is the other party's loss. On the other hand, the constructive process in which mutual advantage is structured through the building of relations with reciprocal content is an essentially social phenomenon and must be deduced from a primary commitment to social values in which the individual may find a threshold of stability. An increasing body of legal theory is taking cognizance of the empirical difference between contract and the adversary bargaining process (the isolated transaction or sale) in which parties take for granted the market or legally structured system of relations which they may individualistically exploit for their own advantage and to the disadvantage of opponents. Two-party contract in legal theory is being increasingly distinguished as a phenomenon where parties with long-term planning objectives are primarily concerned with structuring relational arrangements to provide a continuum of stability productive of reciprocal mutuality. There may be tactical bargaining eddies in the strategic stream of these relational arrangements, but increasingly businesses are so conscious of the triviality of these regressive bargaining issues in the context of long-term planning of relations that they frequently make their resolution secondary and are rather cavalier about detailing rights and duties on specific issues.[32]

This statement of economic relation as the essence of contract may suggest an economic version of the political theory of the social compact. In response to this suggestion, it should be pointed out that the threshold of trust and good faith which supports corporate relations is to be understood in the setting of generalized identification with the system of corporate property in our industrial economy in terms discussed by such writers as Charles Reich and John Kenneth Galbraith.

Reich dealt with elements of the influence of the relational structure on the planning process in his essay, "The New Property."[33] He argued that it was the legal protection of individual rights in property, in other words, the protection of private rights over the future, which historically has made it possible to extend the planning period of production. Reich concedes that the concentration of corporate power over property is a necessary structure for organizing and planning economic activity in a modern, complex society, but he points out that this concentration of power has meant that individuals no longer can rely on private property as the prime guarantee that the production process will serve their own interests as was the case, for example, in freehold subsistence farming. The separation of individual property rights from control over the productive process and the distribution of wealth in the modern corporate economy have resulted in the intervention of government to protect the public interest in the administration of property that was once guaranteed by a more dispersed, individualized control over production. However, even with representative government involved in controlling property through administrative procedures, similar problems of remoteness from individual rights still arise. Reich's recommendation is a new definition of the individual's primary claim on the fruits of social process within the necessary framework of organized and planned corporate and governmental processes.

Theories of entitlement and liability stated from the individualistic point of view may be expected to yield to theories of public interest which are the terms in which modern economic problems are being formulated. The concept of a free market where individual bargains take place in a structure which maximizes individual rights is more applicable in situations of semisubsistence agriculture, where individuals actually have a choice to buy and sell, or to boycott the exchange process. Where the production process is a pervasive structure controlling the economy, the argument that voters' choice and rational self-interest guarantee that the results of political and economic processes will be in the public interest has its shortcomings. It would appear that the political economy of a mixed system can best be correlated with the legal tenets of bargain and sale by considering them special instances of relation which must be structured by society through regulation when the market fails to provide a threshold for protecting individual rights. Relational contract is best seen as an expression of the specialized structuring of relations or private economic planning by participants in an economic continuum. Commitments between businesses are planning and organizing operations which should be viewed in terms of their contribution to social ends, which may include the protection of a zone of arbitrary choice and initiative. Where corporate purposes conflict with widely accepted social ends, the latter unquestionably will take precedence. In this sense, relational contract theory deals with the other end of the spectrum from antitrust law. It has a positive role of enforcing those arrangements found in the public interest, while antitrust regulations strike down and prosecute arrangements antithetical to the public interest.

The current literature takes cognizance of the constructive or planning aspects of economic interaction, on the one hand, and its competitive or zero sum aspects, on the other, in a variety of ways. It is this dichotomy which has been analyzed in terms of economic planning and relational contract versus sale, bargain, and exchange in this discussion. Whether these two aspects are viewed as superimposed layers in an ongoing process, or abutting, discontinuous processes, it is argued that the bargaining transaction is essentially divisive and zero sum, and that it must occur in a contained zone structured by a relational system. On the other hand, the relational structure necessary to an organized economy cannot be derived from an aggregation of bargains, but must be understood as a social construct developed in a setting of widely accepted social values and goals.

## *Notes*

1. *Journal of Law and Economics* 3 (1969): 1–44.
2. Such as Richard A. Posner, *Economic Analysis of Law* (Boston and Toronto: Little, Brown and Company, 1972), pp. 16–21.
3. See H.H. Liebhafsky, " 'The Problem of Social Cost'—An Alternative Approach," *Natural Resources Journal* 13 (1973): 615–76.
4. This point of view is reminiscent of the Roman law doctrine of *causa*, which specified that the public force should not interfere with private transactions except to achieve a public purpose.

5. While Coase's position is somewhat equivocal in that he assumes that the measure of economic efficiency is a result of a total competitive equilibrium of efficiency considerations as well as an accumulation of individual bargains, he logically must derive the efficiency criteria of the market from either a comprehensive social force, individual subjective rationality, or some interaction between the two. He tends to take it for granted that the rational bargain will somehow coincide with a general market equilibrium reflecting total social efficiency. This is shown in his use of unique tort problems as illustrations. The premise that a socially efficient rationalization of tort and contract problems can be postulated in terms of open market criteria and applied as the basis for resolving conflicts, which is also followed by Posner, involves a certain amount of circularity since market relationships are apparently presumed to be expressions of pure bargain rather than some overriding social principle.
6. *The Wealth of Nations* (New York: Modern Library, 1937), pp. 500–501.
7. Gary Becker, "Irrational Behavior and Economic Theory," *Journal of Political Economy* 70 (1962): 1–13. But for opposing views see John F. Muth, "Rational Expectations and the Theory of Price Movements," *Econometrica* 29 (1961): 315–35; G. L. S. Shackle, *Epistemics and Economics* (Cambridge: the University Press, 1972), pp. 15–16, 132, 135–36; and Harold Wolozin, ed., *The Economics of Pollution* (Morristown, N.J.: General Learning Press, 1974), p. 12.
8. Coase does specify that "a system in which the rights of individuals were unlimited would be one in which there were no rights to acquire" ("The Problem of Social Cost," p. 44). He does not explain the apparent contradiction between this statement and his postulated bargain in the absence of liability, under which premise no rights would exist. His discussion of rational bargain is based on the unstated premise of a threshold of socially derived restraint. The problem seems to be, however, that he insists upon evaluating and deriving limitations on rights in terms of a pure theory of rational bargain as the building block of social efficiency expressed in the market. On the other hand, if he derives *limitations* on rights from some generally arrived at social standard, then the scope of bargaining and its results are a by-product of such a social standard, rather than vice versa.
9. If one is inclined to argue that only tortious and not criminal behavior is envisaged in the Coase theorem, it should be pointed out that the definition of torts encompasses acts which are also criminal and that both of these systems assess penalties for antisocial acts. There is an apparent presumption in the Coase theorem of a significant distinction between civil and criminal sanctions from the economic point of view. The only economic difference is that in the case of criminal sanctions, the public has the presumed burden to take the initiative in punishing what is deemed antisocial behavior. In the case of tort or other civil actions, the individual takes the initiative and must assert a claim as a prerequisite to punishment. In both cases, redress is available to the injured party since criminal prosecution does not bar a supplementary civil suit for damages. The real distinction important for the Coasian position is that criminal sanctions are generally publicly known, whereas civil ac-

tions may deal with emerging common law definitions of liability and are frequently debates over whether sanctions achieve a public purpose. In other words, novel issues in tort liability are often marginalist in nature.

10. For the classic eighteenth-century statement, see David Hume, "Of the Original Contract," in *Social Contract*, edited by Ernest Barker (New York: Oxford University Press, 1960).
11. The problem of a threshold which alters relationships was treated by J. M. Buchanan in a general way in "The Coase Theorem and the Theory of the State," *Natural Resources Journal* 13 (1973): 579–94. Ian R. Macneil ("The Many Futures of Contract," *Southern California Law Review* 47 [1974]: 778–79) recognized that allocative arrangements involve zero sum bargaining processes, whereas enterprise relations do not. The distinction between the mutuality implicit in relational arrangements and the zero sum aspect of bargaining has roots going as far back as Book V on justice in Aristotle's *Ethics*. See the author's "Aristotle's Mathematical Analysis of Exchange," *History of Political Economy* 1 (1969): 44–66.
12. The term *contract* is here being used to refer to economic relations which involve a planning function from the economic point of view and are characterized by the exchange of a promise for a promise. It should be pointed out that the legal definition of contract blurs into the definition of sale, which is characterized by instantaneous transactions involving the transfer of title. For a history of the early development of contract law, see E. Allan Farnsworth, "The Past of Promise: An Historical Introduction to Contract," *Columbia Law Review* 69 (1969): 576–607. Modern legal analysis has developed a distinction between transactional contract and relational contract. References to contract in this article should be associated with the theory of relational contract.
13. For a discussion of some of these problems in the modern context of pollution regulation, see Guido Calabresi and A. Douglas Melamed, "Property Rules, Liability Rules, and Inalienability: One View of the Cathedral," *Harvard Law Review* 85 (1972): 1089–1128.
14. This perspective can be applied to the material analyzed in Warren J. Samuels, "Interrelations Between Legal and Economic Processes," *Journal of Law and Economics* 14 (1971): 435–50.
15. See, generally, A. Coddington, "Positive Economics," *Canadian Journal of Economics* 5 (1972): 1–15; and Grant Gilmore, "Legal Realism: Its Cause and Cure," *Yale Law Journal* 70 (1961): 1037–48.
16. For a recent discussion of the influence of Atomist ideas on their contemporaries, see David J. Furley, *Two Studies in the Greek Atomists* (Princeton: Princeton University Press, 1967).
17. Coase recognized the significance of the individual's ability to rely on the market in routine situations in his 1937 article ("The Nature of the Firm," *Economica* 4 [n.s.] [1937]: 386–405) in which he developed the thesis that the firm is an administrative or organizational adjustment to specific efficiencies not available through the market. This view parallels the perspective on contract developed below and suggests an area of analysis in which the emergence of the corporation and the develop-

ment of contract law can both be viewed as supplements to the market structure.

18. For examples of this literature, in addition to that cited below, see E. Allan Farnsworth, "Legal Remedies for Breach of Contract," *Columbia Law Review* 70 (1970): 1145–1216; E. J. Mishan, "The Economics of Disamenity," *Natural Resources Journal* 14 (1974): 55–86; and Benjamin Ward, *What's Wrong With Economics?* (New York: Basic Books, Inc., 1972), pp. 199ff.
19. See Macneil, "Many Futures of Contract," pp. 718–19, for a somewhat parallel discussion of the relational role of contract. Macneil, however, lists exchange as one of the basic roots of contractual relations, characterizing it as the precondition of specialization and the division of labor. He thus assimilates some of the premises of the Coasian tradition. He ignores the overwhelming body of historical evidence from ancient societies which indicates that specialization and division of labor were developed in administrative societies at a stage when bargain and exchange were not significant elements in the allocation of goods, for example, in the centralized, aggregative and distributive Egyptian pharaohates.
20. Adam Smith's recognition that specialization is limited by the extent of the market addresses the problem of the necessity of large-scale economic relations as a prerequisite for mass produced, routinely merchandized goods. It was the need for growth of production on new terms outside the mercantilist market structure which seems to have motivated his analysis.
21. Farnsworth, "The Past of Promise," p. 599. The apparently contradictory statements by Farnsworth on page 604 regarding the intervention of the state in areas "in which the market mechanism was thought to be inadequate" can be explained by their reference to essentially transactional arrangements in the context of market failure rather than relational structures supplementing market limitations.
22. Fritz Pringsheim, *The Greek Law of Sale* (Weimar: Hermann Bohlaus Nachfolger, 1950), pp. 130, 137, 168.
23. *Cyropaedia* I.e. 16–17.
24. See, on Mansfield, S. Todd Lowry, "Lord Mansfield and the Law Merchant: Law and Economics in the Eighteenth Century," *Journal of Economic Issues* 7 (1973): 605–22.
25. Morton J. Horwitz, "The Historical Foundations of Modern Contract Law," *Harvard Law Review* 87 (1974): 917–56.
26. Grant Gilmore, *The Death of Contract* (Columbus: Ohio State University Press, 1974). Gilmore suggests that contract law is moving toward a more flexible system of rulings approximating the frame of reference in which tort decisions are made, an opposite view to the Coasian one that essentially tort problems should be decided in terms approximating traditional bargain theory.
27. Piero V. Mini, *Philosophy and Economics, The Origins and Development of Economic Theory* (Gainesville: University Presses of Florida, 1974).
28. Morris R. Cohen, *Law and the Social Order; Essays in Legal Philosophy* (Hamden, Conn.: Archon Books, 1967 [1933]).

29. See Lawrence M. Friedman and Stewart Macaulay, "Contact Law and Contract Teaching: Past, Present, and Future," *Wisconsin Law Review* 1967 (1967): 805–21.
30. Ian R. Macneil, "Restatement (Second) of Contracts and Presentiation," *Virginia Law Review* 60 (1974): 589–610.
31. The economist should take note of the fact that the measure of damages for breach of contract is generally in terms of the difference between the contractual claim and the currently available open market alternative. It therefore is irrelevant to use legal processes to enforce contractual claims where they parallel stable market conditions. Specific performance of contract is an exceptional remedy and is limited to unique situations.
32. See, for example, Stewart Macaulay, "Non-Contractual Relations in Business: A Preliminary Study," *American Sociological Review* 28 (1963): 55–67.
33. *Yale Law Journal* 73 (1964): 733–87.

# 10

# Price Theory as Jurisprudence: Law and Economics, Chicago Style

*H. H. Liebhafsky*

In 1881, in *The Common Law*, Oliver Wendell Holmes, Jr., wrote: "The life of the law has not been logic: it has been experience. . . . The law embodies the story of a nation's development through many centuries, and it cannot be dealt with as if it contained only the axioms and corollaries of a book of mathematics.[1] In essence, the jurisprudence of the Chicago School of economists is nothing other than the view of Holmes multiplied by "minus 1."[2] More bluntly, the view of the Chicago School is that "the law must be dealt with as if it contained only the assumptions, axioms, and corollaries of *The Theory of Price*."[3]

Consider, for example, the following quotation from the Richard A. Posner version of the law as promulgated by the members of the Chicago School:

> If [Since] the analysis of Part I of this book [*Economic Analysis of Law*] is correct, the ultimate question for decision in many [he cites no exceptions] lawsuits is, what allocation of resources will promote economic efficiency? The market normally decides this question [assuming the hypothetical world conjured up by aggregating the many assumptions encompassed in the general assumption of perfect competition, the Gibraltar

*The author is Professor of Economics, The University of Texas, Austin.* *He is indebted to Wendell Gordon, Carey Thompson, Warren Samuels, and Elizabeth Johnston for their helpful comments on this article and to Jan Crumpton for her work on the manuscript.*

> of Chicago jurisprudence] but *it is given* to the legal system to decide in situations where costs of market determination would exceed those of legal determination [*as it is given to the market* in the reverse situation]. The criteria are the same (italics mine).[4]

And thus is it given unto the Bench and the Bar to adopt the test of "economic efficiency" as a universal rule of decision (*ratio decidendi*) in every case and to apply the test of "which party's interest has the greatest market value" as a universal matter of fact to be found in every case. By adopting these tests universally, the courts will make the "correct" decisions, namely, those which would have been made had the costs of decision in the marketplace not been greater than those of the legal determination. It is assumed, of course, that relative prices are stable and that the economy is operating in the state of equilibrium described by Joseph Schumpeter in chapter 1 of *The Theory of Economic Development,* a stable, static, equilibrium in which there is movement but no change.[5] Otherwise, the answer to the universal factual question would be subject to change while a case was on appeal, and no final answer could be given to the factual question in a court of the first instance. The test thus implies a change in judicial procedure.

Posner also has written:

> If [Although] much of the common law seems informed by an implicit economic logic, the same cannot be said for statute law [which is concerned "primarily with distributional considerations"].
>
> One possible explanation for the difference in the relative emphasis on efficiency and distribution is that the common law rules crystallized in the nineteenth century [a period in which William Blackstone's mystical natural law *Commentaries* served as the leading text for the study of law in this country], while the statutes discussed in this book are for the most part products of this century. The nineteenth century was one of relatively greater scarcity of economic resources than today [1973], and efficiency may be a more highly prized value under conditions of scarcity (at least in Western societies).[6]

Economic efficiency stands here confessed a culturally determined value. All of which raises the interesting question of "how, then, can 'economic efficiency' be advanced as a basis for a universal rule of decision?"

## *The Gospel According to Chicago*

Although I do not propose to restrict the discussion herein to one of his work alone, Posner's book must, I think, be recognized as representative of the word emanating from Chicago for these reasons: Even though he seems to have had no formal training in economics,[7] he has acknowledged his "greatest debt" for the "enrichment of [his] understanding of economic theory and the relationship of economics to law" is owed to his Chicago colleagues Gary S. Becker, Ronald H. Coase, Aaron Director, and George Stigler. He has further acknowledged that "Harold Demsetz, in conversation and a seminar on property rights that he gave at the University of Chicago Law School in 1970, made a significant contribution to the view of the common law developed in Part I of this book."[8] Posner does not confess to having learned anything from non-Chicagoans.

I am not aware that any of the Chicagoans thus credited has filed an action in libel against Posner nor disavowed the credit he has been given. (I have no doubt that the editor of this journal would be willing to publish any such disclaimer as might be forthcoming, should any of the several house organs published by the Chicagoans be unwilling to do so.) To be sure, J. M. Buchanan, who has identified himself as one who "shares a Chicago heritage (pre-empirical)," has characterized Posner's book as "Good Economics—Bad Law."[9] But Buchanan's criticism is largely based on his fear that Posner's universal rule of decision would lead to "creative interpretation" rather than to the impossibility of a "strict interpretation" of our Constitution by the Supreme Court. Thus Buchanan has written: "Mental experiment leads me to think about the potential excesses of a 'Posner' court in the 1980s and 1990s, guided by its extra-legal criterion of maximum value. Would such a court be comparable to the Warren Court in the generation of social unrest and disorder?"[10] (The word *generation* here refers to a process of production rather than to a group of people of about the same age.) Buchanan also has mentioned that Posner has failed to examine critically "the jurisprudential [existing legal] setting" in which the latter's analysis "is placed."[11]

I go further. No Chicagoan, including Buchanan and Gordon Tullock, has examined the place of the theology of the law as it has emanated from Chicago in the field of jurisprudence in general. Chicago jurisprudence is distinguished by the paucity of its references to the ideas of non-Chicago writers. The Chicago "price theory as jurisprudence" approach is a curious mixture, not a compound, of particles of logical positivist methodology suspended randomly in a mythical or secular natural law philosophy. Buchanan's perversion of the vocabulary of the Instrumentalist view of law, in which he has misinterpreted the concept of "law as an instrument of social order" to mean "law is an instrument of *the existing social order,* to wit, The Establishment," is Chicago jurisprudence for all of that.[12] A bill of particulars follows.

Eighteenth-century mystical (supranatural) natural law theories such as those of Blackstone and Justice Story,[13] which stemmed from Aquinas, today have been replaced by the mythical (supernatural) secular law theories of Friedrich Hayek and Ludwig von Mises. The latter's telling sentence, "the reality of the laws of praxology [the science of human choice] is revealed to man by the same signs that reveal the reality of natural law, namely the fact that his power to attain his ends is restricted and conditioned," puts the secular natural law point of view in a nutshell.[14] The transition from the mystical to the mythical or secular natural law point of view resulting from the impact of Newtonian physics is painfully obvious in Thomas Paine's reference to the Almighty as "God, the Great Mechanic of All Creation." Compare the admission by Henry C. Simons that his system rested upon the existence of "a relatively absolute absolute." In 1948, Aaron Director wrote that Simons had been at the time of his death establishing himself as the head of a "School at the University of Chicago."[15]

## *The Chicago Trinity*

The Posner recitation of the catechism recognizes openly and at the outset that Chicago jurisprudence rests upon an Act of Faith, an affirmation of a belief in this trinity: the negatively sloping demand curve, opportunity cost, and "the tendency of resources to gravitate toward their highest valued uses," a tendency "which is also derived from reflection on how self-interested people react to a change in their surroundings" [*provided, however, only* that the conditions exist necessary for such gravitation to occur].[16]

### *The Negatively Sloping Demand Curve*

Chicagoans generally identify the purely analytical concept of the negatively sloping demand curve as a "prediction." Is it a *prediction* or an assumption? Consider the following: It is assumed that consumers maximize nonlinear utility functions subject to budget constraints. Satisfaction of the Marshallian equimarginal principle ("a first order condition") alone is not enough. A "second order condition," depicted graphically by indifference curves convex to the origin, is *necessary* to ensure maximization rather than minimization. This convexity condition is simply the condition that the so-called substitution effect of a price change must operate on purchases in a direction opposite from that of the price change. The same condition is a *necessary* one in the contemporary statement of the conditions under which a demand curve will have a negative slope. Thus, the *necessary* condition for a negatively sloping demand curve is an implicit assumption in the original maximization assumption. The exceptional case in which the income effect of an inferior good is numerically greater than that of the substitution effect is eliminated by casual empiricism: "Such a situation seldom if ever exists."[17] Like all the other ceremonial discoveries of price theory, demand analysis consists of a discovery of the meaning of the assumption originally made.

Given its assumptions, price theory is, at best, an explanation of what the real world is *not* like, a system of purely analytical concepts, a possible basis for classifying information, but not a basis for policy. Gary Becker's attempt[18] to deduce the negatively sloping demand curve from the assumption of scarcity without reliance on the assumption of maximization rests upon his use of Milton Friedman's concept of a Constant Real Income Demand Curve,[19] which is merely a demand curve depicting the substitution effect alone of a price change. Becker's deduction thus rests on the assumption of rational consumer cost-minimizing behavior and amounts merely to a use of the reciprocal of the maximization thesis. The mystical natural law counterpart inversion would seem to be celebration of a Black Mass.

### *Opportunity Cost*

Now consider the second member of the Chicago trinity: opportunity cost, a utility maximization concept derived from the works of the nineteenth-century Austrians. The concept involves an assumption of mutually exclusive alternatives with no middle ground. Reliance upon an opportunity cost concept constitutes at least circumstantial evidence of myopia or of a calculated intention on the part of the analyst to preclude evaluation of the consequences of adoption of free market solutions to policy problems, while pretending to be examining all alternative social policies. It is a condition precedent to the use of the opportunity cost doctrine that all social policies are to be evaluated on the basis of economic considerations only and that philosophico-political objectives are to be assumed to be attained when the economic objectives are attained. Thus price is made a measure of social value, and the distribution of income is assumed to be given. One unrealistic assumption begets another.

Either way, whether the use of the opportunity cost doctrine is the result of myopia or calculation, the effect in any economic analysis of a legal problem is the same: Analysis of the use and an estimation of the consequences of the use of equitable remedies are effectively eliminated, nay, excluded from consideration at the outset in the statement of the problem. I have demonstrated elsewhere, at length,[20] that R. H. Coase's theoretical basis for the Coase Theorem suffers from a fatal defect because he fails to consider the effects of the use of equitable remedies. These remedies developed originally in Courts of Chancery to provide necessary flexibility to the law in adapting to social and technological changes in cases in which "the damage remedy is inadequate," either because of the continuing nature of harmful effects or because damages cannot be measured.

It is a condition precedent to the application of the procedures and rules of equity in a judicial proceeding that the plaintiff carry the burden of showing that the damage remedy is inadequate, in effect, that the assumptions of price theory upon which Chicago jurisprudence rests are irrelevant to the case at bar. Small wonder, then, that either equitable remedies are ignored or the damage remedy is always assumed to be adequate in Chicago jurisprudence (more accurately, Chicago *partial* jurisprudence since it deals only with the special case defined by the assumptions of the price theory upon which it rests and not with the general case). Nowhere is this fact more evident than in Posner's discussion of the remedy of specific performance. In his book he applies his universal *ratio decidendi* of economic efficiency to a case in which a seller refuses to perform his contract:

> The fact that the seller defaulted may indicate that there is another contract which increases value by even more than the sale to me [why not *must,* assuming maximization?]; *if so we want to encourage the breach.* The results of decreeing specific performance are not catastrophic; since the seller can always pay me to surrender my right of specific performance and presumably will do so if a substitute transfer [of the property subject to the contract] would yield him a higher price. But to require the seller to conduct this additional transaction does impose additional transaction costs.[21]

In opening this discussion Posner recognizes that equitable relief is given because damages are difficult to quantify, but in the argument in the quoted passage he switches to the assumption that the parties can quantify the damages. In fact, he assumes that the parties are in a position to estimate the respective values to themselves of compliance or noncompliance with the equitable relief granted with the same degree of certainty that they would enjoy if the case involved liquidated damages (defined as a fixed sum specified in advance in the contract to be paid as damages in the event of a breach).

It thus seems to be a part of the Chicago creed that the damage remedy is always adequate, and discussion of the use of equitable remedies is unnecessary. Equitable remedies, of course, have their counterparts in orders issued by administrative agencies and in statutes enacted by legislative bodies, both of which are "constantly meddling with the natural state of human relationships" encompassed in a laissez-faire system. Equitable remedies, moreover, are available in antitrust proceedings and are used to disturb that state of "economic efficiency" which is achieved under the Stigler "survivorship principle."[22]

Finally, uncritical reliance on the opportunity cost doctrine performs the function in the Chicago dogma of eliminating the necessity for economic analysis of the use of equitable remedies in the judicial process in an apparently, but only apparently, plausible way since few readers who have not studied the law can be expected to know that inadequacy of the damage remedy is a condition precedent to the exercise of equitable jurisdiction by a court, and the Chicago use of the opportunity cost doctrine rests upon an assumption that the damage remedy is always adequate. Thus, the problem of the effect of enforcement of equitable remedies is eliminated by the assumptions inherent in the opportunity cost doctrine. If the damage remedy is inadequate, no basis for bargaining exists.

### *Gravitation of Resources*

The third member of the trinity of the Chicago faith is the assumption of "the tendency of resources to gravitate toward their highest valued uses." This tendency, assuming self-interested maximizing individuals, is a proxy variable energized by the activities of the Unseen Hand, that is, the *allegation* of its existence is offered as circumstantial evidence of the existence of the Unseen Hand. An immaculate conception, the tendency exists primarily in the purely analytical and hence sterile world of perfect competition in which resources freely flow. The tendency performs a role in Chicago price-theory-as-jurisprudence similar to that performed by the Holy Ghost in mystical natural law philosophy, since it is relied upon to exorcise greater than normal profits in the long run.

### *Intermingling of Natural Law and Logical Positivist Preconceptions*

Probably the best example of the use of a natural law philosophy in law is the reliance upon the concept of "substantive due process" by the Supreme Court to establish and maintain judicial superiority with regard to the nature and scope of regulation of economic activities from about the time of the decision in *Munn* v. *Illinois*[23] in 1877 until the decision in *Nebbia* v. *New York*[24] in 1934. Throughout this period, the Court denied to Congress and state legislatures the power to make final determinations in regard to regulation of economic activities. Instead, it substituted its own judgment on the merits of the relevant attempted regulation in making its decisions to uphold or strike down on constitutional grounds the legislation in question. The due process clauses of the Fifth and Fourteenth Amendments were the vehicles used by the Court for this purpose. In *Nebbia* the Court reversed its attitude and declared the principle of legislative superiority in matters of economic regulation. The due process concept was defined as it had been before 1877 to mean, roughly, "reasonable" or "fair" procedure, or essentially, the elements of an adversary proceeding in a nonviolent environment conducted by an impartial umpire. The merits of economic policies adopted by legislatures were declared to be out of the jurisdiction of the courts and considered to be beyond the competence of courts. In the area of civil liberties, however, the Court has retained the doctrine of judicial superiority.[25]

Chicagoans have perceived the windmill of the apparent inconsistency of the Court's positions just described as a giant to be destroyed. The jousting seems to have been opened by Aaron Director in 1964,[26] with subsequent lances tilted by R. H. Coase and J. M. Buchanan (whose views on the Warren Court have been quoted earlier in this article).[27]

In Posner's Lake Michigan scroll it has been written of this question: "While it is said that there was no source for a doctrine of liberty of contract [substantive due process] in the text or history of the relevant constitutional provisions, the same criticism can be (and has been) made of the Court's decisions in a variety of other constitutional areas, such as reapportionment."[28]

Predictably, one finds in his discussion of false advertising the following: "The dichotomy between political and nonpolitical speech is closely related to a larger dichotomy, between the protection of competition in goods and protection of competition in ideas, which is characteristic of constitutional law today.[2] The classical liberals believed that both product markets and political debate should be free. The Court's preference for the latter form of freedom cannot easily be justified on principled grounds."[29] The footnote in this quotation states that the discussion is based on the 1964 piece by Aaron Director in Chicago's *Journal of Law and Economics,* which I have mentioned above.

But a motion for a judgment by the reader in favor of the dichotomy, notwithstanding the adverse verdict of the Chicagoans, easily can be made on principled, instrumentalist, grounds: By adopting a rule of legislative supremacy in regard to matters of economic regulation, the Court has taken the position that it is the will of the voters as expressed by, or to the extent that it is expressed by, elected legislative representatives which should prevail. This position postulates (assumes) the existence of a will (which may change from time to time as voters make self-correcting value judgments) based on information and not upon a demagogic appeal.

By continuing to assert judicial supremacy in the civil liberties area (including, of course, that of voter qualifications and reapportionment) the Court has recognized that it can serve as a brake on what Alexander Hamilton called "dangerous innovations and serious oppressions of the minor party in the community."[30] Contemporary examples of such dangerous innovations are an unwarranted exercise or abuse of presidential power or experimentation by congressional committees with elements of procedural due process (such as have occurred in the 1970s and 1950s, respectively). In other words, the Court has accepted the responsibility of serving as a disinterested party in bringing to reality the assumptions upon which its policy of legislative superiority in matters of economic regulation is based. Absent judicial superiority in regard to civil liberties matters, each legislator or city councilman would be in a position of, to paraphrase James Madison, judging his own cause.

The logical positivist particles which have been mixed up and suspended in the Chicago mythical natural law creed can be illustrated by Posner's definition of *economic theory* as "a system of deductive logic," combined with his redundant qualifying clause, "when correctly applied it yields results that are consistent with one another." To be noted is the implicit conception of logical analysis as "the main business of economics," a view akin to Bertrand Russell's conception of "logical analysis as the main business of philosophy."

Counterparts in jurisprudence of this logical positivist view can be found in the legal positivism of Hans Kelsen[31] and in the analytical jurisprudence of H. L. A. Hart.[32] In Kelsen's view there exists a *Grundnorm*, a basic constitution, whose validity or origin cannot be explained by law but which stands as the first "presupposition." Hart's equivalent basic assumption is that of the existence of "secondary rules." The validity of all subsidiary legal rules is then tested by comparison of their consistency with the *Grundnorm* or secondary rules, respectively, in these two views of law. Thus "the main business of the law" becomes logical analysis. Apostles of the Chicago creed utilize the concept of economic efficiency—defined as "the use of resources where their value is greatest"[33]—to perform a function analogous to that performed by Kelsen's *Grundnorm* or Hart's secondary rules. But there is a difference: The disciples from Chicago rush in where Hart and Kelsen feared to tread. The advocacy of the adoption of the concept of economic efficiency as a universal *ratio decidendi* pretends that the concept is both antecedent and superior to Kelsen's *Grundnorm* and Hart's secondary rules and presumes to explain, validate, and provide a rule for interpreting the *Grundnorm* or secondary rules.

So that I will not be misinterpreted, let me emphasize that I do not question the necessity for internal consistency in any analysis. What I do question is the view that the mere internal consistency of an analysis establishes the validity of its conclusions as a basis for action. Mere tautologies alone are not meaningful bases of policies.

### *The Creed*

Posner's text for each day is that "[economics] explores and tests the implications of the assumption that man is a rational maximizer of his ends in life, his satisfactions—what we shall call his self interest."[34] This attitude *not only* demonstrates the close kinship between the Chicago methodology and that employed by the eighteenth-century philosophers (Descartes, Leibnitz, and Spinoza) in demonstrating by means of deductive reasoning alone the existence of God,[35] but also is amply supported by a study of the visions of property rights of Harold Demsetz and of crime and punishment of Gary Becker and Gordon Tullock.

#### *Demsetz*

The manifestation that the free market safeguards the interests of unborn future generations made its appearance in Demsetz's paper delivered at the 1967 meeting of the American Economic Association.[36] Study of that document reveals that it constitutes a deliverance from the legend that Chicagoans are impeccable logicians. Compare the assumptions underlying the arguments in two quotations taken from consecutive paragraphs.

> If a single [read "individual," not necessarily "unmarried"] person owns land, he will attempt to maximize its present value by taking into account alternative future time streams of benefits and costs and selecting that one which he believes will maximize the present value of his privately-owned land rights. We all know that this means he will attempt to take into account the supply and demand conditions that he thinks will exist after his death.
>
> But with communal rights there is no broker, and the claims of the present generation will be given an uneconomically large weight in determining the intensity with which the land is worked. Future generations might desire to pay present generations enough to change the present intensity of land usage. But they have no living agent to place their claims on the market. Under a communal property system, should a living person pay others to reduce the rate at which they work the land, he would not gain anything of value for his efforts. Communal property means that future generations must speak for themselves. No one has yet estimated the costs of carrying on such a conversation.[37]

Note that in the first paragraph above, either the private owner must carry on a similar conversation with an unconceived foetus to learn its demand function or have access to the occult for the same purpose. Otherwise, any resemblance between his estimated future demand functions and the demand functions of nonexistent persons, living or dead, will be purely coincidental. Demand functions are, after all, a reflection of preferences plus ability to pay; it is elementary price theory that they can be generated from utility or preference functions via the first order conditions, "assuming that second order conditions are met." In short, Demsetz's argument rests upon a switching about of assumptions to produce the desired conclusion. In general, the purely analytical construct of demand employed in static welfare economics eliminates the difficult problem of specifying the chronological age at which the preferences of an individual aggregated into the social welfare function are "to count" by tacitly merging it into an assumption that all individuals have income (or more generally "property") to trade. But Demsetz's fabrication of a market demand function (or a horizontal sum of the individual unconceived foetus's demand functions) cannot rely on this escape hatch unless one takes the view that, in principle, the nonexistent exists.

*Becker*

In "Crime and Punishment: An Economic Approach," Becker has presented an alternative to the views of Feodor Dostoevski. The essence of Becker's pronouncement reads:

> The approach taken here follows the economists' usual analysis of choice and assumes that a person commits an offense if the expected utility to him exceeds the utility he could get by using his time and other resources at other activities [or in plain English, commits an offense because he commits an offense]. Some persons become "criminals," therefore, not because their basic motivation differs from that of other persons, but because their benefits and costs differ. I cannot pause to discuss the many general implications of this approach [the "pause" presumably would be a long one].
>
> This approach implies that there is a function relating the number of offenses by any person to his probability of conviction, to his punishment if convicted, and to other variables, such as the income available to him in legal and other illegal activities, the frequency of nuisance arrests, and his willingness to commit an illegal act. This can be represented as
>
> $$O_j = O_j\ (p_j,\ f_j,\ u_j).$$ [38]

Here $O_j$ represents the crime production function of the $j^{th}$ member of society "during a particular period" of time, $p_j$ the probability of his conviction for each offense, $f_j$ his punishment per offense ("the price he pays" or his "cost"), and "$u_j$ is a portmanteau variable representing all these other factors," including *"his willingness to commit an illegal act* (italics mine)," which I take it is equivalent to the legal concept of "general intent" or *mens rea*. The illegal-activity production function of every member of society includes among its arguments "his willingness to engage in illegal activity" and every man has his price. I leave it to the reader to decide whether or not all this rests upon an acceptance of the doctrine of original sin.

The specification of the production function quite naturally begets a cost function and first and second order conditions. The bones of the orthodox theory of the firm provide the structural basis for the creation of a diagram depicting the continuous "social" marginal revenue and marginal cost functions in which the horizontal (output) axis measures "number of offenses committed." The use of both the calculus and the continuous curves in the diagrams means, of course, that all criminal activities are homogeneous and infinitely divisible.

*Tullock*

Gordon Tullock recently has provided an interesting summary of the testimonials verifying that severity of punishment deters crime. For the most part, these attestations are expressed in unpublished master's theses and doctoral dissertations done at Chicago and under Tullock's direction elsewhere. Among the most powerful sentences written by Tullock, one finds these:

> The first studies in this field, the ones I criticized at the beginning of my survey of the empirical literature, dealt with the death penalty. Recently Ehrlich has returned to this problem and, by using a much more sophisticated method, has demonstrated a very sizeable deterrence payoff to the death penalty for murder.[18] *His figures indicate that each execution prevents between 8 and 20 murders.* Unfortunately, the data available for this study were not what one would hope for. . . . Earlier, and using a quite different set of statistics and a different method, I arranged to have a graduate student do a preliminary study of the same issue; his results showed that each execution prevented two murders. Here again, however, the data were bad and the methods were suitable only for a preliminary examination.[19]
> Even granting the fact that most potential criminals have only a rough idea as to the frequency and severity of punishment, multiple regression studies show that increasing the frequency or severity of the punishment does reduce the likelihood that a given crime will be committed (italics mine).[39]

Even though "the data are bad," Ehrlich's result would seem to apply with particular force to an individual like Bluebeard, particularly if he was executed after killing his first wife, and perhaps in the case of Jack the Ripper, caught after his first homicide. Taking an unweighted arithmetic average of the results in these two studies (since the data are bad in both cases, the results may be assigned equal weights), we have $[(8 + 20)/2 + 2]/2 = 8$ murders prevented by each execution. The results hold at the 0.01 percent level of confidence.

*Posner*

In Posner's version, there appears a criminal's continuous demand curve for criminal activity, with punishment as "the price the criminal pays," all presumably measurable in "appropriate" units of measurement since none are specified. And there is something spiritual to be found in his discussion of the problem of determination of damages in tort cases involving death. He remarks that courts have ignored the problem of "the proper valuation of life," but first presents the reader with this profound thought: "Most people would not exchange their life for anything less than an infinite sum of money if the exchange were to take place *immediately,* since they would have so little time in which to enjoy the proceeds of the sale" (italics mine, otherwise *sic.*).[40] In this discussion he has referred the reader without further comment to E. J. Mishan's article, "The Valuation of Life and Limb: A Theoretical Approach," in which Mishan (tongue-in-cheek?) called attention to the fact that cost benefit studies, undertaken to make estimates of the value of human lives lost for the purpose of determining the optimal rate of accident prevention, should take account of the value to the $j^{th}$ person of the value of the loss of life of the $i^{th}$ person, for example, "an improved chance of losing a dependent or inheriting an asset—or inheriting it sooner" (*sic.*).[41]

The contradiction that breaches of contract are to be encouraged "if they increase value" because the damage remedy is always adequate in such cases but that imprisonment is a proper punishment for rape poses a dilemma. It is resolved in the Chicago dogma in the following pronouncement: "We want to deter only those breaches of contract in which the costs to the victim of the breach are greater than the benefits to the breaching party. . . . But society does not want to deter only those rapes in which the displeasure of the victim is shown to be greater than the satisfaction derived by the rapist from his act. A simple damages remedy would therefore be inadequate."[42]

Chicagoans attempt to except crimes of violence from their universal *ratio decidendi* of economic efficiency by employing a *private* opportunity cost concept in breach of contract and antitrust cases and a concept of *social* opportunity cost in cases of forcible rape and murder. Thus is it revealed that "if the value to the criminal of the criminal conduct exceeds all relevant costs to society, including those of allocation by legal rather than market transactions, the criminal conduct is value maximizing and should be tolerated" (*sic.*).[43]

Chicagoans switch their definitions of opportunity cost from *private* to *social* in these cases because their tacit assumption that social order *always* exists after the test of economic efficiency is applied is contradicted by the very definition of criminal (or antisocial) behavior. Posner's statement that it may be efficient to permit a starving man to steal a loaf of bread is a virtual admission of this point.[44]

Chicagoans cannot be true to their faith in economic efficiency and at the same time commit the heresy of employing the functional concept of law as an instrument of social order. The dilemma in which they find themselves is nowhere more clear than in the concluding paragraph of Posner's *parvum opus*:

> It would appear, therefore, that economic theory ["a system of deductive logic" for which "Bentham's utilitarianism in its positive aspect as a theory of human behavior is another name"], although commonly viewed as an unmoral principle of social order, has ethical implications. It provides unexpected support to those who believe that not all commands backed by state force are entitled to claim obedience as law [*provided however* that it is recognized that those commands which are consistent with the moral and social philosophy embedded in the economic theology promulgated by the Chicago School do have a rightful claim to such obedience].[45]

Reliance upon a mythical natural law philosophy and its constant companion, Bentham's hedonism, or upon a *Grundnorm* or secondary rules, such as the objective of maximization of aggregate preferences in static welfare economics, all have this in common: In each case there is a reliance upon a norm external to the evaluation process and hence to the problem being considered, and inquiry into the consequences of adopting this or that policy or course of action is precluded once the first assumption is satisfied.

### *Instrumentalism as a Theoretical Basis for Law and Institutionalism*

More than four score years ago, John R. Commons put the point clearly:

> Blackstone wished the law to be as he conceived it to be, which to him seemed divine and natural. Bentham wished it to be different and said so. *And this is the only alternative to a theory of change and experiment.* For, in lieu of historic research founded on a theory of the novelty of changes in customs and of experimental adaptation to other changes, wherein the change itself is the subject-matter of investigation and experiment, the only basis left for law and economics is Wish. Blackstone and Bentham were wishers, not scientists (italics mine).[46]

The alternative specified by Commons was based upon the philosophy of C. S. Peirce. In the hands of John Dewey, Peirce's views were fashioned into Instrumentalism, and in the mind of Clarence Ayres, Instrumentalism was recognized to be implicit in Veblen's distinction between the technological and the ceremonial, between "workmanship" and "imbecile institutions." In the work of Ayres, Instrumentalism was formulated into a theoretical basis for Institutionalism.[47] A *process* of self-correcting value judgments—an emphasis upon investigation of the consequences of actions continuously taken and policies adopted—was substituted for the finality of the first assumption of logical positivism and natural law philosophy. Those who have long remembered, and often repeat, the cliché based on the 1932 article by Paul Homan,[48] that Institutionalism has no theory, embarrass knowledgeable listeners by such a naked disclosure of their ignorance of the work of Commons and Ayres. John Galbraith's pregnant sentence, "the enemy of conventional wisdom is not ideas but the march of events,"[49] is Instrumentalism in thirteen words. With apologies to its author, it may be read here as: The enemy of ideas and first assumptions is not other ideas but the consequences of actions taken and policies adopted: The standard of evaluation is inherent in the definition of the problem.

Ayres did not specifically address himself to the problem of the relationship between law and economics, but John R. Commons did do so. The contrast between the Chicago price-theory-as-jurisprudence and the Instrumentalist conception of the judicial process becomes painfully clear when one compares statements made by Posner and Commons. Posner has written:

> Our survey of the major common law fields suggests that the common law exhibits a deep unity that is economic in character. The differences among the law of property, the law of contracts and the law of torts are primarily differences in vocabulary, detail, and subject matter rather than in method or policy [in every case, "economic efficiency" is the externally imposed *ratio decidendi*]. The common law method is to allocate responsibilities between people in interacting activities in such a way as to maximize the joint value, or, what amounts to the same thing, minimize the joint cost of the activities. It may do this by redefining a property right, devising a new rule or liability, or by recognizing a contract right, but nothing fundamental turns on which device is used.[50]

And when the joint value is maximized, that result is reached which satisfies the static standard of evaluation, one external to the problem at hand. If the consequence of water pollution is permanently polluted water, never mind, as long as the joint rent from the use of the water by the parties to the present bargaining is maximized.

Commons correctly described the common law method as historically an experimental one,

> wherein each particular case, when decided, becomes itself a change in the code, constitution, or statute, because it has a lasting effect as a precedent. And then when a new case arises it is not merely a matter of going back to a fixed code or primordial principle that had always existed in law or economics, or even of discovering a previously unknown divine intent applied to that case. It is a matter of reasoning from many conflicting precedents or experiences, some of which would lead to a decision towards one side of the case, and others to a decision on the opposite side of the case. Thus in a common-law country the code, or statute, or constitution, itself changes experimentally with changes in the practices of the people and the decisions of disputes.[51]

In the field of law, the recent tragic death of Wolfgang Friedmann has deprived us of an outstanding Instrumentalist. The judicial process is an instrumentalist process in which decisions follow upon adversary proceedings among parties representing competing social interests, and in this process, as Friedmann wrote,

> the task of the modern judge is increasingly complex. Hardly any major decision can be made without a careful evaluation of . . . conflicting values and interests. . . . Totalitarian government eliminates much of the conflict by dictating what should be done. [And so would adoption of the concept of economic efficiency as a universal *ratio decidendi.*]
> The lot of the democratic judge is nobler and heavier. He cannot escape the burden of individual responsibility, and great as distinct from competent judges have, I submit, been those who have shouldered that burden and made their decisions as articulate a reflection of the conflict before them as possible. [And who have specified clearly their reasons for deciding in favor of the one side rather than the other.][52]

The Instrumentalist conception of law is thus a dynamic, functional one of the making of decisions on the basis of competing social interests in a nonviolent forum subject to rules of procedure which are themselves experimentally or functionally determined and subject to change. The concept is one of law as an instrument of social order.

I have remarked earlier upon Buchanan's perversion of the vocabulary of the Instrumentalist point of view to promote the Chicago "what's good for the free market is good for us all" thesis. He has employed an organic, deified concept of "the market" (defined by Alfred Marshall as "the confluence of supply and demand") and asserted: "Law and legislation that is thoroughly informed by good economics [a term conveniently left undefined, but one understands it to mean *The Theory of Price*] will be based on an understanding of the market's function in maintaining social order which is *not* primarily that of insuring efficiency [which *does* "assume secondary importance in its own right"], or maximizing value, as measured in market-determined-prices."[53]

Buchanan's perversion of the vocabulary of Instrumentalism, or, perhaps more accurately, his bastardization of the concept of an instrument of social order, lies in his bald assertion of a tautology: Reliance on "the market" minimizes the need for internal ethical or external political regulation. This result is achieved by the fact that in the absence of regulation there will be a minimization of the violations of nonexistent regulations. Chicagoans are quick to point to the social costs of regulation and find it convenient to ignore the social costs of nonregulation and the instrumental nature of the regulatory *process*.

Critics of the Chicago price-theory-as-jurisprudence seem habitually to conclude their pieces with a short remark or two purporting to ascribe some merit to that which continues to be promulgated by the Chicago School. I do not propose to do so. In my judgment this literature falls in the category of what Kenneth Boulding has called " 'economics imperialism', which is an attempt on the part of economics to take over all the other social sciences."[54] What Thurman Arnold said of jurisprudence in general in 1934 seems to me an accurate description of the Chicago works: "The writings of [Chicago economists on] jurisprudence should be considered as ceremonial observances rather than as scientific observations."[55] This literature has been produced largely by economists who know no law and a handful of lawyers who have learned their economics from these same economists, all of whom are bound together by their acceptance of eighteenth-century hedonism and a philosophy produced under the influence of two ripe apples—one observed falling by Newton and the other eaten by Adam and Eve. Some of this literature has attained the status of "classic" because it conforms to the Gordon-Liebhafsky Theorem,[56] which states: "Provided that it achieves a certain threshold level of intelligibility, the greater the obscurity of a piece written by an economist, the greater is the likelihood that it will be recognized as a classic or seminal work."

I have been alarmed by the reluctance or inability of economists and lawyers generally to evaluate critically the Chicago literature. My own personal social welfare function calls for a trade-off consisting of a higher rate of unemployment of price theorists writing about jurisprudence and a lower rate of inflation of jurisprudence with price theory. The contrast between the Chicago and the Instrumentalist points of view is sharp and clear, and I have so presented it. The reader is free to take his choice.

## *Notes*

1. Oliver Wendell Holmes, Jr., *The Common Law* (Boston: Little, Brown and Co., 1881), p. 1.
2. With minor modifications, I herein accept the definition of this school provided by H. Lawrence Miller, "On the Chicago School of Economics," *Journal of Political Economy* 70 (February 1962): 64–70. Among the distinguishing characteristics of the group listed by Miller are: They (1) take a "polar position among economists as advocates of an individualistic market economy"; (2) place great emphasis upon the usefulness and relevance of neoclassical economic (price) theory; (3) equate actual and ideal markets; (4) see and apply price theory in and to every nook and cranny of life; and (5) place great emphasis upon the testing of hypotheses (particularly of competing hypotheses) as a neglected element of "positive economics."
3. George Stigler, *The Theory of Price,* 3d ed. (New York: The Macmillan Company, 1966).
4. Richard A. Posner, *Economic Analysis of Law* (Boston: Little, Brown and Co., 1972), p. 320.
5. Joseph A. Schumpeter, *The Theory of Economic Development* (Cambridge, Mass.: Harvard University Press, 1934), chapter 1.
6. Posner, *Economic Analysis,* p. 327.
7. I base this conclusion on Posner's biographical sketch printed in West's 1973 *Directory of Law School Teachers.*
8. Posner, *Economic Analysis,* p. xi.
9. James M. Buchanan, "Good Economics—Bad Law," 60 *Virginia Law Review* 60 (March 1974): 483.
10. Ibid., pp. 491–92.
11. Ibid., p. 484.
12. Ibid. See also my "The Problem of Social Cost—An Alternative Approach," *Natural Resources Journal* 13 (October 1973): 616.
13. *United States* v. *La Jeune Eugenie* 2 Mason 409 (1822).
14. Ludwig von Mises, *Human Action* (New Haven: Yale University Press, 1949), pp. 755–56.
15. Henry C. Simons, *Economic Policy for a Free Society* (Chicago: Uni-

versity of Chicago Press, 1948), pp. v–vi. Director's comment appears in his Preface to this posthumous edition of some of Simons's essays.
16. Posner, *Economic Analysis*, pp. 1–4.
17. See J. R. Hicks, *Value and Capital*, 2d ed. (Oxford: Clarendon Press, 1946), p. 35. "It is *evident* how rare such cases must be," and thus "the simple law of demand—the downward slope of the demand curve—turns out to be almost infallible in its working" (italics mine). A case of the intuitively obvious.
18. Gary S. Becker, *Economic Theory* (New York: Alfred A. Knopf, 1971), pp. 19–23.
19. Milton Friedman, "The Marshallian Demand Curve," *Journal of Political Economy* 57 (December 1949): 463–95, esp. note 6, p. 466.
20. In the reference to my work cited in note 12.
21. Posner, *Economic Analysis*, p. 61.
22. See George J. Stigler, *The Organization of Industry* (Homewood: Richard D. Irwin, Inc., 1968), p. 73, for Stigler's statement of the principle in these words: "The survivor principle avoids both the problems of evaluation of resources and the hypothetical nature of the technological studies. Its fundamental postulate is that the competition of different sizes of firms sifts out the more efficient enterprises." It also avoids content.
23. 94 U. S. 113 (1877).
24. 291 U. S. 502 (1934).
25. For an extended discussion, see my *American Government and Business* (New York: John Wiley & Sons Inc., 1971), p. 114–23.
26. Aaron Director, "The Parity of the Economic Market Place," *Journal of Law and Economics* 7 (October 1964): 1ff.
27. R. H. Coase, "The Market for Goods and the Market for Ideas," Papers and Proceedings of the Eighty-seventh Annual Meeting, *American Economic Review* 65 (May 1975): 384–91.
28. Posner, *Economic Analysis*, p. 266.
29. Ibid., p. 315. His footnote reference is to Director, "Parity."
30. *The Federalist* No. 78 (Hamilton's argument for lifetime tenure for the federal judiciary).
31. Hans Kelsen, *General Theory of Law and the State* (Cambridge, Mass.: Harvard University Press, 1945), p. 115–16.
32. H. L. A. Hart, *The Concept of Law* (London: Oxford University Press, 1961), p. 17 ff.
33. Posner, *Economic Analysis*, p. 4.
34. Ibid., p. 1.
35. Descartes's argument runs: Descartes had a concept of a Perfect Being, but since such an idea could not have come from within himself, it must have been given to him by that Perfect Being. Therefore, the Perfect Being existed. See René Descartes, *Discourse on Method*, trans. by John Veitch (Chicago: Open Court Publishing Co., 1913), pp. 36–39. The statement that man is a "rational maximizer of his ends in life" is equivalent to saying "man does what he does" and has equivalent substantive content.
36. Harold Demsetz, "Toward a Theory of Property Rights," Papers and

Proceedings of the Seventy-Ninth Annual Meeting, *American Economic Review* 57 (May 1967): 347–59.
37. Ibid., p. 355.
38. Gary S. Becker and William M. Landes, eds., *The Economics of Crime and Punishment* (New York: National Bureau of Economic Research, distributed by Columbia University Press, 1974), pp. 9–10.
39. Gordon Tullock, "Does Punishment Deter Crime?" Research Report, *The Public Interest* 36 (Summer 1974): 108 and 109. Footnote references within the quotation are found in the original.
40. Posner, *Economic Analysis*, pp. 82–83.
41. E. J. Mishan, "Evaluation of Life and Limb: A Theoretical Approach," *Journal of Political Economy* 79 (July/August 1971): 687.
42. Posner, *Economic Analysis*, pp. 357–58.
43. Ibid., pp. 358–59.
44. Ibid., p. 359.
45. Ibid., p. 394.
46. John R. Commons, *Institutional Economics*, vol. 1 (Madison: University of Wisconsin Press, 1961), p. 220.
47. For what seems to me to be his clearest statement of his "Technological [instrumental] Theory of Value" see C. E. Ayres, *Toward a Reasonable Society* (Austin: The University of Texas Press, 1961), pp. 113–22.
48. Paul T. Homan, "An Appraisal of Institutional Economics," Papers and Proceedings of the American Economic Association, *American Economic Review* 22 (March 1932): esp. p. 15.
49. John Kenneth Galbraith, *The Affluent Society* (Cambridge, Mass.: The Riverside Press, 1958), p. 13.
50. Posner, *Economic Analysis*, p. 98.
51. Commons, *Institutional Economics*, p. 221.
52. Wolfgang Friedmann, *Law in a Changing Society* (London: Stevens & Sons, Ltd., 1959), p. 67.
53. Buchanan, "Good Economics," p. 483. Interested readers are invited to examine Buchanan's distortion in this piece of the vocabulary I have used in discussing the Instrumentalist view of law in my "Problem of Social Cost" and also to read his piece in that same reference at pp. 580–94.
54. Kenneth Boulding, "Economics as a Moral Science," *American Economic Review* 59 (March 1969):8.
55. Thurman Arnold, *The Symbols of Government* (New York: Harcourt, Brace & Co., Harbinger Edition, 1962), p. 70.
56. Produced by my colleague Wendell C. Gordon and myself. We employed Milton Friedman's methodology, which holds that a theory is to be tested not by the realism of its assumptions but by its ability to predict. Readers wishing the results of our tests of the theorem when applied to the period 1960–1970 should write to Professor Gordon. Even though our data are bad, we have used a sophisticated method, and multiple regression studies show that our theorem is valid.

# 11

# Toward an Expanded Economic Theory of Contract

*Victor P. Goldberg*

The Coase Theorem in its most innocuous form appears to be little more than a restatement of the Pareto criterion. In a zero transaction costs (hereafter ZTC) world, transactions will continue to occur until there remains no possibility for further transactions which would make at least one party better off while making no other party worse off. If transaction costs are defined broadly enough to include all strategic and bargaining costs, then, as Guido Calabresi asserts, the proposition would appear true by definition.[1] It must, as he suggests, hold not only for the short run, but for the long run as well.[2]

However, except by using a very strained characterization of contract (to be discussed below), it can be shown that even this modest version of the Coase Theorem is vulnerable. Before showing this it is worth pausing first to ask whether this trip is really necessary. While exploring all the ramifications of the ZTC assumption may be intellectually challenging, it is not likely that a detailed knowledge of that mythical world will be of much practical use. Indeed, the Coase Theorem—especially in the minimal form presented here—was not proffered as a serious attempt to analyze a ZTC world.[3] Rather, Coase was concerned with showing that the treatment of externalities in the Pigovian tradition implicitly partitioned the world into two categories: those things which the market handled perfectly (normal goods with ZTC) and those which

---

*The author has a joint appointment with the Institute of Governmental Affairs and the Department of Economics, University of California, Davis.*

the market handled not at all (externalities with infinite transaction costs). The world, however, as Coase stressed, lay between these two extremes, with the cost of transactions depending not only upon physical characteristics (as was implicit in the Pigovian formulation), but also upon institutional factors. In particular, Coase showed that a number of problems which appeared to be externalities were, in fact, handled tolerably well by market mechanisms. Since market and nonmarket allocation mechanisms would never work perfectly, the policy problem was to determine which imperfect institutions should govern particular sets of transactions.[4] While Coase posited that this formulation probably would favor a smaller role for the government than that suggested by the Pigovians, he did not insist that that conclusion must follow[5] (although his followers have been less cautious in this regard). The point, however, is that Coase was interested in the ZTC world primarily to highlight the artificial dichotomy implicit in the Pigovian tradition.[6]

In short, analysis of a ZTC world, even if it were to lead to the demolition of the Coase Theorem, would not necessarily impinge on Coase's message. The primary justification for beginning there is that a well-known puzzle (whatever its ultimate merits) can serve as a useful vehicle for introducing new (and more interesting) issues. In this instance, the issues concern a broadened understanding of the nature of contract in economics and in law.

## *Contracts in a ZTC World*

A common definition of *contract* (one we subsequently will argue is too simple) is given in the Restatement of Contracts: "A contract is a promise or set of promises for the breach of which the law gives a remedy, or the performance of which the law in some way recognizes as a duty."[7] The crucial aspects of this definition are "promise" and the consequences of "breach." In the heyday of classical contract theory, Oliver Wendell Holmes put the point clearly: "[T]he only universal consequence of the legally binding promise is that of the law making the promisor pay damages if the promised event does not come to pass."[8] Suppose that Smith promises to deliver a widget to Brown, and Brown pays cash to Smith. Smith then has bound his future options: He either must deliver the widget or suffer the legal consequences of breach.[9] That is, he has, in effect, established transaction costs that would affect his future behavior.[10] Enforceable promises, the very essence of classical contract theory, require that some transaction costs be positive. Or, to turn the argument around, in a ZTC world, contracting parties must be able to breach their agreements costlessly—promises must be legally unenforceable. The only contracts that would be enforceable in the ZTC world would be those in which exchange was completely contemporaneous. Smith's widget must land in Brown's hand at precisely the same moment that Brown's cash lands in Smith's.

Hence, in a ZTC world, promises cannot be exchanged—contracts cannot deal with the future. Present exchange of contingency claims contracts could be arranged costlessly, but such exchange would not take place since the contingent claims themselves are promises which the promisor must be able to breach costlessly.[11] Thus, rather than find, as Calabresi did, that the Coase Theorem must hold in the long run, we must conclude that if the Coase Theorem is to hold, there can be no long run; it can hold only if time stands still. If transaction costs truly are zero, then only a very small subset of desirable transactions will take place. Society would reach the position in which no more costless transactions could be arranged which would make at least one party better off while not making any others worse off, but the locus of such positions would be well within the production possibility frontier that would exist if transactions with positive costs were permitted.

There are two lines of argument which might vitiate this paradoxical result.[12] Suppose that the only permissible penalty for breach of contract were specific performance. Then at precisely the moment that Brown receives Smith's promise, it could be argued that title and control have changed hands. A promise to deliver then would be treated precisely the same as delivery itself; the transaction would be fully presentiated.[13] If Smith attempts to breach, this attempt is to be treated as if Smith attempted to steal Brown's property (and with ZTC, property rights are protected costlessly). If Smith were for some reason to regret the initial transaction, he would have to negotiate (costlessly) with Brown to arrange a new transaction wherein Smith would receive the widget in return for something else, if Brown saw fit. So, if the Coase Theorem is to be salvaged via this route, then the ZTC world would consist of property rights which are costlessly transferrable through fully presentiated exchange, while transaction costs for all other forms of exchange must be infinite. This introduces the same sort of dichotomy as that inherent in the Pigovian approach. It also has the effect of excluding the contracts of classical laissez-faire contract theory from the picture. Since Coase (and the Coasians more so[14]) has tended to use the ZTC model as an argument in favor of common law, freedom of contract, market mechanisms, it is ironic to note that the preferred common law remedy for breach was money damages, not specific performance.[15]

A second means of rescuing the Coase Theorem is to concede that contracts do establish enforceable restrictions (transaction costs) on the promisor's future options, but that these are *voluntarily* determined restrictions. With this interpretation, ZTC means that there are no physical impediments to transactions and no externally imposed (involuntary) transaction costs; voluntary restrictions are acceptable. This redefinition should include not only Smith's promise concerning delivery of his widgets, but also more complex restrictions, such as restrictive covenants running with the land. In fact, we must go much farther. A group of individuals can voluntarily agree to a complex set of restrictions on their future behavior; these restrictions could include the terms upon which these individuals can exit (breach) and upon which others not party to the initial agreement can enter. By adding the appropriate flesh to this abstraction, one can end up with a voluntary agreement to impose a government.[16] Thus, with this conception of a ZTC world, we could end up with a Coasian optimum with a large, active government and with pervasive restrictions on individual behavior. Essentially, private contract blends into social contract. The society will (costlessly) come to unanimous agreement on "constitutional rules" which will establish a pattern of restrictions on the members of society; on *a priori* grounds, there is no reason to suspect that this agreement will lead to "minimal government."[17]

The minimal Coase Theorem can, therefore, be saved, but at a price. Costless bargaining leads to a Pareto optimum only if the classical conception of contract is discarded or if the ZTC world is defined so broadly as to include governmental restrictions. Either tack is awkward for those Coasians who attempt to use ZTC conclusions to justify a laissez-faire freedom of contract policy.

It is important to reiterate that it was never proper for Coasians to draw solace from the apparent conclusion of the ZTC world in the first place. The purpose of the preceding argument was to highlight two aspects of contract that too frequently are suppressed in economic (and legal) analysis, often with deleterious consequences for the analysis. First, contracts have a temporal element and by their very nature impose restrictions (some trivial, some significant) on the future behavior of economic actors. Second, the line between private "voluntary" agreements and public "coerced" agreements is not a clear one;[18] the distinction often is imposed for analytical convenience and then by careless usage elevated to a self-evident truth.

### *Economics and Long-Run Contractual Relations*

The paradigmatic contract of neoclassical economics and of legal analysis is a discrete transaction[19] in which no duties exist between the parties prior to the contract formation and in which the duties of the parties are determined at the formation stage. Prior to their contract, Smith has no duty to Brown; at the time they enter into their agreement, in a single joint exercise of their free choice, they determine their respective duties to each other for the duration of the agreement; completion of the promised performance terminates that party's obligations. In Ian Macneil's words, "sharp in by clear agreement; sharp out by clear performance."[20] While this quite accurately portrays many transactions, there is a large set of contracts for which this is a grotesque caricature. Relations which are to take place over a long period of time and in which the parties will have to deal with each other regularly over a wide range of issues (many of them unknown in advance) often are forced into this discrete transactional mold, both in legal and economic analysis.

The law of contracts to some extent has been forced to come to grips with the complex issues raised by such relationships by the poor fit into the transactional mold of relational fact patterns that are brought before the court. On the other hand, the elegance (and, to be sure, practical merits in many contexts) of analytical models based on choice has led economists to suppress the relational aspects of contracts. Thus, while legal scholars are at least making slow progress toward accommodating long-run complex relations in a broadened theory of contract,[21] economists have, with rare exceptions, not faced up to (or even perceived) the problems.[22] Here, concern will be focused on the economic implications.[23]

It is useful to assume that there exists a point in time at which the relationship comes into existence (the formation stage).[24] We no longer are concerned with the cash sale of a widget for future delivery, but with far more complex transactions: an agreement to construct a new chemical plant incorporating a number of state of the art advances; the sale of a franchise; a long-term management contract. If we focus on "choice" at the formation stage of the agreement, with what will that choice be concerned? This choice problem is very different from the constrained optimization choice problems central to economic analysis. The longer the anticipated relation and the more complexity and uncertainty entailed in that relation, the less significance will be placed upon the price and quantity variables at the formation stage.[25] The emphasis instead will be upon establishing (explicitly or by the incorporation of tacit assumptions[26]) rules to govern the relationship: rules determining the adjustment to factors that will arise in the course of the relationship and rules concerning termination of that relationship.

Central to an ongoing contractual relationship are rules to adjust to the ever-changing needs of the parties. How, for example, will the parties adjust to major alterations in the specifications for the output (an issue that arises regularly in defense contracting)? How should output be allocated if an unforeseen governmental regulation restricts supply? While the economist's initial reaction is that price would (and should) rise to market clearing levels, the contracting parties might well prefer rules for nonprice rationing of the reduced output among the existing customers.[27] It would be possible to go on at great length as to the procedural rules that might be adopted in a long-run relation, but for convenience attention will be confined to some aspects of pricing.

It is conceivable that the parties entering into a long-term contractual relationship might establish a price schedule for the duration of the contract. Indeed, before the Great Depression, long-term business leases commonly fixed the nominal monthly rent at the formation stage.[28] However, the parties might wish to take into account a number of the uncertainties that might arise during the life of the agreement—inflation, temporary shortages of supplies, technological change, the development of substitutes, quality change, changes in specifications, changes in the cost of production (including wage changes, changing legal definitions of liability and the price of insurance therefrom, and decisions by NEPA and OSHA and any other agencies that might come into existence during the life of the agreement), and so on. Rather than leave such elements to chance, or insure against them (if such insurance markets were to exist), or do without, the parties might find it much simpler and more economical to tailor a "flexible pricing" rule to their needs. The rule could be as simple as a cost-of-living escalator or indexing, but there exist many other more complex rules as well. Lon Fuller and Robert Braucher ably summarize the array of options:[29]

> Flexibility is sometimes sought . . . by leaving the price in a supply contract to be set by agreement from time to time. The agreement may contain a general arbitration clause . . . or it may contain a specific provision for arbitration in the event of a failure of the parties to agree on price. Frequently no standard is established for the arbitrator other than the implied one of general fairness and prevailing price levels. At other times the agreement will include a formula that interlocks the price to be paid by the buyer with the price of the same product, or a related product, on some designated market. At other times,

> particularly in agreements between corporations affiliated in ownership or management, price will be determined by actual cost to the seller plus a percentage for profit. In such "cost plus" contracts an elaborate definition of "cost" will usually be required, as well as considerable faith in the processes by which cost accountants purport to allocate costs where more than one product is being manufactured or sold.

Hence, we commonly will observe pricing formulas based on a percentage of gross sales in shopping center leases,[30] franchise contracts, and most royalty arrangements. Cost-plus pricing rules are, of course, commonly used in defense contracting, but also are becoming common in complex, private construction projects.[31] Rate of return regulation in the regulated sector can usefully be viewed as a flexible pricing rule.[32]

When judged by the criteria of the standard neoclassical model, such pricing rules appear inefficient, causing distortions in factor proportions, inducing gold plating, and so forth. The contracts of the private sector have been largely ignored since economists have treated all private sector exchange as presentiated discrete transactions; firms equate marginal cost to marginal revenue, and how they do this is of no great concern to the analyst.[33] However, the "as if" assumptions of the positive analysis of a private market economy have been transmuted into the "ought" conclusions of public economics. "The "inefficiencies" of government contracts and regulation's implicit contracts stand out starkly. The factor proportion bias in regulation (the Averch-Johnson effect[34]) is to be determined with reference to a model based on the discrete transactional framework; the factor proportion bias in a private franchising contract is buried by assuming away the pricing rules.

The point is twofold. First, the argument that regulation gives rise to a factor proportion bias is spurious. What we have is (among other things) a factor proportion *alteration*. The use of one form of flexible pricing (rate of return regulation) can lead to different decisions concerning production methods than would another rule. But given the complexities which led to the need for some flexible pricing rule in the first place, it is not obvious which rule (and therefore which factor proportions) would be best. If the reader can stand a somewhat strained interpretation, the contractual procedures (including the flexible pricing rule) can be viewed as a third factor of production, and a criterion based only on optimizing with respect to the first two factors (that is, capital and labor) will not necessarily yield desirable results. This does not mean, of course, that regulation works optimally (or even tolerably); it simply means that a paradigm suppressing the ongoing nature of the regulatory implicit contract will be misleading. Similarly (and this is the second point), a failure to appreciate the complexity of contractual pricing arrangements in the private sector is apt to leave the analyst unduly sanguine as to the efficacy of private market solutions to many problems.

### *The Blurred Public-Private Distinction*

Suppose that Smith, a tourist with little likelihood of ever again visiting San Francisco, parks his car for one hour in Brown's garage located in that fair city. This would appear to come very close to the discrete transaction ideal. The parties have no expectation of ever seeing each other again, the actual transaction covers a very short period of time, and the basic subject matter seems fairly clearcut. Suppose, however, that when Smith returns there is a large dent in the car which he claims was not there when he left it. He demands compensation, whereupon Brown points to a sign on the wall with the heading: "This contract limits our liability. Read it." The discrete transaction with its apparently unambiguous formation stage—when Smith gave the keys to Brown—is now seen as nested in a longer run contractual relationship between Brown and all his customers. This in turn is conditioned by other contractual (including "social contractual") rules promulgated by private parties, legislatures, and courts. Even an apparently discrete transaction therefore must be looked upon as being part of a longer term relationship.[35] As Judge Jerome Frank noted in *Zell*: "Much of the 'law of contracts' has nothing whatever to do with what the parties contemplated but consists of rules founded on considerations of public policy by which the courts impose on the contracting parties obligations of which the parties were often unaware; this 'objective' perspective discloses that the voluntary act of entering into a contract creates a jural 'relation' or 'status' much in the same way as does being married or holding a public office."[36]

In this sense, all transactions, however well defined they might appear, are nested in a complex pattern of contractual jurisdictions which, taken together, establish the rights, obligations, and ultimately the transaction costs of the respective parties. We can view the problem of designing (and adjusting[37]) the complex pattern of restrictions through two convenient fictions. On the one hand, we can envision people "choosing" the rules in which their behavior is to be embedded.[38] On the other hand, we can view all authority as reposing in a central government which then decentralizes decision making to lower level governments and to private individuals who can write "private legislation" in the form of private contracts.[39] If we ignore the normative overtones of these two approaches (admittedly not an easy task), they are not so terribly different. In both cases we are really saying that the line between private and public rules (restrictions) is blurred, and that to achieve desirable[40] results society will have to erect a set of barriers or restrictions (transaction costs) to channel behavior; this set of barriers will establish a complex admixture of public and private jurisdictions.[41]

The discrete transaction model essentially posits that economic actors can ascertain their long-run self-interest and will in one contractual act exchange promises which will appropriately restrict their future behavior for as long a time as is necessary. In such a world, freedom of choice makes eminent sense. However, if we are concerned with mortal men with bounded rationality pursuing their self-interest as best they can (given their perceived opportunities and constraints), then free choice loses some of its glamour. If faced with a very low price for photocopying or taping, consumers would find it difficult to resist such transactions, even if such behavior would lead to a decreased output of books and records of such magnitude as to make them all worse off. If they had perceived this effect, they might have found it beneficial to band together and collectively restrain their freedom to enter into such contracts.[42] Even if they had not perceived the problem, they might have found it in their interest to employ some agent (perhaps a government) to seek out the existence of such problems and work out solutions; while in some instances the agent's task would be to present his principal with a set of options, in many instances he would simply make decisions, informing his principal neither that the problem existed nor that a solution had been implemented.[43]

In short, situations often will arise in which the individual's short-run, perceived self-interest will conflict with his long-run interests (whether perceived or not), and the choice situation will be so structured as to make it likely that the short-run interest will be pursued. A franchisee, for example, might be sorely tempted to buy cheaper, lower quality chicken if the benefits from the lower prices outweighed the costs to him of the decline in goodwill associated with the franchisor's name. Yet, if all franchisees are free to act in this manner, the value of the franchise itself might well be destroyed. What we have, essentially, is a free rider, or prisoner's dilemma, problem.[44] Unless some restrictions can be imposed on the parties, pursuit of their own self-interest will make all the parties worse off.

The allocational effects of these restrictions can be very difficult to evaluate. If Smith enters into a requirements contract to buy exclusively from Brown for ten years, the choice might appear wise at the formation stage but very inefficient in the eighth year, when Brown's quality or price is no longer competitive. A regulatory agency might, in effect, guarantee an electricity producer a market for a long period by restricting entry and protecting the firm from substitute competition. Again, this clearly would appear inefficient once the generating capacity was installed (bygones are forever bygones), but the ultimate effect on consumers if producers could not attain and rely on such guarantees is more ambiguous.[45] In both examples, the long-term contract places substantial restrictions on at least one party's future pursuit of his short-run self-interest. Whether those restrictions are ultimately beneficial to the contracting parties and society at large is a complex question which requires more than the invocation of "voluntary free choice" or "governmental coercion" for an answer.[46]

### *Conclusions*

The economist's tendency to simplify the environment by treating exchange relationships as if they were discrete transactions has led to a greatly exaggerated view of the virtues of "free choice." Rather than a choice between alternative bundles of goods, the individual is faced with the much more complex problem of a choice from among goods and rules, some of them deep, constitution-like rules. Thus, unless we are willing to bestow the individual with extraordinary analytical powers, there is substantial room for rational, but limited, individuals to develop alternative institutional arrangements—such as regulation or governmentally imposed standards on contractual terms—that will be superior to the private contract, free choice alternative. The explicit recognition of the relational aspects of many transactions not only leads to a broader feasible role of government (in an allocative efficiency framework), but also suggests a very different set of criteria against which to judge efficiency. We must focus on the long-run effects of adjustment processes; concern with factor proportions and short-run marginal costs often will be misplaced.

The spirit of the above argument was ably captured by John R. Commons [1924, p. 137], writing over a half century ago: "Adam Smith was able to start economic theory with the elimination of all associations, corporations, unions, and almost all of the state itself, with their working rules governing the transactions of individuals, and to substitute, in their place, individual units of self-interest, division of labor, liberty, equality, fluidity in the choice of occupaton, and that 'invisible hand' or divine providence which was none other than the working rules of an orderly society as understood by Adam Smith in the middle of the eighteenth century." Commons's "working rules" are the rules governing contractual relations, be they private or social contracts.

We can close by tentatively suggesting that the forces leading to the breakdown of nineteenth-century contract doctrine were the same as those that have given rise to the activist state of the twentieth century, namely, the growing complexity of exchange relationships.[47] Laissez-faire economics and classical contract doctrine both focused on the discrete, impersonal, one-shot transaction. To the extent that this was a reasonable characterization of reality in the commercial sector,[48] it was consonant with a minimal government policy. However, as commerce became more sophisticated and exchange relationships more elaborate and complex, both contract *law* and governmental *institutions* began to adjust to these new forces. Contract and economic *theory*, however, have lagged behind. The legal theory of contract only recently has begun to accommodate this changing reality.[49] It is the goal of this essay to prod economic theory down this same path.

## *Notes*

1. "If people are rational, bargains are costless, and there are no legal impediments to bargains, transactions will *ex hypothesis* occur to the point where bargains can no longer improve the situation; to the point, in short, of optimal resource allocation" [Calabresi, 1968, p. 68].
2. Calabresi [1968, p. 67].
3. This would explain why Coase did not devote any effort to rigorously defining what was meant by zero transaction costs. Similarly, in his earlier article on the nature of the firm [Coase, 1937], his discussion of ZTC was aimed at showing the usefulness of *not* assuming that transactions were costless.
4. For a discussion of why the Coasian formulation of the public policy problem was too narrow, see Samuels [1974].
5. See Coase [1960, p. 18]. Calabresi [1968, p. 73] notes: "Some may take Coase's analysis to suggest that little or no government intervention is usually the best rule. My own conclusions are quite different. His analysis, combined with common intuition or guesses as to the relative costs of transactions, taxation, structural rules and liability rules, can go far to explain various types of heretofore inadequately justified governmental actions." It should be noted, however, that Coase has become much less cautious in recent years. Thus, in commenting on an earlier article by this author, he asserts: "It is now generally accepted by students of the subject that most (perhaps almost all) government regulation is anti-competitive and harmful in its effects." See Coase [1974, p. 493].

6. Another reasonable interpretation of the article is that altering the legal rules of a society often will have surprisingly little effect on the workings of the economy. Liability placed on Smith often can be shifted (by contract or other methods) to someone else. Note that this interpretation is not concerned with the efficiency aspects of either the initial placement of the rights or the means of transferring rights (or liability). In a very different sense, a number of legal scholars (notably Stewart Macaulay [1963]) have stressed the independence of much of the law of contracts from allocational results.
7. Cited by Macneil [1974a, p. 693].
8. Holmes [1881, p. 301]. For a critical discussion of the classical theory of contracts, see Grant Gilmore [1974].
9. We leave aside the extralegal sanctions for breach of an agreement; see note 11 below.
10. Ian Macneil [1974a, p. 714] notes that one element of promise is "the *doing* of something *now* which affects the future by limiting choices which would otherwise be available to the promisor in the future. The promisor thus presently sets in motion forces which may be destructive of what in the future he would otherwise view as in his self-interest, *e.g.*, causing him to repay money lent him earlier where he would prefer to keep the money" (emphasis in original).
11. Conceivably, the contracts could be legally unenforceable but enforced by extralegal means—for example, custom. This would appear to be a particularly inappropriate way of salvaging the Coase Theorem since if such mechanisms could be used for enforcing contractual promises, they equally well could be used for enforcing property right definitions. A Coasian optimum would obtain regardless of the ownership of rights (as the Coasians claim), even if this meant that there were no legally defined rights (which the Coasians would find appalling).

    Nevertheless, the importance of extralegal sanctions should not be overlooked. Consider, for example, Wolfgang Friedmann's [1951, pp. 26–27] discussion of collective bargaining agreements in Great Britain:

    > The strength of trade unionism in most major industries is such that the practical compulsion of union membership is sufficient and also preferable, to legal compulsion. Occasionally, a single trade union is recognized as exclusively entitled to bargain on behalf of the employees, but on the whole, the collective labour agreement, for all its tremendous importance in the lives of millions of people, has remained outside the sphere of the English law courts. It is therefore still on the bare fringe of interest for members of the legal profession and for writers of textbooks. Strictly speaking, the collective contract is not enforceable in the courts. . . . Thus there is no direct enforcement of what, in continental terminology now increasingly familiar in the common law jurisdictions, is termed the contractual or obligatory aspect of collective agreement. The lack of direct legal enforcilibility [*sic*] compares starkly with its social strength, in a society in which group bargaining has almost entirely displaced individual bargaining.

12. A third line of argument would restrict transaction costs to physical costs only. Thus, a restriction on an individual would only be regarded as a change in the relative prices he faces. While this physical interpretation of transaction costs is consistent with recent mathematical treatments of a positive transaction costs world, it fits uneasily in a Coasian framework. In a world in which physical transaction costs were zero, but certain classes of transactions were prohibited (for example, people might be prohibited from contracting out of liability), then the result of the Coase Theorem no longer holds.
13. *Presentiate* is a somewhat archaic word which Ian Macneil has reintroduced into legal analysis. "Presentiation is . . . a recognition that the course of the future is bound by present events, *and* that by those events the future has for many purposes been brought effectively into the present" [Macneil, 1947b, p. 589; emphasis in original].
14. See especially Richard Posner [1973].
15. For a discussion of damage remedies, see Gilmore [1974, pp. 14–15]. While the common law restricted damage remedies to (minimal) monetary compensation, courts of equity did offer specific performance in certain instances. As common law and equity have been merged in most jurisdictions in the twentieth century, the distinction is now primarily of historical interest.
16. Harold Demsetz, in his provocative article on the purported natural monopoly justification for utility regulation, showed that in a ZTC world a private collective contract could yield efficient results. Demsetz, in effect, replaces the public regulatory agency with a private one. See Demsetz [1968] and the discussion of his argument in Goldberg [1975a].
17. See James Buchanan and Gordon Tullock [1962]; while they argue for minimal government, they are concerned with the analytics of voluntary choice of governmental rules and its relation to individual preferences.
18. The blurring of the distinction is similar to that of public and private goods; see Paul Samuelson [1969, pp. 108–10]. However, where that distinction focused on the nature of the *goods*, the distinction in the text concerns the nature of the *agreement*.
19. For a lengthy development of the distinctions between discrete transactions and long-term relations, see Macneil [1974a].
20. Macneil [1974c, p. 15].
21. See especially Macneil [1974a, 1974b, 1974c]. Gilmore [1974, p. 90] suggests that the law of contract might disappear as it is fused with tort law into a "unified theory of civil obligation."
22. Those economists concerned with the implications of "bounded rationality" are among the exceptions. See especially Oliver Williamson's [1971] discussion of long-term contracts and vertical integration. While Demsetz and Posner often allude to some of the problems, they usually dismiss them as something that the market will handle tolerably well. See Demsetz [1968, p. 64] and Posner [1972, pp. 111–16].
23. For a discussion of the legal implications, see Macneil [1974a, 1974b, 1974c, 1975].
24. The common law gradually has come to recognize that contract-like duties can arise before the formation stage—there can be a duty to bargain in good faith, for example. The common law has lagged behind the

European civil codes in this regard; see Friedrich Kessler and Edith Fine [1964]. Just as a common law marriage can give rise to some of the rights and duties of a statutory marriage, an ongoing supply relationship consisting of contractually independent transactions can give rise to some of the same obligations as if there had existed a long-term contract governing the relationship.

25. Even if the price and quantity terms are spelled out, they often are not taken as binding by the contracting parties; see the comments of businessmen concerning the lack of weight they gave to the price and quantity terms in a requirements contract for phosphate in *Columbia Nitrogen Co.* v. *Royster Guano Co.* 451 F.2d 3 (4th Cir. 1971). See Macneil [1974c] for further discussion of that case.
26. See Macneil [1974a, pp. 772–73] for a discussion of the role of tacit assumptions in contracts. For a detailed discussion of the techniques available for providing for flexibility in private contractual relationships, see Macneil [1975].
27. "If, however, on account of shortage of crops, or other causes beyond the control of the seller it is unable to deliver the full amount herein named, it is agreed that the buyer will accept a *pro rata* delivery with other purchasers of all grades of goods covered by this contract, without claim for damages" (disputed term in *Ranney-Davis Mercantile Co.* v. *Shawano Canning Co.* 111 Kan. 68, 206 P. 337 [1922]). See also Uniform Commercial Code 2-615(b) and the unwritten trade "understanding" in *Columbia Nitrogen* (note 25).
28. "The depression between the two World Wars offered a gigantic object lesson in the unwisdom of projecting inflexible legal arrangements too far into the future. At that time, many leases running as long as twenty years stipulated a fixed rental. If such a lease was entered in 1926, by 1932 its rental had usually become completely out of line with prevailing levels. Since times were hard for landlords as well as tenants, landlords tended to hold as long as they could to the old rental. The result was that tenants were thrown into bankruptcy on a wholesale scale and a veritable flood of litigation occurred. It is likely that with the flexible rental provisions that have now become general in leases of business premises the disruptive effect of another decline in prices will be mitigated. Generally, sliding scale pricing in long-term contracts keeps the joints of business flexible." Fuller and Braucher [1964, pp. 78–79].
29. Fuller and Braucher [1964, pp. 77–78]. For a discussion of flexibility in long-term contracts, see Note [1950].
30. In most U.S. shopping centers tenants pay a fixed rent or 5 to 6 percent of the gross, whichever is larger. See "He Builds Shopping Centers around the World," *Business Week*, 1 December 1973, pp. 47–50. Fuller and Braucher [1964, p. 78] note that such arrangements have become very common in long-term leases for commercial real estate generally.
31. For constructing petrochemical plants, *Business Week* notes: "Most of the industry has switched to a negotiated, cost-plus-fixed-fee type of contract from the old fixed-price bid where the contractor with the

lowest bid got the project." See "Fluor Gambles on a Flock of New Orders," *Business Week,* 9 November 1974, p. 128.

32. See Goldberg [1975a].
33. This is not a rehashing of the old "marginal cost controversy"; see Coase [1970, pp. 114–20] for a brief summary. That was concerned with the decision rules of firms selling goods for the broad market, that is, in basically discrete transactions. Here we are concerned with firms that have entered into a long-term contractual relationship embodying a specific pricing rule.
34. Averch and Johnson [1962]. For a more detailed discussion of the general irrelevance of the Averch-Johnson effect, see Goldberg [1975a].
35. The longer run relationship goes well beyond the legal rules, including the social customs which condition exchange patterns in society.
36. *Zell* v. *American Seating Co.* 138 F. 2d 641 (1943).
37. The tendency to look at such problems as if they were discrete once-and-for-all transactions blurs the crucially important point that the rules governing adjustment processes (and the rules governing those rules, ad infinitum) are the significant ones.
38. See especially Buchanan [1972].
39. See, for example, Kessler [1943] and Friedmann [1951].
40. In an earlier article I suggested that this is essentially an optimal jurisdiction or optimal decentralization problem writ large; see Goldberg [1975b]. I have chosen to use "desirable" here rather than "optimal" since there is no reason to assume the risk of misleading someone into thinking that a serious definition of optimality in this context is feasible.
41. The discussion here ignores most distributional issues, although it should be pointed out that in most long-term contractual relationships some localized fairness rules will be developed explicitly or implicitly. See, for example, Macaulay's [1963] discussion of the rules for adjusting to unanticipated conditions in ongoing business relationships; see also the comments of businessmen in the *Columbia Nitrogen* decision (note 25). For a lengthier discussion of localized fairness rules in the context of franchising and the implicit regulatory contract, see Goldberg [1975a].
42. It could be argued that this is not truly a restriction on freedom of contract, but the placement of a property right for reproduction with the owner of the book or music. Reproduction of the materials then would be treated as a form of theft (breach of the social contract).
43. This discussion should not be taken to imply that the adopted solution must be a good one. The point is that, since processing information can be a very costly operation for the individual, he is often better served by being presented with decisions, not options. This is analogous to the delegation of decision making authority by the corporate manager as an information economizing tool.
44. The vulnerability of the franchisor's good will to the individual franchisee's quality degradation is a manifestation of the "Lemon's Principle"; see George Akerlof [1970].
45. See Goldberg [1975a] for a discussion of the possible benefits to consumers of long-term restrictions in the regulatory context.
46. For an extreme example of an individual voluntarily imposing severe restrictions on his future behavior, see *Horwood* v. *Millar's Timber and*

*Trading Co.* 1 K.B. 305 (1917), wherein a man contracted to, among other things, assign his salary to a moneylender without limitation, never terminate his employment without the moneylender's consent, never obtain credit, and never move from his house. (The court voided the agreement.)

47. For a somewhat related discussion of the interconnection between classical contract theory and laissez-faire economics, see Gilmore [1974, p. 95].
48. While many complex, long-term relationships existed in that simpler world, many took place within the nonmonetized sector—within the extended family relationship.
49. See Macneil [1974a, 1974b, 1974c, 1975] and Gilmore [1974].

## *References*


Akerlof, George. 1970. "The Market for 'Lemons': Quality Uncertainty and the Market Mechanism." *Quarterly Journal of Economics* 84 (August): 488-500.

Averch, Harvey, and Leland Johnson. 1962. "Behavior of the Firm under Regulatory Constraint." *American Economic Review* 52 (December): 1052-69.

Buchanan, James. 1972. *The Bases for Collective Action.* New York: General Learning Press.

——— and Gordon Tullock. 1962. *The Calculus of Consent.* Ann Arbor: University of Michigan Press (paperback ed., 1969).

Calabresi, Guido. 1968. "Transaction Costs, Resource Allocation and Liability Rules—A Comment." *Journal of Law and Economics* 11 (April): 67-73.

Coase, Ronald. 1937. "The Nature of the Firm." *Economica* 4 (November): 386-405.

———. 1960. "The Problem of Social Cost." *Journal of Law and Economics* 3 (October): 1-44.

———. 1970. "The Theory of Public Utility Pricing and Its Application." *Bell Journal of Economics and Management Science* 1 (Spring): 113-28.

———. 1974. "The Choice of the Institutional Framework: A Comment." *Journal of Law and Economics* 17 (October): 493-96.

Commons, John R. 1924. *Legal Foundations of Capitalism.* New York: Macmillan.

Demsetz, Harold. 1968. "Why Regulate Utilities?" *Journal of Law and Economics* 11 (April): 55-66.

Friedmann, Wolfgang. 1951. "Changing Functions of Contract in the Common Law." *University of Toronto Law Journal* 9: 15-41.

Fuller, Lon, and Robert Braucher. 1964. *Basic Contract Law.* St. Paul: West Publishing Co.

Gilmore, Grant. 1974. *The Death of Contract.* Columbus: Ohio State University Press.

Goldberg, Victor. 1975a. "Regulation and Administered Contracts." Paper presented at Seminar on Problems of Regulation and Public Utilities at The Amos Tuck School of Business Administration, Dartmouth College, Hanover, New Hampshire, 5 August.

———. 1975b. "Remarks on the State of Orthodoxy." *Journal of Economic Issues* 9 (June): 237-41.

Holmes, Oliver Wendell. 1881. *The Common Law*. Boston: Little, Brown & Co.

Kessler, Friedrich. 1943. "Contracts of Adhesion—Some Thoughts About Freedom of Contract." *Columbia Law Review* 43 (July): 629-42.

——— and Edith Fine. 1964. "'Culpa in Contrahendo,' Bargaining in Good Faith and Freedom of Contract: A Comparative Study." *Harvard Law Review* 77 (January): 401-49.

Macaulay, Stewart. 1963. "Non-Contractual Relations in Business: A Preliminary Study." *American Sociological Review* 28 (February): 55-67.

Macneil, Ian. 1974a. "The Many Futures of Contract." *Southern California Law Review* 47 (May): 691-816.

———. 1974b. "Restatement (Second) of Contracts and Presentiation." *Virginia Law Review* 60 (April): 589-610.

———. 1974c. "Transactional and Relational Contract Law." Manuscript.

———. 1975. "A Primer of Contract Planning." *Southern California Law Review* 48 (January): 627-704.

Note. "Business Practices and the Flexibility of Long-Term Contracts." *Virginia Law Review* 36 (1950): 627-47.

Posner, Richard. 1972. "The Appropriate Scope of Regulation in the Cable Television Industry." *Bell Journal of Economics and Management Science* 3 (Spring): 98-129.

———. 1973. *Economic Analysis of Law*. Boston: Little, Brown & Co.

Samuels, Warren. 1974. "The Coase Theorem and the Study of Law and Economics." *Natural Resources Journal* 14 (January): 1-33.

Samuelson, Paul A. 1969. "Pure Theory of Public Expenditure and Taxation." In *Public Economics*, edited by Julius Margolis and H. Guitton. London: Macmillan. Pp. 98-123.

Williamson, Oliver. 1971. "The Vertical Integration of Production: Market Failure Considerations." *American Economic Review* 61 (May): 112-23.

# 12

# Development Economics from a Chicago Perspective

*W. Paul Strassmann*

A strong Chicago participation in development economics was inevitable during the field's boom years, 1954–1968, because market incentives do have awesome power. The additional psychic spur to participation was abhorrence of the "mischievous fantasies" of protectionists, central planners, "development enthusiasts," or "milennial-minded economists." The early Chicago contributions show little sign of having been kindled directly by a compassionate urge to raise productivity in strange lands.

Perhaps the first participant was Jacob Viner when the Fundaçao Getulio Vargas invited him to Rio de Janeiro for six lectures in July and August 1950. In a disarming way Viner granted that he had not studied Brazilian history, resources, special circumstances, or problems, and indeed lacked "a general theory which enabled me upon demand to supply you with appropriate answers to all or any of your special questions."[1] These lectures were published as *International Trade and Economic Development* in 1953, a part of the first rivulet of books that switched from the term "industrialization."

Later Chicago contributions came from Milton Friedman, Arnold Harberger, Harry G. Johnson, Theodore Schultz, Larry Sjaastad,

---

*The author is Professor of Economics, Michigan State University, East Lansing.* *For detailed, timely, and even helpful suggestions he is indebted to John M. Hunter, Elizabeth Johnston, C. Patric Larrowe, Carl Liedholm, Thomas Mayer, James B. Ramsey, Warren Samuels, Robert Stevens, and Diana Strassmann.*

George Stigler, and others. One could add economists who earned their Ph.D. at Chicago, such as A. G. Hart, and make a much longer list. Philosophy matters more than geography since not all Chicago Ph.D.'s have remained loyal. One renegade, the Marxist Andrew (Andres) Gunder Frank (Ph.D. 1957) recently concluded a nine-page open letter to Arnold Harberger with a sarcastic reference to "calculating the equilibrium conditions of large-scale assassinations and genocide."[2]

Nor are Chicago economists the only hardnosed, laissez-faire exponents writing on development. No one is a more fervent free marketeer than Peter Bauer of the London School of Economics. When Friedman joined C. W. Guillebaud as coeditor of the Cambridge Economic Handbook series in 1956, they decided to commission Bauer and B.S. Yamey to write the development text.[3] We should, however, beware of doing no more than exploring the peculiar talents and prejudices of Group X that has been tautologically selected according to these peculiarities. Nevertheless, it would take us off on too great a tangent to do full justice to all at Chicago, specifically to the pioneering development economist, Bert Hoselitz, long-time director of the Research Center in Economic Development and Cultural Change.

In this article I shall first review the general record of Chicago participants in development economics, appraising the durability of policy recommendations in the light of experience. After that comes a closer look at three specific policy areas that have interested the group: international trade, foreign aid, and the cultivation of market institutions.

### *The Record in General*

Compared with the mainstream and Marxist approaches to economic development in the past quarter of a century, the Chicago anti-interventionists do not come off badly. They have needed to bury fewer conceptual gaffes and to make fewer alibis for bogged down applications. If two-thirds of the time "let markets do it" is the best of a dozen options, unbroken repetition is sure to come off fairly well. But can one do better?

As times changed, and different writers promoted the message, variations in tone and emphasis came about. At first, the whole idea of development economics was treated as an affront. A new body of thought was not needed, the Chicagoans said, to show that market interest rates would raise and deploy capital in an optimal manner, that flexible exchange rates would solve balance-of-payments problems, that inflation and planning were bad, and competitive profits good. A few minor caveats aside, markets and only markets would give any country its peak of efficiency and desirable growth. How infuriating, then, to read Gunnar Myrdal's 1955 Cairo comment that "the price system as a part of a very irrational whole, namely the economy of a backward and stagnating country, can hardly have any great claim on rationality to begin with."[4]

Even more infuriating, because possibly more influential, were early United Nations documents such as *The Economic Development of Latin America and Its Principal Problems* (1949), by Raul Prebisch, and *Measures for the Economic Development of Underdeveloped Countries* (1951). Viner doubted that Prebisch had the "slightest acquaintance with the actual writings of the English classical school" or he would have avoided "the dogmatic identification of agriculture with poverty [or] technological progress [that] tends to confine its blessings to manufacturing" and other "mischievous fantasies."[5] Of course, Viner was correct that technology had no inherent promanufacturing bias and that the terms of trade did not inevitably deteriorate against agriculture. Within two decades, Prebisch, to his credit, came to oppose neglect of agriculture and gave export promotion more weight than import substitution.

During the 1950s came what might be called the Houdini phase of mainstream development economics, and the Chicago group as usual stayed out, avoiding both mistakes and some subsequent learning. In the Houdini phase, national poverty was seen as a vicious circle or "low-level equilibrium trap," and the game was to find some gadget or formula that would allow the country to break out into self-sustaining growth. The rules were to stick to a classical, neoclassical, or Harrod-Domar framework but add one or two complications that (1) caused problems and (2) contained hidden elements for their solution. It was an era of the clever sequence, the proper linkage, the right amount of balance or imbalance, the critical minimum effort, the BIG PUSH, the take-off, and the marginal reinvestment quotient. The possible was often mistaken for the probable, and economic development was still tacitly identified with industrialization. Usually, foreign aid and some planning were recommended for the break-out into the clever sequence.

Today almost none of these concepts is taken seriously, not because of Chicago scorn, but because of empirical disproof or operational irrelevance. The Chicago attack mostly went against the Harrod-Domar framework and its stress on capital, the national savings share, and the incremental capital-output ratio. In an unpublished memorandum for the International Cooperation Administration (an AID predecessor), Milton Friedman wrote in 1955:

> To take it for granted that there is a rigid and mechanical ratio between the amount of investment and additions to output . . . seems to me a serious mistake. At the one extreme, output can increase even without investment . . . the form and distribution of investment are at least as important as its sheer magnitude.
>
> The danger is that concentration on it may lead to policies that increase physical investment at the expense of investment in human capital.[6]

Peter Bauer, who had access to this memorandum, also noted the difference between capital as specified in Harrod-Domar models and as used by Adam Smith and Marx. The classical writers "closely related capital accumulation as an engine of development to the activities of particular groups, organizations and classes . . . to social attitudes, relationships, and institutions, and to changes in these."[7]

In a 1969 report to the Presidential Task Force on International Development, Arnold Harberger likewise stressed that

> while simple theoretical models have been developed in which the bottleneck to progress turns out to be, depending on the circumstances, either a shortage of domestic resources (a "savings gap") or a shortage of imported goods (a "foreign exchange gap") there are at most only a few countries and periods to which such models can be applied in practice. In general, as is well known, the modernization of backward economies is an enormously complex, difficult, and time-consuming process. Barriers to growth abound: social and political elites unreceptive to change, gross deficiencies of the technical skills and capacities required by modernization, markets that are poorly organized and whose proper functioning is further impaired by ill-conceived public policies, systems of fiscal and also of foreign-trade policy that in their present state are if anything impediments to rather than promoters of modernization—these constitute only a partial listing.[8]

What institutional economist could quarrel with that list? Among Chicago economists, Harberger ranks high in actual experience in developing countries. More experience tends to make one more sympathetic, sophisticated, and less doctrinaire. Harberger typically has seen "a great deal of mystery surrounding the problem of growth [although] our technical apparatus does permit us to explain reasonably well the differences in the rates of inflation."[9] Compared with Harberger and Schultz, Friedman and Bauer appear simplistic:

> [Friedman:] What is required in the underdeveloped countries is the release of the energies of millions of able, active, and vigorous people . . . an atmosphere of freedom, of maximum opportunity for individuals to experiment, and of incentive for them to do so in an environment in which there are objective tests of success and failure—in short a vigorous, free capitalistic market.[10]

> [Bauer:] What is required in India is essentially a redirection of the activities of government, away from policies restricting the energies and opportunities of its subjects . . . into directions aimed at releasing the energies of millions of people.[11]

A curious urge made Chicago economists present their veneration of the market as not only logical, but also as novel and exciting. Opposing ideas were labeled old hat. Harrod-Domar models were scorned as a residue from depression Keynesian thought that Keynes himself surely would have disowned. Harry G. Johnson has even traced the Houdini novelties to the interwar period and unmasked them as Balkan imitations of old hat German ideas. Migrating intellectuals such as Kurt Mandelbaum, Nicholas Kaldor, Paul Rosenstein-Rodan, and Thomas Balogh (but not Peter Bauer, Ludwig von Mises, Friedrich von Hayek, Fritz Machlup, William Fellner, and so forth) caused "this infiltration of ideas from Central Europe into the Anglo-Saxon tradition [and] did a great deal to implant the habit of thinking in nationalist rather than cosmopolitan terms. . . . This group of economists was largely responsible for the strong emphasis on the need for industrialization, and the potency of protectionist policies."[12] Despised ideas had an alien and dubious pedigree!

### *Foes of International Barriers*

Apart from doubts about migration from ideologically contaminating countries, as well as from poor countries generally—which Harry Johnson regarded as "obviously . . . impractical"[13]—opposition to international barriers is a consistent Chicago theme. Here the school is at its best. As with many other development economists (Ragnar Nurkse, Albert Hirschman, Richard Eckaus, Henry Bruton, Gerald Meier, Hla Myint, Raymond Mikesell, Jagdish Bhagwati, and so forth), international trade and finance were a primary concern early in professional careers, even the subject of doctoral dissertations. From international trade theory to development theory was a natural step, since blocking trade always has been tempting as a development strategy. Adam

Smith's metaphor of the "invisible hand" occurs in his chapter, "Of Restraints upon the Importation from foreign Countries of such Goods as can be produced at Home." The visible hand of government could promote development of a "particular species of industry. . . . But whether it tends either to increase the general industry of the society, or to give it the most advantageous direction, is not, perhaps, altogether so evident."[14] An impersonal, mechanistic conception of the economy is most apt for its most impersonal, mechanistic sector—the exchange of commodities and financial instruments with numerous and distant foreign partners.

Among the Chicago trophies in this venerable field, Viner's early trouncing of Prebisch, Manoilesco, and Louis Bean has already been cited. Milton Friedman in 1954 criticized compulsory stabilization schemes for primary producers.[15] As usual, he had the courage of his convictions and came out for a unilateral U.S. abolition of "all tariffs, quotas, and other restrictions on trade by a specified date—say, in five or ten years" as the quickest way to help both ourselves and poor countries.[16]

That inflation compels devaluation the sooner the better was another obvious Chicago theme, but less evident were the feedback effects of devaluation on the price level. On the basis of his experience in Chile and Argentina, Harberger modified his views substantially on this issue. His recommendation for a series of small devaluations rather than occasional large ones was adopted by Brazil with dramatic success. Under the circumstances, a doctrinaire insistence on flexible exchange rates would have been rejected.[17]

On this theme of removing trade barriers, Harry Johnson's contributions have been most notable. He did much to promote the distinction between nominal and effective levels of tariff protection. Since advanced countries protect their manufacturing industries more than their raw and semifinished materials producers, the effective rate of protection on value added can be a multiple of that on the commodity. Poor countries should object to differentials *within* the tariff structure of advanced countries more than to the absolute tariff level.[18] Johnson demonstrated as clearly as anyone the cost of using tariffs to correct an imbalance in factor markets. Appropriate tax and subsidy policies can allow greater efficiency and higher consumer welfare. On the other hand, if import dependence has to be decreased for noneconomic reasons, tariffs affecting both producers and consumers are superior to domestic measures that only subsidize import-competing producers or only penalize consumers of imports. In practically all cases, a uniform rate is the least of tariff evils. The essays by Johnson on these topics show great clarity in specifying objectives and estimating the cost of means.

Like most Chicago economists, Johnson has little use for the infant industry or infant economy exception for protective tariffs: His position was that "no serious effort has been made to test and to prove it," and the probability of insufficient scale effects and lack of an "intricate network of input-output relationships" turned him against both infant and fetus.[19] Viner had considered the infant industry or "young-country" argument theoretically valid but destroyed by "weighty objections persuasive as they stand and supported by more than a century of corroborative experience."[20] In a similar vein, Stigler noted the serious lack of externalities from auxiliary industries and educational facilities in poor countries: "At best the small economies that imitate us can follow our methods of doing things this year, but not our methods of changing things next year; therefore, they will be very rigid."[21]

Thus, Chicago economists do not deny the existence or importance of externalities; they merely find them uniformly against policies they oppose and for ones they favor. In the favorable category is the learning experience from consuming imported goods, "participation as consumers in technical progress." Foreign direct investment also brings technology, training, and reinvestment of profits "more or less automatically," according to Johnson.[22] For Friedman, "the activities of International Harvester, Caterpillar Tractor, Singer Sewing Machine, Coca Cola, Hollywood and so on . . . are by all odds the most effective means of disseminating understanding and knowledge of the United States." At least that is more realistic than Johnson's claim that the crucial, modern, and exemplary part of the U.S. economy is small business.[23]

In all of this, Japan is something of an embarrassment for Chicago economists, as it is for Marxists. The Japanese have not only blocked foreign investment, but also, according to Bela Balassa's estimates, had a higher rate of effective protection (29.5 percent) in the early 1960s than the United States (20.0 percent), the Common Market (18.6 percent), Sweden (12.5 percent), or Great Britain (27.8 percent).[24] Certainly the Japanese had not launched their growth by exporting food and raw materials. The Meiji government, as we all know, took the initiative to bring in foreign technology and to found industries. When successful, they were sold for a song to less enterprising nobles and merchants, often as a political payoff. Rights of property and occupational mobility were secured in a pattern that also fits no simple doctrine. That technocratic capitalism, blended with feudalism, might kindle a few wars was seen by Thorstein Veblen, but is nowadays banned from the framework of analysis.

### *Foes of Foreign Aid*

At least Japan had not received foreign aid. The issue of foreign aid splits the school, and nothing is more despised by the most orthodox, except an outright Communist take-over. Indeed, while Marxists think propping up capitalist regimes is the only effect of foreign aid (the way Russia props up Cuba), Friedman sees it as inevitably undermining capitalist democracy. But first let us examine the early views of Jacob Viner.

Viner found it "difficult to overestimate the service to world prosperity that a free and abundant international flow of capital is capable of rendering if it is wisely conducted."[25] It would mean "international discipline directed against national economic plans which operate in such a manner as to produce balance-of-payments deficits."[26] Regretfully, Viner concluded that capital would have to be mobilized domestically because of obstacles to private lending, because expecting much lending from governments was "not realistic" and because there were no "obvious grounds for expectation or hope" of anything from international agencies.[27] Since the U. S. Point Four Program (the Technical Assistance Administration), the Colombo Plan, and the U.N. Technical Assistance Program were already underway, Viner's crystal ball was rather murky. Within a decade, concessionary loans and grants were flowing at annual rates of billions of dollars; economic aid made up a substantial share of the foreign exchange receipts of a number of poor countries; and for advanced countries a one percent share of GNP came to be considered the decent (but rarely attained) minimum contribution.[28]

Horror and outrage were the reactions of Friedman and Bauer to these attempts at sharing the wealth. Such "economic aid . . . can only have disastrous consequences for our country and our way of life," Friedman predicted in 1958.[29] Since foreign aid is naturally channelled through governments that are encouraged to act rationally, that is, to set targets and to make plans for reaching them, it promotes the "all-powerful state" and "implicitly accepts this premise of the Communist ideology. . . . Despite the intentions of foreign economic aid, its major economic effect, insofar as it has any effect at all, will be to speed the Communization of the underdeveloped world."[30]

By strengthening the evil power of bureaucrats, even an aid program that stipulates a major role for the private sector will undermine that sector. Nor will capital formation be encouraged since "the final results of our grants is therefore likely to be a reduction in the amount of capital available from other sources both internally and from the outside."[31]

Nowadays economists would see some validity in a possible savings decline where the capital inflow offsets a "binding trade gap" due to inelasticities in supply and demand for exports. Except for an inability to import key items, a country could conceivably grow because its savings and investment propensities are otherwise adequate. Since the savings-investment gap must equal the import-export gap *ex post facto*, however, a relative fall of savings inevitably will accompany a capital and net import inflow.

But such a macroeconomic approach is not congenial to Friedman. Hollis Chenery and Nicholas Carter have estimated that a binding trade gap stifled Indian growth during the 1960s and that the shortfall of aid by $6 billion (or 45 percent of estimated needs) "was probably the main single factor in her inability to grow more rapidly." It brought India down from a potential 5.3 percent growth rate of GDP to a mere 3.5 percent.[32] Friedman disagreed, claiming in 1974 that "United States aid to India has done India and the United States harm. I think India today would be better off if we had never given them a penny, because the only major effect of our giving them money through foreign aid has been to encourage them to follow economic policies which have aborted a potentially very rapid economic advance in India."[33]

Since foreign aid inhibits growth, international wealth could only be redistributed through voluntary private charity, called a market force by Friedman, or by police forces. The tenor of his discussion invariably implies that police forces and violent autocrats are undesirable; but if so, in early 1975 he managed to qualify this distaste sufficiently for a flight to Santiago and some old-time religion monetarist advice about government budgets to the Chilean *junta*. A little more short-run unemployment should not deter the generals from reducing inflationary government deficits. His basic position remains: "I do not believe the world needs a redistribution of wealth. I think that is wrong" (ibid.). Of course, Chicago economists oppose income and wealth redistribution not only internationally, but also intranationally. From what point of view they consider the existing distributions optimal is never explained.

Harry Johnson generally has shared Friedman's hostility to direct government intervention in economic affairs, but he is less committed to accepting whatever inequality results from letting countries trade and develop as best they can with their own resources. A noninterventionist way of helping poor countries is with international trade preferences in their favor: "the ethical principle embodied in the principle of nondiscrimination is the principle that equals should be treated as equals; and that in international economic relations developed and less developed countries are not equal."[34]

Here we have not the positive summons that the rich and strong should help the poor and weak, a conditioned gut (or guilt) response against suffering. The higher value is "nondiscrimination" as associated with the perfect market, a competition among equals. Dedication to this type of equality is also found in Johnson's worry that "the administration of aid given directly by one country to another places officials of the donor country in the recipient country in a rich-man/poor-man relationship that is scarcely conducive to mutual respect and political amity."[35]

Even this sort of inhibition fades in Schultz (whose most typical contributions do not fall within the three policy areas treated in this article) and Harberger. Schultz has come right out and called for the United States to "do much more than it is doing presently to reduce the inequalities in income among the peoples of the world." Untangling the elements of "humanitarian benevolence, utilitarianism, or a long-run self-interest" behind this program is less important than getting on with the job and being effective.[36] Harberger seems to share his view that concern need be less with justifying generosity by the rich, and more with the conditions for effective use of aid.

Harberger concedes "that the amount of progress that can be generated by a dollar of foreign aid has been greatly exaggerated." Nevertheless, "foreign aid is indeed productive in most cases." The exceptions are likely to be, first, program and sector loans that lead to a resented involvement of foreigners in the domestic affairs of a developing country. A second type of foreign aid failure is due to poorly conceived project loans. In 1969 Harberger doubted "whether any of the less-developed countries have as many as one-twentieth or one-tenth of the trained project evaluators that they could profitably use." Foreign aid for training more of these should be "the first order of business,"[37] one that presumably would inspire more and better aid requests as the second and third order. Harberger helped the process along by collecting his own papers in a volume entitled *Project Evaluation* (London: Macmillan, 1972). The existence of externalities and disequilibria is granted, but the recommended shadow prices are simpler than those of the UNIDO *Guidelines* or the OECD *Manual*. For capital it is the average rate of return before tax, and the shadow price of labor is the wage by skill classification in the unregulated sector of the economy. Foreign aid financing should "run the gamut of types of public-sector projects [and] cover more than the direct foreign exchange costs." Standards, including self-help efforts, should be less rigorous for countries "in greatest poverty."[38]

### *Friends of Markets and Entrepreneurs*

The aim of development policy at Chicago is more competitive markets with brave, more innovative entrepreneurs. Since this goal is identified with rationality itself, its dispassionate study seems oddly irksome. Friedman, as quoted above, simply assumed that "millions of able, active and vigorous people . . . exist in every underdeveloped country" and "require only a favorable environment to transform the face of their countries . . . in short, a vigorous, free capitalistic market."[39] Harry Johnson reverses the causation. The market is not justified by the prior existence of vigorous competitors, but by its ability to create them. "Historical and increasing contemporary evidence suggests that exposure to competition in a large market" inculcates "in those who manage and use capital the habits of seeking constantly to improve efficiency, so that economic growth becomes a self-sustaining process."[40]

But optimizing behavior, while no doubt indispensable, must neither be taken for granted as universally preexisting, nor as easily and automatically generated. Perhaps the most basic human emotion that is relevant here is painful anxiety in the face of uncertainty. To minimize anxiety, all cultures purvey a repertoire of standard fantasies that set the way we see the world. The perfectly competitive market is itself such a fantasy. It allows economists to perceive a determinate world and to pontificate about it with a minimum of anxiety. All missionaries make some converts, but in general the Chicago homilies make little sense to listeners with other fantasies—elitist, parochial, machiavellian, quixotic, evangelical, shamanist, pacifist—the possibilities, while not infinite, are great. Naturally, each fantasy is largely irrational in terms of all others.

Pragmatically, universal market optimizing behavior might be shown as more productive and anxiety-quelling than behavior entailed by the other fantasies. The right kind of optimizing nevertheless remains behavior that has to be learned within a framework of institutions that needs to be built with care. Each higher level of market flexibility needs a buttress of some temporary and some permanent measures for security. At successive stages of entrepreneurial development, a high net income, an adequate minimum income, an assured salvage value, access to markets, guarantees of input quantities and qualities, or various information services may have to be provided. U.S. enterprises would not even set up branches in Puerto Rico without a gamut of carefully tailored financial and qualitative services and guarantees. To the initial surprise of the designers of "Operation Bootstrap," the tax holiday by itself was not enough incentive. Measures that suit small manufacturers may not fit artisans and peasants. The objective may be to condition new psychological responses, more tolerance of anxiety, to encourage learning of simple facts and procedures, or merely to gain participation. Design of measures depends upon the motivation encountered, to gain wealth, to avoid failure, to become modern, to preserve a traditional identity, or various blends. Measures must seem dependable and yet be easily dismantled at the right time. Most difficult and yet essential in market development is weaving a network of financial intermediaries.

Rather obvious in all this is that understanding how markets are built is an interdisciplinary task. Some Chicago writers have indeed recognized that boundaries between disciplines cannot be casually ignored or assumed. Viner thought that experts in neighboring disciplines theoretically could keep economists from "operating on the basis of either too scanty or erroneous premises." Unfortunately, he added, "we have often had to construct them for ourselves, although we had no professional competence or credentials to do so."[41] Bauer concluded his inaugural lecture at the London School of Economics in 1963 with a call for interdisciplinary cooperation. There could be "widely different implications" if certain price differentials were due to "transport costs, inertia, ignorance, custom, lack of response, or quasi-monopoly."[42] But these admonitions have been generally ignored by other Chicago economists, who rarely go so far as to cite the university's own high-level interdisciplinary journal, *Economic Development and Cultural Change*, edited by Bert Hoselitz.

They seem to retain a simple faith that if willful bureaucrats could just somehow be restrained, market behavior and market institutions would proliferate spontaneously. The archaic view that markets started with primitive men bartering fish and furs and seeking a compact medium of exchange has lost no luster for Chicagoans as a valid and profound insight. Some have gone further and cemented market behavior firmly in subconscious foundations. Theodore Schultz has found primitive tillers "not inefficient," but fully capable of attaining "stationary equilibrium." They lack no "essential economic virtues because of some flaws in their culture. . . . Let us cease and desist from maligning farmers in poor countries."[43] Subconscious maximizing not only directs peasants but also leads to equilibrium in education or "human investment," demographic fertility, crime, suicide, and even the level and types of "social interactions."[44]

Harvey Leibenstein has criticized the Chicago approach to human fertility. He notes that people cannot explain or predict much that results from family size. They are aware of group pressures (ignored at Chicago) but unclear about alternatives given up. They are not conscious of having bargained, settled for a price, and transacted an exchange:

> People do not "buy" children. It is not at all clear what the objects traded are. . . . Are we to presume that the market is competitive without any important externalities or collusive arrangements, etc.? It not only strains the imagination to argue that people behave "as if" they are buying consumer durables, but the very nature of the market is vastly different. Even using such words as "market" is questionable in this context. Hence, it is dangerous to presume that the mode of decision making is similar and that we simply have to transfer the well-developed microeconomic mold and its presumed thought processes from one area to another.
>
> We should not use the need to theorize as a license to presume anything we please.[45]

To explain the behavioral changes that constitute economic development in terms of households consciously or subconsciously ("as if") maximizing their utilities seems fanciful. Do non-Western illiterate peasants optimize by subconsciously choosing a system of beliefs that ignores the possibility of comparing the utilities from different beliefs? Can they step outside of their system of beliefs and see it as merely a system? When the subconscious is invoked, as by Freud and Marx, any opponent's critical faculties are discredited and besmirched by what logicians call the gambit of "poisoning the wells." The Chicago doctrine is itself such a closed system of thought. Whether an extenuating bit of insincerity tempers Chicago "as if" theorizing cannot and should not be explored here. But if a system cannot be seen and tested as a system, if it is accepted without reflection and if it is protected against disconfirming evidence by the process of "secondary elaboration,"[46] then we have a form of irrationality among its sincere adherents, even if the system is itself logically consistent and not obviously false in some empirical sense.[47] One can irrationally impute subconscious rationality to all human behavior.

At Chicago, Arnold Harberger stands out as both a genuine member of the school and yet beyond its usual, somewhat petulant, wishful thinking about the latent power of markets. He not only recognizes that markets in poor countries are badly organized, but also once estimated that for Chile their perfection might accomplish no more than a one-time quantum jump in output of 15 percent.[48] Markets will not in any case assure a better distribution of income, so for that there must be waged a pragmatic struggle, "multifaceted, operating on a lot of different fronts at once." If unemployment and underemployment become serious problems, governments may have to become "employers of last resort."[49] Where the government does intervene in the economy, Harberger calls for the "professionalization of the personnel involved" in the process of project evaluation at all levels. He visualizes an "evaluation corps" independent of particular operating agencies and therefore able to resist short-sighted pressures to overstate the case for one's own branch. He cannot be described as guilty of the three misdeeds commonly charged to Chicago work on development: "that it fails to adapt neoclassical theory to the special characteristics of developing countries, that it makes a selective use of evidence in corroboration of its views, and that it holds a 'reactionary' belief in the power of the market to produce 'desirable' solutions in all situations."[50] A Marxist might not detect much difference between Milton Friedman and Arnold Harberger, but it is the latter who actually teaches Economic Development at the University of Chicago and who has come to describe himself as "heterodox."[51]

## *Conclusion*

An inadequate view of rationality and the learning process is perhaps the principal limitation of the Chicago approach to development. Most of these writers do not look far into the past, comparing periods and cultures, nor into the future, projecting population growth and wider income disparities. Joseph Schumpeter was no less a proponent of capitalist markets, but he knew that market rationality could be applied to numerous small decisions and yet be irrelevant to big ones and underlying trends. The establishment and preservation of market institutions is culturally complex, fraught with conflict, and psychologically fragile. A doctrinaire insistence that markets are the quintessence of efficiency, justice, and logic and are inevitable to boot is not the way to cultivate them in the face of equally doctrinaire opposition. For decades, perhaps for centuries, neither markets, nor private property, nor democracy may prevail in many countries today classified as "developing." But their workers, bureaucrats, and military dictators cannot be dismissed as simply demented, unwilling to follow textbooks from Chicago and their own subconscious optimizing drives.

What we really need is rejection of all rational-versus-irrational, optimizing-versus-madness dualisms in development theory. There are gradations in the rationality of belief and the somewhat different matter of rationality in action. In no culture will people accept simple but directly contradictory statements. They can also recognize much that is palpably false empirically. Most of their activities will be goal directed and use the best means that are known. But then comes the gray area involving search for other means and other goals and an examination of the way more complex beliefs have come to be held. This gray area involves learning, which is different from mere choosing and is at the heart of development. In prim jargon, our inability to learn everything can be called "the cognitive limit to rationality." Especially difficult is "deuterolearning"—learning how to learn. We lack time and have a tendency to respond emotionally to culturally conditioned symbols and interpersonal situations. It is much more complex than "comparing net discounted yields subject to an information constraint." That phrase will not take us far toward explaining how we arrive at expenditures, occupations, identities, and social structure itself in a way that puts management of uncertainty via anxiety-quelling fantasies first and optimization second.

## *Notes*

1. Jacob Viner, *International Trade and Economic Development* (London: Oxford University Press, 1953), p. 17.
2. Andres G. Frank, "Las Universidades Norteamericanas y el Fascismo Chileno," *Desarrollo* (November 1974): 59–67.
3. P. T. Bauer and B. S. Yamey, *The Economics of Under-Developed Countries* (Cambridge: the University Press, 1957). For a collection of Bauer's articles, see his *Dissent on Development* (Cambridge, Mass.: Harvard University Press, 1972).
4. Gunnar Myrdal, *Economic Theory and Under-Developed Regions* (London: Duckworth, 1957), p. 90.
5. Viner, *International Trade*, pp. 43–44.
6. Quoted in P.T. Bauer, *Indian Economic Policy and Development* (New York: Praeger, 1961), pp. 71–72.
7. P.T. Bauer, *The Study of Underdeveloped Economies: An Inaugural Lecture* (London: London School of Economics and Political Science, 1963), pp. 12–13.
8. Arnold C. Harberger, "Issues Concerning Capital Assistance to Less-Developed Countries," *Economic Development and Cultural Change* (July 1972), reprinted in *Chicago Essays in Development*, edited by David Wall (Chicago: University of Chicago Press, 1972), p. 354.
9. Arnold C. Harberger, "Some Notes on Inflation," in *Inflation and Growth in Latin America*, edited by Werner Baer and Isaac Kerstenetzky (New Haven: Yale University Press, 1964), reprinted in Wall, ed., *Chicago Essays*, p. 123.

10. Milton Friedman, "Foreign Economic Aid: Means and Objectives," *Yale Review* (Summer 1958): 509.
11. Bauer, *Indian Economic Policy*, p. 141.
12. Harry G. Johnson, "The Ideology of Economic Policy in the New States," in *Economic Nationalism in Old and New States*, edited by Harry G. Johnson (Chicago: University of Chicago Press, 1967), reprinted in Wall, ed., *Chicago Essays*, pp. 30–31.
13. Harry G. Johnson, *Economic Policies Toward Less Developed Countries* (New York: Praeger, 1967), p. 107.
14. Adam Smith, *The Wealth of Nations* (New York: Modern Library, 1937), pp. 420, 423.
15. Milton Friedman, "The Reduction of Fluctuations in the Income of Primary Producers," *Economic Journal* 64 (December 1954).
16. Friedman, "Foreign Economic Aid," p. 514.
17. Harberger, "Some Notes on Inflation," pp. 123–57.
18. Harry G. Johnson, "Tariffs and Economic Development: Some Theoretical Issues," *Journal of Development Studies* (October 1964), reprinted in Wall, ed., *Chicago Essays*, p. 293.
19. Harry G. Johnson, "Trade Preference and Developing Countries," *Lloyd's Bank Review* (April 1966), reprinted in Wall, ed., *Chicago Essays*, pp. 309–10.
20. Viner, *International Trade*, pp. 41–42.
21. George J. Stigler, "The Division of Labor Is Limited by the Extent of the Market," *Journal of Political Economy* 59 (June 1951): 341.
22. Harry G. Johnson, "Fiscal Policy and the Balance of Payments in a Growing Economy," *Malayan Economic Review* (April 1964), reprinted in Wall, ed., *Chicago Essays*, p. 122.
23. Friedman, "Foreign Economic Aid," p. 514; and Johnson, *Economic Policies*, p. 107.
24. Bela Balassa, "Tariff Protection in Industrial Countries: An Evaluation," *Journal of Political Economy* (December 1965), cited in Johnson, "Trade Preferences," pp. 316–17.
25. Viner, *International Trade*, p. 111.
26. Ibid., p. 91.
27. Ibid., p. 110.
28. The Pearson Commission recommended that "official development assistance" should reach 0.70 percent of GNP for industrialized countries by 1975. Official loans should have a grant element between 61 and 70 percent, which at the time meant a 2 percent interest rate, a maturity between 25 and 40 years, and a grace period of 7 to 10 years. Lester B. Pearson et al., *Partners in Development* (New York: Praeger, 1969), pp. 164–67.
29. Friedman, "Foreign Economic Aid," p. 503.
30. Ibid., p. 511.
31. Ibid., p. 507.
32. Hollis B. Chenery and Nicholas G. Carter, "Foreign Assistance and Development Performance, 1960–70," *American Economic Review* 63 (May 1973): 463, 467.
33. Milton Friedman, "Some Thoughts about the Current Economic Scene,"

*University of Chicago Magazine* (Autumn 1974): 13. The statement is not entirely consistent with his earlier view: "I believe that the main reason for the failure of India has been its attempt to repress inflation and particularly to peg the exchange rate." Milton Friedman, *Money and Economic Development: The Horowitz Lectures of 1972* (New York: Praeger, 1972), p. 53. Presumably, more foreign aid would have strengthened the rupee and allowed an anti-inflationary inflow of additional goods. But more foreign aid might simply raise national ambitions, targets, and pressures on central bankers, according to Friedman. "I conclude that the only way to refrain from using inflation as a method of taxation is to avoid having a central bank" (p. 47). What most countries should do, therefore, is to unify their currencies with a large developed country in the manner of Panama or Hong Kong (p. 59). Whether good or bad, monetary policy, he concedes, can merely facilitate but not generate economic development.

34. Johnson, "Trade Preferences," p. 307.
35. Johnson, *Economic Policies*, p. 4.
36. Theodore W. Schultz, "Value of U.S. Farm Surpluses to Underdeveloped Countries," *Journal of Farm Economics* (December 1960), reprinted in Wall, ed., *Chicago Essays*, p. 341.
37. Harberger, "Issues Concerning Capital Assistance," p. 362.
38. Ibid., p. 364.
39. Friedman, "Foreign Economic Aid," pp. 508–509.
40. Johnson, "Trade Preferences," p. 305.
41. Viner, *International Trade*, pp. 13–14.
42. Bauer, *Study of Underdeveloped Economies*, p. 30.
43. Theodore W. Schultz, *Transforming Traditional Agriculture* (New Haven: Yale University Press, 1964), and "Economic Growth from Traditional Agriculture," in Wall, ed., *Chicago Essays*, pp. 4, 15.
44. Gary S. Becker, "A Theory of Social Interactions," *Journal of Political Economy* 82 (November–December 1974): 1063–93; Theodore W. Schultz, *The Economic Value of Education* (New York: Columbia University Press, 1967); Theodore W. Schultz, ed., "Investment in Education: The Equity-Efficiency Quandary," *Journal of Political Economy* 80, Part II (May–June 1972); Gary S. Becker, "An Economic Analysis of Fertility," in National Bureau of Economic Research, *Demographic and Economic Changes in Developed Countries* (Princeton: Princeton University Press, 1960); and Theodore W. Schultz, ed., "New Economic Approaches to Fertility," Supplement to the *Journal of Political Economy* 81 (March–April 1973).
45. Harvey Leibenstein, "An Interpretation of the Economic Theory of Fertility: Promising Path or Blind Alley?" *Journal of Economic Literature* 12 (June 1974): 469–70. See also, Michael C. Keeley, "A Comment," and Harvey Leibenstein, "A Reply," in *Journal of Economic Literature* 13 (June 1975): 461–72.
46. Robin Horton, "African Traditional Thought and Western Science," in *Rationality*, edited by Bryan Wilson (Oxford: Basil Blackwell, 1970), pp. 162–66. For a blatant example of such question-begging, see Gary

Becker, "Irrational Behavior and Economic Theory," *Journal of Political Economy* 70 (February 1962): 1–13.

47. Steven Lukes, "Some Problems about Rationality," in Wilson, ed., *Rationality,* pp. 194–213. See also his essay, "On the Social Determination of Truth," in *Modes of Thought: Essays on Thinking in Western and Non-Western Societies,* edited by Robin Horton and Ruth Finnegan (London: Faber and Faber, 1973).
48. Arnold Harberger, "Using the Resources at Hand More Effectively," *American Economic Review* 49 (May 1959), reprinted in Wall, ed., *Chicago Essays,* p. 41.
49. Arnold Harberger, "Fiscal Policy and Income Redistribution," paper prepared for the Workshop on Income Distribution in Less-Deveolped Countries, Princeton University, 1974 (mimeographed), pp. 26–27.
50. David Wall, "Introduction," in Wall, ed., *Chicago Essays,* p. viii.
51. For example, Arnold Harberger, "The Panamanian Income Tax System—A Heterodox View" (Panama, June 1973, mimeographed).

# 13

# Industrial Organization and Reorganization

*David Dale Martin*

George Stigler began his industrial organization book with this statement:

> Let us start this volume on a higher plane of candor than it will always maintain: there is no such subject as industrial organization. The courses taught under this heading have for their purpose the understanding of the structure and behavior of the industries (goods and service producers) of an economy. These courses deal with the size structure of firms (one or many, "concentrated" or not), the causes (above all the economies of scale) of this size structure, the effects of concentration on competition, the effects of competition upon prices, investments, innovation, and so on. But this is precisely the content of economic theory—price or resource allocation theory, now often given the unfelicitous name of microeconomics.[1]

This article considers not the whole of microeconomics but only a small part of the recent literature closely related to public policy debates on the issue of the adequacy of antitrust enforcement in the United States. The prestige and influence within the economics profession of the Chicago School is sufficiently great that no clear boundaries can be drawn separating "Chicagoans" from industrial organization

*The author is Professor of Business Economics and Public Policy, Graduate School of Business, Indiana University, Bloomington.*

economists generally. This author has chosen to focus attention on a few significant propositions, or themes, that recur and seem to play a central role in the writings of a few industrial organization economists clearly identifiable with the University of Chicago tradition. Chief among them are George J. Stigler and Yale Brozen of the University of Chicago, and Harold Demsetz and J. Fred Weston of the University of California, Los Angeles, although a number of others have also made contributions. No attempt is made herein to critique all of the industrial organization literature or any of the closely related literature on economics and law.

A primary proposition implicit or explicit in the Chicago School industrial organization literature is that those who want *any* action by government must base their case on "scientifically established results" of economic research. A second proposition is that economic science has *not* produced valid research to support the argument that a concentrated structure adversely affects the performance of the U.S. (and presumably the world) economy. The literature consists primarily of refutations of some of the arguments of some antitrust advocates and alternative explanations of the facts and research results of antitrust advocates or others whose work tends to support the need for government action. Because the Chicagoans place the burden of proof on their adversaries, they are willing to rest their case on "muddy waters." Therefore, much of the literature concludes simply that economic science has not yet demonstrated anything about the relation between structure, conduct, and performance of concentrated industries, and therefore the government should not interfere with either the continuance of that structure or changes in it made by "private" power groups.

Thus the Chicago School's chief contributions to industrial organization and competition policy in recent years have had the effect, if not the intent, of supporting the "business position" on that fundamental question of whether "bigness is badness," just as that question is reemerging as a public policy issue in Congress and in public debate.

The optimal degree of centralization of control of society has been, of course, a predominant public policy issue in U.S. society at least since the American Revolution. For one hundred years the centralization of control of industry has been a major policy issue, even though more or less dormant as an explicit election issue since 1912. It has been at issue in the courts all along. The Chicago School has not always been clearly identified with the "no-government" position. The recent literature contains several efforts to distinguish the Henry Simons aberration. The contrast of present-day Chicagoans with Simons will be treated briefly and the implications of the doctrinal change illustrated with the debate about concentration and profits. The interrelation of profits with corporate concentration has played a major role in the debates on the need for stricter enforcement of the merger laws as well as new legislation to accomplish industrial reorganization to remedy the structural consequences of the turn-of-the-century merger movement.

### *On What Simons Says*

The concern about centralization of control of economic activity on the part of U.S. citizens has been so deeply rooted and widespread that it is not surprising that many an economist-qua-citizen would share that concern. Indeed, the concern of Chicago School economists about centralization of control of economic power in government may be explainable in those same terms—as a reflection of their underlying individualist values rather than as a result of the economic research in which they engage.[2] Be that as it may, this writer finds surprising the view recently expressed by Harold Demsetz and Yale Brozen that significant numbers of economists who advocate government action to accomplish a reduction in market concentration have appeared on the scene only since World War II and have arrived at their policy positions primarily on the basis of empirical research by economists. In a 1973 pamphlet aimed at refuting what he perceived to be the "market concentration doctrine" underlying Senator Philip Hart's industrial reorganization bill, Demsetz said:

> The most important sources of the market concentration doctrine are the empirical work done by Gardiner Means and Joe Bain during the 1930s and 1950s, respectively. Means dealt with price flexibility, inflation, and concentration. Bains's studies were concerned with the basic linkage between concentration and monopoly power. Support for the market concentration doctrine became widespread only after these works confronted economists with empirical relationships between market concentration on the one hand and prices and profits on the other that seemed to challenge the notion, then prevalent, that there was little to fear from an industry in which control was dispersed among separate firms, even when very few firms competed in the industry. Prior to World War II, most economists shared a conviction that effective competitive forces would be unleashed by rivalry among even a small number of firms. Leading students of the problem, such as Eliot Jones, J.B. Clark, and A.S. Dewing, subscribed to this conviction, even though some economists of the time, such as Henry C. Simons, were some-

> what less confident about the strength of competition in concentrated industries. But if there existed some concern about market concentration, it was not held with such certainty that it was included in standard classroom fare.[3]

Perhaps "standard classroom fare" was, by definition, the portion of the economics profession's work that supported the existing structure of power. Warren Samuels has said:

> Part of the social control function of economic ideology in any society is to legitimize the particular status quo (or aspects thereof) as preeminent and preexistent to man and man's choice, to reduce and channel choice and thereby avoid fundamental questioning of the established system or details thereof. This is part of the priestly function which economists, a conservative group for the most part, have often been willing to perform.[4]

But the "other part" of the group of economists that has not performed that priestly function has been large and persistent and certainly has roots much deeper than Demsetz recognizes. Almarin Phillips and Rodney Stevenson also recognized a strong conservative force among economists in support of the "natural" origin of big business, but they go on to say:

> There were a few early dissidents for this extreme laissez-faire doctrine. Francis A. Walker and David A. Wells were among them, but they and their school exerted little influence until after the formation of the American Economic Association in 1885. Then the pendulum swung. Edmund J. James advocated public ownership of natural monopolies in 1886. J.B. Clark distinguished between the effects of "conservative competition" in the same year, but subsequently found himself in sympathy with large-scale enterprise and expressed opposition to antitrust laws. Richard T. Ely, however, was an early champion of public ownership for natural monopolies and made a rather limited attack on "artificial" monopolies.[5]

The pendulum has continued to swing. In the 1920s and 1930s it swung back toward the "bigness is not badness" view not only among economists, but also in public policy. Demsetz is correct in his perception of the latest swing of economists toward the anti-trust position and is making a valiant attempt to reverse the direction once again by arguing that recent professional opinion is a temporary departure from a long prevailing view that competition among the few or even combination in the form of trust or otherwise has no demonstrated adverse economic consequences.

Yale Brozen has stated even more strongly this Chicago interpretation of the history of U.S. economic thought on concentration of economic power. He has written:

> In the post-World War II period, the economics profession made a 180 degree turn from its pre-Great Depression position in its view of concentration. In the late nineteenth and early twentieth century, the prevailing view seems to have been that even with only a few firms in an industry, price competition would be persistent and collusion difficult. There was little concern with any probability of successful collusion (shared monopoly or oligopoly) in industries where four firms had, say, 70 percent or more of an industry's capacity or sales.
>
> Even where more than 70 percent of an industry's capacity had been combined to form a *single* firm, no fear was felt by many economists that a monopoly result would ensue. . . . J.B. Clark, for example, pointed to the power of potential competition to produce the same competitive result as a large number of firms or non-colluding behavior of a few.[6]

Brozen goes further than Demsetz in rationalizing the strong pro-competition policy position of Henry C. Simons. Quoting from Simons's generally strong statement of support for government intervention to achieve the requisites of competition,[7] Brozen says:

> As late as the 1930s, after the discussion of administered (rigid) prices in concentrated industries had begun, Professor Simons said: "I am, indeed, not much distressed about private monopoly power. . . . Serious exploitation could be prevented by suppression of lawless violence. . . . The ways of competition are devious, and its vengeance—government intervention apart—will generally be adequate and admirable.[8]

Brozen, in a footnote, went on to say: "Simons spoke out strongly against concentration largely to offset the drive in government and the press at that time to force independent firms into cartels (as under NRA) and combinations."[9]

Thus, Brozen has interpreted Henry Simons so as to make Simons's position appear to be consistent with the currently prevailing Chicago doctrine—that government intervention is inconsistent with economic efficiency, that monopoly power can come only from government intervention, and, therefore, that government intervention to achieve competition is itself anticompetitive. As this author has argued elsewhere,[10] the application of this doctrine to government creation of business corporations would give it more credence, but such a withdrawal of government support of the legal foundations of existing powerful business organizations is not to be found in any of the recent industrial organization literature. It is here that we find the nexus with the "economics and law" work of the Chicago School as well as the basic weakness in the prevailing Chicago School "burden of proof" theme. If governments had not intervened to grant perpetual corporate charters to replace the law of contract with a highly centralized and autocratic legal ordering of relations among the things and persons associated with a corporation, then the burden of proving that the public interest lies in combination and centralization of control would still lie on the business organizations to show by the validated results of economic science that their very existence will improve economic performance.

Simons, it seems to me, was indeed a heretic to the new Chicago doctrine on government policy toward competition, monopoly, and concentration of control. Some of George Stigler's recent work gives support to my position. In a brief sketch of the life and work of Simons Stigler said:

> Simons believed that it was essential to the preservation of personal freedom that a large sector of economic life be organized privately and competitively—this was a fundamental element of the liberal position that many, perhaps even an increasing share of us, still believe. With it, however, he joined an extensive and intricate set of tasks for the state:
>
> 1. The positive pursuit of competition by limitist laws as well as by antitrust policy.
> 2. Public ownership and operation of "natural" monopolies (preferably by local governments where possible).
> 3. Severe restriction of advertising and merchandising.
> 4. Elimination of tariff barriers.
> 5. The elimination of all forms of public debt except long-term bonds and of almost all forms of private debt except short-term credit to strengthen the weapons of monetary policy and eliminate the forced liquidations consequent upon business downturns.

> 6. A monetary authority committed to maintain stability in the quantity or value of money.
>
> All these policies, with the possible exception of the limitation of advertising, could be argued to be necessary to the preservation of a large and efficient private enterprise sector. To this theme, Simons adds a major one which is surely independent: That there should be a large movement toward income equality, achieved primarily by reliance upon a personal income tax.... This strong egalitarian element separated Simons from most conservatives, and indeed one could make a strong case that Simons was a modern liberal who understood price theory. Certainly no other economist accepted so fully Mill's proposition that the distribution of income was a matter of free social choice.[11]

George Stigler thus does not join Brozen and Demsetz in their apparent attempts to sweep Simons "under the rug" or retroactively convert him to a true believer in the contemporary Chicago doctrine on competition policy. Stigler, instead, concludes his sketch of Simons with this statement:

> In forming most present day policy views of Chicago economists, Director and Friedman have been the main intellectual forces.
>
> The evolution of institutions and theories has moved them beyond Simons' positions—and beyond those of contemporaries such as Keynes, Hansen, and Tawney. Yet Simons' central goal is as vital and as irresistible today as it was forty years ago: To devise a decentralized, unpoliticized world in which personal freedom and economic efficiency find wide scope and strong defense.[12]

These words of George Stigler perhaps tell us more about Stigler than Simons. Stigler "still believes" that personal freedom requires an economic structure with a large competitive sector. Stigler implies that he does not still believe that personal freedom requires the set of government tasks which Simons thought essential. Stigler concedes only that most of the tasks "could be argued to be necessary." On regulation of advertising and merchandising, Stigler is not even willing to admit to their arguability, whatever that might mean. Presumably it means that he has closed his mind to any further discussion on that one, but that he entertains at least the shadow of a doubt that present day policy views of Chicago economists may be incorrect—and Simons correct—on the need for government action in the other five areas. Stigler has not rejected Simons out of hand. Indeed, he finds Simons's central goal "as vital and as irresistible today as it was forty years ago."

The need for positive government promotion of competition thus becomes for Stigler as well as for Brozen, Demsetz, and other Chicago economists a very important topic for industrial organization research. Because the Simons interventionist position is "arguable" as a requisite to the preservation of a private, competitive sector, and because such a sector is necessary for freedom, research to settle the issue is relevant. But these economists are not starting from a position of neutrality. That part of Simons's doctrine is no longer believed by Chicagoans, and the research is aimed at moving more and more of the government role into the category of "unarguability" into which Stigler has already placed regulation of advertising and merchandising.

If one believes in Simons's goal, and if one believes that a large, private, competitive sector is requisite, then one might view the role of government more objectively as a means to that end. Running through the Chicago School's writings in all areas of economics, however, is the growing view that government, itself, is undesirable.[13] Simons seems to me to have evaluated combinations of businessmen in the same way as combinations of the citizenry through governmental action, that is, instrumentally with respect to the achievement of personal freedom. Such an attitude toward government is consistent with, and reflected in, his second major theme: Government power should be used to accomplish an egalitarian society. Stigler says this second theme "is purely independent" of Simons's central individualist philosophy. I doubt that it was. If one does not couple one's individualist philosophy with an egalitarian philosophy, then it is much easier to perceive the corporation, no matter how big, as an individual whose freedom from government power must be protected, and to place the burden on the advocate of government action to show that the corporation or combination of corporations interferes with that allocation of resources that would be deemed "efficient," *given* the distribution of wealth, income, and power, rather than placing the burden on the corporation or combination to show that its actions are consistent with the goals of a democratic, egalitarian society.

The recent contributions to industrial organization literature by Chicago School economists seem to me to reflect implicitly a rejection of Simons's egalitarian political philosophy. Whatever one thinks about the "surely independent" question of income distribution, to be working and writing *qua* economist one must be evaluating public policy measures solely in terms of their effects on "efficiency" of resource allocation, given the distribution of wealth, power, and income. That conception of the scope and nature of economic science goes along with accepting Simons's individualism without his egalitarianism. Stigler says that "Simons hardly ever departed from normative economics."[14] The new Chicagoans have become, unlike Simons, positive economists. Thus, they conclude from all that microeconomics teaches that for "a large sector of economic life [to] be organized privately and competitively" is not only "essential to the preservation of personal freedom" but also that it yields "economic efficiency." The larger, and more private the private sector, the better. If the part of the economy that is private, that is, not regulated or managed by government, is by its very nature adequately competitive, then Simons's role for the state as the maintainer of competition is unnecessary. The adequacy of competition without government intervention is thus a chief topic of inquiry by Chicago industrial organization economists. Much of their research has focused on the evidence of others that concentration of control of the private sector has made competition inadequate.

### *Concentration and Competition*

Industrial organization as a subdivision of economics has been given its focus in recent years by the "structure, conduct, performance" analysis developed at Harvard University by Edward S. Mason and his students in the 1930s and 1940s.[15] Out of that tradition much research has come that tends to support the proposition that performance is not adequate and that structure has something to do with it. Also from Harvard came the much more unorthodox work of Gardiner Means on the changing nature of the private sector under corporate control and its effects on pricing, with implications for macro- as well as for microeconomic policies.[16] John Blair, particularly during the thirteen years he was Chief Economist, Senate Subcommittee on Antitrust and Monopoly, directed, encouraged, or published through the committee hearings process an encyclopedic body of facts and analysis in the Means-TNEC tradition.[17] From this large body of literature has come in recent years additional evidence to support the position of the earlier economic dissidents that the corporate form of business organization has resulted in more concentration of control in the private sector than is consistent with the competitive ideal. Demsetz calls this view the "market concentration doctrine."

The need for government intervention either to bring about competition or to substitute public for private control is indicated by research that shows either, in the Mason tradition, that performance is inadequate or, in the Means-Blair tradition, that conduct is contrary to the explanations of the economic theory of a competitive system. The Chicago economists have taken on both groups.

The structure-conduct-performance debate has focused on those topics Stigler lists in the passage quoted at the outset as the typical content of industrial organization courses: the causes and consequences of the size structure of firms. Three specific aspects of this broad question dominate the literature: (1) whether or not the empirical evidence on the relationship between census industry concentration ratios and some measure of industry profits shows inadequate performance attributable to fewness of firms; (2) whether or not census industry concentration ratios are explainable in terms of economies of scale; and (3) whether or not concentration is associated with more or less technological progressiveness. The Means line of development has given rise to a fourth topic: whether or not pricing practices in the concentrated census industries differ from the less concentrated sector in ways that are relevant to the achievement of full employment of resources without inflation. By and large the Chicago School concludes: (1) observed profit-concentration relationships are not inconsistent with the competitive hypothesis; (2) concentration is no greater than the socially desirable degree dictated by economies of scale; (3) no valid evidence exists to prove that concentration has hindered technology; and (4) the evidence on pricing conduct is not inconsistent with the competitive hypothesis. The concentration-profits controversy will serve to illustrate the central issues.

### *The Concentration-Profits Relationship*

The literature is very large and growing on questions associated with the theoretical and observed relationships between the fewness of firms in a market and the profits of the firms. More than two sides exist in the discussions in this literature. The narrow issue that has achieved so much attention is whether or not concentration ratios for census four-digit industries are correlated with profits for those industries. Lurking beneath that question is the relevance of the answer to the need for government intervention to deconcentrate the concentrated industries.

The narrow issue is not as easily settled as might first appear. There are two principle reasons: (1) because divisional reporting of profits of multimarket firms is not required, no data are available on profits of four-digit census industries, and (2) even if simple correlation is found with a proxy data, multiple regression can be attempted with an indefinite number of other variables brought into the statistical models.

This literature seems to have begun with Joe S. Bain's 1951 article on concentration and profits.[18] Demsetz, as mentioned above, gives this empirical work much credit for having persuaded economists that concentrated structures are bad. Although one counter example cannot serve to refute Demsetz's assessment of its influence on the profession generally, this writer can testify that it had no influence on his judgments on the need for government intervention to achieve a more competitive structure of industry. This was because Bain's data and statistical model were so much less adequate than then available information from antitrust litigation and congressional investigations.[19] The data and statistical method problems have not been overcome by either side in the debates that have ensued in the literature in the past quarter century. Fred Weston's testimony on the Hart bill and my questioning of him bring out some, but not all, of these issues.[20] A very careful, concise, and persuasive case for the appropriateness of the statistical method properly used has been made by Lee E. Preston, who has contributed many of the better empirical studies, was a member of the Neal Committee that recommended deconcentration legislation to President Johnson in 1968, and who testified in support of Hart's industrial reorganization bill.[21]

My own reaction to the debate on the narrow issue of statistical interpretation is twofold: The Chicago School economists have not found errors and corrected them so as to constitute the reversal of prevailing professional views that Weston and Demsetz have asserted. They have shown, however, those waters to be quite muddy, like all the other waters in which "economic scientists" fish for laws of nature with multiple regression hooks. Given the epistemological underpinnings of the Chicago School, muddy waters suffice to bring the economics profession in on the side of "bigness is goodness" because they place the burden of proof on the advocates of government intervention rather than on the business interests to show the true relationship.

On the relevance of the profit-concentration empirical work, I find much more of value in the work of the Chicagoans. They have apparently considered the question relevant primarily because of the importance of it to the rest of the profession, particularly to those working in the Mason tradition. Therefore, there is the need on policy grounds to undermine the persuasiveness of the empirical evidence to that portion of the profession which not only sees evidence of this relationship as relevant to the policy issue, but also is willing, if not eager, to accept the limitations of data and statistical method inherent in the work of both sides in the debate. The Chicago position seems to be the following: The relationship between concentration and profits is not a theoretically justifiable basis for a deconcentration policy, but if you think it is, be advised that such a relationship has not been validly demonstrated. My own conclusion is that demonstration of the relationship is relevant, but not by any means necessary or sufficient, to justify government intervention to accomplish a more decentralized structure of control, and that it has been persuasively demonstrated within the limits of the data and the statistical method. The weaknesses of that method seem to me to be greater as it is used by Brozen, Demsetz, and Weston than by Preston, Weiss, and others who have found "evidence" of the relationship.[22] The policy issue certainly should not rest on the empirical findings under circumstances in which the muddy waters leave the power structure intact, and the power structure refuses to divulge the data that might clear up the statistical issue.

Brozen, however, seems quite correct in concluding that "although our theory tells us that economic profits are more likely to persist under monopoly circumstances, it does not tell us that economic profits occur only because of monopoly. They may occur for many other reasons, ranging from disequilibrium to innovation, and they may persist for reasons other than monopoly."[23]

These are valid reasons for not taxing profits to counter the income distribution effects of monopoly.[24] These are also valid reasons, it seems to me, for not making high profits conclusive evidence of monopoly performance and an overly concentrated industry structure. The profit criterion for just these reasons was used in the original version of the Hart bill only as a rebuttable presumption of monopoly powers. If persistent high profits are reported by a corporation (not an industry), the burden would shift to the corporation to demonstrate that their height or their persistence was accounted for by these or other socially desirable "other reasons." "Disequilibrium," however, would be very difficult to distinguish from monopoly power. Granted that high profits may appear for that reason, one must guard against defining away the monopoly problem. It is only in the theory that the equilibrium is significant. Public policy seeks growth and change, and monopoly has its dynamic as well as its static aspects. To show that an industry did not have a static monopoly structure because it was not static is not enough. Monopoly power includes the power to restrict growth in supply relative to growth in demand—by manipulating either blade of the scissors through time. The burden should be on the corporation with persistent high profits to demonstrate that its power is not being used to slow down the movement toward equilibrium naturally from disequilibrium.

A practical reason for not including such a profit criterion in legislation designed to identify and restructure corporations that possess monopoly power is that the powerful ones are likely to be able to manipulate their public accounts to escape the law. Another valid objection for not relying solely on a profit criterion is that monopoly profits may not appear because of the extra costs of the monopolists in maintaining the monopoly, that is, the costs of barriers to entry. These costs include advertising, annual model changes, research to forestall development by others, costly reductions in durability and other measures to increase the rate of growth in demand, and the preemption of resources.

Brozen says: "Even if persistent economic profits were such a signal, we are faced with data which do not tell us whether or not persistent economic profits are occurring. Accounting rates of return may be persistently above average because of accounting conventions which bias reported rates of return persistently upward much more in some industries than in others."[25]

It seems just as likely, if not more so, that the bias will be in the other direction. After lengthy hearings on his industrial reorganization bill, Senator Hart reintroduced it in the 94th Congress with no change except the elimination of the profit criterion from the list of three rebuttable presumptions of monopoly power, retaining the concentration and the pricing practices criteria. That change seems to me to improve the bill, but my reasons are quite unrelated to the empirical evidence on the concentration-profits relationship. Indeed, if that correlation were perfect, the inclusion of a profits criterion would be surplusage.

### *Conclusions*

Present day antitrust advocates within the economics profession by and large seem to me to be aptly described with the phrase Stigler used to describe Henry Simons—as modern liberals who understand price theory. They share the strong egalitarian element that Stigler found to separate Simons from most conservatives. The Chicago School has gone beyond Simons primarily, it seems to me, in embracing concepts of what constitutes knowledge that allow them to "do" economics without having to make commitments to themselves or others on the egalitarian question. If whether or not one is egalitarian becomes irrelevant to policy, however, then one surely is not egalitarian.

The antitrust advocates also share Simons's individualistic philosophy. The Chicagoans profess to do likewise, yet they seem to have no concern that individual rights may be threatened by displacement of market forms with bureaucratic forms of relations between persons or between persons and things in economic activity controlled by large business organizations.

A third group of economists are those who share the egalitarian philosophy so deeply rooted in American culture, but who see "rugged" individualism as outmoded in a modern, industrial economy. With little fear of government per se, such economists tend toward government intervention to achieve egalitarian goals.

By pushing to the extreme the policy implications of individualism without egalitarianism coupled with the positivist epistemological position, the Chicago School is rendering one real service to the economics profession and to society. Confronted with apparent conflicts between the self-evident policy results of such economic advice and the very deeply rooted democratic values of Americans, including economists, the reader is forced to think a little more deeply about his own beliefs and whence they come.

Regression analysis can prove nothing about causal relations. At best it can lead to a statement, given a statistical decision rule chosen either quite arbitrarily and thus irrationally or with normative judgments about probabilities and consequences of errors, that the "evidence" is not inconsistent with the hypothesis. But there are always other hypotheses with which the evidence is also not inconsistent. Some of the latter are likely also not to be inconsistent with the researcher's underlying values, doctrine, and beliefs. Most of the Chicago School industrial organization literature seems to be regression analysis with some new variables or new proxies introduced with which to test alternative hypotheses of that sort. This work is done with brilliance and ingenuity, yet the light this literature throws on the essential emptiness of the whole empirical-statistical method of economic research may turn out to be its greatest contribution. It asks the reader to agree that *knowledge* about causal relationships *means* statistical verification of operationally meaningful propositions. The burden of proof is put upon anyone who would use democratic government action to change the private power structure. Nongovernmental organizations, no matter how large or powerful, are allowed without criticism to make whatever changes in structure their power affords, and their judgments decide with no such burden of scientific proof.

The policy of competition did not originate with the economics profession. It is deeply rooted in the law and other institutions of American society and, fortunately, it does not depend upon universal or even widespread acceptance by professional economists. Indeed, the continued acceptance by society of professional economists as relevant and useful advisers to a democratic government and as teachers of the young is more likely to depend in the years ahead upon the profession's acceptance of democratic, decentralized structures of control of economic activity as a *sine qua non* of economic analysis of public policy issues.

## Notes

1. George J. Stigler, *The Organization of Industry* (Homewood, Ill.: Richard D. Irwin, Inc., 1968), p. 1.
2. Warren Samuels says: "Economics is knowledge, it is social control, and it is psychic balm. . . . Economic ideology has largely replaced theology as the social device for achieving social cohesion, providing a set of moral rules, providing goals for individual internalization and identity-achievement, providing legitimation for the machinations of power players both in and out of government." Warren J. Samuels, "The History of Economic Thought as Intellectual History," *History of Political Economy* 6 (Fall 1974): 314–15.
3. Harold Demsetz, *The Market Concentration Doctrine* (Washington and Stanford: AEI-Hoover Policy Studies, 1973), p. 4.
4. Samuels, "History of Economic Thought," p. 316.
5. Almarin Phillips and Rodney E. Stevenson, "The Historical Development of Industrial Organization," *History of Political Economy* 6 (Fall 1974): 329.
6. Yale Brozen, "Concentration and Profits: Does Concentration Matter?" in *The Impact of Large Firms on the U. S. Economy,* edited by J. Fred Weston and Stanley I. Ornstein (Lexington, Mass.: D. C. Heath and Company, 1973), p. 59.
7. Henry C. Simons, "The Requisites of Free Competition," *American Economic Review* 26 (March 1936, Supplement): 68–76.
8. Brozen, "Concentration and Profits," p. 60.
9. Ibid. p. 265.
10. David Dale Martin, "Beyond Capitalism: A Role for Markets?" *Journal of Economics Issues* 8 (December 1974): 771–84.
11. George J. Stigler, "Henry Calvert Simons," *Journal of Law and Economics* 17 (April 1974): 3.
12. Ibid., p. 5.
13. See Warren J. Samuels, "The Coase Theorem and the Study of Law and Economics," *Natural Resources Journal* 14 (January 1974): 1–33.
14. Stigler, "Henry Calvert Simons," p. 4.
15. Phillips and Stevenson, "Historical Development," pp. 335–40.
16. Ibid., pp. 333–34.
17. This body of evidence is summarized, analyzed, and cited in: John M. Blair, *Economic Concentration* (New York: Harcourt Brace Jovanovich, 1972).
18. J. S. Bain, "Relation of Profit Rate to Industry Concentration, American Manufacturing, 1936–1940," *Quarterly Journal of Economics* 65 (August 1951): 293–324.

19. The article appeared during my last year as a graduate student in residence at UCLA where I was serving as Armen Alchian's teaching assistant in the economic statistics course. On reading it I expressed amazement that Bain would use the statistical methods appropriate for quality control work or laboratory experiment, where both randomness and control of independent variables are possible, to draw inferences about causal relationships from such data as were disclosed and available for analysis. Alchian assured me that economists need not limit their statistical analyses to data from random samples, but on balance I think we would be better off if they did!
20. *The Industrial Reorganization Act, Hearings* before the Subcommittee on Antitrust and Monopoly of the Committee on the Judiciary, United States Senate, 93rd Cong., 1st session, on S. 1167, Part 1, General Views, 27, 28, 29, and 30 March and 7 and 8 May 1973, pp. 234–273. The dialogue occurs at page 243–53.
21. *Industrial Reorganization Act, Hearings,* pp. 294-318.
22. See Yale Brozen, "Significance of Profit Data for Antitrust Policy," in *Public Policy Toward Mergers,* edited by J. Fred Weston and Sam Peltzman (Pacific Palisades: Goodyear Publishing Company, Inc., 1969), pp. 110–27; Harold Demsetz, "Two Systems of Belief about Monopoly," in *Industrial Concentration: the New Learning,* edited by Harvey J. Goldschmid, H. Michael Mann, and J. Fred Weston (Boston: Little, Brown and Company, 1974), pp. 164–84; J. Fred Weston, *Hearings*, pp. 234–73; Lee E. Preston, *Hearings*, pp. 294–318; and Leonard W. Weiss, "The Concentration-Profits Relationship and Antitrust," in *Industrial Concentration,* edited by Goldschmid, Mann, and Weston, pp. 184–232. Professor Weiss's essay constitutes a thorough review of the literature on this subject.
23. Brozen, "Significance of Profit Data," p. 120.
24. A returned earnings tax coupled with a higher progressive income tax on individuals would have advantages over the profits tax on other grounds as well—to broaden the capital market and encourage new ventures by new entrants.
25. Brozen, "Significance of Profit Data."

# 14

# The Chicago School versus Public Utility Regulation

*Harry M. Trebing*

There has been a strong revival of interest in the field of public utility regulation during the past 20 years. Much of this interest has focused on the economic aspects of the direct control of prices and earnings for the regulated firm. As a result, a substantial body of literature has developed dealing with risk-return relationships, the behavior of the firm under regulatory constraints, the development of pricing guidelines, and the adequacy or effectiveness of regulation *per se*. This article focuses on the contribution of representatives of the Chicago School to that portion of the literature devoted to the adequacy of regulation.

Most of the studies of the adequacy of regulation can be placed in four categories. First, there are the case studies which seek to determine the impact of regulation on industry performance. Such studies have been made for electricity, natural gas, and air and surface transport.[1] Second, there are the behavioral studies which attempt to relate the structural and institutional characteristics of the regulatory system to the behavior and effectiveness of the independent agencies. Such studies involve questions of commission practice and procedure, ability to plan, and the appropriateness of the variables selected to achieve regulatory objectives.[2] Third, there are the attacks on regulation by consumer and environmental activists who hold that the commission system is no longer capable of promoting the public interest because it has become too

*The author is Professor of Economics and Director, Institute of Public Utilities, Michigan State University, East Lansing.*

closely identified with the regulated industries. The proposed solutions usually involve a greater reliance on consumer advocacy, more stringent regulation, or the substitution of antitrust for regulation.[3] Fourth, there are the analyses and policy prescriptions of the Chicago School which set forth a neoliberal position that seeks to eliminate government regulation,[4] while at the same time resolving the monopoly problem inherent in high levels of concentration and the existence of economies of scale.

The position of the Chicago School differs in significant respects from that of the others studying the adequacy and effectiveness of regulation. The view of the former is uncompromising regarding the inability of government regulation to promote efficient resource allocation. In contrast, those making industry case studies may argue that deregulation is appropriate for one industry because it is workably competitive, but may argue that continued regulation is necessary for another industry because it displays monopolistic characteristics. Similarly, those studying regulatory behavior usually accept some form of government regulation or control as desirable and focus on the adequacy of existing practices, methods to improve the performance of the commission system, or the desirability of transferring regulatory functions to other agencies or branches of government. Consumer advocates and environmentalists tend to be pragmatic regarding the contribution of regulation and as a result draw criticism from adherents to the Chicago position.[5]

It is not surprising that representatives of the Chicago School should assume a prominent role in challenging the legitimacy of the institution of public regulation. The concept of a commission that is capable of establishing earnings and prices as well as entry and exit conditions for an industry represents an advanced form of government intervention that is in direct conflict with the basic tenets of the Chicago School regarding the role of markets, prices, and profits. But the issues involved are far more complex than a simple confrontation between institutional form and philosophical predisposition. Public utility industries are usually perceived as inherently monopolistic or at least tightly oligopolistic. Therefore, the Chicagoans must come to grips with the problem of reconciling high levels of market concentration with a rejection of direct regulation as a solution. The fashion in which this is accomplished provides an intriguing insight into the Chicago perception of the role of government and the nature of state intervention, the importance of monopoly power, and the changes which have taken place within the Chicago School itself.

## *A Synopsis of the Chicago Viewpoint*

### *The Old Chicago School*

Henry C. Simons was probably the first member of the Chicago School to set forth a detailed criticism of the institution of public utility regulation.[6] In 1934, Simons proclaimed what he felt to be the fundamental challenge to a free society:

> *The great enemy of democracy is monopoly, in all its forms:* gigantic corporations, trade associations and other agencies for price control, trade-unions—or, in general, organization and concentration of power within functional classes. Effectively organized functional groups possess tremendous power for exploiting the community at large and even for sabotaging the system.[7]

Social control of monopoly through regulation was dismissed by Simons as completely unacceptable, and public ownership was prescribed for industries such as public utilities and railroads.

> Public regulation of private monopoly would seem to be, at best, an anomalous arrangement, tolerable only as a temporary expedient. Halfhearted, sporadic, principle-less regulation is a misfortune for all concerned; and systematic regulation, on the basis of any definite and adequate principle, would leave private ownership almost without a significant function or responsibility to discharge. Analysis of the problem, and examination of experience to date, would seem to indicate the wisdom of abandoning the existing scheme of things with respect to the railroads and utilities. . . . Political control of utility charges is imperative, to be sure, for competition simply cannot function effectively as an agency of control. We may endure regulation for a time, on the dubious assumption that governments are more nearly competent to regulate than to operate. *In general, however, the state should face the necessity of actually taking over, owning, and managing directly, both the railroads and the utilities, and all other industries in which it is impossible to maintain effectively competitive conditions.*[8]

Simons not only strenuously rejected regulation, but also called attention to the danger which he perceived in the discretionary authority given to such administrative agencies as a group. To Simons, this broad latitude to determine general policy was a "highroad to dictatorship."[9]

The Simons policy recommendations on regulation had very little impact on the course of public policy in the 1930s and 1940s. Indeed, Simons argued against public regulation during a period which saw the greatest expansion of commission regulation at the federal level. It is clear that Congress was far more influenced by the report of the Federal Trade Commission, *Utility Corporations* (1935),[10] than by Simons's *Positive Program for Laissez Faire* (1934).

### *The New Chicago School*

The interest of the Chicago School in the institution of regulation appears to have been reawakened in the late 1950s when public attention began to focus on the actions of regulators rather than on the actions of the regulated. In part, this interest appears to have stemmed from the worsening problems in transport, scandals associated with the Eisenhower appointments to the commissions, the resignation of Louis Hector from the Civil Aeronautics Board, and the criticisms that Bernstein and others directed at the Interstate Commerce Commission. The time seemed ripe for a new phase of critical regulatory reassessment.

In 1959 Ronald H. Coase presented a lengthy critique of the Federal Communications Commission,[11] and in 1962 George J. Stigler argued that state commissions had little discernible impact on electric utility rates.[12] Stigler's article marked a departure from some of the earlier studies because it focused on the effect of electric utility regulation rather than on the process or procedures of regulation. In the years that followed, a number of articles appeared in the *Journal of Law and Economics* which were critical of the effect of regulation in fields such as transport, broadcasting, natural gas production, and banking.[13]

While Stigler and others examined the economic effects of regulation, Milton Friedman's *Capitalism and Freedom* (1962) proposed a solution to the natural monopoly problem that stood in direct contrast to that proposed earlier by Simons. Friedman observed that when there are "technical conditions [which] make a monopoly the natural outcome of competitive market forces, there are only three alternatives that seem available: private monopoly, or public monopoly, or public regulation. . . . I reluctantly conclude that, if tolerable, private monopoly may be the least of the evils."[14] This is premised on the belief that "the conditions making for technical monopoly frequently change and I suspect that both public regulation and public monopoly are likely to be less responsive to such changes in conditions, to be less readily capable of elimination, than private monopoly."[15]

Thus Friedman had introduced a major change in the Chicago solution to the public utility problem. Private monopoly, subject to the eroding forces of change, was superior to government regulation or public ownership. This shift appears to have had a significant effect on other adherents to the Chicago School, and more detailed arguments were soon offered to demonstrate that unregulated private ownership was superior, that private monopoly could be reconciled with competitive levels of profits without regulation, and that publicly owned utilities would follow pricing policies that maximize voter support rather than efficiency. This change appears to be a significant feature differentiating the new Chicago School from the old as represented by Simons and Frank H. Knight.

Richard A. Posner has argued at length that the evils of unregulated, privately owned natural monopoly have been greatly exaggerated, whether considered in terms of resource misallocation, income distribution, or impact on innovation. He believes that private monopoly will respond to consumer wants and that it represents a much better option than either public ownership or direct regulation. As a positive program, Posner would remove controls on entry and specific rates and substitute an excess profits tax (albeit a modest one) as a limitation on overall profits.[16]

Continuing his criticism of regulation, Posner believes that regulation constitutes a form of taxation. This arises when inefficient rate structures subsidize particular competitors and customers. Such subsidies occur when prices are below marginal cost or when fixed costs are not concentrated on those classes of customers willing to pay them.[17] As a substitute for direct administrative regulation, Posner advocates greater reliance on the common law system of privately enforced rights. Accordingly, the consumer with a grievance against an essentially unregulated private monopolist would look to the common law for relief.

Harold Demsetz has also provided a rationale for private monopoly with no direct price-earnings regulation. He argues that the existence of a natural monopoly can be reconciled with a competitive level of earnings through the auctioning process.[18] A franchise or operating license could be awarded to the highest bidder (agreeing to serve at the lowest price), thereby inducing a competitive pressure among bidders that would force earnings to a competitive market level. Kenneth Dam has also advocated application of the competitive bidding principle in the development of North Sea gas and oil.[19] He is highly critical of British policy which has sought to promote accelerated development of North Sea oil and gas reserves and control of large company dominance through a system of discretionary licenses. Dam would prefer awarding such licenses through a competitive auctioning process that involves royalty bidding. Again, the application of bidding would supposedly reconcile highly imperfect market structures with competitive returns without recourse to discretionary governmental intervention or regulation.

The public ownership option, which was Simons's first choice, has been criticized directly by Sam Peltzman.[20] He argues that the management of a publicly owned utility would behave differently than that of a private utility and that public enterprise would pursue a different set of objectives. The public enterprise, according to Peltzman, would seek to maximize voter support for the firm and continued tenure for management. Furthermore, the government enterprise would design the price structure to buy such votes. As a consequence, rates for public enterprises would tend to ignore the cost of serving particular customer groups because of the political incentive to hold rates down; consumers would be grouped in broader classifications than in the case of private utilities (thereby foregoing profitable opportunities for price discrimination); and public rates would generally be lower than comparable private rates.

Peltzman's arguments and empirical proof (drawn primarily from the electric utility field) are far from convincing.[21] Nevertheless, the allegations do tend, perhaps by inference, to cast doubt on both the idealism of the early public ownership movement and the adequacy of public enterprise as a solution to the monopoly problem.

Although the position of the Chicago School has been overwhelmingly critical of regulation, there was little formal effort to develop a theory of regulation until 1971, when Stigler proposed a theory of economic regulation.[22] He argued that every industry will perceive government regulation either as a potential resource or as a potential threat. By employing regulation to its advantage, an industry can achieve control over entry, substitute goods and services, and prices. However, utilizing government in this fashion involves potential hazards in the form of some loss of control by the dominant firms, procedural delays in effecting changes, and the possible intrusion of outside forces into the decision-making process. Accordingly, an industry is confronted with a trade-off, and it will endeavor to select that degree of regulation which it believes to be optimal for its purposes. What emerges is essentially a perception of regulation in which government involvement is a function of the strategies of various parties, with the result that regulation is apparently incapable of pursuing an independent course to promote the public interest.

Most recently, representatives of the Chicago School have taken a strong stand against the advocates of more direct government controls as a solution to the energy crisis. This confrontation is best exemplified by the differences between the report of the Ford Foundation's Energy Policy Project, *A Time to Choose, America's Energy Future,*[23] and selected rebuttal papers contained in *No Time to Confuse.*[24]

The Ford Foundation report proposes a reduction in the nation's annual rate of growth in energy consumption from 4.5 percent in 1965–1973 to 2 percent for the future. This recommendation is based on the report's assessment of public needs and available energy supplies, and it would be implemented by recourse to government constraints and regulations that transcend the market. Insofar as the electric utilities are concerned, the report calls for the creation of regional rather than state regulatory commissions because electric utilities should operate in regional power pools. Also, the generation and transmission functions should be separated from local distribution to facilitate the formation of regional power systems that would include public representatives as part of their management.

The critical reaction to the Ford Foundation report is clear and unequivocal. Armen A. Alchian claims that the study fails to grasp the nature of market demand and supply and its role in meeting the energy shortage. Alchian further contends that demand and supply will establish a proper balance between lower and higher valued uses in the energy field, and that 'political controls on our use of energy . . . means simply that an elite group is undertaking to limit the options of other people."[25] On the question of monopoly power and restriction of supply, Alchian observes that a "reduction in petroleum availability can result from either a naturally decreasing supply relative to demands or a government cartel, or both."[26] If a cartel of producers attempts to restrict supply to raise price, then Alchian would turn to a variant of the familiar bidding process to grant access to the U. S. market as a means for curbing the economic rents of the cartel.[27] Thomas G. Moore is equally critical of market intervention by government, arguing that regulation cannot assure adequate supplies of energy because lower profit margins are inconsistent with an increase in supply. Market power by private monopolies appears to be largely dismissed, and greater government involvement through the creation of larger regional commissions and other public participation in the management function is viewed by Moore with obvious distaste.[28]

### *A Critique of the Chicago Position*

The foregoing narrative serves to illustrate at least five distinctive features of the Chicago School's position on public utility regulation. These are: (1) a shift in emphasis from concern over private monopoly power to concern over the political power exercised by government; (2) policy proposals which place government in a passive role relative to the enterprise and the consumer; (3) a continuing effort to preserve the efficacy of the market mechanism, even in the face of major structural imperfections; (4) a reliance on a high level of abstraction for purposes of analysis and policy prescriptions; and (5) a belief that the consumer, unassisted by government control or regulation, should be the final arbiter on matters of pollution, abusive practices, and the mix and level of output.

### *The Changing Locus of Power*

The Chicagoans' concern over monopoly power, specifically that associated with private monopoly, has virtually disappeared. In its place has come a preoccupation with the consequences of political power exercised through direct government regulation and intervention.

Whereas monopoly power was a central issue for Simons, and government regulation was either supportive of such power or ineffectual in its control,[29] the thrust of the Chicago argument has now changed so that the adverse effects of monopoly power are either readily reconciled with competitive market criteria or largely ignored. In the case of natural monopoly, private monopoly is the preferred alternative *vis-à-vis* public ownership or public regulation. In the larger oligopolistic context within which the electric, gas, communications, and transport industries function, corporate power is seldom mentioned. For example, the discussion by Edmund W. Kitch of the impact of price controls on natural gas takes the position that such controls discourage the incentive to explore and develop new gas because price is depressed below competitive market levels. There is no in-depth analysis of the alternative possibility that such gas is being withheld by producers in the expectation that prices will rise and that the capacity to withhold is a function of an oligopolistic industry structure.[30]

Similarly, the relationship between market concentration and monopoly power is denigrated,[31] and the problems associated with the imbalance in power between different classes or groups of consumers are either ignored or dismissed. The general distribution of economic power embodied in the existing system of property rights and other institutional arrangements also receives little recognition as a major factor that could distort the outcome of the interaction of market forces.

Instead, concern has come to focus on political power operating through direct government intervention and control. This power is to be feared because it distorts the desires of the market so that high valued uses go unsatisfied, while low valued uses are met and often subsidized. As a consequence, resources are misallocated and inefficiencies are perpetuated. Political power, in the Chicago view, is expressed through regulatory constraints on prices, earnings, and service, through regulatory practices that simulate taxation and promote subsidies, and through public enterprises that buy voter support through pricing strategies.

Furthermore, government regulation will serve to sustain cartel arrangements among private firms since these practices would allegedly be eroded in the absence of government intervention. As a result, the most highly imperfect market structure appears preferable to relying on an administrative agency exercising broad arbitrary authority.

This general change in the position of the Chicago School on the problem of monopoly power can, of course, be viewed as a neoliberal reaction to the growth of big government during the past 40 years. Indeed, it is easy to sympathize with those who argue that a massive, intransigent bureaucracy is more to be feared than a transitory private monopolist operating at the local level. There is, however, a deeper danger inherent in this new position. Government regulation *per se* becomes the culprit, and a new set of biases emerges which tends to preclude consideration of policy options in which government regulation plays an affirmative role. This, in turn, forecloses consideration of the manner in which regulation can be improved and a fuller appreciation of industry structure and the exercise of power in the real world.

### *The Appropriate Role for Government*

Government's role in the public utility industries, according to representatives of the new Chicago School, should be that of a passive participant, following rules which clearly circumscribe its realm of action. This is far from the concept held by reformers and public interest advocates who viewed government intervention as a functional product of public need.

It is not surprising that concern over the ramifications of political power would lead to proposals that place government in a passive, subordinate role. Indeed, the Chicagoans argue that efforts to do otherwise will prove to be abortive or will result in unacceptable welfare-efficiency effects. Stigler's theory of economic regulation portrays commission regulation as vulnerable to manipulation and subversion by firms and special interest groups. Dam's analysis of British experiments in the regulation of North Sea gas sales leads him to conclude that the use of government monopsony and yardsticks is ineffectual. He argues that efforts by the British Gas Council to use its monopsony buying power to depress gas prices and curb economic rents have not been successful. Similarly, he doubts that the government yardstick composed of joint venture on the part of the Gas Council and Amoco has been effective in attracting new gas supplies at yardstick prices.[32] Finally, Peltzman's examination of the behavior of public enterprise leads to the conclusion that government pricing practices reflect political motivation rather than economic criteria.

It is, of course, premature to conclude that government is incapable of playing an affirmative role that promotes the public interest without examining these studies in greater detail.

The theory of economic regulation is essentially a partial explanation of management's position *vis-à-vis* government regulation. As such, it suffers from three major shortcomings if it is to serve as a basis for criticizing the capacity of government to regulate. First, it provides little insight into the entire range of strategies that public utility management can employ to control or manipulate the markets served. Some of these strategies will involve the use of government and others will not. Management may find it far more effective to utilize certain distinctive features of industry structure, such as the division of revenue and common use of facilities, to coordinate efforts, restrict rivalry, and increase stability. An appreciation of the interrelationship between such strategies and the task of regulation is essential. Second, the theory does not take into consideration the fact that the commission system, for better or worse, is the product of a diverse range of promotional interests representing groups with differing economic, political, and social objectives. Any theory which is supposed to serve as a basis for prescribing public policy changes must be capable of reflecting such variables. Clearly, the theory of economic regulation is far from the general theory of regulation that would be required. Third, the theory of economic regulation provides virtually no insight into the alternatives for improving the process of regulation. Regulation is postured essentially as a pawn vulnerable to capture. The only alternative seems to be that of making the burden of regulation so onerous that the prospective gains to management will vanish.

On balance, the economic theory of regulation does not demonstrate that government regulation is inherently impotent or that it cannot be made more effective.

Dam's criticism of British intervention in North Sea gas production also remains an inconclusive basis for criticizing either the effectiveness of regulation or the potential gains from experimenting with other institutional approaches to control. There is insufficient analysis of what the results might have been if the Gas Council had not used its monopsony buying power or its joint venture with Amoco to control prices. A decrease in exploratory drilling for gas in specific fields and the subsequent need to raise yardstick prices, cited by Dam as evidence of apparent failure, may simply indicate that the geological formation where drilling declined was approaching a stage of diminishing returns to scale. Or the decline in drilling and the need to raise prices may reflect the discovery of oil elsewhere in the North Sea and the more lucrative return associated with the sale of petroleum in unregulated markets.[33] Under these circumstances there may be a need to reexamine the return necessary to attract resources for the further exploration of gas, or it may be necessary to investigate the degree of competition in the petroleum industry, but neither action serves as conclusive evidence of a fundamental flaw in the British approach to regulation.

Peltzman's argument that government enterprise will seek to maximize voter support does not provide sufficient evidence to foreclose public ownership as an option. In order to test his hypothesis, Peltzman examines the differences between electric rates for public and privately owned firms, the degree to which rates track costs for public and privately owned firms, and selected measures of differences in corporate behavior, such as the frequency with which both types of firms change rates.

The comparison of public and private electric rates does show that the former are lower than the latter, but these studies are deficient because no attempt was made to control for the many variables, other than customer class and demand volume, which affect price.[34] Such rate comparisons could be affected by differences in fuel costs, customer density in the service areas, the size of different distribution systems, taxes, the availability of hydro power, and many other factors.

To test the extent to which rates track costs, Peltzman regresses selected rates on four variables representing cost, output, customer mix, and average wage. He concludes that cost is less a determinant of price for publicly owned than for privately owned utilities. There is a serious problem with this test, however, because publicly owned firms typically purchase a much larger share of their total power needs than do privately owned firms, and correspondingly they tend to have a much smaller investment in generating plant. Since Peltzman's model uses actual capital employed as a representation of capital costs, the test is biased to show a weaker relationship between costs and prices for public systems than for private systems. The measures of differences in behavior are also beset by shortcomings, and some findings, such as the fact that privately owned electric utilities change their rates more frequently than do publicly owned utilities, explain very little about the relative performance of either group.[35]

One of Peltzman's empirical findings does serve to cast serious doubt on the validity of his basic hypothesis. A review of 31 municipally owned electric utilities that served customers both inside and outside of their political jurisdictions yielded contradictory evidence. If a municipal system were catering to its constituency, one would expect to find that higher rates would be charged to those customers living outside the system's jurisdiction. But in 26 cases, the residential rates were identical to both classes of customers, and in only five cases were rates higher outside the city.[36] In the latter cases, no apparent attempt was made by Peltzman to determine what effect transmission costs might have had on the difference in rates.[37]

Serious reservations can also be expressed about Peltzman's belief that lower rates and broader customer classifications for publicly owned utilities reflect an effort to buy voter support. These features could simply reflect the composition of the service area of the smaller municipal systems, different cost-of-service characteristics, or the effect of lower cost federal power supplied under the public preference clause. Furthermore, any conclusions regarding lower publicly owned utility rates should give sophisticated recognition to payments in lieu of taxes and free services (such as municipal street lighting provided by public systems) as well as the taxes actually paid by private utilities after allowances for investment tax credits and liberalized depreciation. Whether the broader customer classifications of the public systems or the greater use of price discrimination on the part of the private systems represents a superior pattern of behavior in terms of performance remains largely a matter of conjecture.

As a postscript to the Peltzman hypothesis, one must mention Patrick Mann's recent efforts further to quantify the effect of political influence on the rates of publicly owned utilities. Mann found that the more politically active constituencies did not receive price concessions.[38] However, the degree of political dominance by a political party did affect residential electric bills (that is, the higher the degree of dominance, the lower the residential bill). Most important, the political dominance variable emerged as a significant and positive influence on the electric bills of *both the publicly owned and privately owned utilities*.[39] This strongly suggests that private utility management is fully cognizant of political realities and that such forces will tend to influence all utility rates—whether public or private. It also suggests that a regulatory agency, largely independent of political parties, might be capable of making a positive contribution by curbing politically induced distortions.

In summary, the Chicago School's position on the role of government in the public utility industries is far from persuasive. It has not shown government to be impotent as a corrective force. Rather, it has demonstrated a strong desire to reshape government's role in a fashion which is more in accord with its preconception of an idealized laissez-faire society.

### *Efficacy of the Market*

A third feature of the Chicago position is the effort made to preserve the efficacy of the market mechanism no matter how imperfect its structure or operation. Indeed, this desire to maintain the supremacy of the market provides an ideal complement to the desire to relegate government to a passive subordinate role.

The Chicago view appears to classify markets into two categories; those which are essentially competitive, and those which are natural monopolies. In the case of the latter, monopoly is readily reconciled without recourse to extensive government intervention. What is ignored, however, is the possibility that a high level of oligopolistic interdependence between firms might be a dominant characteristic of the public utility industries.

Firms providing electricity, natural gas, and communications face a high degree of interdependence in corporate decision making because of the interrelated nature of technical operations, the shared use of certain types of plant, and the need to apportion revenues stemming from the joint provision of service. Moreover, the movement toward greater reliance on power grids, interconnected communications systems, pooling arrangements, shared reserves, and the joint construction of facilities will reinforce this tendency. The result is an industry structure which is conducive to coordinated corporate planning, continuous interfirm communications that reduce any potential conflicts, and a recognition of the potential hazards associated with tactics that might be viewed as disruptive to the industry. At the same time, each firm is given a high degree of autonomy to adjust to local conditions. To say the least, such structures differ sharply from the simple competitive and natural monopoly models.

The Chicago analysis of public utility regulation also gives little attention to the corporate power inherent in joint ventures, vertical integration, and extensive interlocks which characterize many of the interfirm relationships in this field. Corporate power, as noted earlier, is viewed as a phenomenon dependent on government for its continued existence and something incapable of renewing itself over time on an independent basis.

Perhaps it should come as no surprise, therefore, that there has been little recognition of the fact that these highly interdependent oligopolistic industry structures are conducive to the same type of restrictive practices and forms of cross-subsidization that are commonly attributed to regulation. Recent submissions to the Nuclear Regulatory Commission reveal in great detail how established firms in the electric utility industry have made extensive use of resale restrictions, wheeling contracts, and conditional admittance to power tools to circumscribe the actions of rivals, foreclose entry, and cartelize markets.[40] By the same token, the Bell System has practiced cross-subsidization for more than 70 years through its policies of system-wide averaging, statewide ratemaking, and value-of-service pricing. The results embody the same type of subsidization and taxation that Posner and others associate with regulation. Yet, these actions reflect Bell System policies that in some cases predate the advent of commission regulation and which, until recently, were seldom challenged by regulation.

All of these practices reflect corporate actions in areas that have been of little concern to commissions, so they give some indication of unregulated behavior in a setting of interdependent oligopoly. Yet, the Chicago School representatives propose substantial deregulation or the introduction of competitive bidding in the same setting. Perhaps this indifference to the oligopoly problem also accounts for the dearth of guidelines on what structural reforms must precede the introduction of Chicago-type solutions.

### *Simplifications and Misconceptions*

The Chicago School relies heavily on simplifications of reality in its critique of regulation. One can appreciate the importance of abstractions as part of the positivist's development of analytical constructs. The issue is whether these simplifications bias the validity of the analysis and the relevance of public policy recommendations. There is a basis for argument that the simplifications used to portray commission behavior and the concept of natural monopoly tend to distort the framework of analysis and the options for public policy.

The view of the commission system which emerges from the criticism of the Chicago School is one of a process that induces price and profit rigidity, forecloses entry through licensing and certification, cartelizes industries, and requires the continuance of unwanted services by refusing to authorize expeditious abandonments. As a result, prices do not reflect opportunity costs, inefficiencies are perpetuated, and forces for change are frustrated.

This concept of regulatory behavior is typically contrasted, explicitly or implicitly, with a highly efficient competitive market solution or with a simplistic concept of a natural monopoly whose excess earnings are neutralized by competitive bidding or an excess profits tax. However, the choice between regulation in its worst posture versus a smoothly functioning system of market constraints is inappropriate if the abstractions used to typify regulation and natural monopoly do not reflect reality.

There is no reason to assume that the stereotype of regulation set forth by the Chicagoans accurately reflects either the commission system during its current phase of transition or the form of regulation that might be developed in the future. There has been a surge of vitality at the state commission level as these agencies are compelled to come to grips with "pancaking" applications for price increases, growing consumer resistance, soaring fuel costs, natural gas curtailments, and cutbacks in new plant construction by electric utilities. As a result of these pressures, operational and procedural reforms are being instituted, new ratemaking concepts (such as peak load pricing) are in the process of being introduced or are under serious consideration, and, perhaps most important, the sense of lethargy which has traditionally prevailed among many state commissions has been seriously shaken.

By the same token, there is no reason to assume that federal commissions should remain insensitive to changes in consumer wants, new technology, and the possibility of employing selective competitive pressures to induce superior performance. The best example of such accommodation to change is provided by the decisions of the FCC over the period 1959–1974. The commission has relaxed legal barriers to entry in the specialized carrier and terminal equipment markets to provide a broader basis for consumer choice and to utilize competitive stimuli to spur innovation and change. In addition, the commission has adopted an "open skies" policy for domestic satellites and, conversely, has not extended regulation to the computer industry even though computer technology and common carrier communications are closely interrelated.[41] Although other federal commissions have not displayed the same degree of creativity, there is evidence of change. The FPC has adopted an incremental approach toward the pricing of liquefied natural gas in order to promote a pattern of resource allocation more consistent with the consumer's willingness to pay for the high cost of imported gas. The CAB has also indicated a willingness to experiment with the deregulation of fares and routes on a selected basis.

These changes should not be construed to mean that the commission system has undergone a dramatic transformation or that efforts to promote new pricing concepts, competition, and other regulatory reforms have been an unqualified success. It still remains a highly politicized, imperfect process in need of reform. But these changes do strongly suggest that the simple characterization of commission regulation put forth by the critics does not accurately reflect either its current status or its prospects for improvement.

As mentioned previously, the representatives of the Chicago School tend to classify regulated firms as essentially competitive or as natural monopolies. The difficulty is that the concept of natural monopoly which emerges from such analyses tends to oversimplify the structural problems associated with the public utility industries and bias the nature of government involvement in favor of Chicago-type public policy recommendations.

Stigler and Demsetz accept a definition of natural monopoly in which economies of scale cause unit costs to fall so that competitive interaction among firms will eventually culminate in a single supplier.[42] Posner appears to accept falling fixed unit costs as the cause for natural monopoly, but the outcome is the same, notably, single-firm domination of the market.[43]

This interpretation of natural monopoly tends to correlate the provision of service (that is, supplying electricity, gas, water, or communications) with the establishment and operation of a single firm. Acceptance of this outcome accommodates solutions such as competitive bidding and at the same time eliminates questions of oligopolistic interdependence and other factors which could require extensive government intervention. Under the single-firm outcome, entry and intraindustry rivalry do not become significant problems because falling unit costs make such practices irrational. Posner, for example, relies on this concept of natural monopoly when he argues that entry occurs only because of cross-subsidization due to regulatory constraints and that in the absence of such internal subsidization there would be no new entry.[44]

In practice, this concept of natural monopoly need not be the prevalent case. Particular stages or phases of the supply process may be characterized by economies of scale, while other stages are not. In such situations, there is no need for one firm to provide all services or to perform all functions. It is this interpretation of the place of economies of scale which played an important role in the FCC's efforts to promote competition in the specialized carrier and terminal equipment markets, while retaining a monopoly in the message toll telephone market.

This interpretation complicates the task of regulation much more than the traditional concept of single-firm natural monopoly, for it raises questions about oligopolistic interdependence, the appropriate boundary between regulated and nonregulated activities, the need to take cognizance of system optimization, and the validity of past regulatory tools and practices. On the other hand, such an interpretation reveals new opportunities for improving the capability of the commission system. There is more latitude for commission experimentation in using market structure as a regulatory variable to promote performance. There is also a rationale for resisting increasing concentration in favor of a more pluralistic industry structure in which diversity can be achieved without the prospect of increasing the average unit cost of service or of creating redundant capacity.

The prospect of a regulatory renaissance, on the one hand, and a greater opportunity to improve the effectiveness of regulation by utilizing industry structure, on the other, creates a far different set of public policy options than those associated with the Chicago position. In short, one need not accept the simplification that regulation must be a static, perverse influence on industry performance. Nor is it necessary to accept the simplified belief that decreasing average unit costs must terminate in single-firm monopolies.[45]

### *The Dominant Role of the Consumer*

The Chicago School places great reliance on the role of the consumer in the energy and communications industries. The consumer becomes the ultimate arbiter in the control of pollution, the constraining influence on business practices, and the driving force for establishing priorities and allocating resources. For Alchian and others, the danger lies in distorting the pattern of consumer preferences through regulation and intervention.

The proper procedure for controlling pollution, according to Alchian, is to access the value of the abuse, identify the resource owner, and then be sure that all costs are shifted forward to the user. In this fashion, the consumer will determine the appropriate level of pollution without recourse to government regulation. The consumer would also serve, according to Posner, as an important constraint on the practices of the private monopolist by utilizing common law remedies. Finally, the wishes of the consumer, represented through the familiar demand functions, become a measure of need that relates quantity to price and ultimately becomes a codeterminant of market price and output.

However, it must also be emphasized that a major reason for the establishment of regulation was the protection of the consumer from the potential for extortion inherent in monopoly power. Acceptance of regulation did not imply a denigration of the role of the consumer. Quite the contrary, it was viewed as a means to enhance the freedom of the individual to choose, for as John R. Commons noted, collective action liberates individual action.

The real dilemma becomes one of determining which avenue provides the best means for consumers to express their wishes, whether with respect to the goods and services to be produced, or the control of pollution and other externalities. The selection of a course of action brings one back to a consideration of market power and the effectiveness of government intervention. The lines again become drawn between those sympathetic to an affirmative role for government as a means for curbing abusive practices and monopoly power versus those who sympathize with the Chicago position.

### *An Assessment of Public Policy Prescription*

Just as some members of the Chicago School argue that the validity of a hypothesis is to be judged by its predictive value, so it could be argued that the best test of the Chicago position on regulation lies in the merit of the institutional arrangement that it would substitute for regulation. Expressed somewhat differently, the salient features of the Chicago position, such as the subordination of the role of government, can be debated at length, but the ultimate test is whether the institutional alternatives proposed are demonstrably superior to the institution of regulation.

As noted earlier, the Chicagoans distinguish between regulated industries that are competitive and those that are natural monopolies. The validity of the Chicago proposals can be better evaluated in terms of their ability to handle the monopoly problem. There is nothing particularly distinctive in calling for the deregulation of an industry that supposedly displays the characteristics of workable competition. For purposes of discussion, the traditional public utility industries will be considered as part of the monopoly problem.

Two general solutions are proposed: competitive bidding and the economic deregulation of monopoly augmented by an excess profits tax. The auctioning or bidding proposal would reconcile monopoly with a competitive outcome by utilizing competition for a franchise license or operating authority as a substitute for intraindustry competition. Government need not engage in the direct regulation of prices and output, but instead would confine itself to the selection of a successful bidder—whether defined in terms of agreeing to serve at lowest prices or offering to pay the highest bid price.

### *Deficiencies in the Auctioning Proposal*

The principal conditions for the success of the bidding process, according to Demsetz, are that inputs be readily available to all bidders at competitive prices and that the cost of collusion among bidders be prohibitively high. One need not dwell on the relevance of these conditions for particular utility industries to demonstrate that the bidding process suffers from major deficiencies that severely handicap its application. At least seven important shortcomings should be noted.

First, the establishment of a competitive level of earnings does not provide an adequate constraint on price discrimination. Bidding for a franchise or operating rights may result in the successful bidder receiving only a competitive level of profits, but this would not prevent an undesirable pattern of price discrimination from emerging. In fact, the railroads have had a deficient level of earnings for decades, but they have been continuously involved in issues pertaining to rate structure design and price discrimination.

It might be argued that the pattern of prices could be specified as part of the bidding process, but the consumption of public utility services involves a large number of different users, and the price to each customer would have to be determined at the time that the bidding occurred. The transaction costs associated with such an effort could be phenomenal. In addition, there is the problem of reconciling the outcome with the wishes of consumers (whether present or future) who did not participate in the bidding process.

L. G. Telser has demonstrated that bidding will not reconcile the issue of pricing and efficiency, and that eliminating monopoly profits will not remove the possibility that the actual output of the firm will fall between the monopoly level of output and the socially optimal level of output.[46]

At the applied level, it is quite possible that a competitive rate of return will coexist with a variety of discriminatory prices that promote inefficiency and distort consumer wants. As a consequence, one does not have to become involved in a debate over marginal cost pricing to recognize the need for government to exercise some form of continuous oversight.

Second, recourse to the bidding process can increase uncertainty and its adverse effects, especially when future events cannot be adequately forecasted and discounted. As a result, capital costs may increase significantly. Government may seek to employ various strategies to reduce these uncertainties through the design of different types of franchises, but the prospects for success are not encouraging. If the participants turn to long-term contracts, then the risk of totally unforeseen changes increases, and with it the prospect of a desire on the part of at least one of the parties to renegotiate the contract. This, in turn, will require either a structure of penalties for reopening contracts or administrative machinery to allow arbitration. If the participants turn to short-term contracts, then there is the prospect of excessive transaction costs as properties are sold and resold between successive bidders and of increased risk for the successful bidder if the service is potentially lucrative. In either case, there will be the persistent problem of monitoring the quality of service regardless of the terms of the contract or franchise.

Third, the bargaining agents for the public may lack competence or adequate information. As an example, the British government justifies its rejection of an auctioning or bidding process for the development of North Sea gas, in part, on the grounds that it cannot negotiate or specify a works program for exploration and development without access to the type of information that is in the hands of the large oil companies. On the other hand, the bargaining agents for the public may be too diffused, fragmented, or decentralized to perceive all of the issues involved. The selection of the appropriate public bargaining agent for nationwide message toll telephone service is a case in point.

Fourth, there is the problem of determining whether the bidding process will result in a scale of development that is optimal from the standpoint of society. It is possible that private bidders will be quite willing to serve those portions of the market that are financially attractive, but this scale of development may not correspond with that desired by society. This condition poses a major obstacle for the bidding process. Social objectives or levels of development must be specified, and all parties must have an appreciation of the mix of bids and subsidies needed to achieve these levels. The possibility of error in such a setting is enormous, and the need for regulatory oversight would continue.[47]

Fifth, the bidding process does not establish a clear set of motivations, after the franchise has been awarded, for the successful bidder to undertake long-term experimentation involving new services, new pricing concepts, or new technologies if the results threaten to jeopardize the permissble level of earnings anticipated under the contract. If such experimentation might result in deficits, then the rigidity of the franchise is an obvious deterrent. If the successful bidder anticipates that experimentation might result in excess profits sufficient to bring about a clamor for renegotiating the terms of the franchise, the deterrent effect will still remain. Any attempt to devise a sliding scale schedule for dividing profits and losses faces the disadvantage of forecasting the impact of innovations from that point in time when the bidding takes place. Continuous regulatory surveillance coupled with a flexible system of incentives and penalties appears to be a far more attractive alternative.

Sixth, the bidding process is conducive to the premature abandonment of resources and the failure to develop marginal resources when bidding involves an increase in costs in the form of a royalty payment or the payment of an auction price. This is particularly applicable to the production of natural gas and petroleum. If society wishes to alter the rate of development for these resources, then it must change the cost burden by restructuring royalty payments, allowing credits, or granting remittances. Again, the rigidities of the bidding process would have to be overriden by direct government intervention.

Seventh, the bidding process does not take place in a setting devoid of economic and political power, and the exercise of that power will subvert or utilitize bidding to achieve its goals. Bidding will permit the dominant firm to strengthen its position in the overall market. For example, it could utilize low bids as a form of limit-entry pricing to capture markets, services, functions, or resources to assure its continued dominance. The only condition is that such a firm earn monopoly profits in some markets sufficient to cross-subsidize. Given the imperfections in bidding as a means of control as well as the coverage of a giant multiple-product enterprise supplying utility services, this is not an unrealistic assumption. Perhaps the best example of the use of bidding to assure dominance would involve the radio frequency spectrum. It is not unreasonable to assume that the Bell System would pay a bounty to acquire control of this resource through the bidding process if the result were to foreclose entry by specialized common carriers into the private line market. Thus the Stigler theory of economic regulation could have its counterpart for the bidding process.

The British government has also argued that the bidding-auctioning process fosters corporate power and market dominance. Specifically, the British claim that reliance on bidding favors the largest oil companies in the exploration for oil and gas, and therefore it has been necessary to follow a discretionary licensing system that is designed to encourage a large number of firms to develop reserves. The U. S. experience with auctioning gas and oil leases provides evidence that the bidding process is an ineffectual constraint on corporate power. Oil and gas production on the Louisiana Outer Continental Shelf is dominated by the major oil companies, and the act of bidding or auctioning leases has done little to diminish concentration or to make production more responsive to the substantial price increases for petroleum and gas which have taken place. There is evidence that corporate power is sufficiently strong to permit the majors to withhold production in anticipation of still higher prices.[48]

In summary, the bidding process is not an adequate institutional replacement for direct regulation. The process is vulnerable to crippling deficiencies, and it is not unreasonable to assume that the total cost to society of relying on such a system would be far greater than relying on regulation. Bidding may be appropriate for selected, highly localized services, or it may prove valuable as an adjunct to regulation at particular stages or phases of the process of determining revenue requirements and fixing prices, but it is far from a replacement.

### *Deficiencies in the Deregulation Proposal*

The deregulation of natural monopoly, as recommended by Posner, is premised on the belief that the evils of private monopoly are greatly exaggerated, that abusive practices would be constrained by common law remedies, and that monopoly would be eroded over time by the actions of broader market forces. Although legal barriers to entry would be removed, Posner envisions no entry in practice because of the natural monopoly's cost advantages. Deregulation would also be accompanied by no changes in industry structure.

This type of deregulation suffers from four major deficiencies that make it a poor option for public policy.

First, the effects of unregulated private monopoly on resource allocation, efficiency, innovation, and income distribution should not be minimized despite efforts to deprecate net losses due to allocative and "x" inefficiencies. In the real world, the private monopolist's strategies to maintain a position of dominance through price discrimination, cross-subsidization, entry foreclosure, and political favoritism will set the stage for all of the distortions associated with monopoly power. In addition, such actions are conducive to a redistribution of income from consumers to the monopolist that may become socially and politically intolerable.

Second, the effectiveness of an excess profits tax as a proxy for regulatory control of earnings is dubious, and its superiority is certainly open to challenge. If the objective of the private monopolist is to pay a zero excess profits tax, then expenses will rise to camouflage the monopoly return, thereby producing results similar to those attributed to cost-plus regulation. Furthermore, if the excess profits tax is computed with reference to a normal return on investment, and the monopolist's return is greater than the cost of capital, then the imposition of the tax will produce a nonregulated variant of the familiar Averch-Johnson effect.[49]

If the government proceeds to apply the excess profits tax assiduously, more similarities with the worst features of regulation will appear. It will become necessary to review and approve all legitimate expenses, the application of the tax will require continuous reassessment and refinement, and its administration will ultimately become the basis for lengthy litigation, adversary proceedings, and delays. But even if the excess profits tax is successful in producing a normal or competitive level of earnings for the unregulated firm, the problems associated with price discrimination will still remain to be resolved.

Of course, it is possible to impose a "moderate" excess profits tax. Such a tax would either have a salutary effect or would be conducive to waste and inefficiency, depending upon the tax rate selected. The incidence of whatever tax is imposed will undoubtedly be shifted forward in the long run.

Third, deregulation of monopoly will suffer from many of the problems which plague the bidding process. These include the control of price discrimination, reconciling the imbalance between public and private scales of development, the motivation for superior performance (it is not clear that the retention of greater profits alone will be sufficient), and the impact of corporate and political power. None of these issues can be resolved within the structural context of the public utility industries without some form of government intervention and control.

Fourth, the adequacy of deregulation must be considered in terms of the adequacy of broader constraints on monopoly power which are assumed to be at work. Reliance on common law remedies would appear to be a poor constraint on price discrimination, extortionist pricing, and the restriction of options for consumers. Historically, the inadequacy of this type of solution led to greater government intervention, and the imbalance in power between consumers and suppliers would still appear to be a major obstacle.[50]

With respect to the broader structural, market, and institutional pressures which are supposed to erode monopoly power, it is difficult to discern any changes that might accomplish this task during the coming decade. In fact, deregulation will probably concentrate such power to a greater degree and facilitate control by established firms over those facilities which must be utilized by new entrants or substitute sources of supply.

In the electric power industry, deregulation would facilitate monopoly control of transmission networks and grids. Control of these facilities would foreclose entry by potential rivals into both new and established markets, and it would deny wholesale and industrial buyers access to lower cost sources of power. This could be accomplished by restricting or conditioning admission to the power pools that manage transmission networks or by direct acquisition of transmission facilities through holding companies, joint ventures, and so forth. Deregulation would also encourage intercompany programs for the construction of giant 800–1,200 Mw generating plants which could limit the options for innovation while promoting a community of interest among established firms.[51]

In the natural gas industry, deregulation of production, transmission, and distribution would take place in a setting where prices for gas (a superior fuel) are lower than the prices of alternative fuels. As a result, the demand for gas is inelastic, and deregulation in the short run would do little more than promote price increases without bringing about a corresponding increase in supply. In the long run, deregulation would perpetuate monopoly control over gathering, transmission, and distribution networks by existing firms, thereby performing a restrictive function similar to that noted with respect to electric power networks. Deregulation would also stimulate joint ventures between the major oil companies, pipelines, and distribution companies, with a consequent diminution of arm's-length bargaining. The impact of interindustry competition from other fuels will also be small in the foreseeable future, in part because of the control exercised by energy companies with major investments in gas, oil, coal, shale, and nuclear fuels, and in part because of the higher marginal cost of substitute fuels.

In communications, deregulation would permit AT&T, as the dominant firm with control over all landline transmissions, effectively to control competition. In addition, it is reasonable to assume that intermodal rivalry of the type that might result from IBM's anticipated entry into satellite communications would terminate in tacit oligopolistic coordination and a recognition of mutual interdependence. In both communications and electric power, disruptive innovations would be further minimized by control of transmission facilities, on the one hand, and vertical integration into research and development on the other. Research and development for communications is performed by the Bell Laboratories; that for the electric power industry is financed on a collective basis and centralized in the Electric Power Research Institute.

Deregulation will not be matched by Schumpeterian gales of creative destruction. Rather, it would tend to make the market structure more intransigent and resistant to change. It is possible to argue that enforcement of antitrust laws might cure all of these problems, but it is important to remember that antitrust measures involve long delays and a limited range of solutions in industries with these cost and demand characteristics. A far more productive solution would involve incorporating structural flexibility and the minimization of monopoly power as objectves within the context of regulatory reform. Reliance on deregulation becomes *de facto* reliance on the corporate conscience, and that is a most peculiar culmination of the efforts of the members of the Chicago School.

## *Conclusion*

The position of the Chicago School toward public utility regulation is essentially that of a critic. However, its body of critical analysis is built upon simplifications and biases regarding monopoly power, government intervention, externalities, and the adequacy of markets, all of which are subject to wide differences of opinion and debate. In addition, the institutional alternatives to regulation posed for monopolistic markets are woefully inadequate.

On balance, the contribution of the Chicago School would appear to lie in promoting discussion over the shortcomings of regulation. In this light, its writings should be required reading for regulators and bureaucrats, to shake them out of their sense of indifference and insularity toward reform. The danger is that the output of the Chicagoans may exercise too much influence on a younger generation of academic economists who could make a major contribution toward improving the process of social control.

## *Notes*

1. Representative industry studies include: Ann F. Friedlaender, *The Dilemma of Freight Transport Regulation* (Washington, D.C.: The Brookings Institution, 1969); S. G. Breyer and P. W. MacAvoy, *Energy Regulation by the Federal Power Commission* (Washington, D.C.: The Brookings Institution, 1974); Almarin Phillips, ed., *Promoting Competition in Regulated Markets* (Washington, D.C.: The Brookings Institution, 1975).
2. For example, see: M. H. Bernstein, *Regulating Business by Independent Commission* (Princeton: Princeton University Press, 1955); James M.

Landis, *Report on Regulatory Agencies to the President Elect* (Washington, D. C.: U. S. Government Printing Office, 1960); H. J. Friendly, *The Federal Administrative Agencies: The Need for Better Definition of Standards* (Cambridge, Mass.: Harvard University Press, 1962); and M. H. Bernstein, "Independent Regulatory Agencies: A Perspective on Their Reform," in *A Critique of Administrative Regulation of Public Utilities,* edited by W. J. Samuels and H. M. Trebing (East Lansing: Division of Research, Michigan State University, 1972).

3. For example, see: Mark J. Green, ed., *The Monopoly Makers, Ralph Nader's Study Group Report on Regulation and Competition* (New York: Grossman Publishers, 1973).
4. This article adopts the general definition of the Chicago School used throughout this collection. It is important to note that we are concerned with the work of members of the Chicago School dealing with the adequacy of regulation, and not with their writings in areas such as public utility pricing, and so forth. Of course, adherence to the Chicago position does not imply residence at Chicago, and, of course, not all faculty at Chicago share the same position on regulation. The work of Kenneth Culp Davis in administrative law is a case in point.
5. See: Comments by Ronald H. Coase on Colston E. Warne, "The Muted Voice of the Consumer in Regulatory Agencies," in *Critique*, Samuels and Trebing, eds., pp. 311–16.
6. As background to the Chicago criticism of public utility regulation, it is important to recognize the institutional experimentation that took place as part of the development of the commission system. Historically, all levels of government explored a variety of concepts to regulate those industries affected with the public interest. Throughout much of the nineteenth and early twentieth century there were extensive efforts to refine franchise regulation. These efforts included the use of short-term and long-term franchises, franchises awarded on a competitive, nonexclusive basis, sliding scale franchises, and indeterminate permits which supposedly would facilitate public condemnation of private firms whose performance became unsatisfactory. Legislatures also attempted to fix prices and service standards directly, but with little success. The first independent commission (Interstate Commerce Commission) was established in 1887, and this agency served as a prototype for the modern state commission movement which began in Wisconsin and New York in 1907. Experimentation with other regulatory concepts continued, however, and at one time or another service-at-cost plans, sliding scale profit sharing plans, administrative courts, and public ownership yardsticks were tried with varying degrees of success. Only the independent agency or commission system survived this pragmatic process of searching for a means of imposing social control in the electric, gas, communications, and transport industries. For a more detailed discussion see Martin G. Glaeser, *Public Utilities in American Capitalism* (New York: Macmillan, 1957), particularly pp. 31–154.
7. Henry C. Simons, *Economic Policy for a Free Society* (Chicago: University of Chicago Press, 1948), p. 43. The original paper, "A Positive Program for Laissez Faire, Some Proposals for a Liberal Economic Pol-

icy," appeared as Public Policy Pamphlet No. 15 (Chicago: University of Chicago Press, 1934).
8. Ibid., p. 51.
9. Ibid., p. 322.
10. *Utility Corporations,* Summary Report of the Federal Trade Commission on Economic, Financial and Corporate Phases of Holding and Operating Companies of Electric and Gas Utilities, Document 92, No. 72A. U. S. Senate, 70th Cong., 1st sess. (Washington, D.C.: 1935).
11. R. H. Coase, "The Federal Communications Commission," *Journal of Law and Economics* 2 (October 1959): 1–40.
12. G. J. Stigler and C. Friedland, "What Can Regulators Regulate? The Case of Electricity," *Journal of Law and Economics* 5 (October 1962): 1–16.
13. For example, see R. W. Gerwig, "Natural Gas Production: A Study of the Costs of Regulation," *Journal of Law and Economics* 5 (October 1967): 129–47; A. Dale Tussing, "The Case for Bank Failure," *Journal of Law and Economics* 10 (October 1967): 129–47; and Edmund W. Kitch, "Regulation and the Field Market for Natural Gas," *Journal of Law and Economics* 11 (October 1968): 243–80.
14. Milton Friedman, *Capitalism and Freedom* (Chicago: University of Chicago Press, 1962), p. 28.
15. Ibid.
16. R. A. Posner, "Natural Monopoly and Its Regulation," *Stanford Law Review* 21 (February 1969): 548–643.
17. R. A. Posner, *Economic Analysis of Law* (Boston: Little, Brown and Co., 1972), p. 151.
18. Harold Demsetz, "Why Regulate Utilities?" *Journal of Law and Economics* 11 (April 1968): 55–66.
19. Kenneth W. Dam, "The Evolution of North Sea Licensing Policy in Britain and Norway," *Journal of Law and Economics* 17 (October 1974): 213–63.
20. See Sam Peltzman, "Pricing in Public and Private Enterprise: Electric Utilities in the United States," *Journal of Law and Economics* 14 (April 1971): 109–47.
21. A critique of Peltzman's position is presented on pp. 107–108.
22. See G. J. Stigler, "The Theory of Economic Regulation," *Bell Journal of Economics and Management Science* 2 (Spring 1971): 3–21. See also G. J. Stigler, "Free Riders and Collective Action: An Appendix to Theories of Economic Regulation," *Bell Journal of Economics and Management Science* 5 (Autumn 1974): 359–65.
23. *A Time to Choose, America's Energy Future,* Energy Policy Project of the Ford Foundation (Cambridge, Mass.: Ballinger Publishing Co., 1974).
24. *No Time to Confuse* (San Francisco: Institute for Contemporary Studies, 1975).
25. Ibid., p. 15.
26. Ibid., p. 10.
27. Ibid., pp. 10–11.
28. Ibid., p. 86.

29. The similarity between Simons (as a positive economist) and Horace M. Gray (as an institutional economist) on the question of monopoly power and the inadequacy of regulation, together with the difference in fashion in which they approach the subject, makes an interesting study in comparative methodology. See Simons, *Economic Policy*, and H. M. Gray, "The Passing of the Public Utility Concept," *Journal of Land and Public Utility Economics* 16 (February 1940): 8–20.
30. See Kitch, "Regulation," and for a contrasting analysis of oligopolistic industry structure and the ability to restrict supply, see Statement of David S. Schwartz, *Market Performance and Competition in the Petroleum Industry*, Hearings before the Committee on Interior and Insular Affairs, U. S. Senate, pursuant to S. Resolution 45, The National Fuels and Energy Study, 93 Cong., 1st sess., 12–13 December 1973, pp. 1116–78.
31. See Harold Demsetz, *The Market Concentration Doctrine* (Washington, D. C.: American Enterprise Institute, 1973).
32. See Dam, "Evolution of North Sea Licensing," particularly pp. 223–27.
33. Dam notes these points in passing but does not accept them. Ibid., also pp. 221–22.
34. Peltzman, "Pricing," particularly pp. 122–28.
35. The author benefitted from conversations with William B. O'Neil regarding the shortcomings of Peltzman's econometric analysis.
36. Peltzman, "Pricing," p. 127.
37. Space does not permit a more detailed assessment of the shortcomings inherent in Peltzman's empirical analysis. However, it is appropriate to note that a much more meaningful evaluation of differences in behavior between public and privately owned enterprises could have been developed by analyzing a series of case studies covering comparable systems. For example, comparisons of behavior could be made between the whole range of municipally owned electric systems (from the largest firms serving Los Angeles, Seattle, and so forth, to the smallest municipal distribution plants) and comparable private utilities. An equally valuable case study would involve a comparison of the behavior of the U. S. Postal Service and AT&T when confronted by a mix of markets that range from monopolistic to competitive. The reaction of the U. S. Postal Service to competition from United Parcel Service is remarkably similar to that of AT&T when faced with competition from Datran and MCI. Such a case study would demonstrate the need for regulation to curb price discrimination and at the same time would shed light on the shortcomings of turning to public ownership as a solution for complex problems of industry structure. Peltzman does note postal pricing practices briefly in footnote 46, but he overlooks the parallel nature of the pricing response on the part of both public and privately owned firms.
38. P. C. Mann, "User Power and Electricity Rates," *Journal of Law and Economics* 17 (October 1974): 440.
39. Ibid., pp. 441–42.
40. See Frank W. Frisk, "AEC Begins First Antitrust Hearing in Licensing Case," *Public Power* (November-December 1973): 10–13.
41. For a detailed assessment of FCC entry policy, see H. M. Trebing and W. H. Melody, "Entry Conditions in Telecommunications," in *Regula-*

*tion and Entry*, edited by W. G. Shepherd and Michael W. Klass, forthcoming.

42. Demsetz, *Market Concentration*, and G. J. Stigler, *The Organization of Industry* (Homewood, Ill.: Richard D. Irwin, 1968), pp. 18-19.
43. Posner, *Economic Analysis of Law*, p. 140.
44. Ibid., p. 152; also pp. 146–49.
45. It is important to distinguish between a single-firm monopoly providing the entire service and the case where economies of scale exist at a stage or phase of the production process. The latter will require a single technical system to provide the function (for example, power transmission), but this does not require that a single-firm monopoly dominate the system. It may be jointly owned and managed on a collective basis. The Trans Canada Telecommunications System is an example of this type of arrangement.
46. Telser states that direct regulation of an industry subject to economies of scale is necessary to promote efficiency. He develops the interesting argument that monopolies have an incentive to produce the output at the lowest total cost only if revenue does not depend on the composition of the inputs. To meet this problem, a condition of the bid would require that all bidders indicate the total cost for each level of output. The successful bidder would produce the output most efficiently, but the selection process becomes extremely complex if different bidders have lowest cost schedules for different ranges of output. L. G. Telser, "On the Regulation of Industry: A Note," *Journal of Political Economy* 77 (November/December 1969): 937–52. Also see Harold Demsetz, "On the Regulation of Industry: A Rcply," *Journal of Political Economy* 79 (March/April 1971): 356–63; and L. G. Telser, "On the Regulation of Industry: Rejoinder," *Journal of Political Economy* 79 (March/April 1971): 364–65.
47. Uncertainty in determining the future level of social development would make it difficult to fix subsidies or determine the cost of service at the time of bidding. As a practical matter, the public agent would probably have to choose among a series of least-cost bids for serving a range of output. This selection process is vulnerable to the criticisms noted by Telser (see note 45).
48. See Statement of Dr. Walter S. Measday, Chief Economist, Senate Antitrust and Monopoly Subcommittee, before the Antitrust and Monopoly Subcommittee, 23 September 1975. Measday notes that the Outer Continental Shelf off Louisiana accounts for 12 percent of domestic crude oil production (plus associated natural gas). The region is removed from state conservation and prorationing controls. In a study of production from leases accounting for 94 percent of production on these federal lands, Measday reported that the three majors plus one joint venture accounted for 56 percent of oil production in 1974. Furthermore, Measday states: "Our study of production and development of the OCS Louisiana leases, suggests that these leases could be producing nearly twice as much as they now are. . . . Despite an increase in crude prices of more than 50 percent from early 1970 to the end of 1973 and complete decontrol of new oil prices since then, there has been little or no production response" (p. 10 of mimeographed copy).

49. Harvey Averch and L. L. Johnson, "Behavior of the Firm under Regulatory Constraint," *American Economic Review* 52 (December 1962): 1053–69, and the tenth anniversary reassessment by Johnson in "Behavior of the Firm under Regulatory Constraint: A Reassessment," *American Economic Review, Proceedings* 63 (May 1973): 90–97.
50. There have been cases where environmentalists were successful in delaying or imposing constraints on new construction plans of public utilities, but this is a far cry from intervening in a system-wide rate case involving rates based on second and third degree price discrimination.
51. There is little doubt that deregulation would be conducive to tighter pooling arrangements and joint ventures to construct power generating facilities. Examples of the former were prevalent until government intervention brought about more liberal admissions policies. Power generation would become more concentrated, in part because of the removal of rate base regulation, and in part because of the corporate advantages of such a step. Evidence of the initial move toward consolidated power generation is contained in the 1975 proposal of seven private utilities to form Empire State Power Resources, Inc., to supply a major share of future base load growth for the state of New York. Both the potential efficiencies as well as the opportunity for tacit oligopolistic coordination in such a move must be considered. See H. M. Trebing, "Realism and Relevance in Public Utility Regulation," *Journal of Economic Issues* 8 (June 1974): particularly 223–26.

# 15

# The History of Thought in the Development of the Chicago Paradigm

*John P. Henderson*

My colleagues, who entrepreneured this symposium after having decided there is a *Weltanschauung* which emanates from a particular institution in Chicago, also have correctly concluded that this view includes a place for the history of economic thought. The purpose of this essay, accordingly, is to discuss the role which the history of economic theory has had in the formulation of the "Chicago approach" to economics, a paradigm which stresses the primacy of consumer choice and individual freedom, limited only by the constraint "of the means available to the subject [consumer] and the terms of allocation presented by the facts of his given situation."[1]

### *The Nature of Economics*

At the outset, it should be stressed that the usefulness of the history of thought to the Chicago School has not really been any different than the role that the views of previous economists have played in the formulation of other paradigms, especially ones which seek authority for what Frank H. Knight called "correct economic theorizing."[2] Although Knight probably talked and wrote more about truth in economics than

---

*The author is Professor of Economics, Michigan State University, East Lansing.*
*The consultation of his colleagues Norman P. Obst and Warren J. Samuels on several issues is greatly appreciated. The usual differentiation of responsibility is obviously applicable.*

most members of the profession, always being careful to surround the word with inverted commas, his formalization of the "correct" approach was used as a benchmark against which he measured the relevancy of the contributions of other theorists, contemporary as well as deceased. As A. W. Coats has observed, "in any scholarly and scientific activity the ultimate intellectual authority is truth, and the accepted view of the nature and criteria of valid knowledge can therefore never be a matter of indifference. This, of course, largely explains why methodological disagreements have been so common in economics, for it is a discipline in which the criteria of valid knowledge have been difficult to define and to apply, and in which ideological and other non-logical influences have been highly influential."[3]

The resort to authority always has been one means by which economists have attempted to verify their own views, either by showing some connecting link with previous writers believed to be in the same camp, or by writers pointing up their own break with tradition, so as to differentiate their product. The resort to authority, of course, is not the only means of attempting to verify the correctness of a particular paradigm, and the accelerated use of econometric models has all but relegated the history of thought to the boneyard of economists, especially those born too young to have learned how to program a computer. But in the case of Knight, empiricism actually was incapable of verifying any phenomenon of economic behavior. In one of the more brilliant statements of his position, Knight argued: "It is not conceivably possible to verify any proposition about economic behavior by any empirical procedure, if the key words of this statement are defined as they must be defined to be used with relevance and precision. To form the idea of economy or economizing, one must first know that the end of an action is in general more or less different from its empirical result. Economy involves an intention or intended result, which is not amenable to observation in any admissible use of that term."[4]

The contrast drawn was between an analytical and an empirical proposition; between thinking and doing. According to this view, the most important "epistemological datum for economic theory" is of two parts. On the one hand, Knight alleged, we all know an individual can only achieve maximum efficiency through the ideal allocation of allocable resources against alternative ends; but second, and more important, we "also know that no individual achieves this maximum (or the chances are infinity to one against it)."[5] The divergence between the two propositions, the thinking and doing, arises because of the existence of "ignorance, error and 'prejudice' in innumerable forms."[6]

Unlike the natural scientist, who can rely upon the ultimate decency of the universe for its consistency and repetitiveness, thus making prediction a viable possibility in this area of science, the economist must deal with human action that is constantly groping with uncertainty. The empiricism which always has been the hallmark of the sciences that deal with the forces of nature cannot be employed in economics to verify principles, because the latter are concerned with human conduct, behavior which is ideal only when free from constraint or force.

Man in the process of economizing only knows in some vague way which ends he wants to pursue, and in reality the ends become identified in the very act of the process of their actual realization and achievement. *Ex ante* it is impossible to predict the interests and ends which intelligent maximizing individuals might arrive at in a world of uncertainty. It is for this reason, of course, that economic planning represents the denial of the essence of economics, since the economizing individual in a world of uncertainty is what economics is all about. The individual must never be denied his maximum freedom to grope for ends which only can be achieved *ex post.*

A corollary to the distinction drawn between thinking and doing is that it is impossible to infer from the results of human behavior what the motives or purposes were *ex ante,* or even what the motives were as they emerged in the process of achievement. There is the divergence between the ideal, which economic principles describe, and the actual reality of individual accomplishment. The consumer may never be able to identify just what it is he is trying to maximize, either in terms of utility or satisfaction, but that does not matter; it is the act of striving itself which gives meaning to the economic content of human action, and not the identification of the results accomplished. It is the pursuit and the act of economizing that is important, subject always, of course, to the limited technical facilities available at the moment. Economics, therefore, is the study of psychology (human conduct) and engineering principles.

### *Measuring Utility*

The Knight position, as outlined above, has any number of implications for what might he considered correct theorizing and the identification of error. It may be used to evaluate past economists, as well as to identify which contemporary theorizing is on the right course and which is nonsense. As an example, in his own time Knight was highly critical of the new developments in the theory of demand, for he believed that J. R. Hicks was dealing with a problem which not only was irrelevant but also would lead to confusion as to the very essence of economic theory.[7] At the center of the difference between Knight and Hicks was the significance of the divergence between analytical and empirical propositions, at least that is the way Knight stated the issue. So far as Hicks is concerned, my readings have never turned up anything that deals with the Knight criticisms.

The issue of the measurement of utility is itself a part of the history of economic thought. In what J. M. Keynes referred to as one of "the crevices of Marshall's *Principles*," there is this statement:

> It cannot be too much insisted that to measure directly, or *per se*, either desires or the satisfaction which results from their fulfilment is impossible, if not inconceivable. If we could, we should have two accounts to make up, one of desires, and the other of realized satisfactions. And the two might differ considerably. . . . Some of those desires with which economics is chiefly concerned, and especially those connected with emulation are impulse; many result from the force of habit; some are morbid and lead only to hurt; and many are based on expectations that are never fulfilled [italics in original].[8]

Alfred Marshall was not the only economist associated with the utility theory of value to recognize that human desires could not be measured, but he was the only one who was explicit about stating the case, even if he did bury it in a footnote. But for economists imbued with the need for their discipline to be scientific, the fact that one of the most fundamental propositions of the science was not measurable made them uneasy, to say the least. Going back at least to Galileo, the essence of natural science has been measurement, and Lord Kelvin, the discoverer of the second law of thermodynamics, claimed: "Where you cannot measure your knowledge is meagre and unsatisfactory." So far as Knight was concerned, economists and other social scientists interpreted the Kelvin doctrine to mean that

> "if you cannot measure, measure anyhow!" That is, one either performs some other operation and calls it measurement or measures something else instead of what is ostensibly under discussion, and usually not a social phenomena. To call averaging estimates, or guesses, measurement seems to be merely embezzling a word for its prestige value. And it might be pointed out also that in the field of human interests and relationships much of our most important knowledge is inherently nonquantitative, and could not conceivably be put in quantitative form without being destroyed. Perhaps we do not "know" that our friends really are our friends; in any case an attempt to measure

> their friendship would hardly make the knowledge either more certain or more "satisfactory"![9]

In the case of utility, the Hicks solution for the need to measure was to switch from Marshall's cardinal meaning to Pareto's ordinal principle, and to make use of the diminishing marginal rate of substitution in place of the diminishing marginal utility of the founders of the utility school. Ordinal are superior to cardinal units since they eliminate the need to measure whatever is being consumed, and on the principle of Occam's razor the indifference analysis is preferred. For Knight, however, this amounted to throwing out the baby with the bath water, or it was nonsense. There is no answer to the problem of the quantitative nature of consumer ends. Only intuitively do we *know* that the consumer economizes in the allocation of his income among available alternatives, just as the entrepreneur economizes in the use of numerous inputs. In addition, processes *imply* "quantitative comparisons and declining functional relations between ends and means, hence some 'common denominator.' "[10] It is not only the totality of satisfaction that the consumer considers, but also successive increments of the same good. Therefore:

> The law of diminishing utility, correctly stated and qualified, is valid and useful, *indispensable to a psychologically realistic interpretation of consumers choices.*
>
> The only defensible alternative is altogether to abandon psychology, motivation and valuation, and set up functions and curves in purely objective, "behavioristic" (statistical) terms. This is to take observed behavior as an ultimate fact and give up all pretense of explaining it, except as discovery of uniformities or "laws" passes for explanation. It is no use suggesting that we rank value sensations but do not "quantify" them in the "cardinal" sense. . . . The ranking hypothesis is a compromise without the advantages of either extreme. And it is doubtful whether we ever in fact distinguish (rank) differences in degree without also distinguishing, and estimating, degrees of difference. *Elimination of utility, or "value," in favor of objective, measureable magnitudes, is the recourse of those who worship Science, and the Occam's razor principle.* Unfortunately, there is no way to secure the quantitative data for an indifference curve. . . . It is an inference from hypothetical experimentation, just as the straight-out utility curve is purely introspective.
>
> If we ignore error and values, and stick to objective physical "facts" we are no longer talking about "economics" [italics added].[11]

The formalization of demand theory according to Hicks, in Knight's view, was a step backward, since it called for a new psychology which tended to weaken the importance to economics of analytical propositions regarding individual behavior, in preference to those of the empirical importance of revealed preference. Knight opposed the Hicks interpretation not only because it involved the use of indifference curves, for they were merely the technique of exposition, but also because the Hicks demand curve was generated by keeping the price of all other goods and money income constant, while changing the price of the good in question and thereby changing real income.[12] Such a procedure resulted in a separation of consumption from production, whereas the correct way of viewing their relation was to recognize that production never involves any motivation other than that which is imputed to it by the consumer.

Knight was antipositivist and antiempirical because of the existence of uncertainty in its numerous forms, a position entirely consistent with his philosophical position *vis-à-vis* the nature of economic activity in a laissez-faire system of competition, where individuals engage in the process of maximizing ends; a position initially set forth in *Risk, Uncertainty and Profit*.

The "correct" propositions regarding economic behavior are strictly analytical in character, and it is to the authority of such propositions that economic analysis must ultimately return. The formulation of the Chicago paradigm rests upon unverifiable propositions, except in the sense that together they constitute an internally consistent system of analysis. Not only is the empirical verification of any particular analytical proposition impossible, but also an analytical proposition itself is suspect if derived from empiricism. A number of the "second generation" of Chicago economists have not strayed too far afield from the initial position; analytical propositions are superior to those grounded in empiricism, and there is an overall rejection of a positivist approach to economics. An exception, of course, with respect to empiricism is Milton Friedman, an early Knight protegé. Friedman's positivist approach, however, must be differentiated from the positivist tendencies which Knight attacked so vehemently.

What Knight opposed was the attempt to verify empirically basic propositions such as utility, maximization, or other "economic man concepts." These he correctly said could not be verified by empiricism, and the philosophy of science has moved away from such a position as time passes. Nor does Friedman attempt to verify "basic propositions" of economic analysis, and therefore he is faithful to Knight. The Friedman Chicago empiricism is directed at establishing validity for an entire economic model, what some refer to as Friedman's "little black box." Which analytical propositions are contained within the little black box it is sometimes difficult to tell, as is the manner in which the individual propositions fit together. In this sense, Friedman's little black box is akin to the Ark of the Covenant of Solomon's Temple, which sometimes was thought to contain the Ten Commandments and other times the "divine presence"; in both instances, only the faithful know. What Friedman and his followers do is search for high correlation coefficients for the little black box, and no one really cares about measuring separate or identifiable analytical propositions. In the modern view of the philosophy of science, verification is sought for the "system" and not for any basic postulates. Probably Knight would have found no reason to attempt to verify the analytical system, since if the analytical propositions are themselves "intuitively" correct, then so is the system. Knight's insistence, for example, that the demand curve for investment funds was infinitely elastic, which stood in opposition to empirical findings to the contrary, was the foundation of his system.

While the Friedman positivism is thus different in nature from the early positivist approach in economics, there is still common ground about the necessity for basic analytical postulates and theorems in economic theory. No one disputes, for example, that there are "liquidity" reasons for holding cash, but whether these reasons include a precautionary motive *is* in dispute. But this is a dispute which both Knight and Friedman would argue *cannot* be directly verified through empiricism, since precaution itself is an economic goal, and *ex ante* the individual does not know what the goal means until it has been achieved *ex post*. At night all cats are grey, and to differentiate empirically and isolate the precautionary motive is impossible. It was the analytical character of economic theorems that was important to the development of the Chicago paradigm, and a property which appears to continue to be paramount.

### *The Theory of Value*

The conundrum of the labor theory of value had, of course, been the source of some concern to Knight, since the one classical economist who came the closest to formulating a correct system of individual freedom was David Ricardo. But Ricardo's formulation of value in negative terms (cost), as opposed to positive terms (utility), "clearly shows through in many places as a source of confusion,"[13] and it was the source of Ricardo's "seven aberrations." But this did not bother Knight, since "the history of economic thought is replete with cases in which it seems that the best minds obstinately preferred to talk nonsense when the truth lay open before their eyes, in the world and even on the printed page."[14] After all, Adam Smith had avoided the pitfalls of a labor theory of value,[15] and why did Ricardo not learn more from his master?

In England, of course, W. S. Jevons had found Ricardo to be so much in error on the question of value, he urged his writings be corrected. Meanwhile, Marshall in a futile gesture to retain authority for his own cost of production analysis argued that Ricardo had been misunderstood. Ricardo was "a poor master of language," and to understand him one should ascertain what he should have said and "interpret him as he would have wished to be interpreted." If this approach was employed when reading Ricardo, then he really had a utility theory, and not a labor theory of value.[16] The history of the controversy as to whether Ricardo had a labor theory of value, and whether Marshall or Marx was his residuary legatee, is another article, but Piero Sraffa has said almost all there is to say on the subject,[17] at least in my opinion. But Sraffa's interpretation of Ricardo's theory of value leads to a Cambridge (England) paradigm,[18] and not the one being considered in this article.

So far as the Chicago paradigm is concerned, George Stigler has resolved the issue of Ricardo's theory of value in Knightian terms.

> I can find no basis for the belief that Ricardo had an *analytical* labor theory of value, for quantities of labor are *not* the only determinants of relative values. Such a theory would have to reduce all obstacles to production to expenditures of labor or assert the irrelevance or nonexistence of nonlabor obstacles, and Ricardo does not embrace either view. On the other hand, there is no doubt that he held what may be called an *empirical* labor theory of value, that is, a theory that the relative quantities of labor required in production are the dominant determinants of relative values. Such an empirical proposition cannot be interpreted as an analytical theory, any more than the now popular view that the price level is governed by the wage level and the productivity of labor can possibly be defended as an analytical proposition [italics in original].[19]

Moreover, Stigler continues,

> among economists who were not methodologically self conscious, who did not systematically consider the necessary and sufficient conditions for an equilibrium, the distinction would

> seldom be remarked. Ricardo's emphasis upon the quantitative importance of labor tended to be read as an analytical proposition that labour [sic] quantities were the sole regulators of value.
>
> The failure to distinguish between analytical and empirical propositions has been a source of much misunderstanding in economics. An analytical statement concerns functional relationships; an empirical statement takes account of the quantitative significance of the relationships.[20]

An analytical proposition is superior to an empirical theorem because of the universality of the former, or the limitedness of the latter. In Section IV of his chapter on value, Ricardo analyzes the effect which capital has upon relative values when the degree of capitalization is not uniform throughout the system, or when the ratio of labor to capital varies from industry to industry. Under these circumstances the relative quantities of labor time are no longer the single determinant of relative values, as degrees of capitalization obviously are of significance. So far as Ricardo himself was concerned, this did not matter a great deal since the variation caused by differing degrees of capitalization "could not exceed 6 or 7 per cent [sic]."[21] Ricardo was not looking for universals; what he wanted to do was isolate the principal determinant of relative value, and he was not disturbed at all by the exceptional cases where the theory in effect collapses. But to the Chicago paradigm an empirical proposition cannot have analytical or probative value. Because of the limitedness of the labor theory of value to cases where the degree of capitalization is uniform, which while they may occur are not specified by the ideal properties of pure theory, it must be rejected in favor of the universal and analytical theorem of utility maximization. As the discussion of Knight's thought has revealed, the maximization principle (whether consumer or entrepreneur) is not verifiable because of the presence of uncertainty and the psychology of human behavior when the latter is unfettered by the external control and the constraint of the state.

To indicate that at times the Chicago paradigm may appear to be the product of solipsistic interpretation of economic theory, some comments on the utility principle of value may prove helpful. As the underlying basis for the demand curve, the utility theory of value initially was postulated for the determination of prices when production already had been completed, and "bygones were bygones." In Carl Menger's world, two farmers meet in the forest to exchange their surpluses of grain and wine, to their mutual satisfaction, each employing the incremental principle of maximization.[22] Without tracing the formulation of each of the "founders" of the utility theory, for as Stigler claims they were all hedonists,[23] it is a fact that none of them payed much attention to how the baskets of surplus goods which each carried to market came into existence in the first place. It was, of course, their lack of concern with costs which led Marshall to emphasize that they had supplied but one of the necessary blades of the scissors. Hence, one way of expressing the deficiency in the consideration of costs, by the founders of the utility theory of value, is to argue that they developed a principle to explain the exchange value of Ricardo's "rare statues and pictures, scarce books and coins."[24] If the quantity is given, then utility (demand) determines relative exchange values. What was lacking, according to Knight and Stigler among others, was a theory of distribution. But what the Chicago paradigm refers to as a theory of distribution can just as easily be called a theory of production, except perhaps Knight had some epistemological misgivings about just what is production, so the term may not be interchangeable.

Nevertheless, the deficiency of the originators of the utility school, so far as production, was taken care of by a contingent of troops in the 1890s, of which the *pièce de résistance* was delivered by Philip H. Wicksteed and his *Co-ordination of the Laws of Distribution,* utilizing Euler's theorem.[25] The production function which emerged, and which became one of the analytical propositions of the Chicago paradigm, was homogeneous and linear, appropriate to the *usual assumptions* of economic theory, under perfect competition.[26]

The Wicksteedian production function, and that of neoclassical economics as well, is one which understandably gives emphasis to the law of diminishing returns. Production possibilities for the firm are limited to the second region of its total output curve, that region wherein both the marginal and average products of the variable input both are declining.[27] In region one, in contrast, the average product of the variable factor is rising, and the marginal product of the fixed is negative, while in region three the variable factor has a negative marginal product. Regions one and three are a denial of the maximization principle and therefore have no importance to economic theory under competitive conditions, the latter being essential to the Chicago paradigm.

Region two of the well-behaved production function emerges into the rising marginal cost curve, when the factors acquire prices in their respective resource markets. Hence, the relevant marginal cost curve of the individual entrepreneur lies above the minimum portion of the average variable cost curve, and entrepreneurial output decisions are restricted to the diminishing returns region of the production function. Since the supply schedule to the industry is the arithmetic summation of the rising marginal cost curves of the firms participating in the industry, the utility (demand) curve determines, or imputes, value to the cooperating resources of the production function. No resource, accordingly, has any value other than that imputed to it by the consumer, nor is there a hierarchy of resources, with some being more important than others, that is, labor. The consumer plays no favorites, since at the margin all resources are equally necessary to the fulfillment of his utility. "The distinction between natural agents and artificial, or capital goods, certainly has no general validity . . . and even the distinction between human and non-human rests on non-economic, institutional or sentimental grounds, and economic difference is a matter of degree."[28]

In the neoclassical formulation, the utility theory of value is rescued from its original limited role of determining relative values for Ricardo's rare goods case because of the universality of the law of diminishing returns. For this law has the effect of making *all* goods rare and subject to the general analytical proposition of scarcity. In Ricardo's *Principle*s the law of diminishing returns had a crucial and significant role because of the prevalence of this particular type of production function in the agricultural sector. In agriculture, particularly as found in the England of Ricardo's day, production was limited by land of varying qualities and an overall limit of all land resources. Hence, as population, income, and the demand for goods increased, the relative cost of producing increasing quantities of food rose, leading to the famous Ricardo dictum that "as wages rise profits fall," since food was the primary wage good.

In Ricardo's system, however, the applicability of the law of diminishing returns was limited to agriculture, for in all other instances costs were constant over the range of small variations in output. The value problem for Ricardo was made up of three classes of goods. First, in the cases of the Venus di Milo and the Mona Lisa, cost was of no consequence, for bygones were bygones. In the second instance was agriculture, the special case, where the law of diminishing returns was operative, and costs rose as demand increased. The third category contained all other industries, and here costs were constant because there were no apparent causes which would make them rise or fall, since the relative fertility of land was not a factor in their production. As Piero Sraffa wrote almost fifty years ago, "in normal cases the cost of production of commodities produced competitively . . . must be regarded as constant in respect of small variations in the quantity produced. And so, as a simple way of approaching the problem of competitive value, the old and now obsolete theory which makes it dependent on the cost of production alone appears to hold its ground as the best available."[29]

In order for the utility theory of value to become operational as an analytical proposition, it was necessary for the law of diminishing returns to become generalized from the particular case of land (Ricardo) to every case in which there existed some factor input with a limited quantity. Thus the special case became the general case, and, as Knight claimed, "those who advocate dropping the principle of diminishing utility from economic analysis should logically take the same position with respect to diminishing returns."[30] In the 1890s, theorists like Wicksteed derived a law of supply in the market which could be coordinated with the law of demand (utility) formulated in the 1870s; on the symmetry of these two analytical propositions the modern theory of value was promulgated, with the Chicago paradigm a case in point.

Obviously, in a world of constant costs, demand plays no role in determining price, and it makes no difference whether the respective demand schedules have been derived from an analytical proposition *vis-à-vis* diminishing marginal utility, or from the more modern semiempirical proposition of "revealed preference." Relative prices (values) in a constant cost world are determined solely by relative costs of production, and in the usual Euclidean plane this means that demand is quantity determining along the horizontal axis, but irrelevant to the price axis. In this case, therefore, the utility theory collapses in a fashion similar to the collapse of the labor theory of value when the degree of capitalization is not uniform between industries.

Methodologically it is just as possible to build an economic model based upon an analytical proposition of constant returns as in the case of diminishing returns. But in the Chicago paradigm, interestingly enough, constant returns are a question of empiricism and therefore "not a necessary characteristic of the production function."[31] The reason for the denial of constant returns is that "the learning ability of man . . . is subject to diminishing returns." Stigler says, moreover:

> Quite aside from the difficult problem of expansion itself, large groups are much harder to coordinate than smaller units. For management, and control in general, inherently face a problem: the final authority to make decisions cannot be subdivided or delegated. Large units are, in fact, confronted by a dilemma. At one extreme all authority may be delegated. Then there will be no unity of policy or uniformity of performance. At the other extreme, all decisions may be made by a final center. This system involves bureaucracy in its worst form: "red tape," hopeless delay, decisions based on diluted memoranda. Between these two extremes the large firm attempts to steer a middle course, but it never achieves that compactness, flexibility, and singleness

> of purpose which are possessed by every well-managed medium-sized firm. The growing difficulty of coordination and decision-making eventually stops the growth of every firm.[32]

Empirically speaking, on the other hand, it would be necessary to prove that red tape is of sufficient importance, in a cost and efficiency manner of speaking, to offset the divisibilities of size.

In 1960, when Sraffa published his critique of the marginal theory of value and distribution,[33] by presenting a system of analysis along Ricardian lines, and the avoidance of the traditional demand and supply analysis, the reaction in most quarters was either bewilderment or disdain. In his review, Harry G. Johnson wrote: "Of all the exasperating books that have come out of Cambridge since its emergence as a centre of economic theory, this one might easily be considered the most. . . . And though he differentiates his product by the claim that it is intended as the basis for a critique of neo-classical marginalist theory, he provides only the most allusive hints as to what his criticisms are, while *the complete absence of demand from his system makes it extremely difficult both to formulate these criticisms and to evaluate their significance* [italics added]."[34]

Sraffa's denial of any influence for demand in the determination of prices, and his formulation of distribution theory in terms of Ricardo and Marx, in part contributed to the so-called capital controversy between Cambridge, England, and Cambridge, Massachusetts.[35] In the course of this long debate, representatives from the Chicago paradigm strangely have been silent, even though a recent small volume by Mark Blaug would seem to present an evaluation sympathetic to their viewpoint.[36] According to Blaug's analysis, the neoclassical value and distribution theories emerge unscathed from the criticisms of Joan Robinson, Nicholas Kaldor, Sraffa, and their respective followers.

> Cambridge [England] theories of distribution . . . are all theory without measurement! Its highest aims are to corroborate "stylised facts" rather than to propose falsifiable predictions. . . . Its methods of analysis are deliberately framed to deny the *simultaneous determination of economic variables*: the share of profits, the rate of profits, relative prices, absolute prices and effective demand are all determined in separate compartments and even by separate theories, having little relation with another [sic, italics added].[37]

The unique contribution of the neoclassical system, as formalized and corrected by Stigler in his doctoral dissertation, was the simultaneous determination of all the significant variables in the system of production and distribution under stationary, competitive conditions. There were no loose ends in this system, with production and distribution "so closely interwoven that it would be absurd to attempt to separate them."[38]

### *Role of the History of Thought*

In order for a "school" of thought to come into its own, it appears that a number of essential ingredients are required. The first requirement, of course, is that there must be a founder, and in most instances such a person must be a teacher, with an institution of higher learning serving as a base of operation. Second, it is necessary that there be "students," whose essential role is to perpetuate the basic philosophy of the initial paradigm. Third, the paradigm itself must be prophetic, for as Vilfredo Pareto once claimed, "the person seeking the method of teaching history best calculated to achieve the greatest social benefits must believe, or pretend to believe, that there is but one solution."[39]

So far as Chicago is concerned, Knight was *the* teacher and the major promulgator of its particular point of view. He was not the first economist of note to teach at Chicago, however, for J. Lawrence Laughlin was the first chairman of the department, emigrating there from Cornell in 1891. The following year, Thorstein Veblen joined Laughlin and several others, and by 1900 he had even been promoted to assistant professor. Laughlin and Veblen were highly productive, producing a sizeable number of articles, not only for the new *Journal of Political Economy,* but also for the *Quarterly Journal of Economics. The Index of Economic Journals* for the period of 1886–1924 lists 38 separate articles by Laughlin and 16 for Veblen, although one of Veblen's was in three parts.[40] A sizeable number of the Laughlin and Veblen articles dealt with the history of economic thought. When other Chicagoans such as H. P. Willis are included, Chicago's output exceeded even that of Johns Hopkins, where H. R. Seager, C. W. Mixter, and Jacob Hollander were well-established authorities in the subject. For the several decades both preceeding and following the turn of the century, the history of economic thought was a much more active area of research than it was after mathematics began to assert itself. This was true not only in the United States but also in England, as Edwin Cannan, Henry Higgs, R. H. Tawney, and J. S. Nicholson gave great influence and support to the history of thought. The switch in emphasis to mathematics came in England, however, and Stigler is undoubtedly correct in alleging that Irving Fisher was the only American economist mathematically qualified to participate in the controversy created by Wicksteed's *Co-ordination of the Laws of Distribution,*[41] although he remained silent.

Frank Knight went to Chicago in 1917, a year after Jacob Viner. Both men were new Ph.D.s; Knight from Cornell, and Viner from Harvard. Knight remained only two years, moving in 1919 to the State University of Iowa, where he was joined by Henry Schultz, among others. At Iowa, Knight became one of the more vigorous members of the group of professors protesting the outright censorship of Schultz's research on the nutritional advantages of oleomargarine, and when most of them resigned, Knight returned to Chicago in 1927. For the next 31 years he taught continuously, except for sabbaticals, and it was during this period that he became the moving spirit of the Chicago point of view, fostering not only a strict laissez-faire philosophy, but also the view of economic theory which this article has interpreted as a "paradigm."

Between them, Knight and Viner fashioned economic theory at Chicago and made the *Journal of Political Economy* into an organ for their particular points of view. In the previous listing of the necessary ingredients for the founding of a "school of thought," the need for a journal or forum was not included, since some schools of thought have emerged without the service of a journal. But at Chicago, the *JPE* under the Knight-Viner editorship became essentially a house organ. From 1930 to 1946, the period of their joint editorship, approximately three-quarters of the articles published in the *JPE* were authored by Chicago faculty, their students, or former students. Of course, the same was true of the *QJE* at Harvard, and *Economic Journal* at Cambridge, but these two publications tended to be more catholic in editorial policy. With the exception of Keynes, who is the all-time champion as a journal editor who publishes his own articles, Knight and Viner used the *JPE* to advance their views. Of the 51 articles published by Knight between 1930 and 1946, when Viner left Chicago and the joint editorship, 21 appeared in the *JPE*; during the same period, nine of Viner's 26 articles were published in the *JPE.*

Despite the agreement of Knight and Viner on the necessity of laissez-faire, the Keynesian analysis being all wrong, and the virtues of free trade and neoclassical theory in general, there was sufficient difference in their views to prevent economics at Chicago from being completely procrustean. The contrast between the two men can be appreciated simply from the titles of two of their famous articles on the analysis of cost, the one by Knight characteristically being "Some Fallacies in the Interpretation of Social Cost,"[42] while Viner's title was straightforward: "Cost Curves and Supply Curves."[43]

Besides their general agreement on policy matters, but disagreement over what was important in economic theory (technique versus meaning), Knight and Viner were both students of economic thought. But even in this common interest they contrasted, Viner stressing the details of who said what and when, as exemplified by his opening two chapters on the mercantilists in *Studies in the Theory of International Trade*.[44] Knight, on the other hand, saw a need for the history of economic thought because economics was different from the study of the natural sciences.

The point has been made many times over; the competent natural scientist does not concern himself with the history of science, for it is the current body of theory alone that matters.[45] It is not necessary to study what some so-called physicist in 1885 wrote about atomic structure, since experimentation has verified the exactness of current knowledge. Studying past theory is not only useless, but also counterproductive, so it is off to the cyclotron, and not the archives. But as the discussion above has indicated, the Knight view, or the Chicago view, is that empiricism cannot verify an analytical proposition.[46] This latter function can only be performed by the development of a body of theory based upon postulates which are correct from the standpoint of being internally consistent with one another. The history of economic thought was the means of identifying "fallacies" and "aberrations" which stood in the way of understanding the "correct" view. Thus, Knight wrote in regard to Ricardo:

> On the assumption that the primary interest in the "ancients" in such a field as economics is to learn from their mistakes, the principal theme of this discussion will be the contrast between the "classical" system and "correct" views. . . . While our special interest is distribution theory, it is useful to have in the background clear views of essential doctrines or points of view in the authors' theory of value or price; for these are often closely connected with fallacies in the other field. It will be appropriate to give by way of introduction a kind of formal list of main deficiencies and sources of error in the system as a whole. At least seven such "aberrations" appear to have vital importance.[47]

In more recent times, George Stigler has argued that the major purpose of the history of economic thought is to teach economists how to read.[48] Any economics professor has to know how to read scientific materials, and the best means to acquire this skill is, of course, to read the work of other economists. For this task the writings of past economists are better than the latest professional journal for a variety of reasons. The reader of the work of a past economist can be more neutral, detached, and capable of seeing the errors in the writing.

> Not only can the study of the history of economics teach one how to read, it can also teach us how to react to what we read. Scientific literature is to a considerable degree controversial literature. New ideas are sold very much the way new automobiles are sold: by exaggerating their superiority over the older models.
>
> The role of controversy is indeed to stimulate interest and animosity. Only after a theory has been subjected to hostile review do its weaknesses and limitations become identified and therefore capable of being remedied.[49]

Both the earlier Chicago view of the role of the history of thought, as expressed by Knight, and Stigler's more recent statement share the notion that a body of scientific economic knowledge exists which must serve as a benchmark; against this all past, present, and future economic theory is to be measured. Errors, aberrations, fallacies, weaknesses, and limitations can then be identified and purged and the emerging theory purified. It should be clear, of course, that here we are not talking about mere technique, or the tools of economic analysis, but the whole corpus of an economic framework.

It is not a question of whether a particular writer, past or present, incorrectly expresses the symbolic formula for demand elasticity at a point, since this formula must be written $n = dqp/dpq$, with its negative value expressed. Any technique or analytical task is by its very nature a matter of definition, and there can be no disagreement as to whether an author is correct or not on such matters.

The way that the history of thought was used in the development of the Chicago paradigm was no different methodologically from the manner it has been used by the formulators of other paradigms. In *Theories of Surplus Value,* for example, Marx evaluates the contributions of William Petty through Nassau Senior against his own theoretical framwork,[50] which in this instance is the "correct" view of the operation of the capitalist system. In the case of Smith, Book IV of the *Wealth of Nations* was an evaluation of physiocratic and mercantilist doctrines in terms of showing their relation to Smith's own "correct" view.[51] Keynes, in the *General Theory,* not only relied upon certain misconceptions of the classical economists to point up the uniqueness of his own contribution,[52] but also included a chapter on the "scientific truth" of mercantilist doctrine.[53]

Approaches to the history of economic thought are myriad, ranging from highly interpretative selections[54] to mere compendia of who lived when and where and wrote what;[55] standing alone, of course, is Joseph Schumpeter's magnificent volume,[56] the most outstanding book ever written on the subject. The Knight approach was to use the history of thought to make clear the main characteristics of the "correct view" of economic behavior. In this way, as Patinkin has recently noted,[57] economic theory and the history of economic theory were entwined, as apparently Knight's courses in the two areas overlapped to some considerable degree. Chicago, therefore, was somewhat unique among departments of economics because of the importance attributed to the history of economic thought. It was not a course assigned to professors too old to be retooled as nascent regression runners while they waited out their years to retirement. At perhaps no other university were economic theory and the history of thought combined for the purpose of developing a particular point of view. In his evaluation of why Menger was "correct" Knight wrote:

> It is to the everlasting credit and renown of Menger ... that he not only grasped the utility principle but extended and applied it in two directions: in the field of *complementary* goods and in that of *indirect* goods. He reiterated with emphasis ... the principle that costs are simply the values of cost goods, which values are *derived from* or reflect the value of some final consumption good; and that this value, in turn, is that of the "need satisfaction" *dependent upon* a small portion or increment (Teilquantität) of the final good in question. This is perhaps as accurate a statement as can be put into words (at least such a number of words) of the general principle that explains, as far as it goes, all economic valuation [italics in original].[58]

It is significant that Knight believed this said it *all*, for that is the essence of individualism.

## *Notes*

1. Frank H. Knight, " 'What is Truth' in Economics?" *Journal of Political Economy* 48 (February 1940): 16.
2. The contrast between "correct economic theorizing" and "error,"

"aberrations," or "fallacies" was used repeatedly by Knight, the only question being who was wrong at the moment, since in a Euclidean world there is but one "correct" answer. At this juncture, two examples should suffice to make this point clear. Compare Frank H. Knight, "The Ricardian Theory of Production and Distribution," Parts I–II, *Canadian Journal of Economics and Political Science* 1 (February and May 1935): 3–25 and 171–96; and Knight's review of Marian Bowley, *Nassau Senior: And Classical Economics, Journal of Political Economy* 47 (February 1939): 131–35.

3. A. W. Coats, "The Role of Authority in the Development of British Economics," *Journal of Law and Economics* 7 (October 1964): 86.
4. Knight, " 'What is Truth,' " p. 15. This piece was a review article of T. W. Hutchison's *The Significance and Basic Postulates of Economic Theory* (London: Macmillan, 1938).
5. Ibid., p. 20.
6. Ibid.
7. Frank H. Knight, "Realism and Relevance in the Theory of Demand," *Journal of Political Economy* 52 (December 1944): 289–318.
8. Alfred Marshall, *Principles of Economics*, 8th ed. (London: Macmillan, 1930), pp. 92–93, note 1.
9. Knight, " 'What is Truth,' " p. 18, note 10.
10. Frank H. Knight, Introduction to the English translation of Carl Menger, *Principles of Economics,* translated and edited by James Dingwall and Bert F. Hoselitz (Glencoe, Ill.: The Free Press, 1950), pp. 19–20.
11. Ibid., pp. 20–21.
12. Knight, "Realism and Relevance," pp. 299–301: "It is theoretically impossible for *all* other things to be constant while a change occurs in the expenditure of a given income for a given good at a different price; either other prices or the 'value of money' must change" (italics in original). Knight, "Introduction," p. 21. It should be recognized that in essence this statement is akin to the position of Milton Friedman in "The Marshallian Demand Curve," *Journal of Political Economy* 57 (December 1949): 47–99. Friedman acknowledges the agreement, of course.
13. Knight, "Ricardian Theory," p. 3.
14. Knight, "Introduction," pp. 12–13.
15. "Indeed, Smith—according to Knight—did *not* believe in the labor theory of value (Classnotes, Econ. 302, 1945)." Don Patinkin, "Frank Knight as Teacher," *American Economic Review* 63 (December 1973): 797.
16. Marshall, "Appendix I: Ricardo's Theory of Value," *Principles,* pp. 813–21.
17. Piero Sraffa and Maurice Dobb, eds., "Introduction," *Works and Correspondence of David Ricardo,* vol. 1 (Cambridge: the University Press for the Royal Economic Society, 1952), pp. xxx–lxii.
18. Compare Maurice Dobb, "A Decade of High Criticism," in *Theories of Value and Distribution Since Adam Smith* (Cambridge: the University Press, 1973), chapter 9.

19. George J. Stigler, "Ricardo and the 93% Labor Theory of Value," *American Economic Review* 48 (June 1958): 361.
20. Ibid., p. 366.
21. Ricardo, *Works*, vol. 1, p. 36.
22. Menger, *Principles*, pp. 177–78.
23. George J. Stigler, *Production and Distribution Theories* (New York: Macmillan, 1948), p. 2.
24. "Their value is wholly independent of the quantity of labour necessary to produce them, and varies with the varying wealth and inclinations of those who are desirous to possess them." Ricardo, *Works*, vol. 1, p. 12.
25. Stigler, *Production*, chapter 12.
26. Ibid., p. 332 (italics added).
27. Patinkin, "Frank Knight," pp. 792, 793. See also George Stigler, *The Theory of Price* (New York: Macmillan, 1946), chapter 8.
28. Knight, "Introduction," p. 27.
29. Piero Sraffa, "The Laws of Returns Under Competitive Conditions," *Economic Journal* 36 (December 1926), reprinted in *Readings in Price Theory* (Chicago: American Economic Association, 1952), pp. 186–87. Sraffa's article has probably been reprinted in every collection of articles dealing with value theory in the past fifty years and no bibliography on the subject would be complete without including a citation to it, but few seem to understand that it presents the case for using constant cost as the general rule, rather than increasing costs.
30. Knight, "Introduction," p. 24.
31. Stigler, *Theory of Price*, p.134.
32. Ibid., p. 138.
33. *Production of Commodities by Means of Commodities* (Cambridge: the University Press, 1960).
34. *Canadian Journal of Economics and Political Science* 36 (December 1961): 464. The same criticism about the absence of any demand analysis came from Roy Harrod; see his review of Sraffa, *Economic Journal* 71 (December 1961): 783–87. A more sympathetic review was Ronald L. Meek, "Piero Sraffa's Rehabilitation of Classical Economics," *Scottish Journal of Political Economy* 8 (June 1961): 161–78.
35. G. C. Harcourt, *Some Cambridge Controversies in the Theory of Capital* (Cambridge: the University Press, 1972).
36. *The Cambridge Revolution: Success or Failure?* (London: The Institute of Economic Affairs, 1974).
37. Ibid., p. 81.
38. Stigler, *Production*, p. 6.
39. Vilfredo Pareto, *A Treatise on General Sociology* (New York: Dover Press, 1963), p. 1032.
40. Thorstein Bunde Veblen, "The Preconceptions of Economic Science," Parts I–III, *Quarterly Journal of Economics* 13 (January and July 1899, February 1900): 121–50, 396–426, and 240–69.
41. Stigler, *Production*, p. 321.
42. *Quarterly Journal of Economics* 38 (August 1924): 582–606; reprinted in *Readings in Price Theory*, pp. 160–79.
43. *Zeitschrift für Nationalökonomie* 3 (September 1931): 23–46; reprinted in *Readings in Price Theory*, pp. 198–232.

44. (New York: 1937).
45. For a recent statement, see George J. Stigler, "Does Economics Have a Useful Past," *History of Political Economy* 1 (Fall 1969): 217–18.
46. See Milton Friedman's critical review of Oskar Lange's "casual empiricism" in "Lange on Price Flexibility and Employment: A Methodological Criticism," *American Economic Review* 36 (September 1946): 622–23.
47. Knight, "Ricardian Theory," p. 3.
48. Stigler, "Does Economics Have a Useful Past," pp. 218–19.
49. Ibid., p. 222.
50. Translation by G. A. Bonner and Emile Burns of the Karl Kautsky edition of Marx's *Theorien über den Mehrwert* (New York: International Publishers, 1952).
51. "Of Systems of Political Economy" (New York: Modern Library Edition), pp. 397–652.
52. John Maynard Keynes, *The General Theory of Employment, Interest and Money* (New York: Harcourt, Brace, 1936), chapter 2.
53. Ibid., p. 335.
54. Stigler, *Production.*
55. Lewis H. Haney, *History of Economic Thought* (New York: Macmillan, 1949). Stigler's review of Haney points up a number of instances where authors listed as deceased were still alive, and vice versa.
56. Joseph A. Schumpeter, *History of Economic Analysis* (New York: Oxford University Press, 1954).
57. Patinkin, "Frank Knight," p. 797.
58. Knight, "Introduction," p. 15.

# 16

# Chicago Doctrine as Explanation and Justification

*Warren J. Samuels*

The dual role of economics as explanation and justification is the necessary starting point, and not merely a conclusion, for the interpretation of the Chicago School.[1] The apologist role has been stressed by Joan Robinson, Paul Sweezy, Gunnar Myrdal, John Kenneth Galbraith, and many other heterodox writers in well-known works. But the dual role has been so widely recognized within orthodox economics as well, it does not seem unduly presumptuous to begin with it. Thus, Arrow and Scitovsky have said: "Modern economics developed more or less as the rationalization of the laissez-faire economy, hence its preoccupation with the private sector and the operation of the market in the private sector" [Arrow and Scitovsky 1969, p. 2]. Alfred E. Kahn has written: "Economics emerged in the eighteenth and nineteenth centuries as an attempt to *explain* and to *justify* a market system. This is an oversimplification, but it is a broadly accurate characterization of the mainstream of Western economic thought" [Kahn 1970, p. 1].

With these statements from within the recognized ranks of orthodoxy, economics has lost its naïveté and innocence as well as its pretense of positivist virtue. We must be aware of the close historic association of orthodox economics with certain lines of conservative (nineteenth-century liberal) philosophy. Orthodox economics has long been used as an apologetics, although it has never been solely that; indeed, there has been much historic tension between its ideological and descriptive uses. But there has been the mutual casting of luster between orthodox economics (even with all its transformations) and the market system (such as it evolved). "Economic theory is both the product and the servant of economic ideology" [Randall 1975, p. 84], although it has been other things as well.

The fundamental normative or valuational character of economics abides in contemporary theory, albeit the rationalization element is more subtle and less self-evident. Only rarely has it been so blatantly expressed as in a literary notice for George Opdyke's *Treatise on Political Economy*: "The author undertakes to present a system in perfect harmony with the other portions of our political edifice—a system grounded on the broad principles of justice and equality, and in all its doctrines and legislative applications solely designed to illustrate and enforce those principles" [Anonymous 1851, p. 139]. But this is merely one example of economics allied with the common sense school of rationalization [see Hirsch 1967, p. 75 and passim]. There is, I think, an inevitable normative and faith element in economic theory.

It is fundamentally necessary to envision the Chicago School as one facet of the conservative apologia for the status quo system, or one view of that system. It is a contemporary contribution to a long history of rationalization of the middle class or business system view of the world. *Vis-à-vis* general neoclassicism, there is a greater proportion, or more evident role, of justification and rationalization in Chicago School doctrine.

The fundamental Chicago position is that of a group trying mightily to erect intellectual barriers to what it perceives as the erosion of a business or free market system. Its economic analysis and policy writings are generally a sophisticated rationalization, and description, of its idealized system, as well as a set of defensive counterattacks against lines of reasoning deemed dangerous to the system.

The rationalization or propaganda role was recognized by Frank Knight:

> The original purpose of economics on the classical price-theory line was educational or, one might say, propagandist. It was to show that free co-operation of individuals as consumers and producers, under the guidance of prices fixed by free purchase and sale in markets, is a way, and within wide limits a better way, than tradition and authority, to organize the efficient use of resources to achieve the freely chosen ends of individuals [Knight 1952, p. 49; compare Knight 1951b, pp. 75, 102, 287; and Knight 1956, p. 16 and passim].

More important, its propagandist role has been adopted as a matter of conscious strategy; this is clearly acknowledged by leading members of the school.[2] It is the adoption of the strategy, which explains the ideological extremism perceived in the school's doctrines and writings *vis-à-vis* the realism and limits recognized by Knight. Interestingly, however, the strategy adopted by the current Chicago School is nonetheless fully consistent with Knight's views, for Knight took an almost theological (as well as pessimistic) position in interpreting the social role of economics.

### *Conscious Strategy*

The central strategic goal of the Chicago School is to influence the structure of presumptive reasoning within which professional economic policy recommendations emerge and the public policy area operates. This is done by doctrinaire insistence upon the inevitability and merits of markets and by promoting the role of the neoclassical-libertarian paradigm as a putative force in policy analysis. The school emphasizes those factors which, in its view, will promote and maintain its conception of a free society, a view which centers on its belief that power is more diffused in the market than in any alternative system.

It was Knight, the premier spiritual leader of the current Chicagoans, who emphasized the importance of ideology as the basis for an economic system and the necessity for maintaining that ideology for that purpose. In his view, the reality of limits to the market and to freedom was a less important fact than the maintenance of proper ideology. The goal was to constrain the structural transformation of the system, and for that purpose marginal analysis functions well in obscuring, diverting, and disengaging systemic or structural change. His basic strategy was to establish a presumption in favor of the economic order and thereby minimize the role of government. To promote freedom, a basic ideology was necessary [Knight 1960, pp. 111–12].

In an early article Knight wrote: "Reality is not what is logical, but what it suits our *purposes* to treat as real" [Knight 1951b, p. 95].[3] Later writings support the proposition that the propaganda role has been consciously adopted. Assuming the principles of the system, the business of economics is to explain the system in a favorable light:

> Assuming that men have a right to want and strive to get whatever they do want, and to have the tastes and "higher" values they do have, as long as their conduct does not infringe the equal rights of others, the business of the economics of principles, of utility, and price, is to explain that, and how, the organization through buying-and-selling enables everyone to do whatever he tries to do (whether rational or not, as judged by

> anyone else) many times more effectively than would be possible if each used his own means in a self-sufficient economic life [Knight 1956, p. 263].

Preference determination and resource endowment are less important than explaining the operation of the market: For the propagandist function,

> it does not matter what particular wants the individuals have or what concrete resources they possess or what technical processes are known and available. Taking freedom as a fact and as the norm of policy makes these things irrelevant. The purpose of explaining that this comes about, and how, is not less important than it was in 1776 or at any time in the past [Knight 1952, pp. 49–50].

> The social problem . . . is chiefly a matter of agreement upon ends or, rather, establishing unity of purpose. Again we refer to democracy, a society committed to individual freedom as its primary value. With this much given, the fundamental part of economic analysis, both as explanatory and as a guide to social policy, must—in spite of all sweeping limitations—be the mechanics of instrumental choice, demand and supply, and prices [Knight 1953, pp. 54–55].

Certain considerations must be stressed and others avoided; the role of economic education is societization or internalization of the norms of the system:

> Like-mindedness in beliefs and ideas regarding itself is the really important thing in society, and to produce and maintain it is the really important function of education in the social field. That the unanimity has to do with symbols, and that a part of the task is to keep people from asking what these symbolize in any concrete sense, is a mere corollary; for nothing is more obvious than that any such questioning would turn the likemindedness into universal enmity and conflict. The teaching of social science on any considerable scale must be of this sort, and inevitably will be, and there is simply no problem [Knight 1932, p. 454; compare Knight 1947, p. 79; and Knight 1956, p. 130].

> The modern student of history and social process soon learns that societies have lived in a state of relative peace and order by not raising problems they cannot solve and discussion of which would only stir up antagonism and probably lead to conflict, if not to a social nervous breakdown [Knight 1947, p. 336].

Economic theory has its functional role:

> Education, like other fields of social activity, has this interesting feature, that there are many things about it which are obviously "true," and it may be entirely proper to mention them in friendly conversation, in either a reverent or an irreverent tone, yet to "say" them publicly and officially would simply sink the ship. At least everybody assumes that it would, and the consequence is the same—it must not be and is not done. If this should turn out to be the one general and important principle of methodology in the entire social science field, the fact would undoubtedly be embarrassing to the profession, unless some way were found to keep it dark.
>
> It is incredible that anyone should think education could be other than a part of the system and of a piece with the rest of it, and probably no one really does.
>
> The truth was old when the poet phrased it patly that "man must be taught as if you taught them not." . . . We merely have a new paradox on top of the old; men must be not taught as if you taught them, at the same time that they are taught as if you taught them not. What they are directly given must be a "satisfier," but cannot, like other forms of entertainment, be sold under a descriptive label.
>
> Certainly the large general courses should be prevented from raising any question about objectivity, but should assume the objectivity of the slogans they inculcate as a sacred feature of the system [Knight 1932, pp. 441, 450, 452, 455].
>
> A vitally important fact which is almost systematically ignored by the critics of economic theory . . . is that the subject as expounded in modern times has been developed with definite reference to the practical needs of free society [Knight 1956, p. 144].

The rationality assumption is more than a methodological technique: "A free economic order must assume that men actually tend to be rational in the use of means, that they try to be and tend to succeed" [Knight 1956, p. 25]. But above all the strategy is dependent upon circumstances, and the contemporary problem is statism:

> There was a time, no doubt, when society needed to be awakened to the possibility of remedying evils and stirred to action, mostly negative action, in establishing freedom, but some positive action too. Now, we have found not only that mere individual freedom is not enough but that its excess can have disastrous consequences. And a reaction has set in, so that people have too much faith in positive action, of the nature of passing laws and employing policemen, and the opposite warning is needed [Knight 1956, p. 281].

In many ways, then, Knight's intellectual career comprised a search for "the basis of a propaganda for economic freedom" [Knight 1953, p. 279]. Of course, he was not alone in this. Henry Simons, too, was concerned about "providing a respectable foundation for the older faith of freedom and equality" [Simons 1948, p. v]. Simons wrote his "political credo" in "an endeavor to formulate specifically the political predispositions implicit in his work" [Simons 1948, p. 1n], and his "Positive Program for Laissez Faire" was a somewhat pragmatic effort "to define, for present conditions, the main features of a genuinely liberal program, in the traditional sense of liberalism. Such a program, if it could be realized politically, would suffice to permit tolerable functioning of a free-enterprise system and to prevent (or postpone) revolutionary change in our whole institutional framework" [Simons 1948, p. 56].

It is my hypothesis that the current Chicago School has adopted Knight's mandate, and this quest for the justification of the system has governed their choice of problems, variables, and theoretical formulations. Chicagoans have demonstrated scientific fecundity at the same time that they have sought to perform this role. Their economic science, following the lead of Knight, "is a normative one that provides a solution to his conception of the major social problem of social control." Such a science "is 'educational or, one might say, propagandist,' being a proof that liberalism is a good policy" [Gonce 1972, p. 554]. From Knight's classic 1924 article through Viner's 1931 classic, to Coase's 1960 classic, and Buchanan and Stubblebine's 1962 classic, the strategy has become manifest in the attack on Pigovian externality theory and its progovernmental activism. As Mishan expresses the point in chapter 6, "a more conservative approach was developed . . . which sought to weaken the popular arguments for government intervention, and to strengthen the presumption that unaided market forces would, or could be made to, bring about a proper allocation of resources, at least within the restrictive assumptions of a partial context." The result aimed at is a body of theory from which (again quoting Mishan) "the existence of a *de facto* optimum could then be legitimately inferred." This is but one result of a profound belief in the need to legitimize the market system, to provide part of the consensus of values deemed necessary for a stable market society.

### *Mythic Nature and Role*

There is a mythic quality to Chicago School doctrine, although certainly there is more than myth. The myths serve as the modern equivalent of tribal legends and concern the idols of the tribe. Belief systems are absolutely essential to the organization and operation of society, and each economic system produces a body of myth which tries to present a coherent picture of its way of life; as such it is part of the system's ideology. Myths order and interpret experience. They integrate and provide patterns for human action. They are felt or taken to contribute to the social order with which they are tautological. They comfort against insecurity. They express and evoke attitudes. They mediate the contradictions between actuality and ideal [Barbour 1974, chapters 2 and 4]. "The myth states the social contradictions, restates them in modified fashion until in the final statement the contradictions are resolved, or so modified and masked as to be minimized" [Douglas 1967, p. 57]. Myths serve to rationalize the system; as with theory, the chief function "is the setting of minds at rest" [Shackle 1967, p. 288]. They do this, in part, by masking the truth of disorder and indeterminacy, reducing anxiety, and making life bearable.

The Chicago School doctrine provides an idealized image of business, the business society, and business as a system of power (to use Robert Brady's phrase). Its paradigm corresponds to the major ideology and myths of the capitalist system, a body of metaphysics that is blended with science. It provides for capitalist society "a basic core of value judgments that are unthinkingly accepted by the great bulk of its members" [Friedman 1962, p. 167].[4] Such a body of myth carries the pretense of finality, inexorability, and idealism, all constituting absolutist legitimation, in part through Knight's relatively absolute absolutes. The body of myth casts luster upon the system to render it immune from, if not above, criticism in its fundamentals or to permit criticism only on its own terms. The myths function to legitimize, rationalize, and make authoritative; in sum, to induce the feeling of propriety among those under its captivation. The myths include symbols and verbal phrases and formulas, the code words of the system. These function to create an image of an identicity or equation of the actual (if only proper reforms were effectuated) with the ideal market system [compare Miller 1962, pp. 65, 66, 67, with Stigler 1962, p. 70]. As Charles Wilber and Jon Wisman might express it, myths function to redo the system in its own image (or one of its own images)—the Platonic function of myths. Apropos the Chicago School there is the interesting paradox that its members are the great purveyors of myths, yet also the great demythicizers of myths deemed by other persons—for example, in law and political science—as necessary for social order. The modern Chicagoans are almost Veblenian in the role and the glee with which the demythicizing role is played (quite in contrast to Knight).

The myths in the Chicago doctrine are fairly straightforward and are part of us all. Notice that all have descriptive (empirical) content or explanatory or hueristic value as well as normative significance. Myths may have elements of the unknown and the mysterious, but they also may have concrete and knowable elements as well as grandiose honorific ones. One myth, the reality of capitalism or the market system, is in fact largely an abstraction, multifaceted and kaleidoscopic, with its institutional and valuational characteristics still in dispute. Others are the rationality assumption, the doctrine of consumer sovereignty, the doctrine of the ubiquity and automaticity of markets, methodological individualism, the doctrine of individual autonomy, the premise of given tastes and preferences, business innocence, the idea of a world of fundamental harmony, and so on.

Consumer sovereignty is a myth functioning to legitimize the system. Although it has elements of descriptive accuracy, as is true of most if not all relevant myths, it requires specification and empirical study to determine what it actually means and how it works (for example, which consumers are sovereign). Likewise, the doctrine of individual freedom abstracts from the specification of power structure, which is a partial function of legal-economic interrelations, income and wealth distribution, class structure, and so on. The doctrine of harmony aims at countering the reality of conflict and ubiquitous externalities and non-Pareto optimal changes, and at emphasizing the possibilities of gains from trade. (Compare Buchanan's [1912] emphasis on gains from trade with Foley's [1975] conflict approach.) The Coase theorem projects a ubiquity of markets. The contemporary Chicago doctrine of human capital (not unlike Knight's earlier theory of capital as *the* factor of production) has vast heuristic importance, but it also functions as a myth suppressing the idea of labor as a factor of production: Everyone is a capitalist in his own way; class distinctions are unimportant. (See Dietz [1975].)

Another functional myth is that of productivity ethics, the myth that individuals receive what they create and its associated theory of entitlement. This is an important part of distribution theory, fairly adequate on the demand side, and has sufficient realism to permit accord with experience, given its normative status. Yet it is a recognized fiction to support the status quo and the market, an apologetic economic myth recited by Friedman notwithstanding Knight's rejection of the use of marginal productivity theory to lend ethical support to market system income distribution [Patinkin 1973, pp. 799–800 and references given]. Indeed, Friedman's fascinating discussion of "the instrumental role of distribution according to product" treats the productivity ethic less as an economic principle and more as a functional myth: "No society can be stable unless there is a basic core of value judgments that are unthinkingly accepted by the great bulk of its members. Some key institutions must be accepted as 'absolutes,' not simply as instrumental. I believe that payment in accordance with product has been, and, in large measure, still is, one of these accepted value judgments or institutions" [Friedman 1962, p. 167].

Perhaps the greatest and most powerful myth in the Chicago doctrine is the *market*, a reified abstraction often presented without apparent connection to legal-economic institutions, yet given substantive reality and programming by specific institutions, learned preferences, and power relations such that performance (allocation and distribution) are *pro tanto* specific thereto. The market to which attribution of impersonality is often made is not a neutral black box. Moreover, it is a nonoperational concept, a brilliant metaphysical question-begging organizing principle. The Chicago School, hardly alone in this society, of course, invokes the fantasy of ubiquitous and automatic markets in which the key myth is the market itself. With due allowance for journalistic license, Friedman's statement that "the free market works its magic" [*Newsweek*, 25 August 1975, p. 62] is a good example of the sacerdotal invocation of the myth. The "market works" doctrine will be considered somewhat more technically below (and see Mishan's chapter 6); suffice it to say that the concept explains everything and nothing. Automaticity is an historical fiction or myth: The market gives effect to the power structure, institutions, and preferences operating through it. The doctrine that the market works is a pseudo-scientific myth (again, with empirical and descriptive content) which canonizes both the power structure and forces operating through it and the allocative and distributive performance they create. Yes, there is a market, and it "works," but it is not the magical invisible force preeminent and preexistent to man it is often pictured to be.

The mythic element in economics has to be taken for what it is; inevitably *all* systems of economic thought have that element. The problem is not whether but which myth. It is part of the history of economic thought and the analysis of schools of thought to identify the mythic element. Objectors will perceive nihilism in such agnosticism, which brings us to the next point.

### Character as Religion

It is not surprising that the Chicago School and its doctrine are perceived, and perhaps somewhat deliberately projected, as a secular faith.

The perception is correct.[5] Chicago presents a paradigm clothed in science and offered for acceptance as an act of faith. With the pretense of certitude and finality it nurtures and practices economics imperialism, seeking to extend "the aspect of reality that it sees into a comprehensive vision of the whole" [Campbell 1971, p. 20; see pp. 28, 29], trying always to strengthen its fundamental valuational position. Chicago projects a religion with regard to the meaning of man and of social (especially legal-economic) reality. It offers a utopian picture of conflict and conflict resolution ("through the market"). It offers a theory which presumes to stand above the conflict, indeed, which would minimize conflict, while it is part of the conflict, and a theory whose Pareto rule would remove from consideration (but not reality) most if not all actual fundamental conflicts. The market, preached by Chicago, *does* avoid direct confrontation with and conflict over difficult choices, but it gives effect to the power structure which shapes and operates through it—the very power structure which is the arena and object of conflict. Little wonder that critics see in Chicago a defense of the status quo. Chicago economics preaches the market and thereby tends to be an establishment economics, although it does not have to be. Perhaps it is appropriate to note Knight's dictum that religion may be an opiate of the masses, but it is also a sedative for the classes, thereby controlling the rapacity of all.

Chicagoans operate in a charged theological atmosphere. They are an often fanatical but ever proselytizing group with the gift of faith. They are the contemporary "theologians of the industrial society" [Fusfeld 1972, p. 91], convinced of the market's sufficiency and correctness to the point of dogmatism [see Hochwald 1973, p. 487].

Chicago presents a secular or social religion, à la Karl Mannheim or Vilfredo Pareto, an economic theology which uses economic science with its additional presumption of objectivity and determinate solutions. Contemporary Chicagoans implicitly recognize and administer Knight's mandate that economic principles are religious:

> The point is that the "principles" by which a society or a group lives in tolerable harmony are essentially religious. The essential nature of a religious principle is that not merely is it immoral to oppose it, but to ask what it is, is morally identical with denial and attack.
>
> There must be ultimates, and they must be religious, in economics as anywhere else, if one has anything to say touching conduct or social policy in a practical way. Man is a believing animal and to few, if any, is it given to criticize the foundations of belief and to believe "intelligently" [Knight 1932, p. 448].

> To inquire into the ultimates behind accepted group values is obscene and sacrilegious; objective inquiry is an attempt to uncover the nakedness of man, his soul as well as his body, his deeds, his culture, and his very gods [Knight 1932, p. 449].

It is because of the foregoing that Chicago School doctrine constitutes a significant contribution to the social valuational process or moral philosophy (metaphysics) whose importance is often neglected (that word again!) by a discipline preoccupied with the techniques of positivist science [see Day 1975, p. 232; and Buchanan and Samuels 1975]. The Chicago religion promotes materialism and the commercial spirit as well as its blend of libertarian and social order values. It thus serves the necessary function of an ideology, namely, to provide or serve as a social religion for purposes of social control [Robinson 1962, chapter 1].

## *Casuistry and Argument*

The foregoing analysis should facilitate better comprehension of the character of Chicago School doctrine as argument and, therefore, aspects of its probative status for policy, whether one accepts or rejects the doctrine in whole or in part. A series of points may be made along this line.

### *The Premise*

Everything advocated by the Chicago School rests upon the premise of its paradigm: the propriety of the market system (interpreted, to be sure, as a business system) and the superiority of market solutions. The validity or acceptability of this premise is the hallmark of its intrasystemic meaning. The Chicago School believes this premise and its associated paradigm of market adjustments and solutions to be not only a meaningful but also an adequate, if not complete, representation of economic reality, on positive and normative grounds. Its presumption that the market works, say, in the absence of evidence to the contrary (but with the evidentiary criteria narrowly circumscribed; see below), gives effect to this premise. The great bulk of the work of the Chicago School comprises an articulation of this paradigm and its doctrinal (policy analytic) defense.

The dominant role of its paradigm (as indicated in chapter 5 by Wilber and Wisman) is suggested by the preferred place given to it in the methodology of the school, now generally following Friedman, but with the same effect of following Knight (as indicated in chapter 4 by the

Hirsches): Its truth and propriety are taken for granted. This is achieved by setting up the market model as the maintained hypothesis which is accepted, as it were, by nonrejection. First, evidence is accumulated, none (or not all) of which is inconsistent with the hypothesis that the market works, although it also may be consistent with alternative hypotheses. Second, proof is adduced through counter-example: Market-like behavioral responses are shown to follow from government policy changes which are deemed not only predictable from the market model but which, given the optimality of *market* adjustments, are deemed inferior thereto. The premise of the existence and optimality of market solutions permits the priority of the maintained hypothesis. The premise is critical: The market produces optimal solutions because the latter are defined in terms of the conditions of *market* solutions. The Chicago School well represents that tendency of neoclassical economics to utilize theory's search for the postulates necessary to establish abstractly the conclusions of general and partial equilibrium in order to prove or affirm the optimality of the system. (What is possible theoretically will tend to exist; much Chicago School analysis portrays what *would* happen if the market were left alone to do its job.) The analysis has the patina of logical rigor, but only within the context of the premised paradigm and its valuational basis. Belief in the social advantage of decentralized private enterprise has influenced the choice of substantive, ideological, and methodological presuppositions. (See the chapters by Mishan, Wilber and Wisman, and the Hirsches.) The paradigm and the theory cast luster on each other, and both cast luster on the system.

There are two important limits of the foregoing. First, the Chicago doctrine must be extrasystemically compared with different premises and paradigms, each of which produces a corresponding notion of optimality. Thus, conflicts in Eastern Europe are said to be nonantagonistic due to the harmony reached through the central plan, a view depending upon the optimality presumed for the system [Betz 1974, p. 90]. One also could reason within a paradigm of an equimarginal or market adjustment theory of international relations; a similar route is followed by certain contemporary analyses, including some from the Chicago School, with regard to government as a market. In the case of international relations the veneer easily rubs off: Whether or not one follows Lenin's theory of world wars, international readjustments are a function of power, *inter alia*.

Second, the Chicago doctrine must be both intra- and extrasystemically explored with regard to the various alternative ways of institutionalizing a market system, each of which *pro tanto* produces a corresponding notion of optimality. The market system contemplated by the Chicago School is a business system; one could have a worker system with its own rights and social power structure and with its own optimality rationalizations.[6] Such would appear, of course, as "socialism" to some people.

*On Its Own Terms*

The foregoing serves to indicate that, as G.L.S. Shackle wrote of the older "Grand System" of the economics of tranquillity, the Chicago School has operated with a paradigm "in one sense complete and self-sufficient, able, on its own terms, to answer all questions which those terms allowed."[7] The key is the consultation *on its own terms,* the terms manifesting "a belief in a self-regulating, inherently and naturally self-optimizing, stable and coherent economic system" [Shackle 1967, p. 5]. James Buchanan, for example, firmly believes that "order replaces chaos through the spontaneous coordination (Polanyi's good term) of the market. This is, of course, the central message of economic theory, from Adam Smith onwards, and it is, in fact, about all there is to economics" [Buchanan to Samuels, 30 June 1975]. Thus, "when non-individualistic norms are introduced, the domain of economics, as I define the discipline, is abandoned" [Buchanan 1968, p. 188]. The theory manifests the paradigm, on its own terms. The paradigm governs positive and normative considerations, including the definition of the discipline: "A question will be deemed economic only if it can be formulated in terms of the dominant paradigm" [Jalladeau 1975, p. 4]. This is the case, of course, with all normal science [Jalladeau 1975, p. 10], following Thomas Kuhn [1962]. It is the goal of the Chicago School to establish a framework of economic thought and policy which would consider on its own terms and channel in its approved direction all economic analysis and policy. Meaning is paradigm specific, given inter-systemic analysis (which includes knowledge acceptable, albeit in different contexts, to all relevant persons), for all those unable to step outside its own terms.

*Tautology*

It follows that the analytical and policy conclusions of the Chicago School have meaning only (until otherwise proven) within its own doctrinal paradigm and are in fact tautological therewith. "The conclusions are inherent in the premises, and empirical or historical studies become illustrations of the model. They prove the model and in turn are proven by it, while factors that are excluded from the model do not enter into the discussion."[8] The school's methodological and normative individualist conclusions are tautological with its methodological and normative individualist premises and limits. Thus there is no "shortage" at a market clearing price because *shortage* is defined in such a way as to exclude problems encapsulated in other definitions; this is a good example of the systemic limitation of meaning. Another example of tautology is Knight's theory of risk and uncertainty: Not fully testable (although it has scientific use of substantial merit), it nonetheless functions as a rationalization of profit.

Above all, as already indicated, market solutions enabling the capture of gains from trade are projected as optimal because *optimality* is defined in terms of individuals capturing gains from trade; it is defined in terms of market valuation and adjustment, to prove that markets produce optimal results. Conclusions of optimality are tautological with the terms of the paradigm and the injuries, and so forth, allowed to enter it. With optimality so defined, any valuation and adjustment through the market is presumed optimal, and nonadjustment is deemed evidence of the optimality of extant arrangements, to wit: the tautological optimality of doing nothing. All such reasoning is presumptive, with the conclusions giving effect to the premises. (See the quotations at notes 8 and 9 in the Officer and Stiefel review article, chapter 18.) The system is justified on its own terms; only thus can Demsetz reason that "the valuation power of the institution of property is most effective when it is most private" [Demsetz 1964, p. 19].

It is not surprising, then, that there is close correspondence between the theoretical preferences and ideological beliefs, and between the scientific and policy conclusions, of the Chicago School. The policy conclusions are predetermined by and are largely tautological with the conceptual system from which they emerge.[9] Neoclassical economics, perhaps most especially its Chicago variant, is culture bound [Solow 1973, p. 695]. It studies and gives effect to capitalist institutions, and its conclusions are tautological with the accepted premise of the system. What this ultimately means, of course, is that *all* such systems of thought are tautological: They give effect to the first principles, problem definitions, assumptions, testing techniques, and so on, which are built into them. As Walter Adams remarked to me, most true believers "are mostly acolytes reciting the catechism without understanding the philosophical base of the religion." In the case of Chicago the philosophical base is an image of the market system; everything else of importance follows from that. All this someone such as Knight understood.

### Choice

Notwithstanding the obscured selectivity examined below, tautological systems create the impression of closure and determinateness. They paradoxically seem to neglect the reality of social choice while attempting to channel that very choosing. The conflict of the desire for retention of the decision-making character of the subject matter *vis-à-vis* the demands of deterministic models is a profound methodological problem of policy analysis [Samuels 1975b, p. 68.] It arises, for example, in the neoclassical dualism with regard to the firm, which is projected as both powerless passive responder to market forces and dynamic innovator. Which is to say that the fundamental proposition of scarcity producing a necessity of choice (individual and collective) is awkwardly or incompletely handled. Deterministic models of society fail "to come to grips with the aspect of the social process that, more than any other, sets it apart from physical processes—namely, the display of *social volition* as an integral part of the behavioral forces by which the system is set into motion" [Heilbroner 1970, p. 17.] An example of the general phenomenon is the Harrod-Domar growth model which, as Joan Robinson [1962, p. 105] observed, "seems to suggest that the rate of growth of an economy is determined by technical conditions (which within certain limits fix the ratio of capital to income) and the propensity of the population to save. This leaves out of account the most important element in the whole affair—the decisions governing the rate of accumulation of capital." Chicago growth theory, as Paul Strassmann writes in chapter 12, has not fallen for such oversimplification. However, a main thrust of general Chicago doctrine (especially in the law and economics area dealing with domestic government policy) is to establish "a natural course of events in the absence of conscious human interference" [Gonce 1971, p. 87] and to label as artificial and interference all governmental and collective action not included within its terms.[10] This procedure must inevitably canonize selected aspects of the status quo, in part by obscuring the social choice nature of the system.

### Casuistry

There is more to the limits of the Chicago belief system than the inevitable tautology. Also present is the casuistic manipulation of assumptions and definitions to salvage and protect its putative doctrinal principles and overriding premise. The Chicago School, again, is not alone in this: Orthodox economics has been engaged in the effort to make theory safe for the system for generations.[11] Casuistry is a characteristic of perhaps all intellectual systems, secular as well as sacred. The classic examples in orthodox economics have been Say's Law and marginal productivity theory, the history of both of which evidences the bolstering of their respective chains of reasoning and conclusions by additional qualifying assumptions as new theoretical and/or empirical infirmities were adduced against their policy significance.[12] (See Hutt [1974] and Sowell [1972] for recent contributions in regard to Say's Law.)

Apropos the Chicago School the main casuistic exercises have been aimed at defending the integrity of the fundamental "market works" assumption, thereby diminishing the policy significance of the contrary cases whose existence it perfunctorily or limitedly acknowledges. The main efforts have been in the areas of so-called market failure, to wit: externalities. From Knight [1924] through Buchanan and Stubblebine [1962] (with the effect, intended or not, of making Pareto-irrelevant externalities, so-called, irrelevant for policy purposes) and beyond, the Chicago School has manipulated definitions and assumptions to produce chains of reasoning to support market solutions in theory, practice, and normative status. General neoclassical economics has been quite fecund in this area, too: the Viner-Scitovsky treatment of pecuniary and technological externalities functions to remove the former from policy discussion notwithstanding the non-Pareto optimal changes and losses incurred [see Samuels 1972a].

The Coasian analysis, for example, assumes away initial and consequential income distributions and, in general, holds transaction costs at zero, when in fact it is precisely the effect of positive transaction costs to have allocative effects (and effects varying with the transactional system). The Coasian analysis disingenuously manipulates the assumptions to produce its desired, anti-Pigovian, and promarket solution result, whereas a more accurate and less normatively directed treatment would stress the consequences of actual nonzero transaction cost systems. Instead of rights and liability assignment being allocatively neutral (which paradoxically could result in the inference—not drawn by Chicagoans, I believe—that ethical considerations could be left to dictate placement), the literature represents an exercise in rhetoric: the manipulation of deductive reasoning by excluding undesired or unsafe variables from a critical role.[13] This is an example of what Gustav Bergmann meant when he wrote that "the laws proposed and even the variables entering them may well be determined, at least in part and either consciously or unconsciously, by the values of the author. Practically this is, I believe, one of the most important mechanisms by which scientific ideologies establish themselves as social science" [Brodbeck 1968, p. 137]. Here again is a fine example of Joan Robinson's theme of ideology yielding the formulation of scientific hypothesis. But reading the typical Chicago School article (for example, by Demsetz) one concentrates upon the lines of reasoning producing direct and/or indirect support for the virtue and possibilities of market solutions.[14] In the Coasian literature generally, the limits to the Coase rule are recognized in passing, but are often left behind and the rule overgeneralized. The same is true of the typical Chicago treatment of Pareto optimality.

An interesting example which Chicago shares with general neoclassicism (at least to some extent) is a complex posture with regard to the short and long run. The main emphasis is on the former, for example, endogenous determination of consumer preferences can be ignored and wants taken as given for purposes of economic analysis (for several reasons, including testing problems, but also to further the goal of individual freedom, as noted above). But then there is the peculiar conceit (which we all share to a greater or lesser degree) that the economist is "the special custodian for society of the long view in economic matters" [Viner, quoted by Spengler 1974, p. 536; note that Viner also was quoted there as saying that the view "even in troubled periods . . . is entitled not to undisputed dominance but to a full hearing"]. A theory concentrating upon short-run variables cannot readily specialize in the long run, unless it is the special vision of the premise and its propaganda which the economist is to keep in mind. I add only the general Chicago view, further examined below, that the market is intrinsically competitive in a behavioral sense, such that any problem is a short-run aberration.

Another example of how descriptive-interpretive analysis can be and often is readily turned to normative, presumptive optimality account is the Tiebout model of local governments as competing producers of public goods. As Edel and Sclar [1974, pp. 941–42] have written, "the Tiebout model has since become a source of support for local fiscal autonomy." The *statement* is correct—for the model *has become* a source of such support—but notice that a descriptive analysis is thereby given normative or recommendatory force; a descriptive principle is turned into a principle of policy. The Chicago School takes theories which enlighten us with regard to aspects of economic or legal-economic behavior and performance and endeavors to apply them in such a way as to prove the optimality of certain desired arrangements in idealized circumstances. The effort is to find unassailable, or at least persuasive, grounds for belief in its specific theorems and, ultimately, its promarket premise and paradigm.

The casuistry is also indicated by exclusions. For example, inequality of income, wealth, power, and opportunity is regularly omitted, even in areas where both behavior and (especially) performance are profoundly influenced by such asymmetries.[15] As with most "science," unfortunately, single factor explanations dominate, but there is also the consistent circumscription of the dangerous.

Other areas in which doctrines are purveyed by the Chicago School in order to effectuate its normative message include: the quantity theory of money, the Pigou effect, flexible exchange rates, a free market in gold, methodological individualism, the automaticity of markets, the evil of inflation, and others. Notwithstanding the heuristic significance and status of all of these, they seemingly are used to promote and sanction conservative economic policy. Just as the gold standard was advocated by conservatives as, especially, a device for limiting government activism, Chicago theorists seem to advance the quantity theory of money, constant rate of growth of money supply, and flexible exchange rates (whatever their other merits) for this end as well.

There are still other areas: finessing uncertainty (and protection of the market) by treating it as an aspect of market adjustment through "optimal" information theory; conflicting treatment of rights as having to be fully defined or only minimally delineated; fantasies of ubiquitous markets (perhaps, literally, for everything); strategems to defend the market from the charge that it is not competitive [Rotwein 1973b; and see chapter 17]; the careless use of "efficiency" (see chapter 17); manipulation of micro demand theory to obscure learned (endogenous) preferences and the power of firms; finessing discrimination as a social problem; the sidetracking of methodological collectivist considerations to salvage methodological individualism [Tarascio 1975, p. 881]; the narrowing of issues and the definition of relevant reality away from power structure, class distribution, and conflict topics (ostensibly to make the analysis manageable—and these *are* intractible topics); emphasis upon positivism as value free "in principle"; and so on. Of course, the Chicago School is not alone in much of this in economics (witness the historical antagonism to John Stuart Mill's dichotomy of the laws of production and distribution), and it has provided valuable contributions and insights. But the theological tension is greater in the Chicago School than in general neoclassicism, and the efforts typically are somewhat more pointed, seemingly because of their adoption of the task of providing a propaganda for their conception of economic freedom.[16]

Such casuistry is akin to that found in legal practice through the "dis-precedent and promote the desired end. The practice is inevitable in tinguishing" of case precedents in order to salvage a safe doctrine or moral philosophy, wherein values and facts intertwine, and almost any conclusion can be reached if only the correct starting point be found. Mention of the law elicits a further consideration. Individualism is possible only within legal (and moral) rules. Economic activity requires propitious and facilitating legal arrangements. Taking the logic of individualism to its *reductio ad absurdum* denies such rules or change in such rules. Thus one variant of Chicago School doctrine would have these rules determined once and for all time. The view may have some abstract attraction, but it lacks probative value for real world policy analysis. The doctrine protects an otherwise exposed flank in their argument.

The Chicago School also proceeds along two other tracks. First, it seeks optimality in economic exchange, but fails typically to indicate that there is no unique optimum and that the achieved optimum is a partial function of legal and moral rules. This approach tends to function selectively to reinforce status quo moral and legal rules. Second, the school suggestively and informatively presents an economic analysis of the demand and supply type of forces governing the derivation and operation of legal and moral rules. For example, it projects a model of market determination of legal rules and rights in which the latter are produced through manipulations of the legal system by parties seeking the maximization of calculated advantage. This *is* a very important insight, but notice that it gives effect to the impact of unequal economic power—as the work of Bartlett [1973] and others has shown. It carries the logic of neoclassical theory to its necessary conclusions, given the introduction of unequal economic power or asymmetrical economic position.

The Chicago School therefore both rationalizes the actual optimum, giving effect to the status quo rights structure, and the derivation of the status quo rights structure as a matter of market adjustment. It canonizes market adjustments, which, to another way of thinking, is the legitimation of the results of exercising private economic power (through the market and through government). This is the art of casuistry at its finest, whether one agrees or not with its role and conclusions, although one can see how the school must feel that it is only carrying out the logic of its paradigm (the micro model).

Suffice it to say that there are important insights to be derived from all lines of Chicago analysis. The problem, again, is the optimality judgment added to them, all flowing from their systemic premise. The Chicago School engages in such casuistry, it appears, because of its commitment to the defense of its premise and its supporting paradigm. Justification and rationalization, quite aside from explanatory considerations, require the formulation of lines of reasoning in such a way as to articulate and protect the position. Scientific advance is a by-product of the efforts of interested parties; science is nurtured by ideology.

*The Role of High Priest*

The Chicago School has a deep and abiding belief both in the market system and in the necessity for a spirited defense and justification of the system, that is, for a propaganda for economic freedom. To this end it has assumed the self-appointed role of activist legitimizer of the system, undertaking the burden of articulating its case and defending it against all manner of claimed defects and perceived threats. Chicagoans practice a mixture of science, social control, and psychic balm, including myth, all in the service of the explication and canonization of the market. That they also canonize selectively some of the status quo power structure, including its wealth distribution, may not be the intent, but it is the effect of their doctrine and leaves them exposed to criticism.

The Chicago School thus makes a contribution not only to knowledge but also to ceremony. Members see themselves as the true economists, having the gift of faith, steadfast witnesses to the social glory and redemptive power of the market system. Chicagoans are the proselytizers for the market system; they are its "social or moral philosophers" [Knight 1956, p. 146]. They are the evangelists and theologians of economics. The Chicago School appreciates that ideas do have consequences, that what people believe is important for the evolution of the economic system, that we make the economy in our efforts to apprehend it [Shackle 1967, pp. 116, 130].

The self-appointed role is to provide that propaganda for economic freedom through a constant search for the "respectable foundation" [Simons 1948, p. v] for the faith—the manipulation of the myth(s) deemed necessary for the achievement and preservation of a free society as Chicagoans see it. This role is at the level of manifest function for at least some members: "The precious measure of political and economic freedom which has been won through centuries may soon be lost irreparably; and it falls properly to economists, as custodians of the great liberal tradition out of which their discipline arose, to point the escape from the chaos of political and economic thought which warns of what impends" [Simons 1948, pp. 76–77; compare Knight 1932].

Chicago economics, following Knight, is a science infused with a social control idea [Gonce 1972, pp. 549, 550, 551, 554]. Chicago economics is social engineering at its most subtle level. It is part of the social processes which socialize man along certain lines and not others. The Chicago School economist is both investigator and pleader, both observer and participant. The market is not a mere object of study; it is something which must be shown to work, and evidence to the contrary, while admitted, is narrowly and safely circumscribed.

Much criticism and many limits of the Chicago doctrine arise from the myopia of men of system (to use Adam Smith's felicitous phrase[17]) and especially of high priests. Accuracy requires that the thought not be carried too far, but there is a strong tendency to interpret and evaluate the market on its own terms, effecting a closure with regard to fundamentals taken for granted. Again, one senses the hyperbole of the fanatical devotee in order to create an aura of consistency and compulsion.

There is something to be said for the absolutist formulation of the high priest of all persuasions: It contributes to discourse and social control. Yet, the real world, perhaps fortunately, never resembles any one priest's projected fantasies; no real, pure market system exists. But the reality of the high priest role (through a latent and/or manifest function) is a critical limitation upon positive science and should be deliberated (in my view) by members of the profession, whatever the doctrine which the role seeks to proselytize and advance. This is no less warranted because the Chicago School tends to perceive its own role as a *restraining* and not a justifying influence *vis-à-vis* the status quo, that is, as promoting avoidance of stupid and ineffective (however well intentioned) government policies under twentieth-century liberalism.

What I take as the Chicago argument *is* compelling: The world is a normative arena, and we had best not let it go unattended if we desire to safeguard our values. The problem is not quite that simple (and some Chicagoans, perhaps most notably Knight, Simons, and Buchanan, have been aware of that), but at this point I can only state that, although probably inevitable and (perhaps) necessary, the high priest function and role is something I find objectionable. The high priest is playing God, and this is not an acceptable principle of policy for the economics profession. The advocacy of the high priest role is often rationalized through emphasis on the nondeliberative forces, but notice that this is a manifest and not a latent function: The role is deliberative, not nondeliberative. The role of myth and the high priest function in the modern economic system and in and by economics as a discipline is a key question raised by the Chicago School, and surely it is a limit to their doctrine.

The following also should be considered carefully: a tendency toward the authoritarian. Knight's notion of "relatively absolute absolutes" is manifest in Friedman's statement that "no society can be stable unless there is a basic core of value judgments that are unthinkingly accepted by the great bulk of its members. Some key institutions must be accepted as 'absolutes,' not simply as instrumental" [Friedman 1962, p. 167], and in Simons's: "strong government and an elaborate, stable, and confining structure of law" [Simons 1948, pp. 3–4]. I am reminded of Franz Neumann's frequent statement that the liberal state was always as strong as it had to be. Such a state does attempt to inhibit consolidations of social order deemed adverse by, or to, ruling interests. Chicago thought is power thought [Hutt 1936] and not pure description. Chicago practices *Realpolitik* in its efforts to promote its conception of the system. The school reacts against socialism, and so forth, which it sees as a disguised lust for power; yet, the logic of Chicago's role represents much the same thing. And, alas, perhaps absolutism and authority tend toward fascism. Patinkin acknowledged "the deepest contradiction in Knight's view of human society: on the one hand, he regarded individual freedom as a basic value, and recognized that representative democracy was the only way in which a large society of free individuals could govern itself; on the other, he had basic misgivings about the actual workings of the democratic process—and was accordingly deeply pessimistic about its future" [Patinkin 1973, p. 807]. The same idea is found in the AER obituary for Knight: "A profound distrust of democratic politics . . . was joined to an even more profound fear and dislike of all authoritarian systems: Knight was deeply pessimistic on the rationality of all political processes" [Anonymous 1973, p. 1048]. Capitalism, or the market system, is sorely pressured, and its anxious defenders take solace and find friends where they can. Milton Friedman and Arnold Harberger, and by extension the cachet of the Department of Economics at the University of Chicago, have become identified with the junta currently in power in Chile (and Friedman has had connections with the regime in Brazil) [see Frank 1975]. The meaning of this is uncertain; its significance is being debated within the Chicago School. Friedman has lamented the "destruction of personal freedom in Chile" [*Newsweek*, 17 November 1975, p. 90]. From my point of view, the name of the social game is power, and the advertised pacificism of capitalism should not obscure the struggle for control that marks all nations and all systems.[18]

The foregoing places in perspective the Chicago School argument against making interpersonal utility comparisons and playing God. Surely it is both understandable and congenial that the stated values of the Chicago School would lead to a view antagonistic toward prescribing for others: Such is paternalism, the opposite of self-choice, and presumptuous. Yet, notwithstanding Chicago's outcries against aspects of the welfare state, socialism, social reform, and intervention on this ground, the school itself is engaged, and *necessarily so,* in precisely the same activity, however more subtly. The following may be stated, some of which will be elaborated upon below.

First, the Chicago School has its own agenda for government, its own form of interventionism, in promoting *its* ideal form of economy. It would control law as instrumental for the structuring of economic organization, reworking legal and moral rules to facilitate its conception of the market system [see Samuels 1973, p. 537]. Ensconced within its program for revealing the orderly and rational foundations of the economy is an articulation of the set of principles upon which human control of the economy is to be based, a set of uses of government called "laissez-faire" but hardly constituting "minimal" government in any substantive sense.

Second, Chicago doctrine, including both its normative and positive elements, constitutes its own social welfare function, that is, the superimposition of its determined standards, and makes its own interpersonal utility comparisons. This social welfare function and these comparisons cover, *inter alia,* the following: selective judgments about the relevance of non-Pareto optimal changes; a conception of the social order (its own heavenly city) according to which it prescribes for society, which concept is its structuring of radical indeterminancy; selective judgments concerning which and whose preferences count, for example, in presuming certain definitions and assignments of rights and not others; a strategy of gearing policy to increase profit opportunities; a preoccupation with inflation, or, perhaps, an apparent general preference for a mildly falling than a mildly rising price level (which may be conservative economic policy, but is not laissez-faire); an emphasis on efficiency and Pareto optimality (however selectively), that is, a desire to permit only market adjustment contractarian change—after the system is made right; evaluations of institutional arrangements; the ideology of wealth [see Rotwein 1973a] and economic egoism; an emphasis on consumer sovereignty (both in general and with the extant distribution of wealth) *vis-à-vis* planners' or workers' sovereignty; a tendency to emphasize or be used to emphasize aspects of the established distribution of wealth; an emphasis on preference realization through the market rather than through politics [see Goldberg 1974]—once its system is given effect; specific adherence to certain values and ends (including its specific formulation of the free market); an emphasis on the realization of self-interest, and this through a business system (its tendency to define the market system through business arrangements) and through the status quo distribution of wealth governing *pro tanto* whose interests are to be counted; a specification of freedom and control, or coercion, which is full of interpersonal utility and preference comparisons with regard to freedom and exposure to the freedom of others; and so on.

Third, the Chicago School is playing God in its formulation of economics as the economics of the free enterprise or market system and its quest for a propaganda for its conception of economic freedom.

Fourth, the school refuses to play God with regard to individual economic preferences but does so with regard to its prescriptions of institutional structure, thereby governing the formation of the structure of opportunity sets which is so important to the realization of individual economic preferences and welfare. This is to say, in part, that political and economic preferences are treated differently.

Finally, the Chicago School is making a political judgment—a comparison of interpersonal utilities, its own social welfare function—in its apparent decision that the danger to freedom from government is greater than that from the corporate system.

### *Selectivity*

An additional characteristic of Chicago School doctrine should be specifically indicated, although it is implicit in much that has been said. Chicago emphasizes general principles (for example, Pareto optimality), but in practice it applies those principles selectively. It *is* inevitable for general principles to be selectively applied; such is an aspect of the burden of choice. But given the nature of the school's posture, it is important to make this quite clear. The element of selectivity is an important limit to its doctrines. The theoretical and policy analysis of the Chicago School, for all its heuristic and normative value, cannot and is not immediately and directly applied to policy problems or cases without much selective perception and identification of interests and subsidiary values. I believe Chicagoans know this, but their writings often seem to introduce selectivity inadvertently or without specific explicit acknowledgment thereof. They are more interested in the advancement of their general principles and less in the selectivity necessarily involved in their application. The force with which the Chicago School markets its doctrines, and their actual heuristic value, should not blind economists, who generally should beware of the derivation and attribution of policy and descriptive conclusions going beyond the power of their analysis and tools to provide. The Chicago School, no more and no less than any other, provides no conclusive and objective calculus to determine when selective application is "proper" or "improper," for example, whether or not a change is consonant with the "market system," in part because the market system can be instrumented differently.

The Chicago School is selective, *inter alia,* with regard to recognition of regulation and rights as functional equivalents, and similarly as between property and other rights, and therefore recognition of one side or the other in Alpha-Beta rights conflicts [Samuels 1974a]. It is also selective concerning the following: the specification of relevant legal and moral rules [Lowry's chapter 9; Goldberg 1974]; aspects of economic reality included within their models and the manner of their inclusion; recognition of methodological individualist and methodological collectivist elements of economic life; use of data [Strassmann, chapter 12, p. 290]; perception of government, freedom, coercion, externalities, injuries, power, individuals, public, private, responsibility, rights, interference, necessity of power as a check on power, and so on; use of partial equilibrium models; business *vis-à-vis* nonbusiness uses of government; specification of utility (or objective) and other functions; recognition of facets of interdependence; movements from *is* to *ought* with regard to the status quo through selectively adopted implicit antecedent normative assumptions; interests entering into optimality calculations or determinations; preference registration not amenable to market or pecuniary values, although it does emphasize the role of calculations of advantage and market-like adjustment throughout life, including government; invocation of assumptions, for example, assuming individuals know their interests in the market but not (or not always) in politics [Stigler, in Selden 1975, p. 312]; adoption of an ex post, or winner, approach to optimality in interpreting historical rights conflicts outcomes; specification of pluralism, gradualism, and viability of the market system (including its required institutional arrangements); perception and admission of unintended consequences; use of skepticism about government; the addition of optimality analysis to descriptive or formal neoclassical models; specification of status quo or starting points; specification of individualism and social control, that is, the pattern of freedom and control; separation of resource allocation and income distribution; and so on.

In all these respects, and others, the Chicago School contributes to the social valuational process and the manageability of theory and empirical work. The school is conveying its message, a mixture of science and rationalization. Depending upon one's point of view, Chicago's message, and its valuational contribution, is either clarification or obfuscation, promotive or destructive. Chicago economics alone does not produce specific normative conclusions applicable to policy. In each case implicit antecedent norms are added in one way or another. The result is a powerful but limited, however compelling and attractive, approach to policy analysis. The empty boxes of economic theory are given often very congenial but potentially misleading and always selective and normative packaging. That this is true of all schools of economic thought does not vitiate its importance as a limit to Chicago doctrine.

### *Further Significance*

The argument of this chapter has emphasized the dualism of explanation and rationalization, deliberate strategy, the role of myth, the nature of the Chicago school as a religion, its premise, its casuistic and tautological character, its high priest role, its provision of its own social welfare function and interpersonal utility comparisons, and its intrinsic selectivity. These observations permit a deeper and more meaningful understanding of the Chicago School and certain reactions to its doctrines, especially in certain areas.

#### *In General*

The thrust of the present argument leads to some general conclusions about the Chicago School. Its doctrine is a combination of description explanation and prescription, of brilliant insight and artful canonization, and it lends itself to being reduced to stereotype and caricature. Chicago is a school defined as much by its chosen enemies as by its doctrines and stated values. Its censorial, polemical, adversary economics posture, coupled with its assumption of the high priest role, eclipses its own qualifications of its doctrines. Chicagoans lack a concern for, and even obfuscate, distributional, power, class, and conflict considerations. This attitude and the fact that Chicago takes for granted the solutions to problems that are worked out through policy making in the real world, seemingly in order to channel these solutions along desired or acceptable lines, create a distorted view of the deep decision-making process in society concerning whose interests count and how they are defined and made to count.

#### *Methodolgy*

With regard to methodology, several well-known economists, in personal correspondence, have remarked about Milton Friedman: "The economist who could write with such conviction on 'positive' economics is about the most normative economist of all"; similar comments have been made about James Buchanan. There is a fascinating mixture of science (empirical testing) and metaphysics (values) in Chicago doctrine, and Chicagoans blend the roles of scholar and priest, preaching both value-free economic science and wide-ranging policy prescriptions. Selectivity is used in the school's theory construction and testing; its values masquerade as facts, supported by the sentiments with which the policy analysis accords, and its policy making masquerades as science. Positivism is used to cast luster on and reinforce selected aspects of the status quo. Most current Chicagoans neglect certain deep philosophical-epistemological issues raised by Knight and, to some extent, Buchanan. Adherence to much of the school's belief system and many of its policy positions is not a function of verification, but of consonance with its paradigm, a matter of conversion and colligation [Ward 1972, pp. 95–107, 164–67]. Notwithstanding the general disrepute (even within the Chicago School, I think) of paradigm development, the school's contribution of deepest meaning and greatest value has been at this level. Finally, at Chicago methodological individualism becomes or functions to reinforce a selective normative individualism.

*Ideology*

The image of the economy as projected by the Chicago School has a utopian character. Chicago doctrine is both a chastening of, and an apologia for, business, a catechism to preach its relative blamelessness: Chicago doctrine is conservative propaganda. There is a theological or emotional tone to various writings by Chicagoans and their critics. Technical controversies in economics apparently are viewed by Chicago as arising from and as proxies for ideological differences, which differences these controversies also may mask. Finally, radical and other economists seem to regard the role of Chicago School economics as one of obscuring and rationalizing extant hierarchical and elite rule in the name of democracy, freedom, and the market. Thus, Chicago doctrine is a form of social conditioning, providing a spiritual approach to, and therefore reinforcement of, the dominant power groups in society.

*Economic Theory*

In the channeling of theory by ideology, at Chicago economic theory becomes the handmaid of libertarian social philosophy, a projection of and response to the ideological requirements of the system, with values deeply ensconced in the scientific jargon of that theory. Chicago's formulation of the neoclassical paradigm is conservative, in large part through the superimposition of the Pareto criterion; the school compromises or neglects many standard neoclassical assumptions (competition, knowledge and rationality) and thus the empirical and policy limits thereof. Finally, and perhaps especially, there are the Chicago counterrevolutions. First, there is the desire to defuse if not reverse the effects of A. C. Pigou on externality theory, Edward H. Chamberlin and Joan Robinson on the theory of noncompetitive conditions, and John Maynard Keynes—the *bête noire* of Chicago—on a wide range of topics. Second, and of course not unrelated, is Chicago's effort to absorb (and thereby defuse) macroeconomics and microeconomics and monetary theory, thus avoiding the business cycle, fiscal policy, and the specter of wide-ranging governmental activism, and emphasizing the automaticity of the market (and similarly with industrial organization as a specialized field). All these efforts are designed to reverse the standard criticisms of capitalism, namely, the instability of the private sector, economic injustice or inequity, and the concentration of private economic power, in large part by attributing some or all of these ills to government (which others see as a corrective means). This is a brilliant and logical debating technique and not one without some considerable accuracy.

*Government*

Chicagoans seem artificially to separate the economic and the political, the private and the public. There is the paradox of Chicagoans seeing market-like mechanisms in government and seemingly rejecting politics and government as coercive. The school is preoccupied with policy conclusions, in effect an affirmation of Leo Rogin's principle that the meaning of a theory is in its policy implications. Chicago believes that most problems are nonproblems, and the same is true of crises. The school's doctrine is a system of philosophy with which to counter both majoritarian democracy and, as I suggest in my note on socialism, the use of government to restructure the system of power and privilege in society. Finally, Chicago strives to abort all lines of reasoning deemed to open the doors to governmental activism along unapproved lines and, to that effect, to provide a body of theory of government failure with which to counter theories of market failure.

## Conclusion

The late Ben Seligman wrote of Frank Knight: "pure formalism ... merged with political bias to create the narrowest body of economic theory in modern times." He said of Milton Friedman: "a highly sophisticated but still fallacious collection of arguments upholding all the ancient economic verities" [Seligman 1962, pp. 665, 683]. One may accept or reject this view, but in the light of the argument of this chapter, those opinions do not differ too widely from Stigler's words quoted at the beginning of this book, *given* the difference in evaluation. The Chicago School doctrine is brilliant explanation and brilliant propaganda. It is the mix which is so fascinating, regardless of whether or not one agrees with Chicago in whole or in part.

There is a deep and powerful body of Chicago economics which has certain limits. Some are a result of technical considerations, and others are a function of Chicago's self-assumed role as propagator of the faith. Several of the essays in this volume, including part of the following chapter, explore the technical limits, although chapter 17 is primarily concerned with the way in which the current Chicago School excludes certain considerations, and therefore imposes limits upon its doctrinal reach. These limits, which Knight would understand and applaud (except perhaps in their more extreme forms) are nevertheless so prominent in his work and that of others, including the institutionalists, that at least some of the exclusion seems to be executed with the intent, and certainly with the effect, of producing desired normative consequences (a propaganda for economic freedom), as indicated in this chapter.

## *Notes*

1. It is hardly novel to say that Chicagoans are nineteenth-century liberals or twentieth-century conservatives. Not only is this well known, but also they emphasize it themselves. The problem is to examine how this permeates their doctrines.
2. Specification of the rationalization role and its deliberative adoption will disturb some; it has been raised if not emphasized by Breit and Ransom [1971] in their chapters on Knight, Simons, and Friedman, and by Olson and Clague [1971].
3. Perhaps a modern echo of this is found in the brilliant, candid, and correct statement by Friedman that "a common objection to totalitarian societies is that they regard the end as justifying the means. Taken literally, this objection is clearly illogical. If the end does not justify the means, what does? But this easy answer does not dispose of the objection; it simply shows that the objection is not well put. To deny that the end justifies the means is indirectly to assert that the end in question is not the ultimate end, that the ultimate end is itself the use of the proper means" [Friedman 1962, p. 22].
4. Buchanan [1972a] presents a conception of the role of social contract

theory as a necessary myth for our society. In the comment on a paper by David Landes and Richard Posner presented at the 1975 Universities-NBER Conference, Buchanan wrote: "But the normative abstractions that we impose on the actual workings of an imperfect political world are important themselves in placing limits on action." This is the critical role of myths.

5. Following Joseph Schumpeter [1951, pp. 5, 7], as with Marxism, "Chicago" is a religion:

> In one important sense, Marxism *is* a religion. To the believer it presents, first, a system of ultimate ends that embody the meaning of life and are absolute standards by which to judge events and actions; and, secondly, a guide to those ends which implies a plan of salvation and the indication of the evil from which mankind, or a chosen section of mankind, is to be saved.
>
> Observe how supreme art here succeeds in weaving together those extra-rational cravings which receding religion had left running about like masterless dogs, and the rationalistic and materialistic tendencies of the time, ineluctable for the moment, which would not tolerate any creed that had no scientific or pseudo-scientific connotation.

6. Frank Roosevelt quotes Abram Bergson on Pareto optimality:

> It still does not follow however that this is a universally valid precept, or what comes to the same thing, that it is, as often is supposed, a matter of pure logic. The point is that the derivation of the optimum conditions . . . requires a set of valuations not yet specified, namely that a shift in any factor from one use to another does not make any difference from the point of view of welfare, except in respect of the resulting difference in the value of output. In other words, a zero social value is assigned to such phenomena as . . . differences in a worker's attitude toward different jobs (as distinct from different occupations), etc. Only in this case is it rational to determine the allocation of any factor simply on the basis of a comparison of the value of output in different uses. The condition of equality of marginal value productivity, far from being universally applicable, applies only where the foregoing values prevail [Roosevelt 1969, p. 14].

Roosevelt quotes Daniel Bell to the same effect:

> Clearly here is a "value problem." . . . Which "variable" should one seek to maximize, the satisfaction of the immediate work group or the productivity of the company? Stated more generally: Should work be organized so as to increase output and decrease costs and—assuming the benefits are passed on—so that there is a larger product for society? Or should work be or-

> ganized so as to benefit the individuals on the job? Since relative costs are the variables around which our utilitarian calculi revolve, who shall bear the costs, the consumer or the worker?
>
> Historically, the answer of the market society has been that the consumer should benefit. This underlies our concept of efficiency. In a competitive economy how can any single company take on the burden of increased costs unless all competitors do likewise [Roosevelt 1969, p. 16]?

So the Pareto welfare criterion is based not only on "the 'individualistic' assumption that the only arguments that enter into the social welfare function are the individual levels of welfare" [Levenson 1973, p. 737], but also on the recognition of only certain arguments of individual utility functions or of only certain ways for individual utility to be realized. On this, see Mishan's discussion of the consumer bias of the market in chapter 6; on the Chicago School's social welfare function see below.

7. Shackle [1967, p. 4]. Walter A. Morton, writing of models but with a message applicable to paradigms (and appropriately using an assumer approach), argues:

> A theoretical economic model is a purely abstract hypothetical structure limited by its own postulates. By itself, it proves nothing about the empirical world, but only that certain logical relations hold within the model's assumptions and conclusions. The conclusion may or may not be true of the real world. That is a matter for factual evidence. If, however, one chooses to believe without any evidence or even without sufficient evidence that the model represents reality, then for such a true believer it does. Belief is not truth. Truth, as distinguished from mere internal consistency, depends upon evidence showing the model's consonance with reality. This, the model, by itself, cannot provide and does not purport to provide for any who are able to distinguish between hypothetical and categorical or stochastic judgments. These belong to econometrics [Morton 1971, p. 21].

8. Fusfeld [1974, p. 911]. Roberts [1975, p. 419] recognizes "that verbal analytical arguments, like all theorizing, involve essentially a tautological restatement of the assumptions in a manner which serves to clarify their otherwise unperceived implications."
9. I say "largely" because there is, as I will show below, considerable selectivity of specification possible and practiced within the system's application. Breit and Ransom [1971, pp. 200, 206, 209, 221, 229–30, and 252–53] are unusually candid and lucid on how laissez-faire philosophy and neoclassical economic theory in Chicago doctrine go hand in hand.
10. The choice character of the subject matter arises in an interesting manner in projecting possible reactions to this essay. A strong adverse response, suggesting fanaticism, would tend to confirm the theological characterization given here. But one characteristic of high priest reac-

tions is to minimize public discussion of topics deemed unsafe or to minimize attention to critical lines of reasoning. This reaction, too, tends to confirm the interpretation. But where both a behavior and its opposite are possible under a theory, it is impossible to reject the theory. My point is not that the Popperian criterion may not adequately deal with the social world, although that may be correct, but to emphasize the choice character of the subject matter.

11. See the statements by General Francis A. Walker, discussing what he called "the aristocratic economics of the early part of the century": "I don't think that I exaggerate when I say that, among those who deemed themselves the guardians of the true faith, it was considered far better that a man should know nothing about economic literature, and have no interest whatever in the subject, than that, with any amount of learning and any degree of honest purpose, he should have adopted views varying from the standard that was set up." Ronald Meek, discussing the writings of the Ricardian apologists, has said: "Their fundamental approach, in other words, was determined by a belief that what was socially dangerous could not possibly be true" [both quoted in Samuels 1966, p. 91, n. 126].
12. Seeing what assumptions are necessary to prove a theorem is a fine intellectual or analytical exercise. When made in a policy context, however, it smacks of contrivance: a way of assuming away critical problems or limits.
13. For a critique of the Chicago doctrine that transaction costs should be minimized, see chapter 19 by Allan Schmid. I have discussed this elsewhere in detail [Samuels 1974a], and see Lowry's chapter 9.
14. For an analysis opposite to the Coasian, see Hunt and d'Arge [1973, 346–470].
15. On the "neglect" of distributional inequalities, see Bartlett [1973]; Goldberg [1975, pp. 240–41]; Buchanan and Samuels [1975, p. 34 and passim]; and Bowles and Gintis [1975].
16. To again return to my concern, I suppose that to say these things will inevitably appear to be taking a negative judgmental position. I can only say that I am not.
17. As Adam Smith pointed out,

> the man of system . . . is apt to be very wise in his own conceit, and is often so enamoured with the supposed beauty of his own ideal plan of government, that he cannot suffer the smallest deviation from any part of it. He goes on to establish it completely and in all its parts, without any regard either to the great interests or to the strong prejudices which may oppose it: he seems to imagine that he can arrange the different members of a great society with as much ease as the hand arranges the different pieces upon a chess-board; he does not consider that the pieces upon the chess-board have no other principle of motion besides that which the hand impresses upon them; but that, in the great chess-board of human society, every single piece has a principle of motion of its own, altogether different from that

which the legislature might choose to impress upon it" [Smith 1966, pp. 342–43].

18. There are other considerations raised by the high priest function. First, the role suggests the point posed by Simons concerning scrupulous detachment and dispassionate study:

> Democracy, as viewed by libertarians, is basically a process of government by free, intelligent discussion. It is a means for promoting discussion of obtrusive social problems and for achieving continuous improvement of the moral order through experimental action-out-of-discussion. . . . It also implies, at best, a continuing process of relevant discussion and inquiry among professional truth-seekers or academic problem-solvers, who, though scrupulously detached from active politics and from factional affiliations, subtly and unobtrusively guide or arbitrate political debate by their own discussions. Effective discussion presupposes an elaborate division of labor—between agitators and dispassionate students, between debaters and inquirers, between specialists and philosophers, between political tacticians and statesmen; and, at the highest levels, it presupposes hierarchies of competence, based on the standards of many intellectual disciplines, with groups shifting from the status of arbiter-authorities to that of laymen as different problems arise for discussion [Simons 1948, p. 8].

Knight, too, was somewhat torn by the requisites of free discussion, seemingly having to include its limitation in terms of scope and depth—the latter (and I do not intend to be gratuitous here) characterizing the doctrines of the contemporary Chicago School.

Second, Strassmann, in chapter 12, suggests that "a doctrinaire insistence that markets are the quintessence of efficiency, justice, logic, and inevitable to boot, is not the way to cultivate them in the face of equally doctrinaire opposition." He may or may not be correct in this. It seems to me that the Chicagoans act as if they were attempting to counter extremism on the other side, to force the balance toward their end of the policy spectrum. What is more relevant, this raises the possibility of the dialectic of an Hegelian cunning of reason [Avineri 1972, p. 232] and the eventual (but intended) rise of a left-wing dictatorship following the lead of the present regime. See the discussion of Chile in the text.

The phenomenon was recognized by Knight: "It is along this line that eighteenth- and nineteenth-century liberalism went to an extreme that has provoked a reaction which threatens to engulf all freedom, and justice too, in the modern conception of it, if not to destroy civilization" [Knight 1956, p. 278].

Third, along a different track, the Hegelian result might involve the unintended raising of fundamental questions: the production of debate on issues felt, perhaps, by some best left untouched if not actively quieted.

Fourth, the high priest role (or the general postulate and premise) of the Chicago School is essentially Platonist: revising the system in accordance with a (and I stress the "a") rationalization of itself.

Fifth, recognition of the high priest function raises the question of whether *economics* is a policy science concerned with itself advising the choice of the best or optimal policy alternative. For example: "Economics is a policy science; its ultimate concern is to be able to choose from the set of attainable states of the economic system the 'best' in some defensible sense" [Levenson 1973, p. 736]. Many economists have this view. Is economic science in charge of the economy? In a "free market" system?

Sixth, the high priest function appears to explain the seeming paradox of Friedman's passionate dislike if not hatred of politics coupled with his passion for public arena participation.

Seventh, the Chicago School sees itself, I think, as heterodox dissent from liberal economic orthodoxy. Among other things, this must be juxtaposed to the almost theological concern for the foundations of order held by Knight, Buchanan, and other Chicagoans. But Knight also recognized that "there is no more important prerequisite to clear thinking in regard to economics itself than is recognition of its limited place among human interests at large" [Knight 1951a, p. 3]. He also stressed that "probably the most important fact which students are not made adequately to realize in economics teaching is the utter impossibility of giving anything approaching a 'complete' account of the subject, and the resulting necessity of drastic selection in discussing it" [Knight 1935, p. 803].

Finally, Knight's antagonism toward the absolutist tendencies of religion and religionists is well known [see Patinkin 1973, pp. 806–807 and references given]. Knight balanced his relatively absolute absolutes with an ethical pluralism (the belief that ethical values can coexist in a state of contradiction). Thus the antinomian tendencies of current Chicago School members has some source in Knight himself, although he was relatively less doctrinaire.

# 17

# Further Limits to Chicago School Doctrine

*Warren J. Samuels*

### *The Problem of Order*

The problem of order in any society, following Joseph Spengler [1948], is that of the continuing conflict of autonomy, coordination, continuity, and change. Stated somewhat differently, it is the problem of freedom versus control, including hierarchy versus equality, and continuity versus change. In one respect it is the problem of the organization and control of the economic system, including the distribution of power; in another, it is the creation, revision, and balancing of values to guide organization and conduct. Order is a process, not a condition; it is something which is continually worked out, not achieved once and for all time. Most if not all social and moral philosophy, including speculation and theory with regard to the economic role of government, tends to presume a specific resolution or concept of the "problem" of order. To be ideological in this context is to take a position on the elements of the problem of order.

The Chicago School does not "neglect" the problem. Rather, its doctrines constitute a particular approach, in effect providing for a system of social control and social change. As Frank Knight wrote, "the problem is to find the right proportions between individualism and socialism and the various varieties of each, and to use each in its proper place" [Knight 1951b, p. 58]. Each element of the problem of order is given, more or less ambiguously, a particular formulation. The doctrine supports a certain type of pattern of freedom and control, hierarchy and equality, and continuity and change, that is, those characteristic of the market system with its incentive-reward process, role of authority, and definition of success and conception of identity, as perceived by Chicagoans.

The Chicago School is prescriptive ultimately in its attempt to legitimize its approach to the problem of order. It is descriptive largely to the degree to which the existing order fits the mold of its ideology, but also to the extent to which the behavior processes which it describes (constrained maximization and market or market-like adjustments) characterize all economic systems.

Its propaganda role implies the preaching of the imagery and mythology of freedom, voluntarism, and caution against displacing established property interests. Yet its doctrine inevitably acknowledges the inevitability of control, of methodological and normative collectivist forces larger than and transcending individual choice, and of freedom only within the larger pattern of freedom and control (opportunity set structure). It proposes its own system of freedom and control and mode and direction of continuity and change, including the market as a system of creative destruction. The propaganda role, however, obscures or eclipses all this.

The propaganda role also eclipses certain possibilities of a broader and more open analysis of the problem of order. It channels the study of organization and control of the economic system (including legal-economic interrelations) in accordance with its normative approach, including diminishing the importance of the hierarchy versus equality issue.

The Chicago School envisions market and market-like adjustments as *the* central mode of order, yet it seemingly neglects the institutional and other bases of the market. It fails to integrate two areas where it has made important contributions: the reaching of optimality through market adjustments within existing legal rules and definition and assignment of rights *and* the constrained maximization adjustment of the legal rules themselves. Such an integration produces what I call the joint determination of optimality conditions and the rights structure within and with respect to which optimal results are specific. Explicit consideration needs to be included of the role of the economic power structure operating through the market and through government in an extremely wide process of creative destruction. The Chicago School is preeminently concerned (in addition to providing a defense for the system against what it perceives as government intervention) with the allocation of everything, as it were, but power. As I have repeatedly indicated, the Chicago School neglects power only in that it has a certain approach to its organization. This is an ideologically imposed limit to an otherwise actually and potentially powerful analysis, and it clouds deep social decision making with regard to who counts, that is, the factors and forces governing the distribution and determination of economic welfare.

This is the burden of Chicago's establishmentarian approach to the problem of order. It is a variant of conservative social philosophy, a legitimate and important position and contribution in any society, whether the position is in favor of continuity per se, the status quo power structure, or caution as a general rule.

Further attention should be given at this point to Knight's deep concern with the problems raised by the liberation of the mind from the nondeliberative shackles of past systems of social control. The basic subject, and the basic problem, "is the right to question currently accepted beliefs and patterns of conduct, established by custom and enforced by authority, and to promote changes." According to Knight, "the problem is to find the best compromise between freedom and order—how much to leave to individual free choice and voluntary agreement versus what limits to set by enforced general rules." From his point of view, "the *supreme* value is *order*. This is of the essence of any society, prior to freedom and all others. The question is 'what' order, and how much—since any rigid order excludes all freedom, and all intelligent action, as such" [Knight 1960, pp. 125, 104, 16]. Henry Simons wrote of "responsible freedom" [Simons 1948, p. 8], but individual freedom for Knight was also an absolute value. The explanation is that freedom is a function of the system and its specific structure of freedom and of exposure to the freedom of others, something which Chicago propaganda obscures. The greatest paradox is not what the Chicago School "neglects," for it *is* taking a position on those matters, but that through its efforts to create a propaganda for economic freedom the current Chicago School may well contribute a threat to the *order* which Knight felt was prior to freedom and all other values.

### *Methodological and Normative Individualism*

Chicago's form of methodological individualism is a microcosm of its doctrine with respect to substantive positive content, normative message, and the limits of both. The school interprets *methodological* individualism to mean that individual preferences are to count, a very ambiguous formulation which is as normative as it is methodological in meaningfulness; moreover, it really does not say much in either regard (although it is a professional code term for certain attitudes and a particular paradigm). Such a view begs the reality that individual preferences count in *all* economic systems: In the market system the phrase takes on a particular meaning, but it always is individuals whose preferences count. Moreover, the significant question is not whether individual preferences generally stated are to count, but *which* individuals' preferences are to count and by what means. The market is only *one* means of registering individual preferences, with its own weighting system(s). A more heuristically valuable taxonomy is one in which by *methodological individualism* is meant the view that meaningful knowledge is best or more appropriately derived through the study of individuals. *Methodological collectivism* would be defined as the study of group organizations, forces, processes, and/or problems, and *normative* individualism and collectivism would mean the more or less ambiguous ideologies usually connoted by "individualism" and "collectivism." It is my view that the Chicago School doctrine only selectively uses the methodological individualist approach, that it includes methodological collectivist elements, and that its methodological individualism functions to promote its variant of normative individualism.

One problem involves the recognition of methodological collectivism. A standard criticism leveled at neoclassical economists and Chicagoans, for example, in their adverse reaction to John Kenneth Galbraith's notion of a revised sequence and related Veblenian ideas, such as the endogenous determination of preferences, is the following:

> The psychology of the individual consumer is taken to be not only fundamental but also *given,* that is, its explanation is not considered by the economists. The neoclassical economist assumes that individual consumer preferences come from someplace—from God or innate instincts perhaps—but never considers how society shapes those preferences. It is merely assumed that the highest goal of a well-functioning economy is to follow consumer preferences, not to question their origin. They then proceed to show how consumer preferences in a capitalist economy do indeed determine the prices and amounts produced of all things [Sherman 1975, pp. 244–45].

This view is, I think, a fairly accurate representation of contemporary neoclassical, and especially Chicago School, economic thought, at least insofar as formal economic theory is concerned.

Yet Frank Knight was quite aware of the methodological collectivist (and contrived) character of relevant economic phenomena. Knight will be quoted (from publications spanning his long intellectual career) at some length to establish the basis for the argument to follow, which also rests upon the assumption that current Chicagoans "know their Knight." (See also Patinkin [1973, pp. 796, 799, 803, 804].) In Knight's view, the individual is both determined and constrained by larger forces; voluntary choice takes place only within a larger, and indeed dominating, system of social controls of various types. There really is not much individual freedom and voluntary choice. The individual is not given, but is an artifact:

> Such desires as people have for goods and services are not their own in any original sense, but are the product of social influence of innumerable kinds and of every moral grade, largely manufactured by the competitive system itself [Knight 1951b, p. 235].

> Moreover, the freest individual, the unencumbered male in the prime of life, is in no real sense an ultimate unit or social datum. He is in large measure a product of the economic system, which is a fundamental part of the cultural environment that has formed his desires and needs, given him whatever marketable productive capacity he has, and which largely controls his opportunities. . . . It is plainly contrary to fact to treat the individual as a *datum* [Knight 1951b, pp. 49–50].

> The form of organization also goes far to determine what is to be wanted, and to mould the attitudes of persons toward their work and toward each other [Knight 1951b, p. 102].

> The limitations of individualism are particularly obvious from the standpoint of economic analysis. The theory of market competition takes individuals as given. . . . In sociological terms it may almost be said that the individual is unreal; any nation or other society which acts as a unit in external or internal policy is a complex of "institutions"—traditions, knowledge or belief, and common-interest groupings, rather than an organization of independent individuals. Our "individualistic" society would be more descriptively called "familistic" and—as it has worked out in the past century—nationalistic and "classistic." The individual is not a datum, and social policy cannot treat him as such [Knight 1947, p. 383].

Individual freedom, rationality, and autonomy are rather limited.

> Social order cannot be maintained, especially on the scale demanded by modern technology, in the absence of a *social* religion, in contrast with one of individual "freedom" and "self-expression" [Knight 1951b, p. 320].

> A free society cannot at all get rid of either tradition or authority; the freedom of the individual—besides being limited by his character, a set of habits built up in the milieu of a tradition—is mainly that of choosing the authority he will respect and follow, that is, his boss [Knight 1960, p. 166].

> The essential fact is freedom, or creative activity. But freedom is like other traits of human nature in that it is created by a social situation or, in more technical terms, a complex of institutions. This also sets limits to freedom. The supreme paradox of man, in our civilization, is that he is an individual—unique, creative, and dynamic—yet is the creature of institutions which must be accounted for in terms of historical processes. Nothing could be more false historically than the notion that men are naturally free and equal, or even that they naturally have a right to freedom. In the light of history as a whole, the natural state of man is to live imbedded in a "crust of custom," in which most of his activities, thoughts, and feelings are determined by established patterns [Knight 1947, p. 305].

> The great bulk of individual conduct, bodily and mental, must be conformable to established patterns as a condition of the individual's own effective functioning, specifically as a "free" individual; and this is more pronouncedly true of that part of his conduct which is properly called "social" [Knight 1956, p. 141].

Voluntary choice is thus quite restricted.

> Conscious activity plays a highly various, problematic, and, on the whole, rather limited role. The distinctive interpretive conception would rather be habit, formed in the individual and transmitted in the group by unconscious imitation [Knight 1956, p. 149].

> All rational freedom and the higher life are as much dependent on conduct itself being mostly mechanical as they are on a margin of independent internal determination which makes complete prediction not only impossible (as it is everywhere, even in the best physical laboratory) but also a contradiction in thought [Knight 1956, pp. 239–40].

Contrary to the adverse reactions of the current Chicago School to others' stress upon methodological facets of the economy, I conclude that the school not only holds certain normative individualist values while maintaining a methodological individualist posture, but also that it recognizes the existence, if not the overriding existence, of methodological collectivist forces. For example, Chicagoans realize that resource allocation is only proximately a function of market forces and substantively and ultimately a function of deeper methodological collectivist variables and forces explicitly excluded from their system. Specifically, the Chicago School recognizes (as ultimately governing but largely exogenous to their system) the following: the economy is more than the market; the market is a function of institutions (as well as institutions being a function of market-like adjustments); there are nonmarket adjustment sources of institutional innovation; institutions govern the structure of power operating within, through, and upon the market, including the calculations of costs and benefits; institutions impose limits upon the set of feasible market and policy alternatives; voluntary exchange takes place only within and gives effect to a larger system of institutions and power relations; institutions channel the market and individual choice, governing the weighting of individuals' preferences; property rights are a dependent variable; there are profound limits upon individual freedom imposed, for example, by the opportunity set structure, wealth distribution, law, morals, custom, and social structure; preferences, tastes, and the form and direction of welfare identification and maximization are endogenously generated; the extant structure of power governs the operation of the economy, including resource allocation; the definition of private and public output is a function of the structure of power; social class and conflict characterize the operation of the economy; proper legal and other institutions are necessary to make the market work; there has been an organizational revolution; man is the chief product, as well as producer, of social forces; the reality of social order and societization; the economic system is a blend of intertwined public and private phenomena, that is, of phenomena generally each of which is a mix of private and public elements or aspects; systemic change exists and is endogenously produced; the critical role of power is associated with psychodynamic variables in governing the evolution of the system, including economic growth and development; opportunity sets and power structures are endogenously generated; the morality of self-interested behavior is specified in terms of middle-class values; individual consent is only within the particular system of social control, in other words, individual choice not only is within the composition and structure of opportunity sets but also "the individual in a materialistic community may be formally 'free' to follow many different paths, but he is largely conditioned to follow those paths that bring money rewards" and such "materialism manifestly has the impact of a 'collectivist' force" [Rotwein 1973a, p. 292]; ubiquitous social choice is exercised (both over and through institutions) governing who counts; there is ubiquitous coercion in society; the system of social control enables and governs the operation and performance of markets and the market system; there are preferences which are not amendable to market registration; the social system is the foundation of bargaining and mutual adjustments in the market; and, *inter alia,* the type and size of government is endogenously determined. There is obvious overlapping in the above, and many terms would have to be carefully defined in an analytical inquiry, but I suggest that these and other methodological collectivist facets of economic activity are understood and recognized by the Chicago School.

Nonetheless, the school restricts the scope of its admitted variables and the length of its causal chain. It does this certainly to make its analysis manageable, but also to exclude *methodological* collectivism in order to permit *methodological* individualism to promote *normative* individualism. Although it selectively excludes methodological collectivist phenomena (after all, the market, prices, legal and moral rules, and rights are such phenomena), and although it does examine methodological phenomena from a methodological individualist perspective (for example, government), Chicago primarily seeks to go from methodological individualism to normative individualism, that is, from the individual to individualism. This is a common conceptual bridge [Bergmann, in Brodbeck 1968, p. 136], with individualism defined in terms of selective status quo arrangements. The Chicago School doctrine is a body of theory and policy which takes the system, and its conditioning of individuals, for granted and would function largely to replicate that system. On the very methodological collectivism which it denies, it takes a position, and this treatment serves as a major limit to its analysis and policy conclusions.

The same Frank Knight who argued that the rationality assumption was necessary to promote a free economic order [Knight 1956, p. 25] also wrote: "The idea of a purely individualistic order is a logical device, necessary to separate for study the tendencies of individualism from those of socialism" [Knight 1951b, p. 47n]. The same Milton Friedman who advocated the myth of productivity ethics also wrote: "The final distribution of income and wealth under the full operation of this principle may well depend markedly on the rules of property adopted" [Friedman 1962, p. 162], even going so far as to suggest that perhaps, "in many cases, the existence of a well specified and generally accepted definition of property is far more important than just what the definition is" [Friedman 1962, p. 26]. Methodological collectivism is recognized but selectively invoked; and its invocation, like that of the overriding methodological individualism, functions to promote the Chicago variant of normative individualism. The Chicago School prefers to treat each individual as a "self-contained globule of desire" [Veblen 1948, p. 233]. Recognizing that voluntary choice and therefore resource allocation are a function of larger forces and factors, however, Chicagoans hold ideas—not given prominent display in their propaganda for economic freedom—consonant with Clarence Ayres's proposition:

> The object of dissent is the conception of the market as the guiding mechanism of the economy or, more broadly, the conception of the economy as organized and guided by the market. It simply is not true that scarce resources are allocated among alternative uses by the market. The real determinant of whatever allocation occurs in any society is the organizational structure of that society—in short, its institutions. At most, the market only gives effect to prevailing institutions. By focusing attention on the market mechanism, economists have ignored the real allocational mechanism [Ayres 1957, p. 26].

It appears to me that this ignorance is the presumably intended effect of the myth of the market as allocator of resources. By focusing attention upon the market, other and deeper issues are avoided, all of which is deemed necessary in order to promote the market itself, if nothing else. In the Chicago School doctrine exist the projected ideals of autonomous individual choice and the market mechanism, coupled with a knowledge that these are not and cannot fully be the case. There is the continued Knightian dualism of pure *a priori* theory (more or less modified by Friedman's positivism) and economic behavior conditioned by custom, institutions, and power structure. Nowhere is this clearer than in the case of endogenously determined preferences, yet it is pervasive in Chicago doctrine.

The assessment is inescapable that the Chicago School's presumptive optimality conclusions are based on a narrow and selective methodological individualism. Their view takes for granted the terms on which the social consensus[1] (recognized and emphasized by Knight, Friedman, and Buchanan as so fundamental)—and all the other methodological collectivist processes noted above—constrains the nature and structure of the economic system. Chicago's use of methodological individualism constitutes a fundamental, pervasive, and profound limit to the meaning and probative significance of its substantive analysis and policy conclusions. Because of methodological collectivism, its explanatory value and its support for normative individualism are severely limited, with only more or less slight nonnormative foundation. Its conclusions are restricted to the variables and terms of its model of market adjustment. It simply is inaccurate to say that the market allocates resources. To do so is only to give effect to a limited range of variables, that is, to state a tautology. The market is seen to allocate resources because that which operates through the market is excluded, although apparently understood. Voluntarism, too, is extremely limited by institutions, on which more below.

It is incomplete to say that "indeed, a major aim of the liberal is to leave the ethical problem for the individual to wrestle with. The 'really' important ethical problems are those that face an individual in a free society—what he should do with his freedom" [Friedman 1962, p. 12]. As true as this is, it must be supplemented with *effective* recognition that the scope of choice for the individual—the scope within which the individual exercises freedom—is a function of the larger opportunity set and power structures of society. Similarly, it is misleading to say that "any form of coercion is inappropriate" [Friedman 1962, p. 22], when coercion is ubiquitous, and the problem is to choose between coercions and between systems and structures of social control and power, as Chicagoans versed in Knight so well know. Freedom and voluntary choice exist only within moral and legal rules. By invoking methodological individualism in support of normative individualism, Friedman and other Chicagoans are able to object to introducing notions of social responsibility in business, when in reality what is involved is only a change of the moral and legal rules. One cannot use methodological individualist analysis to evaluate legal change, except in a highly presumptuous and selective fashion. The effect of all these Chicago reasonings is to selectively replicate and reproduce the status quo.

Chicago School doctrine is limited by the fact that although it recognizes methodological collectivist forces and indeed invokes them selectively, its arguments along this line are used to support selectively normative individualist conclusions which beg critical methodological collectivist considerations. The Chicago School, in its formal and policy analysis, assumes autonomous individuals and a free market, whereas the real individual and market are social products, and it is their aspects as social products which are at stake in questions of public policy. On the basis of the assumption of autonomous individuals, however, the school selectively opposes applications and exercises of methodological collectivist processes, which inevitably form the individual, as *violative of individualism*. In doing so, the school is itself participating in these methodologcal collectivist processes: irony of ironies! Such opposition involves inadequate description, uses equivocal normative assumptions (equivocal, not incorrect), is highly selective in its recognition of social control and its ends, and tends to reinforce selective aspects of the status quo power structure. The probative value of such opposition is highly limited: methodological individualist conclusions supporting normative individualist policies which acknowledge but finesse methodological collectivist processes raise the very issue on which they pretend to take a conclusive position. They may be "correct," but only for essentially normative reasons. One cannot study the mechanics and consequences of individual choice and on that basis alone counsel that individual choice is desirable, or that such and such social processes are desirable, or that certain legal changes are undesirable.[2] Methodological individualism cannot properly or conclusively support normative individualism without begging serious questions of methodological collectivism as well as of normative individualism and collectivism. The Chicago School doctrine tends to do all this, seemingly largely because of its dual function as explanation and rationalization. But the analytical and policy significance of its largely normative individualist doctrines are thereby severely limited.

### *Deliberative and Nondeliberative Decision Making*

In addition to these methodological individualism/collectivist problems, there is considerable ambiguity and tension in the Chicago School's position on deliberative *vis-à-vis* nondeliberative decision making. Warren Gramm's chapter evaluates contemporary Chicago doctrine as being the former, in contrast with Hayek's emphasis upon nondeliberative decision making. Hayek's famous and somewhat compelling argument, centering on ignorance as a limit to deliberative collective action and reform of institutions, is also found throughout Knight's writings. To Knight the problem of liberal and democratic society was whether it could survive the liberation of the mind from the constraints of the nondeliberative forces of social control [Knight 1960]. Thus Gonce reminds us of the limits of Knight's tendencies toward institutionalism: "Knight breaks with institutionalism for many reasons. One is because he believes it focuses on deliberately contrived rather than spontaneous or natural institutions" [Gonce 1972, p. 552, n. 44]. Throughout his career Knight stressed nondeliberative over deliberative forces and processes. (See Patinkin [1973, pp. 801, 804–807].) He was often highly explicit as to whether (or how much) open discussion of certain subjects could be borne by society [Knight 1932, p. 441; 1951b, p. 352]. To even pose certain questions "is morally identical with denial and attack" [Knight 1932, p. 448] and to open the door to change. Yet, in 1950, in his AEA Presidential Address, Knight could say: "I incline to the side of 'the slow and silent forces,' slow as in all conscience they are—and though time is fleeting" [Knight 1956, p. 281] and in 1960 could say: "The future can no longer be left to the 'slow and silent forces' of history" [Knight 1960, p. 118].

One not unexpectedly finds, then, a complex blend of deliberative and nondeliberative ideas, themes, and prescriptions in contemporary Chicago thought, a mixed bag of doctrinal positions and stands whose probative significance as both description and, especially, policy is at least selective and at best ambiguous. Listed below, in no particular order, are the elements to be found: emphasis upon subconscious rational maximizing in noneconomic areas of life; stress upon the rational and deliberative in description of and prescription for government policy; belief in the necessity for common values nondeliberatively accepted and held; even more general belief in the virtues of nondeliberative over deliberative policy making and change, although paradoxically such a manifest function treatment of nondeliberative forces tends to convert them to deliberative status; emphasis upon and, of course, legitimation of deliberative decision making in the market; prescription of nondeliberative change coupled with emphasis upon and practice of deliberative study of nondeliberative change, also tending to convert the nondeliberative into the deliberative; caution against excessive faith in deliberative action; the school's own policy activism, perhaps in part brought on by the activism of others; the school's own deliberative critique of certain institutions whose origins were, at least in part, nondeliberative; and emphasis upon deliberatively induced cultural change as a prerequisite for economic devlopment.

In regard to these elements there is, as one would expect, selective invocation of deliberative and nondeliberative decision making, with resulting ambiguity. There is a tension, for example, between the school's contemporary stress upon both predictive power and the importance of unintended consequences (selectively perceived and emphasized). The world is, of course, a blend of deliberative and nondeliberative decision making, and one would expect any adequate body of social theory to reflect that fact. The Chicago School is distinguished, however, by relatively dogmatic emphasis on now one and then the other doctrine, as well as by its departure from the Hayekian-Knightian emphasis upon the nondeliberative, perhaps in part caused—paradoxically—by its self-assumed high priest role. The Chicago School today thus seems to be a good example of the problems caused by the liberation of the mind as perceived by one, such as Knight, who stresses the importance of the predominance of nondeliberative decision making. It is ironic that capitalism, or the market system, has nurtured this habit of deliberative or rational decision making, which has spread into the evaluation of hitherto nondeliberative areas (a phenomenon far more important, in my view and possibly Knight's than the ostensible alienation of certain intellectuals stressed by Hayek, Mises, Friedman, and Buchanan). Capitalism may thus (as Kenneth Boulding has perceived) overly encourage the exchange system at the expense of the integrative system, thereby destroying (in the view of some, at least) the very foundations of capitalism itself [Heilbroner 1975, p. 76].

Possibly the greatest paradox of the current Chicago School is its combination of conservative and establishmentarian doctrines with its threat to the established order through its demythicizing of certain institutions. In its stress upon the role of materialist constrained maximizing in governmental, religious, and other institutions—which, to repeat, is an important analytical contribution—the school is piercing the veil of important institutions. By (more or less accurately) showing the workings of market or market-like forces in the operation of social control institutions, Chicago is destroying myths deemed by many (including Buchanan) as necessary to the existence and functioning of the market system itself and thereby opening up to fundamental inspection, questioning, and attack certain arrangements which some best consider left alone. By showing the extent to which calculations of advantage pervade society, including its moral and legal foundations—and thereby peddling the virtues of its market-mechanism model—the Chicago School may be even more revolutionary, albeit in a more subtle way, than Karl Marx but to the same effect, although this is no part of their intention (except insofar as they desire to question certain twentieth-century liberal trends).[3] Paradox aside, it would be truly ironic if the Chicago School, through its attempts to extend the domain of its model and its efforts to further the rationalization of the system, should contribute to the weakening of the very system it advocates by promoting the substitution of deliberative for ostensibly nondeliberative decision making, that is, by bringing the deliberative element in the latter out in the open, a process I personally commend. Too much, of course, can be made of this threat. While it is relevant and interesting, I would stress the selectivity, and ambiguity, of the Chicago School on the question of deliberative versus nondeliberative decision making in society.

The great question posed by the foregoing is one recognized by Knight: How much change can a society endure? Capitalism itself tends to produce waves of creative destruction, generating problems which in and of themselves and through attempts at solution tend to weaken the system (at least in the view of some). If society cannot handle too much change at once, one wonders how well it could cope with the adoption of the Chicago School agenda for social reform to rehabilitate the market system in the face of what it perceives as accumulated twentieth-century liberal illness. The fact that Chicago considers such governmental action negative does not vitiate its governmental status, nor does it obviate or mitigate the shaking up of society which would ensue.

There are dangers both from an absolute and uncritical acceptance of the status quo and from an absolute and uncritical piercing of the veils and masks of society. Moreover, one person's necessary mask (or security blanket) is another's wart. Hayek's dictum applies to both: "Until we have learnt to recognize the proper limits of reason in the arrangement of social affairs, there is great danger that in trying to force on society what we think is a rational pattern we may smother that freedom which is the main condition for gradual improvement" [Hayek 1967, p. 95]. Hayek is largely correct in this, although the point should not be elevated to an overriding principle of policy. (Also, Hayek is trying to work out his own fortifications for the doctrine of conservatism, and his conception of freedom is equivocal.) The current Chicago School is obviously not of one mind on this,[4] but it is hardly thoroughly Hayekian, as Gramm points out so well in chapter 7. One further problem also involves the nature and degree of "authority" acceptable in order to maintain the market or capitalist system.

### *Rationality, Maximization, Optimality, and Related Topics*

In discussions here and elsewhere [Samuels 1972a, 1974a, 1974d, 1975b; see also Schmid 1974 and below] I have explored many of the limits of the optimality analysis of contemporary welfare economics and legal-economic analysis, particularly of the Chicago School variety. Here a few points will be stated with a minimum of elaboration.

#### *Rationality*

The rationality assumption generally maintains that the individual knows his own ends and acts to pursue them. (The maximization behavior resulting therefrom is discussed below.) The points to be made in regard to the Chicago School and beyond are noted below.

First, if one takes Knight seriously, there is a very limited place for both knowledge of and quest for autonomous self-interest. The Chicago emphasis upon methodological individualism produces conclusions which not only are tautological with the methodological individualist assumptions, but also deal with a very narrow slice of economic reality.

Second, the analysis of formal maximization, assuming rationality, must be differentiated from the substance of objective functions governed by some combination of culture and personal rational choice.

Third, the policy significance of the rationality assumption is ambiguous (it does promote, of course, so-called market versus political solutions to problems). The utility maximizing model explains everything and nothing; the utility or objective function permits any argument to enter, and utility is not defined independent of behavior. Any behavior, if the analyst were willing or desirous, could be included in the utility function by the addition of a new argument, thereby making otherwise irrational behavior rational. (The same is true of profit maximization.) Officer and Stiefel's quote from Paul Samuelson is apropos: "Thus, the consumer's market behavior is explained in terms of preferences, which are in turn defined only by behavior. The result can very easily be circular, and in many formulations undoubtedly is. Often nothing more is stated than the conclusion that people behave as they behave, a theorem which has no empirical implications, since it contains no hypothesis and is consistent with all conceivable behavior, while refutable by none."

Fourth, the foregoing underscores the great opportunity for selective specification of utility functions by policy analysts. In sum, the rationality assumption, so important to Chicago School doctrine, has profound analytical and policy limits.

### *Constrained Maximization*

Neoclassical, and perforce Chicago School, economics is really at least three bodies of theory: the theories of resource allocation, of how markets operate as choosing mechanisms, and of constrained maximization. It is the third which concerns us here. Stigler, Becker, and others within the Chicago School emphasize that most if not all areas of life are subject to maximizing analysis. Although not without limits, such an approach has profound heuristic value. Becker, in particular, has ingeniously applied the behavioral principle of constrained maximization to the analysis of noneconomic or nonmarket institutions in a way that, although it has the usual elements of tautology [see Goode, in Schultz 1974, pp. 346, 347], displays minimal presumptive optimality reasoning. Again certain points should be made.

First, the analysis of constrained maximization involves the study of choice from *within* opportunity sets and says relatively little about the critical role (and almost nothing about the optimality or nonoptimality) of the constraints imposed, for example, by legal and moral social control and by the choices of others, that is, the factors and forces governing the structure and composition of opportunity sets.

Second, the promarket paradigm implies a certain pattern or mode of constraint and rejects others.

Third, the concept of constrained maximization is very fecund: It can be applied to any situation, deliberative or nondeliberative, in which movement (teleological or otherwise) is restricted by conditions. (This permits, for example, the interesting work being done by Tullock in biology.)

Fourth, individuals generally *do* practice constrained maximization, *given* their formulation of the goal or objective function and the constraints exogenously imposed. Individuals *do* adjust to changed constraints in environmental conditions, *given* their objective function. (And, of course, objective functions change through learning.) All this is to say that as a general rule it may be presumed that individuals engage in calculations of advantage, although this does not necessarily imply that observing analysts can specify the objective functions without being presumptive or selective.

Fifth, we must carefully differentiate between (1) individual constrained maximization behavior, including adjustments to changed constraints through recalculated advantage, and (2) the solution of problems through the market system. It is ingenious and insightful to recognize that individuals do engage in constrained maximization in nonmarket situations in a manner quite akin to their activity in market situations, and that mechanisms of choice exist within nonmarket institutions that appear market-like, but it does not follow that the ubiquity of market-like adjustments and mechanisms (which are largely if not entirely sets of constrained maximization interactions) implies the *market system* of neoclassical economics and libertarian ideology. The set of constrained maximization adjustments is larger than the subset of *market* adjustments. For purposes of both analysis and policy, the two are quite different. It is, for example, the case that the fact of constrained maximization, that is, of choice from within the available alternatives upon consideration of the respective opportunity costs thereof, is not the same thing as "consumer sovereignty" [see Mishan 1969, pp. 95–96]. In all social systems or economies, including socialism, individuals operate and putatively act as constrained maximizers. That insight is important and should not be belittled; indeed, it is a powerful analytical technique. But the overriding problems are (1) the choice of system and its power structure and decisional processes and (2) the societization process which *pro tanto* governs individual objective functions. After all, maximization (including rationality) is a behavioral premise, a methodological assumption (to permit determinate solutions), and a rationalization strategem (as above). The foregoing considerations would be important even if presumptive optimality reasoning were not followed; that such reasoning does characterize much of the Chicago School literature makes them even more important.

*Optimality (Economic Efficiency)*

As indicated above, one characteristic of Chicago School application and extension of neoclassical microeconomics and welfare economics is its presumptive optimality reasoning. The Chicago School (not alone, of course) takes the conventional concepts and tools used in describing how markets operate and, with the use of additional selective assumptions, interprets certain arrangements and/or results as optimal. This presumptive optimality reasoning is narrow and selective. Chicagoans are able to reach conclusions of optimality only because of the introduction of antecedent normative premises with which the optimality conclusion is tautological.

For perspective, consider the usual production possibility curve. Let the axes represent any two values (commodities or social values or criteria, such as inflation and unemployment, and so on), and add the actual social welfare function formed by the aggregation of the weighted preferences of the population. Four things are transpiring concurrently in society with regard to what the diagram summarizes: first, the working out of the values to be placed on the axes; second, the formation of the production possibility curve (for example, the forces producing the Phillips curve or, in other cases, enforcement costs); third, the determination of preferences; and, fourth, the formation of the power structure governing, among other things, the weighting of preferences. The momentary equilibrium which results is an episodic resting place in the evolution of the underlying forces. The Chicago School's optimality analysis relates to a very narrow slice of the activity represented on the diagram and in a highly presumptive and selective manner. Several remarks may be made in this connection.

First, such optimality exists only within the model of market valuation and adjustment and is tautological with the limits of the model. Specific optimal solutions are a function of the range and specification of variables introduced; so-called free individual choice produces optimal (or efficient) results because the latter are defined in terms of the former. Such conclusions are, as Mishan states, a function of faith and facts; moreover, they abstract from the provision of specificity arising from methodological collectivist forces.

Second, such optimality is only presumptive: Each efficient solution gives effect only to the interests implicitly or explicitly recognized in the analysis.[5] The key point here is that optimality is a function of rights and of choice within the opportunity set structure, which is a partial function of rights. Maximization of the value of production—a central theme of the Chicago School approach—requires an antecedent specification of whose interests are to count in the maximization of value. The so-called Pareto[6] (or Pareto-Wicksell) approach can produce optimal solutions only by choosing between conflicting rights claimants.[7] Costs themselves are specific to the structure of rights which governs whose interests are to be made a cost to others. (See Schmid's review article, pp. 469–78.)

Third, there is no unique Pareto optimal solution precisely because optimal solutions are a function of the power structure, that is, of the rights governing whose interests and preferences are to count in the market. Institutions weight individuals and, as do rights, operate on *both* the demand side (governing the wherewithal with which demand is made effective, say, through wealth distribution) and the supply side (governing the cost conditions, in part by governing whose interests count as costs and to whom). Thus a change in the law will produce a changed set of Pareto-optimal possibilities. Within both the corporation [Roberts 1975, pp. 415ff] and society, decision making is not and cannot be (except presumptively, depending upon premised power relations or rights) a matter of abstract benefit-cost analysis *independent of* social relations; rather, it is a function of organizational structure, that is, the structure of position and/or rights governing whose interests are to count. (Taking the existing structure for granted will function to contribute to the replication of the system.)

Fourth, because of the foregoing and other limits, the Chicago School optimality analysis is not a self-contained calculus through which policy conclusions can equivocally be reached. What transpires in society are all three of the following and not solely the first: the working out of technical optimal solutions, the determination of the rights in terms of which solutions can be deemed optimal, and the organization and operation of the decisional institutions involved in both. (The Buchanan-Tullock approach to public choice tends to take a once-and-for-all-time position on the latter two.)

Fifth, Chicago School optimality analysis is selective in regard to the externalities, injuries, or costs it introduces *vis-à-vis* ubiquitous and inevitable externalities and opportunity costs.

Sixth, emphasis upon the Pareto criterion selectively promotes the status quo.

Seventh, Chicago School policies themselves introduce non-Pareto optimal changes in legal rules and rights.[8] This is true in such domestic policy areas as deregulation and criminal justice reform, as well as in economic development policy, where such writers as Harberger do not presume the optimality of the results of existing market arrangements but instead propose attacking critical leverage points in order to produce development [Wall 1972, pp. x, xii; and Strassmann, in chapter 12].

Eighth, the Chicago School optimality analysis cannot conclusively resolve the problem of the substance of legal and moral constraints upon individual choice, yet those constraints produce the actual optimal results. For example, casuistic manipulation of the Coase theorem creates the impression that rights and liability placement do not count, but it does so only by excluding the respects in which such placement does matter.

Two general examples will suffice to illustrate the foregoing points. First, as Mishan develops in chapter 6 and as Frank Roosevelt pointed out, in part, through his quotations from Bergson and Bell, there is a consumer bias to the market system. Maximization through consumption actually functions to promote business interests in minimizing registered worker interests (costs) by attributing a zero social value to worker utility, that is, it is a maximizing model which does not register worker job attitudes and security interests except as ordinary commodities. Labor is a commodity, not a human factor whose welfare enters directly into the welfare calculus. To the extent that Chicago School analysis only gives effect to the underlying reality of the business system, it cannot be held responsible; but the cultural specificity (and a rather obscured one at that) does limit the probative value of its optimality analysis. Moreover, the Chicago doctrines do contribute to the reproduction of the system.

The second area involves economic history, where Chicago School revisionism has produced ingenious and controversial reinterpretations. The key characteristic of the work of Douglass North and Robert Fogel, and their respective associates, is the analysis of market and/or market-like mechanisms in the emergence and operation of institutions *coupled with* a highly dubious and at least severely limiting presumptive optimality reasoning. The work of North is a most insightful analysis of the demand for institutional change. (As with the marginal productivity theory, it is primarily a demand side theory, with some illumination of the economics of the supply of institutions, although it too is taken by many as a theory of the whole.) North's approach, which is important in recognizing the role of calculations of advantage in producing institutional innovation and change, is quite similar to that of John R. Commons, who inquired into the legal foundations of the capitalist market and the "demands . . . for new types of private ownership, contract, and organizations to exploit new opportunities and to protect imperiled interests" [Gonce 1971, p. 87]. Commons did not, however, infer the optimality of the actual results or presume the optimality of the system of property as it developed.

North's analysis is an ex post explanation of realized changes from the point of view of the successful demanders of rights. But the actual historic solutions and developments were a function of the structure of power, including differential or asymmetrical access to institutions defining and assigning rights. North is limited by his failure to recognize the dual nature of rights (a right granted to Alpha constitutes Beta's exposure to Alpha, and vice versa); by exclusion of the opportunity set losses by conflicting, losing parties (whether they were active demanders or ignorant victims); and, *inter alia,* by eclipsing other determinants of institutional change, especially power play in the political arena. The results seem to justify the rights which emerged, yet the results are a function of the rights which emerged. If the winners and losers were reversed, the same would be true. The valuation of production is maximized only through or on the basis of rights given legal status; a different maximization would have resulted and appeared optimal ex post if the actual losers in the rights' competition had won. Ex post presumptive optimality is highly limited and question begging. The North approach, moreover, superimposes not only an ex post or winner perspective, but also a proeconomic growth criterion, with growth specified in terms of the marketed economic goods actually realized, in all respects giving optimal status to one set of performance characteristics, the effects actually produced, thereby canonizing the actually produced status quo.

Robert Fogel and Stanley Engerman's [1974] work on American slavery is another example of presumptive optimality reasoning. Even if many of their evaluations are accepted, for example, that slaveowners generally were prudent economic (that is, materialist) maximizers, their conclusions as to efficiency presume and give effect to the structure of rights under slavery, a system in which slave interests were not given economic effect through rights, and the slaves' position was not entered into by them with consent.[9] This is evaluative efficiency analysis carried to an absurd degree: Any situation or arrangement can be canonized as optimal if its own terms are accepted, in this case the terms of the slaveowners.

Presumptive optimality analysis goes unacceptably beyond the quest for the technical conditions of optimality as one facet of equilibrium.[10] Such reasoning serves the evaluative role, giving effect to selective (and often implicit) values, and it adds nothing but the cachet of the discipline to a normative exercise. Economists are not specially equipped to make these judgments and should not make them without explicitly defining the particular choices of interests being given effect and the grounds thereof. The underlying microeconomic analysis of presumptive optimality reasoning has considerable explanatory power, but this use constitutes an unfortunate abuse. Such reasoning also manifests and supports the high priest role, serving as a selective instrument of ideology. That analysts are often not aware of the implicit choices being made does not vitiate the argument.

This is not to reject the Chicago School's splendid emphasis on opportunity cost analysis, which is at the heart of being an economist. But that approach must not be allowed, in the name of a dubious concept of optimality, to beg the issues of opportunity set structure; whose interests are to count, in part as a cost to others; and the power structure governing these, all of which is worked out in the real world economy. In the hands of the Chicago School, opportunity cost analysis is tied selectively, normatively, and presumptively to a certain view of the world of interests.

### *The Market*

What is said here is not intended to denigrate the market, but to confront reality, as I perceive it, and the limits it imposes on the Chicago School doctrines of the market. Needless to say, one could pursue market solutions without discussing these limits (and their respective consequences and alternative evaluations) and that often has been done, but that is not the purpose here. Both the use *and* the rejection of the market (say, because of willingness and unwillingness, respectively, to accept the limits of the use of the market) require an additional normative premise, and such premise is intended. Many fanatical supporters of the market, including the high priests, will find this analysis not only agnostic but sacrilegious. Knight's insight is apropos and bears reiteration: "The essential nature of a religious principle is that not merely is it immoral to oppose it, but to ask what it is, is morally identical with denial and attack. . . . To inquire into the ultimates behind accepted group values is obscene and sacrilegious; objective inquiry is an attempt to uncover the nakedness of man, his soul as well as his body, his deeds, his culture, and his very gods" [Knight 1932, pp. 448, 449]. Discussion of the sacred myth will begin with a perhaps less controversial topic.

*Competition or the Market Per Se: Structure or Behavior*

The Chicago School doctrine is a sophisticated apologia for the market and a brilliant clarification of how markets operate. Both, however, are limited by incomplete consideration of the institutional and power structures forming and operating through markets, but more on that below. The immediate problem is whether the Chicago School means a *competitive market* or simply the *market per se;* or whether it means by "competition" its *structural* or *behavioral* characteristics.[11] "Members of the school devote some attention to defending the market against charges of its noncompetitive structure. It would seem that they believe that competition results from about six firms in an industry and often only three. They believe that existing markets are much more competitive than is believed by "nonmarket" economists, who emphasize imperfections, externalities, and transaction and information costs. Chicagoans also believe that the dynamic effects involving innovation and decreasing inflexibility of resources, and so forth, are more important than mere structural considerations, and they argue that the existing U.S. economy is primarily structurally competitive (and would be more so absent government restrictions).

But it appears that the main emphasis of the Chicago School is on the market per se, rather than on the traditional notions of structural competition. To the Chicago School, the market is an almost magical black box. As they contemplate its operation, it involves competitive, profit-seeking *behavior* (relying, of course, upon the rationality assumption, on which see above). Much analysis stresses that the market works because we can rely upon competitive behavior, meaning thereby that individuals can be counted upon to pursue constrained maximization or calculations-of-advantage adjustments within their extant opportunity sets as market conditions change. If this behavioral approach *is* the market (and it seems largely to be, together with market clearing prices, which makes it difficult to differentiate from individual adjustments to trial-and-error attempts by central planners to set market clearing prices), then the Chicago School stresses a considerably if not radically different conception of the market than does traditional neoclassical economics. It is very close, in effect although not in statement, to the businessman's conception of competing with all others for the consumer's dollar.

As noted before, the Chicago view is that the market is inherently more power diffused, and freer, than any alternative system. Even an imperfect market is the least worse alternative. In the absence of governmental limits upon entry, the market effectively approximates competition or the results of competition abstractly considered; for example, the fear of entry will produce competitive results notwithstanding a less-than-competitive actual industry structure. Moreover, the market works faster than the antitrust laws. Monopoly elements are largely a function of government, not technology or the quest for power and security among businessmen.

The problem is that emphasis upon *competitive behavior* is consistent with or can be and is applied to oligopoly and highly structured noncompetitive markets. Thus game theoretic or strategic moves are a parody of traditional conceptions of competition. While prices are important in making markets work, administered prices are not the same thing as conventional parametric prices. The market may be an arena in which firms try to manipulate the conditions under which they operate; it may be an arena of economic warfare, not beneficent "adjustments." A market not characterized by the free movement of autonomous prices is still a market; goods are produced, consumers buy, and nothing observable fails to "work." But is that "competition"? Is that "the market"? Any *market* result is ipso facto optimal according to Chicago doctrine, inasmuch as it could be different if not, and that other result would be optimal.

The Chicago School response centers on its belief in individual voluntary choice, market organization per se, and its version of competitive behavior, generally regardless of structural considerations (although Chicagoans argue along structural lines as well, seemingly for tactical reasons). (In the foregoing, "structural" is used in the usual industrial organization sense to refer to the firm structure of an industry, not the larger power structure sense used elsewhere in these chapters.) The question of voluntary choice and freedom will be considered below. Here, other than emphasizing the Chicago School's primary reliance upon the market as such and upon behavioral considerations, comparison will be made only between the current Chicago School and the earlier views of Knight and especially Simons, who were much more interested in structural considerations. Simons, indeed, was quite emphatic about the importance of competitive structure and was perhaps supportive of even more radical structural change than that contemplated by Senator Philip Hart's deconcentration bill.[12] He was seriously concerned about the rise of the corporate system. One can project that in something of a dialectic manner Simons's concerns led to the eclipse of competition in the structural sense and to the rise of the market per se (and the behavioral conceptualization of competition) in the Chicago School's propaganda for economic freedom. In any event, contemporary

Chicagoans' behavioral conception of the competitive market is certainly an important limit to the policy significance of their doctrines. Optimal market solutions have a qualitatively different probative value and recommendatory force given a behavioral rather than a structural conception of competition and the market. (I acknowledge, of course, problems of ascertaining structural adequacy.)

*The Market Works, Meaning What?*

The Chicago School believes that the market works and that, absent evidence to the contrary (the reader is reminded of the strategy of the maintained hypothesis), there is or should be a presumption that the market works. The Chicago School believes that markets exist and are a generally less expensive and freer way of solving problems; moreover, markets exist and reveal themselves in simple ways, and they can be observed by using simple market theory and without needlessly esoteric econometric techniques. Given the behavioral approach, ubiquitous economizing implies (or almost implies) the existence of markets and that markets work.

To say that something "works" requires a specification of the thing deemed to work and, in addition to observational data relating to and in some sense describing its working, a normative premise from which the recommendatory force of its actually "working" is derived. The proposition that "the market works" is not only a descriptive (it has such positive elements or aspects) but also a normative statement; it renders approval. In all these respects, the doctrine that the market works has severe limits, and the following points may be suggested.

First, the working of the market has serious technical limits, such as those explored by Mishan and which will not be further summarized here.

Second, the Chicago School provides an ambiguous and certainly equivocal specification of "the market," yet it seems willing to and indeed desirous of granting presumptive optimality status to any market solution. All Chicago doctrines and policy conclusions with regard to the market working presume the superiority of market solutions and that the market works properly (absent evidence to the contrary). This is the central premise, the maintained hypothesis. The market produces optimal solutions because optimal solutions are defined in terms of market solutions. As argued above, both meaning and probative significance for policy rest within and are limited by this cognitive system: The market works within a certain paradigm.

Third, the market does have impact and, among other things, it does serve to allocate resources—given the inputs to the market. The price system does exercise control over production and distribution through market clearing prices (which may or may not be true equilibrium prices; see Gibson [1974, pp. 526–27], discussing the work of Glenn Johnson) and behavioral responses to price changes—within institutions and power structure. The market does in a sense produce determinate results. It does avoid certain terribly important problems of centralized decision making and concentration of power in government. It does minimize, in a sense, the issues to be resolved explicitly through politics, although power is involved in markets, too, and politics does enter even if unobtrusively. There will be maximizing readjustments with allocative consequences in response to government actions or market forces (changes in demand and/or supply conditions). The possibilities for using the market (or markets) as a regulatory system in and for all the foregoing are great [Martin 1974b]. Moreover, the theory of markets is fecund in ferreting out areas of market or market-like adjustments; a powerful heuristic tool.[13]

Fourth, the mere *fact* of market or market-like adjustments, however, is insufficient to derive the normative conclusion that market or market-like processes are desirable. They may be ubiquitous, but in order to say that we *ought* to promote or follow market solutions—particular ones or in general—an additional *normative* premise is required. Even more important is the question of the institutional and power structure within which market and market-like adjustments take place. From my perspective, that *point* is more important than *criticism* of the market (or of market solutions) per se. To true believers (and to others, for example, those interested in rationalizing the extant structure of power and wealth), to raise the point is tantamount to criticism; to still others, it seems like inadequate criticism.

In any event, the statement that "the market works" is distinctively normative (and not strictly positive) due to the normative basis in terms of which the market is said to work. And it is tautological with the limited range of variables and length of causal chain included in the relevant microeconomic model. Normally excluded from the Chicago School analysis is the question of institutional and power structures (except insofar as, one way or another, selective propriety is adduced to or assumed for certain arrangements and not others, as above).[14]

Fifth, in some respects "the market" is a metaphysical or mythical notion, a brilliant question-begging conception at that. Apart from constrained maximization adjustments and responses, seen as an integrated system centering on market prices and in terms of which (variously stated) the market is usually defined, there is no independent confirmation of "the market." The market is not something preexistent and preeminent to man. Rather, it is an artifact (as well as a mental image). Actual markets are formed by institutions and power players. Although market forces can be given an abstract, reified, diagrammatic existence, actual markets do not have an independent existence. They are not given or exogenously determined. There is no independent or transcendent thing called the market. Institutions instrument and channel constrained maximization adjustment behavior. Change the institutions, and the "market" changes; calculations-of-advantage based adjustments will take place, and prices will serve their functions, but performance and operation, and the substance of behavior, likely will change. The market will assume the form and direction of its institutionalization.

Sixth, the market itself is a system of coercion, even independent of one-on-one power relations and general concentrations of power, although coercion through the market is less obtrusive than in other institutions or processes (a situation deemed an advantage by some and a shortcoming by others).

Seventh, the market gives effect to the institutions which form it and the power structure which operates through it, meaning by power the rights and positions, among other things, which enable participation as an economic actor, quite apart from the specific structure of particular industry groupings. Power structure is a partial input and a partial output of the market. The optimality of market solutions is but one statement of an equilibrium condition—representing an equilibrium of power operating in part through the market. The market is not unfettered or neutral: The substance of its operation and performance is a function of the power structure (and not merely the behavioral actions and responses of individual economic actors or units exercising voluntary choice from within their respective extant opportunity sets). Market allocation of resources gives effect to the institutional and power structures constituting and operating through the market, in no small part a function of the distribution of wealth. (See the statement from Ayres, quoted above.) Invocation of "the market" functions to obscure the operation of the power structure and the extant solution to the fundamental problem of the organization and control of the economy, which is what the game ultimately is all about. In other words, the economy as a valuational and allocative process involves more than the market narrowly conceived to be the abstract market mechanism. The Chicago School analysis of the market is about an important but small slice of the economy. In the last decade or so, a deeper knowledge has been acquired, for example, of how specific institutional arrangements "make" the market in securities and commodities. The same generalization applies to all markets.

Eighth, the market can serve as an instrument of power for a ruling class or legal-economic elite. Seidman [1973] has shown how paternal and market arrangements have served as substitute systems of control to organize the labor force to support the ruling class in colonial systems. This is not to say that all market systems so operate, but the market is a vehicle for the exercise of power, perhaps a less repressive means than others, but still a means. Critics of market socialism, so-called, recognize this; free markets, so-called, also are conduits for power, that is, a different power structure. Markets can be an *efficient* way of exercising control—with "efficient" depending upon whose interests are made to count and whose not (as in the case of slavery, discussed earlier).

Finally, the logic of Chicago School market adjustment tends to be independent of any structural considerations. Thus the optimality of the market (of market adjustment and nonadjustment, that is, of doing nothing, too) is an *a priori* or *ipso facto* result or conclusion, a tautology which is not operational, testable, and subject to refutation, but a conclusion giving effect to the premise of the school's paradigm. The exclusion of *structural* considerations (of all kinds) is a severe limit to the doctrines of the Chicago School. Among other things, the doctrines merely state or manifest the tautology of market adjustment. Furthermore, the analysis fails to come to grips with the conflict between private property and competition: Does (or should) property include the right to monopolize or concentrate power? Chicago is less, if at all, concerned with this question, because it feels that it is the *market* and competitive *behavior* which counts. To pygmies in a world of giants and to the objective observer, this view, denigrating structural considerations, is a limit on the probative value of the school's doctrines. The Chicago answer, that the market is effective in controlling and limiting "monopoly" power, not only ignores the larger structure of power but also would be more impressive if it was not caught up with the presumptive optimality of *market* solutions. The fact that there will be market and market-like adjustments does not obviate the importance of power structure, industrial and otherwise. Not unless, of course, power structure is less important than *market per se*.

### *The Status Quo*

Positivist inquiry attempts to explain the status quo, and such explanation is readily put to use to rationalize the status quo. Positive analyses tend to build in and cast luster on the status quo, that is, to give effect to the status quo's answer to the problem of whose interests are to count. The Chicago School is commonly perceived as conservative, as favoring the status quo, although it perceives its own role as restraining, and not justifying, the status quo. There are three points to be made in this connection.

First, the school clearly favors the existing *system*. It assumes the propriety of the established business system, or at least of *a* version of it, and canonizes it.

Second, the school supports *selective* facets or elements of extant arrangements. It is not blindly in favor of whatever exists, but selectively supports and rejects certain parts. It is highly selective in its treatment of the existing structure of power and privilege, in its acceptance of the existing system(s) of social control, in its own role as social control, and in its desires to restrict and promote change and certain modes of change. Apropos government, it favors stable legal rules—so long as the rules are acceptable.

The Pareto criterion, so much stressed by the Chicago School, perhaps especially its Virginia branch, builds in, gives effect to, and reinforces the status quo structures of power and wealth, albeit selectively (although the selectivity is not always obtrusive). The school promotes the imagery of consensus and consent, generally only with regard to certain changes from the status quo and almost never with regard to the nonconsensual origins of existing rights and wealth.[15] (For some changes from the status quo, it substitutes its own social welfare function.) Pareto optimality relates to exchange or gains from trade, or what historically has been called commutative justice, about which Simons remarked: "Commutative justice simply takes for granted an existing distribution of capital, among persons, families, communities, regions, and nations" [Simons, 1948, p. 5]. The use of the Pareto criterion protects the status quo from deep criticism (and from selectively perceived adverse changes). As Knight wrote:

> The theory of maximum freedom if really followed through, ends in a question-begging justification of whatever human relations happen to exist.... Thus the *most* that exchange relations can do is to assure that each individual shall keep, quantitatively unimpaired, the stock of values originally possessed, as measured by free exchange among persons whose original stocks were whatever they happened to be. The principle merely settles the ethical problem by decreeing fixity for all eternity of the *existing* distribution of means of enjoyment [Knight 1947, pp. 4, 5].

To this I would add that the use of the Pareto criterion gives selective protection to interests in the status quo; for example, deregulation enhances or creates certain rights and inhibits or destroys others and thus changes the distribution of wealth and income.

To the extent that the Chicago School accepts and promotes the market or business system, its specific (or a specific) institutionalization thereof, and selected interests in the actual status quo, it is open to criticism, and its position on these points constitutes a limit to its doctrines. Thus, to the extent that the *system* is defined by or identified with the dominant powers and privileged, one can expect antagonism toward and from those advocating a restructuring of the system of power and privilege, the concept of "socialism" discussed in chapter 20.

Third, the Chicago School emphasizes, albeit selectively, the limits to reform and the amount of deliberative change with which society can cope and its political processes handle. The point is not only that they apply the caution selectively, but also that the Schumpeterian creative destruction nurtured by the business system is disruptive of the status quo and is an important cause of the problems which others see as requiring governmental corrective action. But many of the creative destructions are perceived by the Chicago School as merely pecuniary and/or non-Pareto relevant externalities and, one senses, are therefore not important. This too is a limit to the doctrine.

### *Freedom, Power, and Individualism*

The Chicago School supports and would encourage market, or private contractual, solutions to problems. Problems from any other perspective they often do not wish to acknowledge, or treat, as problems; they are redefined in such a way as to suggest how market solutions are feasible substitute conceptions and policies. (And from within their paradigm that is all they feel is necessary to be done: To establish the possibility of a market solution is *ipso facto* to demonstrate its desirability.) Buchanan has given one explanation for what may be taken as the general Chicago School position: "There is an explicit prejudice in favor of previously existing rights, not because this structure possesses some intrinsic ethical attributes, and not because change itself is undesirable, but for the much more elementary reason that only such a prejudice offers incentives for the emergence of voluntarily negotiated settlements among the parties themselves" [Buchanan 1972b, p. 452; see also Buchanan and Samuels 1975, p. 17 and passim].

The topics of freedom, power, and individualism bring together certain themes dissolved in the foregoing. One may interpose to

Buchanan's position the consideration that he does not accept *all* previously existing rights, seemingly only those deemed consonant with a market system, for example, his position is no defense for the continuation of collective bargaining by unions. The problem of selectivity raises the questions of *whose* freedom, *whose* power, and *which* individuals. As Daniel Fusfeld has written [1974, p. 911], there is no "economic equilibrium independent of the organization of power or the structure of social classes."

The crux of the matter is *power,* which here is a neutral, nonpejorative term with which to describe the organization and operation of the economy. Power connotes participation in decision making and, instrumentally, the means or bases (rights, position) thereof. It is necessary to accomplish desired goals, and it is necessary to check others' power. The social task is to distinguish between different possessors and uses and therefore between alternative checking possibilities. The ultimate normative task, in this context, is to differentiate between acceptable and unacceptable power [see Samuels 1972a, 1973a]. The difference, for example, between nineteenth- and twentieth-century liberalism is that, while both desire the diffusion of power, each perceives concentrated power differently, although both are skeptical of state power, at least in some of its uses. The economy as a decision-making process involves a structure of power, that is, of decision-making participation, and the legal-economic arena is the critical locus of the awesome contest for power in the organization and control of the economic system.

The Chicago School typically thinks of power in a one-on-one context and therefore the absence of equivalent alternatives for an individual. It generally is not concerned with the scope of choice open to an individual in terms of the size and composition of individual opportunity sets (*vis-à-vis* the number of alternative parties with whom the individual can contract along any one line of opportunity) and therefore the structure of opportunity sets. Nor is it interested in the factors and forces governing the composition and structure of opportunity sets. It sees and rejects *certain* limits to opportunity sets imposed by government and ignores the limits inherent in property and imposed through the exercise of private power in the market; better, it *accepts* the results of the exercise of private power in the market. It is concerned with explaining and promoting market solutions and therefore choice (and contracting) from within extant opportunity sets as they develop. If there are a few automobile companies from which to buy, and if they constitute substantially equivalent alternatives, the Chicago School is generally satisfied. It matters not that the industry involves a high concentration of power and that other patterns of alternatives might arise from different industry configurations [see Melman 1975]. Whereas others perceive phenomena in terms of power—scope of opportunity to participate in the economy—the Chicago School mind operates in terms of individual constrained maximization adjustments to changed market conditions as the exercise of voluntary choice. To them, that is freedom. To others, the formal opportunity to choose may be hollow if the individual has substantially nothing with which to choose; the distribution of power governs the effectiveness of freedom, and freedom requires the wide diffusion of power.

Actually, the Chicago School, as are all others, is highly selective in its perceptions of government, coercion, freedom, and power, the perceptions tending to be those nurtured by a capitalist or business system. Business participation is not perceived by them as power, but union participation is. Whereas the Chicago School sees property as a defense against government, others see in its concentration and exercise the possibility (if not the fact) of private tyranny and injustice, or at least the domination of the economy. Also, while the Chicago School opposes manifest business restrictionism, other opponents have a broader conception of the phenomenon. In others' view the consumer in the planned system has formal freedom to buy what is available, assuming he has the means with which to buy it; under the market system, the consumer has the same formal freedom. While the consumer in the market system has influence not necessarily shared by the consumer in the planned system (consumer sovereignty, so-called) over the ultimate production of goods, nonetheless the market allocation of resources directed by consumer choice reflects the distribution of wealth, and so forth, that is, power. Without power, the formal freedom is hollow.

Whereas the Chicago School sees the market as a process of equalizing marginal cost and marginal revenue and of adjustments thereto, others perceive marginal cost, and marginal revenue, as a function of the structure of power [Melody 1974, p. 294]. Chicago advocates a system of mutual contractarian advantage through securing gain from trade; others see this process as taking place within and giving effect to the structure of power. These others see certain conservative writers defending explicitly the structure of social power and attempting to limit adverse legal change and egalitarianism and see the Chicago School as ignoring the structure of social power, but addressing sophisticated and subtle doctrines to the same effect. Laissez-faire is a selective means with which dominant interests protect and assert their power. These other writers recognize that the market has its own rationality and represents important and commendable aspects of freedom, but they urge that while it tends to diffuse power it can be and is a vehicle for the exercise of concentrated power. Chicagoans, on the other hand, see less, and less permanently, concentrated business power and fear the systemic injury consequent to government interference with the structure of business. Ultimately, perhaps, the Chicago School is saying that power and concentrated power are inevitable, and freedom is safer under the market (even with *its* governmental uses) than any other system which necessarily would concentrate more power in government, which is less susceptible to checking. In other words, the market is a sophisticated form of checking. The Chicago School sees in others' desire to check corporate power an anticapitalist mentality rather than merely other power players and a necessary or proper exercise of the power-checking role. It holds the latter view, again, because it does not perceive business power as requiring checking beyond what the market would handle. Fixation with the market on such grounds requires willingness to deny the *relative* importance of these other considerations.

The problem is that the market is formed by the structure of business power, and its checking effect, and therefore freedom, is only in terms of, and gives effect to, that structure. Market solutions are specific to the structure of power, for example, wealth-distribution specific and/or industry-structure specific. To members of the Chicago School, such power structure specificity apparently is characteristic of *all* economic systems, and the issue is the *market* organization of economic activity. Some critics would respond that the market may be institutionalized variably and power structured differently, say, with a greater diffusion of power [Martin 1974b], and other critics would simply dismiss the market as such or as a vehicle of the powerful. Many of these critics are concerned about the market as giving effect to the results of past power play over the use of government and power play within the present market. Those who favor the market see in it a maximization of diffusion of opportunity; the Chicago School sees diffusion generic to the market *vis-à-vis* likely alternatives, and others view the market as compatible with both concentrated and diffused structures of social power and prefer the latter. All seem to oppose the arrogance and intransigence of concentrated power, but differ in their perceptions of its reality and location; and some, but not Chicagoans, are concerned about wealth distribution and other dimensions of social power, such as class.

Whether or not resource allocation by market is a synonym for allocation in accordance with power structure is a problem of paradigm choice which has profound normative and potential policy consequences. Emphasis on the market tends to remove attention from power, power structure, and power play, except as selectively deemed hostile to the market system. Emphasis on power tends to eclipse the advantages of a system of gains from trade. The argument on efficiency grounds is tautological with and gives effect to the gains from trade view. For those who accept market organization, the issue involves the best institutionalization of a market system and the best structure of power decentralization. (The Chicagoans seem to have tried to preempt the field and identify the market with *their* version of its institutionalization.) These are normative views and differences, since the differential perception of power is normative-metaphysical, or has essentially normative elements. The Chicago view has the limits inevitably associated with its conception of freedom, power, and related topics. It also suffers from the perceived limit that ideas have systemic meaning relevant to circumstances, and the Chicago School, correctly or incorrectly, is seen as an apologist for not only the market, with which it would not quibble, but also the existing structure of social power, which role it accepts either grudgingly or eagerly.

The positions so far described have not always characterized the Chicago School. Knight and Simons were profoundly concerned with the limits to freedom found in the structure of power, for example, the distribution of wealth and the corporate system. Knight, however, changed his mind. Whereas he formerly believed that freedom without power was empty, he later believed, perhaps as he learned the requirements of an effective propaganda for economic freedom under contemporary conditions (correctly, I think, for the modern U.S. economy is able to operate to no slight degree because the overwhelming majority do not question the structures of rights, power, and wealth), that freedom and power had to be separated as issues. We must preach freedom if we are to have it; or as Buchanan, the most Knightian contemporary Chicagoan, seems to see it, we must preach contractarian exchange in order to have freedom. Inasmuch as the presumption here is that all current Chicago School members (and not solely Buchanan) know their Knight, and inasmuch, too, as Knight's points have not been substantively (as opposed to strategically) rebutted, one may conclude that they feel, as he eventually did, that these considerations are less important than having a market system per se, at least for purposes of rationalizing the system. That may or may not be the ultimate issue, but it is a limit to Chicago doctrines.

We do well to consider Knight's early position for, although he changed his mind about the separability of freedom and power considerations for purposes of a propaganda for economic freedom, he did not repudiate them, but rather reiterated that they were important in proper perspective. In other words, this newer perspective constitutes a limit to the Chicago doctrine, the substance of which is in part formed by Knight's earlier and never repudiated position. Knight argued that economic performance is a function of the structure of power, including wealth distribution, legal rights, and so on [Knight 1947, pp. 7, 10, 152 and passim; 1951b, p. 58 and passim]. He also argued that freedom as an argument functioned to promote the status quo [Knight 1947, p. 4; compare p. 109], a view having its contemporary manifestation in the Pareto criterion and its use. (No wonder economists are trained to be conservative!) Freedom is also quite limited, as was pointed out in the methodological and normative individualism discussion. The justification of the market system is ultimately in terms of power:

> It is in terms of power, then, if at all, that competitive economics and the competitive view of life for which it must be largely accountable are to be justified. Whether we are to regard them as justified at all depends on whether we are willing to accept an ethics of power as the basis of our world view [Knight 1951b, p. 68].

> The business organizations which are the directing divinities of the system are but groups of ignorant and frail beings like the individuals with whom they deal. . . . It is in the field indicated by this summary list of postulates, rather than in that of the mechanics of exchange relations, that we must work out the ultimate critique of free enterprise [Knight 1951b, p. 236].

There is a desire for power to be differentiated from the desire for its fruits: "The situation as regards the self-defeating tendencies of any system of individual liberty is of course aggravated, to the extent that men seek power for 'political' reasons (the desire for power over others for its own sake) rather than for 'economic' reasons (the desire for the fruits of power)" [Knight 1951b, p. 298, n.].

As McKinney says of Knight's view, "what is impressive about the market is not the alleged autonomous nature of individual choice, but the powerful constraints imposed upon economic decision making." Indeed, "it is the *powerlessness*, the opposite of individual autonomy, which is the basis of the market's efficiency." But such powerlessness is a relational concept; in order for freedom to have substance, there must be what we are calling here power (the diffusion of which is responsible for the powerlessness in relational terms).

> In an individualist-utilitarian view of life, freedom means freedom to use power, and economic freedom means freedom to use economic power, without political interference or restraint. Such freedom may in effect become slavery for the per-

> son who has little power at his disposal, since life itself requires practically continuous control of a certain minimum of economic power [Knight 1951b, p. 292].
>
> The question of how much freedom there really was under liberalism at any time and place could of course be argued endlessly. Freedom of expression perhaps tended to outlast economic freedom; but the two affected different groups and strata, and economic liberty also remained up to the actual revolution in any country, for those possessing a sufficient share of power [Knight 1951b, p. 325, n.].
>
> This unexamined, emotional-religious absolute which, objectively viewed, is Property, was generally called by the more appealing name of Liberty. It is a purely negative idea, meaning freedom to use power, and without power, completely empty [Knight 1947, p. 26].
>
> The objective is such a society, made up of such men, that the individual can be trusted with freedom, meaning that he can be trusted with the power which is necessary to give freedom substantial content [Knight 1947, p. 183].
>
> Freedom is a sound ethical idea, but "effective" freedom depends on the possession of power as well as mere absence of interference, at the hands of other individuals or of "society" [Knight 1947, p. 382].
>
> Freedom is empty without *power*, and its effective content depends both on the possession of power (in all these forms) and on what the individual actually wants to do with power [Knight 1956, p. 295].

Knight's later view was different. For example, "freedom as a right presupposes, takes as given, both the means or power possessed by the person and what we may want to do" [Knight 1960, p. 124]. (This statement is a beautiful example of how what is buried in a presupposition or assumption must be taken as a limit of the analysis which follows.) Knight also said: "The major fallacy—doubtless responsible for the inversion referred to in the meaning of liberalism—is to hold that one is not free, unless he has the *power* to do anything he would like to do, or to get anything he wants, and has a right to have, or to be free from, any alleged wrong" [Knight 1960, p. 16]. This last statement ends up as a narrower or weaker rejection of power than it seems to start out: What is rejected is not power per se, but exaggerated claims (which, as the opposite of the power-checking problem, involves equivocal positions).

Knight still maintained that freedom was empty without power:

> Freedom is empty without power to act—though as just shown the two must not be identified [Knight 1960, p. 17].
>
> While freedom is not to be confused with power, it means freedom to use power possessed, and is empty in content without control over means, hence power in some form. That is necessary to make freedom effective. Yet social freedom cannot mean the unlimited right of people possessing great economic power to use it at will, even in free exchange relations, and, in particular, to use it to get more power indefinitely. Freedom, particularly economic freedom, has to be restricted by rules, made and enforced as law by social agencies acting on behalf of the general interest [Knight 1960, p. 113].

This is a remarkable statement coming from Knight. It must be juxtaposed to Buchanan's antipathy toward public interest and social-welfare-function approaches and his preference for his version of methodological individualism, that is, private interest approaches. In comparison, too, Friedman [1962] rejects egalitarian considerations (p. 195) and equates individual liberty with laissez-faire (p. 201). He looks only to individual choice, and stresses the "doctrines relating to a 'free man' which are diametrically opposed to the modern day concept which stresses 'welfare' and equality over freedom. Freedom is the highest value and is the opposite of coercion. It implies the right to make and act on one's own decisions" [quoted in Breit and Ransom 1971, pp. 250–51]. Power, in this context, is irrelevant or secondary; formal equality of right is elevated over the *question* of meaningful participation in the economy as decision maker and beneficiary [Friedman 1962, p. 195].

The crux *is* power. The Chicago School envisions it effectively evaporating or checked in the market system, *ipso facto*. The most severe limit of this view resides in the perception of the market itself as a system of power, again in the neutral, nonpejorative sense. One paradigmatic context of meaning thus challenges another.

But the most practical (and certainly less esoteric) limit to the Chicago School view resides in the perception of the actual market as a system of concentrated power. I have reference to the paradigm denominated by such terms as "the corporate system," "the new industrial state," and so on.

The very idea of the corporate system raises the question of whether or not the market, in its traditional conception, is extinct, or at least largely transcended and ridden by economic giants. (In a sense this is more provocative than the proposition that the market is formed by the structure of business power.) Does the existence of giant firms and of industrial-financial complexes able to exercise considerable (although not complete) control over important elements of their environment signify the eclipse of the "market"? Is the rise of the multinational corporation an extension of the Chicago School concept of the market to the world economy, or is it an indication that the market has been superseded? Can the optimality analysis apply more readily or appropriately to an equilibrium among multinational corporations than among nation-states? The market system may inherently possess greater diffusion of power than any likely alternative system, but do we any longer have a market system? Is "private" business sufficient, or is the giant corporation a *new* phenomenon? Has the defense of the "market" become the defense not only of the existing structure and practice of business power but also of a different economic order? Is there not a high degree of administration of markets through collective private and private-cum-government arrangements, even though it is not acknowledged by the Chicago concept of the market? Is the Chicago gambit of "greater diffusion of power *than any likely alternative system*" an indefinite comparison, not unlike the politicians who say that some policy will keep taxes lower "than they otherwise would be"? Is there not a two-sector "private" economy, one largely competitive and unplanned, as contemplated by traditional thought, including Chicago, and another, dominated by giant corporations, both national and multinational, which, in symbiotic relations among each other and with governments, for all practical purposes administer both their sector and the rest of the "private" economy? Can the "behavior of the existing economic system of the world ... be understood adequately with a theory that treats giant multinational corporations and complex financial interest groups as if they were 'ma and pa' grocery stores" [Martin 1974a, p. 282]?

Robert Aliber argues that the growth of the multinationals is a function of the market, of market adjustments. They develop only because of "the functioning of the market for advantages" and would not have otherwise [Aliber 1972, p. 114]. Ronald Müller [1975, pp. 189–90] finds that the multinationals have negated the social function of the market. I am not conclusively certain what negating the market means, nor am I confident that I know what the market for advantages means, but I do think I know that a market-adjustment rationalization of corporate (multinational) development explains everything and nothing. It is tautological with the market paradigm and lacks an independent test. It is a rationalization of everything which happens, and everything which happens is *ipso facto* a matter of market adjustment. How can we distinguish corporate market adjustments in accordance with a "free market" from businesses' strategic manipulations in a corporate system of power, administering prices, markets, and the future of us all? The individual is able voluntarily to choose the things he will buy, and the corporation can voluntarily choose between manipulations of markets, all within the name of constrained maximization *or* of power play. The Chicago fixation with the rationalization (and explanation) of the market prevents it from accepting the importance of these matters, and their doctrines are limited accordingly.

Is not, in other words, the Chicago School interpreting and rationalizing the economy in terms of the old and venerated *individualist* capitalist ideology, while the world may have changed, and while others have developed a newer, and increasingly accepted and venerated, *managerialist* capitalist ideology? Friedman may exclaim against attribution of social responsibility to the corporation as grant of undeserved power and opportunity for abuse of power, but perhaps the power is already there. Arthur Selwyn Miller thus quotes the Committee for Economic Development:

> In relations with their constituencies and with the larger society, American corporations operate today in an intricate matrix of obligations and responsibilities that far exceed in scope and complexity those of most other institutions and are analogous in many respects to government itself. The great growth of corporations in size, market power, and impact on society has naturally brought with it a commensurate growth in responsibilities; in a democratic society, power sooner or later begets equivalent responsibility [Miller 1972, p. 64].

(I acknowledge that the CED may have been fantasizing and also that the claim for responsibility accepted may simply be a strategem to legitimize power.) Friedman rejects managerialism but not the organizational revolution which produced it; he does not even effectively recognize it [Means 1969, p. 21]. Enterprise concentration of power does not bother him: "In almost any industry that one can mention," he reports, "there are giants and pygmies side by side" [Friedman 1962, p. 121].

Have not the corporations become a system of private governments? Simons [1948, p. 42] referred to them as the organization "of extra-governmental, functional 'states,' " among other things. Are the planning systems of France, West Germany, and Japan "market" systems according to the Chicago conception? What is voluntary choice in the current system compared to individualist capitalism, whatever *its* limits?

At one time Frank W. Taussig [1930, p. 129] could assert: "Better that we should have Napoleons of industry than the blood-guilty Napoleons of history," a view echoed by Simons: "Few of our gigantic corporations can be defended on the ground that their present size is necessary to reasonably full exploitation of production economies: their existence is to be explained in terms of opportunities for promoter profits, personal ambitions of industrial and financial 'Napoleons,' and advantages of monopoly power" [Simons 1948, pp. 59–60]. If the rationalization of the market is to be a subtle device to protect us from the Napoleons of industry, how can we differentiate and support that protection from the legitimacy which the rationalization offers apparently any structure of business? That may be quite a Faustian bargain. And what of my student's remark, upon hearing of Taussig's dictum, that the Napoleons of industry seem to cultivate the Napoleons of history? But, then, imperialism, as are multinationals, is to Chicagoans a matter of market adjustment. The Coasian market for bribes enters international business.

Has the economic system changed such that the endogenous determination of preferences by corporations within the market is eclipsed by the extinction of the market (for at least the planning sector), with the Chicago School's and related doctrines permitting the rationalization of conquest as market adjustment and profit maximizing? In recent years we have seen that the language of politics is more than metaphor in international business: witness ITT in Chile, the foreign marketing practices of aircraft manufacturers and other companies, and so on. Walter Adams describes the oil industry thus:

> The U.S. petroleum industry is a government sanctioned, government supported, government subsidized cartel, reinforced by a honeycomb of private restraints which systematically stifle and suppress competition. The industry is truly an *imperium in imperio*—a sovereign unto itself. It is not subject to effective regulation by the government. It is not subservient to the discipline of the marketplace. It is under no compulsion to promote the public interest. In short, it is effectively immunized by private and public storm shelters from those Schumpeterian gales of creative destruction which are supposed to erode encrusted monopoly power in a dynamic economy [Adams 1975, p. 342].

Moreover, the Mideast oil cartel may be interpreted as having taken over or changed the arrangements of the international cartel hitherto dominated by the oil companies, the governments having changed from their relatively passive role. *Mutatis mutandis,* does not Adams's view also describe what Galbraith and Solo call the planning sector? Is this not a more accurate description than the Chicago School portrayal of the impersonal "market"?

I do not know the answers to these queries, but they do point to potential, if not actual, serious limits to the Chicago School's doctrines for anyone attempting to cope with the realities of the economy as a system of power without the masquerade of ideological rationalization. Granted that rationalization may be put aside in favor of substantive explanation, but these doctrines, if the views suggested by the questions have some accuracy and probative significance, would serve not merely to cloak corporate power, to use Galbraith's phrase, but to obscure the substantive transformation from the traditional market system (with its infirmities and limits) to something else (with perhaps more serious infirmities and limits). The Chicago analysis, which is not without value, it should be remembered, may be so bound by its paradigm that it is unable to even acknowledge the developments raised by the foregoing questions.

Let me quote, with permission, from a letter to me from Horace Gray in which he declined to contribute a paper to this symposium:

> After studying carefully your letter of October 9, 1974, and your paper on the Coase Theorem, I keep asking myself.—Why should it be thought necessary to organize a symposium devoted to a "constructive critique" of the Chicago-Austrian theory—i.e., to identify and fix its limits? Hasn't the profession reached a pretty general consensus reflecting the limitations of this doctrine? Doesn't your Coase paper do all that is really necessary? Hasn't the Chicago School, by its teaching and writing, painted itself into a corner, and defined itself as irrelevant for the modern world—that is, for most of it? My reaction is: "Let the dead bury their dead."

> rather that I reject its general application, its pretensions to uni-
> This does not mean that I reject the Chicago theory in toto, but versality. This theory still has relevance for that minor portion of the private economy where competition still exists, and for a large, but as of now undetermined, area where competition could be functionally viable if society so ordered. Thus, the Chicago theory has a potentiality considerably beyond its present limits. I have argued and fought for years to extend the scope of competition to its feasible limits. But the Chicago School has consistently opposed such efforts on ideological grounds—competition was a naturalistic, universal law, not a manmade, pragmatic, institutional contrivance; it would endure because it was rooted in human nature and in the natural conditions of production. Governmental intervention, therefore, was abhorrent

on both economic and moralistic grounds; it would destroy both economic efficiency and individual freedom.

In America the gradual obsolescence of this mode of thought has been under way for nearly 100 years—that is, from Munn v. Illinois (1876), when the Supreme Court incorporated into our constitutional law the early 19th century doctrine of public interest regulation as developed by English Jurists. Since that feeble beginning governmental intervention has increased with giant strides. Unfortunately, however, this ever-increasing intervention, particularly since the failure of Wilson's New Freedom (1912–16), has not been for the purpose of promoting free competition in the private sector and expanding social production in the public sector but rather to promote monopoly capitalism. In short, our institutional creativity has been perverted to the service of monopoly capitalism, and to the disservice of economic efficiency, individual freedom and social welfare. This monstrosity has developed so rapidly that we don't yet have an agreed name for it. Neo-fascism, the corporative state, multi-national corporativism are not meaningful to the general public; monopoly capitalism undefined sounds too Marxist, my preference for the time being is an awkward but understandable description:—privileged, subsidized, monopoly capitalism organized on an international basis and supported by overwhelming military power. Being an institutionalist, I want to emphasize the *means* by which this system has been created and is held together.

Our present system being what it is the obsolescence and irrelevance of the Chicago theory seems to me self-evident—totally so as a general explanation, potentially of some limited value if we decide to restore free competition insofar as feasible. This being the case, I cannot visualize how a "constructive critique" of the Chicago theory is either possible or worthwhile. Since the Chicago School repudiates "*power*" as a causative factor and defines *positive* economics as a non-power system, I cannot see how a paper on "*power and positive economics*," as you suggest, would be meaningful; the Chicago School would simply ignore it as irrelevant *for their theory*, and they would be right. It is impossible to refute them if they write the ground rules.

The critical task of Institutional Economics today is, as throughout our national history, to devise new, creative, imaginative institutional arrangements for the organization and operation of the economy in the public interest and to preserve democracy. The immediate enemy is monopoly capitalism. To rid ourselves of this octopus we must correct the perversion of institutions that sustains it, and then go on to devise new institutional arrangements to meet new needs. In the process I would expect

> that, among other social benefits, we would get a large increase in competition—more perhaps than the Chicago negativists would approve. They wouldn't want to be made relevant again by governmental action, or by institutional economists [Horace M. Gray to Warren J. Samuels, 31 October 1974].

Henry Simons, as we have seen, held views not entirely dissimilar to those who perceive, and are dissatisfied with, the corporate system, or monopoly capitalism. The current Chicago School reaction to all this, however, would be and is substantially negative, of course. Chicagoans would urge that the market and its conception of freedom *is* correct and that evidence to the contrary either is spurious or fails to penetrate to the essence of the promarket argument and system. One can only reiterate the points that freedom is more complex than the Chicago School contemplates as important; power *is* important and should not be obscured for propaganda reasons; the corporate system is a system of power, indeed of concentrated power that may have superseded the market; and these constitute important limits to the Chicago School doctrine.

And what of individualism? What of extending meaningful participation in the economy to more people? What of extending and diffusing power, in various forms, so that freedom can be made effective for more than a relatively privileged few? In this regard several points may be made.

First, economic ideology speaks of voluntary exchange and laissez-faire; legal ideology speaks of free contract between "legal equals." But individualism, and voluntarism, is always within the structure of power, including the distribution of wealth.[16] Voluntary exchange, the heart of Chicago individualism, always takes place within and gives effect to the relations comprising the social order, within the larger system of institutions and power relations. Individualism and voluntarism exist only within the extant system of social control. The pretenses of ideology must be transcended if the Chicago argument is to be understood; but then the argument may become less attractive and compelling. The Chicago School plays down and denigrates the fact of the hierarchical system of society; its individualism is a rationalization of privilege in the process of, and at least for some the purpose of, rationalizing the market per se.

Second, the real world is predominantly one of adhesion or standardized contracts with the imposition of nonnegotiable and asymmetrical obligations and rights. Such contracts set market relations quite independent of voluntary exchange. One party (typically all sellers) dictates the terms and the others acquiesce, else there is no contract. With (as Lowry shows) private (but governmentally enforced) contracts creating private rights and presentiating the future, voluntarism is accurate enough—individuals *do* choose between the alternatives in their opportunity sets—but this hardly exhausts the description of the choosing process. Asymmetrical power has its day, every day. Government enforcement of adhesion contracts means supporting and giving effect to the structure of power, of advantaged and disadvantaged relationships. (Courts often interpret contracts in favor of the party not having drawn it up, but most contracts never are litigated, and corporate attorneys have learned that lesson too.)

Third, the myths of individualism and voluntarism persist in an increasingly collective and interdependent world. The advocacy of the old individualist ideology seems anachronistic when the business elite itself admits to a managerialist ideology.

Fourth, the Chicago School doctrine, by its subtle finessing of distributional issues, serves inevitably as a defense of the status quo structures of power and wealth. Its commitment to freedom is a commitment to the freedom for the prosperous insofar as it emphasizes economic choice and market exchange. The role of ideology, all establishment and all radical ideology, in the United States and elsewhere, is to obscure hierarchical and elite control and privileged benefits in the name of democracy, freedom, and the market, or whatever linguistic symbolism is practiced.

Fifth, the position of the great mass of the world's population, certainly those in the Western capitalistic or market economies, would be far less salutary today if historical conservatives had had their way in social policy over the last two centuries. Although Chicago doctrine is largely correct in saying that improvement in living conditions is historically attributable to or correlative with industrial capitalism (or the forces which permitted it to flower), the distributional dimension (as John Stuart Mill argued) has been heavily influenced by institutional change and reform tending to permit the pluralization of the economy as well as the polity, making both responsive to a wider range of interests. Conservatives, not incorrectly as definitions go, have called this "socialism," as is discussed in chapter 20. The welfare state and unions have been means of effectuating worker interests. As property equivalents they have protected worker security similar to the way property promotes certain other security interests. Individualism has been spread through institutional change.

Sixth, if that is the case, there remains the problem of whether individualism is to be maximized, as it were, through the number or percentage of the population effectively (freedom plus power) benefited or through the degree of benefit of those most benefited. The Chicago School does not discriminate between these two dimensions of individualism, except that in promoting, intentionally or inadvertently, the status quo structure of power it does support the latter approach; and, of course, current Chicagoans revile egalitarianism. Its formulation of voluntary choice is formally completely independent of the structure of opportunity sets and therefore of the balance between the intensive and extensive margins of individualism. This is a serious problem: individualism yes, but which individuals? What has to be done to promote and protect meaningful widespread individual participation in the economy, to so diffuse power that the incentive system of capitalism so notably stressed by Chicago might better generate wider incentives and to extend the consensual support for the system upon stronger foundations? It is a severe limit to the probative significance of the Chicago School that it would leave all this, after suitable government retrenchment, to the market. The market does produce institutional change—largely as a function of the existing distribution of power; and it may also undermine the consensual foundations of the system itself, as discussed above.

Seventh, ultimately one must consider egalitarianism. Henry Simons again may be juxtaposed to current Chicago doctrine. Simons gave a "special place to liberty (and nearly coordinate place to equality)," saying that "liberal ideas include equality of opportunity—or steadily diminishing inequality," and that "equality of opportunity is an idea that free societies should constantly pursue, even at much cost in terms of other ends. Freedom without power, like power without freedom, has no substance or meaning" [Simons 1948, pp. 2, 4, 6]. One does not have to agree with this. The current Chicago School may be correct in distinguishing "sharply between equality of rights and equality of opportunity, on the one hand, and material equality or equality of outcome" [Friedman 1962, p. 195], although its conception of equality of opportunity is much more restricted than that of Simons. The point is that the concept of an individualism which recognizes the need for power to make freedom and voluntarism widely effective is lacking in the current Chicago view, which constitutes a limit thereto. Moreover, this is not merely a normative matter. As discussed previously, a change in the structure of power will produce a change in resource allocation and output. Because a redistribution of power *may* mean a change (say, a lowering) of income does not necessarily mean that welfare has been reduced, for such a reduction in the size of the pie is in terms of prices and output definitions generated by the previous power structure and cannot, except presumptively, be compared with the new. (This is, moreover, but one example of how reckoning in terms of the existing cost-price structure reinforces and gives effect to the existing structure of power.)

Eighth, without either affirming or denigrating egalitarianism, the issue is more than that alone. Institutions weight individuals, governing who counts how much along either the intensive or the extensive margin of individualism. The Chicago School seems to promote the control of institutions by the already established and privileged interests, or some of them. Existing inequality, for example, is a partial function of certain rights having been granted (and their correlative exposure and disadvantage for others) and not other rights (with the same correlational consequences, but for the other parties), and all this is a function of the asymmetrical access to and use of government. Chicago doctrine canonizes that. Moreover, if I understand correctly what the Chicago School means by economics, it would exclude from economics the study of the factors and forces actually governing the structure and composition of opportunity sets and the determination of economic welfare. For all practical purposes these studies have been eliminated from orthodox economics, but they are viable if difficult endeavors. Furthermore, they can be pursued reasonably objectively without making interpersonal utility comparisons or judgments as to whose interests should count—as the Chicago School says is improper but proceeds to do. Methodological individualism need not abort or channel methodological collectivism, or vice versa.

Finally, perhaps the last word, sadly to say, on the redistribution of power is that the market will not promote greater equality of power and that government will not either. As Bartlett [1973] shows so clearly, the operation of both market and government is a function of private power. *That* may be the ultimate Chicago message.

### *Government*

We are now at the heart of the subject. In my 1957 doctoral dissertation on American business and labor thought on the economic role of government [Samuels 1957, pp. 313ff], I concluded that business (as represented by the major business organizations in this country) prescribed for government the fundamental role of preserving and strengthening the business system (and the variety and depth of things which that entails) and the requirement that everything done by government should be consonant with the theory and practice of the business system. When asked at my defense if this was not essentially the role ascribed by Marx to government in the capitalist system, I responded in the affirmative. There are many differences between business (organized and unorganized) and Chicago School thought on the economic role of government, to be sure, but at bottom the story is much the same. The Chicago School's advocacy of minimal and laissez-faire government is very effective propaganda in the arena of public philosophy and argument, but is analytically meaningful only within the context of a business system and what it takes for granted and implies. There are likewise many differences between Marxism and the Chicago School (and business thought), but at bottom, I think, there is a core of common understanding as to what it is that government does in the business, or capitalist, or market system. To see that, it is necessary to penetrate the ideology, the propaganda, and the affirmative and negative stereotypes.

*The State*

Olson and Clague [1971, p. 769] make this insightful point: "It is surely significant that all three of the great ideologies of the mid-nineteenth century had within them a profound distrust of government." (They refer to laissez-faire liberalism, Marxism, and anarchism.) Not without material cause, and for other reasons, government, as the chief conspicuous institution of social order and control, thereby has become the chief object of civilization's discontents. Quite aside from deeper psychoanalytic explanations, government has been the often justified object for the displacement of frustration and anxiety whenever "things" have been perceived as going "wrong," and in a world of opportunity costs, that is always. Mankind has not conquered its world, its body, and its mind; has not learned to live with conflict; has not given up the quest for fantasies and devils when reality does not measure up to the perfection of ideals which abstract from the conflicts and other problems. It probably never will. Government itself, driven by the lust for power (ego-gratification), is complicated and frustrated by the absence of unequivocal solutions for, as well as definitions of, problems. Creating fictions and fantasies in the process of reaching consensus (or aborting conflict) and keeping order, government is a *cause* of and *conduit* for innumerable *human* problems. Politics is disgusting because of the inevitable dissimulation. Except for those impressed with pomp, circumstance, and nationalism (bear in mind that both Frank Knight and Joan Robinson, unusual allies, do not think much of nationalism), there is not much impressive about the state. But it does exist, and its existence commands our attention, investigation, and analysis, and, I regret to have to add, our loyalty.

*Government and the Market*

The Chicago School adheres to the market system: That is its central premise and paradigm. It also manifests an explicit general antagonism toward governmental activism. It maintains a rigorous, or rigid, adherence to the presumptive propriety of market, or private enterprise and contractarian, solutions to problems.

Not paradoxically, the Chicago School supports change through markets, but such change is characterized in part by government protecting certain interests and not others. As I have shown elsewhere [Samuels 1974e], nonlegal, or market, change actually involves differential government protection of rights as between Alpha and Beta whenever one is able to visit economic injury upon the other, and the right of one (freedom to) is affirmed and the right of the other (freedom from) is denied. The market operates upon the basis of a structure of rights; this structure is a function not of rights fully defined once and for all time, but of continuing differential legal protection of interests. This phenomenon is inevitable, thus the so-called compensation problem is ubiquitous. To support the market, then, is not to avoid government but to engage government in support of one set of interests rather than another, the set supported being selective and, within social structure and asymmetrical access to government, fairly open.

Neither is it paradoxical that the market system, far from eliminating government, actually requires government for its own existence. It seems almost banal to say, but the idea that government will maintain the system of property and contract, and other related legal-economic institutions, *is* important: Take that away, and where is the market system? Government operates to institutionalize the economic order and its processes and arrangements for organizing and controlling economic activity.

*The Use of Government*

I have already applauded the Chicago School view that government (including politics) is subject to constrained maximization analysis and is not an impenetrable black box. This comports with the ideas of government as an economic alternative and of the legal-political system as deliberative processes, ideas which I think are relatively accurate and heuristically valuable. Chicagoans have presented interesting and suggestive interpretations of the bargaining and market-like processes within and over government. But the Chicago School likes to project government as necessarily coercive at the same time that it portrays the operation of market-like processes in government. It thinks of making and exchanging goods as Pareto optimal in the most austere sense, whereas using government is coercive, since it is a mode of imposing one's values upon others. Yet the two processes, market and government, are not all that different: Trades in each are Pareto-better adjustments, by definition, and it is only by emphasizing the externalities of trades and decisions in the government market and by distinguishing away the externalities of trades and decisions in the private market that Chicago, and our ideology generally, is able to distinguish between the two. Both government and the market are used by people. The Chicago School propaganda (which we all share, to lesser or greater degree, by virtue of having been brought up in our civilization) fails explicitly to recognize the nature of its own doctrine as an agenda for government, that is, its use as an economic alternative. It is normatively important and necessary to distinguish between market and government—between private and government markets—but the difference is not such that government is absent from the former; rather, it is critical.

### *Government Decision Making*

The Chicago School also has both profoundly cautioned against over-reliance upon government to solve day-to-day problems and soundly criticized details of government policies and programs. Its greatest concern is that alternative to the market comprised of constant governmental meddling in this and that, even though it acts in response to demands upon it by all comers. Anyone familiar with the history of the U.S. system of government knows that we have preached self-reliance and laissez-faire but practice using government, not all the time but quite often, when we think it will help (us, and therefore, we project, the system).

Two comments: First, the Chicago School here quite properly and accurately points out both that government policies often do not work and, especially, that they have *costs*. This emphasis upon the opportunity cost doctrine, as opposed to emotional wishful thinking (one cause of the criticism directed at the school), is sound; but the choice of the costs must be up to the general decision-making process. As suggested before, the Chicago School interposes or injects its own social welfare function in giving economic policy advice, as its contribution to the process of evaluating the costs and benefits, and in so doing presents its own estimation of whose interests should count.

Second, a fine characterization or example of a Chicago line of reasoning has been given by Murray Weidenbaum [1975, pp. 205–206]: "But, unfortunately, any realistic evaluation of the actual practice of government regulation does not comfortably fit the notion of benign, beneficient, and wise men and women making altogether sensible decisions in the society's greater interests. I must report that, in my study of the subject, I find instead waste, bias, stupidity, arrogance, concentration on trivia, conflicts among the regulators, and, worst of all, arbitrary and often uncontrolled power." This is correct, but its significance requires supplemental recognition that, in contrast to the goods markets where commodities have relatively simple decisions made about them (yet often with externalities galore), the market for governmental decisions is vastly more complex in cognitive structure and perceived conflicts of interest. Without endorsing the bureaucratic mentality, one must insist that what is waste from one point of view can be a desired output from another, a characteristic of the normative evaluation of market goods as well, except there we invoke against making interpersonal utility comparisons. Government decision making must be inferior to market decision making when both are evaluated by the criteria of the latter, notwithstanding the operation of market-like processes in government.

### *Regulation*

The Chicago School reviles against the welfare state, regulation, and assorted policies and actions deemed stupid by its members. Many of these regulatory schemes and policies have been foisted upon government by business itself, and the Chicago School does criticize business abuse of government [see Friedman 1962, pp. 125–26, 131, 137ff]. Chicagoans freely criticize twentieth-century liberals, leftists, welfare staters, and similar undesirables, yet treat with greater circumspection the business use and abuse of government. They *do* criticize, to be sure, but they seem wary of denigrating business (and businessmen) for fear of denigrating the business system, preferring to challenge government per se, as if government were an exogenous or closed system. Chicago's critique, then, is influenced by its normative posture and seeming considerations of strategy. An interesting juxtaposition may be found in Friedman's criticisms of the Federal Reserve System contrasted with Simons's [1948, p. 54] complaint that the private commercial banks had usurped the power of money creation from government. Each takes a different view as to what power configuration is to be taken as given. The two Chicagoans accordingly would derive different lessons from this proposition of Simons: "Laissez faire, to repeat, implies a division of tasks between competitive and political controls; and the failure of the system, if it has failed, is properly to be regarded as a result of failure of the state, especially with respect to money, to do its part" [1948, p. 55].

*Government and Business*

The premier strategy of the Chicago School with regard to government is to prevent and/or disengage alien uses of the state, to destroy the rationales for government action, in part by casting the state as an alien institution, all the while allowing it to perform its valued functions. In the modern world, this means countering the effects of majoritarian use of government to formulate rights, rights equivalents, and other policies which would supplement resource allocation "by the market" in accordance with considerations ostensibly not based solely or primarily on wealth and traditional property, that is, a governmental system in which politicians compete for voter favor with alternative schemes of largesse. Chicago School doctrine may be interpreted as either a perceived necessary defense of the market and/or a serving of the interests of business and property, and the former does tend (as Buchanan acknowledges in his own way) to mean the latter. What Chicago primarily objects to is the use of political rather than goods markets for decision making. This means that it supports the *market* system, which is to say, it supports the *business* system.

*The Chicago Agenda*

The heart of the matter is that the Chicago School has its *own* agenda, or set of uses, for government, which may be summarized as the maintenance and preservation of the existing system of property and the market. The Chicago School by no means "neglects" government: System maintenance is critical, and the school has a distinctive, if necessarily asymmetrical, set of uses for government. Laissez-faire means government protection in fundamentals, and the rest is left, as it were, to the market.

The idea of "minimal" government is utterly fallacious: The responsibility for the economic order is largely given to government (to whom else?) to erect and maintain the system (thus North's economic history suggests some of the processes and devices through which the system of business and property has developed through the use of the state). It also must prevent consolidations of social power, structure, and policy antagonistic to the system of property and business, as Chicago contemplates it. This is why many critics, especially but not only the more radical, see in the minimization of government doctrine a subtle defense of the status quo structure of power functioning to limit legal change deemed antagonistic to the system.

Similarly, the idea of government's "protecting property" is both important and fallacious. It is functional with regard to the protection of the institution of property (as well as specific existing or problematic property rights). But it is fallacious because the rights which government protects are themselves defined through government: They are not protected because they are rights but are rights because they are protected. The key question, then, has to do with the use of government to articulate (and choose between claimants of) rights.

Similarly, the concept of "intervention" is loaded: Government is an important part of the status quo, and legal change ("intervention") does not mean the introduction of government into a situation in which it hitherto has been absent, but a change of the interests to which government is used to give effect and protect.[17] The key problem is not the presence or absence of law but legal change,[18] and on this the Chicago School is, as we have seen, selective.

Finally, government enforcement of contract means, given the power structure, supporting and giving effect to the structure of power. This is in addition to its more conventional and propagandistically useful, as well as accurate (within limits), role of assuring stable, secure, and reliable markets.

Thus, individual liberty is not quite the same as laissez-faire. Not only does a laissez-faire system require *its* legal foundations (to wit: the legal foundations of capitalism), but also, as Jeremy Bentham observed, the law which promotes the liberty of one person likely inhibits the liberty of another. The key question, again, is whose liberty is promoted. Liberty is always liberty within the system and, moreover, is structured by particular liberties. Chicago doctrines on liberty attempt to inculcate acceptance of or identification with certain patterns of liberty.

The terms just discussed (minimal government, protecting property, enforcing contracts, and so on) have empirical and heuristic value, but they also are propaganda terminology serving as code words with systemic meaning and function. More important for present purposes is the recognition by the Chicago School of the necessity for adequate and proper legal institutions to make the system work and which govern, perhaps largely indirectly but nevertheless fundamentally, system performance (resource allocation and income distribution).

The Chicago School doctrine is viable as a defense against a host of special pleaders seeking government largesse. The terms "special pleaders" and "government largesse" are loaded, but they are used to emphasize that all of us are special pleaders and that government is an arena in which largesse is sought after by all of us. We tend to use different words to refer to our own demands and benefits from government, words often reflecting the paradigm within which the fundamental distinctions are posited. Thus, within the market paradigm, business as a system of power is not perceived as the beneficiary of largesse but labor unions are, and vice versa.

The Chicago School makes its own distinctions and identifications as between (1) special pleaders seeking largesse and (2) claims for rights and legal change of rights and of basic economic institutions in a manner deemed consonant with the system. Legal change is an inevitable and important part of the economic or legal-economic process; the Chicago School makes its own differentiations between so-called framework filling and particular intervention activities of government.

Chicago ultimately does not "neglect" the fact that regulation is a functional equivalent of property rights: It designates as property rights the interests it would sanction and decries as either government regulation or feeding at the public trough all other claims. It does not neglect the joint determination process wherein both optimal solutions *and* rights (as well as decisional institutions) governing the substance of optimal solutions are worked out: It would channel them along lines deemed consonant with the system. It does not neglect the police power element in all private property rights: It would guide and channel its exercise. It does not neglect the pressures (in the market and in government) for change of property rights: It would channel both the change and the mode of change. The Chicago School thus makes deep normative judgments in identifying claims for the realization of interests through government as the expression of either property or interference. It makes those judgments on the basis of its selective interpretation of the nature and needs of the business, or market, system.

In all these respects, the fact and substance of the exercise of judgment by the Chicago School constitutes limits to its doctrines. It is playing God with the implementation of the market system and with government.

In all these respects, too, the Chicago School makes an invaluable contribution to the social value-clarification process,[19] for example, in distinguishing between claims upon government as favors or as rights protecting legitimate interests. It is a contribution to the use of "government to establish what shall and what shall not be regarded as property" [Friedman 1962, p. 127]. Most especially it is a contribution to the practice of government not as "a ruler but an intermediary mechanism of group self-control" in a democracy [Knight 1952, p. 49]. The correct meaning of laissez-faire, then, is quite different from its propaganda meaning. This, together with, and indeed as part of, its defense of the system, is the substantive meaning of the Chicago School doctrines with regard to government. Most everything else is propaganda, necessary and instrumental, but not presently useful except as empirical evidence. Its message appears as truth but, quite aside from its descriptive content and normative status, it is tautological with its premise and paradigm and embodies important choices that must be and are made by larger decisional processes which the Chicago School, through its activism in the policy arena, is trying mightily to influence.

The Chicago doctrine is a narrow and selective, albeit important and suggestive, basis from which to reform and conduct the legal, and general governmental, system. As was stressed above, one cannot properly use short-run methodological individualist microeconomic and welfare economics theorems to evaluate conclusively methodological collectivist legal change, including rights. Each use constitutes only *an* informational input, not the result of a precise calculus. Such theories are loaded with recommendatory force—the force of the market paradigm—but their specific content is presumptive and selective, a function of implicit identifications and distinctions, ultimately as to whose interests are to count in instrumenting the market system.

One of the limits of Chicago doctrine has to do with what are *not* recognized as property rights. In our economic system, those interests not recognized as property rights effectively have a disadvantaged position when in competition with interests designated and/or recognized as property rights. Much of the semantics of property and public policy involves eliciting identification in decision makers' minds as to which one of many complex competing interests is to be perceived and protected as a *property* right. The Chicago School literature is replete with such identifications and distinctions.

Another limit involves the selective specification of reality as private or public and power as economic or political. In reality, in the economic system there are private elements in or aspects of everything public and public elements in or aspects of everything private, and political and economic power are typically symbiotic when not coalescent. All private rights and institutions are legal creations, and all law is a partial function of private power play: This is the ultimate relevant general equilibrium system with which the Chicago School (and everyone else) takes positions and makes selective identifications and attributions one way or another. Friedman argues persuasively that capitalism separates economic and political power, but not convincingly if one recognizes that what he contemplates as economic power (and which he also minimizes as power) is itself both an amalgam of and an influence upon political-legal power. The Chicago School takes positions on the checking of power in an area in which economic and political power are both fused and interacting. It is advocating not the separation of economic and political power but a particular, although somewhat ambiguous, set of economic-political interrelations.

In no small part the Chicago School doctrine is asymmetrical with regard to the use of government. It supports a set of business-cum-property and government relations which it denies to nonbusiness and nonproperty interests. This selectivity is important in *any* version of a market system, for it governs whose interests will be given effect, that is, whose system it is. The Chicago view must be compared with a laboristic capitalism, which in the Chicago paradigm is a contradiction of terms or a misconception. Especially striking would be the case (the fact of which I hold in abeyance) of a corporate state in which business and business-government relations are so structured and conducted as to supersede the market (although not market-like adjustments). Absent that eventuality, the problem is neither market versus no market nor government versus no government, but which interests will government be used to support, or which instrumentation of the market system. The Chicago School answer is articulated in terms of the values of a business system. That is one of its most profound limits, whether or not one agrees with Chicago.

Part of the meaning of the Chicago School is its position on the question of maximizing individualism on the intensive versus the extensive margin. There are radically different conceptions of individualism involved, but it should be clear that Chicago would promote the extension of individualism primarily through extending the property system (as conceived of by it) and not through nonproperty (read: welfare state) means. This is perhaps the deepest meaning of its establishmentarian position. Evaluation of the Chicago School turns to no small degree upon where one stands on that issue, given Chicago's tendencies in recognizing interests as property and nonproperty.[20]

*Propaganda*

The Chicago School's often brilliant analyses of government and politics have to be seen as limited by having been informed and channeled by a particular ideology. The school, to its credit, does not appeal to some god of history but makes explicit and proclaims its nineteenth-century liberal ideology. The propaganda role thus has to be seen as both strengthening and weakening its doctrine.

*The Problem of Change*

The Chicago School prefers market solutions, but the market is also a generator of problems which are left to it with only problematic confidence. This was a theme dealt with by Knight. Schumpeterian creative destruction is after all "experimentation by society upon itself," and Knight [1951b, p. 349] said that such "is both limited and terribly dangerous," especially when undertaken through politics, but the principle applies to the market as well. Knight wrote:

> Growth, or any tendency toward cumulative change, is a fundamentally disruptive force, and a conscious effort toward progress further intensifies the problems of order and efficiency almost beyond comparison [Knight 1951b, p. 310].

> Further, the more the society stresses freedom, mobility, change and variety, the more the functions of government are multiplied and elaborated, and the more it inevitably becomes in details a government by men and not of law [Knight 1960, p. 127].

Growth and change produce disruption and a need for social control. "Liberty may bring progress and efficiency, yet disturb order and security, and result in accumulations of power jeopardizing equality of opportunity, justice, and even liberty itself" [Gonce 1972, p. 550, summarizing Knight]. One profound limit of the Chicago School is that its high priestly paradigm, leading to the tautological optimality of doing nothing and leaving everything to the market (which is, of course, its own stereotype), may be unable to handle this Knightian contradiction within the system.[21] Another limit is that its analysis may not even be capable of recognizing the problem, thus leading either to its irrelevance or its self-destructive use.[22] More likely, Chicago will unobtrusively redefine the system in terms of the new corrective action, akin to what it has done to accommodate the growth of giant business.

*The Inadequate Paradigm*

The point is that Chicago School doctrines concerning government are descriptively incomplete. It is necessary to realize that even if one accepts the school's values and its propaganda (role and substance). Much of this essay indicates respects in which the Chicago doctrines are incomplete, question begging, or selective when considered as positive description and analysis. The Chicago analysis of government includes elements of the state as an independent and dependent variable, but its ideology limits its integration of those elements into a comprehensive positive description of government as an economic variable, although it may be moving somewhat in that direction in the work of some of its younger members.

One often must agree with Chicago school criticisms of government. Political decision making and action are often absurd and produce inept and insensitive results. Politicians and bureaucrats seem almost a race apart. Yet the Chicago view of government tends to be simplistic, with a dichotomy of government and business, public and private, and voluntary market exchange and government coercion. But this is its propaganda level; on a deeper level, the school takes positions which blend those seeming opposites. It has its own sense of the structure of private power, of the different essential character of collective decision making, of the "planning system" (a concept no less presumptive than the "market") residing in the corporate system. It has its own sense, too, of the role of the powerful in channeling governmental definition and assignment of rights in favor of some economic actors and not others, and, *inter alia,* of the possible importance of rights to participation, and therefore collective political action, in a large-scale and highly organized world.[23] The problem is not that Chicago School minimization of government is incorrect, because there is fundamental government action and involvement in the market system and the status quo; rather, the bundle of so-called private and governmental interrelations called the market may no longer exist, may have inherent contradictions, may be supportive of too narrow a structure of power, and so on. Perhaps Friedman is correct in suggesting that government will be used to support monopoly and inequality under any system. That, however, is not a sufficient defense against the circulation of the elite, if that is what is involved.[24] As Pareto argued, circulation might bring new vitality to the top.

## *Notes*

1. The problem is that the Chicago School conception of the economic system requires, for its realization, a degree of consensus and agreement about market institutions, processes, and performance that does not and is not likely to exist. Conservatives in all societies wish it were otherwise; consensus sounds nice, but the real question is: On whose terms? The Chicago School appears myopic about the reality of struggle and conflict, yet I think it does recognize the situation, inasmuch as many of its policy doctrines and writings are directed at effectuating particular solutions to the conflicts.
2. Several points may be made. (1) Particular economic functions can be performed by different institutions, within capitalism, each tending to have different performance consequences, and these methodological individualism can only incompletely analyze and evaluate. (2) Methodological individualism is not able conclusively, if at all, to prescribe the best institutional arrangements for a market system. (3) The institutional requirements of the market (as Strassmann suggests) are not entirely clear or given without presumptive reasoning by methodological normative individualism and collectivism. (4) There are considerable institutional variations among actual and among ideal market economies, for example, diverse ways in which the business and financial power of the private sector operates upon, through, and in symbiosis with government. (5) The Chicago School tends to identify capitalism or the market system with certain specific institutions, whereas different technically optimal results can be achieved through many different sets of institutions, and the market system is capable of considerable variety of such arrangements. Most of the points made about methodological individualism also apply to normative individualism.
3. Whether the Chicago School version of economic determinism is closer to Marx than, say, my concentration upon the economy as a system of power is for others to decide, a consideration I raise inasmuch as one member of the school has commented privately to me that in my work with power I was getting perilously close to Marxism. Personally, I think that most such comparisons with Marx(ism) are strained. Perception of the threat to order, however, is a different matter.
4. See, for example, the exchange of ideas between Buchanan and me recorded in my chapter on socialism, below.
5. An early 1974 advertisement received through the mail for the University of Chicago's *Journal of Law and Economics*, edited by Ronald Coase, includes the following: "What influence does the legal framework have on the operation of the economic system? How far are existing, or proposed, laws appropriate to bring about an efficient working of the economic system? These are the underlying questions to which articles in the *Journal of Law and Economics* are directed." The first question is a meaningful one, although its answer may include norma-

tive elements. The second question I think is meaningless: Efficiency is a function of the state of the law, and the law cannot, except through presumptive reasoning, be evaluated by efficiency.

6. Morgenstern [1972, pp. 1169–70] predicts and supports a short life expectancy for Pareto optimality as usually formulated.
7. See Samuels [1974e].
8. Buchanan has criticized other members of the school for not applying the Pareto rule to themselves, although they would impose it upon others. I have made the same criticism of Buchanan.
9. Gramm [chapter 7 at note 40] quotes David and Temin about Fogel and Engerman "making coherent statements about the welfare efficiency of slavery from the standpoint of everyone but the slaves." See also Parker [1974, p. 471]: "The economist—to his discredit—has not been much interested in the material life or psychic welfare of the slaves." Scott [1974, pp. 57–59] stresses that the Fogel and Engerman theory of optimal submission is developed strictly from the slaveowner's point of view and in the context of a particular system of coercion, omitting consideration of the slaves' interests and preferences, as well as of the non-Pareto optimal nature of the original entitlements to the slaves. Scott says that "this insensitivity comes close to passing over into apologetics" [1974, p. 61]. The brilliant thing about the economics of slavery thus far is that it permits much more clear identification of the interests in terms of which optimality is implicitly specified than most previous optimality analysis, although this is apparently no part of the authors' intention.
10. "Therefore, the theory of the existence of such equilibria, which is the heartland of received doctrine, is not a scientific explanation of reality but *is the characterization of a state* which if achieved would have certain desirable properties" [Day 1975, p. 231]. Specification of formal properties must not be confused with articulation of substantive results, which is a matter of presumptive optimality reasoning building upon selective normative premises.
11. As between competition and market per se, most but not all of my colleagues with whom I have discussed the issue thought that the school emphasizes the latter; as between structural and behavioral notions of competition, most felt that the latter were stressed by the school.
12. The following are representative of Simons's approach, concerns, and proposed policies and may be compared with Friedman's [1962, chapter 8] treatment of monopoly. I am not saying, of course, that current Chicagoans like or prefer noncompetitive conditions. The point is that they seem to see very little of it, apart from governmental restrictions on entry. Simons, on the other hand, saw governmental laissez-faire toward the corporation as a form of restrictionism—on others' and the system's freedom. Simons [1948] wrote:

> The central government . . . must systematically prevent, destroy, or control all artificial private monopoly, that is, all extra-governmental organizations with power to restrain trade. Such organizations are not merely an economic evil; they are

also an impairment or usurpation of the state monopoly of coercion and, to repeat, of individual freedom of association (p. 16).

In one respect it is a matter of uncontrolled corporate imperialism and giant enterprise aggregations. The profligate dispensation of privileges under incorporation laws may have accelerated the industrialization of America. Existing corporation laws may have been somewhat appropriate to an agricultural nation bent on rapid change. They may, by their extravagances, have accelerated progress. But they are surely ill designed to sustain progress or tolerable operation of the economy they promoted. Turned loose with inordinate powers, corporations have vastly overorganized most industries.

A heritage of excessive centralization may be a necessary or reasonable price to pay for rapid maturing of new industries and new technology—and the same may be true of some desirable new governmental functions or services. In any case, America should face now an urgent task of deorganizing industry and deconcentrating industrial control. Some direct dismantling of corporate empires seems indispensable. The main concerns of policy, however, should be that of facilitating new enterprise and multiplication of moderate-sized firms (p. 34).

The best single device, in business organization, is to limit the power of officials by keeping their organizations under the severe discipline of competition (p. 37).

Thus, *the great enemy of democracy is monopoly, in all its forms*: gigantic corporations, trade associations and other agencies for price control, trade-unions—or, in general, organization and concentration of power within functional classes. Effectively organized functional groups possess tremendous power for exploiting the community at large and even for sabotaging the system (p. 43).

We may recognize, in the almost unlimited grants of powers to corporate bodies, one of the greatest sins of governments against the free-enterprise system (p. 52).

The corporation is simply running away with our economic (and political) system—by virtue merely of an absurd carelessness and extravagance on the part of the states in granting powers to these legal creatures (p. 58).

13. This is true notwithstanding the uncertain interrelations between faith in the possibility if not existence of competitive markets and faith in the analytical and policy relevance of microeconomics and welfare economics.

14. "I have already mentioned as characteristic a certain Chicago unconcern with distribution as compared with economic freedom and allocative efficiency. This manifests itself in a willingness, even eagerness, to accept whatever results the free market grinds out, with minimal regard for the initial distribution of income and wealth which these results reflect. It also manifests itself in advocacy of policy changes with minimal regard for the distribution of the windfall gains and losses involved in them" [Bronfenbrenner 1962, p. 73].
15. "The distribution of wealth did not arise from economically efficient public policies in an egalitarian society of the past. Today's wealth and income distribution is the result of yesterday's power struggles. Measures used by our ancestors as participants in those power struggles included war, enslavement, and forced migrations; industrial sabotage, strike breaking, monopolization, restraint of trade, and unfair methods of competition; and manipulations of government policy. To accept the distribution of wealth, income, and power now existing, and to argue that measures to redress the unbalance must be consistent with the Pareto optimality condition or else be economically 'inefficient,' are, to me, abuses of economic theory" [Martin 1974, p. 275].
16. Friedman speaks thus of private enterprise: "so that the ultimate contracting parties are individuals," and "that individuals are effectively free to enter or not to enter into any particular exchange, so that every transaction is strictly voluntary" [Freidman 1962, p. 14]. In what modern economic system are "the ultimate contracting parties" *not* individuals? For an extended critique of such lines of reasoning, and of the meaningfulness of "legal equality," see Samuels [1973c].
17. The theory of public goods includes lines of reasoning which conclude both an over- and undersupply. Ideology is important in selection. Similarly, conservative economists of the Chicago variety tend to reason that the growth of government is a function of the logic of bureaucratic maximizing, rejecting, generally without much hard evidence, the alternative hypotheses that voters have wanted government to grow or that the aggregation of political descisions based upon voter preferences has produced governmental growth even though most voters might have opposed growth per se on ideological grounds. (Who wants big government as such?) Contemporary liberals do similar things.

    There is much pretense that socialism is the enemy of the free market, whereas the reality is that most parties within the system use and have to use government to promote their opportunity sets in one way or another. Business in particular is a primary user, again as the work of Commons, North, and many others, such as Carter Goodrich, has shown. If one considers both obtrusive and unobtrusive roles of government, the problem clearly becomes one not of minimizing "intervention," but of determining which interests government is supporting and possible legal change thereof.
18. "The primary difficulty with the notion of law as an ethical principle or norm is that the content of the law itself can never be taken as simply 'given,' or beyond dispute, even at a given moment. In the liberal doctrine in its original form, this problem did not seem serious, because of the limitation of law itself and of its functions to the negative role of

suppressing coercion. But even under this restriction, there was always and inevitably occasion for 'interpreting' the law, in enforcing it, and also for making law outright, i.e., changing it, in consequence of changing conditions and standards" [Knight 1947, pp. 62–63]. Compare, for example, Buchanan [1972a; 1972b] and Buchanan and Samuels [1975].

19. "But since the individual is largely made what he is by institutional processes—notably again with respect to economic wants, means and capacities—the immediate practical problem confronting society at any time is that of progressively remaking its institutional system. But this problem is to be solved in the light of the answer to two other questions; the first is one of fact as to what kind of individuals, and of inter-individual relations, different kinds of institutions will tend to create, while the second is the value problem—what characteristics in individuals and in culture are to be judged good" [Knight 1947, pp. 221–22].
20. I am not interested in doing so here, although I frankly have serious personal doubts about specifying and interpreting capitalism (or *any* economic system) solely on the terms given by a narrow economic elite or already established interests. As a positive proposition, however, I recognize and emphasize that such is the hold which the past has on the present and the future that that is how relevant institutional change takes place (absent revolution, which largely involves the swapping of elites). While the world is possibly better that way, such is in fact largely inevitable. Actual change is gradual, but it does take place, conservatives notwithstanding.
21. "In general and socially speaking, that is, in terms of the instrumental point of view, the political order has, along with other functions, its major role of solving problems that arise in the economic order. Regulation of the latter has come to be much the most controversial and important field for state activity, the function that bulks largest and creates the most controversial issues" [Knight 1960, p. 66].
22. Witness Knight's statement that "many of the vicious aspects of *laissez-faire* were put into effect in the legal system of the common law as interpreted by Blackstone, and in the United States through judicial review, under the Bill of Rights and especially the fourteenth amendment of the Constitution" [Knight 1951b, p. 287, n.].
23. "The concept of social action, or of a society as acting socially, being restricted to democratic process, persons are members of any society to the extent that they are actually free to participate in its process of legal change" [Knight 1947, p. 215].
24. And that is why so much of Vilfredo Pareto's work has been discarded by contemporary Chicago School Paretians. See Samuels [1974d].

# 18

# The New World of Economics: A Review Article

*Lawrence H. Officer*
*and*
*Leanna Stiefel*

In the March 1975 issue of this journal, Alan Randall used four recently published books as leading indicators to delineate certain trends in the presentation of introductory economics.[1] As a companion piece to Randall's article, we examine a work that can be viewed as a culmination of the tendencies noted by him. If we are more critical than he in our assessment, it is because the book under consideration—*The New World of Economics*, by Richard B. McKenzie and Gordon Tullock—is more extreme in its approach to basic economics.[2]

Several features of the publications reviewed by Randall are present in the McKenzie-Tullock volume: a concentration on micro- rather than macroeconomics, a selection of substantive topics that are "relevant" rather than "traditional," and a claim to be pursuing positive rather than normative economics. Yet, McKenzie and Tullock differ from the other authors in three respects. First, they abandon any reference at all to traditional economic topics. Second, they write in an extremely forceful and provocative style, advocating economic concepts and principles above those of all other disciplines. Third, they adopt a single focal

*The authors are, respectively, Professor of Economics, Michigan State University, East Lansing, and Assistant Professor of Economics, Sarah Lawrence College, Bronxville, New York.*

point virtually throughout the volume: individual maximization of utility through the equating of marginal utility or benefit (MU) and marginal cost (MC). They call this "rational behavior."

An outline of the book indicates the full extent of McKenzie-Tullock's abdication of traditional economic topics. The volume consists of 22 chapters divided into 7 parts; these, in addition to the Introduction and Conclusion, are entitled "Sex," "The Family," "Crime and Dishonesty," "Politics, Bureaucracy, and Groups," and "Learning." The authors are proud of their utilization of "far-out" examples as a pedagogical device and of their universal application of the MU = MC rule. They write: "This book attempts to break out of the narrow confines of economic subject matter as traditionally defined, and seek out new and refreshing problems that can be dealt with in a simpler way" (p. ix). They might be distressed to learn that the two principal characteristics of their approach are by no means new. Consider the following description of P. H. Wicksteed's *The Common Sense of Political Economy,* published in 1910.

> Perhaps Wicksteed's greatest contribution was his demonstration that economics is not merely a matter of the market place or of financial dealings, but is one aspect of *all* human activity—namely, the aspect of choice, or the balancing of alternatives one against another, where limited means have to be apportioned among competing ends. His delightful discussions of how much family prayers should be shortened to speed a parting guest to the train, or of the value of a mother-in-law in terms of how high a cliff one would drive off to save her, should open the eyes of every student to the great *generality* of economic principles.[3]

The fact that the McKenzie-Tullock approach is not novel does not detract from its pedagogical value. The book is excellent in its gradual introduction of concepts, usually only one or two in each chapter, and in cleverly discussing them in the context of a particular problem. For example, activities such as walking on the grass, generating a noise level at parties, and reckless driving are used to illustrate the MU = MC rule, opportunity cost, and the private versus social cost dichotomy. Furthermore, market demand and supply curves are introduced using sex as the commodity, consumer surplus is exposited via an exploitation-of-affection model, public goods are discussed with police protection as the example, and bilateral monopoly is considered in the context of Congress purchasing the services of the FBI. Shifting demand and supply curves are presented with student openings in the university as the commodity, and the transformation curve refers to the trade-off not between guns and butter, but between a student's allocation of his study time between French and economics. A final example: Pollution as a case of public disexternalities is not the usual environmental pollution by an industry, but "comment pollution" by members of a committee.

Unfortunately, the explanation of the basic tools of economics in chapter 1 is not adequate for most students with no economics background and therefore will need to be accompanied by a more detailed microeconomics text. The equality of the ratio of marginal utility to price across goods and services (pp. 14–15) is particularly inadequate in its development, given the difficulty many students have with the principle. The "problems" and "questions to ponder" at the end of some chapters are very good. Most chapters, however, are left without such valuable teaching and review devices.

In addition to their pedagogical purposes, the authors hope their book will stimulate instructors to try their hand at applying "economic reasoning outside the traditional field" (p. x). Certainly such efforts, in order to be more than incomplete and misleading games, require an interdisciplinary input. Yet, the authors delight in denigrating previous findings of other disciplines in a rather simplistic fashion (especially those of sociologists and psychologists). It is a difficult task to compare and contrast accurately the approach of two disciplines working in different paradigms. No sociologist or psychologist would prevent economists from studying whatever the latter choose, so why all the protest? Statements such as the following, taken from *The New World,* remind one of films such as *I Want to Live* or *The Wild Bunch* which keep the audience's attention by shocking and bombarding all the senses: "Nevertheless, we cannot escape the feeling that he [a juvenile delinquent] is far better qualified to advise our government on matters of prevention than most professors of criminology" (p. 156).

Part Two, "Sex," requires specific analysis because it is this discussion which changes the text from clever, entertaining, undergraduate instructional material to a sad commentary on the world of today's economists. There are three chapters: "Sexual Behavior," "Exploitation of Affection," and "Equal Pay for Equal Work." The "Equal Pay" chapter, a labor market analysis of male-female differentials in earnings, is not of particular concern in this context. The chapter on "Sexual Behavior," however, is objectionable for several reasons. The authors analyze sex in their usual way—as a service which yields utility and entails costs, leading to a market with downward sloping demand and upward sloping supply schedules. What is gained by such an analysis? The usual criteria for evaluating an economic theory involve the value of the increased understanding in predicting, controlling, or accepting social phenomena. Because the price of sexual interaction other than prostitution is very subjective and individual, the authors' prediction that an increased price will increase the supply and decrease the demand tells us very little. On the other hand, if all sexual encounters are analyzed as prostitution (that is, with a market price), as the authors seem to do despite their denial, then economics would seem to be missing an essential element of the sexual experience.

At the beginning of the "Sexual Behavior" chapter, the authors state: "An attempt will be made to show how the sexual behavior of people other than prostitutes or buyers of services of prostitutes can be discussed, analyzed, and understood within the context of economic concepts and theory" (p. 50). The last section in the chapter presents some quickly collected data from two undergraduate classes to illustrate that the concepts of supply and demand are applicable to the sexual experiences of most people. The "experiment" was conducted with the use of the following problem and questions put to the students:

> Consider the following hypothetical situation: You bump into some female (male) college student on campus whom you do not know. She (he) is about your height, or a little shorter (taller), and you consider her (him) to be reasonably attractive. There is nothing obnoxious about her (him); and you are not, nor do you expect to become, emotionally involved (either negatively or positively) with her (him). If you have sexual intercourse with her (him), there is absolutely no chance of her (your) becoming pregnant or of your contracting any disease, and there is absolutely no possibility that any one else will find out about the relationship.
>
> Given these conditions, we asked the women, "if he were to offer to pay you to engage in light petting (as distinguished from heavy petting and intercourse), what would be the *minimum* amount of money that you would be willing to accept for one and only one session of forty-five minutes?" We asked similar questions concerning heavy petting and intercourse, and each time we stressed that the amount could be as high (infinity) or as low (zero) as they wished.
>
> The men were asked "What would be the *maximum* amount that you would be willing to pay her to engage in light petting for a period of forty-five minutes?" Again, similar questions were posed with regards to heavy petting and intercourse (pp. 61, 62, 63).

Is this what the authors consider to be "sexual behavior of people other than prostitutes"? In addition to the institutional bias of the experimental conditions, we wonder about the propriety of conducting such an experiment and the validity of the results when the transactions were hypothetical (and we are not suggesting a repeat experiment where transactions are carried out!). What will the beginning student of economics learn about the discipline after reading such a discussion? The alternatives are not appealing. He/she might decide to continue study in hopes of one day conducting such studies himself, or to spend time in areas which are contributing knowledge to social problems and forget about economics, or try to ignore the chapter, in which case study time has been wasted.

The following chapter, on "Exploitation of Affection," is no more illuminating, and, in addition, the economic model applied is incorrect. Each partner in a romantic relationship is seen as a potential monopolist in the provision of affection to the other. The ways in which each can drain the surplus value out of the other are analyzed. Such conclusions as the following are reached: "It should, perhaps be noted that male foreplay may be one means by which the women have sexually exploited the men. They in effect say that 'Either you arouse me, or I will not be interested in anything you have in mind' " (p. 72). If both are monopolists, however, we have a bilateral monopoly model, and little can be said about the outcome except that it will depend upon relative bargaining power. But why bother? Does economics used in this way contribute any knowledge, let alone helpful knowledge, to problems of human interaction? Or does such analysis encourage the kind of competitive thinking which makes all but individual actions difficult to undertake?

There are other deficiencies of the book, still within the framework of the authors' approach. For example, in their consideration of wage-rate disparity between men and women, the authors suggest "a strategy for women leaders: equal pay laws should be coupled with quantitative controls to insure against adverse employment effects" (p. 92). Apart from a reference to "the problems associated with controls," the authors do not warn the reader that the wage-rate and employment figures set by *fiat* may be inconsistent (that is, not on the demand curve for female workers), leading to either a failure of the policy or an inefficient outcome for society as a whole.

Nor are the authors clear about the transition from the individual's optimum behavior to a social optimum. They assert that determination of quantity or quality by the rule MU = MC (or demand equals supply) is applicable to the case of *market* demand and supply curves, just as in the case of an individual's curves (providing, of course, that the market is "competitive"). But no explanation is provided, and, in an effort to avoid normative economics, there is no discussion of the value judgments necessary to assume that a market equilibrium produces a social optimum (that is, issues involved in a social welfare function).

More generally, the authors consider each topic separately. General equilibrium is ignored; individual decisions in the various spheres of life are viewed as independent both among spheres and among individuals. Thus, the reader is introduced to partial analysis only.

Furthermore, the work is narrow by its purposeful omission of such traditional issues as inflation, unemployment, pollution, and the impact of government regulations and programs. These omissions are hardly necessary, as demonstrated by other recent texts which achieve similar pedagogical goals without abandoning traditional topics.[4] Katharine Lyall's *Microeconomic Issues of the 70s* is an especially good example of what can be done. She includes, among others, chapters on such relevant topics as "Operation Intercept" (marijuana), "Cram Session," "Rent Subsidies," "Our Ailing Medical System," "ZPG," and "The CIA and Soviet GNP." Her text also is valuable because each issue appears in problem format and requires direct student participation in the learning process.

We now move to a critique of the basic approach taken by McKenzie and Tullock. The application of economic reasoning to traditionally *non*economic problems has its counterpart in the professional literature. To their credit, McKenzie and Tullock are scrupulous in their references, citing, *inter alia,* the basic works of Gary Becker on marriage, Becker and Gordon Tullock on crime, and Wilson Schmidt on charitable exploitation.[5]

We must question whether this all-encompassing view of the scope of economics is a development to be welcomed. In all such applications, people are treated as calculating machines, constantly weighing the costs and benefits of alternative actions. Indeed, McKenzie and Tullock emphasize only *marginal* benefits and costs, ignoring the possibility of *structural* changes. Our criticism, however, is more general. A benefit-cost approach that purports to embrace *all* human behavior leads to sweeping statements that inherently are misapplied, if not incorrect, descriptions of reality. Consider the following assertion: "The law of demand is readily applicable to sex, honesty, dates, highway speeding, babies, and life itself! We predict that if the price of any one of these things goes up, the quantity demanded will diminish and vice-versa" (p. 16).

We are reminded of Isaac Asimov's *Foundation* trilogy, in which "psychohistory" plays the same role for Hari Seldon and his followers that economics does for McKenzie and Tullock:

Seldon: "You say that without thinking. What of psychohistory?"
Novice: "I haven't thought of applying it to the problem."
Seldon: "Before you are done with me, young man, you will learn to apply psychohistory to *all* problems as a matter of course."[6]

Later, however, the men and women of the "Second Foundation" discover that psychohistory fails to predict or to counter the menace of a man with mutant powers, because he is an autonomous force that could not be considered in their calculations.[7]

In a like vein, we challenge economists in the McKenzie-Tullock mold to predict the behavior of, say, an Alexander, a Caesar, or a Hitler. Did these individuals make meticulous calculations of marginal benefits and costs as they pursued their dictatorial goals? Did Caesar carefully compare the marginal utility and marginal cost of crossing the Rubicon? Or did he, rather, have a single-minded goal of achieving supreme power? There is a political observation dating back to Ancient Greece: "Men do not become dictators in order to keep out the cold."

Our counter-examples need not be confined to the behavior of would-be tyrants. What of the great artists in human history? Was it "rational" for Michelangelo to spend years on a work of art? Did Tolstoy put a cost-benefit calculus to work in his decision to write *War and Peace*? A single-minded devotion to a goal is beyond the scope of the MU = MC rule.

McKenzie and Tullock can have recourse to two arguments which defend their approach. First, they can assert that an individual who does not act rationally in *their* terms is "sick." Indeed, this is what they claim: "There is a common notion among lay and professional criminologists and sociologists that certain criminals who commit certain types of crime do not behave rationally. They do not weigh-off the benefits and costs of their actions. . . . we concede the point that there are 'sick' criminals just as we would concede the issue if anyone ever suggested that there are sick plumbers, businessmen, and professors" (p. 134).

An alternative defense would be to categorize an individual's every action as the outcome of an MU = MC calculation. After all, why would one carry out *any* activity unless one *wanted* to do it on a cost-benefit basis, making proper allowance, of course, for the set of feasible outcomes open to an individual and his level of knowledge. Such an argument makes utility maximization true by definition. Our response to this reasoning would be simply to quote Paul Samuelson in the same context and Gottfried Haberler in a related one.

> Thus, the consumer's market behavior is explained in terms of preferences, which are in turn defined only by behavior. The result can very easily be circular, and in many formulations undoubtedly is. Often nothing more is stated than the conclusion that people behave as they behave, a theorem which has no empirical implications, since it contains no hypothesis and is consistent with all conceivable behavior, while refutable by none.[8]

> By hypostasizing every conceivable circumstance which may affect output as a separate factor, the production function can, no doubt, be endowed with constancy, invariance, homogeneity, and what not, but at the price of emptying the theory of all empirical content and reducing it to a useless tautological system.[9]

Our critique of the cost-benefit calculus, which McKenzie and Tullock adopt as the criterion for rational behavior, is not confined to counter-examples based on great actions of great individuals in the history of mankind. McKenzie and Tullock leave no room for behavior founded on *emotion*. For them, love is either a one-way relationship to be exploited (chapter 6) or an element in the definition of an "efficient" marriage (chapter 8). They portray a *joyless* world (for example, people weighing the MU and MC of dating [p. 11]), which culminates in an *absurd* world (for example, women forming a cartel in order to induce men to increase expenditure on dates [pp. 17–18]).

McKenzie and Tullock claim that their approach is amoral, value free (pp. 6–7). The "economic psychohistorian" is concerned purely with positive economics. In fact, however, the value systems of McKenzie and Tullock do affect their analysis. We offer as examples the authors' views on committees and on death.

As usual, "the amount of work a committeeman is willing to undertake" is postulated by the authors to depend "on the perceived benefits from his action and how they compare with the cost of achieving those benefits" (p. 254). *Benefits* then are defined according to the values of McKenzie and Tullock. For example, they state that "decisions [made by a university committee] may have nothing to do with the members' own welfare (but may have a great deal to do with welfare of, say, students)" (p. 254). But what if the committeeman happens to value the welfare of students? Also, they state: "The larger the committee, the smaller the perceived benefits from expended effort" (p. 255). But what of the individual who obtains great utility from persuading and perhaps controlling large groups, but none from small groups?

Another example of the authors' values affecting their conclusions is their assertion that utility maximizing behavior involves using up body organs to the fullest. "The *ideal* exit is to die with a zero bank balance (above that which is planned) and with no surplus capacity in bodily organs (above that which is planned)" (p. 124). The economic psychohistorians view the human body as a good to be fully depreciated as a means of maximizing utility in life. They neglect to mention that keeping the body in good shape (via diet, exercise, and so forth), rather than abusing it, may be a way of increasing *both* the life span and the quality of life. The authors' own view of the world leads them to see only trade-offs when complementary relationships may be present.

While most of the economics profession has been engaged in an effort to minimize the assumptions about consumer preference needed to derive well-behaved demand curves,[10] McKenzie and Tullock seem to be striving for the opposite: a detailed enumeration of the exact nature of each individual's preferences. They certainly will need the aid of psychologists if they want to make valid progress in this direction!

Lest we appear to be unduly critical, we wish to note that when the authors pay attention to real world data their argument becomes quite effective. An example is their discussion of the male-female wage differential and the effect of minimum-wage laws (chapter 7). Also, the analysis of presidential elections (chapter 16) and "bureaucratic entrepreneurs" (chapter 17) makes for fascinating reading. We point out, however, that the analysis in these excellent chapters is only peripherally related to the MU = MC focus of the rest of the book.

Our quarrel is not with the development of "economic psychohistory" as such, but with the *unquestioning* adherence it has received by many members of the profession. The McKenzie-Tullock book is replete with novel and fascinating observations on the human condition, but the approach is a narrow and confining one. As a countermeasure, the principles student requires a work that examines the limitations of the MU = MC model and explores alternatives. Nor are we sanguine about the success of a principles course that fails to examine inflation, unemployment, and similar "traditional" economic issues.

## *Notes*

1. Alan Randall, "Economics and Public Policy for the Undergraduate: A Review Article," *Journal of Economic Issues* 9 (March 1975): 81–86.
2. Richard B. McKenzie and Gordon Tullock, *The New World of*

*Economics: Explorations into the Human Experience* (Homewood, Ill.: Richard D. Irwin, 1975), pp. xi, 269; paper.

3. Kenneth E. Boulding, *Economic Analysis, Volume I, Microeconomics,* 4th ed. (New York: Harper and Row, 1966), p. 701 (italics in original).
4. For example: Katharine C. Lyall, *Microeconomic Issues of the 70s* (New York: Harper and Row, 1974), *Solution Manual* also available; and Douglass C. North and Roger Leroy Miller, *Abortion, Baseball, and Weed: Economic Issues of Our Times* (New York: Harper and Row, 1973).
5. One area that McKenzie and Tullock do not consider is the application of economics to suicide. The basic articles here are Daniel S. Hammermesh and Neal M. Soss, "An Economic Theory of Suicide," *Journal of Political Economy* 82 (January/February 1974): 83–98, and Daniel S. Hammermesh, "The Economics of Black Suicide," *Southern Economic Journal* 41 (October 1974): 188–99.
6. Isaac Asimov, *Foundation* (New York: Avon Books, 1966), p. 18 (italics added). Asimov defines psychohistory as "the quintessence of sociology . . . the science of human behavior reduced to mathematical equations" (*Second Foundation* [New York: Avon Books, 1964], p. vii).
7. Isaac Asimov, *Foundation and Empire* (New York: Avon Books, 1966), Part II, and *Second Foundation,* Part I.
8. Paul A. Samuelson, *Foundations of Economic Analysis* (New York: Atheneum, 1970), pp. 91–92.
9. Gottfried Haberler, *A Survey of International Trade Theory* (Princeton, N. J.: International Finance Section, Department of Economics, Princeton Universtiy, 1961), p. 19, fn. 6.
10. See, for example, James Quirk and Rubin Saposnik, *Introduction to General Equilibrium Theory and Welfare Economics* (New York: McGraw-Hill, 1968), chapter 1. They state: "To summarize, if the consumer has a complete, transitive, and reflexing ranking and preferences are continuous, then we may impute a utility indicator to him" (p. 18).

# 19

# The Economics of Property Rights: A Review Article

*A. Allan Schmid*

The collection begins with Steven Cheung's analysis of market con-
Pigouvian analysis implies that the existence of externalities requires government intervention. This conception seems to reverse the conventional wisdom of economics, which proved the maximization of wealth under competitive market conditions. The writers collected in *The Economics of Property Rights*[1] believe they have found a flaw in the Pigouvian derivations and indeed have turned the externalities conclusion around. Externalities frequently are reduced to their lowest economical level by the market, and, indeed, a good many externalities exist only because we have failed to leave the market alone to do the work for which it is uniquely qualified.

The authors believe they have found an objective benefit-cost analysis which gives answers to the age-old questions of how to choose among alternative property rights systems. The approach involves a conception of welfare improvement (social net benefit), although they specifically deny a social welfare function. The concept of total (social) cost minimization, or maximizing the value of production, enables the authors to critique some property rights rules as inefficient. The entire collection tends to support the glories of market capitalism and the inefficiencies of any other type of business organization, government ownership, or regulation.

---

*The author is Professor of Agricultural Economics, Michigan State University, East Lansing.*

The collection begins with Steven Cheung's analysis of market contracts in the context of the problem of ocean fisheries. This is a situation in which one fisherman's activity affects the return to another's efforts. No one has an incentive to invest and husband the resource, resulting in what some call the "tragedy of the commons." This view of externality leads many to suggest government regulation of numbers and fishing technique. Cheung argues that government is often the cause of the problem, if any, rather than the solution. He notes that the impact of a marginal increment of factor input on intramarginal returns is commonplace in firm economics, but causes no problem to maximizing total firm profit. That insight then forms the calculus of the book. Property rights can be chosen in terms of an aggregative or social view. When individuals do not own a resource, they have no incentive to invest. The answer is not government regulation, but the institution of private ownership rights (right to contract for the use of a resource) and appropriate firm size. The effect of one input on another would be accounted for if the effect were owned and traded. The only allowable consideration is whether it is economical to own and trade. In the case of the sea, it is difficult to police one person's use that steals from the owner. Also, one must have a considerable area before management becomes feasible. This would create high transaction costs in reaching agreement between numerous owners and in policing transgressors. These costs are a matter to be determined empirically. Sometimes the cost of private ownership prohibits exclusive rights and contracting. In that case, and only in that case, government regulation is efficient, says Cheung.

Here we have a microeconomics for determining the efficient system of rights as well as the efficient size of the firm. All is a matter of cost. Firms expand to the point where (among other production cost considerations) the marginal cost of enforcing exclusivity equals the associated marginal gain. If that means monopoly, than so be it, for it fosters efficiency and we all know that everyone is better off with the efficient solution.

The editors believe that property rights analysis as represented in this collection presents a unified approach. This belief is well founded, as the above conception is a common thread in the volume. In essence, all of the knotty problems of public debate over property issues, with all of its interpersonal utility comparisons, can be avoided by an examination of objective costs. Cost is seen as something that exists independent of the property rights system, and it thus can be a guide to choice of that system.

The analysis is used to suggest that a market solution not only is possible in ocean fisheries, but also would solve any problems in allocation of the radio-magnetic spectrum without resorting to the Federal Communications Commission (Ronald Coase). It would solve any problems of land and water use, such as pollution conflicts, without government regulation (Harold Demsetz). The analysis indicates why not-for-profit organizations such as hospitals are likely to be inefficient (M. Pauley and M. Redisch), and why socialist worker-owned firms are likely to underinvest to the detriment of the workers themselves (Eirik Furubotn). It indicates why price controls and licenses are bad since they lead to corruption of officials by bribes (N. Sanchez and A. R. Waters). It is truly a general and powerful conception.

What then are the essentials that these writers suggest in arranging property rights to maximize productivity? Costs and benefits must be brought to bear on those who create them. This is done by private ownership, whereby an actor has the right of residual profit and right of use or sale. This rules out any type of further government regulation or public ownership, which are labeled "rights attenuation."

The right to sell is the key. The authors emphasize that salability is necessary to assure use by the most valuable user. For example, Coase suggests that it prevents the use of the air waves by such deadbeats as the police, military, and educational groups who otherwise might lose out in competitive bidding. This applies to goods such as alternative radio channel uses, but also to bads such as one channel interfering with another. If interference is worthwhile to avoid, the market will so note. The same is true for all so-called negative externalities, such as pollution. Cheung, Demsetz, and others emphasize that sale internalizes all costs (externalities). Internalization is another word for obtaining a trade that allocates the resource to the most valuable use. If a resource or the effect of one aspect of its use has a higher value to another, the latter should be able to bid and obtain it. This makes both the former and new owner better off, while value of output increases. If a harmed party cannot make a sufficient bid, then of course the use is already in its most valued place (and the harmed one can only lick his wounds). We are not asked to inquire what affects the ability of the parties to make bids, as long as the reason is not the "artificial" one of legal barriers to trade or regulations, that is, other status quo rights are assumed.

Economists long have recognized the concept of gains from trade, and these authors have generalized it over a wide range of problems with the concept of internalization of relevant (to them) externalities, or as one author prefers to state it, with the concept of reducing the difference between social and private cost. This classic theme has been supplemented further by the concept of transaction cost.

A person with a better idea (way to increase resource rent) can have the net advantage disappear in a cloud of transaction costs as he tries to work out an exchange of ownership with the present owners. Prohibition of sale makes transaction costs nominally infinite. But even where sale is allowed, there is a particular problem in buying a resource owned in common by many individuals, all of whom must consent to the sale. Therefore, it follows that the world would be better off (rents maximized) if everything could be owned by individuals with unilateral rights to sell, which would keep transaction costs to a minimum. Transaction costs are seen as a pure waste with no benefit to anyone. However, the writers agree that the only valid basis for governmental involvement occurs when, for some resources and products, individual ownership is itself too costly because of exclusion (policing) costs. All of this is a straightforward matter of objective benefit-cost analysis unclouded by any apparent need to resolve interpersonal value questions.

It also follows that the size of the firm is controlled legitimately only by reference to the minimization of these net transaction costs. Unless there are offsetting internal coordination costs, all resources could be owned by one individual or group of stockholders (and this is suggested by Cheung in his analysis of the seas). The writers, notwithstanding their usual devotion to the competitive model, do not appear troubled by any other consequences of concentrated ownership. If costs that they recognize can be saved, the distributive consequences can be handled in a different context. Or, those harmed by monopoly always can try to buy out the monopolist and make it worth his while to act in a competitive manner. Affected people are limited in removing damage to the extent that the damage is not as valuable to them as it is to its creator, and thus society is served, according to several authors.

Closely related to the concept of transaction cost is that of information cost. Armen Alchian and Harold Demsetz present an argument for centralizing ownership of the residual rents and against worker-owned firms. First, there are high transaction-information costs if each resource owner (including labor) must make a simultaneous contract with every other resource owner needed in today's complex industry. These costs can be reduced by having one central contractor contract with all other factor owners individually.

Furthermore, in complex team production it is costly (transaction-information costs again) for everyone involved to determine the marginal product of each worker. It is too costly for each worker to monitor the performance of all other workers and determine the return appropriate for the marginal productivity of each worker. It is assumed that people will shirk if they can get away with it. The only way to prevent it is to make it worth someone's while to monitor their performance as a specialized function. This someone is the owner-directed manager, who will earn a higher income if he can prevent shirking through specialized information gathering. Never mind the problem of distinguishing shirking from revulsion at sweatshop conditions which also might enhance the residual; this is controlled by competition, although the authors do not inquire into how competition is affected by having a few managers dealing with many workers. Thus, again we have a maximization of product (saving of transaction and information cost) rationale for the specialization of ownership and for why worker-owned firms are likely to be uneconomic.

Several of the articles point up the key role of capital markets, which keep managers from shirking, and assure us all of least-cost output of the right products. Forms of business organization other than individual or corporate ownership with capital markets come in for much criticism. Without such a market, managers and residual return owners are not immediately reminded of the effects of decisions on future values, that is, future values are not capitalizable. It is certainly useful for substantive prediction to note what types of gains can be captured by people who make decisions, but the normative policy implications are another matter. What these arguments boil down to is this: If a firm is supposed to maximize those capital values which are seen in a given market, then it is inefficient to account for something else.

But who says that the rights now held and maximized are the correct ones? Could it be that we choose different kinds of business organizations to achieve a type of performance not obtainable in firms reacting to the rights embodied in current capital markets? Perhaps some would like the right to a different set of outputs which result from a different accounting of relevant costs. For example, one author notes that Yugoslav workers cannot sell their share of the firms they work for and shift the capital to a higher profit pizza parlor. But that is the point. Some groups feel that they have the right to direct the main flow of capital, and they prefer heavy industry and education to pizza. Salability is related to mobility, but anyone who has seen a town from which a major industry has moved knows that certain costs were ignored by market choosers as they sought the least cost (to them) location.

The above is a sample of the arguments for private corporate ownership and attendant markets and against rights attenuation in the form of government regulation, communal ownership, socialist and nonprofit firms, or any other form of business organization. Let us now look more closely at the underlying conceptualization.

One must admire the authors for dispassionately extending their logic to passionate areas, one of which is the right to labor power. If you believe that efficiency is unique and dependent upon the existence of a market after the original rights have been vested in one direction or another, you must accept a benefit-cost analysis of a situation beginning with slavery. Demsetz never strays from the logic of his conception and is willing to suggest that subsequent freedom depends upon the value to the slave of his freedom. He can make a bid, and its refusal or acceptance will maximize the value of labor to society. Recall that this analysis takes costs as given, and property rights issues, such as whether or not a market is permitted, follow from these costs. But must we not consider what it is that affects the ability of the slaves to buy their freedom? If the slaves have no other property, they have nothing to offer the owners in exchange, even if slavery is onerous to them. They could go to the capital market and borrow the present value of their future earnings. If the owner has put them to a low value use, this present value may give the owner more profit than if he keeps the slave in his current use. This is what Demsetz means by maximizing the value of product to society at the same time that both parties become better off in a Pareto-better trade. But if the owner already has put the slave in his highest MVP and is enjoying the maximum residual, the slave will not be able to make an effective bid. Well, the logic tells us that no further changes are Pareto-better or can increase the value of the product. Any further change involves a redistribution of income, and we all know that requires a social welfare function solution. But implicit acceptance of the status quo rights also requires a social welfare function.

A slave would not regard the right to buy his freedom as equal to the right to sell his labor. The movement from one rights situation to the other is not Pareto-better. Only if we accept the premise that the man does not own his labor (first order property rights question) can we say that subsequent trade would be viewed as better by both parties; for example, if the owner has the right to create a cost for the worker, then both are better off if second order trades can be made. If we say otherwise, it is equivalent to saying that the owner only has *some* rights as against the worker, who can create certain costs for the owner under the terms of the price regulation, licensing, and so forth. The only Pareto-better solution, given that starting place, is for the owner to buy these attenuations and privileges from the worker. If there are other third parties interested in whether their fellowmen are slaves, they may wish to prevent such sale or take advantage of high transaction costs to discourage sale. (This is a rationale for child labor laws which prevent parents from selling the labor of "their" child instead of sending her/him to school.)

Demsetz says "a primary function of property rights is that of guiding incentives to achieve a greater internalization of externalities." The statement would be more complete if he added: *given* the direction of the externality, namely, the question of who can create a cost for whom.

A person who owns nothing cannot create a cost for anyone else. A logic of cost minimization then will count this person for naught. The lack of human dignity, while an opportunity lost for the slave, is not a cost to the owner. Demsetz keeps our eye on cost minimization, whatever these costs may be. There is an implication that costs exist wholly in nature and technological relationships, but this is false. If the person owns his labor power, he is in a position to place a value on his dignity and other conditions for use of his resource, which then becomes a cost to other would-be users to be again minimized in Demsetz's calculations. *The point is that there is a cost minimization for each alternative property rights distribution. Cost minimization then cannot be a guide to the choice of that distribution.*

But, of course, Demsetz never set out to speak to the choice in initial rights distribution. Inquiry is not addressed to the broader questions of the original and subsequent vestures of property rights among people. It speaks only to the secondary question of carrying out the logic of the costs implicit in a given rights distribution. If we are all agreed that A owns all aspects of a good and may create costs for others with respect to its use, then it is of course illogical and inconsistent with this initial agreement to then reallocate some portion of these rights in the form of prohibitions of sale, price regulation, licensing, and so forth. But that is the point of conflict. People do not agree for all time as to what costs A can create for the B's of the world. When rights are attenuated (read: redistributed) this is not always done because people are stupid and do not know how to minimize given costs, but because they do not agree on what costs to minimize. As rights are changed (not exchanged) over time, the government may not wish to take all of a bundle of rights from A and give them to B, but it may wish to attenuate some of them (perhaps the right to sell or enter business) for the benefit of B.

None of these papers speaks directly to the question of the *distribution* of property as between A and B (except for reference to the Coase Rule). There is no argument as to why A should have much and B little. All attention is given to the *form* of property, such as salability, private versus public, or private stock corporations versus socialist worker-owned or not-for-profit firms. Is it possible to choose among even these limited alternatives without assuming or implying something about the distribution of rights among the A's and B's? The answer already has been suggested. If the nonsalability of a use is itself part of someone's property and income flow, then advocating trade which would ignore the loss of this income is a redistributive choice between A and B. The fact that A and C can make a Pareto-better trade does not tell us about the effect on B.

Third parties are often affected by sales and changes in uses and prices. For example, in Michigan, riparian rights are nonsalable or nonusable separate from the riparian lands. It is important to note that fishermen always support these nonsalable rights whenever they are challenged. Increased sales and diversions of water would affect the interests of fishermen. The fact that sales are prohibited (or that there are high transaction costs in getting the agreement of all communal owners on a stream) is to the benefit of fishermen. Water cannot be made salable without affecting their welfare and making their cost no longer a consideration in any cost minimization. But why not make this an explicit private right of fishermen instead of an indirect effect of the character of landowners' rights or a matter of enforcement by government regulation of migration? Then if someone could pay off the riparian plus all the fishermen and put the water to a higher use, all would be better off than if this is prohibited. The end result is likely to be the same. The transaction costs of dealing with many fishermen would forestall sale anyway. Third party effects have the tendency to be diffuse and nonseparable. If these effects are to be protected by property rights, they are going to be communal or governmentally administered.

The point is that attenuation of one person's rights is not always simply a loss to the world, that is, a waste. One person's attenuation is another person's bread! The right to market is the right to create costs for the parties not represented in the market (that is, to ignore costs not protected by a property right except that of nonmarketability). The right to market cannot be a value-free blanket policy recommendation unless the analysis is a partial one. In other words, the right to sell, and the existence of transaction costs, is like any other right which determines the content and direction of costs and welfare. Licensing, price control, communal ownership, contract rules, and the distribution of ownership between A and B are all alternatives to achieve a certain set of prices and other performance characteristics. Given the different starting places, each has its own subsequent Pareto-better result.

The authors deny that they have found a social welfare function (SWF) which can be used to decide between parties A and B. However, there are two senses to a SWF. One is an explicit weighting which says, for example, that a dollar received by A should count for 50 percent more than one received by B. This type of SWF is not used by these authors. But there is another sense of SWF which is already embodied in any status quo set of property rights which affect which costs count and who has to pay whom. The authors fail to see that this implicit SWF affects relative prices and income just as surely as does an overt weighting scheme. Any acceptance of status quo property rights distribution which is then given effect by the subsequent rights of salability and choice of business organization forms is an acceptance of a social welfare function.

The theoretical arguments supporting private markets, and so forth, dominate the book, but by no means are all of the book. The general empirical model is one of the interconnectedness of ownership rights, incentives, and economic behavior. Another major theme which affects the type of data collected is that people are observed to be utility maximizers with complex ends, of which profit is only one. As already noted, the way in which transaction, information, and policing costs fall are major variables affecting behavior. This produces insights into predicting specific performance characteristics of a host of different situations, some of which have been empirically tested. For example, there is some evidence that mutual savings and loan associations have higher operating costs than do stock firms. Predicting these specific variables is a different matter than proving that society is better or worse because of it.

Publication of this collection of articles, along with the earlier collection, *Theory of Public Choice*, edited by James Buchanan and Robert Tollison,[2] gives students easier access to a rich and useful literature. It would require another review to explore the similarities and differences between what these editors include under the terms *property rights analysis* and *public choice*. One similarity is an attempt to develop a social cost-benefit approach to choice of institutions, whose cost minimization calculus begs the question of what and whose costs are to be considered. Both books also contain articles that forget that one man's attenuated rights are another's bread and that nonsalability is a valuable property right in itself. Both constitute a narrow analysis of property and public choice, focusing as they do on internalization of previously selected rights.

Nevertheless, the two volumes, along with this *Journal*, which has yet to be subject to an anthology, constitute a rising and vibrant neoinstitutional economics addressed to the consequences of alternative institutions and rules of the game. If the pseudo-scientific global efficiency and welfare maximization material can be expunged and the questions broadened, we are well on the way to better informing an individual or like-minded group about which institutions will best further its interests, that is, an individual's calculus of consent.

## *Notes*

1. Eirik Furubotn and Svetozar Pejovich, eds. Cambridge, Mass.: Ballinger Publishing Co., 1974. Pp. 367. $19.50.
2. See A. Allan Schmid, "Theory of Public Choice: A Review Article," *Journal of Economic Issues* 8 (June 1974): 519–24. See also Victor Goldberg, "Public Choice—Property Rights," *Journal of Economic Issues* 8 (September 1974): 555–79.

# 20

# On the Meaning of Socialism

*Warren J. Samuels*

This note presents an interpretation of the historic meaning of the concept *socialism*. In effect, it attempts an answer to the question: What has socialism, and the socialist movement, been about?

Words being artifacts, their definitions depend upon usage, which is a function of nondeliberative and deliberative forces. There have been several definitions of socialism, some of which are simply not helpful or are contradictory in terms of the problem under discussion.[1] I am not trying to prescribe the "correct" or "true" *definition* of socialism, but an *interpretation* of the historical experience with several attempts at definition.

The concept of socialism represents very complex efforts to come to grips with certain fundamental social, economic, and political problems. Any interpretation necessarily involves commenting upon a vast and complex set of social forces, movements, and programs and is not a purely semantic or intellectual exercise. The interpretation presented here may contribute to a deeper comprehension of not only socialism but also the Chicago School of economics (and, by extension, to economic orthodoxy as a whole), which is the subject of this symposium.

The procedure will be to consider in succession the alternative definitions of socialism which have been offered by both advocates and

---

*The author is Professor of Economics, Michigan State University, East Lansing.*
*He is deeply indebted to Royall Brandis, James Buchanan, Howard Sherman, and Paul Strassmann for their reactions to earlier drafts. Some of what they had to say has been incorporated herein.*

critics. For the purpose of brevity, the analysis is very schematic, and I forego documentation. I anticipate that what I have to say will fully satisfy no one.

(1) The primary or traditional definition of socialism has been, of course, public ownership of the means of production or of the principal means of production. Most people who have considered themselves socialist, but by no means all, have thought of socialism in terms of public ownership, in one form or another, whatever else they may have added. Correlative to this definition is another, namely, public production of economic goods and services, and still another, public employment of labor, in each case, say, in rough proportion to the degree of public ownership.

This definition is an emanation and mirror image of the very private ownership system to which the socialist objects.[2] Since private ownership is rejected, the apparent logical alternative is public ownership. If $x$ is bad, then $-x$ must be good.

But public ownership has not been very satisfactory, even to those predisposed in its favor. It has not in practice brought Utopia; it has concentrated power in a few hands; it has exacerbated problems; and, *inter alia,* it sometimes has meant that the previous managers were in office doing much the same thing in much the same way and perhaps with more opportunity to exercise arbitrary power. It promised, or augured, far more than it did—and perhaps could—deliver, even by the criteria of the socialists themselves. By implication, this circumstance (and other experience and reflection) suggests that the dichotomy of private versus public may be misleading, whatever one's preferences. All economic systems are blends of private and public, however perceived and labeled by true believers. In any event, some contemporary socialists have had second thoughts after experience with public ownership.

There is a problem with the undefined concept *public* in public ownership, especially with regard to the concentration of power thereunder. Who is the public: Stalin, Brezhnev, Mao, the planning bureaucracy? As Howard Sherman writes, the public ownership definition "is not useful for the problem posed by socialist analysis, because the whole point of that analysis is to attack and eliminate concentrated power. This definition of socialism muddies the problem of power."[3]

Moreover, this definition is heuristically weak in interpreting socialism historically. After all, was not public ownership a means toward an end? What is its *raison d'être*?

(2) A second common definition (with several variants) has been that any government intervention, especially regulation of business, con-

stitutes socialism. This view is a favorite of critics of socialism, especially businessmen, but it also has been held by individuals who consider themselves socialist(ic). The most sophisticated variant, whose exegesis will do here for the others, identifies socialism with any change of the structure of private rights through law; in short, socialism (and sometimes "coercion," with which socialism is thus definitionally equated) means social change through law.

If the public ownership definition seems unsatisfactory on a combination of historical, normative, and perhaps analytical grounds, the government regulation definition also lacks profound and extensive probative meaning; it is deficient both analytically and empirically, however well it may serve normatively to express one's sentiments about a particular legal change(s).

The reasoning behind this obviously harsh evaluation is as follows. The rights that count in the economy are legal rights; rights are a function of law. In order for the social-change-through-law definition to have analytical and empirical usefulness (I do not say normative utility), one must assume a situation or social order without either law (whatever it is called) or change in and through law. Both of these assumptions lack credibility. The existence of both property rights and business requires a law of property and a law of business. Even aside from changes in values or social power structure, changes produced endogenously within the system will generate opportunity and need for new law, including new rights and new law for business (or market) organization and operation. To postulate the establishment of law on a once-and-for-all-time basis is fanciful. Although it may be useful for modeling purposes, such a postulation has no historical or empirical validity and is utterly useless for understanding the nature of socialism, except as a phantasmagoric invocation, as a propaganda device, that is, as normative rhetoric. I mean this to apply to *both* the libertarian who would dispose of the problem of law and the legal system by putting it behind us and the interventionist who thinks that passing a law will solve the problem which disturbs him.

Yet, such an approach is heuristically valuable, for it is a fairly common characteristic of utopian authors that they posit an ideal system without a mechanism for change. (Interestingly, most, even the antisocialist writers, would use the state to establish their system!) In a sense, that is what the public ownership definition does: It neglects the great complexity and evolutionary dynamics of all modern economic systems. Each of these two approaches (the libertarian and the interventionist) tends to be an escapist effort to establish a comforting situation and one which will remain quiet ever after; perhaps they are sophisticated (Paul

Strassmann suggests that I should say unsophisticated) forms of romanticism. In any case, to define socialism as legal change of law, as government regulation of business, or as intervention (all of which generally only mean legal change of the interests to which government will give effect), does not seem to me to establish the historic meaning of the term. If this definition sufficed, businessmen (and lawyers) would be the leading socialists, for they and their activities have been the major sources of legal change in history. There is a clue here, however, to which I shall return.

(3) The concept of socialism also has been defined in terms of government economic planning. This seems to make some initial sense, inasmuch as the juxtaposition of market and plan as economic organizing mechanisms is fundamental to the modern mind, but it has serious historical and analytical deficiencies. First, it applies to a very limited range of phenomena, unless it is merely a surrogate for legal action (which comes under my second definition). Second, "economic planning" is so heterogeneous—covers, shall we say, such a multitude of sins—as to lack substantive content. The definitions would have to include Soviet comprehensive and mandatory planning; French indicative planning; Swedish macroeconomic-cum-incomes policy planning; German and Japanese business-government relation systems; and, *inter alia,* the "system" described by John Kenneth Galbraith in *The New Industrial State.* Third, it fails to deal adequately with the programmatic nature of law, namely, that market performance is specific to (a function of) the structure (definition and assignment) of rights, which is a partial function of law. Fourth, it fails to deal adequately with the fact that all economic systems are complex and kaleidoscopic blends of nominally private and nominally public participants and activities. In this regard, consider what would be the appropriate name, should this definition be assigned to socialism, if Howard Hughes or some other "private" individual succeeded in acquiring and owning (and/or controlling) all corporate business in the United States.

(4) The latter point raises the possibility of defining socialism as concentrated private ownership. Indeed, some writers have alleged that capitalism, especially the regime of big business and high finance, is *already* socialized. If Hughes did control the economy, it seems to me that the difference between government planning and his (or his executive board's) planning would be nominal so far as "socialism" is concerned. There is another clue here, however, but I shall let it rest for now. Suffice it to say that Swedish planning, which is not dominated by business, seems to be more often cited as socialist than French planning, which is dominated by business.

(5) Still another definition of socialism speaks in terms of macroeconomic supervision of the economy. This idea also makes some initial sense, but lacks heuristic value for several reasons. First, it, too, applies to a very limited range of phenomena. Second, the usual application or invocation of this definition is to fiscal policy (as contrasted with monetary policy or with certain monetary-management systems) and to direct controls, which seems to me to be more in the nature of an expletive or an attempt to condemn through guilt by definitional manipulation or association. In any case, it does not tell us very much about historic socialism, although many socialists, of course, have been concerned about instability and unemployment.[4] Third, and related to the foregoing, such a view either ignores monetary control of the economy or posits only certain monetary rules as nonsocialist, which, among other things, is quite selective and presumptuous to be sure. There is a simple clue here, and it may as well be noted: Certain government macroeconomic regulatory activities are deemed safe and others not.

(6) Another popular definition of socialism specifies welfare state programs, activities, and goals of government. Most socialists who assert public ownership also conjoin welfare state programs with it. These programs hardly require specification, although there is much variety in the manner and degree of their instrumentation and impact: social security retirement, unemployment compensation, workman's compensation and other protective labor legislation, public education, relief programs of various types, and so on. Labor unions (permissive labor relations legislation) can be included. As is the public ownership concept, this is a viable definition, but it is subject to some of the same infirmities as the public ownership and, indeed, some of the other definitions. I shall return to it. Suffice it to say that the juxtaposition of limited liability-cum-property rights to welfare-cum-labor rights raises the question: Since all involve the use of government to secure interests, if the latter constitutes socialism, why not the former?

(7) One specialized definition of socialism refers to a stage in the Marxian schema between the dictatorship of the proletariat and classless communism, sometimes including the former. Except for this role, this usage seems to me to have no heuristic value,[5] although it is one of the most important politically, for example, in the U.S.S.R.

(8) Another definition which has been given to socialism involves government subsidies to private enterprise, both direct and indirect. This concept has normative and rhetorical value as counterpoint to the welfare state definition ("socialism for the rich and laissez-faire for the poor" may be instructive) and perhaps as a correlative of the concen-

trated private ownership definition. However, with one exception given below, I do not find much heuristic value in it for present purposes.

(9) To introduce the definition of socialism which seems to me to have the most heuristic and interpretive value, I shall relate a learning experience of mine. Several years ago, during the period of student activism, a number of students brought certain activities at Michigan State University to the attention of the local police. Before football games, seemingly upstanding citizens would lunch at their cars on campus near the stadium, consuming alcoholic beverages in the process. The students objected, arguing that the campus was dry (at that time), and that the alcoholic beverages were being consumed illegally; even their presence on campus was illegal. They proposed to the police that the violators of the law be made subject to its sanctions and penalties. What first interested me, when I read the accounts in the campus newspaper, were the verbal reactions of the citizen-fans. Reportedly, they cursed the students: In addition to the usual profanities, however, they called the students "communists" and "socialists." My immediate reaction was that these terms had become general if not indiscriminate swear words; as with most dirty names, they meant "I don't like you."

But upon some reflection, it struck me that the alcohol-consuming fans were making (probably unknown to them) a profound point: The students *were* socialists. What the students were saying was that if the campus regulations applied to *students,* they also should apply to *all* persons on campus. There should not be one law for students and another for other persons.

I suggest that socialism, in most if not all of its manifestations over the past two centuries, has meant an attempt to broaden the participation by and of the masses in the economic system and, because of the perception of close interrelations between economic and legal-political processes, in government. Indeed, the importance of participation in government was perceived first; when it was realized that political participation was shallow if economic participation was absent, socialism was self-consciously born. Most other definitions of socialism, including the historic ones of public ownership and the welfare state, have been but means to this end. Socialism has been a response, then, to these questions: Whose economy is it? Whose government is it? Socialism has demanded, and to some extent achieved, the transformation of the "privileges" of the few into the "rights" of the many, of all.

Those who saw socialism in the claims for extension of the franchise, demands of trade unionists, and, *inter alia,* for regulation of business and the welfare state were, according to this interpretation, quite perceptive. (Paul Strassmann tells me that Latin American oligarchs continue to call the property tax socialism.) For what the socialists wanted was a government and an economy which could be responsive to a wider range of interests and conducted toward a broader range of objectives than had been the case under a regime of landed and/or capitalist hegemony, privilege, and exemption. The programs of the welfare state thus were to become the property right equivalents of the otherwise largely unpropertied.

What the foregoing means further is that, to those who opposed socialism, legal change supported by business was acceptable. Concentrated power in the hands of businessmen or of those acceptable to business was permissible, as was the collective action that accompanied it, and, of course, government macroeconomic activity instrumented by those with roots in the financial community was quite safe. Collective private action and accompanying legal change and support for trade unions were unacceptable; collective private action (the corporation) and accompanying legal change and support for corporations were acceptable.

Socialism, then, is a matter of whose interests government is to support. Any legal change deemed antagonistic to established interests and to the business system, however selective all this might be, is considered socialist. Concentrated business power is not socialism, whereas concentrated government power used for non- or antibusiness purposes is; the welfare state is socialism, subsidies to business are not. Antisocialism is now pro business, pro the general status quo, pro the status quo (read: dominant) power structure.

There is much more to this, of course. Many schemes proposed for government action by businessmen have been ill-advised from both a public and their own point of view and an embarrassment to supporters of the business system. Similarly, many schemes proposed by, shall we say, left-wing reformers are wild-eyed and absurd, even to sympathizers who are willing to face economic realities relevant under any system. Furthermore, whether on balance the pluralization of the economy and of government sought by socialists (and by pluralists of all persuasions) has been achieved anywhere is another question and beyond the scope of this note (but see below). There are many other relevant questions: Does the problem of socialism in 1848 remain unchanged in 1975? Is there something called libertarian socialism, just as there are both communist and property anarchism? Is there meaning to the juxtaposition of reform to the radical-revolutionary transformation of the structure of society, or to the idea of the total transformation of society? What is the meaning of the proposition that substantive reform can come only through participation in real social struggles? And so on.

There is a paradox here. Socialism has advocated the use of concentrated government power in order to widen the distribution of economic power and performance. Socialism has connoted both the concentration and the diffusion of power: On the one hand, it has meant public ownership of the means of production and the welfare state and, on the other, the broadened participation by the masses, that is, the establishment of rights for all in place of what hitherto had been the privileges of the few. Perhaps concentrated power is necessary in order to diffuse power; perhaps not. The problem and the paradox are larger than socialism: Capitalism has its power structure too. The future of socialism, and with it the future of the modern economy, will have to come to grips with this paradox. The irony well may be that the choice is between one structure of concentrated power and another. Socialism, as a matter of whose interests government will support, may juxtapose the existing elite to the masses, but it may only take a short while until the leaders of the masses, the new elite, take power. Moreover, substituting a few governmental officials for the oligarchy running industry may not change the concentration of power.[6] The pity is that ideology has so largely clouded our understanding of the details and nuances of the subtle mixes of private and public that mark all actual systems.

I come next to the Chicago School. It would be the ultimate irony if actual capitalism accomplishes the purposes of socialism better than the means of actual socialism, but that is a substantially subjective judgment heavily influenced by ideology governing perception of costs and benefits, among other things. I have more to say on the Chicago School that properly belongs in the Introduction to this symposium, but I shall say the following here. The Chicago School contemplates freedom in the image of the capitalist system. The doctrines of the school represent a purist, ideological definition and defense of the capitalist system, its mode of organizing economic activity, its structure of social power, and its culture. Its doctrine is a rationalization of and presumes the propriety of the status quo of business as a way of life. All of the sophisticated, presumptive optimality reasoning about market solutions and so on, all of the opposition to public ownership, regulation, and the welfare state, is subordinate to, essentially derivative of, and functional to the rationalization or legitimation of these beliefs, quite aside from their value as technical economics and as behavioral predictions about market activity and reactions to government action.

The Chicago School is convinced that the origins and therefore the propriety of existing rights are not very serious problems—at least those of business and property.[7] (Coase theorem addicts would have us believe that rights are really unimportant, and if one sees that it is the *market* which the Chicagoans are stressing, one can understand that more readily. But one does not see Chicagoans assert the theorem in regard to management vis-à-vis labor rights.) Nor do Chicagoans believe that the structure of private (say, corporate) power is very important (again because of the primacy of the market in their system). James Buchanan's emphasis upon exchange, upon starting from the status quo, upon the propriety of existing rights, upon change only through consensual exchange in the market, facilitated by defined rights and so on, including the minimization of externalities, is a variant of this same theme.

The Chicago School ignores or masks the real world of power in a business society. It is convinced of the essential unimportance of the assertion that capitalism—the market system—comprises a power structure and is an arena of power play. Socialists, on the other hand, insist upon the reality of business power. The issue, as they see it, is not an undefined or unspecified status quo, but an economic system dominated by business and wealth; the issue is the *system* of business in which the mass of people are so many pawns. Socialists assert that the performance of the economic system depends upon the structure of power, that is, that results are specific to or a function of the structure of power. "Market socialism," then, would, in the socialist view, comprise a radically different structure of power than the business form of the market.

The Chicago School accepts the business system; socialists reject it and its power structure. What is repression to the one is opportunity to the other, and almost everything else follows from that. Both the defense and the criticism are largely ideological; as such, they comprise the ambiguous if not meaningless abstractions which Vilfredo Pareto (the most narrowly understood of all economists[8]) called "derivations." There are questions of fact involved in the evaluation of economic systems, but they are usually mixed with value judgments. More important, as Pareto realized and insisted, both socialists and libertarians (here the Chicago School) preach ideals, and there is much chimera in each, but they speak the language of power: Each ism is a rationalization of a system of power, and each is instrumental in power play. Each is power-seeking, clothing itself in noble and attractive myths. The stake is the organization and control of the economic system. Both *socialism* and *market* are words without concrete and objective meaning; they are abstractions which move the soul and serve the purposes of rhetoric and power language.

James Buchanan, in his critical reactions to an earlier draft of this note, provided several interesting and incisive insights. He first distinguishes between those who see chaos in the world and those who see order, "or potential order at least." He says that "to the socialist, order must be centrally imposed, and without central imposition all is chaos, necessarily so. To the nonsocialist (restricted to that set relevant to our discussion), it is possible to secure order without central control, without central plan. Order replaces chaos through the spontaneous coordination (Polanyi's good term) of the market. This is, of course, the central message of economic theory, from Adam Smith onwards, and it is, in fact, about all there is to economics."

He goes on to say that, "admittedly, economists have often overlooked, and overlook, the underlying requirements which must be present for their idealized market order to work, to produce results that they postulate. Smith, I think, did recognize this. The market produces order only when property is widely dispersed, decentralized, when collusion is absent, when government does not protect particular groups, and, most importantly, when property is secured within a regime of law. In this context, the libertarian anarchists who defend the market are talking nonsense; I suspect we both agree here."

After indicating that he thinks that one can "go too far in seeing market coordination in everything, and in subjecting all choices to economic dimensions, when noneconomic factors seem clearly to predominate," Buchanan raises what Frank Knight called the problem of deliberative versus nondeliberative decision making. Buchanan says:

> There is a second layer of discourse here, where, under a modified definition, some would call my own position "socialist." I am an acknowledged "constructive rationalist," to use Hayek's pejorative term here. I do not extend the notion of spontaneous order to apply to the evolution of social institutions, and to argue, as Hayek does, that that which evolves without planning is necessarily efficient. Clearly, we may get on evolutionary digressions which can be disastrous. I want positive social control, positive social action, to lay down and to maintain and enforce the constitutional framework or setting within [which] markets can be allowed to produce the order that they are capable of producing. In this, I think I am with Adam Smith, and I think Hayek is seriously wrong, logically, in his misuse of spontaneous order to justify that which evolves. That is to say, I think that we must consciously select, at a constitutional level, the framework within which the order which markets produce can be expected to emerge. Hence, my emphasis on constitutionalism.

Buchanan further explores the question of power: "Regarding power, the key here is dispersion, whether this be for economic units, firms or unions, or for governments. And there is no conceptual difference. A world of muncipally socialized governments, with free migration, comes very close to my ideal (Nozick's utopia is attractive to me), as does the world of genuinely free markets with widely dispersed holdings of private properties. Concentrations are to be avoided, since concentrations will upset the spontaneity of the order that can be produced by markets."[9]

My reactions to these points of Buchanan constitute both an application and an extension of the central agrument given above.

Given a constructive, rationalist position, as he calls it, why not see socialism as an effort (often perhaps misguided) to change the constitutional order so as to produce a greater diffusion of power, that is, greater participation in the economy and polity? Such a view would have profound implications for the juxtaposition of socialist and libertarian (or conservative) positions. Such a socialism does require concentrated power (in the state as an instrument of social control) to produce change. But once so interpreted, socialism becomes not the idea of order centrally imposed, but the use of the state to produce change in social structure, a very different idea, and one which seems to comport well with Buchanan's idea of producing the "right" framework. People could still disagree over details, but such a conception of socialism would not deny the possibility and desirability of spontaneous order; it would raise the question of "on whose terms" and would answer that power should be diffused, as Buchanan stipulates. All this is consonant with the interpretation of socialism given above under definition number nine.

But there is a paradox and a basis for selective perception of power (or of concentrated power): Some see the power in government used to produce legal change (say, diffusion of social structure power); others see power in the status quo (including deliberative change by holders of concentrated "private" power). The historic reaction to the market economy and market economics as a system of business-class domination is certainly a manifestation of the latter perception. Thus, socialism is or represents a desire to diffuse such class power, to convert the economic and political privileges of some to the rights of all.[10] One track is public ownership, another the "socialist market." But others, such as the Chicago School, do not see the power which the socialists would diffuse as being concentrated.

If one accepted Buchanan's constructive rationalism, if one shared the desire for diffusion of power, and if one agreed that socialism could embrace the market if power were diffused (a very important stipulation indeed), there would not be much difference between Buchanan's position and my general interpretation of socialism. But power is not the only facet of interest in Buchanan's reactions. There is also (as is clear from my discussion of power) the matter of constructive rationalism, or deliberative versus nondeliberative social change.

Socialism means deliberative change of institutions. This seems to accord with Buchanan's idea of producing the correct constitution. What Karl Menger termed man's eternal calling, namely, the evaluation and change through reason of institutions that developed nondeliberatively but which became at least in part disastrous or foolish, is exactly what Buchanan proposes and what I see the socialist proposing, namely, reform of social structure institutions.

Anyone may object that I am assuming that, given the right social structure (diffusion of power), the socialists would opt for market system spontaneity and that I may be projecting my own preferences here. At least it is an arguable stipulation or assumption.

An intriguing aspect of the Chicago School is the nondeliberative character of elements of their doctrines, but only in part. Their application of maximizing models to religion, government, and family would seem (to Hayek at least, one would think) to weaken the contributions to social order of those institutions. The paradox is raised: pro market change in some aspects of life and (at least in their own work) the possibility of deliberative change—nonmarket change—in other respects. If the Chicago School can have it both ways, why not the socialists?

There is also a dilemma: Nondeliberative change may mean concentrated power in or through established institutions; deliberative change may mean concentrated power in or through the state to change social structure institutions. (The irony is that social structure dominates in *these* attempts to diffuse power through the state.) "Starting from here," an important injunction of Buchanan's, if I understand his reactions, does not seem to mean the propriety of status quo rights (as he has argued earlier) and that only change through market exchange is permissible (as he also has argued earlier); rather, he seems willing to use the state to create the desired conditions of the spontaneous market, especially diffusion of power. There is a tension, then, between nondeliberative change through the market and deliberative change to produce desirable market conditions. This means that property rights may have to become insecure in order to achieve power diffusion and thus to produce the desired "potential order"—and if such legal change is socialism, then Buchanan's socialism has many followers.

The problem, then, is not two attitudes toward order, but the use of deliberative change to secure power diffusion (which may have its own ironies) and coupled therewith the use of the market. Given the existing concentration of power, the issue is not the status of the status quo power structure. All parties, in terms of power diffusion, are willing to use social control to establish the proper conditions of the market. Moreover, both Buchanan and the socialists (and the classical economists and many others, of course) seem to agree that order—the order that is possible and desirable—is *created*, at least insofar as spontaneity and freedom require the proper institutions and constitution and that the existing institutions and constitution may have to be changed in order to create that order.

But the Chicago School does not recognize the existing concentration of power; thus the issue here *is* the status of the status quo power structure.

## *Notes*

1. Royall Brandis suggests that there seem to be at least three major categories of definitions or usages. *Literary*: Various writers have projected economic and/or social systems (not necessarily utopian) which they have labeled (not pejoratively) "socialism." *Nominal*: Many persons have called systems, events, or proposals they did not like "socialistic," *not* out of any classificatory rationale, but simply to engender opposition to it. Others, in different political situations, have done the same in order to engender support for a system, event, or proposal. *Real*: There exist (or have existed) certain economic arrangements which are designated "socialistic" by *both* those who support them and those who oppose them. In such cases, the arrangements, whatever they are, constitute one definition of "socialism." Royall Brandis to Warren Samuels, 7 July 1975.
2. I am indebted to Royall Brandis for the following: "The function of Socialism is clear. It is a religious reaction going on in an age which thinks in terms of money." John Jay Chapman, *Practical Agitation* (New York: Scribners, 1900).
3. Sherman would define socialism as "ownership and control of industry by the democratically elected federal, state and local governments and the workers in each enterprise. Still ambiguous, but that must be so." Howard Sherman to Warren Samuels, undated (July 1975).

   Royall Brandis writes: "Perhaps the focus should have been, and should be, on *ownership* rather than on public *vs* private. What is origin of concept of 'ownership?' What rights, powers, duties attach to it? Is ownership demanded by economic efficiency? If the basic problem is *power*, then it is rooted in ownership, *not* the private-public question." (Note on earlier draft of this article.) In the light of these remarks I should call attention to Frederic L. Pryor's *Property and Industrial Organization in Communist and Capitalist Nations* (Bloomington: Indiana

University Press, 1973) for many relevant discussions. The book will be given multiple reviews in a future issue of this journal.

In a discussion not related to this note, Robert Solo suggested to me that socialism means control of the processes of production by central planning (political) authority, and (or but?) there can be public ownership without central planning (government serving as a rent collector in re nationalized land and/or leaving enterprise management alone) and central planning without public ownership. The emphasis which Solo urges, and with which I concur, is a decision-making paradigm.

4. Sherman suggests that, except perhaps for a few Swedes, this definition is not the usage of very many socialists.
5. Sherman says that "in the Marxian schema, the point of it is to distinguish two stages. 'Socialism' is public ownership plus wages and prices, where wages are according to work done. 'Communism' is public ownership plus no wages and prices, all goods free. . . . The distinction doesn't seem to me ambiguous or useless, but it does suffer the same problems as [the public ownership definition]" (ibid.).
6. In some if not many respects socialism has been a reaction to individualism, materialism, industrialization, urbanization, competition between men in labor markets under the wage system, and so on. Perhaps, in sum, it has been a reaction to the transformation from *Gemeinschaft* to *Gesellschaft* socioeconomic systems, from a sense of belonging and security, to a feeling of exclusion and alienation. But the old system had its power structure, too, and participation was, in retrospect, illusory.
8. Royall Brandis writes: "My own recent exploration of the question of justice between generations convinces me that, however difficult may be the problem of distribution as of some moment in time, it does not begin to approach the difficulty of the same problem when considered through time. This may be one reason for the Chicago School's fascination with static or comparative statics (Marshallian) models. On the other side, those who attack the status quo usually argue that the path from the past to the present was unfair or unjust to some which sanctifies an arbitrary re-distribution of rights, privileges, etc. Very rarely is the new path from present to future examined in the same light." (Note on earlier draft of this article.) *Vide* E.J. Mishan's treatment of intergenerational equity in his article in this symposium.
8. See Warren J. Samuels, *Pareto on Policy* (New York: American Elsevier, 1974).
9. James Buchanan to Warren Samuels, 30 June 1975. Writes Brandis: "Will one have the right to bequeath an estate? To inherit one or more estates? What about transmission of human capital within the family? These questions are raised just to pose the problem of *time*." (Note on earlier draft of this article.)
10. Brandis writes: "Perhaps the 'true' test of socialism is its attitude toward labor unions. What happens to their economic and political privileges?" (Note on earlier draft of this article.)

# 21

# Book Reviews Relevant to Chicago School Doctrine and Interpretation

THE IMAGE OF AUSTRALIA. PERCEPTIONS OF THE AUSTRALIAN ECONOMY FROM THE EIGHTEENTH TO THE TWENTIETH CENTURY. *By Craufurd D.W. Goodwin.* Durham: Duke University Press, 1974. Pp. 255. $8.75.

Craufurd Goodwin provides a list of questions that guided his research, and these give a fairly accurate general notion of what the book is about. The questions are: "How was information about the Australian economy brought to Great Britain? What were the stimuli for inquiry? How was information given form and meaning by interpretors of the Australian economy? What were the social and economic theories which were brought to bear and how did they influence the economic image of Australia? What did these observers see or think they saw, and what did they convey to their colleagues and readers in the United Kingdom?"

The account that follows is highly thought provoking. One learns how, by the mid-nineteenth century, a pattern had been established which persisted into the twentieth. British observers had relied on economic models to help them understand what was happening in the Australian colonies, gauge its significance, and assess policies that were being pursued. In arguments about such questions as penal policy and colonization, proponents pointed to Australia to bolster their case, their observations often having little relation to reality. Some creative thinking was generated through observation, but on the evidence presented it appears to have been minuscule during the nineteenth century. Generally, economists paid little attention to the special aspects of economic growth in Australia because they felt that they already understood the determinants of growth in any economy.

The debates over self-government for colonies and particularly the gold discoveries in the 1850s increased interest in the country and markedly accelerated the flow of information to Great Britain. But the information transmitted was often distorted. Reporters became increasingly critical as policies adopted in Australia seemed inconsistent with the teachings of economic theory. There were fears that gold mining attracted the wrong kind of people and brought out the worst in those who participated. Australia's criminal origins were invoked, as well as the supposed consequences of the gold rush in contributing to crime and moral degeneration. As the flow of information increased, the image became even more distorted. Observers continued to judge what they saw on the basis of conformity to known and accepted practices and policies, not how well these practices and policies satisfied specific needs, and the conviction grew that the colonies were doing everything wrong. In fact, the impression spread that there was serious social decline, for which convict origins, climate, the cultivation of the gambling propensity, the failure to attract or generate good leaders, and too much democracy were given as reasons. This was the case even in relatively good times. When depression came in the 1890s it was taken as proof (even by Alfred Marshall) that foolish policies were having their expected effects.

Defenders of Australia during the whole period were not silent, but, according to Goodwin, they "replied to theory with facts; and the facts were not taken seriously enough to threaten the theory." By 1914 the defenders had come to prevail, and later the pendulum swung even further in the other direction. The impressive performance of the Australian economy was objectively established by the early twentieth century, the Australians had become less (heterodoxically) innovative, and, most important, British views about proper social policy had undergone drastic change. During the Great Depression the Bank of England issued a report similar to those circulated four decades earlier, but what was by now a minority view was effectively rebutted. More telling was J.M. Keynes's suggestion to the Australians (in 1932) that they be less fervent in their application of the traditionally sanctioned policies. Praise of the country's economic policy had become such a cliché that one Australian reviewer was forced to protest that "Australia's recovery was not quite the neat and ordered thing that . . . [foreign] economic writers have pictured it to be."

The book is very well written and skillfully organized. The material is treated chronologically in general, but for each period the dominant themes are pointed up and serve to give shape to the presentation. Chapter introductions and summaries tie together earlier with later material, making it unusually easy to keep the picture of the whole in mind. Since the material itself is interesting and so well presented, the volume holds one's attention unusually well. Again and again one encounters choice tidbits (such as a quotation which shows Marx's contempt for Australia's convict origins and the account of the Webbs' disillusionment with the country because of bad manners) that make the book a delight to read. I have the impression that the author gives a balanced view of what the data reveal. He has tried, moreover, not only to summarize but also fit the material into a theoretical framework, a process which adds interest and value to the work but also raises some questions.

Goodwin focuses on how social (particularly economic) theory distorts the way social facts are perceived.[1] This enables him to make particularly meaningful some of the facts which his researches have turned up (for example, why economists did not feel that observation of specifics need be undertaken before conclusions about desirable policy were reached). Although he sometimes seems to go out of his way (as in the discussion of the effects of gold discoveries on the world economy) in bringing in material whose pertinence to the main theme is not entirely apparent, the interest of this material is such that it transforms what could be considered a vice into a virtue. In general, Goodwin attempts to show how ideas shape the perception of facts (and can lead to their neglect), and I consider this the volume's most valuable feature. The book is a study of "economic theory in action" in the most meaningful sense, and as such it is a valuable contribution to the history of economic thought.[2]

Goodwin is too able an historian to have forced his material into a narrow theoretical framework. He shows, for example, how economists such as William Newmark, Archibald Alison, Henry Fawcett, and T. E. Cliffe Leslie in their discussion of the effects of gold discoveries transcended the confines of prevailing theory to achieve insights not shared by others.[3] Yet, while praising the author for not wearing theoretical blinders, one wishes that he had given more care to the construction of the framework for the work. No distinction is made between common prejudice, theory, and how theory is used. For example, can doubts about the consequences of convict origins and the gambling propensity be traced to social theory? Was it a change in economic theory in the 1890s which affected the way Australia was viewed, or was it an implicit change in the view that people had of the nature of theory (on the part of laymen, primarily, but change occurred even in the thought of some economists; see, for example, Appendix B of Marshall's *Principles*)? The weakest part of the book is the Introduction; it states what psychologists have to say about memory images, even though in the text no comparisons are made between accounts which were written on the spot and those reconstructed later, and relates how economists affect the kind of data which is collected, even though in the text nothing is said about how data that were collected had any effects. The Introduction tends to throw the reader off balance rather than facilitate his reading.

But these are small weaknesses in a book whose virtues are substantial. It can be recommended to a broad spectrum of readers, who will peruse it with interest, profit, and pleasure.

ABRAHAM HIRSCH
*Brooklyn College*

*Notes*

1. In a sense this book illustrates John Stuart Mill's thesis that "such is the nature of the human understanding—that the very fact of attending with intensity to one part of a thing has a tendency to withdraw the attention from the other parts."
2. It is not enough, I think, for historians of economics to compile summaries of theories or to argue the fine points of David Ricardo's theory of value. We do not have enough understanding of the role that economic theory has played in social affairs, and it is precisely in this area that Goodwin makes his contribution.
3. They were not as convincing as their more rigid brothers, but that is another story.

AN INTRODUCTION TO MODERN ECONOMICS. *By Joan Robinson and John Eatwell.* London: McGraw-Hill Co. Limited, 1973. Pp. 350. $12.50, cloth; $8.95, paper.

A giant among neoclassical economists, Joan Robinson for years has been taxing neoclassical economics for the unreality of its assumptions, the triviality of its theorems, and its capitalist apologetics. In a succession of books written in an inimitable lean, tart, and incisive style, she has addressed herself to the central issues of economics: the concentration of economic power, the instability of income and employment, and the accumulation of capital. Unlike many economists who, in the autumnal years of their career, devote their energies to the defense of their early successes, Robinson is always on the attack, developing her intellectual acuity, so that she better can expose the pretentiousness of the academic model builders. If in consequence she has become the great outsider, those of us who share her agnosticism are the stronger for it. It is impossible to read anything she has written, from *The Economics of Imperfect Competition* through *An Essay on Marxian*

*Economics* to *Freedom and Necessity*, without feeling tremendously in her debt.

The publication of *An Introduction to Modern Economics* therefore whets the appetite as few introductory texts can. Now emeritus at Cambridge, Robinson has been joined by John Eatwell, a Fellow of Trinity College, in bringing to beginning students a volume that attempts to explain the principles of economics while expressing the Robinsonian reservations about them. It must be said at once that the authors have set themselves a difficult task, for one suspects that the vigorously skeptical teacher may communicate to novitiates skepticism without the understanding which gives it its force.

For those who already have experienced a conventional economic education, believers and nonbelievers alike, *An Introduction to Modern Economics* will be a treat. A brief survey of economic doctrine from pre-Adam Smith through the classics, including Marx, to the neoclassical era serves the purpose of raising the great problems of economics. The authors then probe them in the main body of the text in a verbal analysis modestly assisted by graphs, tables, and algebra. The argument is abstract, and there is little institutional, quantitative, or historical data to divert the reader's attention from the structural and aggregative essences of economic organization. While thus developing the familiar analytical concepts of neoclassical economics, Robinson and Eatwell continuously relate them to their classical forebears. They also never let the reader forget that markets are embedded in social relationships which themselves have a profound impact on the distribution of income and wealth. Indeed, unlike most neoclassical textbook writers, they "stress, instead of slurring over, the distinction between income from work and income from property" (p. 99), an emphasis that is given comparative perspective in an analysis of socialist planning (chapter 11, part II), wherein society owns the means of production. The final section of the text deals briefly with the modern problems confronting the capitalist nations, the socialist states, and the Third World.

What makes the book a treat are the pithy, barbed, and no-nonsense observations, a small nonrandom sample of which follows, that one has come to expect from Robinson. On John B. Clark and the marginal productivity of capital: "The analysis was not at all clear but the metaphysic was pleasantly soothing" (p. 42). In an introduction to the Keynesian revolution: "The flimsy intellectual structure of neoclassical theory could appear to stand up because little practical weight was put on it" (p. 46). In a discussion of capital-using bias in technical change: "Ricardo considered a special case of capital-using innovations, and had to admit that it would be unfavourable for the workers. He was reluctant to do so because he was generally strongly in favour of accumulation and technical progress but he was sufficiently candid to accept the logic of the analysis. (In the neo-classical era the point was hushed up; conflicts of interest were rarely mentioned [p. 138])." On revealed preference: "It was argued that the preferences of individuals are revealed by the purchases that they make at various prices. But this concept expresses no more than the notion that consumers can be observed to buy what they can be observed to buy" (p. 202). And finally, in the concluding page of the book: "The orthodox doctrines of the theory of equilibrium and free trade, which are disseminated among the intellectuals of the Third World, are not relevant to their problems" (p. 336).

While introductory texts may be written for the instructors who assign them, they are not likely to make it to the second edition if they do not pass muster with students. I fear that *An Introduction to Modern Economics* may not meet that test, especially with American students. It is a good deal more difficult than the average introductory text because Robinson's style, which is so stimulating to those initiated into the mysteries of economics, is likely to confuse those who are coming to it for the first time. First, it is extremely compressed. There is not much economics that does not appear in the text, but a good deal of it is treated in such brief compass that the beginning student may not always realize what he is getting (or what he is missing). The economics of pollution and incomes policy, for example, are discussed in about two pages each, price discrimination in eight lines, and the theory of games is mentioned, almost as a throwaway, in the concluding paragraph of a chapter on commodities and prices.

Second, an otherwise admirable interlarding of macro- and microeconomics may inhibit an understanding of either one. I make this observation hesitantly because I am probably a victim of conservative economic pedagogy with its macro and micro (or the reverse) quarters. We all know that the distinction is artificial and that economic behavior is constrained both by systemic forces and the organizational characteristics of households and firms. Nonetheless, I am not persuaded that the analysis in quick succession of effective demand (chapter 3, Book II), technical change (chapter 4), and commodities and prices (chapter 5), for example, even when assisted by austere assumptions about the nature of economic reality, will penetrate the average student's mind.

Finally, and this point was alluded to above, if equilibrium analysis has little to recommend it, why put out the effort to understand it? Teachers using the text may not, paradoxically enough, be bringing on the next generation of Joan Robinsons.

*An Introduction to Modern Economics* is best suited for students who already have a knowledge of the historical and institutional background of contemporary economies, some understanding of the methodology of the social sciences, and the intellectual toughness to follow tightly reasoned verbal arguments. It is a text that is not likely to teach itself.

KARL DE SCHWEINITZ, JR.
*Northwestern University*

ECONOMIC ANALYSIS OF LAW. *By Richard A. Posner.* Boston: Little, Brown and Company, 1973. Pp. 415. $10.00.

In reading Professor Richard Posner's book I was struck at the outset by a statement on page 1: "Economics is the *science* of human choice in a world in which resources are limited in relation to human wants" (emphasis added). That recalled Thurman Arnold's oft-repeated blast: "Economics is theology," and sent me back to *The Symbols of Government.* The belief that "economics is a body of scientific fact," as Arnold said, dies hard, and Posner's book is evidence enough of that.

*Economic Analysis of Law* is a text, designed to fill a gap in the pedagogical literature; "it weaves," says the author, "exposition of the relevant economic principles into a systematic (although necessarily incomplete) survey of the rules and institutions of the legal system." Posner devotes chapters to the following: the traditional legal categories of property, contracts, and crimes and torts; regulation of the market through antitrust, labor, and public utility laws; corporations and financial markets; taxation and devolution of property at death; poverty; economic due process, federalism, racial discrimination, and freedom of speech under the Constitution; and, finally, the procedures and enforcement mechanisms of the legal process itself. That is a very large net he throws. Of necessity, therefore, he must be brief. Four hundred pages are scarcely enough to cover much of such a complex subject matter. And he ends his exposition—God save the mark!—by saying that "it may be possible to deduce the basic formal characteristics of law itself from economic theory," and then does so in *two* pages. What *chutzpah*, one might say.

Nonetheless, the book has some limited merit in that, to my knowledge, it is the first attempt to synthesize the technicalities of economics with the value judgments of law. Posner writes in a readable style and does not lard his presentation with incomprehensible (to most lawyers) mathematical formulas. Unique in its field, the book likely will have some adoptions in some of the "better" law schools—those that profess to provide interdisciplinary treatment of traditional legal topics. (I perceive no use of it whatsoever, in either undergraduate or graduate courses in economics.)

Essentially, however, the book is an attempt to consider abstract legal doctrines in the light of abstract laissez-faire economics (as taught by the Chicago School). Posner does not recognize that there is any other variety of that "exact science" known as economics. No doubt, his book will be applauded by those pundits who cluster around Milton Friedman. But one can say with Justice Louis D. Brandeis that a lawyer who knows no economics is a menace to his client and still raise some substantial questions about this effort to mesh the oil of economics with the water of law. Perhaps they will—they can—form a new compound, but surely not by merely throwing them in the same crucible. Something else is required.

That "something," at the very least, is the human (for which read "political") element. Problems of law are problems of political economy, or, as Dean Leon Green once said, all law is public law. The efforts of the Posners of the law school world to reduce the buzzing, booming confusion of life to their neat little economic categories simply will not wash. Jurisprudence was once a branch of theology, and it is only in fairly recent times—the past three or four centuries—that it has broken away from that mindset. But Posner seeks to substitute a modern theology for the ancient variety, and he calls upon the gurus among his colleagues at the University of Chicago for intellectual support.

The book "explores and tests the implications of the assumption that man is a rational maximizer of his ends in life, his satisfactions . . . his 'self interest.' " Posner notes that some may be troubled by what may be considered the "severely unrealistic assumptions that underlie economic theory." He then goes on to say that although those assumptions "are to some extent . . . oversimplified and unrealistic as descriptions of human behavior, there is abundant evidence that theories derived from those assumptions have considerable power in predicting how people in fact behave." For that astonishing statement he cites nothing, apparently in consonance with the Little Abner Rule that "any fool kin plainly see" that what he says is so.

A person not privy to the esoterica of economics, of whatever school, might be permitted to wonder why it is that economists uniformly failed to predict the "stagflation" of 1974. Furthermore, economists are noteworthy for their inability to agree upon the cure(s) for stagflation and other politicoeconomic woes of the day. This should lead those in politics and elsewhere who call upon economists to cure economic ills to look elsewhere for "solutions" or, at least, for help in finding "solutions."

In essence, Posner asks us to believe that having lawyers know a little economics will make better lawyers of them and thus presumably result in better public policies. That just ain't necessarily so. Posner's book may be a first step in that fabled journey of a thousand miles (of seeing law in its social context), but there is a hell of a long way to go.

ARTHUR S. MILLER
*George Washington University*

ECONOMIC FOUNDATIONS OF POLITICAL POWER. *By Randall Bartlett.* New York: The Free Press, 1973. Pp. xiii, 206. $8.95.

Randall Bartlett has produced quite a book. Evolved from a doctoral dissertation at Stanford under John Gurley, Robert Coen, and Michael Boskin, the book is an interesting, suggestive, and important contribution to the economic analysis of government. It is an ingenious use of general neoclassical reasoning to reach Galbraithian conclusions and is an application and extension of the work of Anthony Downs and Mancur Olson. *Inter alia,* it offers an alternative formulation of the economic theory of information. Bartlett emphasizes the economic foundations of politics, but his analysis also incorporates the political foundations of the economy.

The analysis proceeds from three explicit assumptions. First, individuals are assumed to be motivated by their self-interest, not just some but all individuals, specifically, consumers, producers, elected officials, and government bureaucrats. Second, individuals are assumed to act rationally in the sense that their actions will attempt to move them closer to the realization of their chosen goals. Third, individuals are assumed to "suffer from a greater or lesser degree of uncertainty relative to the economic and political decisions they must make" (p. 24). Self-interest as to ends; rationality as to strategy or means; and uncertainty: hardly unconventional assumptions. But there is a fourth assumption unstated *as such* by Bartlett: that individuals are asymmetrical or unequal in their positions and capacities to seek their self-interest, exercise rationality, and counter uncertainty. Asymmetrical positions in markets and access to government: On the basis of this bit of realism Bartlett derives his conclusions about the economic foundations of political power.

The conclusions are hardly novel but are intellectual dynamite in the context of Bartlett's largely, but only largely, conventional assumptions and mode of reasoning. Here are some:

> Relationships are both political and economic in nature (p. 159).
>
> The actions of government influence the distributions of wealth and income, and the distributions of wealth and income influence the actions of government (p. 196).
>
> Governmental actions will reflect a tendency to protect the status quo in terms of the distributions of wealth and property in a society, no matter what the theoretical justification for those actions (p. 196).
>
> The distributions of political power and distributions of wealth are inexorably intertwined, even in a democratically organized state based upon a free market system (p. 198).
>
> To the degree that inequality exists in the distribution of wealth, it implies inequality in both market and political power distributions. . . . It is a basic conclusion of economic theory that the allocation of resources arising from the operation of a market system will reflect the initial distribution of wealth and the structure of the market. . . . It is also the inevitable result of rational, self-interested action on the part of all agents in an uncertain world that the outcomes of decisions in the political realm, even when organized democratically, will also reflect this same distribution. . . . In either the political or the market operations of a society such as the one we have been describing, the wishes of the agents with the greatest wealth will carry the greatest weight. It is not a new "conspiracy" that makes it so. It is merely the action of self-interested rational men (p. 156).

Bartlett strongly urges that these conclusions, as emotionally loaded as they may appear, are nonnormative and strictly positive, whether one likes the situation they describe or not. And he is substantially correct, in the view of this reviewer.

The analysis or mode of reasoning resulting in these and other conclusions is quite straightforward and powerful. Given uncertainty, there is pervasive potential for the production of influence: Private (both consumer and producer) and public policy is partially a function of information, thus policy may be manipulated by the selectively subsidized acquisition of information, information, that is, selected by the subsidizer to be instrumental to his interests. Bartlett's analysis centers on the differential conditions of acquisition and, especially, production of influence, that is, information. The maximizing actors in his drama calculate the costs and gains of acquiring and producing information. The amount of information rationally acquired is less than the amount that one is capable of absorbing, because information may be too large to acquire, and there are substantial costs of acquisition. Parties with an interest in the actions of others may decide to become producers of subsidized information, thereby affecting the flow of information to the others by lowering their price of information and thus influencing the decisions reached. But, whether the influence is of the private or public (and of the voting or nonvoting) variety, actors are differentially (read: unequally) situated both in their capacity to produce influence and in the potential payoffs thereof. In short, the powerful can afford to produce, and have the most to gain from the production of, influence. No wonder that power operates to roughly the same results whether it is exercised through the market or the state.

Bartlett's analysis is quite wide-ranging. The reasoning summarized in the preceeding paragraph is applied to the activities and inactivities of consumers, producers, elected officials, and government bureaucrats; the results are in fact very Galbraithian, for example, the endogenous determination of consumer preferences. As an overview, Part I develops the positive model (*vis-à-vis* the standard normative neoclassical price theory-cum-welfare economics models). Parts II and III present the positive principles of private and public purchasing and of taxation. Part IV explores the forms of nonvoting influence and the choice among alternate forms of influence. Part V brilliantly explores "the system and the long-run structure of society," including social structure, the role of ideology, and the enduring character of inequality, all from the perspective accorded by his formulation of the economics of information.

Bartlett has created a brilliant and seminal application of price theory to the production of information and thence to the operation of both market and government under the conditions of inequality. But Bartlett also has done something of potentially greater profundity: He has shown how neoclassical microeconomics and welfare economics, whether alleged to be positive or normative, tend to rationalize and give effect to the status quo power structure, and he has done this by showing how the careful (shall I say more realistic?) use of conventional neoclassical reasoning *does not have to do so.* Bartlett shows how an analysis of equimarginal calculations of cost and gain, that is, calculations of advantage, can produce a body not of sophisticated ideology but of positive description of basic tendencies. Bartlett's analysis shows how neoclassical economics, and the libertarianism which is so close thereto, rationalizes the market by building in presumptive optimality reasoning, thereby giving effect, first, to selective implicit antecedently specified interests and, second, to a notion of optimality defined in terms of market valuation and adjustment. He does this without criticism of either the market or market solutions, but by demonstrating how the market operates in a purely descriptive and heuristically valuable manner. The conclusions may be radical, but they are descriptively accurate, and all because Bartlett does not fail, as neoclassical theory so typically does, perhaps intentionally, to avoid the specification of power structure and of the causes and consequences of distributional inequality. Compare, for example, Bartlett's economics of information with that of Armen Alchian, Harold Demsetz, and others, most notably of the Chicago School, in whose hands the results of the market take on an aura of sanctity and the operation of asymmetry is obscured. One can prefer inequality *or* equality, one can prefer *or* reject the market, and one still can agree with Bartlett's description.

Bartlett does, however, occasionally slip. There are some subtle normative waves in his sea of positive virtue. He speaks of "those who enjoy a disproportionate share of . . . benefits and those who do not" (p. 162); "artificial alterations in the relative price ratios of goods" (p. 88); certain taxes creating "significant distortions in the allocation of resources within the private sector" (p. 88); indirect taxes introducing "distortions into the system in the form of reduced perceptions of tax burdens" (p. 93); "excessive investment tax credits" (p. 109); "whether or not this excessive power of large agents will be counterbalanced by the actions of small agents acting collectively rather than individually" (p. 150; cf. 154). He also says that "gigantic corporations not only possess excessive control over their markets, but they also possess excessive control over governmental decisions" (p. 156). The problem with these invocations of "disproportionate," "artificial," "distortion," and "excessive" is that they constitute the presumptive optimality reasoning so typical in orthodox economics of both the ostensibly positive and normative variety. Each use tends to give effect to an implicit antecedent normative premise. All can be removed from the book without any injury to his analysis whatsoever; indeed, perhaps it is fortunate that these lapses exist, for they permit the lesson that presumptive optimality reasoning has no place in positive analysis to be so readily observed, identified, and corrected. The slips are so obvious only because the bulk of the text is so strictly positive.

This book, then, deserves serious study and emulation. Bartlett successfully introduces the distributional problem into a positive allocative analysis, specifically, the consequences of an asymmetrical distribution of the resources with and for which to produce influence. The adept introduction of power enables Bartlett to use neoclassical reasoning to indicate the limits of more conventional uses of neoclassicism. The operation of both market and government is shown to give effect to the power structure within the conditions governing the production of influence. The individual is shown not to be autonomous, but to be influenced by others, and the consequences thereof in a world of inequality are elaborated. The state is not the only "coercive" force and is itself "influenced." Preferences are endogenous, that is, the partial result of information production interplay. The logic of collective choice through market and through government can be positively approached through the logic of individual choice, in a context of constrained maximization, *and* inequality can be introduced as it affects the actual answer to the problem as to whose interests are to count in both market and government. Quite an accomplishment. I am tempted to say that Bartlett may have done to neoclassical economics what Karl Marx did to classical economics. What will the next counterrevolution be? What can Bartlett do for an encore?

WARREN J. SAMUELS
*Michigan State University*

INDUSTRIAL CONCENTRATION AND ECONOMIC POWER IN PAKISTAN. *By Lawrence J. White.* Princeton: Princeton University Press, 1974. Pp. xii, 212. $11.00.

The literature on economic development includes a number of studies of the effects of *dirigiste* public policies. But this book is one of the very few—and so far, the most substantial—to use the analytics of industrial organization to study the structure and performance of a less developed economy. Lawrence J. White is an industrial organization economist who was in Pakistan during the turbulent end of the 1960s. By the time of the 1969 coup that brought Yahya Kahn to power, Pakistan's economic progress was appraised as something less than the "success story" which it had been acclaimed earlier in the decade. White suggests that the country's industrial structure and distribution of wealth may have had something to do with this result.

The book's material is largely restricted to the mid- to late 1960s, prior to the secession of East Pakistan. Post-1968 data were mostly unavailable and less reliable than earlier figures. The Pakistani economy was characterized by import licensing and export bonuses (in which there was an organized market), both stemming from an overvalued exchange rate. There were controls on new industrial investments and subsidies for particular investments. Competition was not promoted because it was regarded as disruptive and wasteful. Although "antimonopoly" sentiment was sporadically expressed, three different investigations of business power were suppressed at the behest of the industrialists. A final characteristic of the Pakistani scene was a relative absence of foreign ownership: The problem White addresses is a concentration of *domestic* economic power.

The average Pakistani views economic power as concentrated in "the 22 families." White finds that the 20 largest of these controlled "nearly a third of all large-scale manufacturing and 45% of all private Pakistani-controlled manufacturing." The inclusion of 43 identifiable families of manufacturing groups increased the fractions to 40 percent and 60 percent, respectively. By comparison, many Americans are concerned because 100 companies control slightly less than half of all manufacturing assets.[1] Seven of Pakistan's domestically controlled banks were also under family control and accounted for 60 percent of all bank deposits. Interlocking directorates between family interests were common, although the interlocks may have been more prestigious than powerful.

Not unexpectedly, White finds that industrial concentration was greater in Pakistan than in the United States: The weighted four-firm (capacity) concentration ratio was 51 percent in Pakistan, compared with a U.S. (value of shipments basis) figure of about 38 percent.[2] Among the Pakistani industries sampled here, the 43 families and groups accounted for 38 percent of value added in manufacturing. Despite considerable Pakistani suspicions of monopoly power in retailing, competition in this sector was about as pervasive as in the United States.

It is in conjunction with the pattern of government controls that concentration in Pakistan has had its most substantial effects. Investment subsidies and the structure of tariffs and quotas have underpriced capital relative to its social cost. The result probably has been to encourage techniques of production using too much capital, absorbing too little surplus labor, and giving rise to overstated scale economies and excessive concentration. Import licensing has been defended by Pakistani bureaucrats and politicians as necessary to give small firms and the "little man" a break. It did the opposite: Quotas were granted on the grounds of existing capacity, members of the "families" sat on the control boards, and the already big got bigger. Concentration and protection from imports gave rise to above-normal profits, which were not necessarily reinvested within the country for its growth. The distribution of income was grossly unequal, and the direct taxes that might have mitigated this were substantially evaded. Powerful business families were in fact the beneficiaries of and indeed the prime movers behind the controls.

The book concludes with a narrative description of post-1969 economic reforms. The Pakistani rupee has been devalued, and the import control system largely abandoned. Some industries have been "nationalized" (with government managers, but with private ownership). A Monopolies Control Authority was formed in 1969 with a broad mandate to reduce family power, industrial monopoly, and restrictive trade practices. However, it has just begun to operate. Really progressive taxation is still nowhere in sight.

The book is an impressive piece of work. White has mined available data—of which there was little—for all they are worth. Many of the leading questions and themes in industrial organization are addressed in its less than 200 pages. It turns out that this analysis has quite a bit of relevance for the developing economy. Indeed, the book affords the development specialist whose training omitted industrial organization a remarkably compact and authoritative introduction to the subject. For the industrial organization specialist, the book may serve as a model for similar works on other developing nations. It is also something of a nostalgia trip: Works combining its sweep and pioneering nature have not been seen since the days of the Temporary National Economic Committee and the National Resources Planning Board, or possibly the first edition of J.S. Bain's *Industrial Organization.*[8] Yet, the book's cleanly honed analysis and compact length attest not only to the author's understanding, but also to the vigorous development of his field over the last 35 years. Would that we were as successful in focusing the fears of Americans—or Pakistanis—concerning economic power into relevant and useful public policies.

BRUCE T. ALLEN
*Michigan State University*

## *Notes*

1. Testimony of W. F. Mueller in *Economic Concentration: Hearings,* Subcommittee on Antitrust and Monopoly, Committee on the Judiciary, United States Senate (Washington, D.C.: U.S. Government Printing Office, 1964), pp. 113–15.

2. Reviewer's 1967 estimate for U.S.; details available on request.
3. National Resources Committee, *Structure of the American Economy* (Washington, D.C.: U.S. Government Printing Office; 1939); U.S. Congress, Temporary National Economic Committee, *Hearings* and *Monographs* (Washington, D.C.: U.S. Government Printing Office, 1940–1941), summarized in D. Lynch, *The Concentration of Economic Power* (New York: Columbia University Press, 1946); and J. S. Bain, *Industrial Organization* (New York: John Wiley, 1959).

REDISTRIBUTION THROUGH PUBLIC CHOICE. *Edited by Harold M. Hochman and George E. Peterson.* New York and London: Columbia University Press in cooperation with the Urban Institute, Washington, D.C., 1974. Pp. 341. $12.50.

Questions of tax incidence and the beneficiaries of government spending programs have become increasingly significant to economists in the last few years. The issues are complex, and the literature on the subject is sophisticated and growing. From a public policy standpoint, clarification of these issues becomes vital as governments, responding to electoral pressures, become increasingly interested in devising systems of penalties and rewards to reduce pollution, conserve fuel, build housing, or preserve the environment. It is barely a decade since the U.S. government began to use taxation and spending in an organized, systematic way to regulate the economy. Now ideas abound concerning tax incentives and disincentives to bring about a desired behavior modification. Consequently, a collection of essays on *Redistribution Through Public Choice* is to be welcomed. Unfortunately, the promise is far greater than the performance.

There are some good essays by William J. Baumol, Martin S. Feldstein, David F. Bradford and Wallace E. Oates, Richard Zeckhauser, and others, but in many ways even the good articles seem to be a rehash of work that the authors have done previously. Baumol again raises questions as to who benefits from various public goods programs, particularly in the area of environment. To him, there are serious questions as to whether many of our current environmental programs discriminate against the poor by raising the cost of what they buy, denying them access, in the name of preservation, to many environmental amenities, or by providing public goods from which they derive little benefit. Certainly, if "public choice," whatever it may be, has any merit, it must be in providing more complete information as to the costs and benefits of public projects for a body politic that is becoming increasingly concerned with distributive ethics.

The main criticism of these articles is the trivial nature of the problems they have selected. Some start with larger problems but concede at the end that they are far short of an explanation. Otto A. Davis and John E. Jackson seek to create a model to explain voting behavior in representative assemblies on distributive issues. They begin with a self-interest hypothesis and use the Senate votes on the Family Assistance Plan as a test case. Even with modifications in the model specific to the votes on this proposal, they are still short of explaining the vote of a number of senators and end by speaking of their "guess above." Another author, A. Mitchell Polinsky, discusses the intrapersonal redistribution through time. People generally need more money than their income when they are young and when they approach retirement years. Given imperfect capital markets, they cannot always borrow from those surplus middle years, so the government performs this function for them. The problem is that politicians have known this for years; public health, social security, and other public weal policies have been argued in precisely these terms. Furthermore, Lester C. Thurow has done important empirical research verifying the politician's impressions. Polinsky draws upon this research. The question simply is what more do we know about this policy issue after reading Polinsky's technically proficient article? I would contend, nothing. Some people would rather be rigorous than right or relevant.

The essays originally were presented at a conference at the Urban Institute in Washington, D.C. All are technically proficient, as would be expected from the caliber of the participants and from the quality of the discussants (whose remarks are not included in the volume). Despite some provocative ideas and good articles, overall the volume is disappointing and shows that much work needs to be done.

THOMAS R. DE GREGORI
*University of Houston*

# 22

# Some Notes in Conclusion

*Warren J. Samuels*

Although the contributions to this volume speak for themselves, it seems to me desirable to make certain points and raise certain questions in conclusion. These have to do with the limits of the symposium, especially but not solely in regard to my own contributions; the substance of Chicago doctrine; some further issues raised by the discussion; and a few final points.

### *On the Limits of the Symposium*

First, it should be stressed that although various contributions herein concentrate upon ideology, the real world is an arena *not* fundamentally of intervention versus nonintervention (although such *is* the semantics of policy) but of working out alternative uses of government. The Chicago School doctrine reflects, takes advantage of, and reinforces the long-standing practice of identifying business system use of government as nonintervention or "minimal" government, and all other use as intervention.

Second, it should be clear that this volume is not evaluating Chicago School doctrine as a contribution to Knight's propaganda for economic freedom. Such is a different task than that undertaken here, although the question of the role of such a propaganda is considered below.

Third, there is a canon of historical scholarship which militates against writing a contemporary history of current thought, especially in that area with which one has been associated. Some such is included here as an inevitable incidental facet of the primary task of rendering a constructive critique, for critique informed by history is one of the processes of disciplinary development. As George Stigler has written, "the role of controversy is indeed to stimulate interest and animosity. Only after a theory has been subjected to hostile review do its weaknesses and limitations become identified and therefore capable of being remedied" [Stigler 1969, p. 222]. We have been engaged here in constructive, not hostile, analysis, and the problem of contemporary proximity is not a bar to such work, however much it augurs caution and the existence of interpretive limits.

Finally, the limits adduced to Chicago School doctrines, or analogs to those limits, are relevant to *all* schools of thought. These limits have been stressed in part because they are important and in part to overcome the high priestly exhortation of the Chicago School, so that their presence and importance can be seen. The extrasystemic and matric analysis approach discussed in chapter 1, in which limits are an important part of the analysis, is a valid one.

### *On the Substance of Chicago Doctrines*

The general values of the Chicago School are pluralism with regard to power structure, gradualism with regard to change, and the viability of the business, or capitalist, system. Yet it must be stressed that each of these values is selectively interpreted and applied at Chicago, with the first and second especially influenced by the school's specification of the third.

The libertarian Chicago argument against playing God and for nonintervention is disingenuous; Chicagoans have their own agenda and uses for the state. Theirs is an ideology desiring to mold the social order in accordance with their own prescriptions. They are engaged on the most subtle level of social control available in a free or any society, and ultimately theirs is a propaganda in quest of power. As Knight expressed it, "the real motive back of any political propaganda is largely the quest of power on the part of those who are carrying it on. The propagandist can usually see this clearly in connection with every propaganda except his own" [Knight 1947, p. 260]. The interest here is less with motive than with role or effect; the point applies in both cases, and the mode is always power language [Hutt 1936].

Chicagoans do usefully remind us that society is a civilization, of which government is only one facet, and that the danger from government arises in part from its absolutist legitimation. This danger is a problem relevant to the Chicago School itself. Fundamental choices are made through government, and Chicago, while seeming to discredit government and its use, is really trying to influence those choices. The absolutist legitimation of the free market, so-called, is considerably vitiated by the important agenda for government in such a society.

A strength and weakness of the Chicago message is that it is a variant of a larger doctrine: Beware the concentration of power. The Chicago School emphasizes government (and labor union) power and diminishes the importance of private economic power, especially of business in a corporate system. It is thus selective in its perception of power and in its use of it to check power. The identification of power requiring check is a fundamental valuational task that is only defined but not resolved by Chicago doctrine (nor by any other doctrine, for that matter).

Chicagoans make a political decision that the danger from government is greater than that from the corporate system, which is really a decision that certain uses of government are more dangerous than others. As the quotation from Veblen at the beginning of this volume suggests, Chicago doctrine is an emanation of our economic system. It presents *an* idealized version of the system, but only one of several possible idealizations. The danger is always that emphasis upon one form of power concentration may divert attention away from another and prospectively more important form. The significant issue, in both a positive and normative sense, is the historic rise of the corporate system and its contemporary expansion on a global scale in a manner rivaling the nation-state system itself. Although one may admire the Chicagoans' desire for a free society, one also may feel that in asking us to disregard certain important considerations they are inconclusive in regard to not only some of the foundations of the very market system they embrace but also the severe limits of their own analysis. They also ask us to overlook the propriety and structure of private economic power and its interrelations with government even absent the corporate system. Chicago's ideal "market" and "laissez-faire" are almost complete fictions; perhaps they are acceptable ideals, but they are too readily capable of masking and canonizing concentrations of private power and uses of government which, to say the least, are highly equivocal. Transcending ideology, the real problem and actual practice in society is control of the power structure of the market system and the jockeying for power by status quo interests to use government to maintain and extend their hegemony. Such a statement is essentially positive (descriptive) and requires an additional normative premise before one can read into or from it defense or criticism of the existing system. The point is that the Chicago School's political decision about respective dangers from power concentration (including judgments as to its very existence) must be and, of course, is juxtaposed to other political decisions reaching differing or opposite conclusions.

The ultimate practical problem in a sense is that there are different possible institutionalizations of the market system, different structures of rights with regard to workers, consumers, businessmen, government officials, and subgroups of each. Most relevant domestic policy debates center on the best institutional arrangements for a market system or free economy. (And, of course, there are alternative institutionalizations of market economies found in other countries.) The Chicago School tends to identify the system with certain specific institutional arrangements, whereas technical economic optimality is a function of and can exist with regard to many different sets. Indeed, the answers to such questions as the following are quite open: What is the market system? Whose economy and whose government is it? What change is consistent, in mode and substance, with a market system? How are social answers to these questions worked out? The Chicago School is distinguished by its particular set of responses. One suspects that it does not have a monopoly on the answer to institutionalization: The problem of whose interests are to count is in fact worked out in the legal-economic arena and is not solved conclusively by any one ideology or school. This is true notwithstanding the enormous insight which Chicagoans have provided into how markets operate to govern whose interests really do count, which well may be their most important positive contribution to normative discussion.

Apropos the danger from government, the evil is not government encroachment, in the sense of government as an independent or exogenous force, but of people's use of government *within the system.* Chicago doctrine, however, accepts certain and rejects other uses, which is to make interpersonal utility and value comparisons with regard to both the use of government as a means and the ends and interests served thereby. The Chicago School follows a strategy of denigrating government as a means in hopes of aborting nonacceptable uses.

There is great truth and wisdom in Chicago School strictures concerning a free society and the contribution of the market thereto in conjunction with political democracy (although there is no small amount of Chicago fudging as to just what change democratic—read: majoritarian—government can undertake). But reality differs from the Chicago ideal: The market is manipulated and political democracy is severely circumscribed or channeled by wealth and private power. Chicagoans might explore more thoroughly the consequences of inequality of wealth and related phenomena. The market does work, including giving effect to and reinforcing the status quo structure of social power. One can prefer the market and market solutions but at the same time require more consciousness and attention to positive and normative limits and interpose some skepticism concerning the rationalizing away of problems and the canonizing of established private power and privilege. To better understand how markets work in practice, one can study the forces that operate through the market, for those forces govern both how markets are organized and operated and the results which markets produce. Many neoclassical economists do precisely this, including some work by the Chicago School, as has been stressed above.

The relevant positive and normative problem is the use of government with regard to change of the structure of power and privilege. This is what argument over the status quo is all about, including the reinforcement of positions and arguments by subtle constructions and uses of the neoclassical-Chicago paradigm. No small amount of Chicago argument uses code words with meaning in class conflict. The policy perspective of the Chicago School, whatever else can be said about its doctrine, is that of a group trying mightily to protect the entrenched business and wealth dominated system against the felt inroads of a welfare state or labor oriented system. Just as John Locke's theories of property and government, as well as revolution, were designed to function as an intellectual arsenal against James II, so the modern Chicago libertarian doctrine has its functional role. It is part of the array of conservative movements functioning to defend the existing distribution of wealth and market processes of society. From this point of view others' redistributionist emphasis upon structural issues is anathema. It should not be uncanny, therefore, that all Chicago economics tends to have the same conservative normative implications (whatever the differences among Chicagoans as to details).

It should be reiterated that the Chicago School has made important positive contributions which its equivocal normative posture should not obscure. Moreover, there are complex intellectual problems regarding positive and normative economics, as to their meaning and the role of the status quo, all in relation to the economic role of government [see Buchanan and Samuels 1975]. The Chicago School has made contributions to our understanding of both economic reality and the values by which economic policy is to be conducted. Differences with Chicagoans are a complex admixture of varying positive and normative positions, and hopefully this volume will contribute to the clarification of these.

### *Some Further Questions*

One question which should be raised, and addressed to the economics profession as a whole, involves the prescriptive role of economics. We often declare our science to be value free, and yet we prescribe freely. We often pretend to be observers, yet we strive to be participants. We prefer an image of being above social reality and social struggle, but we are part of it, as Foley [1975, p. 235] has pointed out. As both observers and participants, we are, inevitably, interested parties. We seem to enjoy serving as high, and low, priests, as pleaders more fundamentally than investigators. How far should competence and priestliness be indulged on its own account? How important and necessary is it for economists to be creators and purveyors of systemic myths? More directly, should economics be a policy science specifically concerned with the choice of the best policy alternative? Should economics' self-assignment be as an engineering science? These questions apply to both the Chicago version of policy activism and all other versions. Is economics studying the economy, or is economic science in charge of organizing and controlling the economy, for example, possessed of the oracular capacity to inform all parties as to whether one policy or another is consonant with the "requirements" of the "system"? I for one would be happier to see the profession carefully articulating the complex value premises and performance consequences of alternative institutions and policies rather than invoking the prestige of the profession behind certain policies and against others. My own sins in this regard should not debar me from espousing this view.

A correlated or derived problem concerns the relations of prescription to description and explanation. Among other things which might be said in this connection, let me say only that the propaganda role inhibits the performance of the positive role and constitutes a critical limitation upon positive science (which is difficult enough without the added intentional high priest and legitimation role). Doctrine obscures the factors taken for granted, distorts economics as a science, and confines and constrains positive descriptive and explanatory analysis.

There may be another and more desirable, more austere, role for economists in which there is a strict adherence to clearly separated professional and personal participation. There is an inevitable tension between economics as propaganda (that is, as a secular religion) and as an objective science. A key question, however, concerns the role of myth and high priest in contemporary economics and in the modern economic system. Rationalization of some version of the status quo is a fundamental social process; so is its criticism and the unmasking of both rationalization and of criticism. But is not economics more than that? A profession dominated by the Chicago School would tend to be less of a science and more of a religion than might be preferrable, and this would be true of domination by *any* school. All values cannot be eliminated from economic science, but they can be made explicit, and the work of economists can more involve the open comparison of all relevant alternatives and less the polemical advancement and advertising of selected ones.

The primary self-assumed task of the Chicago School is the marketing of the paradigm within which its work, and the system (or its view of it), makes sense. Chicagoans defend economics, their paradigm, and the system, each to reinforce the others. Yet all three are artifacts, and the element of pure science is quite limited. Beware the role of predictive power casting luster on the status quo it confirms.

However paradoxical may be Friedman's claims to positivism, a major general contribution of the Chicago School is to the valuational process of society. The aim of the school is to influence the value dimensions of economic organization and policy, and this *is* its great role—whether or not one agrees with Chicago in the large or the small.

A chief limit of all schools of thought, including Chicago, is the capacity of its doctrines to serve as a tool of the mean spirited for narrow interests. This is a different point than that made by those who see in Chicago doctrine good intentions but a narrow focus with the same mean results. The use of Chicago's doctrine should be examined with regard to its structural and performance premises and results as independently as possible of evaluation of the interests which those and alternative policies would support or inhibit.

To return to an earlier theme, would the world be better off if we generally understood that government is an economic alternative and that everyone is trying to impose their own agenda on government? Would this be better than pretending that we could adhere—or actually adhere—to a particular exclusivist ideology and its agenda and nonagenda? This is another key problem raised by the previous discussions. Which is the correct question: Can we no longer be the victim of our own ideological illusions? Are our cherished beliefs about government actually illusions? Are these beliefs "merely" our very human way of conducting the social valuational process? Among the instrumental virtues of a proselytizing religion is that it seems to give and in a sense does give a neat set of simple and final answers, an aspect which becomes more attractive yet also more dangerous as the world becomes more complex. Is ideology necessary for social control [Robinson 1962, chapter 1]? Is not "the big job of economics," as Patinkin [1973, p.

791] reports Knight saying in class in 1942, "to divest people of prejudices—to have them see the questions as they are"? Yet, as does Gustav Bergmann [Brodbeck 1969, pp. 137, 138], we need to inquire: *"Is an ideology-free society possible?"* and *"Is an ideology-free society desirable?"* I do not know the answers to these questions, but they are important heuristically.

A closely related issue concerns what is necessary for the achievement and defense of a free society. Central to it, however, are the further matters of whose freedom and over and from what. That is the definition of a free society. Is the deliberate construction and manipulation of myth and high priestly incantations necessary for the promotion of a free society, whichever version is advocated? If we were less ideologically preoccupied and less desirous of reaching or defending normative positions, might we not be more able deliberately and carefully to study the complex and deep problems of hierarchy versus equality, continuity versus change, and freedom versus control? To answer affirmatively, however, may be construed, and may in fact function, to open the door to heterodox or radical ideas. Indeed, it seems that one of the functions of the Chicago School doctrine is to abort investigations which might challenge the system.

### *A Few Final Points*

Just as there is both sophisticated and vulgar Marxism, there is sophisticated and vulgar libertarianism, opposition to libertarianism, and critique of libertarianism. There are stereotyped and sophisticated ways to express and to criticize Chicago School doctrine. Part of the interpretive problem, as indicated in chapter 1, is that the Chicago School's own propagandistic designs and efforts make the task of sophisticated—as opposed to stereotyped and vulgar—critique much more difficult, although the problem is no less acute for those who want to believe the doctrine in its most sophisticated form. The Chicago School has much of value to say without caricaturization, albeit within limits. Both the fanatical devotee and critic will fail to recognize the strength within limits, the former neglecting the limits and the latter the strength. Meaningfulness is a function of both, however much both are equivocal.

What picture of the economy is correct: one emphasizing the possibility of a self-adjusting market mechanism, or one emphasizing the arena of conflict over the organization and control of the economic system? The Chicago School emphasizes the former and takes a normative position on the organization and control of the economic system. The interpretation of the Chicago School in this volume is profoundly influenced by the fact that most authors emphasize the latter problem (without taking a clear-cut position normatively). All contributors emphasize the need to supplement the model of market adjustment with a model of power and therefore the necessity of considering economic inequality and their own version of the realities of the use of government.

Finally, should economics as an intellectual discipline become dominated by an approach or school which, regardless of its other merits, lacks the humility and compassion to consider significant change in the social structure which might permit a wider enjoyment of individualism and its fruits? A concept of optimality which canonizes the existing structure of hierarchy and inequality leaves much to be desired, regardless of the merits of using markets. The Chicago School can inform us of the stupidity of certain reforms, and indeed it has, but it need not stop there. Alas, Chicagoans are not alone in this: Most of us are content to combat policies and solutions offered by others which do not appeal to us, but are unwilling to attend to the underlying problems.

## *References**

Adams, Walter. 1975. "Comment." *Journal of Economic Issues* 9 (June): 341–42.

Aliber, Robert Z. 1972. "Comments on 'The Internationalization of Capital.' " *Journal of Economic Issues* 6 (March): 113–15.

Anonymous. 1851. "Literary Notices." *Harper's* 3 (June): 138–40.

Anonymous. 1973. "In Memoriam: Frank Knight." *American Economic Review* 63 (December): 1047–48.

Arrow, Kenneth J., and Tibor Scitovsky, eds. 1969. *Readings in Welfare Economics*. Homewood, Ill.: Irwin.

Avineri, Shlomo. 1972. *Hegel's Theory of the Modern State*. New York: Cambridge University Press.

Ayres, Clarence E. 1957. "Institutional Economics: Discussion." *American Economic Review* 47 (May): 26–27.

Baran, Paul A. 1963. Book Review. *Journal of Political Economy* 71 (December): 591–94.

Barbour, Ian G. 1974. *Myths, Models and Paradigms*. New York: Harper & Row.

Bartlett, Randall. 1973. *Economic Foundations of Political Power*. New York: Free Press.

Betz, Horst. 1974. "East Germany: The Primacy of Dogma over Reform." *Journal of Economic Issues* 8 (March): 83–96.

Boulding, Kenneth E., and Martin Pfaff, eds. 1972. *Redistribution to the Rich and the Poor*. Belmont, Calif.: Wadsworth.

Bowles, Samuel, and Herbert Gintis. 1975. "The Problem of Human Capital

* *The following are references to chapters 1, 16, 17, and 22 by Warren J. Samuels.*

Theory—A Marxian Critique." *American Economic Review* 65 (May): 74–82.

Breit, William, and Roger L. Ransom. 1971. *The Academic Scribblers*. New York: Holt, Rinehart and Winston.

Brodbeck, May, ed. 1968. *Readings in the Philosophy of the Social Sciences*. New York: Macmillan.

Bronfenbrenner, M. 1962. "Observation on the 'Chicago School(s).'" *Journal of Political Economy* 70 (February): 72–75.

Buchanan, James M. 1968. "What Kind of Redistribution Do We Want?" *Economica* 35 (May): 185–90.

———. 1972a. "Before Public Choice." In *Explorations in the Theory of Anarchy*, edited by Gordon Tullock. Blacksburg: Center for the Study of Public Choice. Pp. 27–37.

———. 1972b. "Politics, Property, and the Law: An Alternative Interpretation of Miller et al v. Schoene." *Journal of Law and Economics* 15 (October): 439–52.

———. 1975. "A Contractarian Paradigm for Applying Economic Theory." *American Economic Review* 65 (May): 225–30.

——— and Warren J. Samuels. 1975. "On Some Fundamental Issues in Political Economy: An Exchange of Correspondence." *Journal of Economic Issues* 9 (March): 15–38.

Buchanan, James M., and William Craig Stubblebine. 1962. "Externality." *Economica* 29 (November): 371–84.

Campbell, William F. 1971. "Economics and the Machiavellian Tradition." *Journal of Economic Issues* 5 (June): 20–30.

Carey, James T. 1975. *The Chicago School*. Beverly Hills, Calif.: Sage.

Coase, R.H. 1960. "The Nature of Social Cost." *Journal of Law and Economics* 3 (October): 1–44.

Day, Richard H. 1975. "Orthodox Economists and Existential Economics." *Journal of Economic Issues* 9 (June): 229–35.

Demsetz, Harold. 1964. "The Exchange and Enforcement of Property Rights." *Journal of Law and Economics* 7 (October): 11–26.

Dietz, James Lowell. 1975. "A Note on *Human Capital*." *Journal of Economic Issues* 9 (September): 525–30.

Douglas, Mary. 1967. "The Meaning of Myth." In *The Structural Study of Myth and Totemism*, edited by Edmund Leach. London: Tavistock Publications.

Edel, Matthew, and Elliott Sclar. 1974. "Taxes, Spending, and Property Values: Supply Adjustment in a Tiebout-Oates Model." *Journal of Political Economy* 82 (September-October): 941–54.

Fogel, Robert William, and Stanley L. Engerman. 1974. *Time on the Cross*. 2 vols. Boston: Little, Brown.

Foley, Duncan J. 1975. "Problems vs. Conflicts: Economic Theory and Ideology." *American Economic Review* 65 (May): 231–36.

Frank, Andre Gunder, 1975. "An Open Letter About Chile to Arnold Harberger and Milton Friedman." *Review of Radical Political Economics* 7 (Summer): 61–76.

Friedman, Milton. 1962. *Capitalism and Freedom*. Chicago: University of Chicago Press.

——. 1974. "Schools at Chicago." *University of Chicago Magazine* (August): 11–16.
Fusfeld, Daniel R. 1972. *The Age of the Economist*. Rev. ed. Glenview, Ill.: Scott, Foresman.
———. 1974. Book Review. *Journal of Economic Issues* 8 (December): 909–11.
Gibson W.L., Jr. 1973. Book Review. *Journal of Economic Issues* 7 (September): 524–27.
Goldberg, Victor P. 1974. "Public Choice—Property Rights." *Journal of Economic Issues* 8 (September): 555–79.
———. 1975. "Remarks on the State of Orthodoxy." *Journal of Economic Issues* 9 (June): 237–41.
Gonce, Richard A. 1971. "John R. Commons's Legal Economic Theory." *Journal of Economic Issues* 5 (September): 80–95.
———. 1972. "Frank H. Knight on Social Control and the Scope and Method of Economics." *Southern Economic Journal* 38 (April): 547–58.
Gray, Horace M. 1973. Book Review. *Journal of Economic Issues* 7 (December): 728–32.
Hayek, F.A. 1967 *Studies in Philosophy, Politics and Economics*. Chicago: University of Chicago Press.
Heilbroner, Robert L. 1970. "On the Possibility of a Political Economics." *Journal of Economic Issues* 4 (December): 1–22.
———. 1975 "Kenneth Boulding, *Collected Papers*: A Review Article." *Journal of Economic Issues* 9 (March): 73–79.
Hirsch, Abraham. 1967. "The American Setting and Wesley Clair Mitchell's View of Traditional Economics." *Journal of Economic Issues* 1 (June): 74–85.
———. 1968. "C.E. Ayres and the Classical Economists: A Comment." *Journal of Economic Issues* 2 (March): 81–86.
Hochwald, Werner. 1973. Book Review. *Journal of Economic Issues* 7 (September): 483–92.
Hook, Sidney, ed. 1967. *Human Values and Economic Policy*. New York: New York University Press.
Hunt, E.K., and Ralph C. d'Arge. 1973. "On Lemmings and Other Acquisitive Animals: Propositions on Consumption." *Journal of Economic Issues* 7 (June): 337–53.
Hutt, W.H. 1936. *Economists and the Public*. London: Cape.
———. 1974. *A Rehabilitation of Say's Law*. Athens: Ohio University Press.
Jalladeau, Joel. 1975. "Restrained or Englarged Scope of Political Economy? A Few Observations." *Journal of Economic Issues* 9 (March): 1–13.
Kahn, Alfred E. 1970. *The Economics of Regulation: Principles and Institutions*. Volume 1. New York: Wiley.
Klein, Philip A. 1973. "Demand Theory and the Economist's Propensity to Assume." *Journal of Economic Issues* 7 (June): 209–43.
Knight, Frank H. 1924. "Some Fallacies in the Interpretation of Social Cost." *Quarterly Journal of Economics* 38 (August): 582–606.

———. 1932. "The Newer Economics and the Control of Economic Activity." *Journal of Political Economy* 40 (August): 433–76.

———. 1935. Book Review. *Columbia Law Review* 35 (May): 803–805.

———. 1947. *Freedom and Reform*. New York: Harper.

———. 1951a. *The Economic Organization*. New York: Kelley.

———.1951b. *The Ethics of Competition*. New York: Kelley.

———. 1952. "Institutionalism and Empiricism in Economics." *American Economic Review* 42 (May): 45–55.

———. 1953. "Theory of Economic Policy and the History of Doctrine." *Ethics* 63 (July): 276–92.

———. 1956. *On the History and Method of Economics*. Chicago: University of Chicago Press.

———. 1957. "Institutional Economics: Discussion." *American Economic Review* 47 (May): 18–21.

———. 1960. *Intelligence and Democratic Action*. Cambridge, Mass.: Harvard University Press.

Krupp, Sherman S. 1968. "Axioms of Economics and the Claim of Efficiency." *Journal of Economic Issues* 2 (September): 273–82.

Kuhn, Thomas S. 1962. *The Structure of Scientific Revolutions*. Chicago: University of Chicago Press.

Levenson, Albert M. 1973. Book Review. *Journal of Economic Issues* 7 (December): 735–38.

Martin, David D. 1974a. "The Uses and Abuses of Economic Theory in the Social Control of Business." *Journal of Economic Issues* 8 (June): 271–85.

———. 1974b. "Beyond Capitalism: A Role for Markets?" *Journal of Economic Issues* 8 (December): 771–84.

Means, Gardiner C. 1969. "The Problems and Prospects of Collective Capitalism." *Journal of Economic Issues* 3 (March): 18–31.

Melman, Seymour. 1975. "The Impact of Economics on Technology." *Journal of Economic Issues* 9 (March): 59–72.

Melody, William H. 1974. "The Marginal Utility of Marginal Analysis in Public Policy Formulation." *Journal of Economic Issues* 8 (June): 287–300.

Miller, Arthur Selwyn. 1972. "Legal Foundations of the Corporate State." *Journal of Economic Issues* 6 (March): 59–79.

Miller, H. Laurence, Jr. 1962. "On the 'Chicago School of Economics.'" *Journal of Political Economy* 70 (February): 64–69.

Mishan, E.J. 1969. *21 Popular Economic Fallacies*. New York: Praeger.

Morgenstern, Oskar. 1972. "Thirteen Critical Points in Contemporary Economic Theory: An Interpretation." *Journal of Economic Literature* 10 (December): 1163–89.

Morton, Walter A. 1971. "Do Utilities Waste Capital?" *Public Utilities Fortnightly* 87 (27 May 1971): 13–24.

Müller, Ronald. 1975. "Global Corporations and National Stabilization Policy: The Need for Social Planning." *Journal of Economic Issues* 9 (June): 181–203.

Olson, Mancur, and Christopher K. Clague. 1971. "Dissent in Economics: The Convergence of Extremes." *Social Research* 38 (Winter): 751–76.

Parker, William N. 1974. "Economists and History." *Reviews in American History* 2 (December): 466–74.
Patinkin, Don. 1973. "Frank Knight as Teacher." *American Economic Review* 63 (December): 787–810.
Randall, Alan. 1975. "Economics and Public Policy for the Undergraduate: A Review Article." *Journal of Economic Issues* 9 (March): 81–86.
Roberts, Marc J. 1975. "An Evolutionary and Institutional View of the Behavior of Public and Private Companies." *American Economic Review* 65 (May): 415–27.
Robinson, Joan. 1962. *Economic Philosophy*. Chicago: Aldine.
Roosevelt, Frank. 1969. "Market Socialism: A Humane Economy?" *Journal of Economic Issues* 3 (December): 3–20.
Rotwein, Eugene. 1973a. "The Ideology of Wealth and the Liberal Economic Heritage: The Neglected View." *Social Research* 40 (Summer): 267–92.
———. 1973b. "Empiricism and Economic Method: Several Views Considered." *Journal of Economic Issues* 7 (September): 361–82.
Samuels, Warren J. 1957. "The Concepts of Major Business and Labor Organizations on the Role of Government in the Economy." Ph.D. diss., University of Wisconsin.
———. 1966. *The Classical Theory of Economic Policy*. Cleveland: World.
———. 1972a. "Welfare Economics, Power and Property." In *Perspectives of Property*, edited by Gene Wunderlich and W.L. Gibson, Jr. University Park: Institute for Research on Land and Water Resources, The Pennsylvania State University. Pp. 61–148.
———. 1972b. "The Scope of Economics Historically Considered." *Land Economics* 48 (August): 248–68.
———. 1972c. "In Defense of a Positive Approach to Government as an Economic Variable." *Journal of Law and Economics* 15 (October): 453–59.
———. 1973a. "Public Utilities and the Theory of Power." In *Perspectives in Public Regulation*, edited by Milton Russell. Carbondale: Southern Illinois University Press. Pp. 1–27.
———. 1973b. "Law and Economics: Introduction." *Journal of Economic Issues* 7 (December): 535–41.
———. 1973c. "The Economy as a System of Power and Its Legal Bases: The Legal Economics of Robert Lee Hale." *University of Miami Law Review* 27 (Spring-Summer): 261–371.
———. 1974a. "The Coase Theorem and the Study of Law and Economics." *Natural Resources Journal* 14 (January): 1–33.
———. 1974b. "The History of Economic Thought as Intellectual History." *History of Political Economy* 6 (Fall): 305–23.
———. 1974c. "Anarchism and the Theory of Power." In *Further Explorations in the Theory of Anarchy*, edited by Gordon Tullock. Blacksburg: University Publications. Pp. 33–57.
———. 1974d. *Pareto on Policy*. New York: American Elsevier.
———. 1974e. "An Economic Perspective on the Compensation Problem." *Wayne Law Review* 21 (November): 113–34.
———. 1975a. "John Henry Beale's Lectures on Jurisprudence, 1909." *University of Miami Law Review* 29 (Winter): 260–333.

———. 1975b. "Approaches to Legal-Economic Policy and Related Problems of Research." In *Policy Studies and the Social Sciences*, edited by Stuart S. Nagel. Lexington: Lexington Books. Pp. 65–73.

Schmid, A. Allan. 1974. "Theory of Public Choice: A Review Article." *Journal of Economic Issues* 8 (June): 519–24.

Schultz, Theodore W., ed. 1974. *Economics of the Family*. Chicago: University of Chicago Press.

Schumpeter, Joseph A. 1951. *Ten Great Economists*. New York: Oxford University Press.

Scott, John Anthony, 1974. "Time on the Cross: The Economics of American Negro Slavery." *Challenge* 17 (November-December): 53–62.

Seidman, Robert B. 1973. "Contract Law, the Free Market, and State Intervention." *Journal of Economic Issues* 7 (December): 553–75.

Selden, Richard T., ed. 1975. *Capitalism and Freedom: Problems and Prospects*. Charlottesville: University Press of Virginia.

Seligman, Ben B. 1962. *Main Currents in Modern Economics*. Glencoe, Ill.: Free Press.

Shackle, G.L.S. 1967. *The Years of High Theory*. New York: Cambridge University Press.

Sherman, Howard. 1975. "The Sad State of Orthodox Economics." *Journal of Economic Issues* 9 (June): 243–50.

Simons, Henry C. 1948. *Economic Policy for a Free Society*. Chicago: University of Chicago Press.

Smith, Adam. 1966. *The Theory of Moral Sentiments*. New York: Kelley.

Solow, Robert M. 1973. Book Review. *Journal of Economic Issues* 7 (December): 694–98.

Sowell, Thomas. 1972. *Say's Law: An Historical Analysis*. Princeton: Princeton University Press.

Spengler, Joseph J. 1948. "The Problem of Order in Economic Affairs," *Southern Economic Journal* 15 (July): 1–29.

———. 1974. "Was 1922–1972 a Golden Age in the History of Economics?" *Journal of Economic Issues* 8 (September): 525–53.

Spiegel, Henry William. 1971. *The Growth of Economic Thought*. Englewood Cliffs, N.J.: Prentice-Hall.

Stigler, George J. 1962. "Comment." *Journal of Political Economy* 70 (February): 70–71.

———. 1965. *Essays in the History of Economics*. Chicago: University of Chicago Press.

———. 1969. "Does Economics Have a Useful Past?" *History of Political Economy* 1 (Fall): 217–30.

Tarascio, Vincent J. 1975. Book Review. *Journal of Political Economy* 83 (August): 880–82.

Taussig, Frank W. 1930. *Inventors and Money-Makers*. New York: Macmillan.

Trebing, Harry M. 1969. "Government Regulation and Modern Capitalism." *Journal of Economic Issues* 3 (March): 87–109.

Veblen, Thorstein. 1948. *The Portable Veblen*, edited by Max Lerner. New York: Viking.

Viner, Jacob. 1931. "Cost Curves and Supply Curves." *Zeitschrift für Nationalökonomie* 3 (September): 23–46.

Wall, David, ed. 1972. *Chicago Essays in Economic Development*. Chicago: University of Chicago Press.

Ward, Benjamin. 1972. *What's Wrong with Economics?* New York: Basic Books.

Witte, Edwin E. 1954. "Institutional Economics as Seen by an Institutional Economist." *Southern Economic Journal* 21 (October): 131–40.

For Product Safety Concerns and Information please contact our EU representative GPSR@taylorandfrancis.com
Taylor & Francis Verlag GmbH, Kaufingerstraße 24, 80331 München, Germany

www.ingramcontent.com/pod-product-compliance
Lightning Source LLC
LaVergne TN
LVHW011101300926
849160LV00008B/243
*9781560006336*